Contents

INTRODUCTION

Many children are able to provide the sounds for phonic patterns when they are presented visually in isolation on single flash cards, or even in a list of single words. Yet some children seem unable to link this knowledge to their reading of a full text or choose the correct patterns automatically when trying to spell words in their free writing.

These simple spelling stories were created to encourage children to recognise those phonic patterns in context, and store strong visual images of those patterns for spelling.

Each story uses words that contain a particular phonic pattern. The intention is that the child will begin to both 'hear' and 'see' words that link to that particular pattern within a story. They are challenged to find words in the story containing that phonic pattern and then make some words using movable letters.

A simple comprehension passage is included for each story where the child is required to write their answers in full sentences. Since every answer will include words containing the focus phonic pattern, then reinforcement in writing (spelling) is encouraged.

The more we use a word within a context in the written form, the more likely we will automate the spelling of that word into our hand. The learner is, therefore, encouraged to write one or two sentences of their own using some of the focus words. Encouraging them to write their own simple stories would also provide repetition.

Once the teacher, or parent working with the learner, is confident that a phonic pattern can be automatically recalled when spelling, then the appropriate section of the clown record sheet can be coloured in. Recording their progress in this way can be motivating.

Lists of the first 200 common words is included as a reference only. Teaching those common words is a National Curriculum requirement and it is assumed they are being taught in school. However, efforts have been made to include a large number of these words in the stories and some simple cumulative dictations are presented at the end of this book for testing automatic recall. These dictations are based on the order of sounds presented in this book, one building upon another to promote continual recall of the patterns taught.

Teaching phonics in 'Word Families' helps to link the sounds and visual patterns to other words that use the same letter strings. Using pictures, stories and writing exercises creates a multi-sensory learning experience to enhance memory.

Teaching a phonic word family

Materials required:

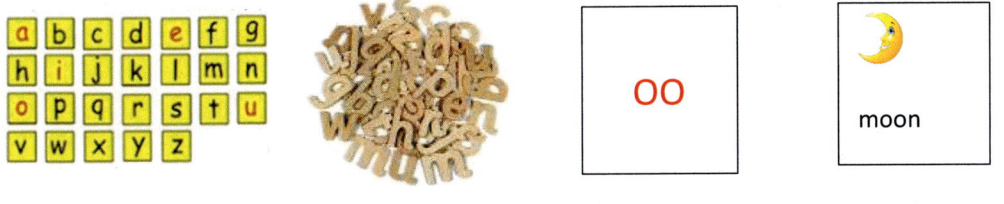

| Letter tiles | or | Wooden letters | | Trigger card front | Trigger card back |

- Wooden letters or tiles - with vowels coloured red
- Trigger cards
- Some additional pictures to reinforce the sounds visually

1. **Set out the wooden alphabet letters in the shape of an arc** or rainbow with 'm' in the middle.

2. **Read the words** presented under the story picture. This introduces the word family being taught. Extension words for each word family can be found in an additional section at the back of this book.

3. **Focus on the sound being taught.** Discuss any unknown words and their meanings. Present more images of the words or ask the learner to draw pictures themselves.

4. **Take the list of words away** and ask the learner what sound they are learning. Can they bring down the letters that make that sound?

5. **Say the words one at a time** and ask the learner to make those words with the letters. Make sure they put all the letters back in the rainbow arc before making the next word. This encourages them to keep thinking about the pattern and also to become familiar and visualise where those letters are placed in the alphabet arc.

6. **Remove the story** and word list and then dictate each word, asking the learner to write the words in their own exercise book. This will test immediate recall of the pattern.

7. **Ask the learner to write over the sound pattern** with a red pencil. Do not use a highlighter pen, rather encourage the writing of the pattern. This reinforces it in motor memory.

8. **Finally make a 'key' word card** that will act as a trigger to open up that sound family in their own memory. Write the sound only on the front of the card and put a picture on the back of the card as illustrated. This begins their own pack of trigger cards for the sounds they will be learning in future lessons. This pack can be drilled regularly for the learner to recall not only the sound but words that are connected to that sound.

The spelling story - Read the story to the learner or ask them to read it. They can then highlight all the words containing the sound being taught. They can colour the picture also.

The comprehension worksheet can then be completed by the learner as an overlearning activity. This encourages them to write the spellings within a meaningful sentence.

The final overlearning worksheets encourage the learner to think and use the knowledge they have gained.

When sufficient practice in spelling and writing is completed and a little time has passed (not immediately after the sound has been taught), administer a simple dictation to test automatic recall. The dictations are structured, cumulative and sequential, building upon the order of sounds presented in the book. Each sound building upon the one before and reinforcing throughout. A 'dip in' approach to using the stories and worksheets can be used depending on which phonic pattern is being taught. However, the dictations are cumulative.

Order of phonic patterns					
1.	a-e	9.	ai	17.	oi
2.	i-e	10.	oa	18.	igh
3.	o-e	11.	ea	19.	ow
4.	u-e ue	12.	ir	20	aw
5.	oo	13.	or	21.	ew
6.	ee	14.	ow (ō)	22.	au
7.	ar	15.	ou		
8.	ay	16.	ur		

Colour the picture as you learn the sounds.

Order of the first lesson

1. Read the a-e story.

2. Look at the picture- read the a-e words under the picture. Focus on the sound.

3. Find words with the pattern in the story.

4. Set out the alphabet in an arc shape.

5. Remove all words from sight.

6. Learner then makes the words with the alphabet letters from memory and an adult prompt.

7. Say each word for learner to write.

8. Learner overwrites the phonic pattern in red.

9. Create a set of trigger cards (see recall cards at the back of the book). The learner chooses a word to write on the back as their prompt.

10. Introduce the over learning activities- colour the picture; answer the comprehension questions; complete the worksheets.

Ideally teach one phonic sound per week with continual reference to that pattern on the trigger card and overlearning materials.

Front    Back

N.B. Each following lesson should begin with the relevant dictation to test automatic recall. Also use the trigger cards to drill the sounds already learnt.

SPELLING STORIES

oo

ee

or

a-e

Grace loved to make cakes. She baked every day and made cakes for all her friends. One day she made a birthday cake for her friend Jade. She scraped Jade's face on the cake with the blade of a knife. She put it on a pretty plate and took it round to Jade.

When Jade saw the cake, she was amazed and excited to see her own face on it. She raced off to tell her friends and they all came to her birthday party. They played games and ate food on pretty party plates.

When it was time to cut the cake, Jade closed her eyes and made a wish. She gave everyone the same size slice. It was delicious. There was not a trace of cake left on that plate when the party ended.

Find the 'a-e' words in this story.

Read the words - listen to the sound for 'a-e'

cake	bake	take	made	face	space
race	lace	ate	hate	shape	cave
name	same	came	brave	age	grape

i-e

Mike loved to ride his bike, so his Dad suggested that they went on a hike together in the countryside. Mike's dad knew where there was a lovely place about ten miles away near a pine forest. The pine forest led down to the sea.

Mike had a very nice bike. It was lime green and he was easy to spot on the road, so his dad would be able to see him if he got lost.

Mike and his dad set off early at nine o'clock and they reached the sea just as the tide was coming in.

Dad bought them both an ice cream and they had a great time riding along the coastline. Dad said, "We must do this again sometime."

'Yes', said Mike with a smile. I would like that.

They were both very tired when they got home and were happy to slide into bed and have a nice rest.

Find the 'i-e' words in this story.

Read the words - listen to the sound for 'i-e'

ice	slice	hide	ride	slide	side
like	hike	mine	fine	pipe	ripe
bite	write	rise	wise	prize	size

o-e

"I hope you don't mind," said Mole to Rabbit. I have stolen your hole for my new home for the night. I lost my own home you see when a pole was poked into it by some naughty children. I nearly jumped out of my bones and choked on all the dust and smoke before my whole home exploded. I am so alone, and I only want to stay here for one night."

"I suppose so", said Rabbit. "You are welcome to stay but do not poke your nose into my things. It is no joke having someone invade your home when you are out."

"I promise I will be very good", said Mole "And I hope to be on my way by the stroke of nine tomorrow".

Find the 'o-e' words in this story.

Read the words - listen to the sound for 'o-e'

rode	rose	smoke	home	hole
joke	mole	hose	globe	rope
bone	phone	hope	throne	slope

u-e / ue

Sue wanted dad to get her a rescue dog because so many people are unkind to animals and she wanted to give one a home.

Dad said it was a good idea and so on Tuesday they went on the Tube up to London. They stood in the queue outside the dog's home for a few minutes before it was time to go in.

The minute Sue saw Luke she fell in love. He was not a huge dog but he had such a cute face and big brown eyes. He was pure black with white tips to his paws.

" I love him, I like him, I want him," said Sue.

Dad did not argue with her, but he said, "Are you sure?"

"Yes, it is true," said Sue. "I am really sure."

The people in the dogs' home had to issue a certificate for Luke and make sure that that he was going to be valued and looked after.

Sue bought a lovely blue collar and a lead for Luke and they all went back home.

Find the 'u-e' and ue words in this story.

13

Read the words - listen to the sound for 'u-e'

cube	tube	rude	huge
use	amuse	fuse	cute
rule	duke	June	tune

oo

There was a foolish man called gloomy Glen. He was always in a mood because he wanted to go to the moon. He thought it would be really cool and it would make him happy. So he trained to be an astronaut. The day soon came when Gloomy Glen went to the moon. On that morning he ate some food and put on his astronaut clothes and boots. His rocket was soon zooming into space and he was on his way. It was a smooth ride and he saw lots of shooting stars.

When he got to the moon he saw some funny looking men. They had spoon shaped heads and they wore big black boots. They made funny hooting sounds. They lived in little houses shaped like igloos.

"Hooray!" said foolish Glen. "I am not so foolish after all. I have got proof now that there are men on the moon. I will soon be famous".

He jumped back into his spaceship and zoomed back to earth. Gloomy Glen was not gloomy anymore.

Find the 'oo' words in this story.

Read the words - listen to the sound for 'oo'

school	fool	pool	moon
boots	soon	spoon	zoom
shoot	gloomy	smooth	food

16

ee

One day Mr. Keen was driving his jeep along a country lane. Suddenly he saw a field of sheep. They were all green! He was so shocked he stopped his jeep and got out. He put his boots on his feet and went across the grass towards the sheep. There were about sixteen sheep. Three of the sheep came up to greet him and he could see that their fur was bright green.

"Well I wonder why you are all green" said Mr. Keen

"I can tell you that," said a voice. A man came out from behind a tree. He said, "I am the farmer. These are my sheep and I have been losing some of them. I think someone is taking them. Last week I painted their coats green so I could find them if they were stolen."

"That is a clever idea,' said Mr. Keen. "They look quite sweet and cheeky in their green coats and of course they can be seen from a long way off."

Find the 'ee' words in this story.

Read the words - listen to the sound for 'ee'

see	bee	three	green
seen	feet	street	heel
peel	feel	week	sheep

ar

Arthur lived on a farm with his mum and dad. He had a dog called Sparky. Sparky loved to play in the barn with his ball and he also loved going on the hay cart with Arthur's dad. He always barked and barked.

One day Arthur and his dad took Sparky in the car to the local farmers' market. There were lots of animals there and lots of food to eat. There were jars of home-made jam, cartons of cream and apple tarts.

Suddenly Sparky spotted another dog and darted off after him, barking and barking. Everyone became alarmed as the dogs knocked over tables sending jam tarts and jars of marmalade into the air. What a mess!

Arthur and his dad were so startled and embarrassed. Arthur grabbed Sparky and held him in his arms until they could put him in the car. Arthur's dad had to pay for all the jam tarts and jars of food. Sparky had to spend the night in the barn for being naughty.

Find the 'ar' words in this story.

Read the words - listen to the sound for 'ar'

bark	barn	car	cart
dart	park	jar	tart
spark	farmer	garden	arm

ay

At the end of May Sanjay went to stay with his friend Ben for a few days. Ben lived on a farm where there were lots of animals to play with. They had lots of fun jumping and playing in the haystacks. One day they found a stray dog. He was very playful. He jumped and played in the hay with them and licked their faces. He stayed with them all day and would not go away.

"Do you think he has run away from home?" said Sanjay.

"No," said Ben "I think he just wants to play with us."

"Shall we give him a name?" said Sanjay "Shall we call him Ray?"

"Yes," said Ben. "We will call him Ray just for today."

Ray stayed with the boys all day and then he ran away back to his own home.

Find the 'ay' words in this story.

Read the words - listen to the sound for 'ay'

day	play	say	may
hay	stray	play	today
stay	clay	spray	way

22

ai

Daisy fell over at school on Monday and sprained her ankle. She went straight home with her mum on the train.

Because it was so painful, she had to stay at home for a few days.

Daisy loved painting so she spent her time painting some pictures.

She painted some snails in the rain. Snails leave silvery trails on the ground.

She also painted a picture of a mermaid and a sailing boat out at sea.

She put a rainbow in the sky because rainbows can often be seen when it is raining and the sun is shining at the same time.

Soon Daisy's painful foot was better and on the next Monday she went straight back to school. She could not wait to show her paintings to Mrs. Main, her teacher.

Find the 'ai' words in this story.

Read the words - listen to the sound for 'ai'

train	brain	chain	again
snail	rain	sail	daisy
stain	strain	fail	rail

oa

Jasmine and her brother Noah were going on their summer holidays.

Dad loaded all the bags into the car and tied their boat to the roof.

Mum made some roast chicken sandwiches for the journey and

brought loads of sweets to eat on the way.

They all had some porridge oats and toast and marmalade for

breakfast. Then they put on their coats and set off early.

On the way to the seaside they saw a toad sitting right in the middle

of the road. Dad had to get out of the car to lift him up. He put him

under an oak tree at the side of the road. The toad croaked and

croaked.

Then Noah started moaning that the journey was taking too long.

Mum said, "Don't moan and groan Noah. We will soon be there."

The sun was roasting hot when they got to the coast, but soon their

boat was floating in the foaming sea.

Find the 'oa' words in this story.

Read the words - listen to the sound for 'oa'

oats	boat	road	toad
toast	roast	moan	oak
coast	groan	throat	goat

ea

Mrs. Mead, our class teacher planned a trip to the beach. We took a beach ball and our swimsuits.

At the beach our teacher sat on a seat and took out her beach bag. She put on her cream sun hat. She reached inside her beach bag and took out a peach for each of us. She put sun cream on us to stop the heat of the sun from burning our skin

We played football with the beach ball in teams of two. Sometimes we had to leap for the ball and would land in a heap on the sand. My team beat the other team and after the game Mrs. Mead treated us all to an ice cream. She had a cup of tea.

When our teacher had finished reading her paper, she took us into the sea for a swim. She told us to stay really close to her to be safe. Suddenly she shouted, "Look there's a seal way out there!"

We all looked and yes there was a seal – what a treat to spot a seal in the ocean.

We all had a really good time at the beach and when I got home, I had my tea and went to bed dreaming of seals.

Find the 'ea' words in this story.

Read the words - listen to the sound for 'ea'

tea	each	teacher	beach
sea	seal	cream	read
meal	peach	heat	peas

ir

It was the third of May and the birds were singing. The sun was shining and Kirk was really happy because it was his birthday. His mum and dad were taking him and his girlfriend Shirley to the circus.

Kirk put on a clean shirt and went down for breakfast. He squirted some milk on his cornflakes and stirred his mug of tea.

On the table was a big red box.

"This is a birthday present from us," said his mum.

"You are thirteen today and I firmly believe you will like this," said Dad.

Kirk was so excited. He opened the box and inside was a virtual reality headset.

"WOW," said Kirk. "This is cool. I can confirm that this is the best birthday present I have ever had!"

Find the 'ir' words in this story.

Read the words - listen to the sound for 'ir'

girl	shirt	bird	fir
first	circus	stir	chirp
thirty	thirteen	skirt	birth

30

or

Mr. Cornwall lived in the forest in a small cottage. He had two horses called Boris and Norman. One stormy night he took his torch when he went out to check that his horses were all safe in their stables.

It was a short walk to the stables but on his way he saw an adorable little pig tied by a cord to a tree.

"Well, well, little porky pig where did you come from?" said Mr. Cornwall. "How would you like to live with me? I will call you Gordon."

"Thank you," said the adorable pig.

Mr. Cornwall was so shocked that the pig could speak and he said, "Goodness me! Some people would give a fortune to hear a little pig speak."

"Well, I will give you a fortune and you can call yourself Lord Cornwall," said Gordon.

The little pig gave three snorts. Suddenly, Mr. Cornwall's cottage turned into a large fort and he had more money than he could count.

So, this is how Lord Cornwall made his fortune and gave Gordon, the talking pig, a home.

Find the 'or' words in this story.

Read the words - listen to the sound for 'or'

born	corn	for	short	fork
horse	torn	pork	snort	story
fort	forty	worn	sport	torch

OW

Dad was mowing the lawn and the grass was blowing all over Mum's snowdrops. She was looking out of the window and yelled.

"My snowdrops will be covered in all the bits of grass blown from your mower. Why don't you put the cover on and mow more slowly?"

A big fat crow was sitting in the tree looking for worms. He was looking at Dad as he put the cover on the mower. Suddenly, he spied a big fat worm slowly wriggling below the mower. He swooped down and lowered his beak to the ground. He picked up the wiggly worm and before long he had flown away to his own nest.

When dad had finished mowing the lawn, lots of birds came to look for worms. There were swallows, crows and sparrows all pecking at the grass.

Find the 'ow' words in this story.

Read the words - listen to the sound for 'ow'

snow	blow	crow	grow	show
low	mow	know	flow	bow
throw	glow	narrow	own	sow

ou

Asif paid three pounds for his pet mouse. He called his mouse Boris.

Boris was so little and only weighed a few ounces.

Asif kept him in a small cage full of mounds of paper to keep him warm and cosy. Boris loved to scrounge around and he made himself a little nest in the paper so he could sleep soundly.

Sometimes Asif let Boris out of his cage to play but his mum told him to be careful.

"I don't want that mouse to run around the house. He is a little scoundrel and he might get lost and not be found."

Asif taught Boris some tricks and soon Boris could spin around, jump over a mound of sand and bounce on top of a ball.

Asif was really proud of Boris.

Find the 'ou' words in this story.

Read the words - listen to the sound for 'ou'

mouse	house	ground	about	out
sound	scrounge	mound	found	loud
shout	spout	bounce	crouch	pound

ur

I met a funny little man in the woods on Thursday. He had curly hair and purple skin and really big furry ears. He had purple fur on his hands and feet.

'Do not be afraid,' I said. 'I will not hurt you.'

He told me his name was Burb and that he had come from another planet called Saturn. He said he was lost and he was looking for his spaceship in the woods. The ship was going to return to his planet on Saturday and so he did not have much time.

I said that if we burn some twigs and make some smoke, the smoke would burst up into the air and his friends from the spaceship would see the smoke curling up and they would come and find him.

Sure enough, when his friends saw the smoke from the burning twigs they turned up and took him back to the spaceship.

On Saturday they all returned to their planet, Saturn.

Find the 'ur' words in this story.

Read the words - listen to the sound for 'ur'

burnt	burn	curl	curly	fur
purple	church	turkey	purse	Thursday
Saturday	hurt	nurse	turn	turnip

oi

Meg and her dad wanted to spoil Mum on her birthday, so they decided to roast a joint for Sunday lunch. Their choice was roasted pork because mum liked pork. They put the loin of pork in the pan and covered it with olive oil. Then they wrapped it in foil to keep it moist. They boiled some potatoes first and then put them in the oven to roast. They also decided to have some boiled carrots and peas.

When the joint was cooked Dad hoisted it out of the oven. It looked delicious and they had not spoilt it. They kept their voices very quiet and did not make a noise as they set the table for lunch. Soon they heard mum's voice.

"Can I join you?" she asked, "Oh my goodness, this looks wonderful!" She was so pleased when she saw the loin of pork on the table.

Find the 'oi' words in this story.

Read the words - listen to the sound for 'oi'

oil	boil	spoil	joint	foil
coil	coin	point	join	toil
toilet	avoid	poison	poilt	soil

igh

It was fireworks night and the children could not wait for night-time to come, when the sky would be dark. Dad was going to light the fireworks in the garden, and they were going to stay right away from them to be safe. He put the dog in the house so he would not be frightened. Mum said they could hold some bright sparklers, but they must hold them tight and not fight with them.

Dad lit the fireworks and it was a beautiful sight to see them brighten up the sky. The rockets went up so high.

When the fireworks were finished, it started to rain and then a storm came. They all went inside and looked through the window. They saw a bright lightning flash in the sky. It was just like having more fireworks. They were not frightened and by midnight they were all tucked up tight in their beds with the moonlight shining through the window.

Find the 'igh' words in this story.

Read the words - listen to the sound for 'igh'

high	sigh	light	knight
bright	night	fight	fright
sight	might	right	frighten

ow

Bozo the clown came into the circus ring. The crowds were howling with laughter at the clowns, but Bozo was not laughing. He was not looking happy. He had a big frown on his face because a circus cow had eaten the flowers on his hat. He walked around the circus ring scowling at the children, but they just laughed and laughed. What Bozo did not see was that there was a big bucket of water hanging from a tower over his head. The cow was walking behind Bozo so he could not see him. However, the children could see the cow and they laughed and laughed. Suddenly, the cow pushed the tower and the bucket of water tipped up and showered down on Bozo. He was drowned in water and the children laughed even more.

Find the 'ow' words in this story.

Read the words - listen to the sound for 'ow'

now	cow	clown	frown	brown
crowd	gown	growl	tower	shower
flower	how	brow	howl	towel

aw

My cat has very soft paws. but her claws are awfully sharp. One morning just as dawn was breaking, I looked out of my bedroom window and I saw her sprawled out on the lawn. She had something in her jaws. She had her claws in it. What was it? Was it some straw from the rabbit hutch? Was it a mouse? No, I could see it was a raw prawn! Where did she get that?

I crept downstairs and saw the fridge door was open. There was a pot of coleslaw on the floor and a bag of prawns. The mess was awful. How did this happen?

I called my mum and then ran into the garden, but my cat was fast and she saw me coming. She ran so fast she slipped and fell in the pond. It was so funny to see her all covered in frogspawn with the prawn still in her mouth. She looked awful as she crawled out of the pond. My mum was not very happy with her.

Find the 'aw' words in this story.

Read the words - listen to the sound for 'aw'

saw	straw	claw	draw	lawn
prawn	raw	dawn	sprawl	crawl
spawn	yawn	squawk	gnaw	awful

46

ew

Mrs. Hewitt took her class on a trip to Kew Gardens. They knew it was going to be fun because lots of strange plants grew there. They all climbed onto the new coach and Mrs. Hewitt said, "No chewing gum on this coach."

They threw their bags onto the luggage racks and a few children dashed for the back seats. Mrs. Hewitt sat at the front and read her newspaper.

Soon they were at Kew Gardens. Mrs. Hewitt showed them a very old yew tree. "Yew trees are often seen in churchyards," she told them. Then the children went into a very warm glass house to view some of the strange plants. Andrew said, "Phew, it's really hot in here."

"Come on Andrew," said Mrs. Hewitt, "We will soon be outside. Look, this plant looks like it is covered in jewels."

At lunchtime the children sat chewing their sandwiches under the yew tree. The next day Mrs. Hewitt asked the children to write about their trip to Kew Gardens and the funny plants that grew there.

Find the 'ew' words in this story.

Read the words - listen to the sound for 'ew'

new	blew	stew	grew	flew
crew	screw	news	chew	knew
threw	jewels	brew	phew	drew

au/augh

Maureen and Audrey were friends. At the end of the lane, where they both lived, was an old house. It was empty, and nobody had lived there for years. People said it was haunted. It was said that on Halloween night you could see the ghost of a witch in the garden stirring her cauldron.

One August evening, in the summer holidays, Maureen and Audrey went to explore the old house. They did not want to get caught so they crept quietly into the garden and up to the front door. Maureen pushed the door and it creaked open. They stepped inside. It was very dark. Suddenly a voice in the dark shouted "Who are you?".

Maureen and Audrey nearly jumped out of their skins. All the lights went on and they could see cameras and spotlights and a person dressed as a witch.

"We have an audience," said the voice. "Come in girls. I am the film director. We are making a film about a haunted house. It will be launched this year."

Maureen and Audrey were really excited. They sat all afternoon watching the actors and got all their autographs before they went home.

Find the 'au' words in this story.

Read the words - listen to the sound for 'au'

August	haunt	Autumn	cause	launch
daughter	author	saucer	autograph	caught
audience	sauce	cauldron	fault	laundry

COMPREHENSION WORKSHEETS

a-e

1. What did Grace love to do?

....

2. What did she make for her friend Jade?

....

3. What did Grace put on the top of the cake?

....

4. What did Grace use to make Jade's face on the cake?

....

5. What did Jade do when she saw the cake?

....

Write two of your own sentences using some of the 'a-e' words.

....

....

i-e

1. Who loved to ride his bike?

....

2. What colour was Mike's bike?

....

3. Where did Mike and his dad go for a ride?

....

4. How far did they ride?

....

5. What time did they set off for their ride?

....

6. What did dad buy Mike when they got to the pine forest?

....

Write two of your own sentences using some of the 'i-e' words.

....

i-e ....

o-e

1. What did Mole ask Rabbit?

....

2. How did Mole lose his home?

....

3. What made Mole choke when his home exploded?

....

4. How did Mole feel when his home was gone?

....

5. What did Rabbit say that Mole must not do in his home?

....

6. What time did Mole say he would be on his way?

....

Write two of your own sentences using some of the 'o-e' words.

....

o-e ....

u-e

1. Why did Sue want a rescue dog?

....

2. How did Dad and Sue get up to London?

....

3. What was the dog's name?

....

4. What colour was the dog?

....

5. What did Dad ask Sue when she said she wanted the dog?

....

6. What colour was the collar that Sue bought for the dog?

....

Write two of your own sentences using some of the 'u-e' words.

....

u-e ....

oo

1. What was the name of the person who went to the moon?

....

2. What did he put on before he went to the moon?

....

3. What did he see on the way?

....

4. What did the moon men look like?

....

5. What did their houses look like?

....

6. Why was Glen so happy?

....

Write two of your own sentences using some of the 'oo' words.

....

....

ee

1. Who was driving his jeep along the country lane?

....

2. What did Mr. Keen see in the field?

....

3. How many sheep came up to Mr. Green?

....

4. Where was the farmer hiding?

....

5. Why did the farmer colour the sheep's coats green?

....

6. How many 'ee' words are there in this story?

....

Write two of your own sentences using some of the 'ee' words.

....

....

ar

Read the story and answer these questions in full sentences.

1. What was the name of Arthur's dog?

....

2. What did Arthur's dog love to do?

....

3. Where did Arthur, his dad and the dog go in the car?

....

4. What things were for sale in the market?

....

5. What did Sparky do when he saw another dog?

....

6. Where did Sparky have to stay the night as a punishment?

....

Write two of your own sentences using some of the 'ar' words.

....

ar ....

ay

Read the story and answer these questions in full sentences.

1. Where does Ben live?

....

2. How did Ben and Sanjay have fun?

....

3. What did Ben and Sanjay find?

....

4. What did they call the dog?

....

5. What did the dog do?

....

6. How long was the dog with Ben and Sanjay?

....

Write two of your own sentences using some of the 'ay' words.

....

ay ....

ai

1. What happened to Daisy on Monday?

....

2. How did Daisy get home?

....

3. How long did Daisy have to stay at home?

....

4. What did Daisy like to do?

....

5. What did Daisy paint?

....

6. Who did Daisy show her pictures to at school?

....

Write two of your own sentences using some of the 'ai' words.

....

....

oa

1. What did Dad do with all the bags?

....

2. What did Dad tie to the roof?

....

3. What kind of food did Mum make to take with them?

....

4. What did everyone have for breakfast?

....

5. What did they see in the road on the way to the seaside?

....

6. What kind of noise did the toad make?

....

Write two of your own sentences using some of the 'oa' words.

....

....

ea

1. Where did the teacher take the children?

....

2. What did the children do on the beach?

....

3. What did the teacher give the children to eat?

....

4. What did the children see in the sea?

....

5. What did the children see in the sky?

....

6. What did the teacher have to drink?

....

Write two of your own sentences using some of the 'ea' words.

....

ea ....

ir

1. What month of the year was it at the start of this story?

....

2. Whose birthday was it?

....

3. What did Kirk put on before he went down to breakfast?

....

4. How old was Kirk?

....

5. What did Kirk get for his birthday present?

....

6. What present would you like for your next birthday?

....

Write two of your own sentences using some of the 'ir' words.

....

ir...

63

or

1. Where did Mr. Cornwall live?

    ....

2. What were the names of his horses?

    ....

3. What did Mr. Cornwall call the little pig?

    ....

4. What noise did the pig make before he turned the cottage into a fort?

    ....

5. What would you have wished for?

    ....

Write two of your own sentences using some of the 'or' words.

....

....

OW

1. What was Dad doing at the beginning of the story?

....

2. Where was all the grass from the mower going?

....

3. Who was sitting in the tree watching Dad?

....

4. Where was the worm?

....

5. How was the worm moving?

....

6. Name the three kinds of birds in this story.

....

Write two of your own sentences using some of the 'ow' words.

....

ow ....

ou

1. What is Boris?

....

2. How much did Asif pay for Boris?

....

3. How much did Boris weigh?

....

4. What did Asif put in the cage for Boris?

....

5. What did Asif's mum say to him?

....

6. Name one trick that Boris could do?

....

Write two of your own sentences using some of the 'ou' words.

....

ou
....

ur

1. What did the funny little man in the woods look like?

....

2. What was his name?

....

3. What planet did the little man come from?

....

4. When did he have to return to his planet?

....

5. How did his friends find him?

....

6. Why do you think the spaceship came to earth?

....

Write two of your own sentences using some of the 'ur' words.

....

ur ....

oi

1. What did Meg and her Dad want to do for Mum?

....

2. What did they plan to cook for lunch?

....

3. How did they cook the carrots and peas?

....

4. What did they do with the potatoes after they boiled them?

....

5. How did they make sure Mum could not hear them?

....

6. How did they know that Mum was coming down the stairs?

....

Write two of your own sentences using some of the 'oi' words.

....

oi ....

igh

1. Why were the children excited?

....

2. What did Mum say they could hold?

....

3. What did Mum say they must not do?

....

4. When Dad lit the rockets where did they go?

....

5. What lit up the sky when the storm came?

....

6. By what time were they all tucked up in bed?

....

Write two of your own sentences using some of the 'igh' words.

....

igh ....

ow

Read the story and answer these questions in full sentences.

1. Who is Bozo?

....

2. How do you know that Bozo was not happy?

....

3. Who had eaten the flowers on his hat?

....

4. What did Bozo do as he walked around the circus ring?

....

5. Where was the bucket of water?

....

6. What happened to Bozo when the bucket fell?

....

Write two of your own sentences using some of the 'ow' words.

....

....

aw

1. What do cats have on the end of their paws?

....

2. What was the cat doing at the beginning of the story?

....

3. What did the cat have in her jaws?

....

4. What was on the floor near the fridge?

....

5. What was the cat covered in when he was in the pond?

....

6. How many words did you find with the sound 'aw' in them.?

....

Write two of your own sentences using some of the 'aw' words.

....

aw ....

ew

1. Where did Mrs. Hewitt take her class for a visit?

....

2. What were they not allowed to do on the coach?

....

3. What did Mrs. Hewitt read on the coach?

....

4. What did Mrs. Hewitt show the children at Kew Gardens?

....

5. Who said it was hot in the glass house?

....

6. What did Mrs. Hewitt ask the children to write about?

....

Write two of your own sentences using some of the 'ew' words.

....

....

au

1. What did people say about the old house?

....

2. In what season of the year is Halloween night?

....

3. What was the witch stirring in the garden?

....

4. In what month of the year did the girls explore the house?

....

5. What did the film director say as the girls walked in?

....

6. What did Maureen and Audrey get from the actors before they went home?

....

Write two of your own sentences using some of the 'au' words.

....

....

OVERLEARNING WORKSHEETS

Overlearning worksheets

These worksheets provide extra practice and encourage the learner to think for themselves rather than just fill in words.
The exercises in this section cover the following thinking activities;

- Word searches which encourage visual recognition of the phonic patterns being taught.

- Fill in missing words to encourage spelling within a meaningful sentence.

- Practice spelling rules associated with these sounds e.g. Add a final 'e' to words with short vowels to create a long vowel sound.

- Match words to their meanings.

- Make decisions about similar phonic sounds.

- Identify real words from non-words.

- Proof reading.

- Identify words from their meaning as in crossword puzzles.

a-e

Unscramble these words. Use your letter tiles to make the words, then write the words you have made.

ames   _____   rabve   _____

ceam   _____   agerp   _____

cefa   _____   pacse   _____

Word Search for a-e words

cake	bake	take	made	space
race	came	name	same	hate

d b p n i x h q b t k c n b

o d m a d e n m r b b c t u

u y q u u q g p g m h a t e

r b a k e s q j j h s i m h

r g t v o t g t e r p a k d

a j g t a k e i n n a m e z

c a k e w a p o a w c h s g

e r c a m e s a m e e o u p

Add an 'e'. Does it make a real word? Say the new word then write it.

cam + e =   cap + e =   sam + e =

tap + e =   mad + e =   hat + e =

Write two sentences using some of the <u>new</u> words you have made.

1 ....

2 ....

Fill in the missing words.

    1. Mum baked a _____ for my birthday.

    2. I do not like peas, I _____ them.

    3. The rocket went into _____ .

    4. Do not leave the garden _____ open, the dog will get out.

Read the story aloud and add an 'e' to the words that need an 'e'

Pam cam into the shop. She wanted to buy some graps but they did not have any left, so she bought some home mad cakes. When she got home, she at two of the cakes.

Draw a plate with some dates and grapes on it.

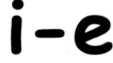 **i-e**

Unscramble these words. Use your letter tiles to make the words, then write the words you have made.

zipre _____

emin _____

iser _____

etirw _____

lcise _____

kihe _____

i-e word search

| ice | like | nice | hide | ride |
| side | write | wise | bite | slide |

```
b v e i y s d t z j x h q u
h j v c o i w b r u q x j j
i s l o i d w w i s e f g y
d w l f s e r s m b k w o t
e r i d e i i l f i h k y i
e l i k e c t i m t p r a g
u a f e m e e d p e y y d e
n i c e i h x e p x k o y r
```

78

Add an 'e'. Does it make a real word? Say the new word then write it.

bit + e =   rip + e =   spin + e =

trip + e =   slim + e =   pip + e =

Write two sentences using some of the <u>new</u> i-e words you have made.

1 ....

2 ....

Fill in the missing words.

1. I like to ride my_____ .

2. Do not slip on the _____ .

3. We played _____ and seek.

4. A clock tells the _____ .

Circle the word that is correct.

1. This apple is very (rip ripe).

2. The teacher told us to stand in a (lin line).

3. This dog can (bite bit).

Draw three mice.

o-e

Unscramble these words. Use your letter tiles to make the words, then write the words you have made.

sore   _____   honpe   _____

olpse   _____   bolge   _____

hrteno _____   msoke   _____

o-e word search

rode	smoke	rose	hope	slope
joke	mole	rope	joke	bone

```
s l o p e b o n e a c n n f
o x y t z h j o k e l h b d
s g b m o l e x m y l k p o
s s b x g y r o d e l r j e
v z r o s e h c j e j o k e
t u a a b o u x s d a p z h
s m o k e x u i g d g e f s
m e b b q o z k n h o p e g
```

80

Add an 'e'. Does it make a real word? Say the new word then write it.

rod + e =   slop + e =   pop + e =

rob + e =   not + e =   hop + e =

Write two sentences using some of the <u>new</u> words you have made.

1 ....

2 ....

Read this sentence and correct the four spelling mistakes you find.

I brok a bon in my hand when I fell down a steep slop. I hop it will be better soon.

How many o-e words can you make with the following letters.
Use your letter tiles to help you.

p s r f j m k s t v n l

	o		e
	o		e
	o		e
	o		e
	o		e
	o		e
	o		e
	o		e
	o		e

Write the words you have made.

....

....

u-e

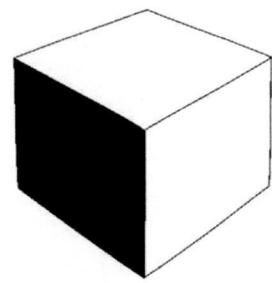

Unscramble these words. Use your letter tiles to make the words, then write the words you have made.

reul   _____   neJu   _____

unte   _____   ucbe   _____

kdue   _____   usef   _____

u-e word search

cube	tube	tune	rude	huge
use	June	excuse	amuse	rule

```
h t u b e y c t t c l w n
t r u d e f a m e k k m x j
a z q f w r q h i g e u s e
m o m y a u m r a e u r c t
u y p j v l q j y m f t u b
s q g y f e g u h q y u b n
e e x c u s e n k k u n e e
s s v c c t t e c t q e q j
```

Add an 'e'. Does it make a real word? Say the new word then write it.

cub + e =   us + e =   cut + e =   hug + e =

Write two sentences using some of the <u>new</u> words you have made.

1 ....

2 ....

Put the right word in the space:

1. The cake is too hot to ....(cute cut clut).

2. Put an ice ....(cub cube crub) in your drink.

Solve this crossword puzzle using magic 'e' (split digraph) words

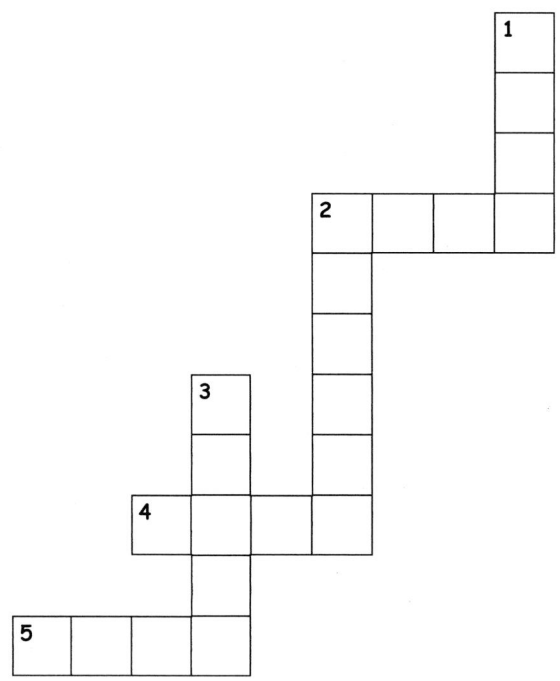

Across

2. You can play this on the piano.

4. You tie things up with this.

5. This months comes after May.

Down

1. We put candles on this on our birthday.

2. A queen sits on this.

3. This comes out of a chimney.

83

oo

Unscramble these words. Use your letter tiles to make the words, then write the words you have made.

poson _____   chosol _____

mostoh _____   obtos _____

nomo _____   ymoglo _____

oo word search

moon	spoon	boom	school	choose
hoot	boot	zoom	pool	fool

t t m b s f o o l v f a r m

m z o o p b o o t d l o s n

k o o o o c h o o s e h a p

l o n m o d a p v x c o b m

q m g m n k a a t v i o q f

u s q h h d j d o p m t y r

p o o l j x q b c z i a r z

s c h o o l q l s o m u i o

84

Unjumble the sentences and write them correctly.

1. day I Every school. to go ....

2. I spoon. my a eat soup with ....

Put a circle around the words that are not real words.

moon   coos   spoon   poon   scoop

shoom   shoot   stool   tool   sprool

Solve this crossword using 'oo' words

Across

3. This is a noise a rocket makes.

4. This is where you go to learn.

5. We sweep the floor with this.

Down

1. Not rough.

2. You can swim in this.

4. Use this to eat soup.

ee

Unscramble these words. Use your letter tiles to make the words, then write the words you have made.

eert _____

ebe _____

ethre _____

sene _____

peseh _____

rgene _____

ee word search

bee	see	deep	feel	sheep
street	green	tree	heel	feet

```
i  x  w  u  v  l  p  e  d  e  e  p  d  i
u  z  h  e  e  l  b  v  f  y  s  p  z  q
x  i  s  t  r  e  e  t  y  f  b  g  v  z
m  s  w  s  h  t  k  c  i  l  s  p  f  q
y  c  t  h  g  r  e  e  n  p  g  c  e  t
t  z  z  e  y  k  s  a  r  o  s  d  e  r
s  f  e  e  t  r  e  w  b  e  e  n  l  e
h  k  l  p  h  q  e  l  k  q  g  p  f  e
```

Fill in the missing 'ee' words

1. There are seven days in a ....

2. I got stung by a ....

3. The grass is .... and the sky is blue.

4. Will you .... this floor with a broom.

5. Here comes the king and ....

Circle the words that are not real words:

queen   creep   greez   green   steep   sreet

heel   feel   peen   speed   geep   bee

Find the words that go together and join them with a line.

pink   sheep

green   cheese

white   seeds

yellow   tree

brown   cheeks

Draw three trees and a queen dressed in green in the box below.

ar

Unscramble these words. Use your letter tiles to make the words, then write the words you have made.

afremr _____   rabk _____

dagren _____   pasrk _____

trat _____   rkda _____

ar word search

car	start	garden	far	park
bark	farm	arm	hard	yard

u f d h t m d o x y x f c j

h a r d g y k o b t x z a q

v r j b a l f z a x x s r z

o y y o r h f a r m v t j a

f x a w d c y i k g e a e v

e a r m e k e w k w r r m v

y z d z n p a r k i s t r a

i d e e d q t j p p x e y m

88

Answer the questions yes or no

1. A farmer lives in the park.   yes   no

2. Sharks have sharp teeth.   yes   no

3. Apple tarts are good to eat.   yes   no

4. All cars are red.   yes   no

5. Cars come in jars.   yes   no

Solve this crossword puzzle for 'ar' words

Across

4. He looks after the land and animals.

6. The noise a dog makes.

Down

1. They sparkle in the sky at night.

2. This fish has a big fin.

3. Someone who is clever.

5. Flowers grow here.

ay

Unscramble these words. Use your letter tiles to make the words, then write the words you have made.

layp _____   alcy _____

tasy _____   ysapr _____

ayw _____   hya _____

ay word search

| pay | day | stay | tray | play |
| clay | hay | may | stray | lay |

z t g y u y j b i b l a y p
s x f q e c l a y h i a x i
c c i t n p l a y a k l l s
h a y a h p j f b e a m m t
v p m d g r b b q l i a a r
g t y p a y x g y a k j y a
t r a y s t a y r w f a i y
d a y b n i z q e n d h a b

90

Fill in the missing words:

1. We go to church on ....

2. I like to .... football.

3. After April comes ....

4. We can make models out of ....

Read the words and put a circle around the real words

chay   play   stay   zay   fay   Sunday

clay   Friday   blay   slay   spray   shray

Circle the correct answers to these questions.

1. Is hay made of clay?   yes   no

2. Should you play in a car park?   yes   no

3. Is Sunday the day after Friday?   yes   no

4. Can you carry cups on a tray?   yes   no

5. Does June come after May?   yes   no

Match the words to the answers:

There are seven of these in a week.   Friday

To squirt water at something.   sway

The day before Saturday.   spray

To move from side to side.   days

91

ai

Unscramble these words. Use your letter tiles to make the words, then write the words you have made.

ilsa _____   inar _____

siparn _____   riban _____

siyad _____   tirna _____

ai word search

daisy	rain	paint	train	again
snail	brain	mermaid	trail	straight

```
t r a i n h l y t d m v n x
p u k c j v m u h o t o b d
p b d c k w r m e r m a i d
u q y t e p n u g x m g v p
a g a i n b r a i n r c f a
l l s i y g p s n a i l w i
r a i n v y t r a i l i q n
s t r a i g h t d a i s y t
```

Fill in the missing words:

1. The .... is in the station.

2. A fox has a bushy ....

3. My tummy hurts; I have a ....

4. A .... moves very slowly in the garden.

How many 'ai' words can you make with these letters?

p   t   r   s   n   l   m   f   a   i

....

Solve this crossword puzzle for 'ai' words

Across

2. Artists do this.

4. A lady with a fish tail.

6. This creature moves very slowly.

Down

1. You think with this.

3. This travels on rails.

5. A small white flower with a yellow centre.

oa

Unscramble these words. Use your letter tiles to make the words, then write the words you have made.

ogta   _____   obta   _____

ocats   _____   dota   _____

hotrat   _____   rogan   _____

oa word search

road	toad	toast	roast	throat
goat	moat	moan	groan	float

```
m f l o a t m o a t u g j v
o t h r o a t g c p v r l z
a t z x e n i o h q w o u h
n g x t d c e a y y h a r q
m y p d w a r t d k d s k l
g r o a n w o o r j d t q e
u o m y w t a a l c y m r a
i e g d e x d d l t o a s e
```

Fill in the missing words:

1. A boat can .... on water.

2. You drive a car on the ....

3. We have a .... dinner on Sunday.

4. I have a cold and a sore ....

Find the spelling mistakes in the following sentences.

There was a hoal in my boat. The boat did not flote. It sank to the bottom of the pond. I hoap I can fix it.

Unscramble these sentences and write them out correctly.

toad A in sat road. the ....

boat Can this on float water? ....

I soap. wash face my with ....

toast had I breakfast. my for ....

Write the answers.

This farm animal has a beard.   ....

This sails on water.   ....

Wear this to keep you warm.   ....

The sound a frog makes.   ....

What is porridge made with?   ....

ea

Unscramble these words. Use your letter tiles to make the words, then write the words you have made.

recam _____   epach _____

lesa _____   becah _____

psea _____   daer _____

ea word search

tea	teacher	beach	seal	cream
sea	meal	read	meat	speak

```
s e a l m e a l h p w c y q
f u m p e r s e a m m s c o
k b l n t e l s p u s p r k
y z t n e a x m e a t e e x
i h r f a d d s d a p a a z
y m x e m q i m i r f k m x
n c v t e a c h e r t s g m
c b q h y m b e a c h s b e
```

Fill in the missing words:

1. I can sit on this ....

2. I like to eat ice ....

3. Fish live in the ....

4. Sometimes when we sleep we ....

Unscramble these words and write the sentence correctly.

cup tea. like a I of ....

nice. teacher Our is...

like I read beach. to the on ....

Match the words to their meanings. Draw a line to connect them.

A drink with sugar and milk.   sea

Another word for ocean.   tea

When you say something.   read

What you do with a book.   speak

Circle the correct spellings.

- I feal/feel sick.

- Do not steel/steal my sweets.

- Pleese/please may I have another cake?

- I like to reed/read books.

ir

Unscramble these words. Use your letter tiles to make the words, then write the words you have made.

ifrts _____   krits _____

irgl _____   yrtiht _____

icucrs _____   thbri _____

ir word search

shirt	birthday	fir	sir	stir	circus
girl	firm	thirty	thirteen	thirsty	

```
c i r c u s g i r l v n d j
t h i r t e e n s k d s j o
f e t v x z f i r t j r e f
l z t h i r s t y u a d g i
f b k k w l s h i r t s i r
p f b a s d p t h i r t y m
c u z q k j f p n x d i h w
b i r t h d a y z l n r b k
```

98

Fill in the missing words:

1. The man wore a white .... and a blue tie.

2. The .... made a nest in the tree.

3. I came .... in the race.

4. It is my .... today. I am having a party.

Solve this crossword puzzle for 'ir' words

Across

2. The day you were born.

5. This creature can fly.

6. Clowns work here.

Down

1. The number that comes after twenty nine.

3. When you need a drink you are this.

4. The number that comes after twelve.

or

Unscramble these words. Use your letter tiles to make the words, then write the words you have made.

sohrt _____   prsot _____

ofrk _____   yosrt _____

yofrt _____   nbro _____

Or word search

for	fort	corn	born	story
horse	port	pork	snort	cord

c b o r n r n x q s y h r

o y p o r t i q p g q m o q

r p v j e u p g c j w h r d

d x p o r k h p r v g d s q

y o z h h d e f m w h v e i

w h w w x v n o e g f o r t

c o r n n s t o r y k u h h

s n o r t l a z z f o r g t

Write in the missing words:

1. I use a knife and .... to eat my dinner.

2. We had roast .... for Sunday lunch.

3. Can you take the dog .... a walk?

4. I hate thunder ....

Look at these words. Fill in the correct sound. Is it 'ar' or is it 'or' ?

c......   sh........k   c......n   n......th

p......k   sp......k   st......m   c......k

sh......t   f......m   sh......p   sn......t

Join the words to their meanings

These creatures sleep in a stable.   morning

The meat we get from a pig.   horses

The time of day when we wake up.   story

We read this in a book.   pork

Unscramble these sentences and write them correctly.

a Can eat horse corn? ....

I horse. a ride to like...

ship The sailed port. into ....

101

ow

Unscramble these words. Use your letter tiles to make the words, then write the words you have made.

oknw _____   norwra _____

hotrw _____   oflw _____

olsw _____   rarwo _____

ow word search

blow	bow	crow	snow	grow
sparrow	arrow	mow	glow	slow

```
w  l  a  u  b  o  w  o  v  g  i  y  s  t
k  s  p  a  r  r  o  w  v  y  x  w  l  f
f  x  h  j  f  n  f  s  n  o  w  s  o  a
g  l  o  w  c  o  j  m  f  g  r  o  w  r
c  r  o  w  m  a  m  v  n  n  w  y  j  r
g  u  t  a  o  l  f  u  v  a  p  n  k  o
i  b  l  o  w  b  s  c  v  t  w  j  f  w
w  a  d  n  i  i  p  p  n  g  w  t  e  m
```

Write in the missing words:

1. I can catch and .... a ball really well.

2. Flowers .... in the garden.

3. Can you .... up a balloon?

4. A snail moves very .... ly.

5. .... drops are spring flowers.

Draw a snowman and a crow sitting on a fence.

Circle the correct answers.

Is a sparrow a type of bird?	yes	no
Can you eat an arrow?	yes	no
Does a horse bark?	yes	no
Is snow white?	yes	no

ou

Unscramble these words. Use your letter tiles to make the words, then write the words you have made.

moesu _____   dnofu _____

uhose _____   cebuno _____

npudo _____   rocuhc _____

ou word search

out	shout	round	ground	mouse
pound	sound	loud	found	about

c u j o n l r q k q d h g t

s z r o f v m r o u n d g i

o o g u q f w w o f b s o s

u j b t a b o u t b f b b n

n v e m z y y c a s h o u t

d g r o u n d p o u n d b t

l o u d f o u n d p h z w d

d h n e l s m m o u s e a r

Fill in the missing words:

1. I can see fluffy .... in the sky.

2. My cat chased a ....

3. Come .... side in the garden.

4. My .... has three bedrooms.

Tick what a scout would take camping

His scout hat   A pet mouse   A ground sheet

A large house   A sour lemon   A pound of beef

Solve this crossword for 'ou' words

Across

2. A small creature that squeaks.

5. A place you live in.

6. The shape of a circle.

Down

1. Not inside.

3. One hundred pence.

4. To speak really loudly.

ur

Unscramble these words. Use your letter tiles to make the words, then write the words you have made.

brnu   _____   ufr   _____

dasutrya   _____   suenr   _____

uprse   _____   cyulr   _____

ur word search

burn	burnt	curl	fur	Thursday
Saturday	church	turn	turnip	turkey

```
c t u r k e y a b i c n v z
u q y j e o t z u n h t n i
r m n r a d u n r y r u g n
l c j f t l f q n t u r n n
w r b e s u x l t y e n f f
s t u s a t u r d a y i f p
x i r t h u r s d a y p u v
w x n c h u r c h t a w r o
```

Write in the missing words:

1. Fire is hot it can ....

2. We eat .... at Christmas.

3. A .... works in the hospital.

4. Sally does not have straight hair, she has .... hair.

5. We play football on .... mornings.

Draw a burglar with curly hair, wearing a purple jumper and fur boots.

Fill in the correct spellings. Is it 'ur' or is it 'ir' ?

b.......d   c.........l   b.........n   st.........   g........l

Th........sday   sk.......t   ch.........ch   b.........thday   t.........n

oi

Unscramble these words. Use your letter tiles to make the words, then write the words you have made.

pisol _____   loci _____

polits _____   loib _____

vodai _____   ojint _____

oi word search

boil	coil	soil	spoil	coin
joint	avoid	ointment	foil	join

a t a e k j v s o i l m j v

v n w c o i l e w u x i b z

o j o i n t m e n t m s e o

i f k p t d o a d t h z p w

d p w g c s a t x c m v t g

b o i l s p o i l p u a o x

e x m t k f o i l f b v n j

l y s o d c c o i n j o i n

Fill in the missing words:

1. Eating sweets will .... your dinner.

2. We fry chips in cooking ....

3. I can .... up my writing.

4. We plant seeds in .... so they will grow.

5. I do not like swimming, I try to .... it.

Write two sentences of your own using some of these words:

boil   toilet   joint   joining   spoilt   oil   avoid   ointment

1...

2...

Link the words to their meanings.

When hot water starts to bubble.   spoilt

To put two things together.   oil

When something is ruined.   coil

At snake does this.   boil

We cook chips in this.   join

When we hear the sound 'oi' at the end of a word we always use 'oy'. Read the following words to check this out:

boy   toy   joy   annoy   destroy   enjoy   cowboy

igh

Unscramble these words. Use your letter tiles to make the words, then write the words you have made.

inhgt _____

ihgh _____

ikgnht _____

ibrght _____

sghit _____

gfhti _____

igh word search

high	sigh	light	knight	bright
night	fright	sight	might	right

```
j  v  v  v  n  k  n  m  i  g  h  t  t
t  p  d  a  g  f  h  i  c  l  m  i  a  o
c  i  x  k  h  z  p  v  u  i  j  g  k  l
x  u  b  b  r  i  g  h  t  g  s  h  h  y
u  s  z  t  c  k  l  q  q  h  i  g  l  j
r  i  g  h  t  t  v  q  d  t  g  g  s  c
n  i  g  h  t  d  f  r  i  g  h  t  c  q
k  n  i  g  h  t  s  i  g  h  t  a  h  t
```

Fill in the missing words:

1. I go to bed at ....

2. The sun is very ....

3. I have at left hand and at .... hand.

4. A mountain is very ....

5. The .... slayed the dragon.

Unscramble the sentences and write them correctly.

right after Turn shop. the pet ....

had I fright a the in night. ....

Solve this crossword for 'igh' words

Across

1. Not dull.

3. He wears a suit of armour.

6. To scare someone.

Down

2. Not low.

4. This follows day.

5. Take a deep breath and then release it.

ow

Unscramble these words. Use your letter tiles to make the words, then write the words you have made.

wcrod _____

folwre _____

who _____

eltwo _____

wlcon _____

nfrwo _____

ow word search

cow	now	brow	frown	clown
crown	drown	growl	how	brown

```
f r o w n v k a v c e o b z
d h q b d m m w d o n l l b
w i h q p e h o w w n b n r
y e d o k o c d d g o r g o
g o f e w u q b z w w o r w
c l o w n k g g x b o w o n
b s c r o w n i z b j o w a
v n i h n d r o w n r b l t
```

Fill in the missing words:

1. We get milk from a ....

2. Dogs .... when they are angry.

3. The queen wears a ....

4. Can you show me .... to do this?

Read these words and draw a circle around the real words.

growl   prown   browt   brown   prowt

crowd   slowt   down   scowl   row

Can you guess the answers using 'ow' words?

You stand under this to get clean. ....

When you are cross you do this. ....

What are roses, tulips, daffodils called? ....

A word for many people in one place. ....

Draw a colourful clown

113

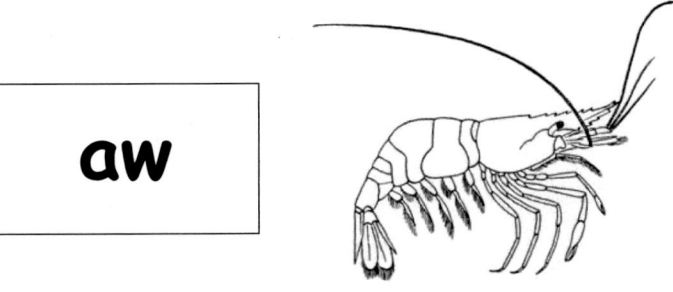

aw

Unscramble these words. Use your letter tiles to make the words, then write the words you have made.

wparn _____   pslawr _____

wrcal _____   aulwf _____

wcal _____   sawrt _____

aw word search

saw	straw	awful	lawn	prawn
yawn	dawn	gnaw	claw	draw

s l c l a w d r a w u z o g

t a d s y a w n y a r u k f

r w a h l q q i t s i s g v

a n w z p s f p v z l i g e

w m n p r a w n v e q j r m

m p g c u w j n e n a n q a

d q t g n a w g o l a r o k

u s a w f u l t v m f o r b

114

Fill in the missing words:

1. This food tastes ....

2. .... are small shellfish.

3. When someone .... they are often very tired.

4. The parrot gave a loud ....

Correct the spelling mistakes in this story. Can you find 7 mistakes? Write the correct spelling over the words in a red pen.

When we went on holiday to Spayn, we sor so many beeches. It was really hot and we had to put on sun creem in case we got birnt. Some of the food was nice but some of it was orful.

Unscramble these sentences and write them correctly.

I prawn. saw pink a ....

The sprawled on cat the lawn. ....

....

Draw lion a sharp with claws. ....

Match the sentences to their meanings:

Something that is not nice.	draw
These are rules.	paws
Delicious red fruit.	awful
Cats have four of them.	laws
An artist can do this.	strawberries

115

ew

Unscramble these words. Use your letter tiles to make the words, then write the words you have made.

ehcw _____   wcrse _____

ejlesw _____   ehrtw _____

efwl _____   kenw _____

ew word search

new	blew	stew	grew	flew
crew	screw	chew	threw	jewels

```
f o y s v d s r k y e j g n
n h q b m x l b e l z b s e
e r b l e w n l g i f q c w
s c r e w x k x m k c r e w
c h e w y j b e v v u s p q
u s t e w y z a j e w e l s
g r e w t h r e w v k f m l
n n a g e f l e w q q c p v
```

116

Fill in the missing words:

1. The burglar grabbed the .... from the shop window.

2. I .... a ball into the water.

3. I .... all the answers to the questions.

4. The bird .... away when we got close to him.

Is it 'oo' or is it 'ew'? Fill in the correct letters.

bl......   kn.......   br......m   thr......

dr......p   sh......t   st......   j......el

Solve this crossword puzzle for 'ew' words

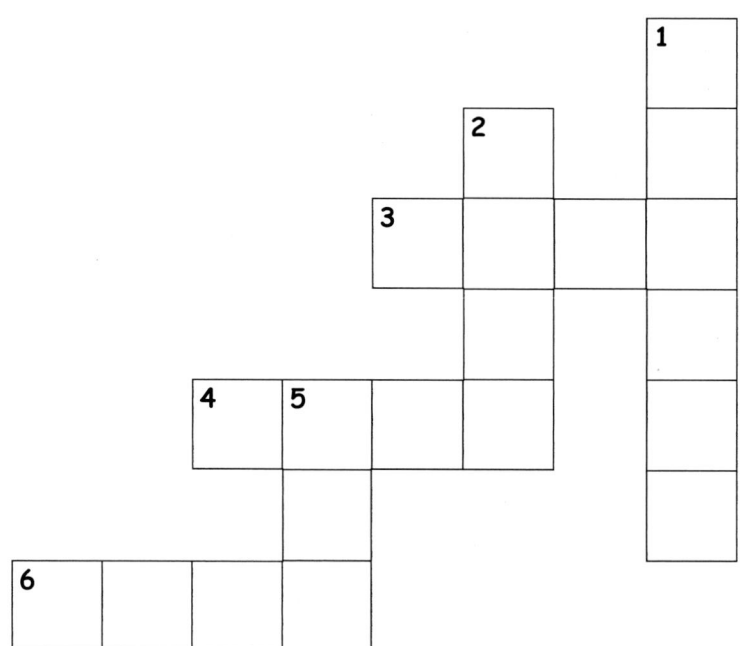

Across

3. How you put the candles out.

4. He understood how to do it.

6. To munch your food.

Down

1. These are sparkling gems.

2. How the bird left the tree.

5. Not old.

au

au word search

caught	sauce	haunt	August	Autumn
daughter	cause	author	launch	saucer

```
p t y l h b c y c a u g h t
l p j l a u n c h q b e x a
n a u g u s t s a u c e r u
h e i v n d a u g h t e r t
a f p r t l w w m y s z t u
p u i g f l j h y z i n u m
c a u s e z p t a t s y e n
s a u c e a u t h o r z d a
```

Join the words to their meanings:

A season of the year.   saucer

A month of the year.   audience

People who are watching a show.   Autumn

You rest your cup on this.   August

118

Fill in the missing words:

1. The house was .... by a ghost.

2. The month after July is ....

3. My dad .... a large fish with his fishing rod.

4. The food tastes ....

5. I like tomato .... on my burger.

Is it 'or' 'aw' or 'au' ? Fill in the correct letters.

h......nted   f......k   l......   s......ce   p......k

pr......n   str......   st......y   l......n   ......gust

Draw: A flying saucer   **A haunted house**

OVERLEARNING GAMES

Snakes and ladders game

Aim: To practise spellings from word families taught.

Material required: A base board/coloured counters/ a dice/ a pile of word cards using words from the phonic families that have been taught.

How to play: Each player chooses a coloured counter and then throws the dice. They must move their counter along the equivalent number of spaces.

If a player lands on a red circle the teacher takes a card from the pile of cards and reads it out. The player must spell or write the word. It the player is successful they can move two spaces forward. If they land on a square with a ladder, they can go up the ladder and claim their two extra spaces as well.

If a player lands on a snake they must slither down the snake.

Use this game board for practice when several word families have been taught or to reinforce one or two of them.

Snakes and ladders game

Finish

spoil

Start

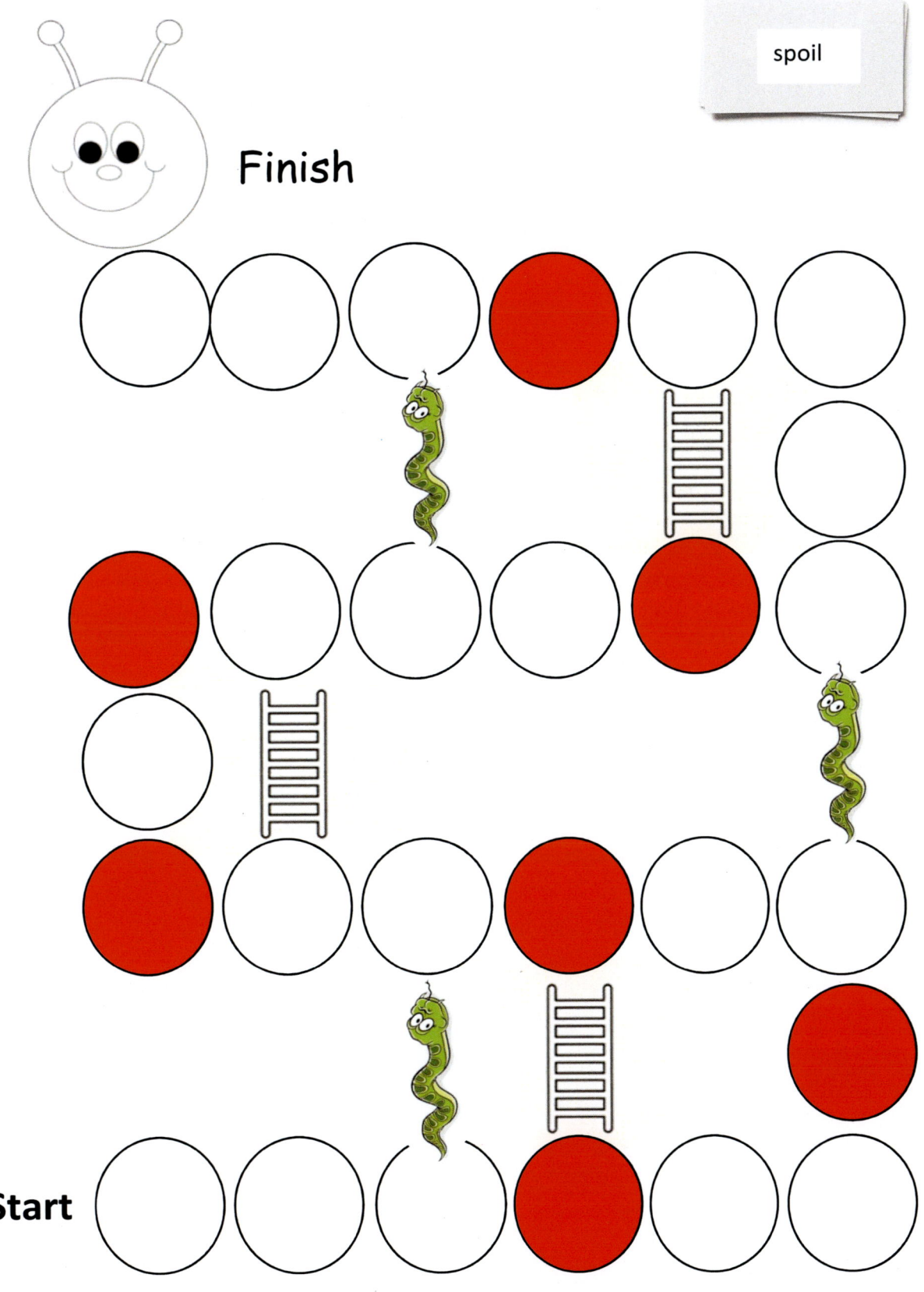

122

Bingo

Aim: To encourage the learner to make spelling choices.

Materials: Create bingo boards with a variety of phonic sounds

How to Play: The teacher calls out a word and players must put a counter on the sound pattern they think is in that spoken word. They must spell or write the word.

Three correct answers in a row wins the game

ai	ee	ou
or	a-e	oo
oa	ea	o-e

ur	au	or
ar	ew	oi
oa	ea	ai

ay	au	or
ar	u-e	oi
oa	ea	ee

Split Digraph Game

Aim: To encourage the learner to listen for the vowel sound and how it changes with the addition of an 'e'.

Materials: 2 sets of cards. One set uses only three letter (CVC) words. The second set uses split digraph words.

How to Play: Deal 8 cards to each player. The player must sort their cards into sets saying the three -letter word and then the word with the additional 'e'. If they cannot match their cards they must ask another player if they have a matching card. The winner is the one to get rid of all their cards.

sam	rip	rat	same	ripe	rate
rod	bit	cub	rode	bite	cube
tub	pip	pop	tube	pipe	pope
cut	hop	slid	cute	hope	slide
mad	hat	cop	made	hate	cope

CUMULATIVE SEQUENTIAL DICTATIONS

How to administer the dictations.

These simple dictations are presented in the order of the phonic patterns in the spelling stories.

Dictations are useful as a 'test' of automatic recall and should be administered at least one week after the word family has been taught and over learnt, and retention checked before moving onto a new word family. The dictation will test the learner's ability to retrieve phonic patterns without prompts.

N.B. ALWAYS use a pencil to write the dictation

1. Read the whole sentence aloud to the learner- do not read one word at a time as meaning is lost.

2. Ask the learner to repeat the sentence out loud keeping it active in short term memory - the sentences have been kept short to reduce load on auditory memory.

3. Ask the learner to write the sentence they have repeated - saying each word aloud as they write thus reinforcing the sounds they are recalling.

4. Ask the learner to read back what they have written looking for any spelling errors.

5. The teacher/helper can now read the learner's work and point out any missed errors- can the learner correct them?

6. If errors are found- rub out the whole word and write it again; this helps to reinforce the correct spelling.

a-e

1. 'Will you bake a cake for me?", said Sam.
2. I ate the grape on my plate.
3. I hate snakes but I love dates.
4. I put on a brave face when I cut my hand.

i-e

1. Can I have a nice slice of pie?
2. What is ice made of?
3. I like to ride my bike and win a prize.
4. Can I write with this red pen?

o-e

1. I broke the bone in my leg.
2. Smoke rose from the grate.
3. The slope on the slide was very wet.
4. I am late. Can I phone home?

u-e

1. There was a huge ice cube in my drink.
2. We went for a ride on the tube.
3. I like the hot sun in June.
4. I can play a tune on my flute.

oo

1. Soon we will be going to school.

2. Is it cool on the moon?

3. I have some red boots.

4. Cake is the best food.

ee

1. A bee sat on my boot.

2. The Duke came to my school.

3. I can see three green trees.

4. The queen sat on the throne.

ar

1. There is a green car in the car park.

2. The farmer had three sheep in his barn.

3. I had a scar on my arm.

4. We have a large garden.

ay

1. May I play in the yard?

2. Stay away from the park on Sunday.

3. Can you see your way in the dark?

4. Can I stay and play in the hay?

ai

1. I went to school on the train today.

2. I can see snails in the garden.

3. Wait for me, I will be there soon.

4. Can I swim in the pool again today?

oa

1. We can see a toad in the road.

2. Bob saw a goat in the zoo today.

3. My boat can float on the pond.

4. We have toast every Friday.

ea

1. I eat my meal with a fork.

2. We like to read with the teacher in school.

3. Ice cream is the best thing to eat.

4. A peach tart is really good with a cup of tea.

ir

1. The girl had dirt on her skirt.

2. My birthday is on the thirteenth of June.

3. The first bird I saw today was a robin.

4. There are lots of fir trees in the park.

or

1. I need a torch to see in the dark.

2. My horse loves sweet corn.

3. This fork is for your food.

4. I love all sorts of sports.

ow

1. Snow fell on the ground.

2. I know I can spell goat.

3. "Do not throw food at the crows," said Mum.

4. I grow snowdrops in my garden.

ou

1. There was a mouse in the house.

2. I found a pound on the ground.

3. Do not run around and shout in the playground.

4. The dog ran around the hay cart.

ur

1. Dad burnt the toast today.

2. The church is not open on Thursdays.

3. The nurse had some fur boots.

4. We eat turkey and turnips on Saturday.

oi

1. We must put some oil in the car.

2. You can boil peas in a pan..

3. Flowers grow in soil.

4. The boy had oil paints in his box.

igh

1. I had a fright in the night.

2. The moon was bright tonight.

3. I might see you on Saturday.

4. "Do not fight," said the teacher.

ow

1. There are lots of flowers in my garden.

2. Can you train a cow to frown?

3. How do you sail a boat on the sea?

4. Dogs bark and growl when they are cross.

aw

1. The dog clawed the straw with his paw.

2. Raw prawns are awful to eat.

3. I yawn when I need to go to bed.

4. "Draw a clown yawning," said the teacher

ew

1. The bird flew out of the tree.

2. Can I have a few boiled sweets please?

3. The wind blew the clouds across the sky.

4. I knew how to sail the boat

au

1. "Please can I have your autograph," said the nurse.

2. The old house was haunted.

3. The boys caught lots of fish.

4. The teacher taught her daughter how to swim.

EXTENSION WORDS FOR EACH PHONIC FAMILY

Extension words for each phonic family

a-e	i-e	o-e / oe
awake blame blaze brave bracelet chase date flame game rage stage strange female pavement safety stale waste disgrace misplace engage rampage inflame inflate irritate isolate mistake exchange accommodate immediate exaggerate evaporate estimate	chime crime arrive divide invite dislike nineteen ninety beside whine white twice advice device admire acquire desire expire inspire retire require excitement definite definitely subside recognise incline pantomime crocodile	alone broke choke telephone wrote whole compose disclose episode explode impose scope tomatoes potatoes expose oboe toes revoke globe hopeless clothes stroke compose

u-e / ue	oo	ee
accuse acute amuse argue capsule compute consume continue issue include refuse dispute exclude execute reduce subdue presume queue reduce salute subdue	hoof hooves loot bedroom bloom boon boost booze groom noodles poodle roost scoop snooze choose goose loose	bee bleed bleep creep greedy indeed weekend committee disagree exceed freedom greeting proceed screech breeze Greece squeeze anti-freeze cheese sleeve reed wheel

ar	ay	ai
arc arctic alarm artist cardigan carpet carton harmless darkness scarves scarlet Denmark marble department garlic harness harvest jargon larder marmalade margarine Parliament regard remarkable sarcastic sharpener startle	today holiday Monday Wednesday crayon display ashtray bayonet bray decay Norway relay repay x-ray railway	painful afraid against bargain claim complain daily explain frail faint faith maize mountain plaice remain saint Spain sprain training acquainted bailiff braise captain contain detain sic entail maiden maisonette prevail praise quaint raise raisin refrain restrain retain vain waive tainted

oa	ea	ir
cloak cloakroom foam goal poach roam toadstool approach bloated foal gloat goad hoax loam loathe oath reproach shoal	jeans leaves mean treatment beacon bleak cease creature defeat eagle eavesdrop feast feasible freak grease ideal league least leave peace sheaf tease treason treaty veal wheat wreath yeast zeal sneak treacle seam	circle circuit circular circulate circumstances confirm girdle girth mirth shirt skirmish squirm twirl virtual virtue virtuoso virtuous whirl whirlpool

or	ow	oi
acorn sword transport absorb afford assorted deport import important export evaporate boring forbid morbid normal northern orbit orchard organ organise ordinary portrait reform resort worn support transform opportunity ornament perform performance	arrow narrow below borrow bowler elbow follow growth hollow marrow meadow owe pillow yellow window shallow sorrow widow tow lowly sallow willow tomorrow disown know	avoid choice noise ointment appoint poison toilet voice boiler exploit hoist loin moist moisture poise void disappointment
ou	**igh**	**ur**
about aloud cloud count blouse bounce hound mountain pouch pounce thousand trout account announce bound crouch discount grouse recount flour hour sour slouch surround noun lounge	delight delighted sigh tight tights alight mighty slight thigh twilight eyesight blight plight	burglar burst churn disturb furnish further hurt murder purr surface surgeon surprise urgent absurd curb curse curve purchase slur surgical urn Turkey survive urchin urge surly turban surf
aw	**ew**	**ow (ō)**
awkward bawl dawn dawdle drawn hawk hawthorn jaw lawful thaw yawned awe awning flaw withdrawn lawyer	crew nephew screw brew ewe Jew Jewish pew pewter review shrew shred skewer steward view	drown drowsy tower owl town allow gown prowler coward eyebrow endow fowl however howl power powder prowl renown scowl trowel vowel vow sow frowned rowdy
au		
astronaut author automatic cause fault laundry auction audacity audible audition authentic authorise automobile caustic clause daub daunted faultless flaunt gaudy gauze launch maul trauma traumatic undaunted vault		

NATIONAL CURRICULUM WORDS FOR YEARS 1, 2, 3, 4

National Curriculum Word Lists for:

Years one and two

the	come	go	mind	clothes	past	sugar
a	some	so	floor	cold	father	could
do	one	by	because	gold	class	would
to	once	my	kind	hold	water	Sure
today	ask	here	behind	told	again	Eye
of	friend	there	whole	every	grass	should
said	school	where	any	great	pass	who
say	put	love	child	break	plant	Mr
your	are	push	wild	steak	path	Mrs
they	were	pull	most	busy	bath	parents
be	was	full	both	people	hour	Christmas
he	is	house	children	pretty	move	everybody
me	his	our	climb	beautiful	prove	even
she	as	door	only	after	half	
we	I	poor	old	fast	money	
no	you	find	many	last	improve	

Years three and four

accident(ally)	early	knowledge	purpose
actual(ly)	earth	learn	quarter
address	eight/eighth	length	question
answer	enough	library	recent
appear	exercise	material	regular
arrive	experience	medicine	reign
believe	experiment	mention	remember
bicycle	extreme	minute	sentence
breath	famous	natural	separate
breathe	favourite	naughty	special
build	February	notice	straight
busy/business	forward(s)	occasion(ally)	strange
calendar	fruit	often	strength

caught	grammar	opposite	suppose
centre	group	ordinary	surprise
century	guard	particular	therefore
certain	guide	peculiar	though/although
circle	heard	perhaps	thought
complete	heart	popular	through
consider	height	position	various
continue	history	possess(ion)	weight
decide	imagine	possible	woman/women
describe	increase	potatoes	disappear
different	important	pressure	Island
difficult	interest	probably	promise

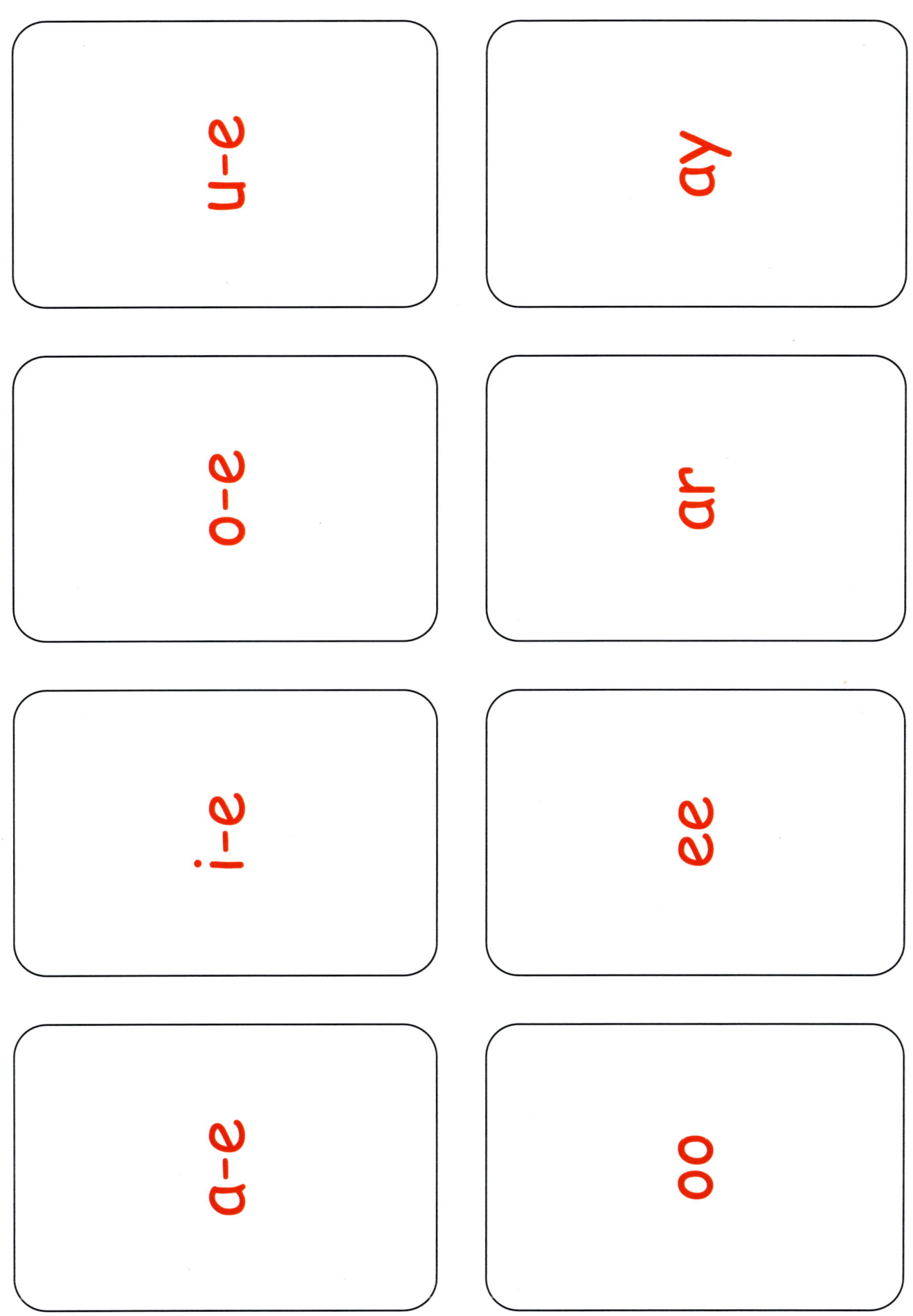

u-e

ay

o-e

ar

i-e

ee

a-e

oo

139

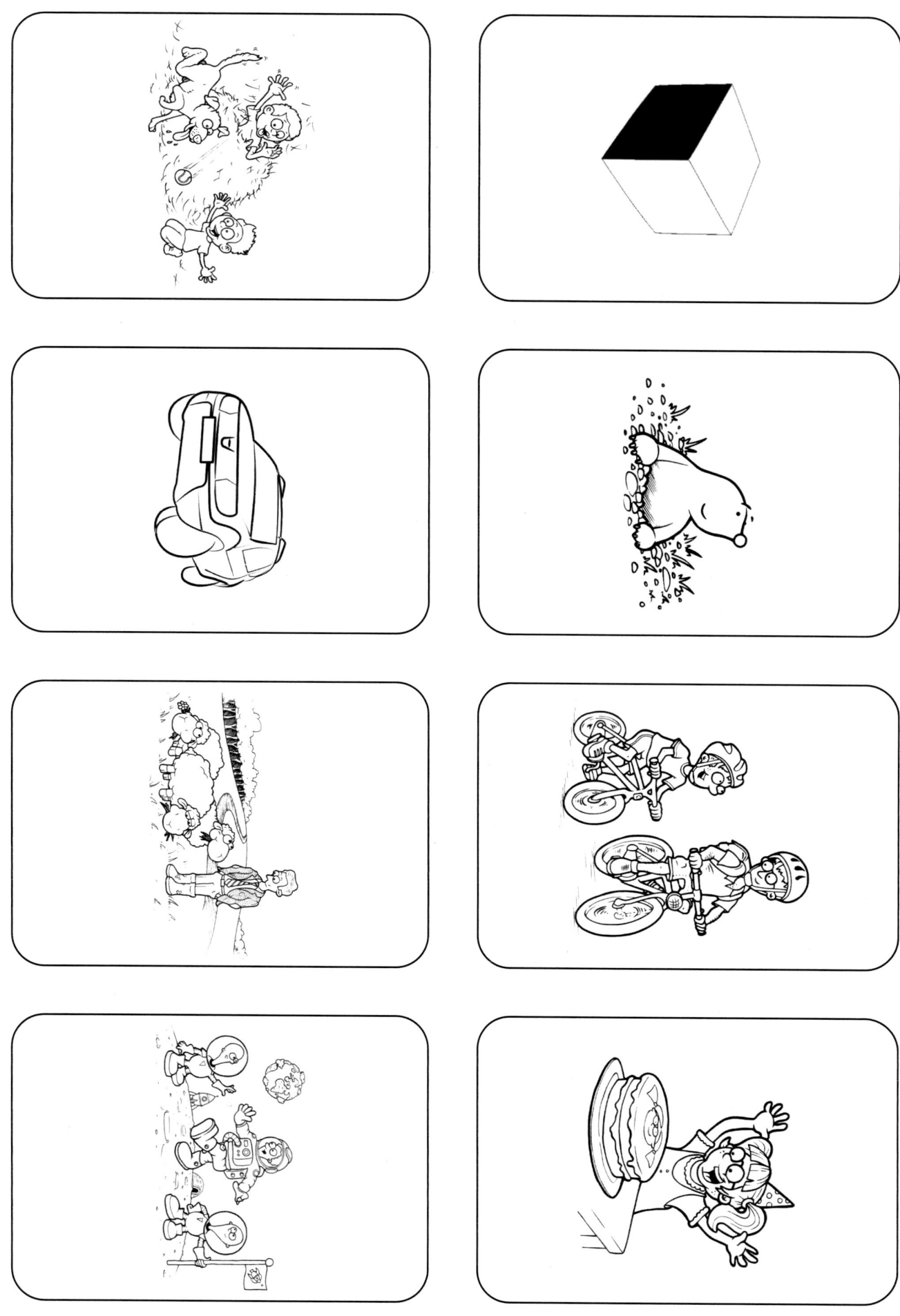

ir

ur

ea

no

oa

ow

ai

or

141

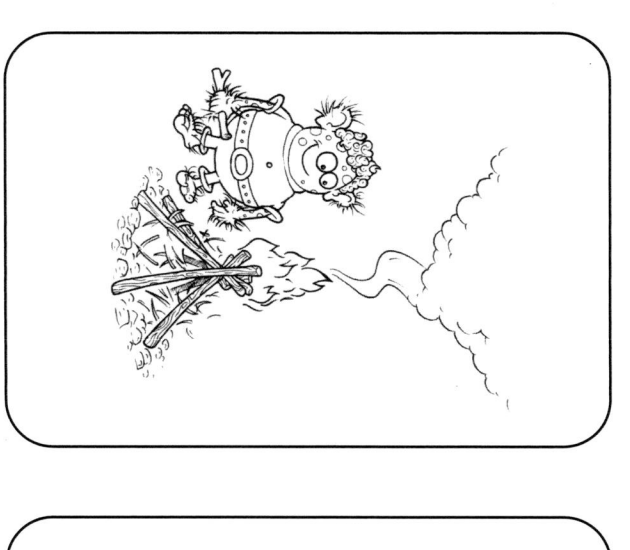

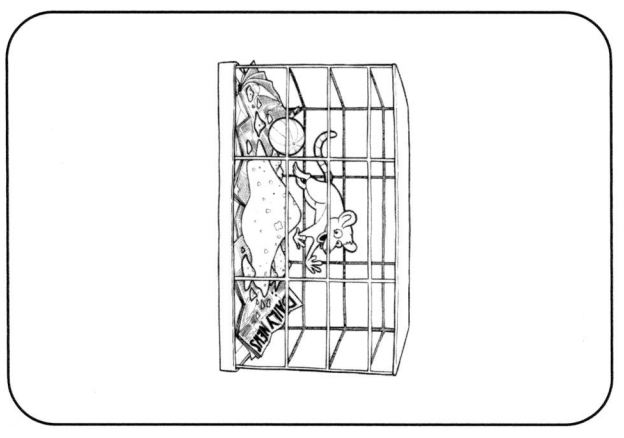

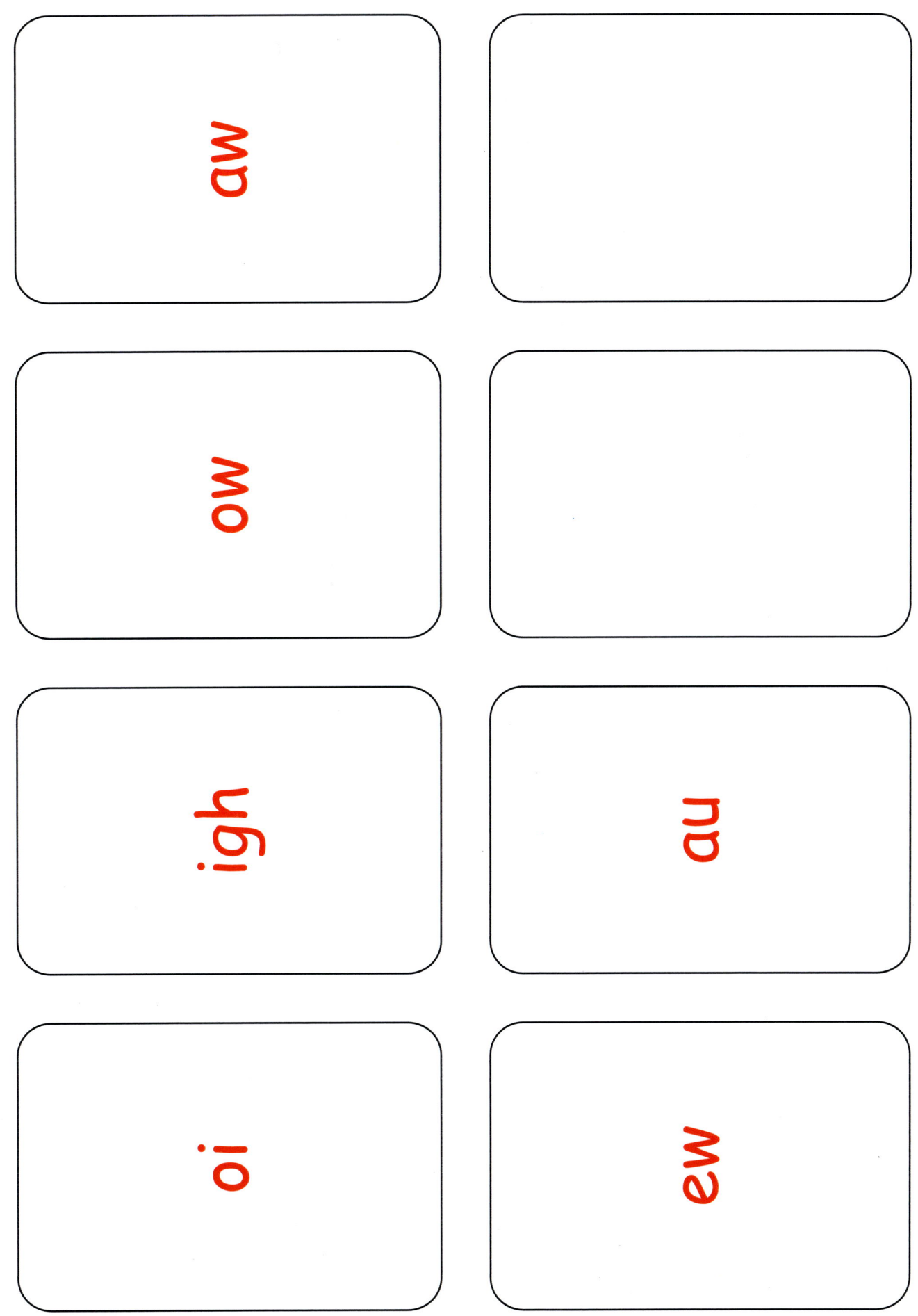

aw

ow

igh

oi

au

ew

Cruise First Class

VOLVO PENTA
Power

NCESS 500

First class accommodation, first class comfort, a first class ride and first class quality. A Princess is a beautiful example of the current state of the art in power cruising.

The highest standards of design, comfort and finish are matched by a formidable offshore performance derived from years of experience and innovation.

RINCESS 406 RIVIERA

The pleasure of driving a Princess gracefully and effortlessly across the water is hard to match. Quick onto the plane, fast, smooth riding and immensely capable even in the most severe conditions, these are qualities that clearly demonstrate the remarkable all-round performance of Princess' advanced deep vee hull designs.

With over 20 years experience as Europe's number one Princess dealer, nobody knows Princess better than Marine Secol. For the best sales and after-sales service, including private tuition, export advice, finance and insurance facilities, contact any of our offices, and let us show you what first class cruising really means.

DISTRIBUTORS FOR
UK AND EXPORT SALES

BRIGHTON
Marine Secol, Brighton Marina
Tel: 0273 686168 Fax: 0273 600043

HAMBLE
Solent Powerboat Sales, Swanwick Marina
Tel: 0489 885656 Fax: 0489 886681

POOLE
Marine Secol, Salterns Marina
Tel: 0202 709402 Fax: 0202 709061

PLYMOUTH
Marine Secol, Queen Anne's Battery Marina
Tel: 0752 600657 Fax: 0752 600658

LOCAL AGENTS

PORT SOLENT Crest Marine
TORQUAY Torquay Marine Sales
WINDERMERE Waterhead Marine

EUROPEAN OFFICE

GIBRALTAR
Marine Secol, 10 The Square, Marina Bay
Tel: (350) 40060 Fax: (350) 40061

HEAD OFFICE
Marine Secol Trading Co Limited
Billing Wharf, Cogenhoe, Northampton, England
Tel: 0604 890559 Fax: 0604 891202

Marine Secol

PRINCESS
EXCLUSIVE DISTRIBUTOR

BRIDGE MOTOR YACHTS · 66 · 58 · 500 · 470 · 440 · 410 · 380 · 360   RIVIERA SPORTS YACHTS · 46 · 406 · 366 · 32

RMA

A new entry at the top of the charts

Dataline Chart

The latest in a string of hits, it's more than just a plotter, it's a complete navigation system.

Versatility? Its unique keyboard/tracker ball allows the widest possible number of installation options - from flush mounted next to the monitor to handheld for maximum ease of use.

Featuring powerful navigation software, entering waypoints couldn't be simpler. The special 'rubber banding' feature allows for fast editing of waypoints, while the number keys allow for quick manual entry.

In a group with other navigation equipment, the Dataline Chart provides one of the most powerful integrated systems available. All the Dataline products such as GPS, Autopilot and instruments are designed to work in close harmony. As a supporting act the Chart is also available in a fully waterproof version for outdoor events.

Check out the Dataline Chart entry at your nearest stockist.

The hand held controller adds convenience to the alread[y] simple data entry system

MARINECALL

THE SPECIALIST WEATHER SERVICE
KEEPING SAILORS IN THE PICTURE

FOR A DETAILED 24 HOUR LOCAL FORECAST
PHONE 0891·500·PLUS AREA NUMBER
FOR A 2 DAY LOCAL FORECAST AND CHARTS
FAX 0336·400·PLUS AREA NUMBER

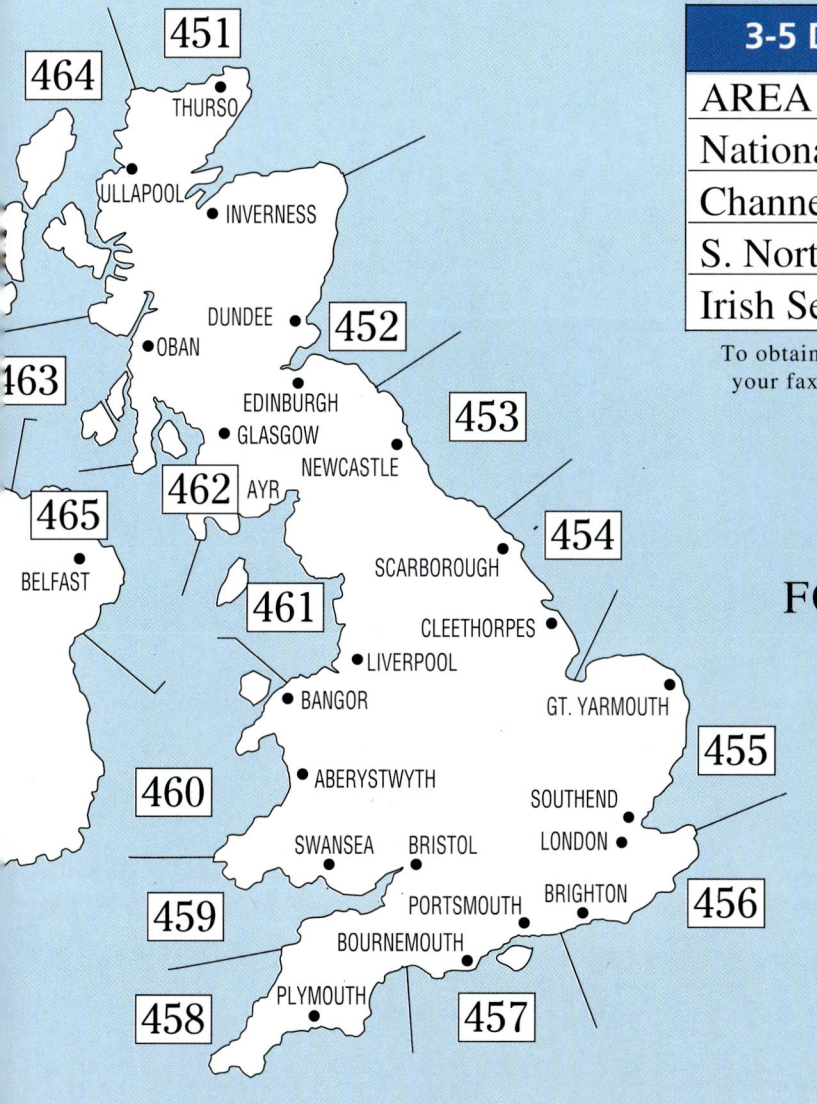

3-5 DAY FORECASTS AND CHARTS		
AREA	FAX	TEL
National Inshore Waters	450	450
Channel Waters	471	992
S. North Sea Waters	472	991
Irish Sea	473	942

To obtain fax - simply dial the 0336·400·plus area number on
your fax machine and press the start button when prompted

Information Supplied by
The Met. Office

FOR CURRENT WEATHER REPORTS FREQUENTLY UPDATED CALL MARINECALL SELECT
0891·505·200

For a free Marinecall card call
071·236·3500. Problems using the
fax – fax our helpline with your fax
machine details on **0344·854·018**
or phone **0344·854·435**

telephone information services plc

24 West Smithfield, London EC1A 9DL. Tel 071 975 9000.
Calls cost 36p per minute cheap rate and 48p per minute at all other times (as at August '93).

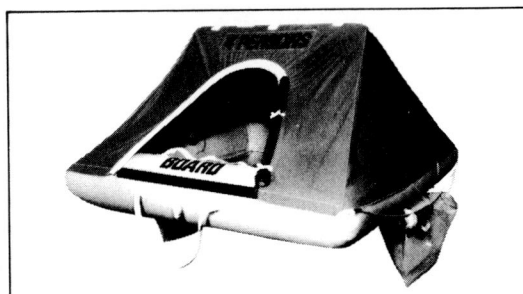

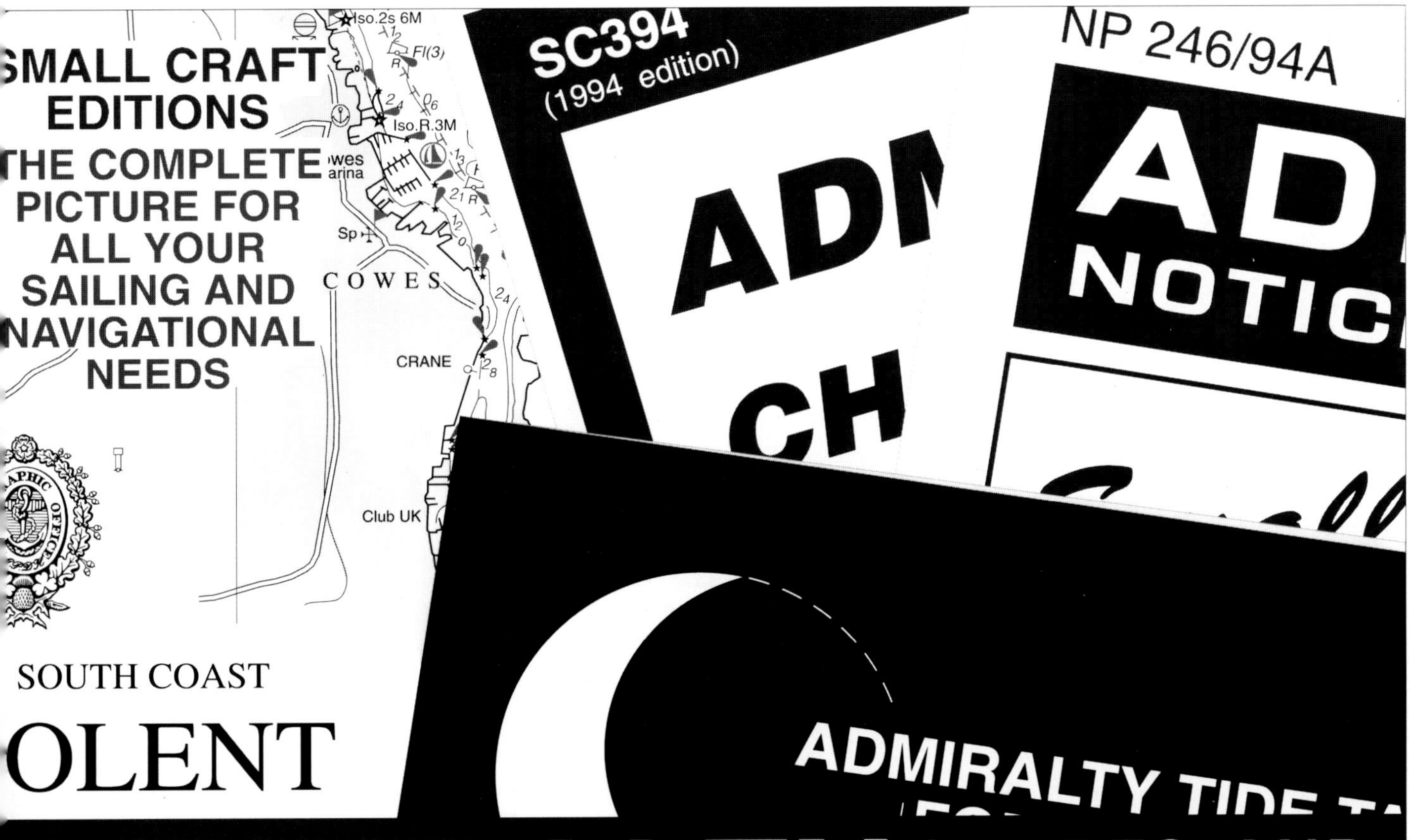

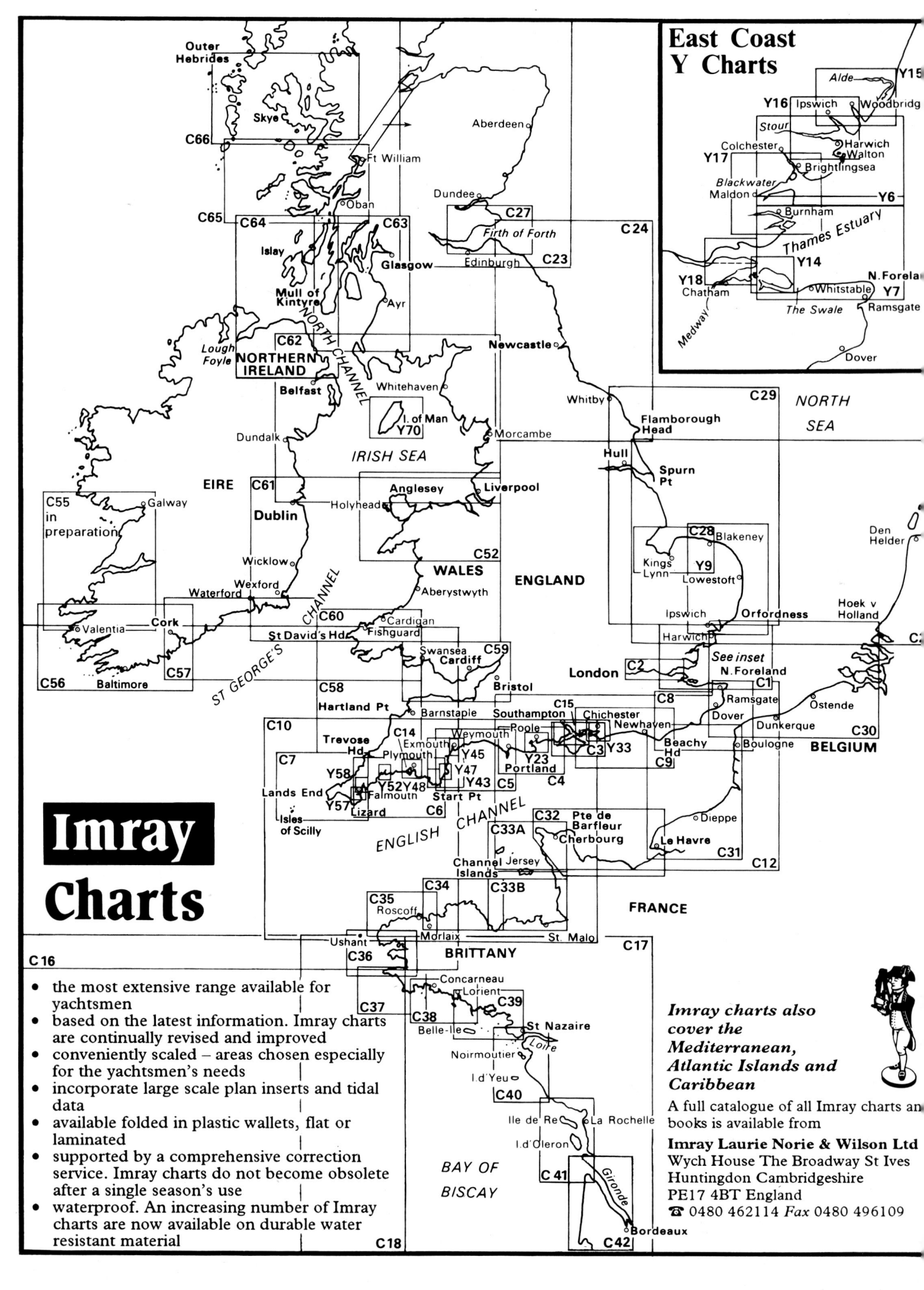

East Coast Y Charts

Imray Charts

- the most extensive range available for yachtsmen
- based on the latest information. Imray charts are continually revised and improved
- conveniently scaled – areas chosen especially for the yachtsmen's needs
- incorporate large scale plan inserts and tidal data
- available folded in plastic wallets, flat or laminated
- supported by a comprehensive correction service. Imray charts do not become obsolete after a single season's use
- waterproof. An increasing number of Imray charts are now available on durable water resistant material

Imray charts also cover the Mediterranean, Atlantic Islands and Caribbean

A full catalogue of all Imray charts and books is available from

Imray Laurie Norie & Wilson Ltd
Wych House The Broadway St Ives
Huntingdon Cambridgeshire
PE17 4BT England
☎ 0480 462114 *Fax* 0480 496109

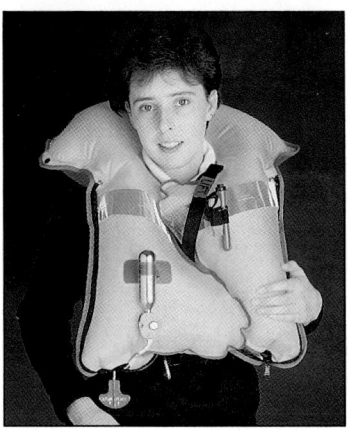

THE CHANNEL WEST
& SOLENT ALMANAC
1994

INTRODUCTION

This 14th edition of CHANNEL WEST and SOLENT has a new look with the introduction of chartlets illustrating the port information on Channel Island and French ports. This feature has long been requested and the continued support of Kelvin Hughes has allowed its inclusion. The charts, drawn by the editor, are based, for the most part, on the work he did for Adlard Coles Nautical in their Pilot Packs but also include new material based on Admiralty and other official publications. The excellent titling and labelling are the work of Roger Maber and Associates.

If this new feature is as well received as we hope, it will be extended in the 1995 edition.

For the 1994 edition we are most grateful for the support of Marina Developments, who own and manage many of Britain's top marinas.

We continue to be grateful to readers who draw attention to errors or ommissions and who make suggestions for improvement. Please make sure that your copy is up to date by requesting an amendment sheet, using the form at the back of the book.

Brian Goulder
Editor

Supported by Marina Developments

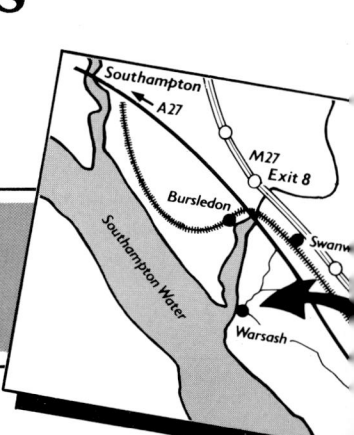

As Britain's leading marina operator we aim to provide services and facilities that are second to none. We work harder than anyone to ensure

The pick of Britain's marinas

that our marinas are the most attractive, the most welcoming, the most convenient and the most secure.

MARINA BERTH RENTALS

Berths are available on annual rental terms, entitling berth holders to complimentary membership of Club Outlook which provides free short-stay and half-price overnight berthing at all other Marina Developments marinas.*

MARINA BERTH PURCHASE

The berth purchase option offers a choice of berths with leasing terms over various periods. An owner has exclusive use of the berth, the freedom to sublet, and Gold Card membership of Club Outlook which entitles him to free visitors berthing at all other Marina Developments marinas.*

MARINA BUSINESS

Retail, office, workshop and light industrial premises are available on leasing terms at most Marina Developments marinas. They offer the opportunity for a wide variety of marine and non-marine business activities, in very attractive, waterfront environments.

MARINA EVENTS

Marina Developments marinas are host to some of the worlds most prestigious sailing events, including The Whitbread and British Steel Challenge. Among the many other popular events are new and used boat shows, and opportunities for newcomers to try boating at first hand.

Marina Developments Ltd

**Outlook House, Hamble Point,
School Lane, Hamble,
Southampton SO3 5NB, England**

**Tel +44 (0)703 457155/457152
Fax +44 (0)703 457154**

*Subject to availability and Club Outlook conditions

JUST SOME OF THE MANY BOATS
WHICH HAVE VISITED OUR MARINAS
IN 1993:

Aacatoule Abalone Abraxas Absolutely Adonno Adriennemay Aegir Aelous of Exe Ailish III Aithina Alderney Alex 11 Alexandra Jayne Alison Allez-Cat Allo Allo Aloisius Alpha Altair Alvine Amadeus Amanda Amanzi Amethyst Amity Amokura of Hamble Amphlette Amy II Anahita III Ananda Anctora Andante Andrella Andromeda Angele Anish Mell Anita Maria Anna Annie Antares Antipodes Any Way Apollo April Lady Aqua Vitae Aqua-Libra Aquagem Aquaholic Aquelia Ar-Y-Mor Arcadian Archiu Arcoloa Arcturus Arenarga Ariane Ariel of Hamble Arrivadecchi Artemis II Arturus •Astra Attacker of Hornet Aubade Auberge Audovin Autumn Gold Avalon of Langstone Aviator Ayacocho Ayli Azrar Babs Bagpuss Balletto Bally Hoo Barbican Barella III Basil the Viking Bavarian Lady Bay Bee Beakey Bear Necessity Bee-Tiar Beel Bellerophon Bellsdown Benguella Beowulf Bergander Bernadette Bertie Beta of Burnham Bethan Betsinda Beautifull Dreamer "Best of Boingo" Bevorlac Bhanshu Bianca Bianca D Bigwig Bimbler Bimbling About Black Duck Black Max Black Rose Black Tie Blue Bear Blue Eagle Blue Flamingo Blue Hat Blue Marlin Blue Melody Blue Moon Blue Nun Blue Sapphir Blue Sapphire Blue Scherzo Bluebird Bluefin Bodea Bolero Bon Viveur Bonito Brave Wolf Breakaway Breeze of Meon Bright Sparks Brimble British Steel II Britsea Broadsword Brock Bruma Bryher Bugle Call Bula 3 Bungay Belle Burkesque Burlesque Busker Byfrost Ca Va Cabaret Cachoucha Cadellin Caiety of Lymington Calaisto Calina Caller 'Ou Calypso Camelot Cameo Candra II Cantata Caper Caprice Captain Nash Captain Simon Careless Whisper Cari Cariad Caribbean Breaze Carla Vanessa Carleen Carolina Moon Carouse III Carra Carrice Cascade Catchfly Catherine Cats Castle Caurus Cavalier Celticist Cenzar Chakis Chalfont Lady Channel Cutter Channel Ghost Chantelle Chantik Chardonnay of Solent Charlie Charlotte Amalie Charmed Life Chazey Lady Cheap Thrill Chere Cherkin Chesara Cheval de Mer Cheyenne Chic Alors Chilli Chill Chimera Chiron Chloris IV Christines Gold Christmas Rose Christolyn Cicero Civette Claire Louise Clairella Clannad Clarionet Clio Cloud 9 Cloud Nine Cloud Ten Cloudruster Cluck Coaster Cockney Spirit Cocobella II Colludor Columbra Commercial Union Assurance Conchy Joe Concordia Contended Soul Contessa Catherine Coopers & Lybrand Coppice Two Coreopsis Corinth Mistral Coriolis Coromondez Quest Coronis Coryphaena Cossack Cotton Blossom Counterpoise Crazy Hen Creola Cresset Crest Hawk Crestline Lady Crew Cats Cringle Crystal Ship Culprit Curlew Currentbun II Cyan Cyndyca Cyra Czardas Dabchick Dacia Dalheath Dalveen Damaris Danae Dans La Rouge Dansewde Zon Dark & Stormy Dark Star Darus Salam Dasler of Lymington Daus Salam Dawarjo Dawdle Dawn Chaser Dawn Runner Dawn Seeker Dazzler Delfine Delft Delphin Delphinus Delta Lady Demelza Demelza Jade Denaria Denebola Desperado 11 Deva Diamond White Diaton Dibbey Diddle Dee Diddlers Dream Diela II Dimple Dimuka Distant Dream Diva Dolfin Dolphin & Youth W60 Dominee Domino Donabella Donnella Double M Dragonfly Dragonsong Dragonstar Dreamtime Drummer Eager Beaver Eagles Wings Earendil Earl of Essex Echo Eclipse Edd the Duck Eeng Shui El Grande El-Oh-Ay Elan Elfin Elidor Elizabethan Lady Ellandonan II Elsker Elusiff Emily Alma Emma J Enchantress Enchantressof Enjoyer Enshaialla Ensis Enza Eos Epik Erica Escapade Escape Esmeralda Esselle Estella Esther Ruth III Ethel Eureka Evenstar Expresser Extasie Extempore Eygnus II Ezebreeze Fable of Hamford Fair Rover Fair Share Fairmaura Faith Fancy Free Fandango Fantasy Farfelu Fast Escape Faustina Feeling Feeling Good Fidelius Fidenza Fifty Fifty Filanda First Drawdown First Kiss Fiscal Fistral Five K Fizgig Flair Flame of Avon Fletcher Fletcher (White) Fletcher 0281 Fleur De La Mer Fleur Elyse Fleuret Flipsam Florestan Flying Boat Flying Dreamer Flying Fox Flying Spirit Flyover Footbad Fortuna Fortuna II Foy Joy Freda Free Spirit Freebee Freebird Freedom of Wight Freelance Freeway French Connection Freya Friska Frisky Fritha Fulani Fuz-E-Duk Gael Galliuanti Gamekeeper Ganesh Garance Gatablanca Gay Charges Gees Ja Van Urk Gem Gemini Gemini Girl Gemini II Gemma Genie Germaine II Gimik Ginao Gipgi Gladiateur Gloria Go-Between Going Krakkers Gold Script Golden Shadow Great Escape Grebe Green Pepper Grese Grey Heron Grey Magil Grey Wolf Groggs Mob Group 4 Securitas Grumpy Skipper Guildford Duke Guilemot Gumdrops Gunshot Gwen II Gwendoline Gypsy Rose Hagar Halcyon Halic Hamara Hanamada Hannah Louise Harika Haveajar Haven Gem Havoc Hayaku Haymaker Heart of Glass Heath Insured Hebridean Girl Heck-Meck Helen Mary R Helena Hellsbells Helms Angel Helmwige Hereth Heretique Heron of Heybridge Herrag Hiccatee Hofbrau Lager Hoodoo Huff & Puff Hungry Tiger Hunny Pot Hurrying Angel Hussar Hypnos Idle Wish Idlehorse Image Impromptu of Hamble Impulse Inca Incus Indred Infocus Innocents Abroad Inothe Inshallah Inspiration of Hastings Interspray Intrum Justica Invicta Irene Isis Islamorada Island Breeze Islander Isle of Pentarchy Ivory Moon Jabberwocky Jacanty Jackdaw Jackie Jaelen Jaks Jameelah Jamie Bump Janneil Too Jasmine Jaunty II Jay Jay of Beaulieu Jay-Gr-M Jazzy II Jeazel Jenanto Jenni Ann Jennie M Jenny Wren Jetstream Jill 'n' Fay Jimara Jo-Jo Joante Jobella Joffer Marieke John B John Riley Johns Folly Joke Jon Jon Jonchawa Jos of Hamble Juicy Kipper Julia Juliain Julio Juluka June Junica Juniper Junkette Jupiter Kaarina Kabisa Kajye II Kalaboo Kale Vala Kalema Kalmar Kandy Kaos Karen Marie Kate Katerina Kathryn of Colne Katinka Two Katrina Kaywana Kaywana of Essex Keimar Kerenza Kiama Kiebitz Kifaru Kilcreggan King Royal Kirmarcy Kiron Kirsten Faye Kisadee Kismet Kita Kitch Kithros Kittiwake Kitty of Pocrvan Kittywake Kiwi Kleco Konspiracy Kookaburra Korri III Kotari Kotick Kraken Kruggerrand Kukarei Kukakoo Kylara L'Iroise L. Ming Hong La Lagune La Nef 11 La Paix La Santa de Avila La Sargque Ladark Ladies Event Lady Anne Lady B Lady Beaverbrook Lady Beefeater Lady Camelot Lady Camlot Lady Dorothy Lady Eowyn Lady Mine Lady Seamouse Lady Valerie Ladybird Laetitia Laga Lass Lambada Lancashire Witch Larc Larrikin Larson Laughing Water Laurel Lavanco Layla Le Monde Le Poulpe Le Sacre du Printemps II Lefkada Legal Eye Leisure II Lelika Lerici Levante Liberty of Dartmouth Libra III Lilentious Lady Lilly Lang Lincolnshire Poacher Lionheart Little Auk Little Lizzy Lizzie Isobel Lone Gerd Longbow Look Far Lorena Lou Lou Loucha Lua Lucy Lucy II Lyra Lysander of Topsham Macken II Macnab Madajar Madhatter Maelstrom Magaluf Magaredella Magewind Maggie Magic Donut Magrethe Mainstream Makita Mia Malayan Moon Malkin Mallard Mando Maplin Maplin Mapulen Margaret Alice Marie of Malew Marigold Marisa Marsv Martimique Mary Gloag Mary May Medoc Meglomania Melady Fair Mellow Yellow Melody & Wiston Meridian Merit Cup Merlani Merlin II Mersea Memsahib Mickey's Magic Midnight Blue Midnight Dance Mikador Mike Millers Damsel Min II Minerva Minestrong Minstral Minuet Mirage Mirelune Mischievous Mood Miss Helena Miss Molly Miss Nobody Miss Peppercorn Miss Piggy Miss Samantha Missuann III Mistral Mistress Quickly Misty Morn Misty Wight Mithril III Mirua Mogalorie Momentum Monemvasia Monksfoot Moody Blues Moody Music Moonglow Moonlight Moonshine Moonstroak II Moray Morgenrote Morning All Morning Gift Morning Mist Morning Star Mouche Mr Beam Mranda Too Mstress Nell Muirgen Mulberry Muna Musketeer My Fair Lady Mylinda Mystique Nagaina Nagoya Nampara Naomidee II Naruhall 360 Natasha of Burnam Nauicular Nausicaa Nauti Bear Navere Nebula Nedos II Nelli Kim Nellie Jane Nellson's Pride Nepos Nereid Neutrino New Dawn New Morning New Zealand Endeavour Nice One Nice One Too Nicolyan Nidders Nikita Nikomis Nillson Nimbus II Nimrod Nina Nirvana Nizwa Nokomis Nordtrold Nore Light Norma Ann North Eagle Northern Rose Norvad Nouvelle Now Wait A Minute Nuada Nuage Nuclear Electric Nutting Girl Obsession Ocean Flame II Ocean Fox Ocean Ovation Ocean Slipper Octavia October Girl Octogan Odessa Odyssey Offshore Olive J Omatere Onanon Ondine Onny-Maja Onyva Opus 1 Orissa Oriwoco Orthodixie Oscatoo Osina Osprey of Portland Out of the Blue Oyster Boot Oyster River P146 Pacific High Padi Painted Lady Pal Joey Palikonda II Pallas Panda Pandora Paperchase Paperchase II Pappilon Paprika Paradis Paranda Paris-B Parsival Paulnova Peace of Lawrenny Pebbles Pedroma Pellegrina Pandragon Pengelly Pennepedia Penny Lane Pennywise H Pentangle Perdita Peregrine Periquita Permata Phaestus Phoenix Phyllis Phyllis Mabel Pican Picaroon Pickle Pierrot Pilot Pacer Pinstripe Piper Pirate Jess Pisces Platypus Playmate Polarlys Polo IV Pop Corn Poppa-M Port Bridge Pracere Presto Pride of Teesside Prime Time Princess Ruslka Privateer Promises Proten Prufrock Pslam of Life Puffin Quadrille Queen Esther Quesera Quintet Quirina Racy Lady II Ragged Edge Raggy Ragtrade Rain Goose Rainbow Raincheck Rapida Raposa Rascal II Ratter Razouli Reading King Reality Rebel Red Gull Red Rose Red Ted Redskin Reflection Reflections of St He Regina Resolis Revenger Reverie of Gosport Rhone-Poulenc Rhubard II Rifiki Right Royal Riobamba Rioy of Blue Rippon Riva Robanda Robsons Choice Rogette Rolly Polly Romanza Ron Bhan Rosa Mytstica Rosache Roseta of Wykeham Rosie Rosmarin Rowena Roxanne Royal Rozwante Rubicon Ruffin Runcible Moon Rusalka Sabrina Fair Sadiq Sadler Holiday Sae Orn Saedraca Sagitta Sagitta of Colne Sahira Salacia Sally Salty Salty Dog Sam Samatal Samphire Samylou San Haze San Souci Sanctacaris Sandpiper Sanibel Sanjika Seascape Seatern of Rockley Seathwaite Seatoller Seatrix Seaval Seawyf Sedona Selene Selma Senta September Song Serendipity Sergius Sesamee Sevon-o-Seven Shadow Shady Lady 3 Shaka Zulu Shaker Shaliad Shande Shapes IV Shauonne Shearwater Sheenar Shenaloah Sheorta Sheree Sherpa Shillianaire Shimmer III Shiralee Shiraz Shofa Short Fuse Shukuran Si-Trois Sian II Sigducer Sikat Silent Falcon Silk Purse Silvarne Silver Ann Silver Cobra Silver Crown Silver Dawn Silver Image II Silver Sonnet Simoon Simply Blue Simply Red Singa Sinope Sir Cloudsley Sirius of Upnor Sirone Sirrah Sirrius Skald III Skerry Ski Mer Skibeereen Sky Gypsy Slam Slingshot Slowcoach Slowhand Smokey Bear Snork Maiden Soleil Solent Falcon Solent Privateer Solent Trader Solitaire II Sonsibility Sorry Ghark Sorry Shark Southern Mist Spangle Spare Trader Special K Spellbinder W.S.C. Spinalong Spin 'Sula' Tempest Termagant Tern Thalamege The Dog House The Other Woman Thea Thestral Third Encounter Thoma Thor Three Seasons Tia-Maria Ticker Tiga Tigermoon Tillygreig Timari Two Time Out Time Warp Timoa Tinga Tire Bouchon Tobermory Tobipus Tomlyn Tommy Topsy Total Eclipse Touvh N Go Touvh of Tar Trade Secret Trader Jo Tranquilla Trapeze Travelling Light Tregastel Treligga Trenova Treuanna Bay Trigger Trilogy Trio Triptych D'Vasco Velore Vencedor Verity of Mylor Veronica Vigilante Viking of Mersea Virinia Warrior Visa Vivacious Vivia Vixen Volante Volare Volunta Voodoo Vulcana Wagtail Wallbanger Warna Carina Waterman Waveney Weaverbird Welsh Dragon II Wendreda Westely Centaur Westerley Skytrain Westerly Maid Whisker Whisky Mac Whisper Whispy Whistler White Aster White Fox White Lady White Magic White Rose White Satin White Ski Winston US Women's Challenge Yamaha

Try our marinas for yourself, and discover what Marina Developments has to offer.
You may find this Almanac of assistance in finding your way to these marinas.

Marina Developments Ltd Outlook House, Hamble Point, School Lane, Hamble, Southampton SO3 5NB Tel 0703 457155/457152 Fax 0703 457154

CONTENTS

ABBREVIATIONS

Some abbreviations used in this Almanac and in Admiralty publications.
For a complete list, see Chart 5011, Symbols and Abbreviations.

h	Hour	FFl( ) or FGp Fl	Fixed and group flashing
min	Minute (of time)	Mo(A)	Morse code (e.g. sounding or flashing · –)
sec	Second (of time)		
m	Metres	Bl	Blue
ft	Foot, feet	G	Green
M	Sea mile(s)	Or	Orange
°	Degree	R	Red
'	Minute (of arc)	W	White
"	Second (of arc)	Dia	Diaphone
No	Number	HW	High water
Lt	Light	LW	Low water
Lt Ho	Lighthouse	MHWS	Mean high water springs
Lt V	Light-vessel	MHWN	Mean high water neaps
F	Fixed	MLWS	Mean low water springs
Oc or Occ	Occulting	MLWN	Mean low water neaps
Fl	Flashing	HAT	Highest astronomical tides
Iso	Isophase	LAT	Lowest astronomical tides
Q or Qk Fl	Quick flashing		
IQ or Int Qk Fl	Interrupted quick flashing		Marina
Al or Alt	Alternating		
Oc( ) or Gp Occ	Group occulting		Harbour Master
Fl( ) or Gp Fl	Group flashing		
FFl	Fixed and flashing		Yacht Club

Acknowledgements

Tidal and navigational information is based on Admiralty tide tables and charts, Crown Copyright, reproduced with permission of the Controller of HM Stationery Office, the Hydrographer of the Navy. Copyright reserved. Tide Tables for Dieppe, Le Havre, Cherbourg, St Malo and Brest are taken from the tidal yearbook Vol 1 – Ports of France – of the Service Hydrographique et Océanographique de la Marine and reproduced with their authorisation. Tidal predictions for Dover, Shoreham, Southampton, St Helier, St Mary's Scilly Isles, Falmouth, Salcombe, Lymington and Chichester have been computed by the Proudman Oceanographic Laboratory: copyright reserved.

List of lights is drawn from information published by the Hydrographic Service and is reproduced with the permission of the Controller of HM Stationery Office, the Hydrographer of the Navy.

Astronomical and calendarial information is reproduced, with permission of the Controller of HM Stationery Office, from data supplied by the Science and Engineering Research Council.

Tidal stream charts, Ushant, on pp. 105-107, are © 1974 Service Hydrographique et Océanographique de la Marine, France. Reproduced by permission.

Disclaimer

The greatest possible care has been taken with the compilation of this almanac and all the information is, at the time of going press, accurate to the best of the publisher's knowledge and belief.

Neither the publisher, nor his agents, can, however, accept any responsibility for any errors, omissions or subsequent changes, nor for the consequences of any incident in which the users of the almanac may be involved.

© Compilation: Geoffrey Chapman 1990
© 1994 Kelvin Hughes Ltd.

ISBN 0 9517096 3 1

Produced by Roger Maber & Associates, Fareham, Hampshire.
Printed in England.

SECTION 1
YACHTSMAN'S ALMANAC

ALMANAC 1994

All times are GMT. ADD ONE HOUR for BST between 0100 on March 27th and 0100 on October 23rd (provisional). Heights in metres.

Rising and setting times

These are based on Latitude 50°N on the Greenwich meridian and are therefore a fair compromise for the area covered by this book. The times given are when the upper limb of the sun, or moon, is just on the visible horizon as seen from sea level. ADD 4 minutes (of time) for every degree WEST of Greenwich.

JANUARY

		Dover Tides HW				Rising and Setting Moon		Rising and Setting Sun	
		time	ht	time	ht	rise	set	rise	set
1	Sa	0038	6.7	1254	6.5	2047	0936	0759	1610
2	Su	0118	6.7	1335	6.5	2203	1001	59	10
3	M	0202	6.6	1422	6.3	2320	1025	59	10
4	Tu	0252	6.5	1516	6.1	2437	1050	58	13
5	W	0348	6.2	1620	5.8	0037	1117	58	13
6	Th	0455	6.0	1740	5.6	0155	1148	0758	1613
7	F	0613	5.8	1901	5.6	0311	1225	57	17
8	Sa	0731	5.8	2014	5.7	0424	1310	57	17
9	Su	0842	6.0	2117	6.0	0529	1404	57	17
10	M	0944	6.2	2210	6.3	0626	1506	56	21
11	Tu	1036	6.4	2256	6.5	0712	1615	0756	1621
12	W	1120	6.5	2336	6.7	0749	1726	56	21
13	Th	1200	6.6	----		0819	1836	54	25
14	F	0015	6.8	1238	6.8	0845	1946	54	25
15	Sa	0054	6.8	1314	6.4	0907	2053	54	25
16	Su	0130	6.3	1351	6.3	0928	2158	0751	1629
17	M	0205	6.1	1427	6.1	0949	2302	51	29
18	Tu	0239	5.8	1505	5.8	1010	2406	51	29
19	W	0315	5.9	1550	5.5	1032	0006	49	34
20	Th	0401	5.6	1651	5.3	1058	0109	49	34
21	F	0507	5.3	1801	5.1	1129	0212	0749	1634
22	Sa	0622	5.2	1908	5.2	1206	0314	45	39
23	Su	0730	5.3	2010	5.4	1251	0412	45	39
24	M	0829	5.6	2102	5.7	1344	0505	45	39
25	Tu	0919	5.9	2147	6.1	1447	0552	42	44
26	W	1002	6.2	2227	6.4	1557	0633	0742	1644
27	Th	1043	6.4	2305	6.6	1712	0708	42	44
28	F	1121	6.6	2343	6.8	1829	0738	38	49
29	Sa	1159	6.7	----		1947	0805	38	49
30	Su	0021	6.9	1238	6.7	2106	0830	38	49
31	M	0102	7.0	1319	6.7	2225	0856	0734	1654

FEBRUARY

		Dover Tides HW				Rising and Setting Moon		Rising and Setting Sun	
		time	ht	time	ht	rise	set	rise	set
1	Tu	0144	6.9	1403	6.5	2343	0922	0734	1654
2	W	0230	6.7	1453	6.3	2500	0952	34	59
3	Th	0323	6.4	1553	5.9	0100	1027	30	59
4	F	0427	5.9	1709	5.5	0214	1109	30	59
5	Sa	0548	5.8	1838	5.4	0321	1159	30	59
6	Su	0717	5.5	2002	5.5	0419	1257	0725	1704
7	M	0840	5.7	2111	5.8	0508	1401	25	04
8	Tu	0945	6.0	2203	6.1	0547	1510	25	04
9	W	1033	6.2	2246	6.4	0620	1620	20	09
10	Th	1112	6.4	2324	6.6	0647	1729	20	09
11	F	1147	6.5	----		0711	1836	0720	1709
12	Sa	0000	6.7	1220	6.5	0733	1943	15	15
13	Su	0035	6.7	1252	6.5	0753	2048	15	15
14	M	0106	6.6	1322	6.4	0814	2152	15	15
15	Tu	0133	6.5	1349	6.2	0837	2255	09	20
16	W	0156	6.0	1413	6.0	0901	2358	0709	1720
17	Th	0221	6.1	1440	5.8	0930	2459	09	20
18	F	0255	5.8	1521	5.4	1003	0059	04	25
19	Sa	0344	5.4	1645	5.1	1043	0158	04	25
20	Su	0528	5.1	1826	5.0	1132	0252	04	25
21	M	0654	5.1	1935	5.2	1229	0342	0658	1730
22	Tu	0800	5.4	2033	5.6	1334	0425	58	30
23	W	0855	5.8	2121	6.0	1446	0502	58	30
24	Th	0941	6.2	2203	6.4	1602	0535	52	35
25	F	1022	6.5	2243	6.7	1721	0604	52	35
26	Sa	1101	6.7	2322	7.0	1842	0631	0652	1735
27	Su	1140	6.9	----		2003	0657	46	40
28	M	0001	7.1	1219	6.9	2125	0725	46	40

MARCH

		Dover Tides HW				Rising and Setting Moon		Rising and Setting Sun	
		time	ht	time	ht	rise	set	rise	set
1	Tu	0042	7.1	1300	6.9	2245	0754	0646	1740
2	W	0125	7.0	1345	6.7	2402	0829	40	45
3	Th	0210	6.8	1434	6.4	0002	0909	40	45
4	F	0303	6.3	1533	5.9	0112	0957	40	45
5	Sa	0408	5.8	1648	5.5	0214	1053	34	50
6	Su	0531	5.4	1815	5.3	0305	1155	0634	1750
7	M	0707	5.3	1946	5.4	0347	1302	34	50
8	Tu	0838	5.5	2057	5.7	0422	1410	27	55
9	W	0935	5.9	2147	6.1	0450	1518	27	55
10	Th	1018	6.1	2227	6.4	0515	1625	27	55
11	F	1053	6.3	2304	6.6	0537	1731	0621	1800
12	Sa	1125	6.5	2338	6.6	0558	1836	21	00
13	Su	1156	6.5	----		0620	1940	21	00
14	M	0011	6.6	1226	6.5	0641	2043	14	04
15	Tu	0039	6.6	1253	6.4	0705	2146	14	04
16	W	0101	6.5	1314	6.3	0732	2248	0614	1804
17	Th	0119	6.4	1333	6.2	0804	2347	08	09
18	F	0143	6.2	1401	6.0	0841	2442	08	09
19	Sa	0216	6.0	1439	5.7	0925	0042	08	09
20	Su	0300	5.6	1533	5.3	1018	0133	01	14
21	M	0408	5.2	1741	5.0	1118	0217	0601	1814
22	Tu	0621	5.1	1859	5.2	1224	0256	01	14
23	W	0731	5.4	2001	5.6	1336	0330	0555	19
24	Th	0828	5.8	2052	6.0	1452	0400	55	19
25	F	0916	6.2	2137	6.4	1611	0428	55	19
26	Sa	0959	6.5	2219	6.8	1732	0455	0548	1824
27	Su	1039	6.8	2259	7.0	1855	0522	48	24
28	M	1119	7.0	2340	7.2	2019	0552	48	24
29	Tu	1200	7.0	----		2140	0625	42	28
30	W	0022	7.2	1243	7.0	2256	0704	42	28
31	Th	0107	7.0	1329	6.8	2404	0751	0542	1828

ALMANAC 1994

All times are GMT. ADD ONE HOUR for BST between 0100 on March 27th and 0100 on October 23rd (provisional). Heights in metres.

Rising and setting times

These are based on Latitude 50°N on the Greenwich meridian and are therefore a fair compromise for the area covered by this book.

The times given are when the upper limb of the sun, or moon, is just on the visible horizon as seen from sea level. ADD 4 minutes (of time) for every degree WEST of Greenwich.

APRIL

Day		Dover Tides HW time	ht	HW time	ht	Rising Moon rise	set	Setting Sun rise	set
1	F	0154	6.7	1420	6.5	0004	0846	0535	1833
2	Sa	0249	6.3	1519	6.0	0100	0948	35	33
3	Su	0355	5.8	1629	5.6	0146	1055	35	33
4	M	0513	5.4	1747	5.4	0223	1203	29	38
5	Tu	0648	5.3	1916	5.4	0254	1310	29	38
6	W	0817	5.5	2029	5.7	0319	1417	0529	1838
7	Th	0911	5.8	2119	6.0	0342	1523	22	42
8	F	0952	6.0	2201	6.3	0404	1627	22	42
9	Sa	1026	6.2	2237	6.4	0425	1731	22	42
10	Su	1058	6.4	2312	6.5	0446	1834	16	47
11	M	1128	6.4	2343	6.5	0510	1937	0516	1847
12	Tu	1158	6.4	----	---	0536	2039	16	47
13	W	0010	6.4	1226	6.4	0606	2139	10	52
14	Th	0033	6.4	1248	6.3	0641	2236	10	52
15	F	0052	6.3	1309	6.3	0723	2327	10	52
16	Sa	0117	6.3	1338	6.2	0812	2413	0504	1856
17	Su	0152	6.1	1418	5.9	0908	0013	04	56
18	M	0237	5.8	1512	5.6	1011	0053	04	56
19	Tu	0340	5.4	1644	5.3	1118	0128	0458	1901
20	W	0543	5.3	1818	5.4	1230	0159	58	01
21	Th	0657	5.5	1923	5.7	1345	0226	0458	1901
22	F	0757	5.8	2019	6.1	1502	0253	52	06
23	Sa	0848	6.2	2108	6.5	1623	0319	52	06
24	Su	0934	6.5	2154	6.8	1745	0347	52	06
25	M	1017	6.8	2238	7.0	1909	0418	46	11
26	Tu	1100	6.9	2322	7.1	2030	0455	0446	1911
27	W	1143	7.0	----	---	2144	0539	46	11
28	Th	0006	7.1	1229	7.0	2248	0632	41	15
29	F	0053	6.9	1317	6.8	2340	0733	41	15
30	Sa	0142	6.6	1408	6.5	2422	0841	41	15

MAY

Day		Dover Tides HW time	ht	HW time	ht	Rising Moon rise	set	Setting Sun rise	set
1	Su	0238	6.3	1504	6.2	0022	0951	0435	1920
2	M	0339	5.9	1605	5.9	0055	1100	35	20
3	Tu	0447	5.5	1712	5.6	0123	1208	35	20
4	W	0605	5.4	1827	5.5	0147	1315	30	24
5	Th	0732	5.4	1943	5.6	0209	1420	30	24
6	F	0832	5.6	2041	5.8	0230	1523	0430	1924
7	Sa	0916	5.9	2127	6.1	0252	1627	25	29
8	Su	0953	6.1	2206	6.2	0314	1730	25	29
9	M	1027	6.2	2241	6.3	0339	1832	25	29
10	Tu	1059	6.3	2313	6.3	0408	1932	20	33
11	W	1131	6.4	2342	6.3	0442	2030	0420	1933
12	Th	----	---	1202	6.4	0522	2124	20	33
13	F	0009	6.3	1229	6.4	0609	2212	16	38
14	Sa	0035	6.3	1256	6.3	0703	2254	16	38
15	Su	0103	6.2	1328	6.2	0803	2330	16	38
16	M	0140	6.1	1409	6.1	0908	2401	0412	1942
17	Tu	0225	5.9	1502	5.9	1017	0001	12	42
18	W	0324	5.7	1609	5.7	1128	0029	12	42
19	Th	0446	5.5	1728	5.7	1242	0054	08	46
20	F	0614	5.6	1841	5.8	1358	0120	08	46
21	Sa	0721	5.8	1944	6.1	1517	0146	0408	1946
22	Su	0818	6.1	2040	6.4	1638	0214	04	50
23	M	0910	6.4	2131	6.6	1759	0247	04	50
24	Tu	0959	6.6	2221	6.8	1917	0326	04	50
25	W	1046	6.8	2309	6.9	2028	0415	01	53
26	Th	1133	6.9	----	---	2127	0513	0401	1953
27	F	1220	6.9			2215	0619	01	53
28	Sa	0044	6.8	1307	6.8	2253	0730	0358	57
29	Su	0133	6.6	1355	6.6	2325	0843	58	57
30	M	0224	6.3	1446	6.4	2351	0954	58	57
31	Tu	0318	6.0	1539	6.1	2414	1102	0356	2000

JUNE

Day		Dover Tides HW time	ht	HW time	ht	Rising Moon rise	set	Setting Sun rise	set
1	W	0415	5.7	1635	5.8	0014	1209	0356	2000
2	Th	0515	5.5	1735	5.6	0035	1314	56	0C
3	F	0622	5.4	1842	5.6	0057	1418	54	03
4	Sa	0732	5.5	1948	5.6	0119	1521	54	03
5	Su	0829	5.6	2044	5.8	0143	1623	54	03
6	M	0915	5.8	2129	5.9	0210	1724	0352	2006
7	Tu	0954	6.0	2208	6.1	0242	1824	52	06
8	W	1030	6.2	2243	6.2	0320	1919	52	06
9	Th	1105	6.3	2317	6.2	0405	2010	51	08
10	F	1139	6.4	2350	6.3	0457	2054	51	08
11	Sa	----	---	1211	6.4	0556	2132	0351	2008
12	Su	0021	6.3	1244	6.4	0700	2205	50	10
13	M	0054	6.3	1319	6.4	0808	2234	50	10
14	Tu	0131	6.2	1400	6.4	0918	2300	50	10
15	W	0215	6.1	1447	6.3	1030	2324	50	11
16	Th	0306	6.0	1543	6.1	1144	2349	0350	2011
17	F	0409	5.8	1647	6.0	1300	2415	50	11
18	Sa	0524	5.7	1759	6.0	1417	0015	50	12
19	Su	0643	5.7	1911	6.0	1536	0045	50	12
20	M	0752	5.9	2017	6.2	1653	0120	50	12
21	Tu	0854	6.1	2118	6.4	1806	0203	0351	2013
22	W	0950	6.4	2214	6.6	1910	0255	51	13
23	Th	1040	6.6	2306	6.7	2004	0356	51	13
24	F	1127	6.8	----	---	2048	0506	51	13
25	Sa			1212	6.8	2123	-0619	52	13
26	Su	0038	6.7	1256	6.8	2152	0732	0352	2013
27	M	0122	6.6	1339	6.7	2217	0844	53	13
28	Tu	0206	6.4	1423	6.5	2240	0953	53	13
29	W	0251	6.1	1508	6.3	2302	1100	53	13
30	Th	0338	5.9	1556	6.0	2324	1205	55	13

ALMANAC 1994

All times are GMT. ADD ONE HOUR for BST between 0100 on March 27th and 0100 on October 23rd (provisional). Heights in metres.

Rising and setting times

These are based on Latitude 50°N on the Greenwich meridian and are therefore a fair compromise for the area covered by this book.

The times given are when the upper limb of the sun, or moon, is just on the visible horizon as seen from sea level. ADD 4 minutes (of time) for every degree WEST of Greenwich.

JULY

Date	Day	HW time	ht	time	ht	Moon rise	set	Sun rise	set
1	F	0430	5.6	1648	5.7	2347	1309	0355	2013
2	Sa	0526	5.4	1745	5.5	2413	1412	55	13
3	Su	0628	5.3	1849	5.4	0013	1514	57	11
4	M	0733	5.4	1952	5.5	0043	1614	57	11
5	Tu	0832	5.6	2049	5.7	0118	1711	57	11
6	W	0921	5.8	2135	5.9	0200	1804	0359	2010
7	Th	1002	6.0	2216	6.1	0249	1851	59	10
8	F	1040	6.2	2253	6.2	0346	1932	59	10
9	Sa	1116	6.4	2330	6.3	0449	2007	0402	08
10	Su	1151	6.5	----		0557	2038	02	08
11	M	0004	6.4	1227	6.6	0708	2105	0402	2008
12	Tu	0040	6.4	1303	6.6	0820	2131	05	06
13	W	0117	6.5	1343	6.6	0934	2155	05	06
14	Th	0158	6.5	1427	6.5	1049	2221	05	06
15	F	0246	6.3	1518	6.4	1204	2249	08	03
16	Sa	0341	6.0	1617	6.1	1321	2321	0408	2003
17	Su	0451	5.8	1729	5.9	1437	2359	08	00
18	M	0615	5.6	1849	5.8	1550	2446	12	00
19	Tu	0736	5.7	2007	5.9	1656	0046	12	00
20	W	0846	5.9	2116	6.1	1753	0141	12	00
21	Th	0946	6.2	2216	6.4	1841	0246	0415	1957
22	F	1036	6.5	2305	6.5	1920	0356	15	57
23	Sa	1120	6.7	2348	6.6	1952	0509	15	57
24	Su	1200	6.8	----		2019	0622	19	53
25	M	0027	6.7	1240	6.8	2043	0733	19	53
26	Tu	0104	6.6	1319	6.8	2106	0842	0419	1953
27	W	0141	6.4	1357	6.6	2128	0949	23	49
28	Th	0219	6.2	1434	6.4	2151	1054	23	49
29	F	0258	6.0	1513	6.1	2216	1158	23	49
30	Sa	0342	5.7	1557	5.8	2244	1301	27	44
31	Su	0436	5.4	1654	5.5	2317	1401	0427	1944

AUGUST

Date	Day	HW time	ht	time	ht	Moon rise	set	Sun rise	set
1	M	0539	5.2	1801	5.3	2356	1500	0427	1944
2	Tu	0646	5.2	1909	5.3	2441	1554	32	40
3	W	0752	5.3	2012	5.5	0041	1644	32	40
4	Th	0848	5.6	2106	5.8	0135	1728	40	40
5	F	0934	6.0	2150	6.1	0236	1806	0436	1935
6	Sa	1013	6.3	2230	6.3	0342	1839	0436	1935
7	Su	1051	6.5	2307	6.5	0453	1908	36	35
8	M	1127	6.7	2343	6.6	0606	1935	40	30
9	Tu	----		1204	6.8	0721	2001	40	30
10	W	0019	6.7	1242	6.9	0836	2027	40	30
11	Th	0057	6.7	1322	6.9	0953	2054	0445	1924
12	F	0138	6.6	1406	6.8	1110	2125	45	24
13	Sa	0224	6.4	1455	6.5	1226	2201	45	24
14	Su	0319	6.1	1554	6.1	1339	2244	49	19
15	M	0430	5.7	1711	5.7	1447	2336	49	19
16	Tu	0600	5.5	1839	5.6	1546	2435	0449	1919
17	W	0727	5.5	2005	5.7	1636	0035	54	13
18	Th	0841	5.8	2119	6.0	1717	0142	54	13
19	F	0939	6.1	2213	6.3	1751	0252	54	13
20	Sa	1026	6.5	2256	6.5	1820	0404	58	07
21	Su	1106	6.7	2333	6.6	1845	0515	0458	1907
22	M	1143	6.8	----		1909	0625	58	07
23	Tu	0007	6.6	1220	6.8	1932	0732	0502	01
24	W	0041	6.6	1254	6.8	1955	0838	02	01
25	Th	0113	6.5	1327	6.6	2019	0943	02	01
26	F	0144	6.3	1356	6.4	2046	1047	0507	1855
27	Sa	0213	6.1	1423	6.2	2117	1148	07	55
28	Su	0244	5.8	1455	5.8	2153	1247	07	55
29	M	0325	5.5	1546	5.5	2235	1343	11	49
30	Tu	0450	5.2	1718	5.2	2324	1434	11	49
31	W	0607	5.1	1835	5.1	2421	1520	0511	1849

SEPTEMBER

Date	Day	HW time	ht	time	ht	Moon rise	set	Sun rise	set
1	Th	0715	5.2	1940	5.4	0021	1600	0516	1843
2	F	0815	5.6	2037	5.7	0124	1636	16	43
3	Sa	0904	6.0	2124	6.1	0233	1707	16	43
4	Su	0945	6.4	2204	6.4	0345	1735	20	36
5	M	1024	6.7	2242	6.7	0500	1802	20	36
6	Tu	1102	6.9	2319	6.8	0617	1829	0520	1836
7	W	1140	7.1	2356	6.9	0735	1857	25	30
8	Th	----		1219	7.1	0854	1927	25	30
9	F	0035	6.9	1300	7.1	1012	2003	25	30
10	Sa	0118	6.8	1344	6.9	1128	2044	29	23
11	Su	0205	6.5	1435	6.5	1238	2134	0529	1823
12	M	0302	6.1	1538	6.0	1340	2231	29	23
13	Tu	0417	5.7	1701	5.6	1433	2335	34	16
14	W	0545	5.5	1831	5.5	1516	2443	34	16
15	Th	0713	5.5	2004	5.6	1552	0043	34	16
16	F	0829	5.8	2111	5.9	1622	0153	0538	1810
17	Sa	0924	6.2	2159	6.2	1648	0302	38	10
18	Su	1007	6.5	2237	6.5	1712	0411	38	10
19	M	1044	6.7	2310	6.6	1735	0519	43	03
20	Tu	1120	6.8	2341	6.6	1758	0625	43	03
21	W	1154	6.8	----		1822	0730	0543	1803
22	Th	0012	6.6	1227	6.7	1848	0834	47	1757
23	F	0043	6.5	1255	6.6	1918	0936	47	57
24	Sa	0110	6.4	1317	6.4	1952	1036	47	57
25	Su	0132	6.2	1337	6.2	2031	1133	52	50
26	M	0153	6.0	1406	6.0	2117	1225	0552	1750
27	Tu	0226	5.8	1446	5.8	2210	1313	52	50
28	W	0318	5.4	1601	5.4	2309	1354	56	43
29	Th	0526	5.1	1801	5.1	2413	1431	56	43
30	F	0638	5.3	1909	5.4	0013	1503	56	43

ALMANAC 1994

All times are GMT. ADD ONE HOUR for BST between 0100 on March 27th and 0100 on October 23rd (provisional).
Heights in metres.

Rising and setting times

These are based on Latitude 50°N on the Greenwich meridian and are therefore a fair compromise for the area covered by this book.
The times given are when the upper limb of the sun, or moon, is just on the visible horizon as seen from sea level. ADD 4 minutes (of time) for every degree WEST of Greenwich.

OCTOBER

Day		Dover Tides HW time ht		time ht		Rising Moon rise	set	Setting Sun rise	set
1	Sa	0740	5.6	2006	5.7	0122	1533	0601	1737
2	Su	0831	6.0	2055	6.1	0235	1600	01	37
3	M	0915	6.4	2137	6.5	0350	1627	01	37
4	Tu	0956	6.8	2216	6.8	0508	1655	06	30
5	W	1035	7.1	2254	7.0	0628	1725	06	30
6	Th	1115	7.2	2334	7.1	0749	1759	0606	1730
7	F	1156	7.2	----		0909	1840	10	24
8	Sa	0016	7.1	1240	7.1	1024	1928	10	24
9	Su	0101	6.9	1327	6.9	1131	2024	15	18
10	M	0151	6.6	1420	6.5	1228	2128	15	18
11	Tu	0250	6.2	1527	6.0	1315	2235	0615	1718
12	W	0402	5.8	1647	5.6	1354	2345	15	18
13	Th	0521	5.6	1815	5.5	1425	2454	20	12
14	F	0646	5.6	1945	5.6	1452	0054	20	12
15	Sa	0802	5.8	2048	5.8	1517	0202	20	12
16	Su	0857	6.1	2133	6.1	1540	0309	0625	1705
17	M	0940	6.4	2209	6.3	1603	0415	25	05
18	Tu	1018	6.6	2242	6.5	1626	0520	25	05
19	W	1053	6.7	2313	6.6	1651	0624	29	00
20	Th	1126	6.7	2344	6.6	1720	0726	29	00
21	F	1157	6.6	----		1752	0827	0629	1700
22	Sa	0014	6.6	1225	6.5	1830	0925	34	54
23	Su	0042	6.5	1247	6.4	1913	1019	34	54
24	M	0103	6.3	1308	6.3	2003	1108	34	54
25	Tu	0126	6.2	1337	6.1	2058	1151	39	48
26	W	0200	6.0	1417	5.8	2159	1229	0639	1648
27	Th	0248	5.7	1514	5.5	2305	1302	39	48
28	F	0413	5.4	1718	5.3	2413	1331	44	43
29	Sa	0554	5.4	1833	5.4	0013	1359	44	43
30	Su	0659	5.6	1932	5.7	0125	1425	44	43
31	M	0755	6.0	2023	6.1	0240	1452	0649	1637

NOVEMBER

Day		Dover Tides HW time ht		time ht		Rising Moon rise	set	Setting Sun rise	set
1	Tu	0843	6.4	2109	6.5	0357	1520	0649	1637
2	W	0928	6.8	2151	6.8	0518	1552	49	37
3	Th	1011	7.0	2233	7.0	0639	1630	54	32
4	F	1054	7.2	2316	7.1	0759	1715	54	32
5	Sa	1138	7.2	----		0913	1810	54	32
6	Su	0001	7.1	1225	7.1	1017	1913	0659	1628
7	M	0048	7.0	1314	6.8	1110	2021	59	28
8	Tu	0139	6.7	1408	6.5	1153	2133	59	28
9	W	0236	6.4	1512	6.1	1227	2244	0704	23
10	Th	0339	6.1	1622	5.7	1256	2354	04	23
11	F	0447	5.8	1738	5.5	1322	2501	0704	1623
12	Sa	0601	5.7	1901	5.5	1345	0101	09	19
13	Su	0717	5.7	2008	5.7	1408	0207	09	19
14	M	0818	5.9	2057	5.9	1431	0312	09	19
15	Tu	0907	6.2	2137	6.1	1455	0416	14	15
16	W	0948	6.3	2212	6.3	1522	0518	0714	1615
17	Th	1025	6.4	2245	6.4	1553	0620	14	15
18	F	1059	6.5	2318	6.5	1629	0719	19	12
19	Sa	1130	6.5	2350	6.5	1710	0814	19	12
20	Su	1200	6.4	----		1758	0905	19	12
21	M	0019	6.5	1226	6.4	1852	0950	0723	1608
22	Tu	0045	6.4	1252	6.3	1951	1029	23	08
23	W	0112	6.3	1322	6.2	2054	1104	23	08
24	Th	0146	6.2	1401	6.1	2200	1134	28	06
25	F	0231	6.0	1451	5.8	2308	1201	28	06
26	Sa	0329	5.8	1600	5.6	2419	1227	0728	1606
27	Su	0447	5.7	1738	5.5	0019	1252	32	03
28	M	0608	5.7	1851	5.7	0132	1318	32	03
29	Tu	0714	6.0	1950	6.0	0249	1347	32	03
30	W	0811	6.3	2042	6.3	0407	1420	36	01

DECEMBER

Day		Dover Tides HW time ht		time ht		Rising Moon rise	set	Setting Sun rise	set
1	Th	0903	6.6	2131	6.6	0527	1501	0736	1601
2	F	0952	6.8	2218	6.8	0644	1550	36	01
3	Sa	1040	7.0	2305	7.0	0755	1650	40	00
4	Su	1127	7.0	2352	7.0	0856	1758	40	00
5	M			1215	6.9	0945	1911	40	00
6	Tu	0039	7.0	1304	6.8	1025	2025	0744	1559
7	W	0128	6.8	1355	6.5	1058	2138	44	59
8	Th	0218	6.6	1450	6.2	1125	2249	44	59
9	F	0312	6.3	1549	5.9	1150	2357	47	58
10	Sa	0409	6.0	1650	5.6	1213	2502	47	58
11	Su	0511	5.8	1756	5.5	1236	0102	0747	1558
12	M	0617	5.6	1906	5.5	1300	0207	50	58
13	Tu	0726	5.7	2010	5.6	1326	0310	50	58
14	W	0826	5.8	2101	5.8	1355	0412	50	58
15	Th	0916	6.0	2143	6.1	1429	0511	53	59
16	F	0957	6.1	2220	6.2	1508	0608	0753	1559
17	Sa	1033	6.2	2255	6.4	1554	0701	53	59
18	Su	1106	6.3	2328	6.5	1646	0749	55	59
19	M	1139	6.3	2359	6.5	1744	0830	55	59
20	Tu			1209	6.3	1846	0907	55	59
21	W	0029	6.5	1239	6.3	1951	0938	0756	1601
22	Th	0059	6.5	1310	6.3	2058	1006	56	01
23	F	0133	6.4	1347	6.2	2207	1032	56	01
24	Sa	0213	6.4	1431	6.1	2318	1057	58	03
25	Su	0302	6.2	1525	5.9	2431	1122	58	03
26	M	0401	6.0	1633	5.7	0031	1148	0758	1603
27	Tu	0513	5.8	1759	5.6	0145	1218	58	05
28	W	0633	5.8	1918	5.7	0302	1253	58	05
29	Th	0745	6.0	2023	6.0	0418	1336	58	05
30	F	0847	6.3	2121	6.3	0531	1429	59	07
31	Sa	0944	6.5	2213	6.6	0636	1531	0759	1607

TIDES

DEFINITIONS

Definitions of the various states of level of the sea and heights of land features which relate to it are illustrated below. Springs occur just after full and new moons and neaps about on the quarters; this is illustrated in Part 1, The Yachtsman's Calendar. Note especially:

1 Chart Datum, on most modern charts, is LAT, therefore there will almost always be more water than the chart shows.
2 The height of water, as calculated, should be added to the sounding on the chart to give the predicted depth of water.
3 The height of drying rocks (shown underlined on the chart) relates to Chart Datum.
4 Heights of light houses are given above MHWS.
5 At new and full moons, the time of high water is roughly constant for a particular locality throughout the year. This time, High Water, Full and Change, is about 1130 (GMT) for Portsmouth. Knowing this, a seaman can look at the moon and have a very good idea of the state of the tide without consulting any tables.

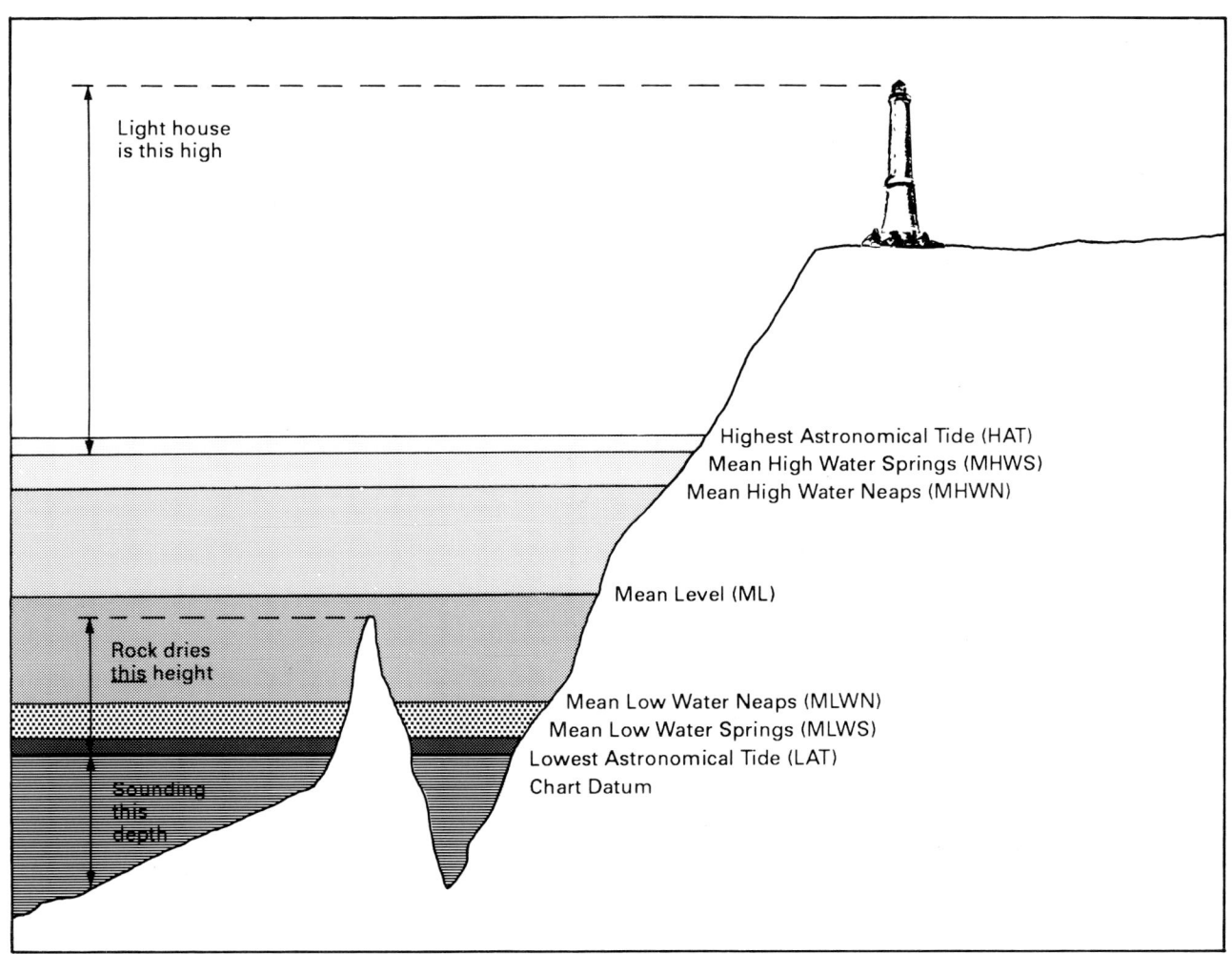

Light house is this high

Highest Astronomical Tide (HAT)
Mean High Water Springs (MHWS)
Mean High Water Neaps (MHWN)

Mean Level (ML)

Rock dries this height

Mean Low Water Neaps (MLWN)
Mean Low Water Springs (MLWS)
Lowest Astronomical Tide (LAT)
Chart Datum

Sounding this depth

HOW TO USE THE TIDE TABLES

The standard ports are arranged:
(1) English ports from east to west
(2) Channel Islands
(3) French ports from east to west

The tables show the times and heights of HW and LW for each day of the year. The times are GMT for English and Channel Island ports and GMT PLUS ONE HOUR for French ports. The heights are in metres.

Remember that calculated heights must be added to the charted depth to give the actual depth of water.

STANDARD PORTS

Times of HW and LW are read directly from the tables. To determine heights at intermediate times (or vice versa) you can either apply the 'twelfths' rule or use the tidal curves which are printed for each standard port. The 'twelfths' rule states that changes in height or speed take place as follows: $1/12$ in the first hour, $2/12$ in the second hour, $3/12$ in the third hour, $3/12$ in the fourth hour, $2/12$ in the fifth hour and $1/12$ in the sixth hour.

The tidal curves give much greater accuracy and the new layout allows very quick working and is therefore strongly recommended.

Using the example below, supposing one requires the height of tide at Shoreham at 1000 when HW is 0735 (5.0m) and LW is 1404 (1.7m).

1. Mark 5.0m on the top line and 1.7m on the bottom line and connect the two points.

2. Write in the time of HW in the box below the curve and extend the times so that it is easy to see where 1000 appears (2 hrs and 25 mins after HW).

3. Rule a line up from this time until it meets the tidal curve and then rule horizontally until the sloping line connecting HW and LW is met, then rule vertically to the HW line which is cut at 3.8m.

4. Height of tide at 1000 is then 3.8m.

5. By reversing the process, the time for a particular height of tide can be obtained.

6. Note that some curves have separate Spring and Neap lines; some, in the Solent area have an intermediate line between. Use the most appropriate one.

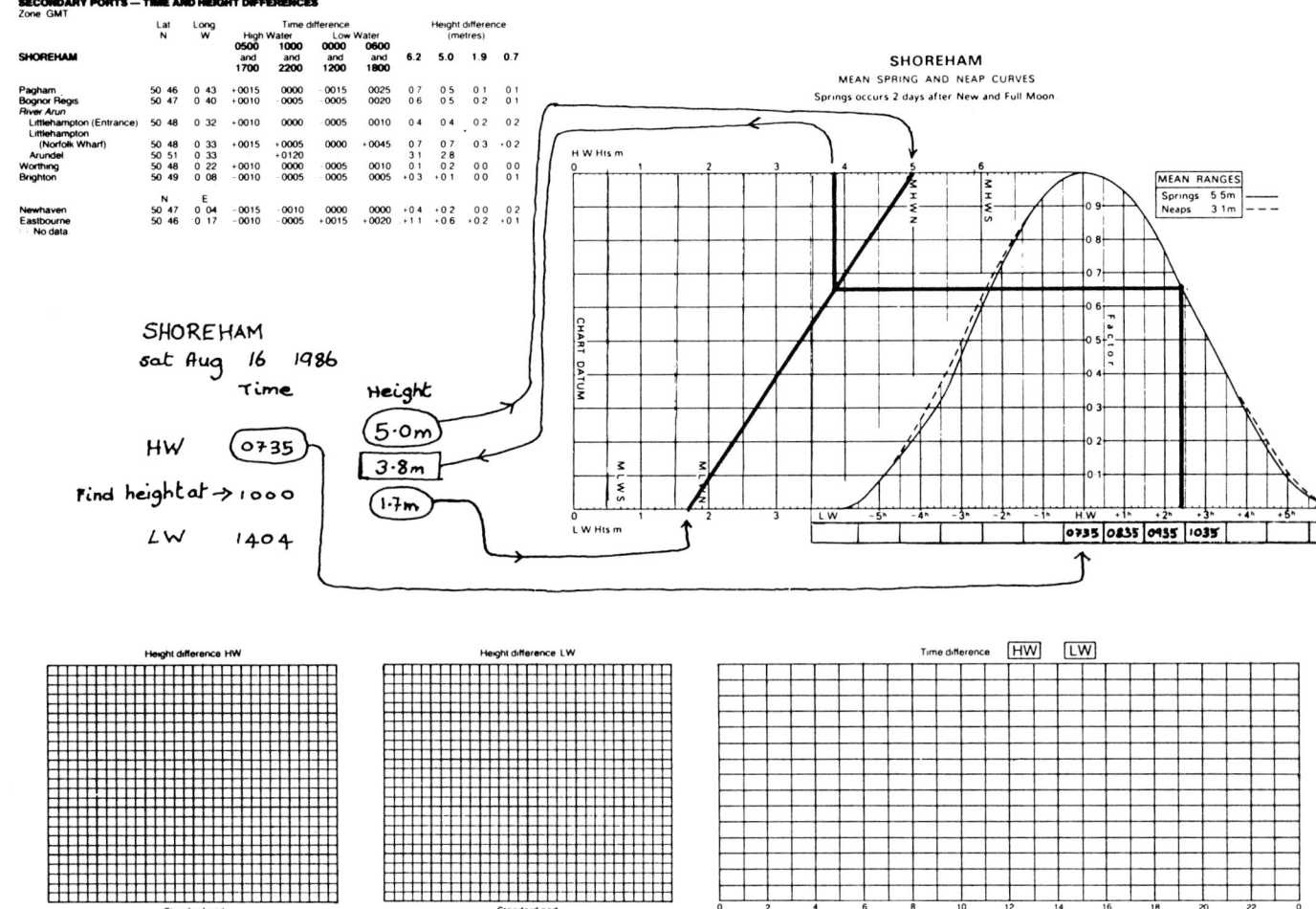

SECONDARY PORTS — TIME AND HEIGHT DIFFERENCES
Zone GMT

SHOREHAM	Lat N	Long W	High Water 0500 and 1700	High Water 1000 and 2200	Low Water 0000 and 1200	Low Water 0600 and 1800	6.2	5.0	1.9	0.7
Pagham	50 46	0 43	+0015	0000	-0015	0025	0 7	0 5	0 1	0 1
Bognor Regis	50 47	0 40	+0010	0005	-0005	0020	0 6	0 5	0 2	0 1
River Arun										
Littlehampton (Entrance)	50 48	0 32	+0010	0000	-0005	0010	0 4	0 4	0 2	0 2
Littlehampton (Norfolk Wharf)	50 48	0 33	+0015	+0005	0000	+0045	0 7	0 7	0 3	+0 2
Arundel	50 51	0 33		+0120			3 1	2 8		
Worthing	50 48	0 22	+0010	0000	0005	0010	0 1	0 2	0 0	0 0
Brighton	50 49	0 08	-0010	0005	0005	0005	+0 3	+0 1	0 0	0 1
	N	E								
Newhaven	50 47	0 04	-0015	-0010	0000	0000	+0 4	+0 2	0 0	0 0
Eastbourne	50 46	0 17	-0010	-0005	+0015	+0020	+1 1	+0 6	+0 2	+0 1
No data										

SHOREHAM
MEAN SPRING AND NEAP CURVES
Springs occurs 2 days after New and Full Moon

HW Hts m

CHART DATUM

MEAN RANGES
Springs   5 5m ———
Neaps   3 1m - - -

LW Hts m

LW -5ʰ -4ʰ -3ʰ -2ʰ -1ʰ HW +1ʰ +2ʰ +3ʰ +4ʰ +5ʰ LW

| 0735 | 0835 | 0935 | 1035 |

SHOREHAM
sat Aug 16 1986

Time   Height

HW 0735   5·0m
            3·8m
Find height at → 1000
            1·7m
LW 1404

Height difference HW	Height difference LW	Time difference [HW] [LW]

Standard port   Standard port

0   2   4   6   8   10   12   14   16   18   20   22   0
Standard port

SECONDARY PORTS

Using the example shown below, supposing one requires the height of tide at Eastbourne at 0600.

The principle is exactly the same as for a standard port but the time of high water and the height of tide at HW and LW must first be interpolated from the table which, for convenience, is now alongside the standard port tidal curve.

Interpolation can be done by eye and, for most yachtsmen's purposes, this is quite good enough. Indeed the differences are often so small that the standard port curve can be used directly.

Where the differences are large or where the navigator likes to work accurately, interpolation is necessary. This operation can be done by a simple arithmetic, by using a programmed calculator or graphically. Usually only HW time difference is needed to operate the curve but LW may be required specifically or the tidal curve, such as those for the Solent, may be based on LW in which case the work area should be used for LW.

Looking at HW height difference, and bearing in mind that it takes much longer to explain than to do, mark on the spring and neap heights of the standard port on the horizontal axis (6.2m and 5.0m). The scale is left to the navigator to fix himself. Then mark on the height differences, again selecting a suitable scale, which may not be the same as the horizontal axis scale, at springs and neaps on the vertical axis (+1.1m and +0.6m). Mark the intersections of the two axes and draw a line between them. This will allow height differences at Eastbourne to be read for any height of tide at Shoreham.

Suppose for the day in question, the tide table gives HW height at Shoreham is 5.5m. Ruling up to the sloping line and then across, show that the difference at Eastbourne is +0.8m. Hence height at HW is 5.5 + 0.8 = 6.3m.

Similarly, plot LW heights at Shoreham (1.9m and 0.7m) against differences at Eastbourne (+0.2m and +0.1m). If the tide table gives LW height at Shoreham as 1.4m, the difference at Eastbourne is +0.2m (to the nearest 0.1m). Hence height at LW is 1.4 + 0.2 = 1.6m.

The sloping line can now be drawn on the tidal curve connecting 6.3m with 1.6m.

Time differences for HW can now be plotted. The horizontal scale is fixed to cover 24 hours and the points plotted: −0010 at 0500, −0005 at 1000, −0010 at 1700 and −0005 at 2200; and connected.

With the time of HW at Shoreham, from the tide table, of 0246, strike up from this time and across to the vertical axis to show that the time difference at Eastbourne is −0009, hence HW Eastbourne is 0246 − 0009 = 0237.

0237 can now be inserted in the HW box under the tidal curve and extended to 0600, showing that the height of HW at Eastbourne will be 3.6m.

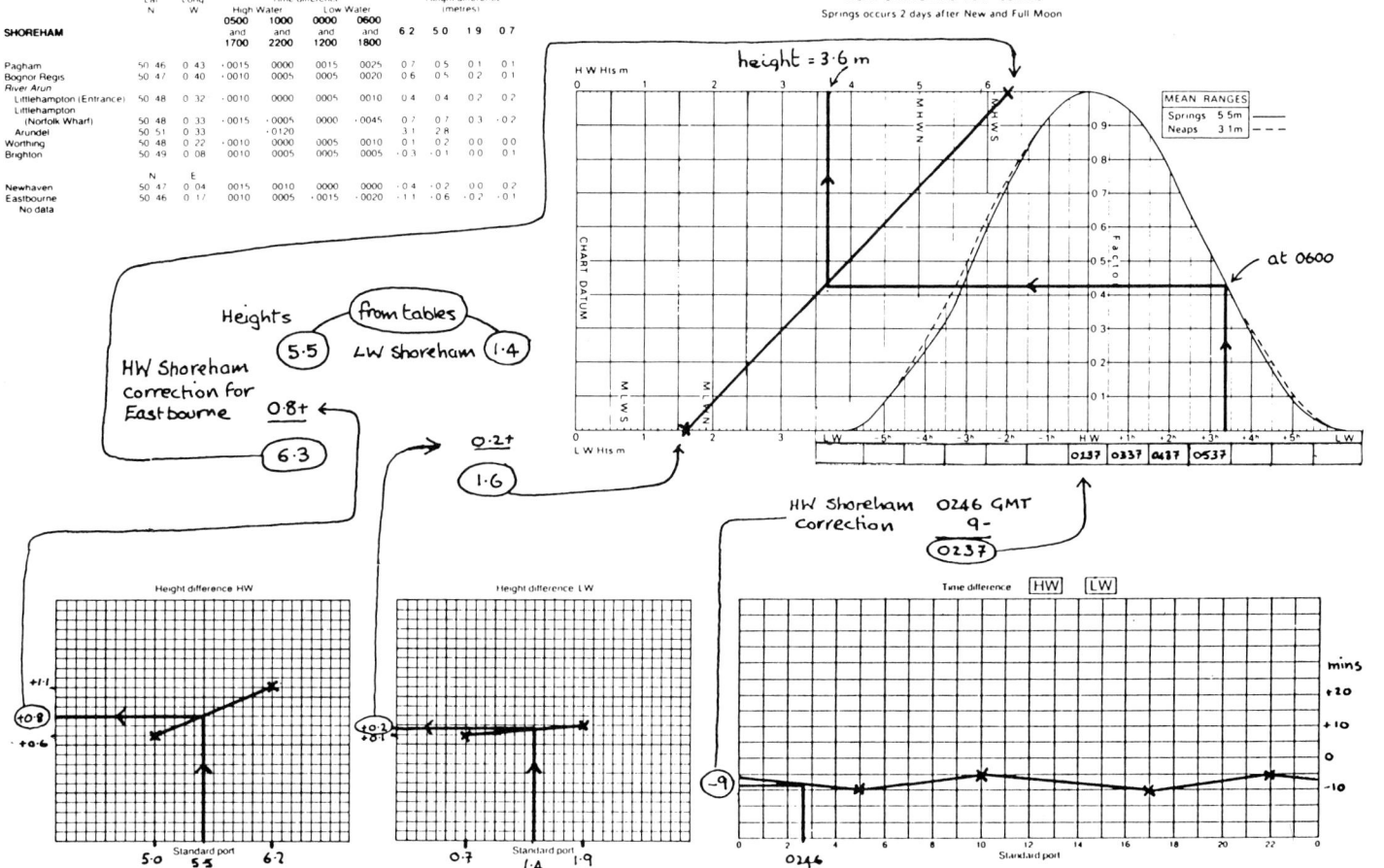

SECONDARY PORTS — TIME AND HEIGHT DIFFERENCES

Zone GMT

SHOREHAM	Lat N	Long W	High Water 0500 and 1700	High Water 1000 and 2200	Low Water 0000 and 1200	Low Water 0600 and 1800	Height difference (metres) 6.2	5.0	1.9	0.7
Pagham	50 46	0 43	·0015	0000	0015	0025	0.7	0.5	0.1	0.1
Bognor Regis	50 47	0 40	·0010	0005	0005	0005	0.6	0.5	0.2	0.1
River Arun										
Littlehampton (Entrance)	50 48	0 32	·0010	0000	0005	0010	0.4	0.4	0.2	0.2
Littlehampton (Norfolk Wharf)	50 48	0 33	·0015	·0005	0000	·0045	0.7	0.7	0.3	·0.2
Arundel	50 51	0 33		·0120			3.1	2.8		
Worthing	50 48	0 22	·0010	0000	0005	0010	0.1	0.2	0.0	0.0
Brighton	50 49	0 08	0010	0005	0005	0005	·0.3	·0.1	0.0	0.1
	N	E								
Newhaven	50 47	0 04	0015	0010	0000	0000	·0.4	·0.2	0.0	0.2
Eastbourne No data	50 46	0 17	0010	0005	·0015	·0020	·1.1	·0.6	·0.2	·0.1

SHOREHAM
MEAN SPRING AND NEAP CURVES
Springs occurs 2 days after New and Full Moon

height = 3·6 m

MEAN RANGES
Springs 5 5m
Neaps   3 1m

at 0600

Heights   from tables
HW Shoreham (5·5) LW Shoreham (1·4)
Correction for Eastbourne 0·8+
(6·3)   0·2+
         (1·6)

HW Shoreham 0246 GMT
correction   9−
             (0237)

Height difference HW   Height difference LW   Time difference [HW] [LW]

5·0 Standard port 6·2   0·7 Standard port 1·9   0246 Standard port
     5·5   1·4

DOVER

MEAN SPRING AND NEAP CURVES
Springs occur 2 days after New and Full Moon.

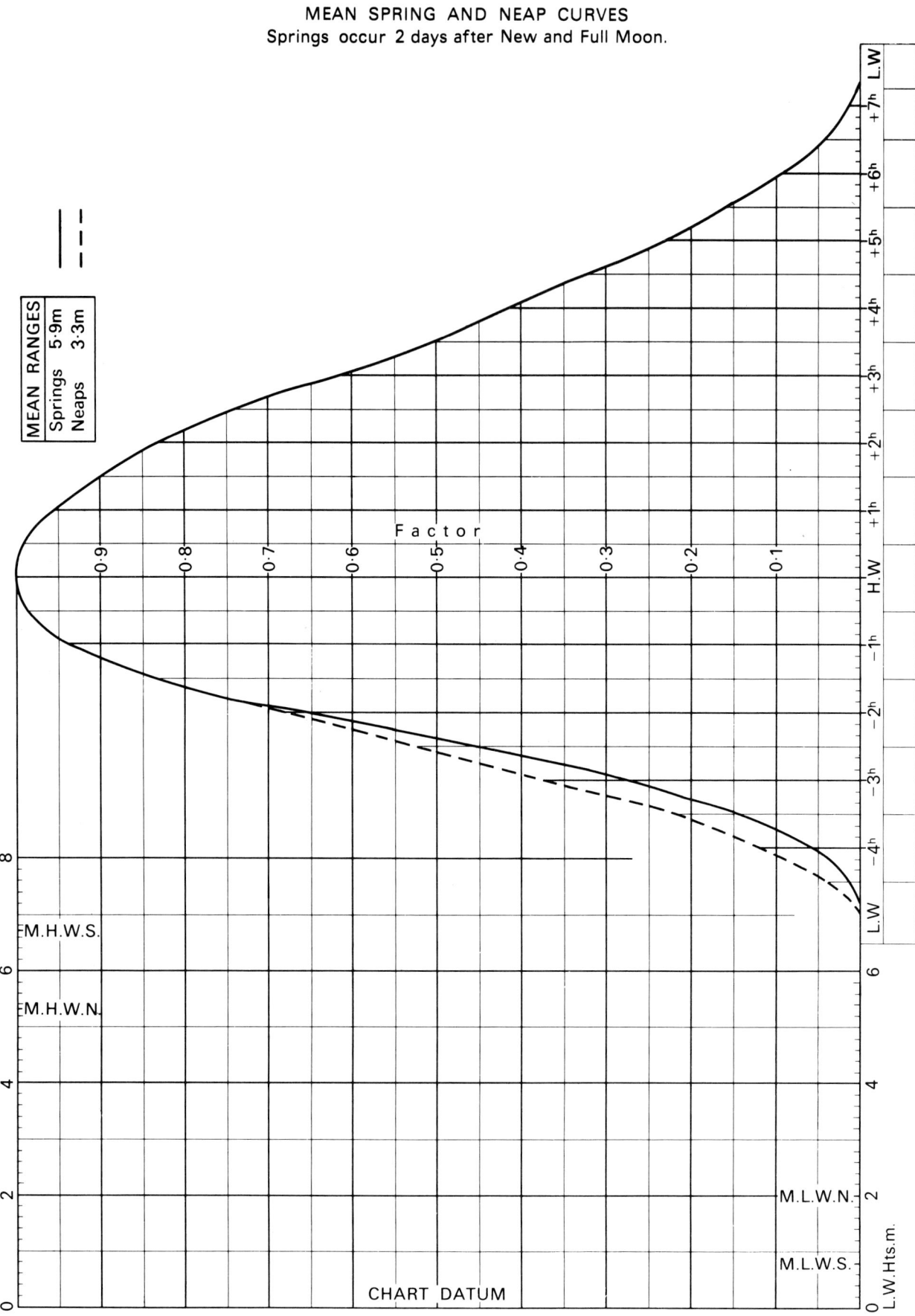

DOVER

51°07′N 1°19′E

Times and heights (in metres) of high and low water 1994
Time: GMT. For BST, ADD ONE HOUR in the shaded area
High Water, full and change, 1110

JANUARY

Day	Time	m	Time	m	Time	m	Time	m
1 SA	0038	6.7	0813	0.9	1254	6.5	2028	1.1
2 SU	0118	6.7	0854	1.0	1335	6.5	2107	1.2
3 M	0202	6.6	0937	1.1	1422	6.3	2149	1.3
4 TU	0252	6.5	1022	1.2	1516	6.1	2237	1.5
5 W	0348	6.2	1114	1.4	1620	5.8	2333	1.7
6 TH	0455	6.0	1214	1.6	1740	5.6		
7 F	0042	1.9	0613	5.8	1325	1.7	1901	5.6
8 SA	0159	1.9	0731	5.8	1439	1.6	2014	5.7
9 SU	0316	1.7	0842	6.0	1556	1.5	2117	6.0
10 M	0433	1.4	0944	6.2	1708	1.2	2210	6.3
11 TU ●	0537	1.1	1036	6.4	1805	1.0	2256	6.5
12 W	0629	0.9	1120	6.5	1853	0.9	2336	6.7
13 TH	0714	0.8	1200	6.6	1933	0.9		
14 F	0015	6.8	0753	0.8	1238	6.5	2007	1.0
15 SA	0054	6.8	0828	0.9	1314	6.4	2037	1.1
16 SU	0130	6.7	0859	1.0	1351	6.3	2103	1.3
17 M	0205	6.5	0927	1.2	1427	6.1	2127	1.4
18 TU	0239	6.2	0953	1.4	1505	5.8	2156	1.7
19 W	0315	5.9	1026	1.7	1550	5.5	2235	1.9
20 TH	0401	5.6	1109	1.9	1651	5.3	2325	2.2
21 F	0507	5.3	1211	2.1	1801	5.1		
22 SA	0042	2.3	0622	5.2	1335	2.2	1908	5.2
23 SU	0208	2.3	0730	5.3	1446	2.0	2010	5.4
24 M	0315	2.0	0829	5.6	1545	1.7	2102	5.7
25 TU	0410	1.6	0919	5.9	1638	1.4	2147	6.1
26 W	0501	1.3	1002	6.2	1727	1.2	2227	6.4
27 TH O	0549	1.0	1043	6.4	1813	1.0	2305	6.6
28 F	0636	0.8	1121	6.6	1857	0.9	2343	6.8
29 SA	0721	0.7	1159	6.7	1939	0.8		
30 SU	0021	6.9	0803	0.6	1238	6.7	2017	0.8
31 M	0102	7.0	0843	0.6	1319	6.7	2055	0.8

FEBRUARY

Day	Time	m	Time	m	Time	m	Time	m
1 TU	0144	6.9	0923	0.7	1403	6.5	2135	0.9
2 W	0230	6.7	1004	0.9	1453	6.3	2218	1.2
3 TH	0323	6.4	1050	1.2	1553	5.9	2309	1.5
4 F	0427	5.9	1146	1.6	1709	5.5		
5 SA	0013	1.9	0548	5.6	1256	1.8	1838	5.4
6 SU	0132	2.0	0717	5.5	1418	1.9	2002	5.5
7 M	0259	1.9	0840	5.7	1547	1.7	2111	5.8
8 TU	0428	1.5	0945	6.0	1702	1.3	2203	6.1
9 W	0530	1.1	1033	6.2	1757	1.1	2246	6.4
10 TH ●	0619	0.9	1112	6.4	1840	0.9	2324	6.6
11 F	0701	0.7	1147	6.5	1916	0.9		
12 SA	0000	6.7	0735	0.7	1220	6.5	1946	0.9
13 SU	0035	6.7	0805	0.8	1252	6.5	2010	1.0
14 M	0106	6.6	0829	0.9	1322	6.4	2030	1.1
15 TU	0133	6.5	0850	1.1	1349	6.2	2051	1.2
16 W	0156	6.3	0913	1.2	1413	6.0	2120	1.4
17 TH	0221	6.1	0943	1.4	1440	5.8	2155	1.6
18 F	0255	5.8	1020	1.7	1521	5.4	2237	1.9
19 SA	0344	5.4	1108	2.1	1645	5.1	2334	2.3
20 SU	0528	5.1	1226	2.3	1826	5.0		
21 M	0114	2.4	0654	5.1	1409	2.2	1935	5.2
22 TU	0239	2.1	0800	5.4	1517	1.9	2033	5.6
23 W	0341	1.6	0855	5.8	1613	1.5	2121	6.0
24 TH	0436	1.2	0941	6.2	1704	1.2	2203	6.4
25 F	0527	0.9	1022	6.5	1753	0.9	2243	6.7
26 SA O	0617	0.6	1101	6.7	1840	0.7	2322	7.0
27 SU	0704	0.4	1140	6.9	1922	0.6		
28 M	0001	7.1	0747	0.3	1219	6.9	2001	0.5

MARCH

Day	Time	m	Time	m	Time	m	Time	m
1 TU	0042	7.1	0827	0.3	1300	6.9	2039	0.5
2 W	0125	7.0	0905	0.5	1345	6.7	2118	0.7
3 TH	0210	6.8	0945	0.8	1434	6.4	2200	1.0
4 F	0303	6.3	1029	1.2	1533	5.9	2250	1.5
5 SA	0408	5.8	1124	1.7	1648	5.5	2353	1.9
6 SU	0531	5.4	1236	2.0	1815	5.3		
7 M	0114	2.1	0707	5.3	1403	2.0	1946	5.4
8 TU	0249	1.9	0838	5.5	1538	1.8	2057	5.7
9 W	0417	1.5	0935	5.9	1648	1.4	2147	6.1
10 TH	0514	1.1	1018	6.1	1738	1.1	2227	6.4
11 F	0601	0.9	1053	6.3	1818	1.0	2304	6.6
12 SA ●	0639	0.8	1125	6.5	1852	0.9	2338	6.6
13 SU	0711	0.8	1156	6.5	1919	0.9		
14 M	0011	6.6	0736	0.9			1940	1.0
15 TU	0039	6.6	0757	1.0	1253	6.4	1958	1.0
16 W	0101	6.5	0817	1.0	1314	6.3	2022	1.1
17 TH	0119	6.4	0841	1.2	1333	6.2	2051	1.2
18 F	0143	6.2	0911	1.4	1401	6.0	2125	1.5
19 SA	0216	6.0	0946	1.6	1439	5.7	2204	1.8
20 SU	0300	5.6	1029	2.0	1533	5.3	2255	2.1
21 M	0408	5.2	1129	2.3	1741	5.0		
22 TU	0015	2.3	0621	5.1	1324	2.3	1859	5.2
23 W	0201	2.1	0731	5.4	1444	2.0	2001	5.6
24 TH	0310	1.6	0828	5.8	1544	1.5	2052	6.0
25 F	0407	1.2	0916	6.2	1637	1.2	2137	6.4
26 SA	0502	0.8	0959	6.5	1729	0.9	2219	6.8
27 SU O	0555	0.5	1039	6.8	1818	0.6	2259	7.0
28 M	0644	0.3	1119	7.0	1903	0.5	2340	7.2
29 TU	0729	0.3	1200	7.0	1944	0.4		
30 W	0022	7.2	0809	0.3	1243	7.0	2023	0.5
31 TH	0107	7.0	0848	0.5	1329	6.8	2103	0.7

APRIL

Day	Time	m	Time	m	Time	m	Time	m
1 F	0154	6.7	0928	0.8	1420	6.5	2146	1.0
2 SA	0249	6.3	1013	1.3	1519	6.0	2237	1.4
3 SU	0355	5.8	1109	1.7	1629	5.6	2340	1.8
4 M	0513	5.4	1221	2.1	1747	5.4		
5 TU	0059	2.0	0648	5.3	1344	2.1	1916	5.4
6 W	0227	1.8	0817	5.5	1506	1.8	2029	5.7
7 TH	0346	1.5	0911	5.8	1612	1.5	2119	6.0
8 F	0443	1.2	0952	6.0	1703	1.3	2201	6.3
9 SA	0529	1.1	1026	6.2	1744	1.1	2237	6.4
10 SU	0607	1.0	1058	6.4	1819	1.1	2312	6.5
11 M ●	0637	1.0	1128	6.4	1846	1.1	2343	6.5
12 TU	0702	1.0	1158	6.4	1908	1.1		
13 W	0010	6.4	0724	1.1	1226	6.4	1931	1.1
14 TH	0033	6.4	0749	1.1	1248	6.3	1959	1.1
15 F	0052	6.3	0817	1.2	1309	6.3	2030	1.2
16 SA	0117	6.3	0848	1.4	1338	6.2	2104	1.4
17 SU	0152	6.1	0923	1.6	1418	5.9	2143	1.7
18 M	0237	5.8	1005	1.9	1512	5.6	2232	1.9
19 TU	0340	5.4	1100	2.1	1644	5.3	2341	2.1
20 W	0543	5.3	1227	2.2	1818	5.4		
21 TH	0119	2.0	0657	5.5	1405	2.0	1923	5.7
22 F	0234	1.6	0757	5.8	1509	1.6	2019	6.1
23 SA	0335	1.2	0848	6.2	1606	1.2	2108	6.5
24 SU	0433	0.9	0934	6.5	1701	0.9	2154	6.8
25 M O	0530	0.6	1017	6.8	1754	0.7	2238	7.0
26 TU	0623	0.4	1100	6.9	1843	0.5	2322	7.1
27 W	0711	0.4	1143	7.0	1928	0.5		
28 TH	0006	7.1	0754	0.4	1229	7.0	2010	0.5
29 F	0053	6.9	0835	0.6	1317	6.8	2053	0.7
30 SA	0142	6.6	0917	0.8	1408	6.5	2138	1.0

DOVER

51°07′N 1°19′E

Times and heights (in metres) of high and low water 1994
Time: GMT. For BST, ADD ONE HOUR in the shaded area
High Water, full and change, 1110

MAY

Day	Time	m		Day	Time	m
1 SU	0238	6.3	16 M	0140	6.1
	1003	1.3		0909	1.5
	1504	6.2		1409	6.1
	2228	1.4		2132	1.5
2 M	0339	5.9	17 TU	0225	5.9
	1056	1.7		0951	1.7
	1605	5.9		1502	5.9
	2328	1.7		2220	1.7
3 TU	0447	5.5	18 W	0324	5.7
	1201	2.0		1042	1.9
	1712	5.6		1609	5.7
				2321	1.8
4 W	0036	1.8	19 TH	0446	5.5
	0605	5.4		1150	2.0
	1312	2.0		1728	5.7
	1827	5.5			
5 TH	0148	1.8	20 F	0040	1.7
	0732	5.4		0614	5.6
	1418	1.9		1318	1.9
	1943	5.6		1841	5.8
6 F	0253	1.6	21 SA	0156	1.5
	0832	5.6		0721	5.8
	1518	1.7		1430	1.6
	2041	5.8		1944	6.1
7 SA	0351	1.5	22 SU	0301	1.2
	0916	5.9		0818	6.1
	1612	1.5		1532	1.3
	2127	6.1		2040	6.4
8 SU	0441	1.3	23 M	0403	1.0
	0953	6.1		0910	6.4
	1659	1.4		1633	1.1
	2206	6.2		2131	6.6
9 M	0522	1.2	24 TU	0505	0.8
	1027	6.2		0959	6.6
	1738	1.3		1732	0.8
	2241	6.3		2221	6.8
10 TU ●	0557	1.2	25 W O	0604	0.6
	1059	6.3		1046	6.8
	1810	1.2		1827	0.7
	2313	6.3		2309	6.9
11 W	0628	1.2	26 TH	0656	0.6
	1131	6.4		1133	6.9
	1839	1.2		1916	0.6
	2342	6.3		2357	6.9
12 TH	0657	1.2	27 F	0743	0.6
	1202	6.4		1220	6.9
	1909	1.1		2002	0.6
13 F	0009	6.3	28 SA	0044	6.8
	0728	1.2		0827	0.7
	1229	6.4		1307	6.8
	1942	1.2		2046	0.7
14 SA	0035	6.3	29 SU	0133	6.6
	0800	1.2		0909	1.0
	1256	6.3		1355	6.6
	2016	1.2		2130	0.9
15 SU	0103	6.2	30 M	0224	6.3
	0833	1.3		0952	1.2
	1328	6.2		1446	6.4
	2052	1.3		2217	1.2
			31 TU	0318	6.0
				1039	1.5
				1539	6.1
				2306	1.5

JUNE

Day	Time	m		Day	Time	m
1 W	0415	5.7	16 TH	0306	6.0
	1130	1.8		1028	1.5
	1635	5.8		1543	6.1
	2303	1.4			
2 TH	0001	1.7	17 F	0409	5.8
	0515	5.5		1124	1.7
	1228	2.0		1647	6.0
	1735	5.6			
3 F	0100	1.8	18 SA	0006	1.5
	0622	5.4		0524	5.7
	1328	2.0		1235	1.7
	1842	5.6		1759	5.9
4 SA	0159	1.8	19 SU	0117	1.5
	0732	5.5		0643	5.7
	1426	1.9		1350	1.7
	1948	5.6		1911	6.0
5 SU	0254	1.7	20 M	0228	1.4
	0829	5.6		0752	5.9
	1520	1.8		1500	1.5
	2044	5.8		2017	6.2
6 M	0347	1.6	21 TU	0337	1.2
	0915	5.8		0854	6.1
	1611	1.6		1609	1.3
	2129	5.9		2118	6.4
7 TU	0434	1.5	22 W	0446	1.0
	0954	6.0		0950	6.4
	1656	1.4		1715	1.0
	2208	6.1		2214	6.6
8 W	0518	1.3	23 TH O	0550	0.8
	1030	6.2		1040	6.6
	1736	1.3		1815	0.8
	2243	6.2		2306	6.7
9 TH ●	0557	1.3	24 F	0645	0.7
	1105	6.3		1127	6.8
	1814	1.2		1907	0.6
	2317	6.2		2353	6.7
10 F	0634	1.2	25 SA	0734	0.7
	1139	6.4		1212	6.8
	1851	1.1		1954	0.6
	2350	6.3			
11 SA	0711	1.2	26 SU	0038	6.7
	1211	6.4		0817	0.8
	1929	1.1		1256	6.8
				2036	0.7
12 SU	0021	6.3	27 M	0122	6.6
	0747	1.2		0856	0.9
	1244	6.4		1339	6.7
	2007	1.1		2116	0.8
13 M	0054	6.3	28 TU	0206	6.4
	0824	1.2		0934	1.1
	1319	6.4		1423	6.5
	2045	1.2		2155	1.0
14 TU	0131	6.2	29 W	0251	6.1
	0901	1.3		1010	1.4
	1400	6.4		1508	6.3
	2126	1.2		2234	1.3
15 W	0215	6.1	30 TH	0338	5.9
	0942	1.4		1048	1.6
	1447	6.3		1556	6.0
	2211	1.3		2316	1.6

JULY

Day	Time	m		Day	Time	m
1 F	0430	5.6	16 SA	0341	6.0
	1132	1.9		1101	1.5
	1648	5.7		1617	6.1
	2337	1.4			
2 SA	0005	1.8	17 SU	0451	5.8
	0526	5.4		1203	1.7
	1228	2.1		1729	5.9
	1745	5.5			
3 SU	0103	2.0	18 M	0044	1.6
	0628	5.3		0615	5.6
	1331	2.1		1318	1.8
	1849	5.4		1849	5.8
4 M	0205	2.0	19 TU	0200	1.6
	0733	5.4		0736	5.7
	1433	2.0		1437	1.7
	1952	5.5		2007	5.9
5 TU	0303	1.8	20 W	0319	1.5
	0832	5.6		0846	5.9
	1530	1.8		1554	1.4
	2049	5.7		2116	6.1
6 W	0357	1.6	21 TH	0435	1.3
	0921	5.8		0946	6.2
	1621	1.6		1707	1.1
	2135	5.9		2216	6.4
7 TH	0446	1.4	22 F O	0542	1.0
	1002	6.0		1036	6.5
	1707	1.4		1807	0.9
	2216	6.1		2305	6.5
8 F ●	0531	1.3	23 SA	0636	0.8
	1040	6.2		1120	6.7
	1751	1.2		1858	0.7
	2253	6.2		2348	6.6
9 SA	0614	1.2	24 SU	0722	0.7
	1116	6.4		1200	6.8
	1833	1.1		1942	0.6
	2330	6.3			
10 SU	0656	1.1	25 M	0027	6.7
	1151	6.5		0801	0.8
	1915	1.0		1240	6.8
				2020	0.6
11 M	0004	6.4	26 TU	0104	6.6
	0735	1.1		0835	0.9
	1227	6.6		1319	6.8
	1956	0.9		2054	0.8
12 TU	0040	6.4	27 W	0141	6.4
	0814	1.0		0906	1.0
	1303	6.6		1357	6.6
	2036	0.9		2124	1.0
13 W	0117	6.5	28 TH	0219	6.2
	0852	1.1		0933	1.3
	1343	6.6		1434	6.4
	2116	0.9		2153	1.2
14 TH	0158	6.4	29 F	0258	6.0
	0930	1.1		0957	1.5
	1427	6.5		1513	6.1
	2157	1.0		2221	1.5
15 F	0246	6.3	30 SA	0342	5.7
	1012	1.3		1027	1.8
	1518	6.4		1557	5.8
	2243	1.2		2256	1.8
			31 SU	0436	5.4
				1111	2.0
				1654	5.5
				2350	2.1

AUGUST

Day	Time	m		Day	Time	m
1 M	0539	5.2	16 TU	0018	1.8
	1219	2.3		0600	5.5
	1801	5.3		1256	2.0
				1839	5.6
2 TU	0110	2.2	17 W	0142	1.9
	0646	5.2		0727	5.5
	1346	2.3		1423	1.9
	1909	5.3		2005	5.7
3 W	0226	2.1	18 TH	0311	1.7
	0752	5.3		0841	5.8
	1454	2.0		1552	1.6
	2012	5.5		2119	6.0
4 TH	0327	1.8	19 F	0432	1.4
	0848	5.6		0939	6.1
	1551	1.7		1702	1.2
	2106	5.8		2213	6.3
5 F	0419	1.5	20 SA	0533	1.1
	0934	6.0		1026	6.5
	1641	1.4		1757	0.9
	2150	6.1		2256	6.5
6 SA	0508	1.3	21 SU O	0622	0.9
	1013	6.3		1106	6.7
	1728	1.1		1843	0.7
	2230	6.3		2333	6.6
7 SU ●	0554	1.1	22 M	0703	0.8
	1051	6.5		1143	6.8
	1814	0.9		1923	0.7
	2307	6.5			
8 M	0638	1.0	23 TU	0007	6.6
	1127	6.7		0737	0.8
	1859	0.8		1220	6.8
	2343	6.6		1955	0.7
9 TU	0719	0.9	24 W	0041	6.6
	1204	6.8		0807	0.9
	1942	0.7		1254	6.8
				2023	0.9
10 W	0019	6.7	25 TH	0113	6.5
	0758	0.8		0831	1.1
	1242	6.9		1327	6.6
	2021	0.6		2047	1.0
11 TH	0057	6.7	26 F	0144	6.3
	0836	0.8		0849	1.2
	1322	6.9		1356	6.4
	2100	0.7		2106	1.2
12 F	0138	6.6	27 SA	0213	6.1
	0913	0.9		0910	1.4
	1406	6.8		1423	6.2
	2138	0.9		2130	1.5
13 SA	0224	6.4	28 SU	0244	5.8
	0953	1.1		0941	1.7
	1455	6.5		1455	5.8
	2221	1.1		2203	1.8
14 SU	0319	6.1	29 M	0325	5.5
	1040	1.4		1021	2.0
	1554	6.1		1546	5.5
	2312	1.5		2247	2.1
15 M	0430	5.7	30 TU	0450	5.2
	1139	1.7		1114	2.3
	1711	5.7		1718	5.2
				2353	2.4
			31 W	0607	5.1
				1247	2.4
				1835	5.1

DOVER
51°07'N 1°19'E

Times and heights (in metres) of high and low water 1994
Time: GMT. For BST, ADD ONE HOUR in the shaded area
High Water, full and change, 1110

SEPTEMBER

Date	Day	Time	m	Time	m	Time	m	Time	m
1	TH	0145	2.4	0715	5.2	1419	2.2	1940	5.4
16	F	0307	1.9	0829	5.8	1547	1.6	2111	5.9
2	F	0257	2.0	0815	5.6	1521	1.8	2037	5.7
17	SA	0420	1.5	0924	6.2	1649	1.2	2159	6.2
3	SA	0353	1.7	0904	6.0	1614	1.4	2124	6.1
18	SU	0515	1.2	1007	6.5	1739	0.9	2237	6.5
4	SU	0443	1.3	0945	6.4	1704	1.1	2204	6.4
19	M	0559	1.0	1044	6.7	1821	0.8	2310	6.6
5	M	0530	1.1	1024	6.7	1752	0.8	2242	6.7
20	TU	0637	1.0	1120	6.8	1857	0.8	2341	6.6
6	TU	0616	0.9	1102	6.9	1839	0.6	2319	6.8
21	W	0708	1.0	1154	6.8	1925	0.9		
7	W	0659	0.8	1140	7.1	1922	0.5	2356	6.9
22	TH	0012	6.6	0733	1.1	1227	6.7	1948	1.0
8	TH	0739	0.7	1219	7.1	2002	0.5		
23	F	0043	6.5	0752	1.2	1255	6.6	2007	1.2
9	F	0035	6.9	0816	0.7	1300	7.1	2040	0.6
24	SA	0110	6.4	0811	1.3	1317	6.4	2027	1.3
10	SA	0118	6.8	0854	0.8	1344	6.9	2119	0.8
25	SU	0132	6.2	0836	1.4	1337	6.2	2054	1.5
11	SU	0205	6.5	0935	1.1	1435	6.5	2201	1.2
26	M	0153	6.0	0909	1.6	1406	6.0	2128	1.7
12	M	0302	6.1	1023	1.5	1538	6.0	2252	1.6
27	TU	0226	5.8	0948	1.9	1446	5.6	2210	2.1
13	TU	0417	5.7	1123	1.9	1701	5.6		
28	W	0318	5.4	1036	2.2	1601	5.2	2303	2.4
14	W	0000	2.0	0545	5.5	1242	2.1	1831	5.5
29	TH	0526	5.1	1147	2.5	1801	5.1		
15	TH	0131	2.1	0713	5.5	1418	2.0	2004	5.6
30	F	0045	2.5	0638	5.3	1337	2.3	1909	5.4

OCTOBER

Date	Day	Time	m	Time	m	Time	m	Time	m
1	SA	0222	2.2	0740	5.6	1449	1.9	2006	5.7
16	SU	0350	1.6	0857	6.1	1621	1.3	2133	6.1
2	SU	0322	1.8	0831	6.0	1545	1.4	2055	6.1
17	M	0443	1.4	0940	6.4	1710	1.1	2209	6.3
3	M	0414	1.4	0915	6.4	1637	1.1	2137	6.5
18	TU	0526	1.2	1018	6.6	1750	1.1	2242	6.5
4	TU	0503	1.1	0956	6.8	1727	0.8	2216	6.8
19	W	0603	1.2	1053	6.7	1824	1.1	2313	6.6
5	W	0551	0.9	1035	7.1	1816	0.6	2254	7.0
20	TH	0634	1.2	1126	6.7	1850	1.1	2344	6.6
6	TH	0636	0.7	1115	7.2	1901	0.5	2334	7.1
21	F	0658	1.2	1157	6.6	1913	1.2		
7	F	0718	0.7	1156	7.2	1943	0.5		
22	SA	0014	6.6	0719	1.3	1225	6.5	1933	1.3
8	SA	0016	7.1	0758	0.7	1240	7.1	2022	0.7
23	SU	0042	6.5	0743	1.3	1247	6.4	1959	1.4
9	SU	0101	6.9	0839	0.9	1327	6.9	2102	0.9
24	M	0103	6.3	0813	1.4	1308	6.3	2030	1.5
10	M	0151	6.6	0922	1.1	1420	6.5	2146	1.3
25	TU	0126	6.2	0847	1.6	1337	6.1	2104	1.7
11	TU	0250	6.2	1011	1.5	1527	6.0	2238	1.8
26	W	0200	6.0	0926	1.8	1417	5.8	2145	2.0
12	W	0402	5.8	1112	1.9	1647	5.6	2347	2.1
27	TH	0248	5.7	1012	2.1	1514	5.5	2234	2.2
13	TH	0521	5.6	1231	2.1	1815	5.5		
28	F	0413	5.4	1113	2.3	1718	5.3	2343	2.4
14	F	0115	2.2	0646	5.6	1403	2.0	1945	5.6
29	SA	0554	5.4	1247	2.2	1833	5.4		
15	SA	0242	2.0	0802	5.8	1523	1.6	2048	5.9
30	SU	0133	2.3	0659	5.6	1409	1.9	1932	5.7
31	M	0244	1.9	0755	6.0	1511	1.5	2023	6.1

NOVEMBER

Date	Day	Time	m	Time	m	Time	m	Time	m
1	TU	0341	1.5	0843	6.4	1607	1.1	2109	6.5
16	W	0444	1.5	0948	6.3	1709	1.3	2212	6.3
2	W	0434	1.2	0928	6.8	1701	0.9	2151	6.8
17	TH	0525	1.4	1025	6.4	1744	1.3	2245	6.4
3	TH	0525	1.0	1011	7.0	1753	0.7	2233	7.0
18	F	0559	1.3	1059	6.5	1814	1.3	2318	6.5
4	F	0615	0.8	1054	7.2	1841	0.6	2316	7.1
19	SA	0627	1.3	1130	6.5	1842	1.3	2350	6.5
5	SA	0701	0.7	1138	7.2	1926	0.6		
20	SU	0655	1.3	1200	6.4	1910	1.3		
6	SU	0001	7.1	0745	0.7	1225	7.1	2008	0.8
21	M	0019	6.5	0725	1.3	1226	6.4	1941	1.4
7	M	0048	7.0	0829	0.9	1314	6.8	2051	1.0
22	TU	0045	6.4	0758	1.4	1252	6.3	2014	1.5
8	TU	0139	6.7	0914	1.1	1408	6.5	2136	1.4
23	W	0112	6.3	0834	1.5	1322	6.2	2049	1.6
9	W	0236	6.4	1004	1.4	1512	6.1	2228	1.7
24	TH	0146	6.2	0912	1.6	1401	6.0	2128	1.8
10	TH	0339	6.1	1102	1.7	1622	5.7	2330	2.0
25	F	0231	6.0	0956	1.8	1451	5.8	2213	2.0
11	F	0447	5.8	1210	1.9	1738	5.5		
26	SA	0329	5.8	1050	1.9	1600	5.6	2310	2.1
12	SA	0042	2.2	0601	5.8	1324	1.9	1901	5.5
27	SU	0447	5.7	1200	2.0	1738	5.5		
13	SU	0154	2.1	0717	5.7	1434	1.8	2008	5.7
28	M	0031	2.2	0608	5.7	1322	1.9	1851	5.7
14	M	0300	1.9	0818	5.9	1535	1.6	2057	5.9
29	TU	0157	2.0	0714	6.0	1432	1.6	1950	6.0
15	TU	0356	1.7	0907	6.2	1626	1.4	2137	6.1
30	W	0304	1.7	0811	6.3	1535	1.3	2042	6.3

DECEMBER

Date	Day	Time	m	Time	m	Time	m	Time	m
1	TH	0404	1.4	0903	6.6	1634	1.0	2131	6.6
16	F	0445	1.6	0957	6.1	1705	1.5	2220	6.2
2	F	0503	1.1	0952	6.8	1732	0.8	2218	6.8
17	SA	0525	1.4	1033	6.2	1742	1.4	2255	6.4
3	SA	0558	0.9	1040	7.0	1826	0.7	2305	7.0
18	SU	0601	1.3	1106	6.3	1818	1.3	2328	6.5
4	SU	0649	0.7	1127	7.0	1915	0.7	2352	7.0
19	M	0636	1.2	1139	6.3	1852	1.3	2359	6.5
5	M	0737	0.7	1215	6.9	2001	0.8		
20	TU	0711	1.2	1209	6.3	1928	1.3		
6	TU	0039	7.0	0823	0.8	1304	6.8	2044	1.0
21	W	0029	6.5	0748	1.2	1239	6.3	2003	1.3
7	W	0128	6.8	0909	0.9	1355	6.5	2127	1.2
22	TH	0059	6.5	0825	1.2	1310	6.3	2039	1.4
8	TH	0218	6.6	0955	1.2	1450	6.2	2213	1.5
23	F	0133	6.4	0903	1.3	1347	6.2	2116	1.5
9	F	0312	6.3	1044	1.4	1549	5.9	2302	1.8
24	SA	0213	6.4	0944	1.4	1431	6.1	2156	1.6
10	SA	0409	6.0	1137	1.7	1650	5.6	2358	2.0
25	SU	0302	6.2	1030	1.6	1525	5.9	2245	1.8
11	SU	0511	5.8	1235	1.9	1756	5.5		
26	M	0401	6.0	1125	1.7	1633	5.7	2346	1.9
12	M	0100	2.1	0617	5.6	1336	1.9	1906	5.5
27	TU	0513	5.8	1234	1.7	1759	5.6		
13	TU	0203	2.1	0726	5.7	1435	1.9	2010	5.6
28	W	0105	2.0	0633	5.8	1350	1.7	1918	5.7
14	W	0302	1.8	0826	5.8	1531	1.7	2101	5.8
29	TH	0225	1.8	0745	6.0	1503	1.5	2023	6.0
15	TH	0357	1.8	0916	6.0	1621	1.6	2143	6.1
30	F	0337	1.5	0847	6.3	1612	1.2	2121	6.3
31	SA	0444	1.2	0944	6.5	1717	1.0	2213	6.6

13

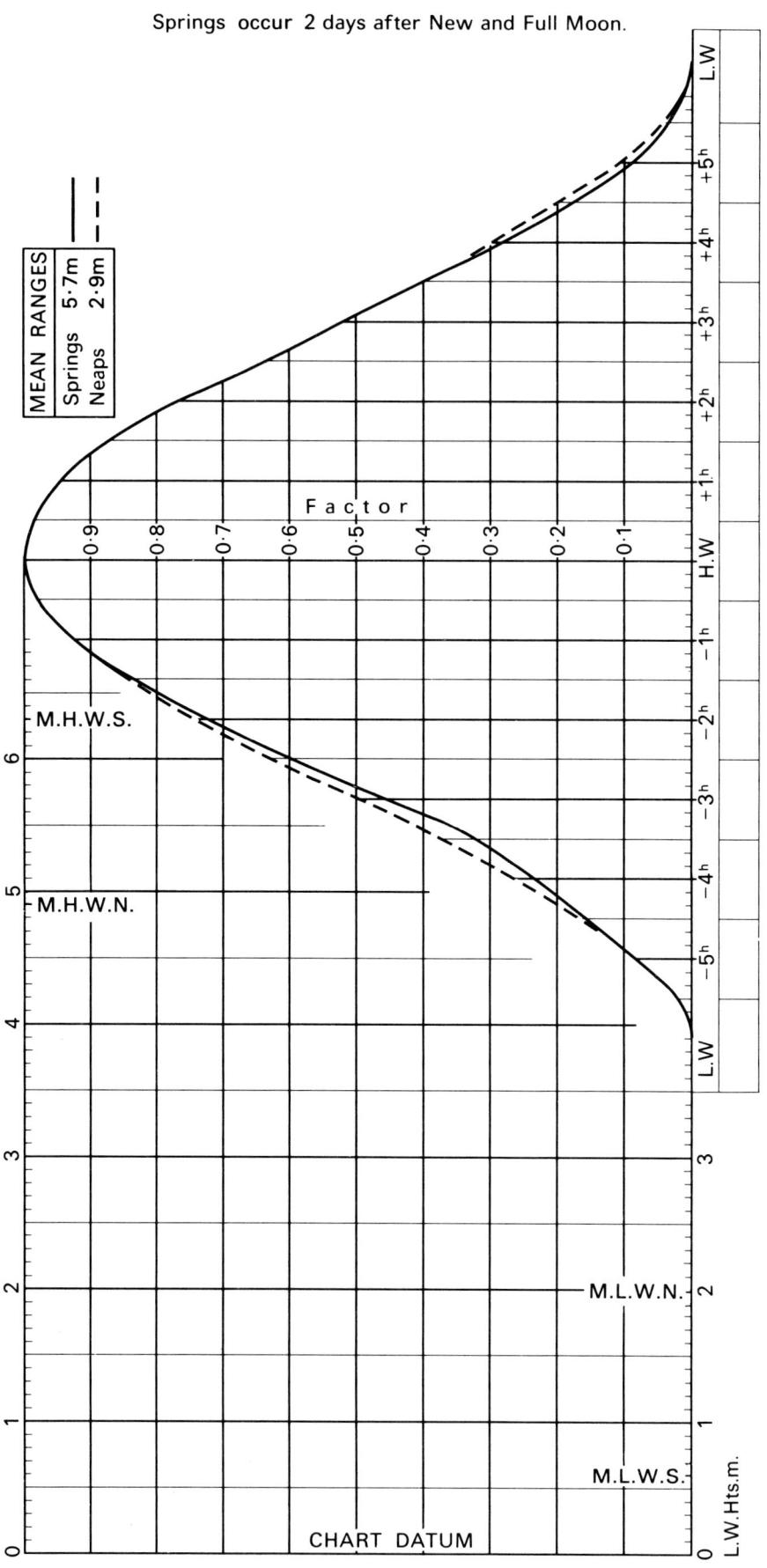

SHOREHAM

MEAN SPRING AND NEAP CURVES

Springs occur 2 days after New and Full Moon.

SHOREHAM
50°50′N 0°15′W

Times and heights (in metres) of high and low water 1994
Time: GMT. For BST, ADD ONE HOUR in the shaded area
High Water, full and change, 1122

JANUARY

Day	Time	m	Time	m	Time	m	Time	m
1 SA	0057	6.2	0705	0.8	1309	6.2	1929	0.6
16 SU	0148	6.1	0746	1.0	1359	5.9	2005	0.9
2 SU	0137	6.2	0747	0.8	1352	6.1	2011	0.7
17 M	0219	5.9	0821	1.1	1429	5.7	2040	1.1
3 M	0220	6.1	0834	0.9	1437	5.9	2058	0.8
18 TU	0246	5.7	0858	1.4	1458	5.4	2117	1.3
4 TU	0307	5.9	0926	1.1	1528	5.7	2150	1.1
19 W	0314	5.4	0940	1.6	1534	5.1	2200	1.6
5 W	0401	5.6	1027	1.3	1626	5.4	2252	1.3
20 TH	0354	5.1	1030	1.9	1627	4.8	2251	1.9
6 TH	0505	5.4	1139	1.5	1735	5.2		
21 F	0500	4.8	1130	2.1	1758	4.6	2356	2.1
7 F	0006	1.5	0621	5.3	1256	1.5	1902	5.1
22 SA	0630	4.8	1242	2.1	1910	4.7		
8 SA	0125	1.5	0744	5.4	1405	1.3	2024	5.3
23 SU	0114	2.1	0736	4.9	1403	1.9	2012	4.9
9 SU	0232	1.3	0854	5.6	1505	1.1	2129	5.6
24 M	0231	1.9	0833	5.2	1507	1.6	2107	5.3
10 M	0330	1.1	0952	5.9	1559	0.8	2223	5.9
25 TU	0327	1.5	0923	5.6	1554	1.2	2155	5.7
11 TU ●	0421	0.9	1042	6.1	1648	0.7	2312	6.1
26 W	0412	1.2	1008	5.9	1636	0.9	2239	6.0
12 W	0508	0.8	1129	6.2	1733	0.6	2356	6.3
27 TH O	0453	0.9	1051	6.1	1716	0.7	2320	6.2
13 TH	0553	0.7	1211	6.3	1816	0.6		
28 F	0532	0.7	1133	6.3	1755	0.5		
14 F	0037	6.3	0633	0.8	1251	6.2	1855	0.6
29 SA	0001	6.4	0611	0.6	1215	6.4	1834	0.4
15 SA	0114	6.3	0711	0.8	1326	6.1	1931	0.7
30 SU	0042	6.5	0652	0.5	1257	6.5	1914	0.4
31 M	0123	6.5	0734	0.5	1338	6.4	1956	0.4

FEBRUARY

Day	Time	m	Time	m	Time	m	Time	m
1 TU	0204	6.4	0818	0.6	1421	6.2	2040	0.6
16 W	0200	5.8	0822	1.1	1415	5.6	2040	1.2
2 W	0247	6.1	0906	0.8	1508	5.9	2129	0.9
17 TH	0228	5.6	0857	1.4	1447	5.4	2116	1.5
3 TH	0336	5.8	1001	1.1	1601	5.5	2225	1.3
18 F	0305	5.3	0938	1.7	1529	5.0	2200	1.8
4 F	0435	5.4	1109	1.5	1707	5.1	2340	1.6
19 SA	0352	4.9	1034	2.0	1628	4.7	2303	2.1
5 SA	0548	5.1	1233	1.6	1836	4.9		
20 SU	0505	4.6	1149	2.1	1828	4.5		
6 SU	0108	1.7	0725	5.0	1350	1.6	2015	5.0
21 M	0027	2.2	0658	4.6	1315	2.0	1939	4.8
7 M	0221	1.6	0847	5.3	1454	1.3	2122	5.4
22 TU	0153	1.9	0803	5.0	1431	1.7	2038	5.2
8 TU	0320	1.3	0945	5.6	1547	1.0	2215	5.8
23 W	0257	1.5	0858	5.4	1525	1.3	2129	5.6
9 W	0410	1.0	1034	5.9	1634	0.8	2301	6.1
24 TH	0346	1.1	0946	5.8	1609	0.9	2215	6.0
10 TH ●	0455	0.8	1117	6.1	1717	0.6	2341	6.2
25 F	0428	0.8	1031	6.2	1651	0.6	2259	6.4
11 F	0536	0.7	1156	6.2	1757	0.6		
26 SA O	0510	0.5	1115	6.4	1732	0.4	2342	6.6
12 SA	0018	6.3	0613	0.7	1232	6.2	1832	0.6
27 SU	0551	0.3	1159	6.6	1814	0.2		
13 SU	0052	6.3	0647	0.7	1303	6.2	1905	0.6
28 M	0024	6.7	0633	0.2	1242	6.7	1855	0.2
14 M	0120	6.2	0718	0.8	1329	6.0	1936	0.8
15 TU	0141	6.0	0749	0.9	1350	5.8	2007	0.9

MARCH

Day	Time	m	Time	m	Time	m	Time	m
1 TU	0105	6.7	0716	0.2	1323	6.6	1938	0.2
16 W	0105	6.0	0720	0.8	1320	5.9	1937	0.9
2 W	0146	6.5	0801	0.4	1406	6.4	2022	0.5
17 TH	0127	5.9	0750	0.9	1346	5.7	2007	1.1
3 TH	0228	6.2	0847	0.6	1451	6.0	2110	0.8
18 F	0156	5.7	0821	1.2	1418	5.5	2040	1.3
4 F	0315	5.8	0939	1.0	1543	5.5	2205	1.3
19 SA	0232	5.4	0858	1.4	1457	5.2	2123	1.6
5 SA	0413	5.3	1044	1.5	1649	5.1	2319	1.7
20 SU	0316	5.0	0950	1.7	1550	4.8	2222	1.9
6 SU	0525	4.9	1214	1.7	1818	4.8		
21 M	0418	4.6	1102	2.0	1726	4.5	2345	2.1
7 M	0054	1.8	0710	4.7	1334	1.7	2002	4.9
22 TU	0615	4.5	1229	1.9	1906	4.8		
8 TU	0208	1.7	0835	5.0	1437	1.4	2108	5.3
23 W	0113	1.9	0731	4.9	1350	1.6	2007	5.2
9 W	0306	1.3	0932	5.4	1530	1.1	2158	5.7
24 TH	0222	1.5	0830	5.3	1449	1.2	2100	5.7
10 TH	0354	1.0	1018	5.8	1614	0.9	2241	6.0
25 F	0315	1.0	0921	5.8	1537	0.8	2149	6.1
11 F	0435	0.8	1058	6.0	1655	0.7	2319	6.2
26 SA	0400	0.7	1009	6.2	1621	0.5	2235	6.4
12 SA ●	0513	0.7	1131	6.1	1732	0.6	2353	6.2
27 SU O	0444	0.4	1055	6.5	1705	0.3	2320	6.7
13 SU	0549	0.6	1208	6.1	1806	0.6		
28 M	0528	0.2	1141	6.6	1750	0.1		
14 M	0023	6.2	0620	0.6	1236	6.1	1837	0.6
29 TU	0004	6.8	0612	0.1	1226	6.7	1834	0.1
15 TU	0047	6.1	0651	0.7	1259	6.0	1908	0.7
30 W	0047	6.7	0657	0.1	1309	6.6	1919	0.2
31 TH	0129	6.6	0743	0.3	1353	6.4	2005	0.4

APRIL

Day	Time	m	Time	m	Time	m	Time	m
1 F	0212	6.2	0830	0.6	1439	6.0	2053	0.8
16 SA	0134	5.7	0755	1.0	1358	5.5	2015	1.2
2 SA	0300	5.7	0922	1.0	1532	5.6	2148	1.3
17 SU	0210	5.4	0833	1.2	1438	5.3	2058	1.5
3 SU	0356	5.2	1024	1.4	1635	5.1	2301	1.7
18 M	0254	5.1	0924	1.5	1530	5.0	2156	1.7
4 M	0506	4.8	1151	1.7	1756	4.8		
19 TU	0352	4.8	1029	1.7	1644	4.8	2309	1.8
5 TU	0034	1.8	0643	4.6	1311	1.7	1935	4.9
20 W	0520	4.6	1146	1.7	1825	4.9		
6 W	0146	1.7	0811	4.9	1413	1.5	2041	5.3
21 TH	0031	1.7	0653	4.9	1307	1.5	1933	5.2
7 TH	0243	1.4	0907	5.3	1504	1.2	2131	5.6
22 F	0144	1.4	0758	5.3	1411	1.2	2029	5.7
8 F	0329	1.1	0953	5.6	1548	1.0	2213	5.9
23 SA	0241	1.0	0853	5.7	1504	0.8	2121	6.1
9 SA	0409	0.9	1033	5.8	1627	0.8	2250	6.0
24 SU	0331	0.6	0944	6.1	1552	0.5	2210	6.4
10 SU	0446	0.8	1108	5.9	1703	0.8	2323	6.1
25 M O	0418	0.3	1034	6.4	1640	0.3	2258	6.6
11 M ●	0521	0.7	1140	6.0	1738	0.7	2351	6.0
26 TU	0505	0.1	1122	6.5	1727	0.2	2345	6.7
12 TU	0554	0.7	1207	6.0	1811	0.7		
27 W	0552	0.1	1210	6.6	1815	0.2		
13 W	0013	6.0	0625	0.7	1232	5.9	1842	0.8
28 TH	0030	6.6	0639	0.1	1257	6.5	1901	0.3
14 TH	0036	5.9	0656	0.7	1257	5.8	1912	0.9
29 F	0115	6.5	0726	0.3	1343	6.3	1949	0.5
15 F	0103	5.8	0725	0.9	1325	5.7	1941	1.0
30 SA	0200	6.1	0815	0.5	1430	6.0	2038	0.8

SHOREHAM

50°50'N 0°15'W

Times and heights (in metres) of high and low water 1994
Time: GMT. For BST, ADD ONE HOUR in the shaded area
High Water, full and change, 1122

MAY

Day		Time	m	Time	m	Time	m	Time	m
1	SU	0248	5.7	0906	0.9	1522	5.7	2131	1.2
16	M	0156	5.5	0817	1.1	1427	5.4	2041	1.3
2	M	0341	5.3	1004	1.3	1619	5.3	2236	1.6
17	TU	0240	5.3	0905	1.2	1517	5.2	2134	1.4
3	TU	0443	4.9	1118	1.6	1725	5.0	2359	1.7
18	W	0335	5.1	1004	1.4	1619	5.1	2239	1.5
4	W	0556	4.7	1236	1.6	1843	5.0		
19	TH	0444	4.9	1111	1.4	1736	5.1	2353	1.5
5	TH	0112	1.7	0726	4.8	1338	1.6	1958	5.1
20	F	0606	5.0	1225	1.4	1853	5.3		
6	F	0210	1.5	0830	5.0	1430	1.4	2053	5.4
21	SA	0105	1.3	0721	5.2	1335	1.1	1956	5.6
7	SA	0257	1.3	0918	5.3	1516	1.2	2137	5.6
22	SU	0209	1.0	0824	5.6	1434	0.9	2053	5.9
8	SU	0339	1.1	0959	5.5	1556	1.1	2214	5.7
23	M	0304	0.7	0921	5.9	1528	0.6	2147	6.2
9	M	0418	0.9	1035	5.7	1635	1.0	2247	5.8
24	TU	0356	0.4	1015	6.1	1619	0.5	2238	6.4
10	TU ●	0454	0.8	1107	5.8	1711	0.9	2316	5.9
25	W O	0446	0.3	1107	6.3	1709	0.4	2328	6.5
11	W	0529	0.8	1138	5.8	1746	0.9	2344	5.9
26	TH	0536	0.2	1157	6.4	1758	0.3		
12	TH	0604	0.7	1208	5.8	1820	0.9		
27	F	0016	6.5	0624	0.2	1246	6.4	1846	0.4
13	F	0013	5.8	0636	0.8	1239	5.8	1851	0.9
28	SA	0103	6.3	0712	0.5	1333	6.3	1934	0.6
14	SA	0044	5.8	0706	0.8	1311	5.7	1922	1.0
29	SU	0148	6.1	0759	0.5	1419	6.1	2021	0.8
15	SU	0118	5.7	0738	0.9	1346	5.6	1957	1.1
30	M	0234	5.8	0847	0.8	1506	5.8	2110	1.1
31	TU	0323	5.4	0937	1.1	1556	5.5	2202	1.4

JUNE

Day		Time	m	Time	m	Time	m	Time	m
1	W	0415	5.1	1032	1.4	1648	5.3	2302	1.6
16	TH	0318	5.4	0941	1.1	1555	5.5	2213	1.2
2	TH	0512	4.9	1137	1.6	1745	5.1		
17	F	0416	5.2	1041	1.2	1657	5.4	2320	1.3
3	F	0016	1.8	0613	4.8	1248	1.7	1844	5.0
18	SA	0524	5.1	1151	1.3	1809	5.4		
4	SA	0125	1.7	0720	4.8	1349	1.7	1946	5.1
19	SU	0033	1.3	0642	5.2	1306	1.2	1922	5.5
5	SU	0220	1.6	0824	5.0	1441	1.5	2042	5.3
20	M	0143	1.1	0758	5.4	1412	1.1	2029	5.7
6	M	0307	1.4	0914	5.2	1526	1.4	2128	5.4
21	TU	0245	0.8	0904	5.6	1511	0.9	2129	5.9
7	TU	0349	1.2	0956	5.4	1608	1.2	2207	5.6
22	W	0340	0.6	1002	5.9	1605	0.7	2224	6.1
8	W	0428	1.0	1035	5.6	1647	1.1	2244	5.7
23	TH O	0432	0.4	1056	6.1	1656	0.6	2316	6.3
9	TH ●	0506	0.9	1112	5.7	1724	1.0	2319	5.8
24	F	0522	0.3	1147	6.3	1746	0.5		
10	F	0543	0.8	1147	5.8	1800	0.9	2354	5.8
25	SA	0004	6.3	0610	0.3	1235	6.4	1832	0.5
11	SA	0619	0.8	1222	5.8	1835	0.9		
26	SU	0051	6.3	0656	0.4	1320	6.3	1918	0.6
12	SU	0029	5.8	0652	0.8	1258	5.8	1908	0.9
27	M	0134	6.1	0741	0.5	1403	6.2	2001	0.8
13	M	0106	5.8	0725	0.8	1335	5.8	1943	0.9
28	TU	0216	5.9	0823	0.8	1444	6.0	2043	1.0
14	TU	0145	5.7	0803	0.9	1416	5.7	2025	1.0
29	W	0257	5.6	0904	1.0	1525	5.7	2124	1.2
15	W	0229	5.6	0848	1.0	1502	5.6	2115	1.1
30	TH	0341	5.3	0946	1.3	1609	5.4	2208	1.5

JULY

Day		Time	m	Time	m	Time	m	Time	m
1	F	0429	5.0	1033	1.6	1658	5.2	2259	1.7
16	SA	0352	5.5	1015	1.1	1628	5.5	2252	1.2
2	SA	0525	4.8	1127	1.8	1753	5.0		
17	SU	0454	5.2	1123	1.4	1735	5.3		
3	SU	0000	1.9	0624	4.7	1237	1.9	1851	4.9
18	M	0007	1.4	0610	5.1	1245	1.5	1853	5.3
4	M	0120	1.9	0727	4.8	1356	1.9	1950	5.0
19	TU	0125	1.3	0742	5.1	1359	1.4	2014	5.4
5	TU	0230	1.7	0827	5.0	1455	1.7	2045	5.2
20	W	0232	1.1	0855	5.4	1501	1.1	2120	5.7
6	W	0321	1.4	0920	5.3	1542	1.4	2134	5.4
21	TH	0330	0.8	0956	5.8	1556	0.9	2216	6.0
7	TH	0404	1.2	1006	5.5	1624	1.2	2217	5.6
22	F O	0421	0.6	1049	6.1	1646	0.7	2307	6.1
8	F ●	0444	0.9	1048	5.7	1703	1.0	2257	5.8
23	SA	0509	0.5	1137	6.3	1733	0.6	2353	6.2
9	SA	0522	0.9	1127	5.9	1741	0.9	2335	5.9
24	SU	0555	0.4	1221	6.4	1817	0.6		
10	SU	0600	0.7	1204	6.0	1817	0.8		
25	M	0036	6.2	0637	0.5	1303	6.4	1858	0.7
11	M	0013	6.0	0635	0.6	1242	6.1	1853	0.8
26	TU	0116	6.2	0717	0.6	1341	6.3	1936	0.8
12	TU	0052	6.0	0710	0.6	1321	6.1	1929	0.7
27	W	0152	6.0	0754	0.7	1416	6.1	2011	0.9
13	W	0132	6.0	0748	0.6	1401	6.1	2010	0.8
28	TH	0227	5.8	0828	1.0	1449	5.9	2046	1.1
14	TH	0214	5.9	0831	0.7	1444	5.9	2056	0.9
29	F	0300	5.5	0905	1.2	1522	5.6	2125	1.4
15	F	0300	5.7	0919	0.9	1532	5.8	2149	1.0
30	SA	0336	5.2	0946	1.5	1558	5.2	2210	1.7
31	SU	0427	4.9	1035	1.8	1655	4.9	2304	1.9

AUGUST

Day		Time	m	Time	m	Time	m	Time	m
1	M	0539	4.6	1137	2.1	1807	4.7		
16	TU	0553	4.9	1232	1.7	1837	5.0		
2	TU	0012	2.0	0648	4.6	1256	2.1	1912	4.8
17	W	0113	1.5	0736	5.0	1350	1.6	2009	5.2
3	W	0138	1.9	0752	4.8	1421	1.9	2013	5.0
18	TH	0222	1.3	0851	5.3	1453	1.3	2115	5.5
4	TH	0250	1.6	0850	5.2	1517	1.6	2106	5.3
19	F	0319	1.0	0949	5.8	1546	1.0	2208	5.9
5	F	0338	1.3	0939	5.5	1600	1.3	2152	5.6
20	SA	0409	0.7	1038	6.1	1633	0.8	2255	6.1
6	SA	0419	1.0	1023	5.8	1640	1.0	2234	5.9
21	SU O	0453	0.5	1123	6.3	1716	0.7	2337	6.2
7	SU ●	0458	0.8	1104	6.1	1719	0.8	2315	6.1
22	M	0535	0.5	1202	6.4	1756	0.6		
8	M	0536	0.6	1143	6.3	1756	0.7	2355	6.2
23	TU	0016	6.3	0614	0.5	1239	6.4	1833	0.7
9	TU	0614	0.5	1223	6.4	1834	0.6		
24	W	0052	6.2	0649	0.6	1313	6.3	1906	0.8
10	W	0035	6.3	0651	0.5	1303	6.4	1912	0.5
25	TH	0123	6.0	0722	0.7	1342	6.1	1938	0.9
11	TH	0116	6.3	0730	0.5	1343	6.4	1953	0.6
26	F	0150	5.8	0753	0.9	1404	5.9	2010	1.1
12	F	0157	6.2	0813	0.6	1424	6.2	2038	0.7
27	SA	0212	5.6	0827	1.2	1424	5.6	2046	1.3
13	SA	0241	5.9	0859	0.8	1510	5.9	2128	1.0
28	SU	0239	5.3	0905	1.5	1455	5.3	2127	1.6
14	SU	0331	5.6	0954	1.2	1604	5.5	2229	1.3
29	M	0317	5.0	0950	1.8	1539	5.0	2218	1.9
15	M	0433	5.2	1103	1.5	1711	5.2	2347	1.5
30	TU	0415	4.6	1052	2.1	1654	4.6	2327	2.1
31	W	0612	4.5	1212	2.3	1838	4.6		

SHOREHAM
50°50′N 0°15′W

Times and heights (in metres) of high and low water 1994
Time: GMT. For BST, ADD ONE HOUR in the shaded area
High Water, full and change, 1122

SEPTEMBER

Day	Time	m	Time	m	Time	m	Time	m
1 TH	0050	2.1	0721	4.7	1339	2.1	1943	4.9
16 F	0209	1.4	0840	5.4	1440	1.4	2104	5.5
2 F	0213	1.8	0820	5.1	1445	1.7	2038	5.3
17 SA	0304	1.1	0934	5.8	1531	1.1	2153	5.8
3 SA	0307	1.4	0911	5.6	1532	1.3	2126	5.7
18 SU	0351	0.8	1019	6.1	1614	0.8	2237	6.1
4 SU	0350	1.0	0956	6.0	1613	1.0	2210	6.0
19 M O	0432	0.7	1100	6.3	1654	0.7	2316	6.2
5 M ●	0430	0.7	1038	6.3	1652	0.7	2253	6.3
20 TU	0511	0.6	1137	6.4	1731	0.7	2352	6.2
6 TU	0509	0.5	1120	6.5	1731	0.5	2335	6.4
21 W	0547	0.6	1211	6.3	1806	0.7		
7 W	0549	0.4	1201	6.6	1811	0.4		
22 TH	0024	6.2	0620	0.7	1241	6.2	1837	0.8
8 TH	0017	6.5	0629	0.3	1242	6.6	1852	0.4
23 F	0052	6.0	0651	0.8	1304	6.1	1908	0.9
9 F	0058	6.5	0711	0.4	1323	6.5	1935	0.4
24 SA	0114	5.9	0722	0.9	1322	5.9	1939	1.0
10 SA	0140	6.4	0755	0.5	1405	6.3	2021	0.6
25 SU	0136	5.7	0754	1.2	1346	5.7	2012	1.2
11 SU	0224	6.1	0843	0.8	1451	5.9	2111	1.0
26 M	0204	5.5	0829	1.4	1419	5.4	2049	1.5
12 M	0315	5.6	0938	1.2	1546	5.5	2212	1.3
27 TU	0241	5.2	0911	1.8	1501	5.0	2137	1.8
13 TU	0419	5.2	1049	1.6	1656	5.1	2332	1.6
28 W	0331	4.8	1010	2.1	1600	4.7	2244	2.1
14 W	0545	4.9	1221	1.8	1829	4.9		
29 TH	0521	4.5	1132	2.2	1758	4.6		
15 TH	0100	1.7	0728	5.0	1339	1.7	2001	5.1
30 F	0006	2.1	0646	4.7	1256	2.1	1911	4.8

OCTOBER

Day	Time	m	Time	m	Time	m	Time	m
1 SA	0128	1.8	0747	5.1	1406	1.7	2008	5.3
16 SU	0241	1.3	0909	5.7	1508	1.2	2130	5.7
2 SU	0230	1.4	0840	5.6	1457	1.3	2059	5.7
17 M	0327	1.0	0953	6.0	1550	0.9	2213	6.0
3 M	0316	1.0	0927	6.0	1541	0.9	2145	6.1
18 TU	0408	0.9	1033	6.2	1629	0.8	2251	6.1
4 TU	0359	0.7	1011	6.4	1622	0.6	2230	6.2
19 W O	0445	0.8	1108	6.2	1705	0.8	2325	6.1
5 W ●	0440	0.5	1055	6.6	1704	0.4	2314	6.6
20 TH	0521	0.8	1140	6.2	1739	0.8	2355	6.1
6 TH	0523	0.3	1138	6.7	1748	0.3	2358	6.7
21 F	0554	0.8	1206	6.1	1812	0.8		
7 F	0607	0.3	1222	6.7	1832	0.3		
22 SA	0021	6.0	0625	0.9	1229	6.0	1843	0.9
8 SA	0041	6.6	0651	0.3	1305	6.6	1917	0.4
23 SU	0046	5.9	0656	1.0	1252	5.9	1914	1.0
9 SU	0126	6.4	0738	0.5	1349	6.3	2005	0.6
24 M	0111	5.8	0728	1.2	1320	5.7	1945	1.2
10 M	0212	6.1	0828	0.9	1437	5.9	2056	1.0
25 TU	0141	5.6	0801	1.4	1354	5.5	2021	1.4
11 TU	0305	5.7	0924	1.3	1533	5.5	2156	1.4
26 W	0218	5.3	0842	1.6	1435	5.2	2106	1.7
12 W	0409	5.3	1035	1.6	1642	5.0	2314	1.7
27 TH	0305	5.0	0937	1.9	1530	4.9	2206	1.9
13 TH	0530	5.0	1205	1.8	1813	4.9		
28 F	0412	4.8	1050	2.1	1650	4.7	2319	1.9
14 F	0040	1.7	0705	5.0	1319	1.7	1940	5.0
29 SA	0601	4.8	1210	2.0	1830	4.8		
15 SA	0147	1.5	0816	5.4	1419	1.4	2042	5.4
30 SU	0037	1.8	0710	5.2	1321	1.7	1934	5.2
31 M	0145	1.5	0806	5.6	1419	1.3	2028	5.7

NOVEMBER

Day	Time	m	Time	m	Time	m	Time	m
1 TU	0239	1.1	0856	6.0	1508	0.9	2118	6.0
16 W	0340	1.2	1002	5.9	1603	1.0	2223	5.8
2 W	0327	0.8	0944	6.4	1554	0.6	2207	6.4
17 TH	0420	1.0	1036	6.0	1641	0.9	2256	5.9
3 TH ●	0413	0.5	1031	6.6	1640	0.4	2254	6.6
18 F O	0456	1.0	1106	6.0	1716	0.9	2326	6.0
4 F	0500	0.4	1117	6.7	1727	0.3	2341	6.7
19 SA	0531	0.9	1134	6.0	1751	0.9	2356	6.0
5 SA	0547	0.3	1204	6.7	1814	0.3		
20 SU	0605	1.0	1201	6.0	1824	0.9		
6 SU	0028	6.6	0634	0.4	1250	6.6	1901	0.4
21 M	0025	5.9	0637	1.0	1231	5.9	1856	1.0
7 M	0115	6.5	0723	0.6	1337	6.3	1950	0.6
22 TU	0055	5.8	0708	1.1	1302	5.8	1927	1.1
8 TU	0204	6.2	0814	0.9	1426	6.0	2042	0.9
23 W	0127	5.7	0741	1.3	1338	5.6	2001	1.2
9 W	0256	5.9	0910	1.2	1520	5.6	2138	1.2
24 TH	0203	5.6	0819	1.4	1418	5.4	2042	1.4
10 TH	0355	5.5	1015	1.5	1623	5.2	2246	1.6
25 F	0247	5.4	0909	1.6	1507	5.2	2135	1.6
11 F	0502	5.2	1134	1.8	1736	5.0		
26 SA	0343	5.2	1011	1.8	1609	5.0	2237	1.7
12 SA	0005	1.7	0621	5.1	1248	1.7	1901	5.0
27 SU	0454	5.1	1123	1.8	1727	5.0	2347	1.6
13 SU	0113	1.7	0737	5.3	1348	1.6	2008	5.2
28 M	0620	5.2	1236	1.6	1849	5.2		
14 M	0210	1.5	0835	5.5	1439	1.4	2100	5.4
29 TU	0100	1.5	0728	5.5	1342	1.3	1956	5.5
15 TU	0258	1.3	0921	5.7	1523	1.2	2144	5.7
30 W	0204	1.2	0826	5.9	1439	1.0	2053	5.9

DECEMBER

Day	Time	m	Time	m	Time	m	Time	m
1 TH	0300	0.9	0920	6.2	1531	0.7	2147	6.2
16 F	0356	1.3	1001	5.7	1619	1.1	2227	5.7
2 F ●	0352	0.7	1011	6.5	1622	0.5	2239	6.4
17 SA	0435	1.2	1035	5.9	1657	1.0	2301	5.8
3 SA	0442	0.5	1101	6.6	1711	0.3	2329	6.5
18 SU O	0512	1.1	1108	5.9	1733	0.9	2335	5.9
4 SU	0532	0.4	1150	6.6	1800	0.3		
19 M	0547	1.0	1140	6.0	1808	0.9		
5 M	0018	6.6	0621	0.5	1238	6.6	1848	0.4
20 TU	0007	6.0	0621	1.0	1214	6.0	1842	0.9
6 TU	0107	6.5	0710	0.6	1326	6.4	1937	0.5
21 W	0040	6.0	0653	1.0	1248	5.9	1913	0.9
7 W	0154	6.3	0759	0.8	1413	6.1	2025	0.8
22 TH	0113	5.9	0724	1.1	1324	5.9	1945	1.0
8 TH	0242	6.1	0850	1.1	1502	5.8	2115	1.1
23 F	0150	5.8	0800	1.2	1403	5.7	2023	1.1
9 F	0332	5.8	0944	1.4	1554	5.4	2208	1.4
24 SA	0231	5.7	0844	1.3	1447	5.6	2108	1.2
10 SA	0425	5.5	1045	1.7	1650	5.1	2309	1.7
25 SU	0318	5.6	0938	1.4	1539	5.4	2202	1.3
11 SU	0523	5.2	1157	1.8	1752	4.9		
26 M	0415	5.4	1042	1.5	1642	5.2	2306	1.5
12 M	0021	1.8	0626	5.1	1306	1.8	1903	4.9
27 TU	0524	5.3	1155	1.6	1756	5.1		
13 TU	0128	1.8	0735	5.2	1404	1.7	2014	5.0
28 W	0020	1.5	0645	5.4	1310	1.4	1921	5.3
14 W	0225	1.7	0837	5.3	1454	1.5	2108	5.3
29 TH	0136	1.4	0758	5.6	1417	1.2	2033	5.6
15 TH	0313	1.5	0923	5.5	1539	1.3	2150	5.5
30 F	0241	1.1	0901	5.9	1515	0.9	2134	5.9
31 SA	0338	0.9	0957	6.2	1609	0.6	2229	6.2

CHICHESTER HARBOUR

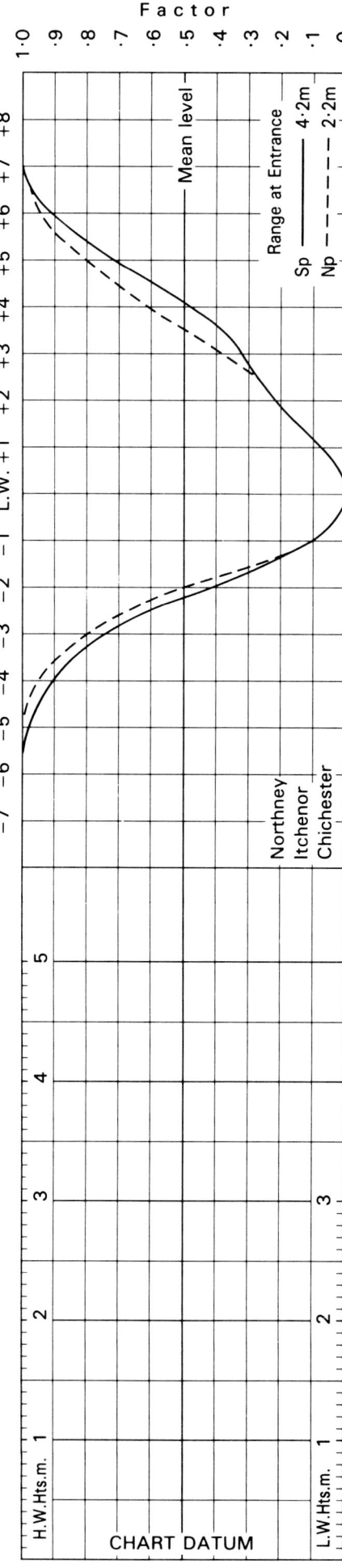

18

CHICHESTER
50°47′N 0°56′W

Times and heights (in metres) of high and low water 1994
Time: GMT. For BST, ADD ONE HOUR in the shaded area

JANUARY

Day	Time	m	Day	Time	m
1 SA	0108	4.9	**16** SU	0147	4.9
	0651	1.1		0732	1.2
	1317	4.8		1354	4.7
	1915	0.9		1949	1.1
2 SU	0147	4.9	**17** M	0219	4.8
	0734	1.1		0804	1.4
	1357	4.8		1428	4.6
	1956	1.0		2021	1.3
3 M	0229	4.8	**18** TU	0253	4.7
	0818	1.2		0838	1.5
	1440	4.7		1502	4.4
	2042	1.1		2054	1.5
4 TU	0314	4.7	**19** W	0330	4.5
	0908	1.4		0916	1.7
	1528	4.5		1540	4.2
	2133	1.3		2134	1.7
5 W	0406	4.6	**20** TH	0412	4.4
	1004	1.5		1002	2.0
	1625	4.4		1629	4.0
	2233	1.4		2227	2.0
6 TH	0508	4.5	**21** F	0507	4.2
	1112	1.6		1110	2.2
	1738	4.2		1738	3.9
	2344	1.6		2345	2.2
7 F	0625	4.5	**22** SA	0619	4.2
	1231	1.6		1244	2.1
	1903	4.3		1907	3.9
8 SA	0102	1.6	**23** SU	0111	2.1
	0740	4.5		0735	4.2
	1349	1.5		1357	1.9
	2022	4.4		2025	4.1
9 SU	0213	1.5	**24** M	0216	1.9
	0849	4.7		0842	4.4
	1454	1.4		1451	1.6
	2129	4.6		2125	4.3
10 M	0314	1.4	**25** TU	0307	1.6
	0949	4.8		0937	4.5
	1549	1.1		1536	1.4
	2226	4.8		2214	4.6
11 TU ●	0406	1.2	**26** W	0351	1.4
	1041	4.9		1022	4.7
	1637	1.0		1618	1.1
	2314	4.9		2254	4.7
12 W	0454	1.1	**27** TH ○	0433	1.2
	1126	5.0		1103	4.8
	1723	0.8		1700	0.9
	2358	5.0		2334	4.9
13 TH	0538	1.0	**28** F	0515	1.0
	1208	5.0		1143	4.9
	1805	0.8		1740	0.7
14 F	0038	5.0	**29** SA	0013	5.0
	0619	1.0		0557	0.9
	1246	4.9		1223	5.0
	1843	0.8		1820	0.6
15 SA	0114	4.9	**30** SU	0051	5.0
	0656	1.1		0638	0.8
	1322	4.8		1303	5.0
	1917	0.9		1900	0.6
			31 M	0130	5.0
				0719	0.8
				1344	5.0
				1941	0.7

FEBRUARY

Day	Time	m	Day	Time	m
1 TU	0211	5.0	**16** W	0217	4.7
	0801	0.9		0759	1.4
	1426	4.8		1431	4.5
	2023	0.9		2014	1.4
2 W	0253	4.9	**17** TH	0249	4.6
	0847	1.1		0830	1.5
	1511	4.7		1504	4.3
	2111	1.1		2047	1.6
3 TH	0340	4.7	**18** F	0325	4.4
	0939	1.4		0909	1.8
	1605	4.4		1544	4.1
	2208	1.4		2131	1.9
4 F	0436	4.4	**19** SA	0409	4.2
	1044	1.5		1000	2.0
	1713	4.2		1641	3.9
	2321	1.7		2236	2.2
5 SA	0551	4.3	**20** SU	0514	4.0
	1206	1.7		1125	2.2
	1844	4.1		1809	3.9
6 SU	0047	1.8	**21** M	0023	2.3
	0718	4.3		0639	4.0
	1333	1.6		1317	2.0
	2014	4.2		1943	4.0
7 M	0206	1.7	**22** TU	0149	2.0
	0838	4.4		0803	4.2
	1444	1.4		1422	1.7
	2126	4.5		2056	4.3
8 TU	0309	1.4	**23** W	0245	1.7
	0942	4.6		0908	4.4
	1539	1.2		1512	1.4
	2220	4.7		2149	4.5
9 W	0359	1.3	**24** TH	0332	1.4
	1032	4.8		1000	4.6
	1625	1.0		1555	1.1
	2304	4.8		2233	4.8
10 TH ●	0443	1.1	**25** F	0414	1.1
	1115	4.8		1043	4.8
	1707	0.8		1637	0.8
	2343	4.9		2313	5.0
11 F	0523	1.0	**26** SA ○	0457	0.8
	1151	4.9		1124	5.0
	1744	0.7		1719	0.5
				2352	5.1
12 SA	0017	4.9	**27** SU	0538	0.6
	0600	0.9		1206	5.1
	1226	4.9		1801	0.4
	1819	0.8			
13 SU	0048	4.9	**28** M	0032	5.2
	0633	0.9		0620	0.5
	1257	4.8		1248	5.1
	1850	0.8		1842	0.4
14 M	0117	4.9			
	0703	1.0			
	1328	4.7			
	1919	1.0			
15 TU	0147	4.8			
	0732	1.2			
	1359	4.6			
	1947	1.2			

MARCH

Day	Time	m	Day	Time	m
1 TU	0112	5.1	**16** W	0116	4.8
	0701	0.5		0701	1.0
	1329	5.1		1333	4.7
	1923	0.5		1915	1.2
2 W	0152	5.1	**17** TH	0146	4.7
	0744	0.7		0727	1.2
	1412	5.0		1405	4.6
	2006	0.8		1943	1.4
3 TH	0234	4.9	**18** F	0216	4.6
	0828	0.9		0756	1.4
	1459	4.7		1438	4.4
	2054	1.1		2015	1.5
4 F	0319	4.6	**19** SA	0248	4.4
	0918	1.2		0832	1.5
	1551	4.5		1515	4.2
	2150	1.4		2056	1.8
5 SA	0412	4.3	**20** SU	0328	4.2
	1021	1.5		0919	1.8
	1656	4.2		1607	4.0
	2305	1.7		2154	2.1
6 SU	0525	4.1	**21** M	0426	4.0
	1145	1.7		1028	2.0
	1831	4.1		1723	3.9
				2330	2.2
7 M	0033	1.8	**22** TU	0548	3.9
	0702	4.0		1218	2.0
	1315	1.7		1857	4.0
	2004	4.2			
8 TU	0157	1.7	**23** W	0112	2.0
	0829	4.2		0718	4.0
	1429	1.5		1342	1.7
	2114	4.4		2017	4.3
9 W	0300	1.4	**24** TH	0216	1.6
	0932	4.4		0833	4.3
	1523	1.3		1438	1.4
	2207	4.7		2116	4.6
10 TH	0347	1.3	**25** F	0306	1.3
	1020	4.6		0930	4.6
	1606	1.0		1526	1.0
	2247	4.8		2205	4.8
11 F ●	0426	1.0	**26** SA	0350	1.0
	1058	4.7		1019	4.8
	1643	0.9		1610	0.7
	2320	4.9		2248	5.0
12 SA ●	0502	0.9	**27** SU ○	0433	0.7
	1132	4.8		1103	5.0
	1719	0.8		1654	0.5
	2351	4.9		2329	5.2
13 SU	0535	0.8	**28** M	0516	0.5
	1202	4.8		1147	5.1
	1752	0.8		1737	0.4
14 M	0018	4.9	**29** TU	0011	5.2
	0607	0.8		0600	0.4
	1232	4.8		1232	5.2
	1822	0.9		1822	0.4
15 TU	0047	4.8	**30** W	0053	5.2
	0635	0.9		0644	0.4
	1303	4.7		1316	5.1
	1850	1.0		1906	0.5
			31 TH	0135	5.0
				0727	0.6
				1401	5.0
				1951	0.8

APRIL

Day	Time	m	Day	Time	m
1 F	0218	4.8	**16** SA	0150	4.6
	0812	0.8		0733	1.3
	1448	4.8		1418	4.5
	2040	1.1		1953	1.4
2 SA	0304	4.6	**17** SU	0224	4.4
	0902	1.1		0810	1.4
	1540	4.5		1457	4.3
	2137	1.4		2036	1.6
3 SU	0356	4.3	**18** M	0304	4.2
	1002	1.4		0856	1.6
	1643	4.3		1546	4.2
	2247	1.7		2132	1.9
4 M	0504	4.0	**19** TU	0357	4.1
	1119	1.6		0958	1.8
	1811	4.1		1650	4.1
				2250	2.0
5 TU	0010	1.8	**20** W	0508	4.0
	0640	3.9		1124	1.8
	1246	1.7		1813	4.1
	1939	4.2			
6 W	0133	1.7	**21** TH	0021	1.9
	0807	4.0		0633	4.0
	1401	1.5		1252	1.6
	2046	4.4		1933	4.3
7 TH	0236	1.5	**22** F	0135	1.6
	0909	4.2		0752	4.2
	1456	1.4		1358	1.4
	2139	4.6		2037	4.6
8 F	0322	1.3	**23** SA	0231	1.3
	0958	4.4		0856	4.5
	1537	1.2		1452	1.0
	2220	4.7		2131	4.8
9 SA	0359	1.1	**24** SU	0321	0.9
	1035	4.5		0951	4.8
	1613	1.0		1540	0.7
	2252	4.8		2220	5.0
10 SU	0433	0.9	**25** M ○	0408	0.7
	1107	4.6		1040	5.0
	1647	0.9		1627	0.6
	2321	4.8		2306	5.2
11 M ●	0507	0.9	**26** TU	0454	0.5
	1136	4.7		1127	5.1
	1721	0.9		1715	0.5
	2348	4.8		2350	5.2
12 TU	0538	0.9	**27** W	0541	0.4
	1206	4.7		1216	5.1
	1753	1.0		1803	0.5
13 W	0017	4.8	**28** TH	0036	5.1
	0608	0.9		0627	0.5
	1238	4.7		1303	5.1
	1822	1.1		1850	0.6
14 TH	0048	4.7	**29** F	0121	5.0
	0635	1.0		0713	0.6
	1310	4.7		1349	5.0
	1850	1.2		1937	0.8
15 F	0120	4.7	**30** SA	0205	4.8
	0702	1.1		0759	0.8
	1344	4.6		1439	4.8
	1919	1.3		2026	1.1

CHICHESTER

50°47′N 0°56′W

Times and heights (in metres) of high and low water 1994
Time: GMT. For BST, ADD ONE HOUR in the shaded area

MAY

Day	Time	m	Day	Time	m
1 SU	0251 / 0848 / 1529 / 2120	4.6 / 1.1 / 4.6 / 1.4	**16** M	0208 / 0757 / 1442 / 2023	4.5 / 1.3 / 4.5 / 1.4
2 M	0340 / 0943 / 1626 / 2221	4.3 / 1.4 / 4.4 / 1.6	**17** TU	0248 / 0843 / 1529 / 2116	4.4 / 1.4 / 4.4 / 1.6
3 TU	0440 / 1047 / 1737 / 2334	4.1 / 1.5 / 4.2 / 1.8	**18** W	0338 / 0939 / 1625 / 2220	4.2 / 1.5 / 4.3 / 1.7
4 W	0601 / 1203 / 1856	3.9 / 1.7 / 4.2	**19** TH	0437 / 1047 / 1735 / 2335	4.2 / 1.5 / 4.3 / 1.7
5 TH	0050 / 0725 / 1317 / 2003	1.8 / 3.9 / 1.6 / 4.3	**20** F	0554 / 1203 / 1851	4.2 / 1.5 / 4.4
6 F	0156 / 0832 / 1415 / 2058	1.6 / 4.1 / 1.5 / 4.4	**21** SA	0049 / 0713 / 1316 / 1959	1.5 / 4.3 / 1.4 / 4.6
7 SA	0244 / 0922 / 1500 / 2142	1.4 / 4.2 / 1.4 / 4.6	**22** SU	0156 / 0822 / 1418 / 2059	1.4 / 4.5 / 1.1 / 4.8
8 SU	0325 / 1004 / 1538 / 2219	1.3 / 4.4 / 1.2 / 4.6	**23** M	0253 / 0923 / 1513 / 2155	1.1 / 4.7 / 0.9 / 5.0
9 M	0401 / 1037 / 1614 / 2249	1.1 / 4.5 / 1.1 / 4.7	**24** TU	0345 / 1020 / 1604 / 2244	0.8 / 4.9 / 0.7 / 5.1
10 TU ●	0435 / 1109 / 1650 / 2319	1.0 / 4.6 / 1.1 / 4.7	**25** W O	0435 / 1111 / 1656 / 2332	0.6 / 5.0 / 0.7 / 5.1
11 W	0510 / 1141 / 1724 / 2351	1.0 / 4.6 / 1.1 / 4.7	**26** TH	0525 / 1201 / 1746	0.6 / 5.1 / 0.7
12 TH	0543 / 1215 / 1757	1.0 / 4.6 / 1.2	**27** F	0019 / 0614 / 1250 / 1835	5.1 / 0.6 / 5.1 / 0.7
13 F	0024 / 0614 / 1250 / 1829	4.7 / 1.0 / 4.6 / 1.2	**28** SA	0107 / 0701 / 1338 / 1922	5.0 / 0.6 / 5.0 / 0.9
14 SA	0058 / 0645 / 1326 / 1902	4.6 / 1.1 / 4.6 / 1.3	**29** SU	0151 / 0747 / 1425 / 2009	4.9 / 0.8 / 4.9 / 1.1
15 SU	0132 / 0718 / 1402 / 1940	4.6 / 1.2 / 4.5 / 1.4	**30** M	0236 / 0831 / 1511 / 2057	4.7 / 1.0 / 4.7 / 1.3
			31 TU	0320 / 0918 / 1600 / 2148	4.4 / 1.3 / 4.5 / 1.5

JUNE

Day	Time	m	Day	Time	m
1 W	0408 / 1010 / 1652 / 2246	4.2 / 1.5 / 4.3 / 1.7	**16** TH	0320 / 0921 / 1601 / 2154	4.5 / 1.3 / 4.5 / 1.4
2 TH	0507 / 1111 / 1757 / 2351	4.0 / 1.7 / 4.2 / 1.8	**17** F	0414 / 1019 / 1701 / 2259	4.3 / 1.4 / 4.4 / 1.5
3 F	0621 / 1219 / 1904	3.9 / 1.8 / 4.2	**18** SA	0522 / 1128 / 1813	4.3 / 1.4 / 4.5
4 SA	0100 / 0735 / 1324 / 2005	1.8 / 4.0 / 1.7 / 4.3	**19** SU	0011 / 0639 / 1240 / 1925	1.5 / 4.3 / 1.4 / 4.6
5 SU	0158 / 0836 / 1417 / 2056	1.7 / 4.1 / 1.6 / 4.4	**20** M	0124 / 0755 / 1352 / 2032	1.4 / 4.4 / 1.3 / 4.7
6 M	0245 / 0924 / 1502 / 2139	1.5 / 4.2 / 1.4 / 4.5	**21** TU	0230 / 0903 / 1454 / 2132	1.2 / 4.6 / 1.2 / 4.9
7 TU	0327 / 1006 / 1542 / 2218	1.4 / 4.4 / 1.4 / 4.6	**22** W	0329 / 1005 / 1550 / 2227	1.0 / 4.8 / 1.0 / 5.0
8 W	0406 / 1043 / 1621 / 2252	1.2 / 4.5 / 1.3 / 4.6	**23** TH O	0422 / 1058 / 1642 / 2318	0.8 / 4.9 / 0.9 / 5.1
9 TH ●	0444 / 1118 / 1659 / 2328	1.1 / 4.6 / 1.2 / 4.7	**24** F	0513 / 1149 / 1733	0.7 / 5.0 / 0.8
10 F	0522 / 1154 / 1736	1.1 / 4.6 / 1.2	**25** SA	0005 / 0602 / 1238 / 1821	5.0 / 0.7 / 5.0 / 0.8
11 SA	0004 / 0558 / 1232 / 1813	4.7 / 1.1 / 4.6 / 1.2	**26** SU	0051 / 0648 / 1323 / 1905	5.0 / 0.7 / 5.0 / 0.9
12 SU	0041 / 0633 / 1309 / 1850	4.7 / 1.0 / 4.7 / 1.2	**27** M	0134 / 0729 / 1405 / 1948	4.9 / 0.8 / 4.9 / 1.1
13 M	0116 / 0708 / 1347 / 1928	4.6 / 1.1 / 4.7 / 1.2	**28** TU	0214 / 0808 / 1445 / 2028	4.8 / 1.0 / 4.8 / 1.2
14 TU	0154 / 0748 / 1427 / 2010	4.6 / 1.1 / 4.6 / 1.3	**29** W	0253 / 0847 / 1525 / 2109	4.6 / 1.2 / 4.6 / 1.4
15 W	0235 / 0831 / 1510 / 2059	4.5 / 1.2 / 4.6 / 1.4	**30** TH	0333 / 0928 / 1606 / 2154	4.4 / 1.4 / 4.5 / 1.6

JULY

Day	Time	m	Day	Time	m
1 F	0416 / 1015 / 1652 / 2249	4.1 / 1.7 / 4.3 / 1.8	**16** SA	0354 / 0955 / 1632 / 2231	4.5 / 1.4 / 4.5 / 1.4
2 SA	0510 / 1115 / 1752 / 2357	4.0 / 1.9 / 4.2 / 2.0	**17** SU	0456 / 1100 / 1740 / 2344	4.3 / 1.5 / 4.4 / 1.5
3 SU	0621 / 1226 / 1859	3.9 / 2.0 / 4.2	**18** M	0616 / 1218 / 1858	4.3 / 1.6 / 4.5
4 M	0107 / 0738 / 1333 / 2003	1.9 / 4.0 / 1.9 / 4.3	**19** TU	0104 / 0738 / 1337 / 2012	1.5 / 4.3 / 1.5 / 4.6
5 TU	0207 / 0843 / 1428 / 2059	1.7 / 4.1 / 1.7 / 4.4	**20** W	0217 / 0853 / 1444 / 2118	1.4 / 4.5 / 1.4 / 4.7
6 W	0257 / 0936 / 1515 / 2147	1.5 / 4.3 / 1.5 / 4.5	**21** TH	0319 / 0958 / 1542 / 2216	1.2 / 4.7 / 1.2 / 4.9
7 TH	0341 / 1020 / 1557 / 2229	1.4 / 4.5 / 1.4 / 4.6	**22** F O	0412 / 1050 / 1633 / 2305	0.9 / 4.9 / 1.0 / 5.0
8 F ●	0422 / 1058 / 1637 / 2307	1.2 / 4.6 / 1.3 / 4.7	**23** SA	0502 / 1138 / 1720 / 2350	0.8 / 5.0 / 0.9 / 5.0
9 SA	0502 / 1137 / 1718 / 2345	1.1 / 4.7 / 1.2 / 4.7	**24** SU	0547 / 1222 / 1805	0.7 / 5.0 / 0.9
10 SU	0541 / 1215 / 1757	1.0 / 4.7 / 1.1	**25** M	0033 / 0629 / 1303 / 1845	5.0 / 0.7 / 5.0 / 0.9
11 M	0022 / 0619 / 1252 / 1836	4.7 / 0.9 / 4.8 / 1.0	**26** TU	0111 / 0705 / 1339 / 1921	4.9 / 0.8 / 5.0 / 1.0
12 TU	0101 / 0656 / 1329 / 1914	4.8 / 0.9 / 4.8 / 1.0	**27** W	0147 / 0740 / 1412 / 1955	4.8 / 1.0 / 4.9 / 1.2
13 W	0139 / 0734 / 1409 / 1955	4.8 / 0.9 / 4.8 / 1.1	**28** TH	0221 / 0812 / 1446 / 2030	4.6 / 1.2 / 4.7 / 1.4
14 TH	0219 / 0815 / 1450 / 2040	4.7 / 1.0 / 4.8 / 1.2	**29** F	0255 / 0845 / 1521 / 2106	4.5 / 1.4 / 4.6 / 1.5
15 F	0303 / 0902 / 1537 / 2132	4.6 / 1.1 / 4.7 / 1.3	**30** SA	0333 / 0923 / 1601 / 2149	4.3 / 1.6 / 4.4 / 1.8
			31 SU	0418 / 1010 / 1648 / 2248	4.1 / 1.9 / 4.2 / 2.0

AUGUST

Day	Time	m	Day	Time	m
1 M	0518 / 1122 / 1754	3.9 / 2.1 / 4.1	**16** TU	0601 / 1207 / 1839	4.2 / 1.8 / 4.3
2 TU	0013 / 0640 / 1252 / 1911	2.1 / 3.9 / 2.2 / 4.1	**17** W	0052 / 0732 / 1332 / 2001	1.6 / 4.3 / 1.7 / 4.4
3 W	0130 / 0803 / 1400 / 2021	1.9 / 4.1 / 2.0 / 4.2	**18** TH	0209 / 0850 / 1441 / 2111	1.4 / 4.5 / 1.5 / 4.6
4 TH	0229 / 0907 / 1452 / 2119	1.7 / 4.3 / 1.7 / 4.4	**19** F	0311 / 0952 / 1536 / 2208	1.2 / 4.7 / 1.3 / 4.8
5 F	0317 / 0958 / 1537 / 2206	1.4 / 4.5 / 1.5 / 4.6	**20** SA	0401 / 1041 / 1622 / 2253	1.0 / 4.9 / 1.1 / 4.9
6 SA	0400 / 1039 / 1618 / 2247	1.2 / 4.7 / 1.3 / 4.7	**21** SU O	0445 / 1123 / 1705 / 2334	0.8 / 5.0 / 0.9 / 4.9
7 SU ●	0440 / 1117 / 1658 / 2324	1.0 / 4.8 / 1.1 / 4.8	**22** M	0526 / 1201 / 1743	0.7 / 5.0 / 0.9
8 M	0520 / 1154 / 1738	0.8 / 4.9 / 0.9	**23** TU	0011 / 0603 / 1237 / 1819	4.9 / 0.7 / 5.0 / 0.9
9 TU	0003 / 0600 / 1233 / 1817	4.9 / 0.7 / 5.0 / 0.8	**24** W	0045 / 0637 / 1308 / 1851	4.9 / 0.8 / 4.9 / 1.0
10 W	0043 / 0638 / 1310 / 1856	4.9 / 0.7 / 5.0 / 0.8	**25** TH	0117 / 0708 / 1338 / 1922	4.8 / 1.0 / 4.8 / 1.2
11 TH	0123 / 0717 / 1349 / 1938	4.9 / 0.7 / 5.0 / 0.9	**26** F	0148 / 0737 / 1409 / 1951	4.7 / 1.2 / 4.7 / 1.3
12 F	0203 / 0758 / 1430 / 2021	4.9 / 0.9 / 4.9 / 1.0	**27** SA	0221 / 0805 / 1440 / 2023	4.5 / 1.4 / 4.6 / 1.5
13 SA	0247 / 0843 / 1515 / 2111	4.7 / 1.1 / 4.7 / 1.2	**28** SU	0255 / 0838 / 1515 / 2100	4.4 / 1.6 / 4.4 / 1.7
14 SU	0338 / 0936 / 1607 / 2209	4.5 / 1.4 / 4.5 / 1.4	**29** M	0336 / 0919 / 1558 / 2149	4.2 / 1.9 / 4.2 / 2.0
15 M	0439 / 1043 / 1714 / 2325	4.3 / 1.6 / 4.3 / 1.6	**30** TU	0429 / 1018 / 1655 / 2308	4.0 / 2.2 / 4.1 / 2.2
			31 W	0548 / 1205 / 1817	3.9 / 2.3 / 4.0

CHICHESTER
50°47′N 0°56′W

Times and heights (in metres) of high and low water 1994
Time: GMT. For BST, ADD ONE HOUR in the shaded area

SEPTEMBER

Day	Time	m		Day	Time	m
1 TH	0053 / 0721 / 1331 / 1942	2.1 / 4.0 / 2.1 / 4.1		**16** F	0157 / 0842 / 1432 / 2103	1.5 / 4.5 / 1.5 / 4.5
2 F	0201 / 0836 / 1428 / 2048	1.8 / 4.3 / 1.8 / 4.3		**17** SA	0257 / 0939 / 1523 / 2156	1.3 / 4.7 / 1.4 / 4.7
3 SA	0252 / 0930 / 1514 / 2140	1.4 / 4.5 / 1.5 / 4.6		**18** SU	0343 / 1024 / 1605 / 2237	1.1 / 4.9 / 1.1 / 4.8
4 SU	0335 / 1015 / 1555 / 2222	1.2 / 4.7 / 1.2 / 4.8		**19** M	0423 / 1102 / 1642 / 2314	0.9 / 4.9 / 1.0 / 4.9
5 M	0415 / 1053 / 1635 / 2302	0.9 / 4.9 / 1.0 / 4.9		**20** TU	0500 / 1136 / 1717 / 2346	0.8 / 5.0 / 0.9 / 4.9
6 TU	0456 / 1131 / 1715 / 2343	0.7 / 5.0 / 0.8 / 5.0		**21** W	0534 / 1206 / 1751	0.8 / 4.9 / 0.9
7 W	0536 / 1210 / 1756	0.6 / 5.1 / 0.7		**22** TH	0016 / 0606 / 1236 / 1821	4.8 / 0.9 / 4.9 / 1.0
8 TH	0023 / 0617 / 1250 / 1837	5.1 / 0.6 / 5.1 / 0.7		**23** F	0047 / 0637 / 1305 / 1850	4.8 / 1.0 / 4.8 / 1.2
9 F	0106 / 0657 / 1330 / 1919	5.1 / 0.6 / 5.0 / 0.7		**24** SA	0118 / 0704 / 1335 / 1918	4.7 / 1.2 / 4.7 / 1.3
10 SA	0148 / 0741 / 1411 / 2003	5.0 / 0.8 / 4.9 / 0.9		**25** SU	0150 / 0732 / 1406 / 1948	4.6 / 1.4 / 4.6 / 1.4
11 SU	0234 / 0828 / 1457 / 2053	4.8 / 1.1 / 4.7 / 1.2		**26** M	0224 / 0803 / 1439 / 2023	4.5 / 1.6 / 4.4 / 1.6
12 M	0325 / 0923 / 1550 / 2153	4.6 / 1.4 / 4.4 / 1.4		**27** TU	0303 / 0842 / 1517 / 2108	4.3 / 1.9 / 4.3 / 1.9
13 TU	0428 / 1032 / 1656 / 2310	4.3 / 1.7 / 4.2 / 1.7		**28** W	0351 / 0936 / 1610 / 2214	4.1 / 2.1 / 4.1 / 2.1
14 W	0552 / 1158 / 1828	4.2 / 1.8 / 4.1		**29** TH	0502 / 1106 / 1727	4.0 / 2.3 / 4.0
15 TH	0038 / 0725 / 1324 / 1955	1.7 / 4.3 / 1.8 / 4.3		**30** F	0000 / 0634 / 1252 / 1858	2.1 / 4.0 / 2.2 / 4.1

OCTOBER

Day	Time	m		Day	Time	m
1 SA	0123 / 0756 / 1356 / 2013	1.9 / 4.3 / 1.9 / 4.3		**16** SU	0232 / 0914 / 1500 / 2134	1.4 / 4.7 / 1.4 / 4.6
2 SU	0218 / 0855 / 1444 / 2108	1.5 / 4.6 / 1.5 / 4.6		**17** M	0317 / 0959 / 1540 / 2216	1.3 / 4.8 / 1.2 / 4.7
3 M	0304 / 0943 / 1527 / 2156	1.2 / 4.8 / 1.2 / 4.8		**18** TU	0355 / 1035 / 1615 / 2249	1.1 / 4.9 / 1.1 / 4.8
4 TU	0346 / 1026 / 1608 / 2238	0.9 / 5.0 / 0.9 / 5.0		**19** W	0429 / 1107 / 1649 / 2319	1.0 / 4.9 / 1.0 / 4.8
5 W	0427 / 1107 / 1650 / 2320	0.7 / 5.1 / 0.7 / 5.1		**20** TH	0503 / 1136 / 1721 / 2348	1.0 / 4.8 / 1.0 / 4.8
6 TH	0511 / 1147 / 1733	0.5 / 5.2 / 0.6		**21** F	0536 / 1204 / 1753	1.0 / 4.8 / 1.1
7 F	0004 / 0555 / 1230 / 1817	5.2 / 0.5 / 5.2 / 0.6		**22** SA	0019 / 0607 / 1235 / 1823	4.8 / 1.1 / 4.8 / 1.2
8 SA	0049 / 0640 / 1313 / 1901	5.1 / 0.6 / 5.1 / 0.7		**23** SU	0052 / 0637 / 1307 / 1851	4.7 / 1.3 / 4.7 / 1.3
9 SU	0135 / 0725 / 1356 / 1949	5.0 / 0.8 / 4.9 / 0.9		**24** M	0126 / 0706 / 1339 / 1922	4.6 / 1.4 / 4.6 / 1.4
10 M	0222 / 0815 / 1443 / 2039	4.9 / 1.1 / 4.7 / 1.2		**25** TU	0201 / 0739 / 1411 / 1957	4.5 / 1.5 / 4.5 / 1.5
11 TU	0315 / 0911 / 1537 / 2139	4.6 / 1.4 / 4.4 / 1.4		**26** W	0240 / 0818 / 1450 / 2041	4.4 / 1.8 / 4.3 / 1.7
12 W	0416 / 1019 / 1642 / 2251	4.4 / 1.7 / 4.2 / 1.7		**27** TH	0325 / 0909 / 1538 / 2140	4.3 / 2.0 / 4.2 / 1.9
13 TH	0537 / 1139 / 1812	4.2 / 1.8 / 4.1		**28** F	0426 / 1020 / 1643 / 2300	4.1 / 2.2 / 4.1 / 2.0
14 F	0014 / 0707 / 1302 / 1938	1.7 / 4.3 / 1.8 / 4.2		**29** SA	0546 / 1152 / 1808	4.1 / 2.1 / 4.1
15 SA	0132 / 0818 / 1410 / 2043	1.6 / 4.5 / 1.6 / 4.4		**30** SU	0027 / 0708 / 1310 / 1928	1.9 / 4.3 / 1.9 / 4.3
				31 M	0134 / 0814 / 1407 / 2032	1.6 / 4.6 / 1.5 / 4.6

NOVEMBER

Day	Time	m		Day	Time	m
1 TU	0227 / 0908 / 1456 / 2125	1.3 / 4.8 / 1.3 / 4.8		**16** W	0322 / 1004 / 1545 / 2223	1.4 / 4.7 / 1.3 / 4.6
2 W	0314 / 0957 / 1541 / 2215	1.0 / 5.0 / 1.0 / 5.0		**17** TH	0358 / 1037 / 1620 / 2255	1.2 / 4.8 / 1.2 / 4.7
3 TH	0400 / 1042 / 1626 / 2300	0.8 / 5.2 / 0.8 / 5.1		**18** F	0433 / 1107 / 1655 / 2325	1.2 / 4.8 / 1.1 / 4.7
4 F	0446 / 1126 / 1713 / 2347	0.6 / 5.2 / 0.7 / 5.2		**19** SA	0509 / 1138 / 1729 / 2357	1.2 / 4.8 / 1.1 / 4.7
5 SA	0534 / 1211 / 1801	0.6 / 5.2 / 0.7		**20** SU	0543 / 1210 / 1802	1.2 / 4.8 / 1.2
6 SU	0035 / 0623 / 1257 / 1848	5.2 / 0.7 / 5.1 / 0.7		**21** M	0032 / 0616 / 1245 / 1833	4.7 / 1.3 / 4.7 / 1.3
7 M	0123 / 0711 / 1343 / 1936	5.1 / 0.9 / 4.9 / 0.9		**22** TU	0108 / 0648 / 1318 / 1905	4.7 / 1.4 / 4.6 / 1.4
8 TU	0212 / 0802 / 1431 / 2026	4.9 / 1.1 / 4.7 / 1.1		**23** W	0143 / 0722 / 1352 / 1941	4.6 / 1.5 / 4.6 / 1.4
9 W	0304 / 0856 / 1522 / 2122	4.7 / 1.4 / 4.5 / 1.4		**24** TH	0221 / 0801 / 1429 / 2022	4.6 / 1.6 / 4.4 / 1.5
10 TH	0401 / 0956 / 1621 / 2224	4.5 / 1.6 / 4.3 / 1.6		**25** F	0305 / 0848 / 1513 / 2113	4.5 / 1.8 / 4.3 / 1.7
11 F	0508 / 1105 / 1738 / 2336	4.4 / 1.8 / 4.1 / 1.7		**26** SA	0356 / 0947 / 1608 / 2217	4.4 / 1.9 / 4.2 / 1.8
12 SA	0627 / 1221 / 1901	4.3 / 1.8 / 4.1		**27** SU	0501 / 1058 / 1719 / 2331	4.3 / 2.0 / 4.2 / 1.7
13 SU	0051 / 0738 / 1331 / 2008	1.7 / 4.4 / 1.7 / 4.2		**28** M	0618 / 1215 / 1841	4.4 / 1.8 / 4.3
14 M	0154 / 0837 / 1426 / 2103	1.6 / 4.5 / 1.5 / 4.4		**29** TU	0043 / 0730 / 1326 / 1954	1.6 / 4.6 / 1.6 / 4.5
15 TU	0241 / 0924 / 1508 / 2147	1.4 / 4.7 / 1.4 / 4.5		**30** W	0149 / 0832 / 1425 / 2056	1.4 / 4.8 / 1.4 / 4.7

DECEMBER

Day	Time	m		Day	Time	m
1 TH	0244 / 0927 / 1518 / 2152	1.2 / 5.0 / 1.1 / 4.9		**16** F	0329 / 1008 / 1555 / 2234	1.4 / 4.7 / 1.3 / 4.6
2 F	0337 / 1020 / 1608 / 2244	1.0 / 5.2 / 0.9 / 5.1		**17** SA	0408 / 1042 / 1633 / 2307	1.4 / 4.7 / 1.2 / 4.6
3 SA	0427 / 1107 / 1659 / 2334	0.8 / 5.2 / 0.7 / 5.1		**18** SU	0446 / 1116 / 1711 / 2341	1.3 / 4.8 / 1.2 / 4.7
4 SU	0518 / 1154 / 1748	0.8 / 5.2 / 0.7		**19** M	0523 / 1150 / 1746	1.3 / 4.8 / 1.1
5 M	0023 / 0609 / 1243 / 1837	5.2 / 0.8 / 5.1 / 0.7		**20** TU	0016 / 0559 / 1225 / 1820	4.7 / 1.3 / 4.7 / 1.1
6 TU	0112 / 0658 / 1329 / 1924	5.1 / 0.9 / 5.0 / 0.8		**21** W	0051 / 0633 / 1300 / 1852	4.7 / 1.3 / 4.7 / 1.2
7 W	0200 / 0747 / 1414 / 2010	5.0 / 1.1 / 4.8 / 1.0		**22** TH	0128 / 0708 / 1335 / 1927	4.7 / 1.4 / 4.7 / 1.2
8 TH	0247 / 0835 / 1501 / 2058	4.9 / 1.3 / 4.6 / 1.2		**23** F	0204 / 0746 / 1411 / 2005	4.7 / 1.4 / 4.6 / 1.3
9 F	0336 / 0926 / 1550 / 2148	4.7 / 1.5 / 4.4 / 1.4		**24** SA	0243 / 0828 / 1452 / 2050	4.7 / 1.5 / 4.5 / 1.4
10 SA	0428 / 1022 / 1646 / 2247	4.5 / 1.7 / 4.2 / 1.7		**25** SU	0329 / 0919 / 1540 / 2144	4.6 / 1.6 / 4.4 / 1.5
11 SU	0531 / 1128 / 1800 / 2353	4.4 / 1.9 / 4.0 / 1.8		**26** M	0423 / 1019 / 1640 / 2247	4.5 / 1.7 / 4.3 / 1.6
12 M	0641 / 1238 / 1919	4.3 / 1.9 / 4.0		**27** TU	0531 / 1131 / 1758	4.5 / 1.8 / 4.2
13 TU	0102 / 0746 / 1342 / 2023	1.8 / 4.4 / 1.8 / 4.2		**28** W	0001 / 0648 / 1249 / 1920	1.6 / 4.5 / 1.7 / 4.3
14 W	0200 / 0842 / 1433 / 2116	1.7 / 4.5 / 1.6 / 4.3		**29** TH	0116 / 0759 / 1402 / 2034	1.5 / 4.7 / 1.4 / 4.5
15 TH	0248 / 0928 / 1516 / 2159	1.6 / 4.6 / 1.4 / 4.5		**30** F	0223 / 0903 / 1503 / 2138	1.4 / 4.9 / 1.2 / 4.8
				31 SA	0322 / 1001 / 1558 / 2233	1.2 / 5.0 / 1.0 / 4.9

TIDAL CURVES—RYDE TO SELSEY

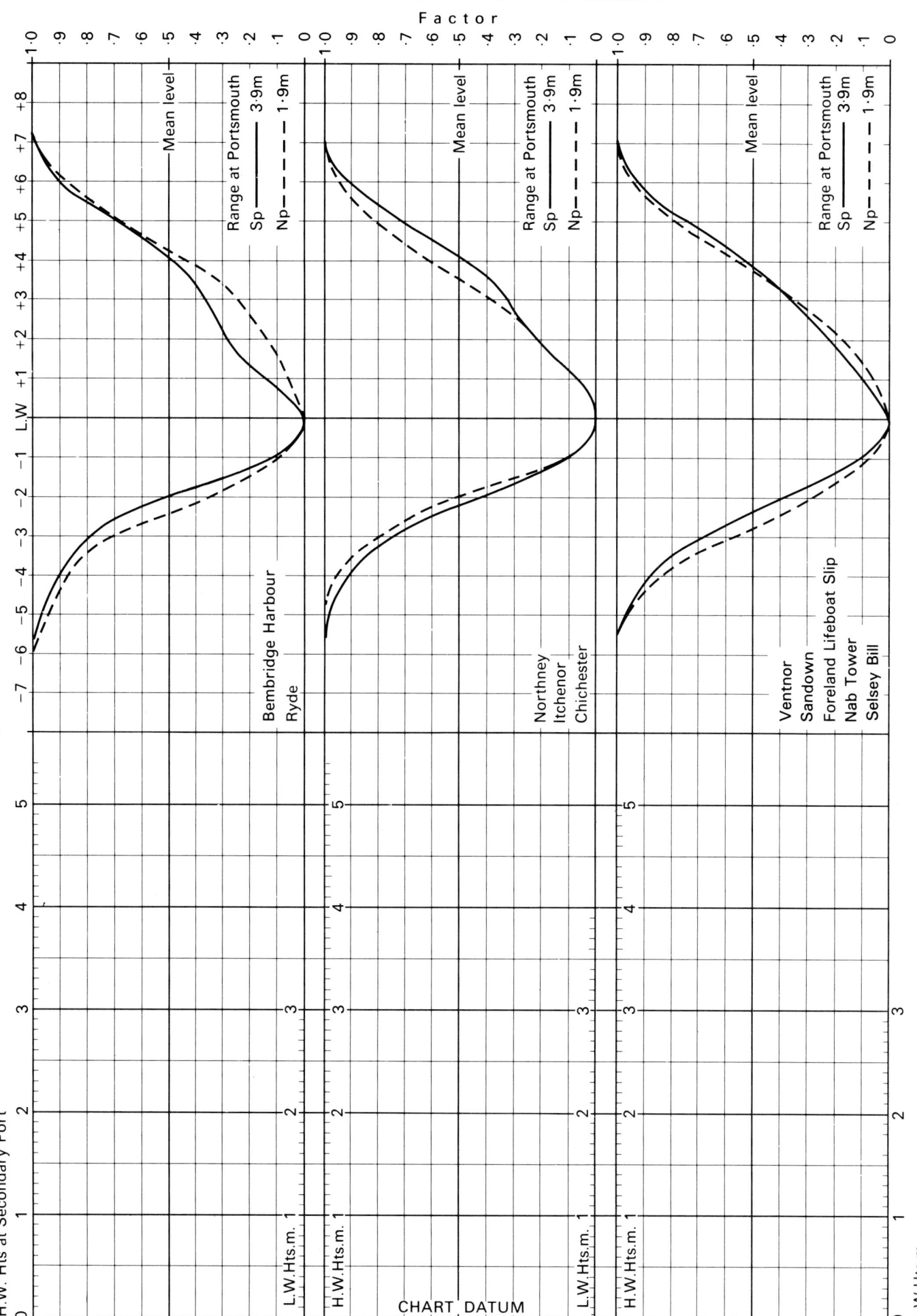

Factor

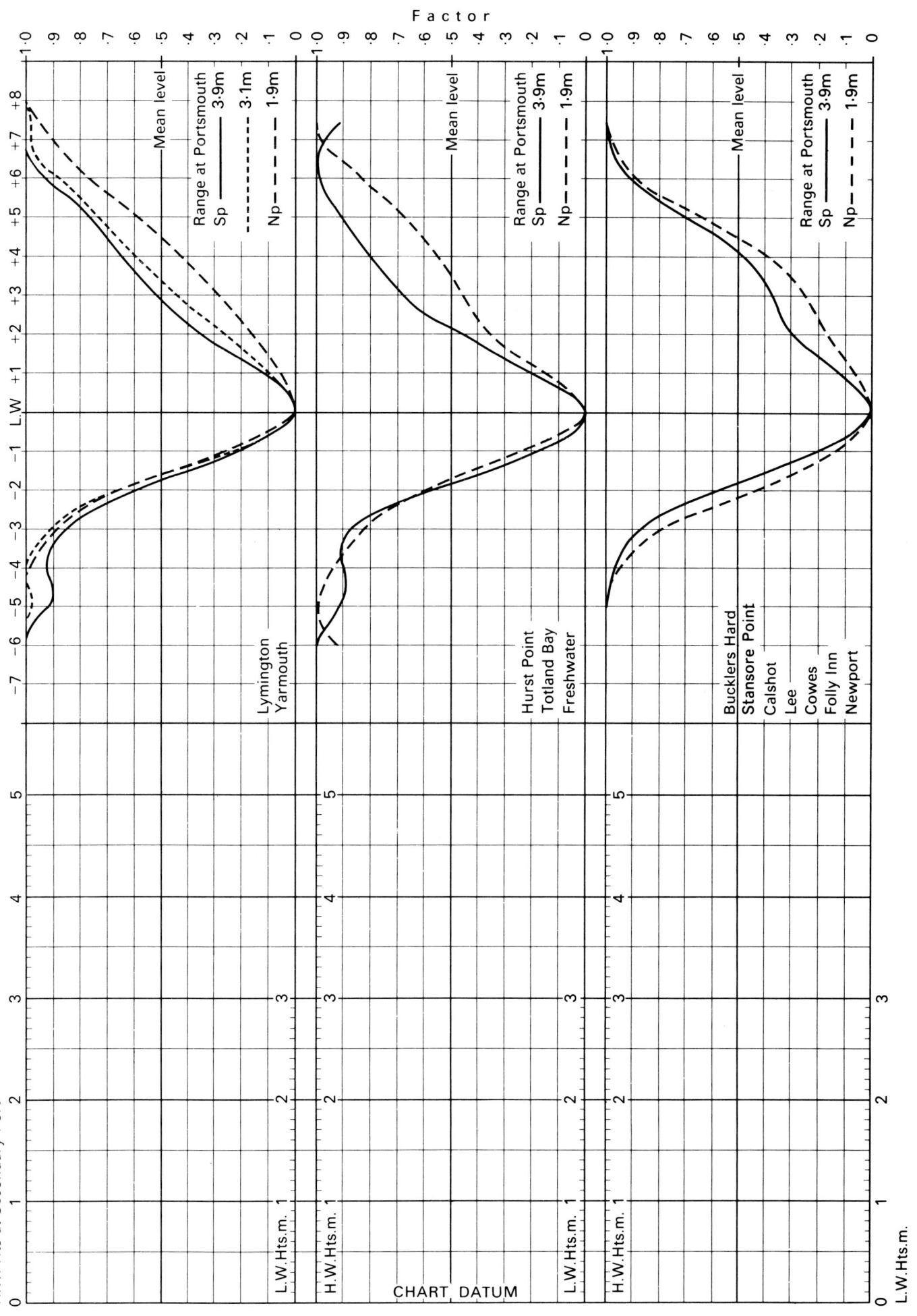

PORTSMOUTH

MEAN SPRING AND NEAP CURVES
Springs occur 2 days after New and Full Moon

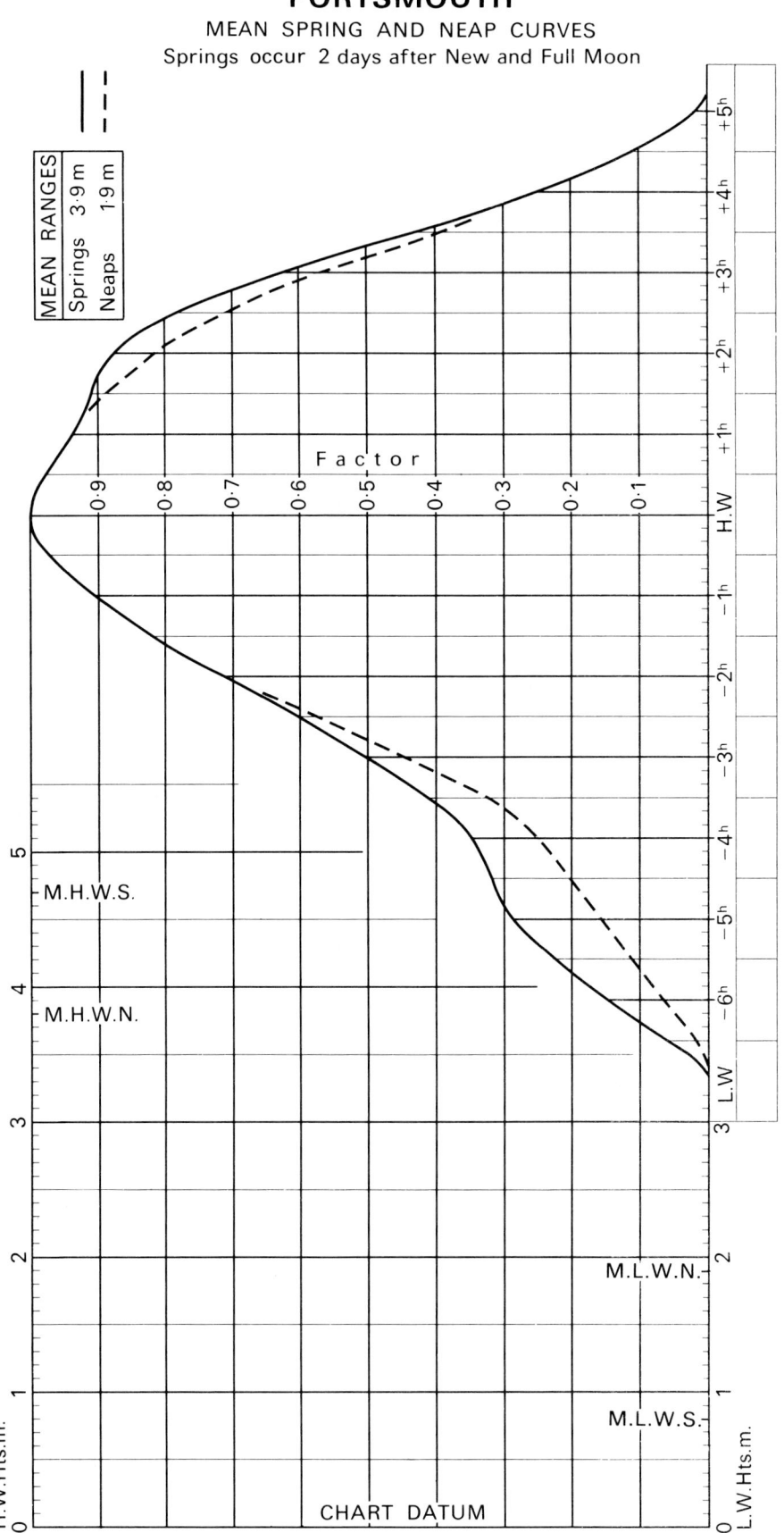

MEAN RANGES
Springs 3·9 m
Neaps 1·9 m

Factor

0·9 0·8 0·7 0·6 0·5 0·4 0·3 0·2 0·1

H.W.

+5ʰ +4ʰ +3ʰ +2ʰ +1ʰ H.W −1ʰ −2ʰ −3ʰ −4ʰ −5ʰ −6ʰ L.W

M.H.W.S.

M.H.W.N.

M.L.W.N.

M.L.W.S.

CHART DATUM

H.W.Hts.m.

L.W.Hts.m.

PORTSMOUTH
50°48′N 1°07′W

Times and heights (in metres) of high and low water 1994
Time: GMT. For BST, ADD ONE HOUR in the shaded area
High Water, full and change, 1133

JANUARY

#	Time	m	Time	m	#	Time	m	Time	m
1 SA	0109 / 0632 / 1319 / 1856	4.7 / 1.0 / 4.6 / 0.8			16 SU	0151 / 0713 / 1358 / 1931	4.7 / 1.1 / 4.5 / 1.0		
2 SU	0150 / 0715 / 1401 / 1938	4.7 / 1.0 / 4.6 / 0.9			17 M	0224 / 0746 / 1433 / 2003	4.6 / 1.3 / 4.4 / 1.2		
3 M	0234 / 0800 / 1445 / 2024	4.6 / 1.1 / 4.5 / 1.0			18 TU	0259 / 0820 / 1508 / 2036	4.5 / 1.5 / 4.2 / 1.5		
4 TU	0321 / 0850 / 1535 / 2115	4.5 / 1.3 / 4.3 / 1.2			19 W	0337 / 0858 / 1548 / 2116	4.3 / 1.7 / 4.0 / 1.7		
5 W	0414 / 0947 / 1634 / 2216	4.4 / 1.5 / 4.2 / 1.4			20 TH	0421 / 0945 / 1638 / 2210	4.2 / 2.0 / 3.8 / 2.0		
6 TH	0517 / 1056 / 1746 / 2328	4.3 / 1.6 / 4.0 / 1.6			21 F	0516 / 1054 / 1746 / 2329	4.0 / 2.2 / 3.7 / 2.2		
7 F	0630 / 1216 / 1907	4.3 / 1.6 / 4.1			22 SA	0625 / 1229 / 1910	4.0 / 2.1 / 3.7		
8 SA	0046 / 0742 / 1332 / 2022	1.6 / 4.3 / 1.5 / 4.2			23 SU	0055 / 0737 / 1340 / 2025	2.1 / 4.0 / 1.9 / 3.9		
9 SU	0156 / 0848 / 1436 / 2126	1.5 / 4.5 / 1.3 / 4.4			24 M	0159 / 0841 / 1433 / 2122	1.9 / 4.2 / 1.6 / 4.1		
10 M	0256 / 0945 / 1531 / 2222	1.3 / 4.6 / 1.0 / 4.6			25 TU	0249 / 0933 / 1518 / 2209	1.6 / 4.3 / 1.3 / 4.4		
11 TU ●	0348 / 1037 / 1619 / 2311	1.1 / 4.7 / 0.9 / 4.7			26 W	0333 / 1018 / 1600 / 2251	1.4 / 4.5 / 1.0 / 4.5		
12 W	0435 / 1124 / 1704 / 2357	1.0 / 4.8 / 0.7 / 4.8			27 TH ○	0415 / 1100 / 1641 / 2332	1.1 / 4.6 / 0.8 / 4.7		
13 TH	0519 / 1207 / 1745	0.9 / 4.8 / 0.7			28 F	0456 / 1141 / 1721	0.9 / 4.7 / 0.6		
14 F	0038 / 0559 / 1247 / 1823	4.8 / 0.9 / 4.7 / 0.7			29 SA	0012 / 0537 / 1223 / 1800	4.8 / 0.8 / 4.8 / 0.5		
15 SA	0116 / 0637 / 1324 / 1858	4.7 / 1.0 / 4.6 / 0.8			30 SU	0052 / 0618 / 1304 / 1841	4.8 / 0.7 / 4.8 / 0.5		
					31 M	0133 / 0700 / 1347 / 1922	4.8 / 0.7 / 4.8 / 0.6		

FEBRUARY

#	Time	m	Time	m	#	Time	m	Time	m
1 TU	0215 / 0743 / 1431 / 2005	4.8 / 0.8 / 4.6 / 0.8			16 W	0222 / 0741 / 1436 / 1956	4.5 / 1.3 / 4.3 / 1.3		
2 W	0259 / 0829 / 1518 / 2053	4.7 / 1.0 / 4.5 / 1.0			17 TH	0255 / 0812 / 1510 / 2029	4.4 / 1.5 / 4.1 / 1.6		
3 TH	0348 / 0921 / 1613 / 2151	4.5 / 1.3 / 4.2 / 1.4			18 F	0332 / 0851 / 1552 / 2113	4.2 / 1.8 / 3.9 / 1.9		
4 F	0446 / 1027 / 1722 / 2305	4.2 / 1.5 / 4.0 / 1.7			19 SA	0418 / 0943 / 1651 / 2219	4.0 / 2.0 / 3.7 / 2.2		
5 SA	0558 / 1151 / 1849	4.1 / 1.7 / 3.9			20 SU	0523 / 1109 / 1815	3.8 / 2.2 / 3.7		
6 SU	0031 / 0721 / 1317 / 2014	1.8 / 4.1 / 1.6 / 4.0			21 M	0008 / 0644 / 1301 / 1945	2.3 / 3.8 / 2.0 / 3.8		
7 M	0149 / 0837 / 1427 / 2123	1.7 / 4.2 / 1.4 / 4.3			22 TU	0132 / 0804 / 1405 / 2054	2.0 / 4.0 / 1.7 / 4.1		
8 TU	0251 / 0938 / 1521 / 2216	1.4 / 4.4 / 1.1 / 4.5			23 W	0228 / 0906 / 1454 / 2145	1.7 / 4.2 / 1.3 / 4.3		
9 W	0341 / 1028 / 1607 / 2301	1.2 / 4.6 / 0.9 / 4.6			24 TH	0314 / 0955 / 1537 / 2229	1.3 / 4.4 / 1.0 / 4.6		
10 TH ●	0425 / 1112 / 1648 / 2341	1.0 / 4.6 / 0.7 / 4.7			25 F	0356 / 1039 / 1619 / 2310	1.0 / 4.6 / 0.7 / 4.8		
11 F	0504 / 1150 / 1725	0.9 / 4.7 / 0.6			26 SA ○	0438 / 1122 / 1700 / 2351	0.7 / 4.8 / 0.4 / 4.9		
12 SA	0017 / 0540 / 1226 / 1759	4.7 / 0.8 / 4.7 / 0.7			27 SU	0519 / 1205 / 1741	0.5 / 4.9 / 0.3		
13 SU	0049 / 0613 / 1258 / 1831	4.7 / 0.8 / 4.6 / 0.7			28 M	0032 / 0600 / 1249 / 1822	5.0 / 0.4 / 4.9 / 0.3		
14 M	0119 / 0644 / 1330 / 1900	4.7 / 0.9 / 4.5 / 0.9							
15 TU	0150 / 0713 / 1403 / 1928	4.6 / 1.1 / 4.4 / 1.1							

MARCH

#	Time	m	Time	m	#	Time	m	Time	m
1 TU	0114 / 0642 / 1332 / 1904	4.9 / 0.4 / 4.9 / 0.4			16 W	0118 / 0642 / 1336 / 1856	4.6 / 0.9 / 4.5 / 1.1		
2 W	0156 / 0725 / 1417 / 1948	4.9 / 0.6 / 4.8 / 0.7			17 TH	0149 / 0708 / 1409 / 1924	4.5 / 1.1 / 4.4 / 1.3		
3 TH	0239 / 0810 / 1505 / 2036	4.7 / 0.8 / 4.5 / 1.0			18 F	0221 / 0738 / 1443 / 1957	4.4 / 1.3 / 4.2 / 1.5		
4 F	0326 / 0900 / 1559 / 2133	4.4 / 1.1 / 4.3 / 1.4			19 SA	0254 / 0814 / 1522 / 2038	4.2 / 1.5 / 4.0 / 1.8		
5 SA	0421 / 1004 / 1706 / 2249	4.1 / 1.5 / 4.0 / 1.7			20 SU	0335 / 0901 / 1615 / 2137	4.0 / 1.8 / 3.8 / 2.1		
6 SU	0533 / 1129 / 1836	3.9 / 1.7 / 3.9			21 M	0435 / 1011 / 1731 / 2314	3.8 / 2.0 / 3.7 / 2.2		
7 M	0018 / 0706 / 1259 / 2005	1.8 / 3.8 / 1.7 / 4.0			22 TU	0555 / 1203 / 1901	3.7 / 2.0 / 3.8		
8 TU	0140 / 0829 / 1412 / 2111	1.7 / 4.0 / 1.5 / 4.2			23 W	0056 / 0721 / 1326 / 2017	2.0 / 3.8 / 1.7 / 4.1		
9 W	0242 / 0929 / 1505 / 2202	1.4 / 4.2 / 1.2 / 4.5			24 TH	0159 / 0832 / 1421 / 2113	1.6 / 4.1 / 1.3 / 4.4		
10 TH	0329 / 1016 / 1548 / 2243	1.2 / 4.4 / 0.9 / 4.6			25 F	0248 / 0927 / 1508 / 2200	1.2 / 4.4 / 0.9 / 4.6		
11 F	0408 / 1055 / 1625 / 2318	0.9 / 4.5 / 0.8 / 4.7			26 SA	0332 / 1014 / 1552 / 2244	0.9 / 4.6 / 0.6 / 4.8		
12 SA ●	0443 / 1130 / 1700 / 2350	0.8 / 4.6 / 0.7 / 4.7			27 SU ○	0415 / 1100 / 1635 / 2327	0.6 / 4.8 / 0.5 / 5.0		
13 SU	0516 / 1201 / 1732	0.7 / 4.6 / 0.7			28 M	0457 / 1145 / 1718	0.4 / 4.9 / 0.3		
14 M	0018 / 0547 / 1232 / 1802	4.7 / 0.7 / 4.6 / 0.8			29 TU	0010 / 0540 / 1232 / 1802	5.0 / 0.3 / 5.0 / 0.3		
15 TU	0048 / 0615 / 1304 / 1830	4.6 / 0.8 / 4.5 / 0.9			30 W	0054 / 0624 / 1318 / 1847	5.0 / 0.3 / 4.9 / 0.4		
					31 TH	0138 / 0708 / 1405 / 1933	4.8 / 0.5 / 4.8 / 0.7		

APRIL

#	Time	m	Time	m	#	Time	m	Time	m
1 F	0223 / 0754 / 1454 / 2022	4.6 / 0.7 / 4.6 / 1.0			16 SA	0154 / 0714 / 1423 / 1935	4.4 / 1.2 / 4.3 / 1.4		
2 SA	0310 / 0844 / 1548 / 2119	4.4 / 1.0 / 4.3 / 1.4			17 SU	0229 / 0752 / 1503 / 2018	4.2 / 1.3 / 4.1 / 1.6		
3 SU	0404 / 0945 / 1653 / 2231	4.1 / 1.4 / 4.1 / 1.7			18 M	0310 / 0838 / 1554 / 2114	4.0 / 1.6 / 4.0 / 1.9		
4 M	0513 / 1103 / 1817 / 2355	3.8 / 1.6 / 3.9 / 1.8			19 TU	0405 / 0941 / 1700 / 2234	3.9 / 1.8 / 3.9 / 2.0		
5 TU	0645 / 1230 / 1941	3.7 / 1.7 / 4.0			20 W	0517 / 1108 / 1819	3.8 / 1.8 / 3.9		
6 W	0117 / 0808 / 1344 / 2045	1.7 / 3.8 / 1.5 / 4.2			21 TH	0006 / 0638 / 1236 / 1935	1.9 / 3.8 / 1.6 / 4.1		
7 TH	0219 / 0907 / 1438 / 2135	1.5 / 4.0 / 1.3 / 4.4			22 F	0119 / 0753 / 1341 / 2036	1.6 / 4.0 / 1.3 / 4.4		
8 F	0304 / 0953 / 1519 / 2215	1.2 / 4.2 / 1.1 / 4.5			23 SA	0214 / 0854 / 1434 / 2128	1.2 / 4.3 / 0.9 / 4.6		
9 SA	0341 / 1031 / 1555 / 2249	1.0 / 4.3 / 0.9 / 4.6			24 SU	0303 / 0947 / 1522 / 2216	0.8 / 4.6 / 0.6 / 4.8		
10 SU	0415 / 1104 / 1629 / 2319	0.8 / 4.4 / 0.8 / 4.6			25 M ○	0350 / 1036 / 1609 / 2303	0.6 / 4.8 / 0.5 / 5.0		
11 M ●	0448 / 1134 / 1702 / 2347	0.8 / 4.5 / 0.8 / 4.6			26 TU	0435 / 1125 / 1656 / 2349	0.4 / 4.9 / 0.4 / 5.0		
12 TU	0519 / 1205 / 1733	0.8 / 4.5 / 0.9			27 W	0522 / 1215 / 1743	0.3 / 4.9 / 0.4		
13 W	0017 / 0548 / 1238 / 1802	4.6 / 0.8 / 4.5 / 1.0			28 TH	0036 / 0607 / 1304 / 1830	4.9 / 0.4 / 4.9 / 0.5		
14 TH	0049 / 0615 / 1312 / 1830	4.5 / 0.9 / 4.5 / 1.1			29 F	0123 / 0654 / 1353 / 1918	4.8 / 0.5 / 4.8 / 0.7		
15 F	0122 / 0643 / 1347 / 1900	4.5 / 1.0 / 4.4 / 1.2			30 SA	0209 / 0741 / 1444 / 2008	4.6 / 0.7 / 4.6 / 1.0		

PORTSMOUTH

50°48′N 1°07′W

Times and heights (in metres) of high and low water 1994
Time: GMT. For BST, ADD ONE HOUR in the shaded area
High Water, full and change, 1133

MAY

Date	Time	m	Time	m	Time	m	Time	m
1 SU	0257	4.4	0830	1.0	1536	4.4	2102	1.3
2 M	0348	4.1	0925	1.3	1635	4.2	2204	1.6
3 TU	0450	3.9	1031	1.5	1745	4.0	2318	1.8
4 W	0608	3.7	1148	1.7	1900	4.0		
5 TH	0034	1.8	0728	3.7	1301	1.6	2004	4.1
6 F	0139	1.6	0831	3.9	1358	1.5	2056	4.2
7 SA	0227	1.4	0919	4.0	1442	1.3	2138	4.4
8 SU	0307	1.2	0959	4.2	1520	1.1	2214	4.4
9 M	0343	1.0	1033	4.3	1556	1.0	2246	4.5
10 TU ●	0417	0.9	1106	4.4	1631	1.0	2317	4.5
11 W	0451	0.9	1139	4.4	1705	1.0	2350	4.5
12 TH	0524	0.9	1214	4.4	1737	1.1		
13 F	0024	4.5	0554	0.9	1251	4.4	1809	1.1
14 SA	0059	4.4	0625	1.0	1328	4.4	1843	1.2
15 SU	0135	4.4	0659	1.1	1406	4.3	1921	1.3
16 M	0212	4.3	0739	1.2	1448	4.3	2005	1.4
17 TU	0254	4.2	0825	1.3	1536	4.2	2058	1.6
18 W	0345	4.0	0921	1.5	1634	4.1	2203	1.7
19 TH	0447	4.0	1031	1.5	1743	4.1	2319	1.7
20 F	0601	4.0	1148	1.5	1855	4.2		
21 SA	0033	1.5	0716	4.1	1300	1.3	2000	4.4
22 SU	0139	1.3	0822	4.3	1401	1.0	2057	4.6
23 M	0235	1.0	0920	4.5	1455	0.8	2150	4.8
24 TU	0327	0.7	1015	4.7	1546	0.6	2240	4.9
25 W O	0417	0.5	1108	4.8	1637	0.6	2330	4.9
26 TH	0506	0.5	1200	4.9	1727	0.6		
27 F	0019	4.9	0554	0.5	1251	4.9	1815	0.6
28 SA	0108	4.8	0642	0.5	1341	4.8	1903	0.8
29 SU	0155	4.7	0728	0.7	1430	4.7	1951	1.0
30 M	0241	4.5	0813	0.9	1518	4.5	2039	1.2
31 TU	0327	4.2	0900	1.2	1608	4.3	2130	1.5

JUNE

Date	Time	m	Time	m	Time	m	Time	m
1 W	0417	4.0	0953	1.5	1702	4.1	2229	1.7
2 TH	0516	3.8	1055	1.7	1804	4.0	2336	1.8
3 F	0627	3.7	1204	1.8	1908	4.0		
4 SA	0044	1.8	0737	3.8	1308	1.7	2006	4.1
5 SU	0141	1.7	0835	3.9	1400	1.6	2054	4.2
6 M	0228	1.5	0921	4.0	1444	1.4	2135	4.3
7 TU	0309	1.3	1001	4.2	1524	1.3	2213	4.4
8 W	0348	1.1	1039	4.3	1603	1.2	2249	4.4
9 TH ●	0426	1.0	1116	4.4	1640	1.1	2326	4.5
10 F	0503	1.0	1153	4.4	1717	1.1		
11 SA	0003	4.5	0538	1.0	1232	4.4	1753	1.1
12 SU	0041	4.5	0613	0.9	1311	4.5	1830	1.1
13 M	0118	4.4	0649	1.0	1350	4.5	1909	1.1
14 TU	0158	4.4	0729	1.0	1432	4.4	1952	1.2
15 W	0240	4.3	0813	1.1	1517	4.4	2041	1.3
16 TH	0327	4.3	0903	1.2	1609	4.3	2137	1.4
17 F	0423	4.1	1002	1.3	1710	4.2	2243	1.5
18 SA	0530	4.1	1112	1.4	1819	4.3	2356	1.5
19 SU	0644	4.1	1225	1.4	1928	4.4		
20 M	0108	1.4	0756	4.2	1335	1.2	2031	4.5
21 TU	0213	1.1	0901	4.4	1436	1.1	2129	4.7
22 W	0311	0.9	1000	4.6	1532	0.9	2223	4.8
23 TH O	0404	0.7	1055	4.7	1624	0.8	2315	4.9
24 F	0454	0.6	1148	4.8	1714	0.7		
25 SA	0004	4.8	0542	0.6	1238	4.8	1801	0.7
26 SU	0052	4.8	0628	0.6	1325	4.8	1846	0.8
27 M	0137	4.7	0710	0.7	1409	4.7	1929	1.0
28 TU	0219	4.6	0750	0.9	1451	4.6	2010	1.1
29 W	0259	4.4	0829	1.1	1532	4.4	2051	1.4
30 TH	0340	4.2	0910	1.4	1614	4.3	2137	1.6

JULY

Date	Time	m	Time	m	Time	m	Time	m
1 F	0425	3.9	0958	1.7	1702	4.1	2233	1.8
2 SA	0519	3.8	1059	1.9	1759	4.0	2342	2.0
3 SU	0627	3.7	1211	2.0	1903	4.0		
4 M	0051	1.9	0740	3.8	1317	1.9	2004	4.1
5 TU	0150	1.7	0842	3.9	1411	1.7	2057	4.2
6 W	0239	1.5	0932	4.1	1457	1.5	2143	4.3
7 TH	0323	1.3	1015	4.3	1539	1.4	2225	4.4
8 F ●	0404	1.1	1055	4.4	1619	1.2	2304	4.5
9 SA	0443	1.0	1135	4.5	1659	1.1	2343	4.5
10 SU	0522	0.9	1214	4.5	1737	1.0		
11 M	0022	4.5	0559	0.8	1253	4.6	1816	0.9
12 TU	0102	4.6	0637	0.8	1332	4.6	1855	0.9
13 W	0142	4.6	0715	0.8	1413	4.6	1937	1.0
14 TH	0224	4.5	0757	0.9	1456	4.6	2022	1.1
15 F	0309	4.4	0844	1.0	1544	4.5	2114	1.2
16 SA	0402	4.3	0938	1.3	1641	4.3	2214	1.4
17 SU	0506	4.1	1044	1.5	1748	4.2	2328	1.5
18 M	0622	4.1	1203	1.6	1902	4.3		
19 TU	0048	1.5	0740	4.1	1321	1.5	2012	4.4
20 W	0200	1.3	0851	4.3	1427	1.3	2115	4.5
21 TH	0301	1.1	0953	4.5	1524	1.1	2211	4.7
22 F O	0354	0.8	1047	4.7	1615	0.9	2302	4.8
23 SA	0443	0.7	1136	4.8	1701	0.8	2349	4.8
24 SU	0528	0.6	1222	4.8	1745	0.8		
25 M	0033	4.8	0609	0.6	1304	4.8	1825	0.8
26 TU	0113	4.7	0646	0.7	1342	4.8	1902	0.9
27 W	0150	4.6	0721	0.9	1417	4.7	1937	1.1
28 TH	0226	4.4	0754	1.1	1452	4.5	2012	1.3
29 F	0301	4.3	0827	1.3	1528	4.4	2048	1.5
30 SA	0340	4.1	0905	1.6	1609	4.2	2132	1.8
31 SU	0427	3.9	0953	1.9	1658	4.0	2232	2.0

AUGUST

Date	Time	m	Time	m	Time	m	Time	m
1 M	0527	3.7	1106	2.1	1801	3.9	2358	2.1
2 TU	0645	3.7	1236	2.2	1914	3.9		
3 W	0114	1.9	0804	3.9	1343	2.0	2021	4.0
4 TH	0212	1.7	0905	4.1	1434	1.7	2116	4.2
5 F	0259	1.4	0953	4.3	1519	1.5	2201	4.4
6 SA	0342	1.1	1035	4.5	1600	1.2	2243	4.5
7 SU ●	0422	0.9	1114	4.6	1639	1.0	2322	4.6
8 M	0501	0.7	1153	4.7	1719	0.8		
9 TU	0002	4.7	0540	0.6	1233	4.8	1757	0.7
10 W	0043	4.7	0618	0.6	1312	4.8	1837	0.7
11 TH	0125	4.7	0658	0.6	1353	4.8	1919	0.8
12 F	0207	4.7	0740	0.8	1435	4.7	2003	0.9
13 SA	0253	4.5	0825	1.0	1522	4.5	2053	1.1
14 SU	0345	4.3	0918	1.3	1616	4.3	2152	1.4
15 M	0449	4.1	1026	1.6	1723	4.1	2309	1.6
16 TU	0608	4.0	1152	1.8	1844	4.1		
17 W	0036	1.6	0734	4.1	1316	1.7	2002	4.2
18 TH	0152	1.4	0849	4.3	1424	1.5	2109	4.4
19 F	0253	1.1	0948	4.5	1518	1.2	2203	4.6
20 SA	0343	0.9	1037	4.7	1604	1.0	2250	4.7
21 SU O	0427	0.7	1121	4.8	1646	0.8	2332	4.7
22 M	0507	0.6	1200	4.8	1724	0.8		
23 TU	0010	4.7	0543	0.6	1237	4.8	1759	0.8
24 W	0045	4.7	0617	0.7	1309	4.7	1832	0.9
25 TH	0119	4.6	0649	0.9	1341	4.6	1903	1.1
26 F	0152	4.5	0718	1.1	1413	4.5	1933	1.2
27 SA	0226	4.3	0747	1.3	1446	4.4	2005	1.5
28 SU	0301	4.2	0820	1.6	1522	4.2	2042	1.7
29 M	0343	4.0	0901	1.9	1606	4.0	2132	2.0
30 TU	0438	3.8	1001	2.2	1705	3.9	2252	2.2
31 W	0555	3.7	1150	2.3	1823	3.8		

PORTSMOUTH

50°48'N 1°07'W

Times and heights (in metres) of high and low water 1994
Time: GMT. For BST, ADD ONE HOUR in the shaded area
High Water, full and change, 1133

SEPTEMBER

Day	Time	m	Time	m	Day	Time	m	Time	m
1 TH	0037 / 0724 / 1315 / 1944	2.1 / 3.8 / 2.1 / 3.9			16 F	0140 / 0841 / 1415 / 2101	1.5 / 4.3 / 1.5 / 4.3		
2 F	0144 / 0835 / 1411 / 2047	1.8 / 4.1 / 1.8 / 4.1			17 SA	0239 / 0935 / 1505 / 2151	1.2 / 4.5 / 1.3 / 4.5		
3 SA	0234 / 0927 / 1456 / 2136	1.4 / 4.3 / 1.5 / 4.4			18 SU	0325 / 1020 / 1547 / 2233	1.0 / 4.7 / 1.0 / 4.6		
4 SU	0317 / 1010 / 1537 / 2218	1.1 / 4.5 / 1.1 / 4.6			19 M O	0405 / 1059 / 1624 / 2311	0.8 / 4.7 / 0.9 / 4.7		
5 M ●	0357 / 1050 / 1617 / 2259	0.8 / 4.7 / 0.9 / 4.7			20 TU	0441 / 1134 / 1658 / 2344	0.7 / 4.8 / 0.8 / 4.7		
6 TU	0437 / 1129 / 1656 / 2341	0.6 / 4.8 / 0.7 / 4.8			21 W	0515 / 1205 / 1731	0.7 / 4.7 / 0.8		
7 W	0517 / 1209 / 1736	0.5 / 4.9 / 0.6			22 TH	0016 / 0546 / 1236 / 1801	4.6 / 0.8 / 4.7 / 0.9		
8 TH	0023 / 0557 / 1251 / 1817	4.9 / 0.5 / 4.9 / 0.6			23 F	0048 / 0617 / 1306 / 1830	4.6 / 0.9 / 4.6 / 1.1		
9 F	0107 / 0638 / 1333 / 1900	4.9 / 0.5 / 4.8 / 0.6			24 SA	0120 / 0645 / 1338 / 1859	4.5 / 1.1 / 4.5 / 1.2		
10 SA	0152 / 0722 / 1416 / 1945	4.8 / 0.7 / 4.7 / 0.8			25 SU	0154 / 0713 / 1410 / 1929	4.4 / 1.3 / 4.4 / 1.4		
11 SU	0239 / 0810 / 1503 / 2035	4.6 / 1.0 / 4.5 / 1.1			26 M	0229 / 0745 / 1444 / 2005	4.3 / 1.6 / 4.2 / 1.6		
12 M	0332 / 0905 / 1558 / 2136	4.4 / 1.3 / 4.2 / 1.4			27 TU	0309 / 0824 / 1524 / 2050	4.1 / 1.9 / 4.1 / 1.9		
13 TU	0437 / 1015 / 1706 / 2254	4.1 / 1.7 / 4.0 / 1.7			28 W	0359 / 0918 / 1619 / 2157	3.9 / 2.1 / 3.9 / 2.1		
14 W	0559 / 1143 / 1833	4.0 / 1.8 / 3.9			29 TH	0511 / 1050 / 1735 / 2345	3.8 / 2.3 / 3.8 / 2.1		
15 TH	0023 / 0728 / 1308 / 1956	1.7 / 4.1 / 1.8 / 4.1			30 F	0639 / 1236 / 1902	3.8 / 2.2 / 3.9		

OCTOBER

Day	Time	m	Day	Time	m
1 SA	0107 / 0757 / 1339 / 2013	1.9 / 4.1 / 1.9 / 4.1	16 SU	0215 / 0911 / 1442 / 2130	1.4 / 4.5 / 1.4 / 4.4
2 SU	0201 / 0853 / 1427 / 2106	1.5 / 4.4 / 1.5 / 4.4	17 M	0259 / 0954 / 1522 / 2211	1.2 / 4.6 / 1.1 / 4.5
3 M	0246 / 0939 / 1509 / 2151	1.1 / 4.6 / 1.1 / 4.6	18 TU	0337 / 1031 / 1557 / 2246	1.0 / 4.7 / 1.0 / 4.6
4 TU	0328 / 1022 / 1550 / 2234	0.8 / 4.8 / 0.8 / 4.8	19 W O	0411 / 1104 / 1630 / 2317	0.9 / 4.7 / 0.9 / 4.6
5 W ●	0409 / 1104 / 1631 / 2318	0.6 / 4.9 / 0.6 / 4.9	20 TH	0444 / 1134 / 1702 / 2347	0.9 / 4.6 / 0.9 / 4.6
6 TH	0452 / 1146 / 1714	0.4 / 5.0 / 0.5	21 F	0517 / 1203 / 1733	0.9 / 4.6 / 1.0
7 F	0003 / 0535 / 1230 / 1757	5.0 / 0.4 / 5.0 / 0.5	22 SA	0019 / 0547 / 1235 / 1803	4.6 / 1.0 / 4.6 / 1.1
8 SA	0050 / 0620 / 1315 / 1842	4.9 / 0.5 / 4.9 / 0.6	23 SU	0053 / 0617 / 1308 / 1832	4.5 / 1.2 / 4.5 / 1.2
9 SU	0138 / 0706 / 1400 / 1930	4.8 / 0.7 / 4.7 / 0.8	24 M	0128 / 0647 / 1342 / 1903	4.4 / 1.3 / 4.4 / 1.4
10 M	0227 / 0757 / 1449 / 2021	4.7 / 1.0 / 4.5 / 1.1	25 TU	0205 / 0720 / 1416 / 1939	4.3 / 1.5 / 4.3 / 1.5
11 TU	0322 / 0853 / 1544 / 2121	4.4 / 1.4 / 4.2 / 1.4	26 W	0245 / 0800 / 1456 / 2023	4.2 / 1.8 / 4.1 / 1.7
12 W	0425 / 1002 / 1652 / 2235	4.2 / 1.7 / 4.0 / 1.7	27 TH	0332 / 0851 / 1546 / 2122	4.1 / 2.0 / 4.0 / 1.9
13 TH	0545 / 1123 / 1818 / 2359	4.0 / 1.8 / 3.9 / 1.7	28 F	0435 / 1003 / 1653 / 2244	3.9 / 2.2 / 3.9 / 2.0
14 F	0710 / 1246 / 1940	4.1 / 1.8 / 4.0	29 SA	0553 / 1137 / 1814	3.9 / 2.1 / 3.9
15 SA	0116 / 0818 / 1353 / 2042	1.6 / 4.3 / 1.6 / 4.2	30 SU	0012 / 0711 / 1254 / 1930	1.9 / 4.1 / 1.9 / 4.1
			31 M	0118 / 0814 / 1350 / 2031	1.6 / 4.4 / 1.5 / 4.4

NOVEMBER

Day	Time	m	Day	Time	m
1 TU	0210 / 0906 / 1438 / 2122	1.2 / 4.6 / 1.2 / 4.6	16 W	0304 / 0959 / 1527 / 2219	1.3 / 4.5 / 1.2 / 4.4
2 W	0256 / 0952 / 1523 / 2210	0.9 / 4.8 / 0.9 / 4.8	17 TH	0340 / 1033 / 1602 / 2252	1.1 / 4.6 / 1.1 / 4.5
3 TH ●	0342 / 1038 / 1608 / 2257	0.7 / 5.0 / 0.7 / 4.9	18 F O	0415 / 1104 / 1636 / 2323	1.1 / 4.6 / 1.0 / 4.5
4 F	0428 / 1124 / 1654 / 2346	0.5 / 5.0 / 0.6 / 5.0	19 SA	0450 / 1136 / 1710 / 2356	1.1 / 4.6 / 1.0 / 4.5
5 SA	0515 / 1210 / 1741	0.5 / 5.0 / 0.6	20 SU	0524 / 1209 / 1742	1.1 / 4.6 / 1.1
6 SU	0035 / 0603 / 1258 / 1828	5.0 / 0.6 / 4.9 / 0.6	21 M	0032 / 0556 / 1245 / 1813	4.5 / 1.2 / 4.5 / 1.2
7 M	0125 / 0652 / 1346 / 1917	4.9 / 0.8 / 4.7 / 0.8	22 TU	0109 / 0628 / 1320 / 1846	4.5 / 1.3 / 4.4 / 1.3
8 TU	0217 / 0744 / 1436 / 2008	4.7 / 1.0 / 4.5 / 1.0	23 W	0146 / 0703 / 1356 / 1922	4.4 / 1.5 / 4.4 / 1.4
9 W	0310 / 0838 / 1529 / 2104	4.5 / 1.3 / 4.3 / 1.3	24 TH	0226 / 0743 / 1434 / 2004	4.4 / 1.6 / 4.2 / 1.5
10 TH	0409 / 0939 / 1630 / 2207	4.3 / 1.6 / 4.1 / 1.6	25 F	0311 / 0830 / 1520 / 2055	4.3 / 1.8 / 4.1 / 1.7
11 F	0517 / 1049 / 1746 / 2320	4.2 / 1.8 / 3.9 / 1.7	26 SA	0404 / 0929 / 1617 / 2200	4.2 / 1.9 / 4.0 / 1.8
12 SA	0632 / 1206 / 1905	4.1 / 1.8 / 3.9	27 SU	0510 / 1042 / 1728 / 2315	4.1 / 2.0 / 4.0 / 1.7
13 SU	0035 / 0740 / 1315 / 2009	1.7 / 4.2 / 1.7 / 4.0	28 M	0624 / 1200 / 1846	4.2 / 1.8 / 4.1
14 M	0137 / 0836 / 1409 / 2101	1.6 / 4.3 / 1.5 / 4.2	29 TU	0028 / 0732 / 1310 / 1955	1.6 / 4.4 / 1.6 / 4.3
15 TU	0224 / 0921 / 1450 / 2143	1.4 / 4.5 / 1.3 / 4.3	30 W	0132 / 0831 / 1408 / 2054	1.3 / 4.6 / 1.3 / 4.5

DECEMBER

Day	Time	m	Day	Time	m
1 TH	0227 / 0924 / 1500 / 2148	1.1 / 4.8 / 1.0 / 4.7	16 F	0311 / 1003 / 1537 / 2230	1.4 / 4.5 / 1.2 / 4.4
2 F ●	0319 / 1015 / 1550 / 2240	0.9 / 5.0 / 0.8 / 4.9	17 SA	0350 / 1038 / 1615 / 2304	1.3 / 4.5 / 1.1 / 4.4
3 SA	0409 / 1104 / 1640 / 2332	0.7 / 5.0 / 0.6 / 4.9	18 SU O	0428 / 1113 / 1652 / 2339	1.2 / 4.6 / 1.1 / 4.5
4 SU	0459 / 1153 / 1729	0.7 / 5.0 / 0.6	19 M	0504 / 1149 / 1727	1.2 / 4.6 / 1.0
5 M	0023 / 0549 / 1243 / 1817	5.0 / 0.7 / 4.9 / 0.6	20 TU	0015 / 0539 / 1225 / 1800	4.5 / 1.2 / 4.5 / 1.0
6 TU	0114 / 0639 / 1332 / 1905	4.9 / 0.8 / 4.8 / 0.7	21 W	0052 / 0613 / 1301 / 1833	4.5 / 1.2 / 4.5 / 1.1
7 W	0204 / 0728 / 1419 / 1952	4.8 / 1.0 / 4.6 / 0.9	22 TH	0130 / 0649 / 1338 / 1908	4.5 / 1.3 / 4.5 / 1.1
8 TH	0253 / 0817 / 1507 / 2040	4.7 / 1.2 / 4.4 / 1.1	23 F	0208 / 0727 / 1416 / 1947	4.5 / 1.4 / 4.4 / 1.2
9 F	0343 / 0908 / 1558 / 2131	4.5 / 1.5 / 4.2 / 1.4	24 SA	0249 / 0810 / 1458 / 2032	4.5 / 1.5 / 4.3 / 1.3
10 SA	0437 / 1005 / 1656 / 2230	4.3 / 1.7 / 4.0 / 1.7	25 SU	0336 / 0901 / 1548 / 2126	4.4 / 1.6 / 4.2 / 1.5
11 SU	0539 / 1112 / 1807 / 2338	4.2 / 1.9 / 3.8 / 1.8	26 M	0432 / 1002 / 1650 / 2231	4.3 / 1.7 / 4.1 / 1.6
12 M	0646 / 1223 / 1922	4.1 / 1.9 / 3.8	27 TU	0539 / 1115 / 1805 / 2346	4.3 / 1.8 / 4.0 / 1.6
13 TU	0046 / 0748 / 1326 / 2023	1.8 / 4.2 / 1.8 / 4.0	28 W	0652 / 1233 / 1923	4.3 / 1.7 / 4.1
14 W	0143 / 0841 / 1416 / 2113	1.7 / 4.3 / 1.6 / 4.1	29 TH	0100 / 0800 / 1345 / 2033	1.5 / 4.5 / 1.4 / 4.3
15 TH	0230 / 0925 / 1458 / 2154	1.6 / 4.4 / 1.4 / 4.3	30 F	0206 / 0901 / 1445 / 2134	1.3 / 4.7 / 1.1 / 4.6
			31 SA	0304 / 0956 / 1540 / 2229	1.1 / 4.8 / 0.9 / 4.7

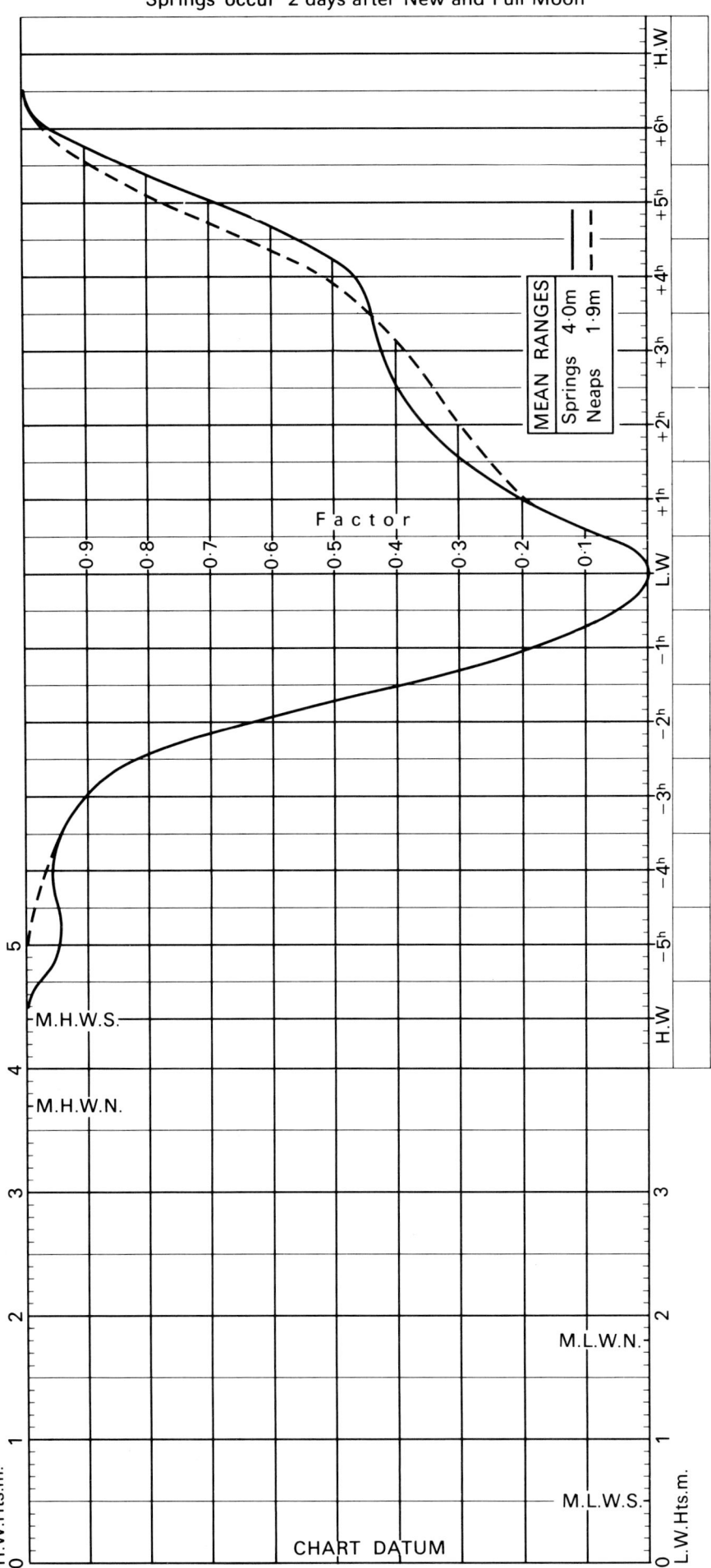

SOUTHAMPTON

MEAN SPRING AND NEAP CURVES

Springs occur 2 days after New and Full Moon

MEAN RANGES
Springs 4·0m
Neaps 1·9m

Factor

H.W.Hts.m.

L.W.Hts.m.

M.H.W.S.

M.H.W.N.

M.L.W.N.

M.L.W.S.

CHART DATUM

HIGH WATERS - IMPORTANT NOTE
Double high waters occur at Southampton. The predictions are for the first high water.

SOUTHAMPTON
50°54′N 1°24′W

Times and heights (in metres) of high and low water 1994
Time: GMT. For BST, ADD ONE HOUR in the shaded area
High Water, full and change, 1103 (first) and 1303 (second)

JANUARY

Day	Time	m	Time	m		Day	Time	m	Time	m
1 SA	0029 / 0624 / 1245 / 1846	4.5 / 0.7 / 4.6 / 0.6				**16** SU	0110 / 0703 / 1321 / 1919	4.4 / 0.9 / 4.4 / 0.8		
2 SU	0111 / 0706 / 1328 / 1928	4.5 / 0.8 / 4.5 / 0.7				**17** M	0147 / 0736 / 1358 / 1950	4.4 / 1.1 / 4.2 / 1.1		
3 M	0156 / 0751 / 1415 / 2014	4.4 / 0.9 / 4.4 / 0.9				**18** TU	0225 / 0810 / 1437 / 2023	4.2 / 1.3 / 4.1 / 1.3		
4 TU	0246 / 0842 / 1507 / 2106	4.4 / 1.0 / 4.2 / 1.1				**19** W	0307 / 0849 / 1522 / 2103	4.1 / 1.6 / 3.9 / 1.6		
5 W	0342 / 0940 / 1608 / 2206	4.3 / 1.2 / 4.1 / 1.3				**20** TH	0354 / 0938 / 1616 / 2156	4.0 / 1.8 / 3.7 / 1.9		
6 TH	0447 / 1048 / 1719 / 2316	4.2 / 1.3 / 3.9 / 1.4				**21** F	0452 / 1043 / 1726 / 2309	3.9 / 2.0 / 3.6 / 2.1		
7 F	0559 / 1204 / 1836	4.1 / 1.4 / 3.9				**22** SA	0603 / 1207 / 1847	3.8 / 2.0 / 3.6		
8 SA	0032 / 0712 / 1319 / 1951	1.4 / 4.2 / 1.3 / 4.0				**23** SU	0034 / 0716 / 1324 / 2000	2.1 / 3.9 / 1.8 / 3.8		
9 SU	0143 / 0820 / 1425 / 2056	1.3 / 4.3 / 1.1 / 4.1				**24** M	0146 / 0819 / 1423 / 2057	1.9 / 4.0 / 1.5 / 3.9		
10 M	0246 / 0918 / 1522 / 2151	1.1 / 4.4 / 0.8 / 4.2				**25** TU	0241 / 0910 / 1512 / 2142	1.6 / 4.2 / 1.2 / 4.2		
11 TU ●	0340 / 1008 / 1612 / 2238	0.9 / 4.5 / 0.6 / 4.4				**26** W	0328 / 0952 / 1555 / 2220	1.2 / 4.4 / 0.8 / 4.3		
12 W	0429 / 1052 / 1657 / 2320	0.7 / 4.6 / 0.4 / 4.4				**27** TH O	0411 / 1031 / 1636 / 2257	0.9 / 4.5 / 0.5 / 4.5		
13 TH	0513 / 1132 / 1737 / 2358	0.6 / 4.6 / 0.4 / 4.5				**28** F	0452 / 1108 / 1715 / 2334	0.6 / 4.7 / 0.3 / 4.6		
14 F	0553 / 1209 / 1815	0.6 / 4.5 / 0.4				**29** SA	0531 / 1147 / 1754	0.4 / 4.8 / 0.2		
15 SA	0034 / 0629 / 1245 / 1848	4.5 / 0.7 / 4.5 / 0.6				**30** SU	0012 / 0610 / 1227 / 1832	4.7 / 0.3 / 4.8 / 0.2		
						31 M	0052 / 0650 / 1309 / 1912	4.7 / 0.4 / 4.7 / 0.4		

FEBRUARY

Day	Time	m		Day	Time	m
1 TU	0135 / 0733 / 1355 / 1954	4.6 / 0.5 / 4.6 / 0.6		**16** W	0147 / 0731 / 1402 / 1943	4.3 / 1.1 / 4.2 / 1.2
2 W	0222 / 0819 / 1445 / 2042	4.5 / 0.8 / 4.3 / 0.9		**17** TH	0223 / 0802 / 1441 / 2016	4.2 / 1.4 / 4.1 / 1.5
3 TH	0314 / 0913 / 1543 / 2139	4.3 / 1.1 / 4.1 / 1.3		**18** F	0304 / 0841 / 1526 / 2059	4.0 / 1.6 / 3.9 / 1.8
4 F	0416 / 1020 / 1654 / 2251	4.1 / 1.4 / 3.9 / 1.6		**19** SA	0352 / 0934 / 1626 / 2201	3.9 / 1.9 / 3.7 / 2.1
5 SA	0531 / 1142 / 1820	4.0 / 1.5 / 3.8		**20** SU	0458 / 1054 / 1747 / 2337	3.7 / 2.1 / 3.6 / 2.2
6 SU	0016 / 0656 / 1305 / 1947	1.7 / 3.9 / 1.5 / 3.8		**21** M	0621 / 1235 / 1917	3.7 / 2.0 / 3.7
7 M	0135 / 0813 / 1416 / 2055	1.6 / 4.1 / 1.3 / 4.0		**22** TU	0110 / 0741 / 1350 / 2026	2.0 / 3.8 / 1.6 / 3.9
8 TU	0239 / 0914 / 1512 / 2147	1.3 / 4.2 / 1.0 / 4.2		**23** W	0215 / 0841 / 1445 / 2117	1.6 / 4.0 / 1.2 / 4.1
9 W	0332 / 1002 / 1559 / 2230	1.0 / 4.4 / 0.7 / 4.4		**24** TH	0306 / 0928 / 1532 / 2158	1.2 / 4.3 / 0.8 / 4.4
10 TH ●	0416 / 1042 / 1641 / 2306	0.8 / 4.5 / 0.5 / 4.4		**25** F	0350 / 1009 / 1615 / 2236	0.8 / 4.6 / 0.4 / 4.6
11 F	0456 / 1116 / 1718 / 2338	0.6 / 4.5 / 0.4 / 4.5		**26** SA O	0432 / 1048 / 1655 / 2313	0.4 / 4.8 / 0.1 / 4.8
12 SA	0533 / 1148 / 1752	0.5 / 4.5 / 0.4		**27** SU	0513 / 1128 / 1735 / 2352	0.1 / 4.9 / 0.0 / 4.9
13 SU	0009 / 0605 / 1220 / 1823	4.5 / 0.6 / 4.5 / 0.5		**28** M	0553 / 1208 / 1814	0.0 / 4.9 / 0.0
14 M	0040 / 0635 / 1252 / 1850	4.5 / 0.7 / 4.5 / 0.7				
15 TU	0113 / 0703 / 1326 / 1916	4.4 / 0.9 / 4.4 / 1.0				

MARCH

Day	Time	m		Day	Time	m
1 TU	0032 / 0632 / 1251 / 1854	4.9 / 0.1 / 4.9 / 0.2		**16** W	0041 / 0633 / 1258 / 1845	4.5 / 0.7 / 4.4 / 0.9
2 W	0114 / 0714 / 1336 / 1935	4.8 / 0.2 / 4.7 / 0.5		**17** TH	0115 / 0658 / 1334 / 1912	4.4 / 0.9 / 4.3 / 1.2
3 TH	0159 / 0758 / 1426 / 2021	4.5 / 0.6 / 4.4 / 0.9		**18** F	0150 / 0728 / 1411 / 1943	4.2 / 1.2 / 4.2 / 1.4
4 F	0250 / 0849 / 1524 / 2117	4.3 / 1.0 / 4.1 / 1.4		**19** SA	0227 / 0804 / 1454 / 2025	4.1 / 1.5 / 4.0 / 1.7
5 SA	0350 / 0954 / 1636 / 2232	4.0 / 1.3 / 3.8 / 1.7		**20** SU	0312 / 0851 / 1549 / 2121	3.9 / 1.7 / 3.8 / 2.0
6 SU	0508 / 1119 / 1810	3.8 / 1.6 / 3.7		**21** M	0411 / 0959 / 1702 / 2247	3.7 / 1.9 / 3.7 / 2.1
7 M	0005 / 0643 / 1248 / 1939	1.8 / 3.7 / 1.6 / 3.8		**22** TU	0530 / 1137 / 1829	3.6 / 1.9 / 3.7
8 TU	0128 / 0805 / 1400 / 2045	1.7 / 3.9 / 1.4 / 4.0		**23** W	0028 / 0655 / 1305 / 1946	2.0 / 3.7 / 1.6 / 3.9
9 W	0230 / 0903 / 1455 / 2133	1.4 / 4.1 / 1.1 / 4.2		**24** TH	0141 / 0805 / 1408 / 2043	1.6 / 3.9 / 1.2 / 4.2
10 TH	0317 / 0948 / 1538 / 2212	1.1 / 4.3 / 0.8 / 4.4		**25** F	0236 / 0858 / 1500 / 2129	1.1 / 4.2 / 0.7 / 4.5
11 F	0357 / 1025 / 1617 / 2244	0.8 / 4.4 / 0.6 / 4.5		**26** SA	0325 / 0943 / 1547 / 2210	0.7 / 4.5 / 0.3 / 4.7
12 SA ●	0433 / 1056 / 1652 / 2313	0.6 / 4.5 / 0.4 / 4.5		**27** SU O	0409 / 1026 / 1631 / 2250	0.3 / 4.8 / 0.0 / 4.9
13 SU	0508 / 1124 / 1725 / 2340	0.5 / 4.5 / 0.5 / 4.5		**28** M	0452 / 1107 / 1713 / 2331	0.0 / 4.9 / -0.1 / 5.0
14 M	0539 / 1153 / 1755	0.5 / 4.5 / 0.6		**29** TU	0533 / 1150 / 1755	-0.2 / 4.9 / -0.1
15 TU	0009 / 0607 / 1225 / 1821	4.5 / 0.6 / 4.5 / 0.7		**30** W	0012 / 0614 / 1235 / 1835	4.9 / -0.1 / 4.9 / 0.1
				31 TH	0055 / 0656 / 1321 / 1918	4.8 / 0.1 / 4.7 / 0.5

APRIL

Day	Time	m		Day	Time	m
1 F	0141 / 0740 / 1412 / 2005	4.5 / 0.4 / 4.4 / 0.9		**16** SA	0124 / 0704 / 1350 / 1923	4.2 / 1.1 / 4.2 / 1.4
2 SA	0231 / 0830 / 1511 / 2101	4.2 / 0.9 / 4.1 / 1.4		**17** SU	0203 / 0741 / 1434 / 2005	4.1 / 1.3 / 4.1 / 1.6
3 SU	0330 / 0931 / 1623 / 2215	3.9 / 1.3 / 3.9 / 1.7		**18** M	0248 / 0828 / 1527 / 2101	3.9 / 1.5 / 3.9 / 1.8
4 M	0447 / 1051 / 1752 / 2345	3.7 / 1.5 / 3.8 / 1.9		**19** TU	0343 / 0930 / 1632 / 2217	3.8 / 1.7 / 3.8 / 1.9
5 TU	0621 / 1217 / 1916	3.6 / 1.6 / 3.9		**20** W	0454 / 1052 / 1748 / 2345	3.7 / 1.7 / 3.9 / 1.8
6 W	0106 / 0741 / 1329 / 2018	1.8 / 3.8 / 1.5 / 4.1		**21** TH	0612 / 1216 / 1902	3.7 / 1.5 / 4.0
7 TH	0207 / 0839 / 1424 / 2105	1.5 / 4.0 / 1.3 / 4.2		**22** F	0100 / 0723 / 1326 / 2004	1.5 / 3.9 / 1.1 / 4.2
8 F	0251 / 0924 / 1507 / 2143	1.2 / 4.1 / 1.0 / 4.4		**23** SA	0201 / 0823 / 1424 / 2056	1.1 / 4.2 / 0.7 / 4.5
9 SA	0330 / 1000 / 1545 / 2215	0.9 / 4.3 / 0.8 / 4.4		**24** SU	0255 / 0914 / 1516 / 2143	0.7 / 4.4 / 0.4 / 4.7
10 SU	0405 / 1030 / 1621 / 2243	0.7 / 4.3 / 0.7 / 4.5		**25** M O	0344 / 1002 / 1605 / 2227	0.3 / 4.6 / 0.1 / 4.9
11 M ●	0439 / 1059 / 1655 / 2311	0.5 / 4.4 / 0.6 / 4.5		**26** TU	0430 / 1048 / 1651 / 2311	0.0 / 4.8 / 0.0 / 4.9
12 TU	0512 / 1128 / 1727 / 2341	0.5 / 4.4 / 0.7 / 4.5		**27** W	0515 / 1133 / 1736 / 2355	-0.1 / 4.8 / 0.0 / 4.9
13 W	0541 / 1200 / 1755	0.6 / 4.4 / 0.8		**28** TH	0558 / 1220 / 1820	-0.1 / 4.8 / 0.2
14 TH	0014 / 0607 / 1235 / 1821	4.4 / 0.7 / 4.4 / 1.0		**29** F	0039 / 0641 / 1309 / 1904	4.7 / 0.1 / 4.6 / 0.5
15 F	0048 / 0634 / 1311 / 1849	4.3 / 0.9 / 4.3 / 1.2		**30** SA	0127 / 0726 / 1401 / 1952	4.5 / 0.4 / 4.4 / 0.9

SOUTHAMPTON

50°54′N 1°24′W

Times and heights (in metres) of high and low water 1994
Time: GMT. For BST, ADD ONE HOUR in the shaded area
High Water, full and change, 1103 (first) and 1303 (second)

MAY

Day	Time	m	Day	Time	m
1 SU	0217	4.2	**16** M	0146	4.1
	0814	0.8		0729	1.2
	1459	4.2		1418	4.1
	2046	1.3		1955	1.4
2 M	0314	3.9	**17** TU	0232	4.0
	0911	1.2		0816	1.3
	1605	4.0		1509	4.0
	2152	1.7		2049	1.6
3 TU	0423	3.7	**18** W	0325	3.9
	1018	1.4		0913	1.4
	1721	3.9		1608	4.0
	2309	1.8		2154	1.6
4 W	0544	3.6	**19** TH	0426	3.8
	1133	1.6		1022	1.4
	1835	3.9		1714	4.0
				2307	1.6
5 TH	0024	1.8	**20** F	0535	3.9
	0700	3.7		1135	1.3
	1243	1.6		1823	4.1
	1937	4.0			
6 F	0126	1.6	**21** SA	0019	1.4
	0801	3.8		0645	3.9
	1341	1.4		1245	1.1
	2027	4.2		1927	4.3
7 SA	0215	1.3	**22** SU	0126	1.1
	0849	4.0		0749	4.1
	1428	1.2		1349	0.8
	2108	4.3		2025	4.4
8 SU	0256	1.1	**23** M	0225	0.8
	0928	4.1		0847	4.3
	1510	1.1		1447	0.5
	2142	4.3		2118	4.6
9 M	0334	0.9	**24** TU	0320	0.5
	1002	4.2		0940	4.5
	1549	0.9		1541	0.3
	2214	4.4		2207	4.7
10 TU ●	0410	0.7	**25** W O	0411	0.2
	1033	4.3		1031	4.6
	1625	0.8		1632	0.2
	2245	4.4		2254	4.7
11 W	0445	0.7	**26** TH	0459	0.1
	1105	4.3		1120	4.6
	1700	0.8		1720	0.2
	2317	4.4		2341	4.7
12 TH	0517	0.7	**27** F	0545	0.1
	1138	4.3		1208	4.6
	1732	0.9		1807	0.4
	2351	4.3			
13 F	0548	0.8	**28** SA	0027	4.6
	1214	4.3		0630	0.2
	1803	1.0		1258	4.5
				1852	0.6
14 SA	0027	4.3	**29** SU	0114	4.4
	0617	0.9		0714	0.4
	1252	4.3		1348	4.4
	1834	1.2		1938	0.9
15 SU	0106	4.2	**30** M	0202	4.2
	0650	1.0		0759	0.7
	1333	4.2		1441	4.2
	1911	1.3		2027	1.2
			31 TU	0254	4.0
				0847	1.1
				1538	4.1
				2120	1.5

JUNE

Day	Time	m	Day	Time	m
1 W	0352	3.8	**16** TH	0306	4.1
	0941	1.4		0857	1.2
	1639	4.0		1543	4.1
	2221	1.7		2131	1.4
2 TH	0457	3.7	**17** F	0402	4.0
	1042	1.6		0956	1.3
	1744	3.9		1644	4.1
	2328	1.8		2235	1.4
3 F	0607	3.7	**18** SA	0506	4.0
	1148	1.7		1103	1.3
	1846	4.0		1750	4.1
				2345	1.4
4 SA	0033	1.7	**19** SU	0614	4.0
	0711	3.7		1213	1.2
	1251	1.6		1857	4.2
	1940	4.0			
5 SU	0130	1.6	**20** M	0055	1.2
	0806	3.8		0722	4.0
	1346	1.5		1322	1.0
	2028	4.1		2000	4.3
6 M	0218	1.4	**21** TU	0201	1.0
	0853	4.0		0826	4.1
	1434	1.4		1426	0.8
	2109	4.2		2058	4.4
7 TU	0301	1.2	**22** W	0302	0.7
	0933	4.1		0925	4.3
	1518	1.2		1524	0.6
	2146	4.3		2152	4.5
8 W	0342	1.0	**23** TH O	0357	0.5
	1009	4.2		1019	4.4
	1558	1.1		1618	0.5
	2222	4.3		2242	4.6
9 TH ●	0421	0.9	**24** F	0447	0.4
	1044	4.2		1109	4.5
	1637	1.0		1708	0.4
	2257	4.3		2329	4.5
10 F	0457	0.8	**25** SA	0534	0.3
	1119	4.2		1157	4.5
	1713	1.0		1755	0.5
	2332	4.3			
11 SA	0532	0.8	**26** SU	0014	4.5
	1155	4.2		0618	0.4
	1748	1.0		1243	4.4
				1838	0.6
12 SU	0010	4.3	**27** M	0058	4.4
	0606	0.9		0659	0.5
	1234	4.2		1328	4.4
	1823	1.0		1920	0.8
13 M	0049	4.2	**28** TU	0142	4.2
	0641	1.0		0739	0.7
	1315	4.2		1414	4.3
	1902	1.1		2001	1.1
14 TU	0131	4.2	**29** W	0227	4.1
	0720	1.0		0819	1.0
	1359	4.2		1501	4.1
	1945	1.2		2044	1.4
15 W	0216	4.1	**30** TH	0314	3.9
	0805	1.1		0901	1.3
	1448	4.2		1551	4.0
	2034	1.3		2131	1.6

JULY

Day	Time	m	Day	Time	m
1 F	0407	3.8	**16** SA	0339	4.1
	0950	1.6		0933	1.2
	1646	3.9		1615	4.1
	2226	1.8		2208	1.3
2 SA	0507	3.7	**17** SU	0442	4.0
	1049	1.8		1038	1.3
	1746	3.9		1722	4.1
	2332	1.9		2318	1.4
3 SU	0613	3.7	**18** M	0552	3.9
	1157	1.9		1151	1.4
	1847	3.9		1833	4.1
4 M	0039	1.8	**19** TU	0034	1.4
	0718	3.8		0706	4.0
	1304	1.8		1307	1.3
	1945	3.9		1944	4.1
5 TU	0139	1.7	**20** W	0147	1.2
	0816	3.9		0817	4.0
	1402	1.7		1415	1.1
	2037	4.0		2048	4.2
6 W	0231	1.5	**21** TH	0250	1.0
	0905	4.0		0919	4.2
	1451	1.5		1515	0.9
	2122	4.1		2144	4.3
7 TH	0317	1.2	**22** F O	0346	0.7
	0947	4.1		1012	4.3
	1535	1.3		1608	0.7
	2201	4.2		2233	4.4
8 F ●	0359	1.0	**23** SA	0435	0.6
	1025	4.2		1059	4.4
	1617	1.1		1656	0.6
	2238	4.3		2317	4.5
9 SA	0439	0.9	**24** SU	0520	0.4
	1100	4.2		1142	4.4
	1656	0.9		1740	0.5
	2314	4.3		2358	4.4
10 SU	0516	0.8	**25** M	0601	0.4
	1136	4.3		1222	4.4
	1733	0.8		1820	0.6
	2351	4.3			
11 M	0553	0.8	**26** TU	0036	4.4
	1213	4.3		0638	0.6
	1811	0.8		1301	4.4
				1856	0.7
12 TU	0030	4.4	**27** W	0114	4.3
	0630	0.8		0713	0.8
	1254	4.3		1339	4.3
	1849	0.8		1930	1.0
13 W	0111	4.3	**28** TH	0153	4.2
	0708	0.8		0746	1.0
	1336	4.3		1419	4.2
	1930	0.9		2004	1.2
14 TH	0156	4.3	**29** F	0233	4.0
	0750	0.9		0819	1.3
	1423	4.3		1501	4.1
	2015	1.0		2041	1.5
15 F	0244	4.2	**30** SA	0319	3.9
	0838	1.1		0858	1.6
	1516	4.1		1549	3.9
	2107	1.2		2126	1.8
			31 SU	0411	3.8
				0948	1.9
				1644	3.8
				2224	2.0

AUGUST

Day	Time	m	Day	Time	m
1 M	0515	3.7	**16** TU	0540	3.9
	1056	2.1		1140	1.6
	1750	3.7		1820	3.9
	2341	2.0			
2 TU	0628	3.7	**17** W	0023	1.5
	1219	2.1		0703	3.9
	1900	3.8		1301	1.5
				1938	4.0
3 W	0059	1.9	**18** TH	0138	1.4
	0739	3.8		0816	4.0
	1331	1.9		1409	1.3
	2004	3.9		2044	4.1
4 TH	0201	1.7	**19** F	0241	1.1
	0838	3.9		0915	4.2
	1427	1.7		1507	1.1
	2056	4.0		2137	4.3
5 F	0252	1.4	**20** SA	0333	0.9
	0925	4.1		1004	4.3
	1514	1.4		1555	0.8
	2139	4.2		2222	4.4
6 SA	0337	1.1	**21** SU O	0419	0.7
	1003	4.3		1045	4.4
	1556	1.1		1639	0.6
	2217	4.3		2300	4.4
7 SU ●	0418	0.8	**22** M	0500	0.5
	1039	4.3		1121	4.5
	1636	0.8		1718	0.5
	2253	4.4		2335	4.4
8 M	0457	0.6	**23** TU	0537	0.5
	1114	4.4		1155	4.5
	1714	0.6		1755	0.6
	2329	4.5			
9 TU	0535	0.5	**24** W	0008	4.4
	1151	4.5		0611	0.6
	1753	0.5		1228	4.4
				1827	0.7
10 W	0008	4.5	**25** TH	0042	4.3
	0612	0.5		0642	0.8
	1230	4.5		1302	4.4
	1831	0.5		1857	0.9
11 TH	0049	4.5	**26** F	0117	4.3
	0650	0.6		0710	1.0
	1312	4.5		1338	4.3
	1911	0.6		1925	1.1
12 F	0133	4.5	**27** SA	0154	4.2
	0732	0.7		0738	1.3
	1358	4.4		1416	4.1
	1955	0.8		1956	1.4
13 SA	0222	4.3	**28** SU	0235	4.0
	0817	1.0		0811	1.6
	1449	4.3		1458	4.0
	2045	1.1		2033	1.7
14 SU	0317	4.1	**29** M	0323	3.9
	0911	1.2		0854	1.9
	1549	4.1		1549	3.8
	2145	1.3		2123	2.0
15 M	0423	4.0	**30** TU	0422	3.7
	1019	1.5		0954	2.1
	1700	4.0		1653	3.7
	2300	1.5		2237	2.1
			31 W	0537	3.7
				1126	2.2
				1810	3.7

SOUTHAMPTON
50°54'N 1°24'W

Times and heights (in metres) of high and low water 1994
Time: GMT. For BST, ADD ONE HOUR in the shaded area
High Water, full and change, 1103 (first) and 1303 (second)

SEPTEMBER

Day	Time	m	Time	m	Time	m	Time	m
1 TH	0012	2.1	0658	3.7	1256	2.1	1926	3.8
16 F	0126	1.4	0810	4.1	1359	1.4	2034	4.1
2 F	0127	1.8	0806	3.9	1358	1.8	2025	3.9
17 SA	0225	1.2	0904	4.3	1452	1.1	2124	4.3
3 SA	0222	1.5	0856	4.1	1447	1.4	2111	4.2
18 SU	0313	1.0	0947	4.4	1536	0.9	2204	4.4
4 SU	0309	1.1	0937	4.3	1531	1.0	2150	4.4
19 M ○	0355	0.7	1023	4.5	1615	0.7	2238	4.4
5 M ●	0351	0.7	1014	4.5	1612	0.6	2227	4.5
20 TU	0433	0.6	1055	4.5	1652	0.6	2308	4.4
6 TU	0432	0.4	1050	4.6	1651	0.4	2305	4.7
21 W	0508	0.6	1125	4.5	1726	0.6	2338	4.4
7 W	0511	0.3	1127	4.7	1731	0.3	2344	4.7
22 TH	0541	0.6	1155	4.5	1757	0.7		
8 TH	0551	0.2	1207	4.7	1810	0.3		
23 F	0010	4.4	0610	0.8	1228	4.4	1825	0.9
9 F	0026	4.7	0630	0.4	1249	4.7	1851	0.4
24 SA	0044	4.3	0636	1.0	1303	4.3	1851	1.1
10 SA	0111	4.6	0712	0.6	1335	4.5	1935	0.6
25 SU	0120	4.2	0702	1.3	1339	4.2	1919	1.3
11 SU	0201	4.4	0758	0.9	1426	4.3	2025	1.0
26 M	0159	4.1	0734	1.5	1420	4.0	1954	1.6
12 M	0258	4.2	0853	1.3	1527	4.1	2127	1.3
27 TU	0244	3.9	0815	1.8	1506	3.9	2040	1.9
13 TU	0408	3.9	1004	1.6	1642	3.9	2246	1.6
28 W	0339	3.8	0910	2.1	1606	3.7	2146	2.1
14 W	0534	3.8	1130	1.7	1811	3.8		
29 TH	0450	3.7	1032	2.2	1720	3.7	2317	2.1
15 TH	0012	1.6	0701	3.9	1253	1.7	1931	3.9
30 F	0612	3.7	1207	2.1	1839	3.7		

OCTOBER

Day	Time	m	Time	m	Time	m	Time	m
1 SA	0041	1.8	0724	3.9	1317	1.8	1944	3.9
16 SU	0159	1.3	0840	4.3	1427	1.2	2101	4.2
2 SU	0143	1.5	0820	4.2	1412	1.4	2035	4.2
17 M	0245	1.1	0922	4.4	1509	1.0	2139	4.3
3 M	0234	1.0	0905	4.4	1459	0.9	2119	4.4
18 TU	0325	0.9	0957	4.5	1547	0.8	2212	4.4
4 TU	0320	0.6	0946	4.6	1544	0.6	2200	4.6
19 W ○	0402	0.8	1027	4.5	1623	0.7	2242	4.4
5 W ●	0404	0.3	1025	4.8	1627	0.3	2241	4.8
20 TH	0438	0.7	1056	4.5	1657	0.6	2311	4.4
6 TH	0447	0.1	1105	4.9	1709	0.1	2323	4.8
21 F	0511	0.7	1127	4.5	1729	0.7	2342	4.4
7 F	0528	0.1	1146	4.9	1751	0.1		
22 SA	0541	0.8	1159	4.5	1758	0.9		
8 SA	0007	4.8	0610	0.2	1230	4.8	1833	0.3
23 SU	0016	4.3	0609	1.0	1235	4.4	1824	1.1
9 SU	0054	4.6	0654	0.5	1317	4.6	1919	0.5
24 M	0053	4.3	0637	1.2	1312	4.3	1853	1.3
10 M	0145	4.4	0742	0.9	1408	4.3	2010	0.9
25 TU	0133	4.2	0709	1.4	1351	4.1	1929	1.5
11 TU	0243	4.2	0838	1.3	1509	4.1	2111	1.3
26 W	0216	4.0	0750	1.7	1436	4.0	2013	1.7
12 W	0355	4.0	0948	1.6	1625	3.9	2227	1.5
27 TH	0307	3.9	0843	1.9	1530	3.8	2112	1.8
13 TH	0520	3.9	1111	1.8	1753	3.8	2348	1.6
28 F	0410	3.8	0953	2.0	1636	3.8	2229	1.9
14 F	0643	4.0	1231	1.7	1912	3.9		
29 SA	0524	3.9	1115	1.9	1749	3.8	2349	1.7
15 SA	0101	1.5	0749	4.1	1336	1.5	2013	4.1
30 SU	0637	4.0	1230	1.7	1859	3.9		
31 M	0057	1.4	0738	4.2	1332	1.3	1957	4.2

NOVEMBER

Day	Time	m	Time	m	Time	m	Time	m
1 TU	0155	1.0	0831	4.4	1426	0.9	2048	4.4
16 W	0252	1.2	0927	4.4	1517	1.0	2147	4.3
2 W	0248	0.6	0917	4.7	1516	0.6	2135	4.6
17 TH	0331	1.0	1000	4.5	1555	0.8	2219	4.3
3 TH ●	0336	0.3	1002	4.9	1603	0.3	2220	4.7
18 F ○	0409	0.9	1031	4.5	1631	0.8	2249	4.3
4 F	0423	0.1	1045	4.9	1649	0.1	2306	4.8
19 SA	0444	0.9	1103	4.5	1705	0.8	2322	4.3
5 SA	0509	0.1	1129	4.9	1734	0.1	2352	4.8
20 SU	0518	0.9	1137	4.5	1737	0.9	2356	4.3
6 SU	0554	0.2	1214	4.8	1819	0.2		
21 M	0549	1.0	1212	4.4	1807	1.0		
7 M	0040	4.7	0640	0.4	1302	4.7	1905	0.4
22 TU	0033	4.3	0620	1.1	1250	4.3	1837	1.2
8 TU	0133	4.5	0728	0.8	1353	4.4	1955	0.8
23 W	0112	4.2	0654	1.3	1329	4.2	1912	1.3
9 W	0229	4.3	0822	1.2	1451	4.1	2051	1.1
24 TH	0154	4.1	0734	1.4	1412	4.1	1955	1.5
10 TH	0335	4.1	0925	1.5	1559	3.9	2157	1.4
25 F	0241	4.1	0823	1.6	1500	4.0	2047	1.6
11 F	0450	4.0	1037	1.7	1718	3.8	2309	1.6
26 SA	0336	4.0	0922	1.7	1557	3.9	2150	1.6
12 SA	0607	4.0	1152	1.7	1836	3.8		
27 SU	0440	4.0	1031	1.7	1703	3.9	2301	1.5
13 SU	0019	1.6	0712	4.1	1259	1.6	1939	4.0
28 M	0549	4.1	1144	1.6	1814	4.0		
14 M	0120	1.5	0806	4.2	1352	1.4	2030	4.1
29 TU	0012	1.4	0656	4.2	1253	1.3	1920	4.1
15 TU	0209	1.3	0850	4.3	1437	1.2	2112	4.2
30 W	0118	1.1	0757	4.4	1355	1.0	2020	4.3

DECEMBER

Day	Time	m	Time	m	Time	m	Time	m
1 TH	0217	0.8	0851	4.6	1452	0.7	2114	4.5
16 F	0303	1.3	0935	4.4	1530	1.0	2200	4.2
2 F ●	0313	0.5	0941	4.8	1544	0.4	2205	4.6
17 SA	0344	1.1	1010	4.4	1609	0.9	2234	4.3
3 SA	0404	0.3	1029	4.9	1634	0.2	2254	4.7
18 SU ○	0423	1.0	1044	4.5	1647	0.8	2306	4.3
4 SU	0454	0.2	1116	4.9	1722	0.1	2342	4.7
19 M	0500	1.0	1118	4.5	1722	0.8	2340	4.3
5 M	0542	0.3	1202	4.8	1808	0.1		
20 TU	0534	0.9	1154	4.5	1754	0.9		
6 TU	0030	4.7	0628	0.4	1249	4.7	1853	0.3
21 W	0015	4.3	0607	1.0	1231	4.4	1826	1.0
7 W	0120	4.5	0715	0.7	1337	4.5	1939	0.6
22 TH	0053	4.3	0642	1.1	1309	4.4	1900	1.0
8 TH	0211	4.4	0803	1.0	1428	4.2	2027	0.9
23 F	0133	4.3	0720	1.1	1349	4.3	1938	1.1
9 F	0306	4.2	0855	1.3	1524	4.0	2119	1.3
24 SA	0216	4.3	0803	1.3	1434	4.2	2023	1.3
10 SA	0407	4.0	0953	1.6	1629	3.8	2218	1.5
25 SU	0305	4.2	0854	1.4	1525	4.1	2117	1.3
11 SU	0513	4.0	1059	1.7	1741	3.7	2324	1.7
26 M	0401	4.2	0954	1.5	1625	4.0	2220	1.4
12 M	0620	4.0	1208	1.7	1852	3.8		
27 TU	0507	4.1	1104	1.5	1734	3.9	2332	1.4
13 TU	0030	1.7	0720	4.0	1310	1.6	1952	3.9
28 W	0617	4.2	1219	1.4	1848	4.0		
14 W	0129	1.7	0812	4.2	1403	1.4	2042	4.0
29 TH	0045	1.3	0726	4.3	1331	1.2	1958	4.1
15 TH	0219	1.5	0856	4.3	1449	1.2	2124	4.1
30 F	0154	1.0	0830	4.5	1435	0.9	2100	4.3
31 SA	0256	0.8	0926	4.6	1532	0.5	2156	4.5

LYMINGTON

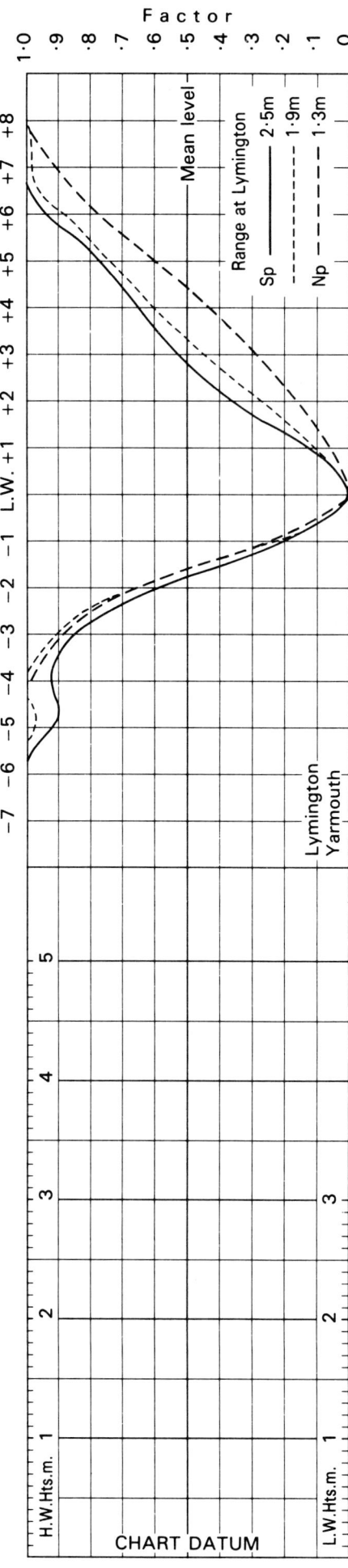

LYMINGTON
50°46′N 1°32′W

Sea Level is above Mean Tide Level from 4.0 hours after L.W. to 2.0 hours before the next L.W. and H.W. will occur between 6.5 hours after L.W. and 4.0 hours before the next L.W.

Times of low water and heights (in metres) of high and low water 1994
Time: GMT. For BST, ADD ONE HOUR in the shaded area

JANUARY

Day	Time	m	Time	m		Day	Time	m	Time	m
1 SA	0612	3.0 / 0.8	1836	3.0 / 0.7		**16** SU	0653	3.0 / 0.9	1911	2.9 / 0.8
2 SU	0655	3.0 / 0.8	1918	3.0 / 0.8		**17** M	0726	3.0 / 1.0	1943	2.9 / 1.0
3 M	0740	3.0 / 0.9	2004	2.9 / 0.8		**18** TU	0800	2.9 / 1.1	2016	2.8 / 1.1
4 TU	0830	2.9 / 1.0	2055	2.8 / 1.0		**19** W	0838	2.8 / 1.3	2056	2.7 / 1.3
5 W	0927	2.9 / 1.1	2156	2.8 / 1.1		**20** TH	0925	2.8 / 1.5	2150	2.6 / 1.5
6 TH	1036	2.8 / 1.2	2308	2.7 / 1.2		**21** F	1034	2.7 / 1.6	2309	2.6 / 1.6
7 F	1156	2.8 / 1.2 / 2.7				**22** SA	1209	2.7 / 1.5 / 2.6		
8 SA	0026	1.2 / 2.8	1312	1.1 / 2.8		**23** SU	0035	1.5 / 2.7	1320	1.4 / 2.6
9 SU	0136	1.1 / 2.9	1416	1.0 / 2.9		**24** M	0139	1.4 / 2.8	1413	1.2 / 2.7
10 M	0236	1.0 / 3.0	1511	0.8 / 3.0		**25** TU	0229	1.2 / 2.8	1458	1.0 / 2.9
11 TU ●	0328	0.9 / 3.0	1559	0.8 / 3.0		**26** W	0313	1.1 / 2.9	1540	0.8 / 2.9
12 W	0415	0.8 / 3.0	1644	0.6 / 3.0		**27** TH ○	0355	0.9 / 3.0	1621	0.7 / 3.0
13 TH	0459	0.8 / 3.0	1725	0.6 / 3.0		**28** F	0436	0.8 / 3.0	1701	0.6
14 F	0539	3.0 / 0.8	1803	3.0 / 0.6		**29** SA	0517	3.0 / 0.7	1740	3.0 / 0.5
15 SA	0617	3.0 / 0.8	1838	3.0 / 0.7		**30** SU	0558	3.0 / 0.6	1821	3.0 / 0.5
						31 M	0640	3.0 / 0.6	1902	3.0 / 0.6

FEBRUARY

Day	Time	m	Time	m		Day	Time	m	Time	m
1 TU	0723	3.0 / 0.7	1945	3.0 / 0.7		**16** W	0721	2.9 / 1.0	1936	2.8 / 1.0
2 W	0809	3.0 / 0.8	2033	2.9 / 0.8		**17** TH	0752	2.9 / 1.1	2009	2.7 / 1.2
3 TH	0901	2.9 / 1.0	2131	2.8 / 1.1		**18** F	0831	2.8 / 1.3	2053	2.6 / 1.4
4 F	1007	2.8 / 1.1	2245	2.7 / 1.3		**19** SA	0923	2.7 / 1.5	2159	2.6 / 1.6
5 SA	1131	2.7 / 1.3 / 2.6				**20** SU	1049	2.6 / 1.6	2348	2.6 / 1.7
6 SU	0011	1.3 / 2.7	1257	1.2 / 2.7		**21** M	1241	2.6 / 1.5 / 2.6		
7 M	0129	1.3 / 2.8	1407	1.1 / 2.8		**22** TU	0112	1.5 / 2.7	1345	1.3 / 2.7
8 TU	0231	1.1 / 2.9	1501	0.9 / 2.9		**23** W	0208	1.3 / 2.8	1434	1.0 / 2.8
9 W	0321	1.0 / 3.0	1547	0.8 / 3.0		**24** TH	0254	1.0 / 2.9	1517	0.8 / 3.0
10 TH ●	0405	0.8 / 3.0	1628	0.6 / 3.0		**25** F	0336	0.8 / 3.0	1559	0.6 / 3.0
11 F	0444	0.8 / 3.0	1705	0.6		**26** SA ○	0418	0.6 / 3.0	1640	0.4 / 3.1
12 SA	0520	3.0 / 0.7	1739	3.0 / 0.6		**27** SU	0459	0.5 / 3.1	1721	0.4
13 SU	0553	3.0 / 0.7	1811	3.0 / 0.6		**28** M	0540	3.1 / 0.4	1802	3.1 / 0.4
14 M	0624	3.0 / 0.8	1840	2.9 / 0.8						
15 TU	0653	3.0 / 0.9	1908	2.9 / 0.9						

MARCH

Day	Time	m	Time	m		Day	Time	m	Time	m
1 TU	0622	3.1 / 0.4	1844	3.1 / 0.4		**16** W	0622	3.0 / 0.8	1836	2.9 / 0.9
2 W	0705	3.1 / 0.6	1928	3.0 / 0.6		**17** TH	0648	2.9 / 0.9	1904	2.9 / 1.0
3 TH	0750	3.0 / 0.7	2016	2.9 / 0.8		**18** F	0718	2.9 / 1.0	1937	2.8 / 1.1
4 F	0840	2.9 / 0.9	2113	2.8 / 1.1		**19** SA	0754	2.8 / 1.1	2018	2.7 / 1.3
5 SA	0944	2.7 / 1.1	2229	2.7 / 1.3		**20** SU	0841	2.7 / 1.3	2117	2.6 / 1.5
6 SU	1109	2.6 / 1.3	2358	2.6 / 1.3		**21** M	0951	2.6 / 1.5	2254	2.6 / 1.6
7 M	1239	2.6 / 1.3 / 2.7				**22** TU	1143	2.6 / 1.5 / 2.6		
8 TU	0120	1.3 / 2.7	1352	1.1 / 2.8		**23** W	0036	1.5 / 2.6	1306	1.3 / 2.7
9 W	0222	1.1 / 2.8	1445	1.0 / 2.9		**24** TH	0139	1.2 / 2.7	1401	1.0 / 2.9
10 TH	0309	1.0 / 2.9	1528	0.8 / 3.0		**25** F	0228	1.0 / 2.9	1448	0.8 / 3.0
11 F	0348	0.8 / 2.9	1605	0.7 / 3.0		**26** SA	0312	0.8 / 3.0	1532	0.6 / 3.0
12 SA ●	0423	0.7 / 3.0	1640	0.6 / 3.0		**27** SU ○	0355	0.6 / 3.0	1615	0.4 / 3.1
13 SU	0456	0.6 / 3.0	1712	0.6		**28** M	0437	0.4 / 3.1	1658	0.4
14 M	0527	3.0 / 0.6	1742	3.0 / 0.7		**29** TU	0520	3.1 / 0.4	1742	3.1 / 0.4
15 TU	0555	3.0 / 0.7	1810	2.9 / 0.8		**30** W	0604	3.1 / 0.4	1827	3.1 / 0.4
						31 TH	0648	3.0 / 0.5	1913	3.0 / 0.6

APRIL

(shaded area — add one hour for BST)

Day	Time	m	Time	m		Day	Time	m	Time	m
1 F	0734	3.0 / 0.6	2002	3.0 / 0.8		**16** SA	0654	2.9 / 1.0	1915	2.8 / 1.1
2 SA	0824	2.9 / 0.8	2059	2.8 / 1.1		**17** SU	0732	2.8 / 1.0	1958	2.7 / 1.2
3 SU	0925	2.7 / 1.1	2211	2.7 / 1.3		**18** M	0818	2.7 / 1.2	2054	2.7 / 1.4
4 M	1043	2.6 / 1.2	2335	2.6 / 1.3		**19** TU	0921	2.6 / 1.3	2214	2.6 / 1.5
5 TU	1210	2.6 / 1.3 / 2.7				**20** W	1048	2.6 / 1.3	2346	2.6 / 1.4
6 W	0057	1.3 / 2.6	1324	1.1 / 2.8		**21** TH	1216	2.6 / 1.2 / 2.7		
7 TH	0159	1.1 / 2.7	1418	1.0 / 2.9		**22** F	0059	1.2 / 2.7	1321	1.0 / 2.9
8 F	0244	1.0 / 2.8	1459	0.9 / 2.9		**23** SA	0154	1.0 / 2.8	1414	0.8 / 3.0
9 SA	0321	0.8 / 2.8	1535	0.8 / 3.0		**24** SU	0243	0.7 / 3.0	1502	0.6 / 3.0
10 SU	0355	0.7 / 2.9	1609	0.7 / 3.0		**25** M ○	0330	0.6 / 3.0	1549	0.5 / 3.1
11 M ●	0428	0.7 / 2.9	1642	0.7 / 3.0		**26** TU	0415	0.4 / 3.1	1636	0.4 / 3.1
12 TU	0459	0.7 / 2.9	1713	0.8		**27** W	0502	0.4 / 3.1	1723	0.4
13 W	0528	3.0 / 0.7	1742	2.9 / 0.8		**28** TH	0547	3.1 / 0.4	1810	3.1 / 0.5
14 TH	0555	2.9 / 0.8	1810	2.9 / 0.9		**29** F	0634	3.0 / 0.5	1858	3.0 / 0.6
15 F	0623	2.9 / 0.8	1840	2.9 / 1.0		**30** SA	0721	3.0 / 0.6	1948	3.0 / 0.8

LYMINGTON

50°46′N 1°32′W

Times of low water and heights (in metres) of high and low water 1994
Time: GMT. For BST, ADD ONE HOUR in the shaded area

> Sea Level is above Mean Tide Level from 4.0 hours after L.W. to 2.0 hours before the next L.W. and H.W. will occur between 6.5 hours after L.W. and 4.0 hours before the next L.W.

MAY

Day	Heights / Time(LW)	Day	Heights / Time(LW)
1 SU	2.9 · 0810 0.8 · 2.9 · 2042 1.0	16 M	0719 2.8 1.0 · 2.8 · 1945 1.1
2 M	2.7 · 0905 1.0 · 2.8 · 2144 1.2	17 TU	0805 2.8 1.0 · 2.8 · 2038 1.2
3 TU	2.6 · 1011 1.1 · 2.7 · 2258 1.3	18 W	0901 2.7 1.1 · 2.7 · 2143 1.3
4 W	2.6 · 1128 1.3 · 2.7	19 TH	1011 2.7 1.1 · 2.7 · 2259 1.3
5 TH	0014 1.3 · 1241 2.6 1.2 · 2.7	20 F	1128 2.7 1.1 · 2.8
6 F	0119 1.2 · 1338 2.7 1.1 · 2.8	21 SA	0013 1.1 · 1240 2.7 1.0 · 2.9
7 SA	0207 1.1 · 1422 2.7 1.0 · 2.9	22 SU	0119 1.0 · 1341 2.8 0.8 · 3.0
8 SU	0247 1.0 · 1500 2.8 0.9 · 2.9	23 M	0215 0.8 · 1435 2.9 0.7 · 3.0
9 M	0323 0.8 · 1536 2.8 0.8 · 2.9	24 TU	0307 0.6 · 1526 3.0 0.6 · 3.1
10 TU ●	0357 0.8 · 1611 2.9 0.8 · 2.9	25 W ○	0357 0.5 · 1617 3.0 0.6 · 3.1
11 W	0431 0.8 · 1645 2.9 0.8 · 2.9	26 TH	0446 0.5 · 1707 3.1 0.6
12 TH	0504 0.8 · 1717 2.9 0.9	27 F	0534 3.1 · 1755 0.5 0.6
13 F	0534 2.9 · 1749 2.9 0.9	28 SA	0622 3.0 · 1843 0.5 0.7
14 SA	0605 2.9 0.8 · 1823 2.9 1.0	29 SU	0708 3.0 · 1931 0.6 0.8
15 SU	0639 2.9 0.9 · 1901 2.8 1.0	30 M	0753 2.9 · 2019 0.8 1.0
		31 TU	0840 2.8 · 2110 1.0 1.1

JUNE

Day	Heights / Time(LW)	Day	Heights / Time(LW)
1 W	0933 2.7 1.1 · 2.7 · 2209 1.3	16 TH	0843 2.8 1.0 · 2.8 · 2117 1.1
2 TH	1035 2.6 1.3 · 2.7 · 2316 1.3	17 F	0942 2.7 1.0 · 2.8 · 2223 1.1
3 F	1144 2.6 1.3 · 2.7	18 SA	1052 2.7 1.1 · 2.8 · 2336 1.1
4 SA	0024 1.3 · 1248 2.6 1.3 · 2.7	19 SU	1205 2.7 1.1 · 2.9
5 SU	0121 1.3 · 1340 2.6 1.2 · 2.8	20 M	0048 1.1 · 1315 2.6 1.0 · 2.9
6 M	0208 1.1 · 1424 2.7 1.1 · 2.8	21 TU	0153 0.9 · 1416 2.7 0.9 · 3.0
7 TU	0249 1.0 · 1504 2.8 1.0 · 2.9	22 W	0251 0.8 · 1512 2.8 0.8 · 3.0
8 W	0328 0.9 · 1543 2.8 1.0 · 2.9	23 TH ○	0344 0.6 · 1604 2.8 0.7 · 3.1
9 TH ●	0406 0.8 · 1620 2.9 0.9 · 2.9	24 F	0434 0.6 · 1654 2.9 0.6
10 F	0443 0.8 · 1657 2.9 0.9	25 SA	0522 3.0 · 1741 0.6 0.6
11 SA	0518 2.9 · 1733 0.8 0.9	26 SU	0608 3.0 · 1826 0.6 0.7
12 SU	0553 2.9 · 1810 0.8 0.9	27 M	0650 3.0 · 1909 0.6 0.8
13 M	0629 2.9 · 1849 0.8 0.9	28 TU	0730 3.0 · 1950 0.8 0.9
14 TU	0709 2.9 0.8 · 1932 2.9 1.0	29 W	0809 2.9 · 2031 0.9 1.1
15 W	0753 2.8 0.9 · 2021 2.9 1.0	30 TH	0850 2.8 1.1 · 2117 2.8 1.2

JULY

Day	Heights / Time(LW)	Day	Heights / Time(LW)
1 F	0938 2.6 1.3 · 2.7 · 2213 1.3	16 SA	0918 2.8 1.0 · 2.8 · 2154 1.1
2 SA	1039 2.6 1.4 · 2.7 · 2322 1.5	17 SU	1024 2.7 1.1 · 2.8 · 2308 1.1
3 SU	1151 2.6 1.5 · 2.7	18 M	1143 2.7 1.2 · 2.8
4 M	0031 1.4 · 1257 2.6 1.4 · 2.7	19 TU	0028 1.1 · 1301 2.7 1.1 · 2.9
5 TU	0130 1.3 · 1351 2.6 1.3 · 2.8	20 W	0140 1.0 · 1407 2.8 1.0 · 2.9
6 W	0219 1.1 · 1437 2.7 1.1 · 2.8	21 TH	0241 0.9 · 1504 2.9 0.9 · 3.0
7 TH	0303 1.0 · 1519 2.8 1.1 · 2.9	22 F ○	0334 0.7 · 1555 3.0 0.8 · 3.0
8 F ●	0344 0.9 · 1559 2.9 1.0 · 2.9	23 SA	0423 0.6 · 1641 3.0 0.7 · 3.0
9 SA	0423 0.8 · 1639 2.9 0.9 · 2.9	24 SU	0508 0.6 · 1725 3.0 0.7
10 SU	0502 0.8 · 1717 2.9 0.8	25 M	0549 3.0 · 1805 0.6 0.7
11 M	0539 2.9 · 1756 0.7 0.8	26 TU	0626 3.0 · 1842 0.6 0.8
12 TU	0617 3.0 · 1835 0.7 0.8	27 W	0701 3.0 · 1917 0.8 0.9
13 W	0655 3.0 0.7 · 1917 3.0 0.8	28 TH	0734 2.9 · 1952 0.9 1.0
14 TH	0737 2.9 0.8 · 2002 3.0 0.9	29 F	0807 2.8 1.0 · 2028 2.9 1.1
15 F	0824 2.9 0.8 · 2054 2.9 1.0	30 SA	0845 2.7 1.2 · 2112 2.8 1.3
		31 SU	0933 2.6 · 2212 2.7 1.4 1.5

AUGUST

Day	Heights / Time(LW)	Day	Heights / Time(LW)
1 M	1046 2.6 1.5 · 2.6 · 2338 1.5	16 TU	1132 2.7 1.3 · 2.7
2 TU	1216 2.6 1.6 · 2.6	17 W	0016 1.2 · 1256 2.7 1.3 · 2.8
3 W	0054 1.4 · 1323 2.6 1.5 · 2.7	18 TH	0132 1.1 · 1404 2.8 1.1 · 2.9
4 TH	0152 1.3 · 1414 2.7 1.3 · 2.8	19 F	0233 0.9 · 1458 2.9 1.0 · 3.0
5 F	0239 1.1 · 1459 2.8 1.1 · 2.9	20 SA	0323 0.8 · 1544 3.0 0.8 · 3.0
6 SA	0322 0.9 · 1540 2.9 1.0 · 2.9	21 SU ○	0407 0.6 · 1626 3.0 0.7 · 3.0
7 SU ●	0402 0.8 · 1619 3.0 0.8 · 3.0	22 M	0447 0.6 · 1704 3.0 0.7
8 M	0441 0.6 · 1659 3.0 0.7	23 TU	0523 3.0 · 1739 0.6 0.7
9 TU	0520 0.6 · 1737 3.0 0.6	24 W	0557 3.0 · 1812 0.6 0.8
10 W	0558 0.6 · 1817 3.0 0.6	25 TH	0629 3.0 · 1843 0.8 0.9
11 TH	0638 3.0 · 1859 0.6 0.7	26 F	0658 2.9 · 1913 0.9 1.0
12 F	0720 3.0 0.7 · 1943 3.0 0.8	27 SA	0727 2.8 · 1945 1.0 1.1
13 SA	0805 2.9 0.8 · 2033 2.9 0.9	28 SU	0800 2.8 · 2022 1.2 1.3
14 SU	0858 2.8 1.0 · 2132 2.8 1.1	29 M	0841 2.7 1.4 · 2112 2.7 1.5
15 M	1006 2.7 1.2 · 2249 2.7 1.2	30 TU	0941 2.6 1.6 · 2232 2.6 1.6
		31 W	1130 2.6 1.7 · 2.6

LYMINGTON
50°46′N 1°32′W

> Sea Level is above Mean Tide Level from 4.0 hours after L.W. to 2.0 hours before the next L.W. and H.W. will occur between 6.5 hours after L.W. and 4.0 hours before the next L.W.

Times of low water and heights (in metres) of high and low water 1994
Time: GMT. For BST, ADD ONE HOUR in the shaded area

SEPTEMBER

Day	DoW	Times & heights (m)
1	TH	0017 1.5 / 2.6 · 1255 1.5 / 2.6
2	F	0124 1.3 / 2.7 · 1351 1.3 / 2.7
3	SA	0214 1.1 / 2.8 · 1436 1.1 / 2.9
4	SU	0257 0.9 / 2.9 · 1517 0.9 / 3.0
5	M ●	0337 0.7 / 3.0 · 1557 0.8 / 3.0
6	TU	0417 0.6 / 3.0 · 1636 0.6 / 3.0
7	W	0457 0.5 / 3.1 · 1716 0.6
8	TH	3.1 · 0537 0.5 / 3.1 · 1757 0.6
9	F	3.1 · 0618 0.5 / 3.0 · 1840 0.6
10	SA	3.0 · 0702 0.6 / 3.0 · 1925 0.7
11	SU	3.0 · 0750 0.8 / 2.9 · 2015 0.9
12	M	2.9 · 0845 1.0 / 2.8 · 2116 1.1
13	TU	2.7 · 0955 1.3 / 2.7 · 2234 1.3
14	W	2.7 · 1123 1.3 / 2.6
15	TH	0003 1.3 / 2.7 · 1248 1.3 / 2.7
16	F	0120 1.1 / 2.8 · 1355 1.1 / 2.8
17	SA	0219 1.0 / 2.9 · 1445 1.0 / 2.9
18	SU	0305 0.8 / 3.0 · 1527 0.8 / 3.0
19	M O	0345 0.7 / 3.0 · 1604 0.8 / 3.0
20	TU	0421 0.6 / 3.0 · 1638 0.7 / 3.0
21	W	0455 0.6 / 3.0 · 1711 0.7
22	TH	3.0 · 0526 0.7 · 1741 0.8
23	F	3.0 · 0557 0.8 · 1810 0.9
24	SA	2.9 · 0625 0.9 · 1839 1.0
25	SU	2.9 · 0653 1.0 · 1909 1.1
26	M	2.8 · 0725 1.2 · 1945 1.2
27	TU	2.7 · 0804 1.4 · 2030 1.4
28	W	2.6 · 0858 1.5 · 2137 1.5
29	TH	2.6 · 1030 1.7 · 2325 1.5
30	F	2.6 · 1216 1.6

OCTOBER

Day	DoW	Times & heights (m)
1	SA	0047 1.4 / 2.7 · 1319 1.4 / 2.7
2	SU	0141 1.1 / 2.9 · 1407 1.1 / 2.9
3	M	0226 0.9 / 3.0 · 1449 0.9 / 3.0
4	TU	0308 0.7 / 3.0 · 1530 0.7 / 3.0
5	W ●	0349 0.6 / 3.1 · 1611 0.6 / 3.1
6	TH	0432 0.4 / 3.1 · 1654 0.5
7	F	3.1 · 0515 0.4 / 3.1 · 1737 0.5
8	SA	3.1 · 0600 0.5 / 3.1 · 1822 0.6
9	SU	3.0 · 0646 0.6 / 3.0 · 1910 0.7
10	M	3.0 · 0737 0.8 / 2.9 · 2001 0.9
11	TU	2.9 · 0833 1.1 / 2.8 · 2101 1.1
12	W	2.8 · 0942 1.3 / 2.7 · 2215 1.3
13	TH	2.7 · 1103 1.3 / 2.6 · 2339 1.3
14	F	2.7 · 1226 1.3 / 2.7
15	SA	0056 1.2 / 2.8 · 1333 1.2 / 2.8
16	SU	0155 1.1 / 2.9 · 1422 1.1 / 2.9
17	M	0239 1.0 / 3.0 · 1502 0.9 / 2.9
18	TU	0317 0.8 / 3.0 · 1537 0.8 / 3.0
19	W O	0351 0.8 / 3.0 · 1610 0.8 / 3.0
20	TH	0424 0.8 / 3.0 · 1642 0.8 / 3.0
21	F	0457 0.8 / 3.0 · 1713 0.8
22	SA	3.0 · 0527 0.8 · 1743 0.9
23	SU	2.9 · 0557 1.0 · 1812 1.0
24	M	2.9 · 0627 1.0 · 1843 1.1
25	TU	2.8 · 0700 1.1 · 1919 1.1
26	W	2.8 · 0740 1.3 · 2003 1.3
27	TH	2.7 · 0831 1.5 · 2102 1.4
28	F	2.6 · 0943 1.6 · 2224 1.5
29	SA	2.6 · 1117 1.5 · 2352 1.4
30	SU	2.7 · 1234 1.4 · 2.7
31	M	0058 1.2 / 2.9 · 1330 1.1 / 2.9

NOVEMBER

Day	DoW	Times & heights (m)
1	TU	0150 1.0 / 3.0 · 1418 1.0 / 3.0
2	W	0236 0.8 / 3.0 · 1503 0.8 / 3.0
3	TH ●	0322 0.6 / 3.1 · 1548 0.6 / 3.1
4	F	0408 0.5 / 3.1 · 1634 0.6 / 3.1
5	SA	0455 0.5 / 3.1 · 1721 0.6
6	SU	3.1 · 0543 0.6 / 3.1 · 1808 0.6
7	M	3.1 · 0632 0.7 / 3.0 · 1857 0.7
8	TU	3.0 · 0724 0.8 / 2.9 · 1948 0.8
9	W	2.9 · 0818 1.0 / 2.8 · 2044 1.0
10	TH	2.8 · 0919 1.2 / 2.7 · 2147 1.2
11	F	2.8 · 1029 1.3 / 2.6 · 2300 1.3
12	SA	2.7 · 1146 1.3 / 2.6
13	SU	0015 1.3 / 2.8 · 1255 1.3 / 2.7
14	M	0117 1.2 / 2.8 · 1349 1.1 / 2.8
15	TU	0204 1.1 / 2.9 · 1430 1.0 / 2.8
16	W	0244 1.0 / 2.9 · 1507 1.0 / 2.9
17	TH	0320 0.9 / 3.0 · 1542 0.9 / 2.9
18	F O	0355 0.9 / 3.0 · 1616 0.8 / 2.9
19	SA	0430 0.9 / 3.0 · 1650 0.8 / 2.9
20	SU	0504 0.9 / 3.0 · 1722 0.9
21	M	2.9 · 0536 1.0 · 1753 1.0
22	TU	2.9 · 0608 1.0 · 1826 1.0
23	W	2.9 · 0643 1.1 · 1902 1.1
24	TH	2.9 · 0723 1.2 · 1944 1.1
25	F	2.8 · 0810 1.3 · 2035 1.3
26	SA	2.8 · 0909 1.4 · 2140 1.3
27	SU	2.7 · 1022 1.5 · 2255 1.3
28	M	2.8 · 1140 1.3 · 2.7
29	TU	0008 1.2 / 2.9 · 1250 1.2 / 2.8
30	W	0112 1.0 / 3.0 · 1348 1.0 / 2.9

DECEMBER

Day	DoW	Times & heights (m)
1	TH	0207 0.9 / 3.0 · 1440 0.8 / 3.0
2	F ●	0259 0.8 / 3.1 · 1530 0.7 / 3.1
3	SA	0349 0.6 / 3.1 · 1620 0.6 / 3.1
4	SU	0439 0.6 / 3.1 · 1709 0.6
5	M	3.1 · 0529 0.6 / 3.1 · 1757 0.6
6	TU	3.1 · 0619 0.7 / 3.0 · 1845 0.6
7	W	3.0 · 0708 0.8 / 3.0 · 1932 0.8
8	TH	3.0 · 0757 1.0 / 2.9 · 2020 0.9
9	F	2.9 · 0848 1.1 / 2.8 · 2111 1.1
10	SA	2.8 · 0945 1.3 / 2.7 · 2210 1.3
11	SU	2.8 · 1052 1.4 / 2.6 · 2318 1.3
12	M	2.7 · 1203 1.4 / 2.6
13	TU	0026 1.3 / 2.8 · 1306 1.3 / 2.7
14	W	0123 1.3 / 2.8 · 1356 1.2 / 2.7
15	TH	0210 1.2 / 2.9 · 1438 1.1 / 2.8
16	F	0251 1.1 / 2.9 · 1517 1.0 / 2.9
17	SA	0330 1.0 / 2.9 · 1555 0.9 / 2.9
18	SU O	0408 1.0 / 3.0 · 1632 0.9 / 2.9
19	M	0444 1.0 / 3.0 · 1707 0.8
20	TU	2.9 · 0519 1.0 · 1740 0.8
21	W	2.9 · 0553 1.0 · 1813 0.9
22	TH	2.9 · 0629 1.0 · 1848 0.9
23	F	2.9 · 0707 1.1 · 1927 1.0
24	SA	2.9 · 0750 1.1 · 2012 1.0
25	SU	2.9 · 0841 1.2 · 2106 1.1
26	M	2.8 · 0942 1.3 · 2211 1.2
27	TU	2.8 · 1055 1.3 · 2326 1.2
28	W	2.8 · 1213 1.3 · 2.7
29	TH	0040 1.1 / 2.9 · 1325 1.1 / 2.8
30	F	0146 1.0 / 3.0 · 1425 0.9 / 3.0
31	SA	0244 0.9 / 3.0 · 1520 0.8 / 3.0

TIDAL CURVES—SWANAGE TO CHRISTCHURCH

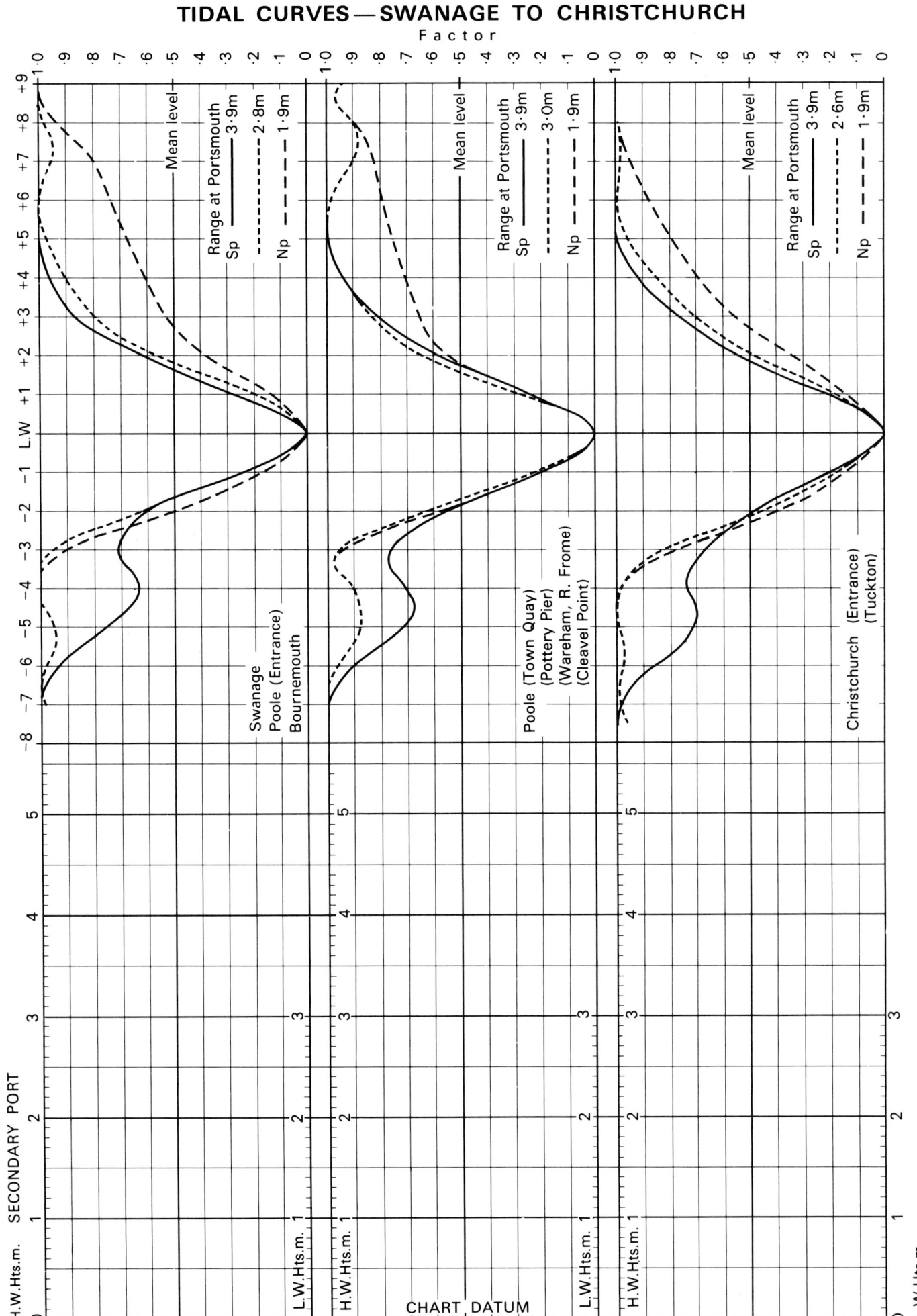

Sea Level is above Mean Tide Level from 2.0 hours after L.W. to 2.0 hours before the next L.W. and H.W. will occur between 5.0 hours after L.W. and 3.0 hours before the next L.W.

POOLE
50°43′N 1°59′W

Times of low water and heights (in metres) of high and low water 1994
Time: GMT. For BST, ADD ONE HOUR in the shaded area

JANUARY

Date	Time	m	Date	Time	m
1 SA	0620 / 1844	2.1 0.7 2.0 0.6	16 SU	0701 / 1920	2.1 0.8 2.0 0.7
2 SU	0704 / 1927	2.1 0.7 2.0 0.7	17 M	0736 / 1953	2.0 0.9 1.9 0.8
3 M	0750 / 2015	2.0 0.8 2.0 0.7	18 TU	0811 / 2027	2.0 1.0 1.8 1.0
4 TU	0842 / 2107	2.0 0.9 1.9 0.8	19 W	0850 / 2108	1.9 1.1 1.7 1.1
5 W	0940 / 2210	1.9 1.0 1.8 0.9	20 TH	0938 / 2203	1.8 1.3 1.6 1.3
6 TH	1051 / 2322	1.9 1.0 1.7 1.0	21 F	1049 / 2323	1.7 1.4 1.5 1.4
7 F	1209	1.9 1.0 1.8	22 SA	1222	1.7 1.3 1.5
8 SA	0038 / 1323	1.0 1.9 1.0 1.8	23 SU	0047 / 1331	1.3 1.7 1.2 1.7
9 SU	0146 / 1425	1.0 2.0 0.9 1.9	24 M	0149 / 1422	1.2 1.8 1.0 1.8
10 M	0244 / 1518	0.9 2.0 0.7 2.0	25 TU	0237 / 1506	1.0 1.9 0.9 1.9
11 TU ●	0335 / 1605	0.8 2.1 0.7 2.1	26 W	0320 / 1547	0.9 2.0 0.7 2.0
12 W	0421 / 1649	0.7 2.2 0.5 2.2	27 TH O	0402 / 1627	0.8 2.0 0.6 2.1
13 TH	0505 / 1732	0.7 2.2 0.5	28 F	0441 / 1707	0.7 2.1 0.5
14 F	0546 / 1810	2.2 0.7 2.1 0.5	29 SA	0523 / 1747	2.2 0.6 2.2 0.4
15 SA	0625 / 1846	2.1 0.7 2.0 0.6	30 SU	0605 / 1829	2.2 0.5 2.2 0.4
			31 M	0648 / 1911	2.2 0.5 2.2 0.5

FEBRUARY

Date	Time	m	Date	Time	m
1 TU	0732 / 1955	2.2 0.6 2.0 0.6	16 W	0730 / 1946	2.0 0.9 1.9 0.9
2 W	0820 / 2045	2.1 0.7 2.0 0.7	17 TH	0802 / 2020	1.9 1.0 1.8 1.0
3 TH	0913 / 2144	2.0 0.9 1.8 0.9	18 F	0843 / 2105	1.8 1.1 1.7 1.2
4 F	1021 / 2300	1.8 1.0 1.7 1.1	19 SA	0936 / 2213	1.7 1.3 1.5 1.4
5 SA	1144	1.8 1.1 1.7	20 SU	1104	1.6 1.4 1.5
6 SU	0023 / 1308	1.1 1.8 1.0 1.7	21 M	0001 / 1253	1.4 1.6 1.3 1.6
7 M	0139 / 1416	1.1 1.8 0.9 1.9	22 TU	0123 / 1355	1.3 1.7 1.1 1.8
8 TU	0239 / 1509	0.9 1.9 0.8 2.0	23 W	0217 / 1442	1.1 1.8 0.9 1.9
9 W	0328 / 1554	0.8 2.0 0.7 2.0	24 TH	0302 / 1524	0.9 1.9 0.7 2.0
10 TH ●	0411 / 1633	0.7 2.0 0.5 2.1	25 F	0343 / 1605	0.7 2.0 0.5 2.2
11 F	0449 / 1711	0.7 2.1 0.5	26 SA O	0424 / 1645	0.5 2.2 0.4 2.2
12 SA	0526 / 1746	2.1 0.6 2.1 0.5	27 SU	0505 / 1727	0.4 2.2 0.3
13 SU	0600 / 1819	2.1 0.6 2.0 0.5	28 M	0547 / 1809	2.3 0.4 2.2 0.3
14 M	0632 / 1848	2.1 0.7 2.0 0.7			
15 TU	0701 / 1917	2.0 0.8 1.9 0.8			

MARCH

Date	Time	m	Date	Time	m
1 TU	0630 / 1852	2.2 0.4 2.2 0.4	16 W	0630 / 1844	2.0 0.7 2.0 0.8
2 W	0714 / 1938	2.2 0.5 2.2 0.5	17 TH	0656 / 1913	2.0 0.8 1.9 0.9
3 TH	0800 / 2027	2.1 0.6 2.0 0.7	18 F	0727 / 1947	1.9 0.9 1.8 1.0
4 F	0852 / 2126	1.9 0.8 1.9 0.9	19 SA	0804 / 2029	1.8 1.0 1.7 1.1
5 SA	0957 / 2244	1.8 1.0 1.7 1.1	20 SU	0853 / 2130	1.7 1.1 1.6 1.3
6 SU	1123	1.7 1.1 1.7	21 M	1004 / 2309	1.6 1.3 1.5 1.4
7 M	0011 / 1251	1.1 1.6 1.1 1.7	22 TU	1156	1.5 1.3 1.6
8 TU	0131 / 1402	1.1 1.7 1.0 1.8	23 W	0048 / 1317	1.3 1.6 1.1 1.8
9 W	0231 / 1453	0.9 1.8 0.8 2.0	24 TH	0149 / 1410	1.0 1.8 0.9 1.9
10 TH	0317 / 1535	0.8 1.9 0.7 2.0	25 F	0236 / 1456	0.8 1.9 0.7 2.0
11 F	0355 / 1611	0.7 2.0 0.6 2.1	26 SA	0319 / 1539	0.7 2.0 0.5 2.2
12 SA ●	0429 / 1645	0.6 2.0 0.5 2.1	27 SU O	0402 / 1621	0.5 2.2 0.4 2.3
13 SU	0502 / 1718	0.5 2.0 0.5	28 M	0442 / 1704	0.4 2.2 0.3
14 M	0534 / 1749	2.1 0.5 2.0 0.6	29 TU	0526 / 1749	2.3 0.3 2.3 0.3
15 TU	0602 / 1818	2.0 0.6 2.0 0.7	30 W	0611 / 1835	2.3 0.3 2.2 0.4
			31 TH	0656 / 1922	2.2 0.4 2.2 0.5

APRIL

Date	Time	m	Date	Time	m
1 F	0744 / 2013	2.0 0.5 2.0 0.7	16 SA	0702 / 1924	1.9 0.8 1.9 0.9
2 SA	0835 / 2111	1.9 0.7 1.9 0.9	17 SU	0742 / 2009	1.8 0.9 1.8 1.0
3 SU	0938 / 2225	1.8 0.9 1.8 1.1	18 M	0829 / 2106	1.7 1.0 1.7 1.2
4 M	1058 / 2348	1.6 1.0 1.7 1.1	19 TU	0934 / 2228	1.7 1.1 1.7 1.3
5 TU	1223	1.5 1.1 1.7	20 W	1103 / 2359	1.6 1.1 1.7 1.2
6 W	0108 / 1335	1.1 1.6 1.0 1.8	21 TH	1228	1.6 1.0 1.8
7 TH	0208 / 1427	1.1 1.7 0.9 1.9	22 F	0110 / 1332	1.0 1.7 0.9 1.9
8 F	0252 / 1507	0.8 1.8 0.8 2.0	23 SA	0204 / 1423	0.8 1.9 0.7 2.0
9 SA	0328 / 1542	0.7 1.9 0.7 2.0	24 SU	0251 / 1510	0.6 2.0 0.5 2.2
10 SU	0402 / 1615	0.6 1.9 0.6 2.0	25 M O	0337 / 1556	0.5 2.2 0.4 2.3
11 M ●	0433 / 1647	0.6 2.0 0.6 2.0	26 TU	0421 / 1641	0.4 2.2 0.4 2.3
12 TU	0505 / 1719	0.6 2.0 0.7	27 W	0508 / 1729	0.3 2.2 0.4
13 W	0535 / 1749	2.0 0.6 2.0 0.7	28 TH	0554 / 1818	2.2 0.4 2.2 0.4
14 TH	0602 / 1818	2.0 0.7 2.0 0.8	29 F	0642 / 1907	2.2 0.4 2.2 0.5
15 F	0631 / 1848	2.0 0.7 1.9 0.8	30 SA	0730 / 1958	2.0 0.5 2.0 0.7

POOLE
50°43′N 1°59′W

Sea Level is above Mean Tide Level from 2.0 hours after L.W. to 2.0 hours before the next L.W. and H.W. will occur between 5.0 hours after L.W. and 3.0 hours before the next L.W.

Times of low water and heights (in metres) of high and low water 1994
Time: GMT. For BST, ADD ONE HOUR in the shaded area

MAY

Date	Day	Times	Heights (m)
1	SU	0821 / 2054	1.9, 0.7, 1.9, 0.9
2	M	0917 / 2157	1.8, 0.9, 1.8, 1.0
3	TU	1025 / 2312	1.7, 1.0, 1.7, 1.1
4	W	1141	1.5, 1.1, 1.7
5	TH	0026 / 1253	1.1, 1.5, 1.0, 1.8
6	F	0130 / 1348	1.0, 1.7, 1.0, 1.8
7	SA	0216 / 1431	0.9, 1.7, 0.9, 1.9
8	SU	0255 / 1508	0.8, 1.8, 0.8, 1.9
9	M	0330 / 1543	0.7, 1.9, 0.7, 2.0
10	TU ●	0403 / 1617	0.7, 1.9, 0.7, 2.0
11	W	0436 / 1650	0.7, 1.9, 0.7, 2.0
12	TH	0510 / 1723	0.7, 1.9, 0.8
13	F	0541 / 1756	2.0, 0.7, 1.9, 0.8
14	SA	0612 / 1831	1.9, 0.7, 1.9, 0.8
15	SU	0647 / 1910	1.9, 0.8, 1.9, 0.9
16	M	0728 / 1955	1.9, 0.8, 1.9, 0.9
17	TU	0816 / 2050	1.8, 0.9, 1.8, 1.0
18	W	0913 / 2156	1.7, 1.0, 1.8, 1.1
19	TH	1025 / 2313	1.7, 1.0, 1.8, 1.1
20	F	1141	1.7, 1.0, 1.8
21	SA	0025 / 1252	1.0, 1.8, 0.9, 1.9
22	SU	0130 / 1351	0.9, 1.9, 0.7, 2.0
23	M	0224 / 1443	0.7, 2.0, 0.6, 2.2
24	TU	0315 / 1533	0.5, 2.1, 0.5, 2.2
25	W O	0403 / 1623	0.4, 2.2, 0.5, 2.2
26	TH	0451 / 1713	0.4, 2.2, 0.5
27	F	0541 / 1802	2.2, 0.4, 2.2, 0.5
28	SA	0630 / 1851	2.2, 0.4, 2.2, 0.6
29	SU	0717 / 1941	2.1, 0.5, 2.1, 0.7
30	M	0803 / 2030	2.0, 0.7, 2.0, 0.8
31	TU	0852 / 2123	1.8, 0.8, 1.9, 1.0

JUNE

Date	Day	Times	Heights (m)
1	W	0946 / 2223	1.7, 1.0, 1.8, 1.1
2	TH	1050 / 2330	1.6, 1.1, 1.7, 1.1
3	F	1157	1.5, 1.1, 1.7
4	SA	0036 / 1300	1.1, 1.6, 1.1, 1.8
5	SU	0132 / 1350	1.1, 1.7, 1.0, 1.8
6	M	0217 / 1433	1.0, 1.7, 0.9, 1.9
7	TU	0257 / 1512	0.9, 1.8, 0.9, 1.9
8	W	0335 / 1550	0.8, 1.9, 0.8, 1.9
9	TH ●	0412 / 1626	0.7, 1.9, 0.8, 2.0
10	F	0448 / 1703	0.7, 1.9, 0.8
11	SA	0524 / 1740	2.0, 0.7, 1.9, 0.8
12	SU	0600 / 1818	2.0, 0.7, 2.0, 0.8
13	M	0637 / 1857	1.9, 0.7, 2.0, 0.8
14	TU	0718 / 1942	1.9, 0.7, 1.9, 0.8
15	W	0803 / 2032	1.9, 0.8, 1.9, 0.9
16	TH	0855 / 2130	1.9, 0.8, 1.9, 0.9
17	F	0955 / 2237	1.8, 0.9, 1.8, 1.0
18	SA	1107 / 2349	1.8, 0.9, 1.9, 1.0
19	SU	1218	1.8, 0.9, 1.9
20	M	0100 / 1326	0.9, 1.8, 0.8, 2.0
21	TU	0203 / 1425	0.8, 1.9, 0.8, 2.1
22	W	0259 / 1519	0.7, 2.0, 0.7, 2.2
23	TH O	0351 / 1610	0.5, 2.1, 0.6, 2.2
24	F	0439 / 1659	0.5, 2.2, 0.5
25	SA	0528 / 1748	2.2, 0.5, 2.2, 0.5
26	SU	0615 / 1834	2.2, 0.5, 2.2, 0.6
27	M	0658 / 1918	2.1, 0.5, 2.1, 0.7
28	TU	0740 / 2000	2.0, 0.7, 2.0, 0.8
29	W	0820 / 2043	1.9, 0.7, 1.9, 0.9
30	TH	0902 / 2130	1.8, 0.9, 1.9, 1.0

JULY

Date	Day	Times	Heights (m)
1	F	0951 / 2227	1.7, 1.1, 1.8, 1.1
2	SA	1054 / 2336	1.6, 1.2, 1.7, 1.3
3	SU	1204	1.5, 1.3, 1.7
4	M	0043 / 1308	1.2, 1.6, 1.2, 1.8
5	TU	0140 / 1401	1.1, 1.7, 1.1, 1.8
6	W	0228 / 1445	1.0, 1.8, 1.0, 1.9
7	TH	0311 / 1526	0.9, 1.9, 0.9, 1.9
8	F ●	0351 / 1605	0.8, 1.9, 0.8, 2.0
9	SA	0429 / 1644	0.7, 2.0, 0.8, 2.0
10	SU	0508 / 1723	0.7, 2.0, 0.7
11	M	0546 / 1803	2.0, 0.6, 2.0, 0.7
12	TU	0625 / 1843	2.0, 0.6, 2.0, 0.7
13	W	0704 / 1926	2.0, 0.6, 2.0, 0.7
14	TH	0747 / 2013	2.0, 0.7, 2.0, 0.8
15	F	0835 / 2106	1.9, 0.7, 2.0, 0.8
16	SA	0931 / 2207	1.9, 0.9, 1.9, 0.9
17	SU	1038 / 2322	1.8, 1.0, 1.8, 1.0
18	M	1156	1.8, 1.0, 1.9
19	TU	0040 / 1312	1.0, 1.8, 1.0, 1.9
20	W	0150 / 1416	0.9, 1.9, 0.9, 2.0
21	TH	0249 / 1512	0.8, 2.0, 0.8, 2.1
22	F O	0341 / 1602	0.6, 2.1, 0.7, 2.2
23	SA	0429 / 1646	0.5, 2.2, 0.6, 2.2
24	SU	0514 / 1732	0.5, 2.2, 0.6
25	M	0556 / 1812	2.2, 0.5, 2.2, 0.6
26	TU	0634 / 1850	2.1, 0.5, 2.2, 0.7
27	W	0710 / 1926	2.0, 0.7, 2.1, 0.8
28	TH	0744 / 2002	1.9, 0.8, 2.0, 0.9
29	F	0818 / 2040	1.9, 0.9, 1.9, 1.0
30	SA	0857 / 2125	1.8, 1.0, 1.8, 1.1
31	SU	0946 / 2226	1.7, 1.2, 1.7, 1.3

AUGUST

Date	Day	Times	Heights (m)
1	M	1101 / 2351	1.5, 1.3, 1.7, 1.3
2	TU	1228	1.5, 1.4, 1.7
3	W	0106 / 1334	1.2, 1.7, 1.3, 1.7
4	TH	0202 / 1423	1.1, 1.8, 1.1, 1.8
5	F	0247 / 1507	0.9, 1.9, 1.0, 1.9
6	SA	0329 / 1547	0.8, 2.0, 0.8, 2.0
7	SU ●	0408 / 1625	0.7, 2.0, 0.7, 2.0
8	M	0446 / 1705	0.5, 2.1, 0.6
9	TU	0526 / 1744	2.1, 0.5, 2.2, 0.5
10	W	0605 / 1825	2.1, 0.5, 2.2, 0.5
11	TH	0646 / 1908	2.1, 0.5, 2.2, 0.6
12	F	0729 / 1953	2.1, 0.6, 2.1, 0.7
13	SA	0816 / 2045	2.0, 0.7, 2.0, 0.8
14	SU	0910 / 2145	1.9, 0.9, 1.9, 0.9
15	M	1020 / 2304	1.8, 1.0, 1.8, 1.0
16	TU	1145	1.7, 1.1, 1.8
17	W	0028 / 1307	1.0, 1.8, 1.1, 1.8
18	TH	0142 / 1413	0.9, 1.9, 1.0, 1.9
19	F	0241 / 1506	0.8, 2.0, 0.8, 2.0
20	SA	0330 / 1551	0.7, 2.1, 0.7, 2.1
21	SU O	0413 / 1631	0.5, 2.2, 0.6, 2.1
22	M	0452 / 1710	0.5, 2.2, 0.6
23	TU	0529 / 1746	2.1, 0.5, 2.2, 0.6
24	W	0604 / 1820	2.1, 0.5, 2.1, 0.7
25	TH	0637 / 1851	2.0, 0.7, 2.0, 0.8
26	F	0707 / 1922	2.0, 0.8, 2.0, 0.8
27	SA	0737 / 1955	1.9, 0.9, 1.9, 1.0
28	SU	0811 / 2033	1.8, 1.0, 1.8, 1.1
29	M	0853 / 2125	1.7, 1.2, 1.7, 1.3
30	TU	0954 / 2247	1.6, 1.4, 1.7, 1.4
31	W	1143	1.5, 1.4, 1.6

POOLE
50°43′N 1°59′W

> Sea Level is above Mean Tide Level from 2.0 hours after L.W. to 2.0 hours before the next L.W. and H.W. will occur between 5.0 hours after L.W. and 3.0 hours before the next L.W.

Times of low water and heights (in metres) of high and low water 1994
Time: GMT. For BST, ADD ONE HOUR in the shaded area

SEPTEMBER

Day	Time	m		Day	Time	m
1 TH	0029 / 1307	1.3 1.6 1.3 1.7		16 F	0131 / 1405	1.0 1.9 1.0 1.9
2 F	0135 / 1401	1.1 1.8 1.1 1.8		17 SA	0228 / 1453	0.8 2.0 0.9 2.0
3 SA	0223 / 1444	0.9 1.9 1.0 1.9		18 SU	0313 / 1534	0.7 2.1 0.7 2.0
4 SU	0305 / 1524	0.8 2.0 0.8 2.0		19 M ○	0352 / 1610	0.6 2.1 0.7 2.0
5 M ●	0344 / 1603	0.6 2.1 0.7 2.1		20 TU	0427 / 1643	0.5 2.2 0.6 2.1
6 TU	0423 / 1641	0.5 2.2 0.5 2.2		21 W	0501 / 1717	0.5 2.1 0.6 2.2
7 W	0503 / 1722	0.4 2.2 0.5		22 TH	0533 / 1748	2.0 0.6 2.1 0.7
8 TH	0544 / 1804	2.2 0.4 2.2 0.5		23 F	0604 / 1818	2.0 0.7 2.0 0.8
9 F	0626 / 1848	2.2 0.4 2.2 0.5		24 SA	0633 / 1847	2.0 0.8 2.0 0.8
10 SA	0711 / 1935	2.2 0.5 2.1 0.6		25 SU	0701 / 1918	1.9 0.9 1.9 0.9
11 SU	0800 / 2026	2.0 0.7 2.0 0.8		26 M	0735 / 1955	1.9 1.0 1.8 1.0
12 M	0857 / 2129	1.9 0.9 1.8 0.9		27 TU	0815 / 2042	1.8 1.2 1.8 1.2
13 TU	1009 / 2249	1.8 1.1 1.7 1.1		28 W	0910 / 2150	1.7 1.3 1.7 1.3
14 W	1137	1.7 1.1 1.7		29 TH	1045 / 2339	1.6 1.4 1.6 1.3
15 TH	0016 / 1300	1.1 1.8 1.1 1.8		30 F	1228	1.6 1.4 1.7

OCTOBER

Day	Time	m		Day	Time	m
1 SA	0059 / 1330	1.2 1.8 1.2 1.8		16 SU	0205 / 1431	0.9 2.0 0.9 1.9
2 SU	0151 / 1416	1.0 1.9 1.0 1.9		17 M	0247 / 1510	0.8 2.0 0.8 2.0
3 M	0234 / 1457	0.8 2.0 0.8 2.0		18 TU	0324 / 1544	0.7 2.1 0.7 2.0
4 TU	0316 / 1537	0.6 2.2 0.6 2.2		19 W ○	0358 / 1616	0.7 2.1 0.7 2.0
5 W ●	0356 / 1617	0.5 2.2 0.5 2.2		20 TH	0430 / 1647	0.7 2.0 0.7 2.0
6 TH	0437 / 1659	0.4 2.3 0.4		21 F	0503 / 1719	2.0 0.7 2.0 0.7
7 F	0521 / 1744	2.3 0.4 2.3 0.4		22 SA	0534 / 1750	2.0 0.4 2.0 0.8
8 SA	0607 / 1830	2.2 0.4 2.2 0.5		23 SU	0604 / 1820	2.0 0.5 2.0 0.9
9 SU	0654 / 1919	2.2 0.5 2.1 0.6		24 M	0635 / 1851	1.9 0.6 1.9 0.9
10 M	0747 / 2012	2.1 0.7 2.0 0.8		25 TU	0709 / 1928	1.9 0.7 1.9 1.0
11 TU	0845 / 2113	1.9 0.9 1.8 0.9		26 W	0750 / 2014	1.8 0.9 1.8 1.1
12 W	0955 / 2229	1.8 1.1 1.7 1.1		27 TH	0843 / 2114	1.8 1.3 1.7 1.2
13 TH	1117 / 2352	1.7 1.1 1.7 1.1		28 F	0956 / 2238	1.7 1.4 1.7 1.3
14 F	1238	1.8 1.1 1.7		29 SA	1131	1.7 1.3 1.7
15 SA	0107 / 1343	1.0 1.9 1.0 1.8		30 SU	0005 / 1246	1.2 1.8 1.2 1.8
				31 M	0109 / 1340	1.0 1.9 1.0 1.9

NOVEMBER

Day	Time	m		Day	Time	m
1 TU	0200 / 1427	0.8 2.0 0.8 2.0		16 W	0252 / 1515	0.9 2.0 0.8 1.9
2 W	0244 / 1511	0.7 2.2 0.7 2.2		17 TH	0327 / 1549	0.8 2.0 0.8 2.0
3 TH ●	0329 / 1555	0.5 2.3 0.5 2.2		18 F ○	0402 / 1622	0.8 2.0 0.7 2.0
4 F	0414 / 1639	0.4 2.3 0.5 2.3		19 SA	0435 / 1655	0.8 2.0 0.7 2.0
5 SA	0501 / 1727	0.4 2.3 0.5		20 SU	0510 / 1728	0.8 2.0 0.8
6 SU	0550 / 1815	2.3 0.5 2.2 0.5		21 M	0543 / 1800	2.0 0.8 2.0 0.8
7 M	0640 / 1906	2.2 0.6 2.1 0.6		22 TU	0615 / 1834	2.0 0.9 1.9 0.9
8 TU	0733 / 1958	2.1 0.7 2.0 0.7		23 W	0651 / 1911	1.9 1.0 1.9 0.9
9 W	0829 / 2056	2.0 0.9 1.9 0.9		24 TH	0732 / 1954	2.0 1.0 1.8 1.0
10 TH	0932 / 2200	1.9 1.0 1.8 1.0		25 F	0821 / 2047	1.9 1.1 1.8 1.1
11 F	1044 / 2314	1.8 1.1 1.7 1.1		26 SA	0921 / 2153	1.8 1.2 1.7 1.1
12 SA	1159	1.8 1.1 1.7		27 SU	1036 / 2310	1.8 1.3 1.7 1.1
13 SU	0027 / 1307	1.1 1.8 1.1 1.7		28 M	1153	1.8 1.1 1.8
14 M	0128 / 1359	1.0 1.9 1.0 1.8		29 TU	0021 / 1302	1.0 1.9 1.0 1.9
15 TU	0213 / 1438	0.9 2.0 0.9 1.9		30 W	0123 / 1358	0.9 2.0 0.9 2.0

DECEMBER

Day	Time	m		Day	Time	m
1 TH	0216 / 1448	0.8 2.2 0.7 2.1		16 F	0259 / 1524	0.9 2.0 0.8 1.9
2 F ●	0307 / 1537	0.7 2.3 0.6 2.2		17 SA	0337 / 1602	0.9 2.0 0.8 1.9
3 SA	0356 / 1626	0.5 2.3 0.5 2.2		18 SU ○	0414 / 1637	0.8 2.0 0.8 2.0
4 SU	0444 / 1715	0.5 2.3 0.5		19 M	0449 / 1713	0.8 2.0 0.7
5 M	0536 / 1804	2.3 0.5 2.2 0.5		20 TU	0525 / 1747	2.0 0.8 2.0 0.7
6 TU	0627 / 1853	2.2 0.6 2.2 0.5		21 W	0600 / 1821	2.0 0.8 2.0 0.8
7 W	0717 / 1942	2.2 0.7 2.0 0.7		22 TH	0637 / 1856	2.0 0.9 2.0 0.8
8 TH	0808 / 2031	2.1 0.8 1.9 0.8		23 F	0716 / 1937	2.0 0.9 1.9 0.8
9 F	0900 / 2124	2.0 1.0 1.8 0.9		24 SA	0800 / 2023	2.0 1.0 1.9 0.9
10 SA	0958 / 2224	1.9 1.1 1.7 1.1		25 SU	0853 / 2118	1.9 1.0 1.8 1.0
11 SU	1107 / 2332	1.8 1.2 1.6 1.1		26 M	0955 / 2225	1.9 1.1 1.8 1.0
12 M	1216	1.8 1.2 1.6		27 TU	1110 / 2339	1.9 1.1 1.7 1.0
13 TU	0038 / 1317	1.1 1.9 1.1 1.7		28 W	1225	1.9 1.1 1.8
14 W	0134 / 1405	1.1 1.9 1.0 1.8		29 TH	0052 / 1336	1.0 2.0 0.9 1.9
15 TH	0219 / 1446	1.0 1.9 0.9 1.9		30 F	0156 / 1434	0.9 2.1 0.8 2.0
				31 SA	0252 / 1527	0.8 2.2 0.7 2.1

PORTLAND

MEAN SPRING AND NEAP CURVES

Springs occur 2 days after New and Full Moon

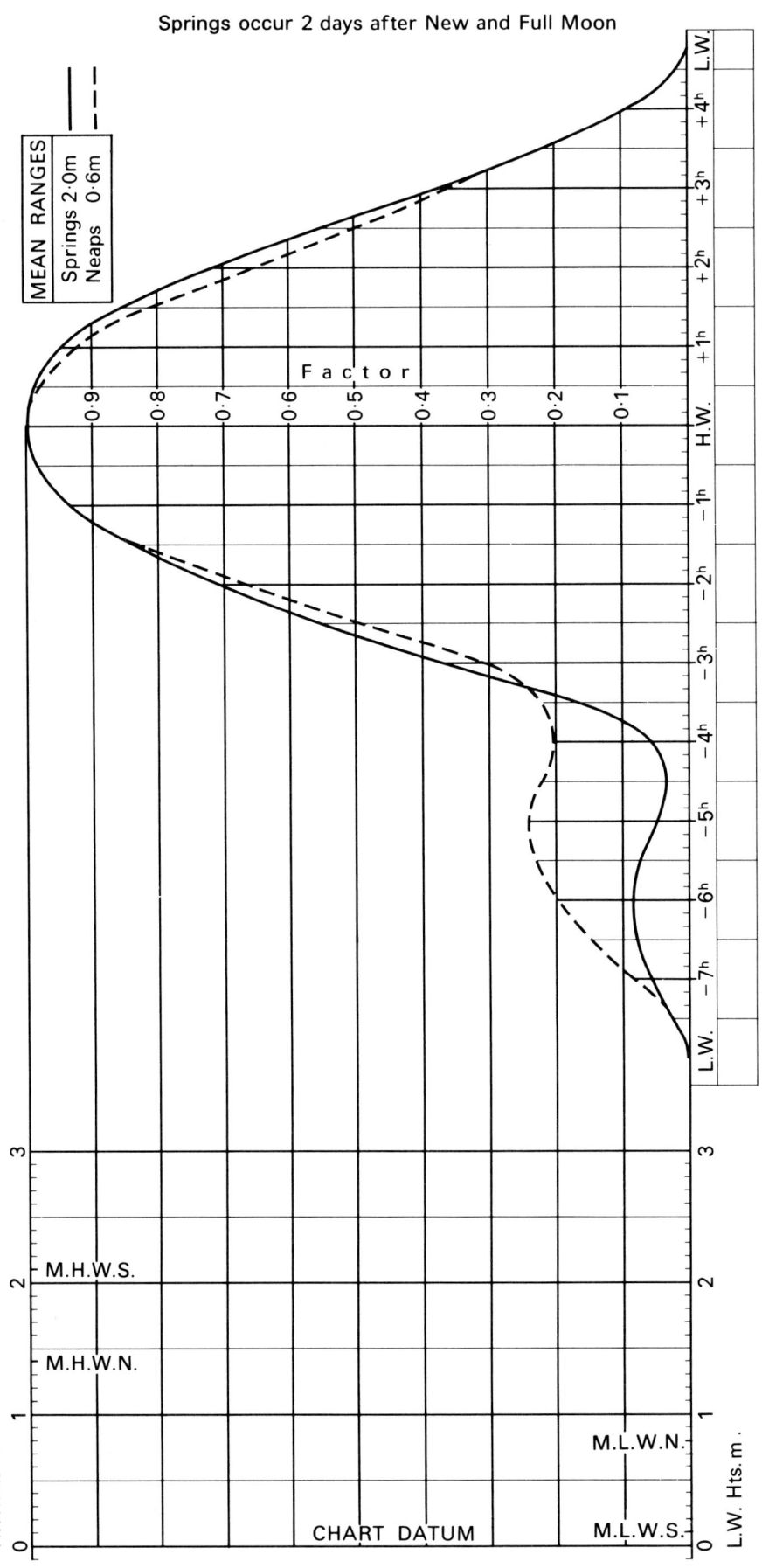

PORTLAND

50°34′N 2°26′W

Times and heights (in metres) of high and low water 1994
Time: GMT. For BST, ADD ONE HOUR in the shaded area
High Water, full and change, 0711

JANUARY

	Time	m		Time	m
1 SA	0123 0839 1348 2109	0.2 2.1 0.2 1.9	**16** SU	0204 0909 1433 2125	0.3 2.0 0.3 1.7
2 SU	0205 0916 1430 2147	0.3 2.0 0.2 1.8	**17** M	0238 0937 1505 2153	0.4 1.9 0.3 1.6
3 M	0246 0955 1513 2229	0.3 1.9 0.3 1.7	**18** TU	0304 1006 1527 2224	0.5 1.7 0.4 1.6
4 TU	0329 1037 1601 2316	0.4 1.8 0.4 1.6	**19** W	0325 1035 1547 2259	0.6 1.6 0.5 1.5
5 W	0418 1124 1659	0.6 1.7 0.5	**20** TH	0353 1105 1618 2343	0.6 1.4 0.6 1.4
6 TH	0011 0521 1220 1810	1.6 0.7 1.6 0.6	**21** F	0435 1145 1707	0.7 1.4 0.6
7 F	0120 0642 1331 1933	1.6 0.8 1.6 0.6	**22** SA	0043 0541 1253 1833	1.4 0.8 1.3 0.7
8 SA	0246 0809 1506 2044	1.6 0.8 1.6 0.6	**23** SU	0205 0746 1441 2018	1.4 0.8 1.3 0.6
9 SU	0404 0919 1630 2142	1.8 0.7 1.7 0.5	**24** M	0331 0901 1614 2122	1.5 0.7 1.4 0.5
10 M	0507 1016 1733 2233	1.9 0.6 1.8 0.4	**25** TU	0444 0957 1721 2214	1.7 0.5 1.6 0.4
11 TU ●	0600 1106 1825 2319	2.1 0.4 1.9 0.3	**26** W	0541 1045 1814 2302	1.9 0.4 1.8 0.2
12 W	0646 1152 1911	2.2 0.3 2.0	**27** TH O	0630 1130 1900 2346	2.1 0.2 1.9 0.1
13 TH	0003 0728 1235 1951	0.2 2.3 0.2 2.0	**28** F	0714 1213 1942	2.2 0.1 2.0
14 F	0046 0806 1317 2027	0.2 2.2 0.2 1.9	**29** SA	0029 0755 1255 2022	0.0 2.2 0.0 2.0
15 SA	0126 0839 1356 2058	0.2 2.1 0.2 1.9	**30** SU	0111 0834 1336 2059	0.0 2.2 0.0 2.0
			31 M	0152 0911 1417 2136	0.0 2.1 0.0 1.9

FEBRUARY

	Time	m		Time	m
1 TU	0231 0948 1458 2214	0.1 2.0 0.1 1.8	**16** W	0233 0939 1447 2150	0.3 1.7 0.3 1.6
2 W	0312 1026 1541 2254	0.2 1.9 0.3 1.7	**17** TH	0252 1003 1506 2216	0.4 1.6 0.4 1.5
3 TH	0355 1108 1629 2341	0.4 1.7 0.4 1.6	**18** F	0317 1024 1535 2248	0.5 1.4 0.4 1.4
4 F	0450 1156 1735	0.6 1.6 0.6	**19** SA	0352 1056 1616 2337	0.6 1.3 0.5 1.4
5 SA	0040 0610 1259 1904	1.5 0.7 1.4 0.6	**20** SU	0444 1154 1722	0.7 1.2 0.6
6 SU	0206 0756 1441 2028	1.5 0.8 1.4 0.6	**21** M	0049 0625 1334 1936	1.3 0.8 1.2 0.7
7 M	0348 0913 1625 2131	1.6 0.7 1.5 0.5	**22** TU	0236 0836 1547 2058	1.4 0.7 1.3 0.5
8 TU	0459 1010 1728 2222	1.8 0.5 1.7 0.4	**23** W	0415 0938 1703 2154	1.6 0.5 1.5 0.3
9 W	0550 1057 1817 2307	2.0 0.4 1.8 0.3	**24** TH	0520 1027 1757 2243	1.8 0.3 1.8 0.2
10 TH ●	0634 1140 1858 2349	2.1 0.2 1.9 0.2	**25** F	0611 1112 1842 2328	2.1 0.1 2.0 0.0
11 F	0713 1219 1935	2.2 0.1 2.0	**26** SA O	0657 1155 1925	2.2 -0.1 2.1
12 SA	0029 0747 1258 2008	0.1 2.2 0.1 2.0	**27** SU	0011 0738 1238 2005	-0.1 2.3 -0.1 2.1
13 SU	0107 0819 1334 2036	0.1 2.1 0.1 1.9	**28** M	0053 0818 1319 2043	-0.2 2.3 -0.2 2.1
14 M	0142 0846 1406 2101	0.2 2.0 0.1 1.8			
15 TU	0212 0913 1431 2125	0.2 1.9 0.2 1.7			

MARCH

	Time	m		Time	m
1 TU	0134 0857 1359 2120	-0.1 2.2 -0.1 2.0	**16** W	0144 0847 1358 2059	0.2 1.9 0.2 1.8
2 W	0214 0934 1439 2158	0.0 2.1 0.0 1.9	**17** TH	0205 0913 1416 2122	0.3 1.7 0.3 1.7
3 TH	0254 1012 1520 2236	0.1 1.9 0.2 1.7	**18** F	0226 0936 1437 2144	0.3 1.6 0.3 1.6
4 F	0336 1052 1605 2319	0.3 1.7 0.4 1.6	**19** SA	0251 1000 1505 2214	0.4 1.4 0.4 1.5
5 SA	0430 1138 1706	0.5 1.5 0.6	**20** SU	0324 1035 1541 2300	0.5 1.3 0.5 1.4
6 SU	0012 0552 1239 1836	1.5 0.7 1.3 0.7	**21** M	0412 1133 1643	0.6 1.2 0.6
7 M	0134 0749 1437 2009	1.4 0.7 1.3 0.7	**22** TU	0006 0547 1304 1854	1.4 0.7 1.2 0.7
8 TU	0332 0904 1619 2114	1.5 0.6 1.4 0.6	**23** W	0137 0810 1517 2031	1.4 0.6 1.3 0.6
9 W	0443 0957 1716 2205	1.7 0.5 1.6 0.4	**24** TH	0335 0914 1636 2129	1.6 0.4 1.5 0.4
10 TH	0531 1041 1759 2249	1.9 0.3 1.8 0.3	**25** F	0450 1004 1731 2219	1.8 0.2 1.8 0.2
11 F	0612 1119 1837 2329	2.0 0.2 1.9 0.2	**26** SA	0544 1050 1818 2305	2.0 0.0 2.0 0.0
12 SA ●	0649 1156 1912	2.1 0.1 2.0	**27** SU O	0632 1134 1902 2349	2.2 -0.1 2.2 -0.1
13 SU	0007 0722 1233 1942	0.1 2.1 0.0 2.0	**28** M	0716 1216 1943	2.3 -0.2 2.2
14 M	0044 0752 1307 2010	0.1 2.1 0.0 2.0	**29** TU	0031 0758 1258 2023	-0.1 2.3 -0.2 2.2
15 TU	0117 0820 1336 2035	0.1 2.0 0.1 1.9	**30** W	0114 0839 1339 2103	-0.1 2.2 -0.1 2.1
			31 TH	0155 0918 1420 2142	0.0 2.1 0.0 2.0

APRIL

	Time	m		Time	m
1 F	0237 0958 1501 2221	0.1 1.8 0.2 1.8	**16** SA	0206 0918 1417 2123	0.3 1.6 0.4 1.6
2 SA	0323 1039 1547 2302	0.3 1.6 0.4 1.6	**17** SU	0234 0948 1446 2155	0.4 1.4 0.4 1.6
3 SU	0419 1126 1645 2352	0.5 1.4 0.6 1.5	**18** M	0309 1029 1524 2240	0.4 1.4 0.5 1.5
4 M	0537 1228 1806	0.6 1.3 0.7	**19** TU	0359 1128 1627 2341	0.5 1.3 0.6 1.5
5 TU	0107 0725 1428 1936	1.4 0.7 1.3 0.7	**20** W	0526 1248 1817	0.6 1.3 0.7
6 W	0303 0841 1555 2046	1.4 0.6 1.4 0.6	**21** TH	0059 0728 1439 1956	1.5 0.6 1.4 0.6
7 TH	0413 0932 1648 2139	1.6 0.5 1.6 0.5	**22** F	0246 0841 1600 2059	1.6 0.4 1.6 0.5
8 F	0502 1014 1730 2222	1.8 0.3 1.8 0.4	**23** SA	0412 0935 1659 2151	1.8 0.3 1.8 0.3
9 SA	0543 1051 1808 2302	1.9 0.2 1.9 0.3	**24** SU	0513 1023 1750 2240	2.0 0.1 2.1 0.1
10 SU	0620 1127 1842 2340	2.0 0.1 2.0 0.2	**25** M O	0605 1109 1836 2326	2.2 0.0 2.2 0.0
11 M	0653 1202 1913	2.0 0.1 2.0	**26** TU	0653 1154 1921	2.3 -0.1 2.3
12 TU	0016 0723 1236 1941	0.2 2.0 0.1 2.0	**27** W	0010 0737 1237 2004	0.0 2.3 -0.1 2.3
13 W	0050 0753 1306 2009	0.2 1.9 0.2 1.9	**28** TH	0055 0821 1320 2046	0.0 2.2 0.0 2.2
14 TH	0118 0823 1330 2035	0.2 1.8 0.2 1.8	**29** F	0139 0904 1402 2127	0.1 2.0 0.1 2.0
15 F	0141 0851 1352 2059	0.3 1.7 0.3 1.7	**30** SA	0224 0946 1446 2208	0.2 1.8 0.3 1.8

PORTLAND

50°34'N 2°26'W

Times and heights (in metres) of high and low water 1994
Time: GMT. For BST, ADD ONE HOUR in the shaded area
High Water, full and change, 0711

LOW WATERS - IMPORTANT NOTE
Double low waters occur at Portland. The predictions are for the first low water. The second low water occurs from 3 to 4 hours later and may, at springs, on occasions be lower than the first.

MAY

Day	Time	m	Time	m		Day	Time	m	Time	m
1 SU	0312	0.3	1029	1.6		16 M	0226	0.4	0944	1.5
	1532	0.4	2249	1.7			1443	0.5	2148	1.7
2 M	0406	0.5	1115	1.5		17 TU	0305	0.4	1027	1.5
	1627	0.6	2335	1.5			1525	0.6	2231	1.6
3 TU	0513	0.6	1214	1.3		18 W	0355	0.5	1121	1.4
	1734	0.7					1623	0.6	2325	1.6
4 W	0034	1.4	0630	0.6		19 TH	0504	0.6	1229	1.4
	1346	1.3	1848	0.7			1744	0.7		
5 TH	0207	1.4	0750	0.6		20 F	0033	1.6	0634	0.6
	1512	1.4	1959	0.7			1356	1.5	1912	0.7
6 F	0327	1.5	0849	0.5		21 SA	0158	1.6	0800	0.5
	1609	1.5	2058	0.6			1519	1.6	2024	0.6
7 SA	0422	1.6	0934	0.4		22 SU	0333	1.7	0903	0.4
	1653	1.7	2146	0.5			1626	1.8	2123	0.4
8 SU	0507	1.7	1014	0.4		23 M	0443	1.9	0957	0.3
	1732	1.8	2229	0.4			1722	2.0	2216	0.3
9 M	0546	1.8	1053	0.3		24 TU	0541	2.1	1047	0.2
	1808	1.9	2309	0.4			1813	2.2	2306	0.2
10 TU ●	0622	1.9	1130	0.2		25 W O	0633	2.2	1134	0.1
	1842	2.0	2347	0.3			1901	2.3	2353	0.2
11 W	0657	1.9	1205	0.2		26 TH	0722	2.2	1220	0.1
	1915	2.0					1947	2.3		
12 TH	0022	0.3	0731	1.9		27 F	0040	0.1	0808	2.1
	1238	0.3	1947	2.0			1305	0.1	2031	2.2
13 F	0053	0.3	0805	1.8		28 SA	0127	0.2	0852	2.0
	1308	0.3	2017	1.9			1349	0.2	2114	2.1
14 SA	0123	0.3	0837	1.7		29 SU	0213	0.2	0935	1.9
	1337	0.4	2046	1.8			1433	0.3	2155	1.9
15 SU	0153	0.3	0909	1.6		30 M	0300	0.3	1017	1.7
	1408	0.4	2114	1.7			1518	0.4	2234	1.8
						31 TU	0348	0.4	1058	1.6
							1607	0.6	2313	1.6

JUNE

Day	Time	m	Time	m		Day	Time	m	Time	m
1 W	0441	0.5	1143	1.4		16 TH	0347	0.4	1110	1.6
	1701	0.7	2356	1.5			1613	0.6	2314	1.7
2 TH	0540	0.6	1237	1.4		17 F	0442	0.5	1206	1.6
	1802	0.7					1715	0.6		
3 F	0048	1.4	0642	0.6		18 SA	0011	1.6	0553	0.6
	1346	1.4	1906	0.8			1316	1.6	1831	0.7
4 SA	0156	1.4	0744	0.6		19 SU	0122	1.6	0717	0.6
	1502	1.5	2008	0.7			1438	1.6	1952	0.7
5 SU	0314	1.4	0840	0.6		20 M	0252	1.7	0834	0.5
	1602	1.6	2104	0.7			1554	1.8	2101	0.6
6 M	0418	1.5	0931	0.5		21 TU	0417	1.8	0936	0.4
	1650	1.7	2153	0.6			1659	1.9	2200	0.5
7 TU	0509	1.6	1017	0.5		22 W	0524	1.9	1030	0.3
	1733	1.8	2238	0.5			1756	2.1	2254	0.4
8 W	0553	1.7	1059	0.4		23 TH O	0620	2.0	1120	0.3
	1814	1.9	2319	0.4			1847	2.2	2343	0.3
9 TH ●	0635	1.8	1139	0.3		24 F	0711	2.1	1207	0.2
	1854	2.0	2357	0.3			1934	2.3		
10 F	0715	1.8	1216	0.3		25 SA	0031	0.2	0757	2.1
	1931	2.0					1253	0.2	2018	2.3
11 SA	0033	0.3	0754	1.8		26 SU	0117	0.2	0841	2.0
	1253	0.3	2007	2.0			1336	0.2	2100	2.2
12 SU	0109	0.3	0830	1.8		27 M	0201	0.2	0921	1.9
	1328	0.3	2040	1.9			1419	0.3	2138	2.0
13 M	0144	0.3	0906	1.8		28 TU	0243	0.3	0958	1.8
	1405	0.4	2113	1.8			1500	0.4	2213	1.9
14 TU	0222	0.3	0942	1.7		29 W	0325	0.4	1031	1.7
	1443	0.4	2147	1.8			1541	0.5	2244	1.7
15 W	0302	0.3	1023	1.6		30 TH	0407	0.5	1104	1.5
	1524	0.5	2227	1.7			1623	0.6	2316	1.6

JULY

Day	Time	m	Time	m		Day	Time	m	Time	m
1 F	0449	0.6	1144	1.5		16 SA	0422	0.4	1143	1.6
	1710	0.7	2355	1.4			1649	0.6	2352	1.6
2 SA	0537	0.7	1233	1.4		17 SU	0523	0.5	1242	1.6
	1809	0.8					1801	0.7		
3 SU	0045	1.4	0637	0.7		18 M	0053	1.6	0646	0.6
	1334	1.4	1916	0.8			1401	1.6	1933	0.7
4 M	0152	1.3	0744	0.7		19 TU	0219	1.5	0816	0.6
	1446	1.5	2021	0.8			1530	1.7	2053	0.7
5 TU	0312	1.4	0847	0.7		20 W	0401	1.6	0924	0.5
	1559	1.6	2120	0.7			1645	1.9	2155	0.6
6 W	0430	1.5	0942	0.6		21 TH	0515	1.8	1020	0.4
	1701	1.7	2210	0.6			1745	2.0	2248	0.4
7 TH	0530	1.6	1031	0.5		22 F O	0613	1.9	1109	0.3
	1751	1.8	2256	0.5			1835	2.2	2335	0.3
8 F ●	0619	1.7	1116	0.4		23 SA	0701	2.0	1155	0.2
	1836	2.0	2337	0.3			1920	2.3		
9 SA	0703	1.8	1157	0.3		24 SU	0020	0.2	0744	2.1
	1919	2.0					1238	0.2	2002	2.3
10 SU	0016	0.2	0744	1.9		25 M	0103	0.2	0824	2.1
	1238	0.2	1958	2.1			1319	0.2	2040	2.2
11 M	0055	0.2	0823	1.9		26 TU	0143	0.2	0859	2.0
	1317	0.2	2035	2.0			1359	0.2	2114	2.1
12 TU	0134	0.2	0859	1.9		27 W	0222	0.2	0930	1.9
	1355	0.2	2110	2.0			1436	0.3	2144	1.9
13 W	0213	0.2	0935	1.8		28 TH	0257	0.3	0957	1.7
	1434	0.3	2144	1.9			1510	0.4	2210	1.8
14 TH	0253	0.3	1012	1.8		29 F	0328	0.4	1024	1.6
	1513	0.3	2221	1.8			1538	0.5	2236	1.6
15 F	0334	0.3	1054	1.7		30 SA	0349	0.5	1056	1.5
	1556	0.5	2303	1.7			1558	0.6	2305	1.4
						31 SU	0409	0.6	1134	1.4
							1629	0.7	2337	1.3

AUGUST

Day	Time	m	Time	m		Day	Time	m	Time	m
1 M	0444	0.7	1226	1.4		16 TU	0033	1.5	0627	0.7
	1726	0.8					1334	1.5	1932	0.8
2 TU	0031	1.3	0550	0.8		17 W	0205	1.4	0807	0.7
	1341	1.4	1940	0.8			1516	1.6	2051	0.7
3 W	0210	1.2	0805	0.7		18 TH	0359	1.5	0914	0.6
	1508	1.4	2051	0.7			1635	1.8	2149	0.6
4 TH	0353	1.3	0913	0.6		19 F	0511	1.7	1008	0.5
	1629	1.6	2147	0.6			1732	2.0	2238	0.4
5 F	0508	1.5	1007	0.5		20 SA	0601	1.9	1054	0.4
	1729	1.8	2234	0.4			1818	2.2	2321	0.3
6 SA	0601	1.7	1053	0.3		21 SU O	0644	2.0	1137	0.3
	1817	2.0	2317	0.3			1900	2.3		
7 SU ●	0646	1.9	1137	0.2		22 M	0002	0.2	0723	2.1
	1901	2.1	2358	0.1			1218	0.2	1938	2.3
8 M	0728	2.0	1218	0.1		23 TU	0041	0.1	0758	2.1
	1943	2.2					1257	0.2	2013	2.2
9 TU	0038	0.1	0807	2.1		24 W	0118	0.1	0830	2.0
	1258	0.0	2021	2.2			1334	0.2	2043	2.1
10 W	0118	0.0	0844	2.1		25 TH	0154	0.2	0856	1.9
	1338	0.1	2057	2.2			1408	0.3	2109	2.0
11 TH	0158	0.0	0920	2.0		26 F	0224	0.3	0919	1.8
	1417	0.1	2133	2.0			1436	0.4	2133	1.8
12 F	0237	0.1	0957	1.9		27 SA	0246	0.4	0943	1.7
	1456	0.2	2209	1.9			1454	0.5	2157	1.6
13 SA	0318	0.3	1036	1.8		28 SU	0301	0.5	1009	1.6
	1538	0.4	2249	1.8			1513	0.6	2219	1.5
14 SU	0403	0.4	1121	1.7		29 M	0323	0.5	1038	1.5
	1628	0.6	2335	1.6			1543	0.7	2245	1.3
15 M	0500	0.6	1216	1.6		30 TU	0356	0.6	1121	1.4
	1743	0.7					1629	0.8	2334	1.3
						31 W	0450	0.7	1228	1.4
							1829	0.8		

PORTLAND
50°34′N 2°26′W

Times and heights (in metres) of high and low water 1994
Time: GMT. For BST, ADD ONE HOUR in the shaded area
High Water, full and change, 0711

SEPTEMBER

Day	Time	m	Day	Time	m
1 TH	0107 / 0722 / 1414 / 2027	1.2 / 0.8 / 1.4 / 0.7	**16** F	0356 / 0859 / 1617 / 2134	1.5 / 0.7 / 1.8 / 0.5
2 F	0321 / 0846 / 1552 / 2123	1.3 / 0.7 / 1.6 / 0.6	**17** SA	0455 / 0950 / 1710 / 2218	1.7 / 0.6 / 1.9 / 0.4
3 SA	0442 / 0941 / 1700 / 2210	1.5 / 0.5 / 1.8 / 0.4	**18** SU	0539 / 1034 / 1753 / 2257	1.9 / 0.4 / 2.1 / 0.3
4 SU	0536 / 1028 / 1751 / 2253	1.8 / 0.3 / 2.0 / 0.2	**19** M	0618 / 1114 / 1832 / O 2335	2.0 / 0.3 / 2.2 / 0.2
5 M	0621 / 1112 / 1837 / ● 2335	2.0 / 0.2 / 2.2 / 0.1	**20** TU	0654 / 1152 / 1908	2.1 / 0.2 / 2.2
6 TU	0703 / 1154 / 1919	2.1 / 0.0 / 2.3	**21** W	0011 / 0726 / 1230 / 1940	0.1 / 2.1 / 0.2 / 2.2
7 W	0016 / 0743 / 1236 / 1959	0.0 / 2.2 / 0.0 / 2.3	**22** TH	0047 / 0754 / 1305 / 2008	0.1 / 2.1 / 0.2 / 2.1
8 TH	0057 / 0822 / 1316 / 2038	-0.1 / 2.2 / 0.0 / 2.2	**23** F	0120 / 0818 / 1337 / 2033	0.2 / 2.0 / 0.3 / 1.9
9 F	0137 / 0859 / 1356 / 2116	0.0 / 2.1 / 0.1 / 2.1	**24** SA	0148 / 0842 / 1403 / 2059	0.3 / 1.9 / 0.4 / 1.8
10 SA	0217 / 0937 / 1437 / 2154	0.1 / 2.0 / 0.2 / 1.9	**25** SU	0207 / 0906 / 1421 / 2124	0.4 / 1.8 / 0.5 / 1.6
11 SU	0258 / 1016 / 1521 / 2234	0.3 / 1.8 / 0.4 / 1.7	**26** M	0225 / 0930 / 1442 / 2148	0.5 / 1.7 / 0.5 / 1.5
12 M	0343 / 1100 / 1614 / 2321	0.5 / 1.7 / 0.6 / 1.6	**27** TU	0248 / 0957 / 1512 / 2221	0.6 / 1.6 / 0.6 / 1.4
13 TU	0441 / 1154 / 1737	0.6 / 1.6 / 0.7	**28** W	0319 / 1038 / 1557 / 2314	0.7 / 1.5 / 0.7 / 1.3
14 W	0023 / 0611 / 1314 / 1931	1.4 / 0.8 / 1.5 / 0.7	**29** TH	0411 / 1140 / 1727	0.8 / 1.4 / 0.8
15 TH	0215 / 0753 / 1503 / 2041	1.4 / 0.8 / 1.6 / 0.7	**30** F	0041 / 0621 / 1310 / 1955	1.3 / 0.9 / 1.4 / 0.7

OCTOBER

Day	Time	m	Day	Time	m
1 SA	0250 / 0815 / 1507 / 2053	1.4 / 0.8 / 1.6 / 0.5	**16** SU	0427 / 0924 / 1638 / 2147	1.7 / 0.7 / 1.8 / 0.4
2 SU	0409 / 0912 / 1623 / 2140	1.6 / 0.6 / 1.8 / 0.4	**17** M	0508 / 1007 / 1721 / 2225	1.9 / 0.5 / 2.0 / 0.3
3 M	0504 / 1000 / 1719 / 2224	1.8 / 0.4 / 2.0 / 0.2	**18** TU	0546 / 1045 / 1759 / 2301	2.0 / 0.4 / 2.1 / 0.2
4 TU	0551 / 1045 / 1807 / 2307	2.1 / 0.2 / 2.2 / 0.0	**19** W	0620 / 1123 / 1834 / O 2337	2.1 / 0.4 / 2.1 / 0.2
5 W	0634 / 1128 / 1852 / ● 2349	2.2 / 0.1 / 2.3 / 0.0	**20** TH	0650 / 1200 / 1905	2.2 / 0.3 / 2.1
6 TH	0716 / 1210 / 1935	2.3 / 0.0 / 2.3	**21** F	0012 / 0717 / 1236 / 1934	0.2 / 2.1 / 0.3 / 2.0
7 F	0031 / 0756 / 1253 / 2016	0.0 / 2.3 / 0.0 / 2.3	**22** SA	0045 / 0744 / 1308 / 2003	0.3 / 2.1 / 0.4 / 1.9
8 SA	0113 / 0836 / 1335 / 2056	0.0 / 2.2 / 0.1 / 2.1	**23** SU	0113 / 0811 / 1333 / 2032	0.4 / 2.0 / 0.4 / 1.8
9 SU	0155 / 0916 / 1418 / 2138	0.2 / 2.1 / 0.2 / 1.9	**24** M	0136 / 0837 / 1355 / 2100	0.5 / 1.9 / 0.5 / 1.6
10 M	0237 / 0956 / 1506 / 2221	0.3 / 1.9 / 0.4 / 1.7	**25** TU	0158 / 0902 / 1420 / 2130	0.6 / 1.8 / 0.5 / 1.5
11 TU	0324 / 1039 / 1603 / 2311	0.5 / 1.8 / 0.6 / 1.5	**26** W	0224 / 0932 / 1452 / 2210	0.6 / 1.7 / 0.6 / 1.4
12 W	0422 / 1132 / 1723	0.7 / 1.6 / 0.7	**27** TH	0256 / 1012 / 1538 / 2305	0.7 / 1.6 / 0.6 / 1.4
13 TH	0019 / 0544 / 1249 / 1906	1.4 / 0.8 / 1.5 / 0.7	**28** F	0349 / 1110 / 1656	0.8 / 1.5 / 0.7
14 F	0212 / 0723 / 1436 / 2015	1.4 / 0.9 / 1.6 / 0.6	**29** SA	0022 / 0534 / 1226 / 1901	1.4 / 0.9 / 1.5 / 0.7
15 SA	0333 / 0833 / 1547 / 2105	1.5 / 0.8 / 1.7 / 0.5	**30** SU	0210 / 0732 / 1409 / 2012	1.5 / 0.8 / 1.6 / 0.6
			31 M	0330 / 0837 / 1541 / 2105	1.7 / 0.7 / 1.8 / 0.4

NOVEMBER

Day	Time	m	Day	Time	m
1 TU	0429 / 0928 / 1644 / 2152	1.9 / 0.5 / 2.0 / 0.2	**16** W	0510 / 1012 / 1724 / 2224	1.9 / 0.6 / 1.9 / 0.4
2 W	0519 / 1016 / 1737 / 2238	2.1 / 0.3 / 2.2 / 0.1	**17** TH	0544 / 1052 / 1800 / 2303	2.1 / 0.5 / 1.9 / 0.3
3 TH	0606 / 1101 / 1825 / ● 2322	2.3 / 0.2 / 2.3 / 0.1	**18** F	0616 / 1131 / 1834 / O 2340	2.1 / 0.4 / 1.9 / 0.3
4 F	0650 / 1146 / 1911	2.4 / 0.1 / 2.3	**19** SA	0647 / 1208 / 1908	2.1 / 0.4 / 1.9
5 SA	0006 / 0733 / 1231 / 1955	0.1 / 2.4 / 0.1 / 2.2	**20** SU	0015 / 0719 / 1242 / 1941	0.3 / 2.1 / 0.4 / 1.9
6 SU	0050 / 0815 / 1316 / 2039	0.1 / 2.3 / 0.2 / 2.1	**21** M	0047 / 0750 / 1311 / 2014	0.4 / 2.0 / 0.4 / 1.8
7 M	0134 / 0857 / 1403 / 2123	0.2 / 2.2 / 0.3 / 1.9	**22** TU	0116 / 0820 / 1339 / 2047	0.5 / 1.9 / 0.4 / 1.7
8 TU	0218 / 0938 / 1452 / 2208	0.4 / 2.0 / 0.4 / 1.7	**23** W	0145 / 0849 / 1409 / 2121	0.5 / 1.8 / 0.5 / 1.6
9 W	0306 / 1021 / 1548 / 2258	0.5 / 1.8 / 0.5 / 1.6	**24** TH	0216 / 0921 / 1443 / 2202	0.6 / 1.8 / 0.5 / 1.5
10 TH	0401 / 1109 / 1654	0.7 / 1.7 / 0.6	**25** F	0253 / 1001 / 1527 / 2252	0.7 / 1.7 / 0.5 / 1.5
11 F	0000 / 0508 / 1209 / 1810	1.5 / 0.8 / 1.6 / 0.7	**26** SA	0342 / 1051 / 1629 / 2356	0.8 / 1.6 / 0.6 / 1.5
12 SA	0131 / 0626 / 1338 / 1923	1.4 / 0.9 / 1.5 / 0.6	**27** SU	0457 / 1154 / 1752	0.8 / 1.6 / 0.6
13 SU	0251 / 0743 / 1500 / 2020	1.5 / 0.9 / 1.6 / 0.6	**28** M	0117 / 0629 / 1313 / 1919	1.5 / 0.8 / 1.6 / 0.6
14 M	0347 / 0844 / 1558 / 2105	1.7 / 0.8 / 1.7 / 0.5	**29** TU	0243 / 0752 / 1450 / 2026	1.7 / 0.7 / 1.7 / 0.5
15 TU	0431 / 0931 / 1644 / 2145	1.8 / 0.7 / 1.8 / 0.4	**30** W	0352 / 0855 / 1608 / 2121	1.9 / 0.6 / 1.9 / 0.4

DECEMBER

Day	Time	m	Day	Time	m
1 TH	0449 / 0949 / 1709 / 2212	2.1 / 0.5 / 2.0 / 0.3	**16** F	0510 / 1022 / 1731 / 2233	1.9 / 0.6 / 1.7 / 0.4
2 F	0541 / 1039 / 1803 / ● 2300	2.2 / 0.3 / 2.1 / 0.2	**17** SA	0549 / 1105 / 1812 / 2314	2.0 / 0.5 / 1.8 / 0.4
3 SA	0629 / 1128 / 1853 / 2347	2.3 / 0.2 / 2.2 / 0.1	**18** SU	0627 / 1144 / 1852 / O 2353	2.1 / 0.4 / 1.9 / 0.3
4 SU	0716 / 1215 / 1940	2.4 / 0.2 / 2.2	**19** M	0704 / 1220 / 1930	2.1 / 0.4 / 1.9
5 M	0032 / 0800 / 1303 / 2025	0.2 / 2.3 / 0.2 / 2.1	**20** TU	0030 / 0740 / 1254 / 2006	0.3 / 2.1 / 0.3 / 1.8
6 TU	0118 / 0843 / 1350 / 2109	0.2 / 2.2 / 0.2 / 2.0	**21** W	0105 / 0814 / 1327 / 2041	0.4 / 2.0 / 0.3 / 1.8
7 W	0203 / 0925 / 1438 / 2153	0.3 / 2.1 / 0.3 / 1.8	**22** TH	0139 / 0846 / 1401 / 2115	0.4 / 1.9 / 0.3 / 1.7
8 TH	0249 / 1005 / 1527 / 2236	0.5 / 1.9 / 0.4 / 1.7	**23** F	0214 / 0919 / 1437 / 2152	0.5 / 1.9 / 0.4 / 1.7
9 F	0337 / 1045 / 1620 / 2321	0.6 / 1.8 / 0.5 / 1.5	**24** SA	0250 / 0956 / 1516 / 2235	0.5 / 1.8 / 0.4 / 1.6
10 SA	0431 / 1128 / 1718	0.7 / 1.6 / 0.6	**25** SU	0332 / 1039 / 1605 / 2327	0.6 / 1.7 / 0.5 / 1.6
11 SU	0014 / 0532 / 1220 / 1818	1.5 / 0.8 / 1.5 / 0.6	**26** M	0425 / 1131 / 1708	0.7 / 1.7 / 0.5
12 M	0122 / 0639 / 1325 / 1918	1.5 / 0.9 / 1.5 / 0.6	**27** TU	0029 / 0537 / 1235 / 1827	1.6 / 0.8 / 1.6 / 0.6
13 TU	0239 / 0745 / 1444 / 2013	1.5 / 0.8 / 1.5 / 0.6	**28** W	0147 / 0704 / 1355 / 1950	1.6 / 0.8 / 1.6 / 0.6
14 W	0340 / 0844 / 1553 / 2104	1.6 / 0.8 / 1.5 / 0.6	**29** TH	0312 / 0825 / 1532 / 2057	1.7 / 0.7 / 1.7 / 0.5
15 TH	0428 / 0936 / 1645 / 2150	1.8 / 0.7 / 1.6 / 0.5	**30** F	0423 / 0930 / 1648 / 2154	1.9 / 0.6 / 1.8 / 0.4
			31 SA	0523 / 1026 / 1748 / 2246	2.1 / 0.4 / 2.0 / 0.3

SALCOMBE

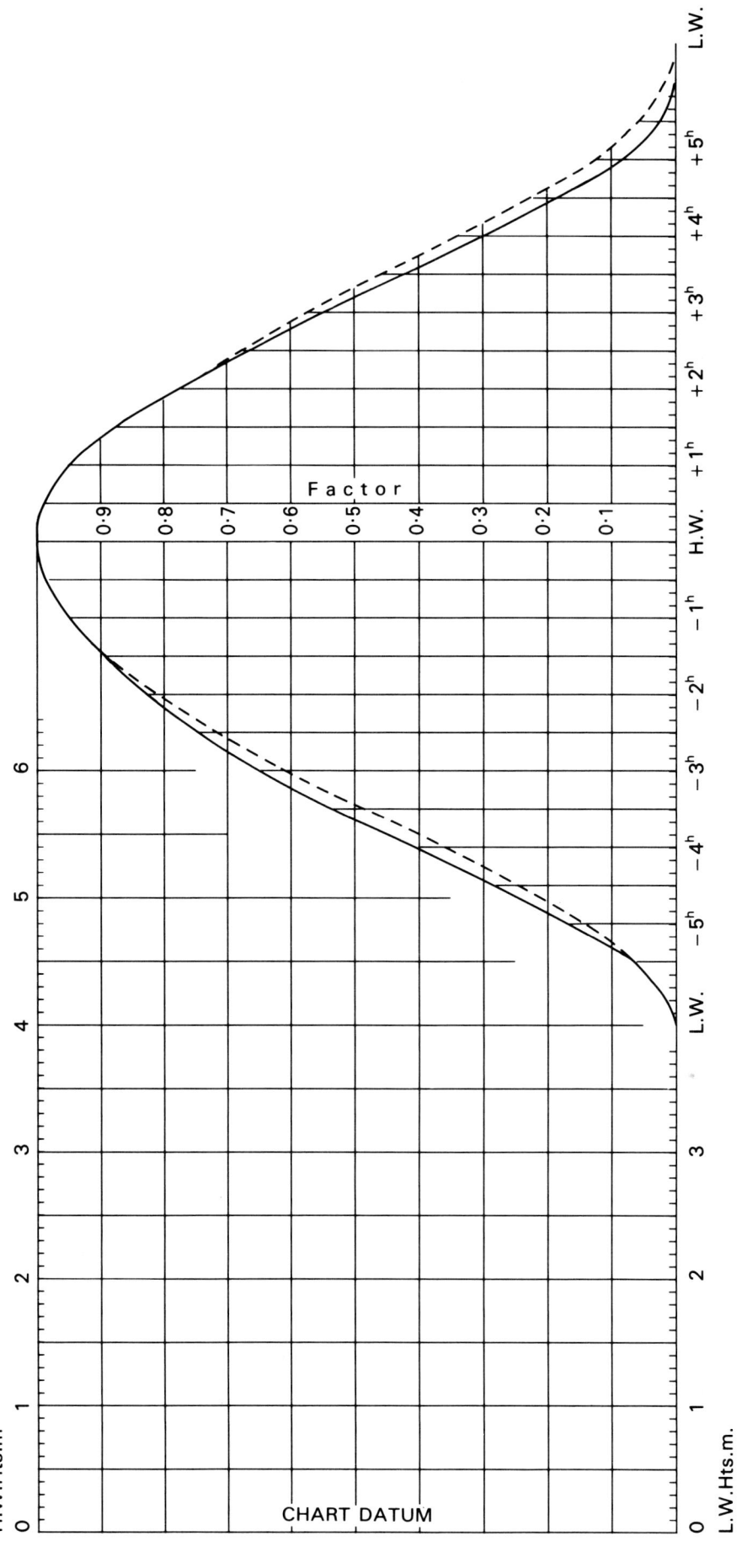

H.W.Hts.m

Factor

CHART DATUM

L.W.Hts.m.

SALCOMBE

50°13′N 3°47′W

Times and heights (in metres) of high and low water 1994
Time: GMT. For BST, ADD ONE HOUR in the shaded area

JANUARY

Day	Time	m	Time	m	Time	m	Time	m
1 SA	0143	0.9	0759	5.2	1408	0.8	2025	5.0
16 SU	0225	0.9	0824	5.1	1444	0.9	2041	4.8
2 SU	0220	0.9	0838	5.2	1446	0.9	2104	4.9
17 M	0253	1.1	0850	5.0	1511	1.2	2110	4.6
3 M	0258	1.0	0919	5.1	1523	1.0	2145	4.8
18 TU	0319	1.4	0921	4.8	1539	1.5	2143	4.4
4 TU	0339	1.2	1001	4.9	1606	1.2	2230	4.5
19 W	0347	1.7	0955	4.5	1609	1.8	2221	4.2
5 W	0426	1.4	1051	4.6	1658	1.5	2325	4.4
20 TH	0421	2.0	1037	4.2	1653	2.0	2311	4.1
6 TH	0526	1.7	1153	4.4	1809	1.7		
21 F	0522	2.2	1131	4.0	1804	2.2		
7 F	0035	4.3	0650	1.8	1309	4.3	1939	1.8
22 SA	0016	4.0	0644	2.3	1247	3.9	1920	2.2
8 SA	0156	4.4	0819	1.7	1431	4.4	2058	1.6
23 SU	0148	4.1	0759	2.1	1428	4.1	2030	1.9
9 SU	0311	4.6	0933	1.5	1543	4.6	2204	1.3
24 M	0308	4.3	0906	1.8	1539	4.3	2133	1.6
10 M	0415	4.9	1035	1.2	1644	4.8	2300	1.1
25 TU	0405	4.6	1007	1.5	1632	4.6	2229	1.3
11 TU ●	0509	5.1	1128	0.9	1736	5.0	2351	0.9
26 W	0454	5.0	1100	1.1	1719	4.9	2321	1.0
12 W	0558	5.3	1217	0.7	1824	5.1		
27 TH O	0539	5.2	1150	0.8	1806	5.0		
13 TH	0037	0.7	0640	5.3	1302	0.6	1906	5.1
28 F	0009	0.8	0623	5.3	1237	0.6	1849	5.1
14 F	0119	0.7	0721	5.3	1340	0.6	1944	5.0
29 SA	0054	0.6	0706	5.4	1320	0.5	1931	5.2
15 SA	0153	0.8	0755	5.3	1414	0.7	2015	4.9
30 SU	0134	0.5	0748	5.4	1357	0.4	2012	5.2
31 M	0211	0.5	0828	5.4	1433	0.5	2050	5.1

FEBRUARY

Day	Time	m	Time	m	Time	m	Time	m
1 TU	0247	0.6	0906	5.3	1509	0.7	2128	5.0
16 W	0247	1.2	0853	4.8	1501	1.3	2111	4.6
2 W	0323	0.8	0946	5.0	1546	1.0	2209	4.8
17 TH	0308	1.4	0923	4.5	1520	1.5	2144	4.4
3 TH	0405	1.2	1031	4.6	1631	1.4	2259	4.4
18 F	0329	1.7	0958	4.2	1547	1.8	2224	4.1
4 F	0457	1.6	1129	4.3	1732	1.8		
19 SA	0407	2.0	1046	4.0	1641	2.1	2321	4.0
5 SA	0007	4.2	0612	1.9	1248	4.1	1909	2.0
20 SU	0546	2.3	1152	3.8	1835	2.2		
6 SU	0131	4.2	0801	1.9	1415	4.1	2044	1.8
21 M	0040	3.9	0719	2.2	1335	3.9	1954	2.1
7 M	0253	4.4	0923	1.6	1533	4.3	2153	1.5
22 TU	0226	4.1	0834	1.9	1511	4.2	2103	1.7
8 TU	0400	4.6	1024	1.3	1634	4.6	2248	1.2
23 W	0336	4.5	0939	1.4	1609	4.5	2206	1.3
9 W	0453	5.0	1114	0.9	1721	4.9	2336	0.9
24 TH	0429	4.9	1037	1.0	1658	4.9	2300	0.9
10 TH ●	0538	5.2	1201	0.7	1804	5.0		
25 F	0515	5.2	1129	0.6	1744	5.1	2350	0.6
11 F	0019	0.7	0619	5.3	1243	0.5	1841	5.0
26 SA O	0602	5.4	1216	0.4	1829	5.2		
12 SA	0059	0.6	0656	5.3	1320	0.5	1915	5.0
27 SU	0036	0.3	0646	5.5	1301	0.2	1911	5.3
13 SU	0132	0.6	0728	5.2	1349	0.6	1944	5.0
28 M	0118	0.2	0729	5.5	1340	0.2	1952	5.4
14 M	0200	0.7	0756	5.1	1417	0.8	2012	4.9
15 TU	0225	0.9	0824	5.0	1440	1.0	2040	4.8

MARCH

Day	Time	m	Time	m	Time	m	Time	m
1 TU	0155	0.2	0811	5.5	1417	0.3	2032	5.3
16 W	0157	0.9	0758	5.0	1409	1.0	2013	4.9
2 W	0231	0.4	0851	5.3	1452	0.5	2110	5.1
17 TH	0218	1.1	0828	4.8	1428	1.2	2042	4.6
3 TH	0308	0.7	0930	5.0	1529	0.9	2150	4.9
18 F	0237	1.3	0857	4.5	1447	1.4	2113	4.4
4 F	0348	1.1	1014	4.6	1611	1.4	2236	4.4
19 SA	0259	1.6	0930	4.2	1514	1.7	2150	4.2
5 SA	0438	1.6	1111	4.2	1708	1.9	2344	4.2
20 SU	0335	1.8	1016	4.0	1558	2.0	2243	4.0
6 SU	0548	2.0	1233	3.9	1845	2.1		
21 M	0442	2.1	1119	3.8	1747	2.2	2354	4.0
7 M	0111	4.1	0746	2.0	1403	4.0	2030	2.0
22 TU	0643	2.1	1243	3.8	1920	2.1		
8 TU	0234	4.3	0908	1.7	1520	4.2	2136	1.6
23 W	0128	4.1	0801	1.8	1434	4.1	2033	1.7
9 W	0340	4.5	1006	1.3	1616	4.5	2228	1.2
24 TH	0257	4.4	0908	1.4	1539	4.5	2137	1.3
10 TH	0432	4.9	1054	0.9	1700	4.8	2313	0.9
25 F	0357	4.9	1009	0.9	1630	4.9	2234	0.8
11 F	0514	5.1	1137	0.7	1738	5.0	2356	0.7
26 SA	0447	5.2	1102	0.6	1717	5.1	2325	0.5
12 SA ●	0553	5.2	1217	0.6	1813	5.1		
27 SU O	0536	5.4	1152	0.3	1804	5.3		
13 SU	0032	0.6	0628	5.2	1253	0.6	1844	5.1
28 M	0012	0.2	0623	5.5	1238	0.1	1847	5.4
14 M	0106	0.6	0659	5.2	1322	0.6	1915	5.1
29 TU	0058	0.1	0709	5.6	1320	0.1	1931	5.5
15 TU	0133	0.7	0729	5.1	1347	0.8	1944	5.0
30 W	0138	0.1	0753	5.5	1359	0.3	2012	5.4
31 TH	0217	0.3	0836	5.3	1437	0.6	2052	5.2

APRIL

Day	Time	m	Time	m	Time	m	Time	m
1 F	0255	0.6	0918	5.0	1516	1.0	2132	4.9
16 SA	0217	1.3	0837	4.4	1426	1.4	2049	4.5
2 SA	0337	1.1	1001	4.5	1558	1.4	2218	4.5
17 SU	0244	1.5	0912	4.3	1457	1.6	2127	4.4
3 SU	0425	1.5	1058	4.2	1652	1.9	2323	4.2
18 M	0321	1.7	0957	4.1	1544	1.9	2219	4.2
4 M	0532	1.9	1220	3.9	1816	2.1		
19 TU	0424	1.9	1057	3.9	1706	2.1	2323	4.1
5 TU	0049	4.1	0717	2.0	1341	4.0	1959	2.0
20 W	0606	1.9	1210	3.9	1843	2.0		
6 W	0207	4.2	0839	1.7	1452	4.2	2107	1.7
21 TH	0040	4.2	0725	1.7	1340	4.1	1958	1.7
7 TH	0311	4.4	0937	1.4	1546	4.4	2200	1.3
22 F	0207	4.4	0834	1.3	1458	4.4	2104	1.3
8 F	0402	4.8	1024	1.1	1630	4.8	2245	1.0
23 SA	0317	4.8	0936	0.9	1556	4.9	2204	0.9
9 SA	0444	5.0	1107	0.8	1707	4.9	2326	0.8
24 SU	0415	5.1	1033	0.6	1647	5.1	2258	0.5
10 SU	0522	5.1	1145	0.7	1741	5.0		
25 M O	0508	5.3	1125	0.4	1737	5.3	2349	0.3
11 M ●	0003	0.7	0558	5.1	1220	0.7	1815	5.1
26 TU	0600	5.4	1214	0.2	1825	5.5		
12 TU	0036	0.8	0631	5.1	1251	0.8	1846	5.1
27 W	0037	0.2	0649	5.4	1301	0.2	1911	5.5
13 W	0105	0.8	0704	5.0	1317	0.9	1919	5.0
28 TH	0122	0.2	0736	5.4	1344	0.4	1955	5.4
14 TH	0130	1.0	0736	4.9	1341	1.0	1950	4.9
29 F	0205	0.4	0822	5.2	1425	0.6	2037	5.3
15 F	0153	1.1	0807	4.6	1403	1.2	2019	4.8
30 SA	0246	0.6	0906	4.9	1506	1.0	2120	5.0

SALCOMBE

50°13′N 3°47′W

Times and heights (in metres) of high and low water 1994
Time: GMT. For BST, ADD ONE HOUR in the shaded area

MAY

Day	Time	m		Day	Time	m
1 SU	0328 / 0950 / 1548 / 2202	1.0 / 4.5 / 1.4 / 4.6		**16** M	0240 / 0902 / 1454 / 2115	1.3 / 4.3 / 1.5 / 4.5
2 M	0414 / 1044 / 1637 / 2259	1.4 / 4.2 / 1.7 / 4.3		**17** TU	0320 / 0945 / 1540 / 2201	1.4 / 4.2 / 1.6 / 4.4
3 TU	0512 / 1154 / 1741	1.7 / 4.0 / 2.0		**18** W	0414 / 1038 / 1642 / 2259	1.6 / 4.1 / 1.8 / 4.3
4 W	0016 / 0628 / 1306 / 1906	4.2 / 1.9 / 4.0 / 2.0		**19** TH	0529 / 1142 / 1801	1.6 / 4.1 / 1.8
5 TH	0129 / 0752 / 1411 / 2022	4.2 / 1.8 / 4.1 / 1.8		**20** F	0006 / 0646 / 1255 / 1919	4.3 / 1.5 / 4.2 / 1.6
6 F	0232 / 0855 / 1506 / 2121	4.3 / 1.6 / 4.3 / 1.6		**21** SA	0123 / 0758 / 1412 / 2030	4.4 / 1.3 / 4.4 / 1.3
7 SA	0325 / 0947 / 1553 / 2209	4.5 / 1.3 / 4.5 / 1.3		**22** SU	0239 / 0903 / 1521 / 2134	4.6 / 1.1 / 4.8 / 1.0
8 SU	0410 / 1030 / 1633 / 2251	4.6 / 1.1 / 4.8 / 1.1		**23** M	0345 / 1005 / 1619 / 2233	5.0 / 0.8 / 5.0 / 0.7
9 M	0449 / 1109 / 1709 / 2329	4.9 / 1.0 / 5.0 / 1.0		**24** TU	0444 / 1100 / 1713 / 2327	5.1 / 0.6 / 5.3 / 0.5
10 TU ●	0527 / 1145 / 1745	4.9 / 1.0 / 5.0		**25** W O	0539 / 1154 / 1805	5.2 / 0.5 / 5.4
11 W	0004 / 0605 / 1218 / 1822	1.0 / 4.9 / 1.0 / 5.0		**26** TH	0019 / 0632 / 1244 / 1853	0.4 / 5.3 / 0.4 / 5.4
12 TH	0037 / 0641 / 1249 / 1858	1.0 / 4.9 / 1.0 / 5.0		**27** F	0109 / 0722 / 1331 / 1941	0.3 / 5.2 / 0.5 / 5.3
13 F	0107 / 0718 / 1319 / 1931	1.0 / 4.8 / 1.1 / 4.9		**28** SA	0153 / 0810 / 1414 / 2025	0.4 / 5.1 / 0.6 / 5.3
14 SA	0137 / 0753 / 1348 / 2003	1.1 / 4.6 / 1.2 / 4.8		**29** SU	0236 / 0854 / 1454 / 2106	0.6 / 4.9 / 0.9 / 5.1
15 SU	0207 / 0826 / 1418 / 2036	1.2 / 4.5 / 1.3 / 4.6		**30** M	0317 / 0937 / 1534 / 2144	0.9 / 4.6 / 1.2 / 4.8
				31 TU	0358 / 1020 / 1615 / 2224	1.2 / 4.3 / 1.5 / 4.5

JUNE

Day	Time	m		Day	Time	m
1 W	0443 / 1110 / 1703 / 2316	1.5 / 4.1 / 1.8 / 4.2		**16** TH	0400 / 1022 / 1620 / 2237	1.2 / 4.3 / 1.4 / 4.5
2 TH	0536 / 1213 / 1801	1.8 / 4.0 / 2.0		**17** F	0455 / 1117 / 1723 / 2337	1.4 / 4.3 / 1.5 / 4.4
3 F	0031 / 0641 / 1318 / 1913	4.1 / 1.9 / 4.0 / 2.0		**18** SA	0605 / 1222 / 1840	1.5 / 4.3 / 1.6
4 SA	0140 / 0752 / 1418 / 2023	4.1 / 1.8 / 4.2 / 1.9		**19** SU	0048 / 0723 / 1336 / 1957	4.4 / 1.4 / 4.4 / 1.4
5 SU	0239 / 0853 / 1509 / 2122	4.2 / 1.6 / 4.3 / 1.6		**20** M	0208 / 0835 / 1451 / 2108	4.5 / 1.3 / 4.6 / 1.2
6 M	0331 / 0944 / 1556 / 2210	4.4 / 1.5 / 4.5 / 1.4		**21** TU	0322 / 0941 / 1556 / 2213	4.6 / 1.0 / 4.9 / 1.0
7 TU	0416 / 1028 / 1638 / 2253	4.5 / 1.3 / 4.8 / 1.3		**22** W	0426 / 1042 / 1654 / 2311	4.9 / 0.8 / 5.1 / 0.7
8 W	0459 / 1108 / 1719 / 2333	4.6 / 1.2 / 4.9 / 1.1		**23** TH O	0522 / 1138 / 1747	5.0 / 0.7 / 5.3
9 TH ●	0541 / 1146 / 1801	4.8 / 1.1 / 5.0		**24** F	0006 / 0616 / 1230 / 1838	0.5 / 5.1 / 0.5 / 5.4
10 F	0011 / 0622 / 1225 / 1840	1.1 / 4.8 / 1.1 / 5.0		**25** SA	0057 / 0707 / 1319 / 1925	0.4 / 5.1 / 0.5 / 5.4
11 SA	0049 / 0703 / 1303 / 1918	1.0 / 4.8 / 1.1 / 5.0		**26** SU	0142 / 0754 / 1400 / 2009	0.4 / 5.0 / 0.6 / 5.3
12 SU	0125 / 0742 / 1338 / 1954	1.0 / 4.6 / 1.1 / 4.9		**27** M	0222 / 0837 / 1438 / 2047	0.5 / 4.9 / 0.7 / 5.1
13 M	0200 / 0820 / 1414 / 2029	1.0 / 4.5 / 1.1 / 4.9		**28** TU	0259 / 0913 / 1514 / 2118	0.7 / 4.8 / 1.0 / 4.9
14 TU	0237 / 0856 / 1450 / 2106	1.1 / 4.5 / 1.2 / 4.8		**29** W	0334 / 0943 / 1548 / 2146	1.0 / 4.5 / 1.3 / 4.6
15 W	0315 / 0936 / 1532 / 2148	1.1 / 4.4 / 1.3 / 4.6		**30** TH	0410 / 1014 / 1625 / 2219	1.3 / 4.3 / 1.6 / 4.4

JULY

Day	Time	m		Day	Time	m
1 F	0449 / 1055 / 1710 / 2304	1.6 / 4.1 / 1.9 / 4.2		**16** SA	0427 / 1053 / 1652 / 2313	1.2 / 4.4 / 1.4 / 4.4
2 SA	0539 / 1151 / 1806	1.9 / 4.0 / 2.0		**17** SU	0528 / 1154 / 1802	1.5 / 4.3 / 1.6
3 SU	0007 / 0640 / 1307 / 1914	4.0 / 2.0 / 4.0 / 2.1		**18** M	0023 / 0650 / 1309 / 1931	4.3 / 1.6 / 4.3 / 1.6
4 M	0139 / 0747 / 1421 / 2022	4.0 / 1.9 / 4.1 / 1.9		**19** TU	0148 / 0814 / 1429 / 2052	4.3 / 1.5 / 4.4 / 1.5
5 TU	0252 / 0850 / 1520 / 2125	4.1 / 1.7 / 4.4 / 1.7		**20** W	0307 / 0927 / 1539 / 2202	4.4 / 1.3 / 4.8 / 1.2
6 W	0347 / 0946 / 1610 / 2217	4.3 / 1.5 / 4.6 / 1.4		**21** TH	0413 / 1030 / 1639 / 2301	4.6 / 1.0 / 5.0 / 0.8
7 TH	0435 / 1036 / 1656 / 2305	4.5 / 1.3 / 4.9 / 1.2		**22** F O	0510 / 1126 / 1732 / 2355	4.9 / 0.8 / 5.2 / 0.6
8 F ●	0520 / 1122 / 1740 / 2350	4.6 / 1.1 / 5.0 / 1.0		**23** SA	0602 / 1216 / 1821	5.0 / 0.6 / 5.3
9 SA	0605 / 1206 / 1823	4.8 / 1.0 / 5.0		**24** SU	0043 / 0648 / 1302 / 1906	0.4 / 5.0 / 0.5 / 5.3
10 SU	0033 / 0647 / 1249 / 1904	0.9 / 4.8 / 0.9 / 5.1		**25** M	0125 / 0731 / 1342 / 1946	0.4 / 5.0 / 0.5 / 5.3
11 M	0115 / 0729 / 1328 / 1943	0.8 / 4.8 / 0.8 / 5.1		**26** TU	0202 / 0809 / 1417 / 2020	0.4 / 5.0 / 0.6 / 5.2
12 TU	0151 / 0808 / 1405 / 2020	0.7 / 4.8 / 0.8 / 5.1		**27** W	0235 / 0838 / 1447 / 2045	0.6 / 4.8 / 0.8 / 5.0
13 W	0227 / 0845 / 1441 / 2056	0.7 / 4.8 / 0.8 / 5.0		**28** TH	0305 / 0904 / 1516 / 2111	0.9 / 4.6 / 1.1 / 4.8
14 TH	0302 / 0922 / 1517 / 2135	0.8 / 4.6 / 1.0 / 4.9		**29** F	0333 / 0932 / 1545 / 2141	1.2 / 4.4 / 1.5 / 4.5
15 F	0342 / 1003 / 1600 / 2219	1.0 / 4.5 / 1.2 / 4.6		**30** SA	0404 / 1007 / 1620 / 2217	1.6 / 4.2 / 1.8 / 4.2
				31 SU	0444 / 1052 / 1712 / 2306	1.9 / 4.1 / 2.1 / 4.0

AUGUST

Day	Time	m		Day	Time	m
1 M	0544 / 1152 / 1821	2.1 / 3.9 / 2.2		**16** TU	0007 / 0626 / 1252 / 1916	4.1 / 1.9 / 4.2 / 1.8
2 TU	0017 / 0657 / 1323 / 1935	3.8 / 2.1 / 4.0 / 2.1		**17** W	0138 / 0805 / 1415 / 2046	4.1 / 1.8 / 4.3 / 1.6
3 W	0211 / 0807 / 1446 / 2044	3.9 / 1.9 / 4.2 / 1.9		**18** TH	0301 / 0920 / 1528 / 2154	4.3 / 1.5 / 4.6 / 1.2
4 TH	0323 / 0910 / 1544 / 2147	4.2 / 1.7 / 4.5 / 1.5		**19** F	0407 / 1020 / 1626 / 2249	4.5 / 1.1 / 5.0 / 0.9
5 F	0414 / 1008 / 1633 / 2240	4.4 / 1.4 / 4.8 / 1.2		**20** SA	0459 / 1111 / 1715 / 2338	4.9 / 0.8 / 5.2 / 0.6
6 SA	0501 / 1059 / 1718 / 2329	4.6 / 1.1 / 5.0 / 0.9		**21** SU O	0544 / 1158 / 1801	5.0 / 0.6 / 5.3
7 SU ●	0545 / 1147 / 1803	4.9 / 0.9 / 5.2		**22** M	0022 / 0625 / 1241 / 1840	0.4 / 5.1 / 0.5 / 5.3
8 M	0015 / 0628 / 1232 / 1844	0.7 / 5.0 / 0.7 / 5.2		**23** TU	0103 / 0702 / 1319 / 1917	0.4 / 5.1 / 0.5 / 5.3
9 TU	0058 / 0710 / 1314 / 1926	0.5 / 5.0 / 0.6 / 5.3		**24** W	0137 / 0734 / 1350 / 1947	0.5 / 5.0 / 0.6 / 5.2
10 W	0136 / 0750 / 1350 / 2005	0.5 / 5.0 / 0.5 / 5.3		**25** TH	0206 / 0801 / 1418 / 2012	0.7 / 4.9 / 0.8 / 5.0
11 TH	0212 / 0828 / 1425 / 2042	0.5 / 5.0 / 0.6 / 5.2		**26** F	0232 / 0829 / 1444 / 2038	0.9 / 4.8 / 1.1 / 4.8
12 F	0246 / 0906 / 1501 / 2121	0.6 / 4.9 / 0.8 / 5.0		**27** SA	0255 / 0857 / 1507 / 2108	1.2 / 4.6 / 1.4 / 4.5
13 SA	0322 / 0945 / 1542 / 2201	0.9 / 4.8 / 1.1 / 4.8		**28** SU	0317 / 0930 / 1530 / 2142	1.5 / 4.4 / 1.7 / 4.4
14 SU	0404 / 1032 / 1630 / 2253	1.2 / 4.6 / 1.4 / 4.4		**29** M	0340 / 1009 / 1602 / 2225	1.9 / 4.2 / 2.1 / 4.0
15 M	0500 / 1132 / 1737	1.6 / 4.3 / 1.7		**30** TU	0426 / 1102 / 1732 / 2325	2.2 / 4.0 / 2.3 / 3.8
				31 W	0613 / 1218 / 1857	2.3 / 3.9 / 2.3

SALCOMBE

50°13′N 3°47′W

Times and heights (in metres) of high and low water 1994
Time: GMT. For BST, ADD ONE HOUR in the shaded area

SEPTEMBER

Day	Time	m	Time	m	Day	Time	m	Time	m
1 TH	0116 / 0732 / 1407 / 2011	3.8 / 2.1 / 4.1 / 2.0			**16** F	0255 / 0907 / 1514 / 2139	4.2 / 1.6 / 4.6 / 1.3		
2 F	0257 / 0841 / 1516 / 2117	4.1 / 1.8 / 4.4 / 1.6			**17** SA	0357 / 1003 / 1609 / 2230	4.5 / 1.2 / 5.0 / 0.9		
3 SA	0353 / 0941 / 1608 / 2214	4.4 / 1.4 / 4.8 / 1.2			**18** SU	0442 / 1051 / 1655 / 2315	4.9 / 0.9 / 5.2 / 0.7		
4 SU	0438 / 1035 / 1654 / 2304	4.8 / 1.1 / 5.1 / 0.8			**19** M	0522 / 1134 / 1736 / 2357 O	5.1 / 0.7 / 5.3 / 0.5		
5 M	0521 / 1124 / 1738 / 2351 ●	5.0 / 0.7 / 5.3 / 0.5			**20** TU	0559 / 1214 / 1813	5.1 / 0.6 / 5.3		
6 TU	0605 / 1209 / 1822	5.2 / 0.5 / 5.4			**21** W	0035 / 0631 / 1251 / 1845	0.5 / 5.2 / 0.6 / 5.2		
7 W	0035 / 0646 / 1253 / 1904	0.4 / 5.3 / 0.4 / 5.5			**22** TH	0108 / 0701 / 1321 / 1915	0.6 / 5.1 / 0.8 / 5.2		
8 TH	0116 / 0727 / 1332 / 1946	0.3 / 5.3 / 0.4 / 5.4			**23** F	0135 / 0729 / 1348 / 1943	0.8 / 5.1 / 1.0 / 5.0		
9 F	0153 / 0807 / 1409 / 2026	0.4 / 5.3 / 0.5 / 5.3			**24** SA	0159 / 0757 / 1411 / 2011	1.0 / 5.0 / 1.2 / 4.9		
10 SA	0228 / 0847 / 1446 / 2106	0.6 / 5.1 / 0.7 / 5.1			**25** SU	0219 / 0828 / 1432 / 2040	1.3 / 4.8 / 1.4 / 4.5		
11 SU	0305 / 0927 / 1526 / 2148	0.9 / 4.9 / 1.1 / 4.8			**26** M	0236 / 0859 / 1449 / 2114	1.6 / 4.5 / 1.7 / 4.3		
12 M	0346 / 1013 / 1614 / 2239	1.3 / 4.6 / 1.5 / 4.3			**27** TU	0256 / 0936 / 1517 / 2154	1.8 / 4.3 / 2.0 / 4.1		
13 TU	0441 / 1115 / 1721 / 2357	1.8 / 4.3 / 1.9 / 4.0			**28** W	0333 / 1026 / 1614 / 2252	2.1 / 4.1 / 2.3 / 3.9		
14 W	0610 / 1238 / 1908	2.1 / 4.2 / 2.0			**29** TH	0517 / 1132 / 1820	2.4 / 4.0 / 2.3		
15 TH	0132 / 0756 / 1404 / 2037	4.0 / 2.0 / 4.3 / 1.7			**30** F	0013 / 0657 / 1304 / 1937	3.8 / 2.3 / 4.1 / 2.0		

OCTOBER

Day	Time	m	Time	m	Day	Time	m	Time	m
1 SA	0220 / 0809 / 1436 / 2044	4.0 / 1.9 / 4.4 / 1.6			**16** SU	0331 / 0937 / 1543 / 2203	4.5 / 1.4 / 4.9 / 1.2		
2 SU	0322 / 0911 / 1535 / 2143	4.4 / 1.5 / 4.9 / 1.2			**17** M	0416 / 1024 / 1629 / 2247	4.9 / 1.1 / 5.1 / 0.9		
3 M	0410 / 1007 / 1624 / 2236	4.9 / 1.1 / 5.2 / 0.8			**18** TU	0455 / 1106 / 1708 / 2327	5.1 / 0.9 / 5.2 / 0.8		
4 TU	0455 / 1057 / 1710 / 2324	5.1 / 0.7 / 5.4 / 0.5			**19** W	0529 / 1145 / 1743 O	5.2 / 0.8 / 5.2		
5 W	0538 / 1144 / 1757 ●	5.3 / 0.5 / 5.5			**20** TH	0004 / 0601 / 1221 / 1816	0.8 / 5.2 / 0.9 / 5.2		
6 TH	0010 / 0622 / 1230 / 1842	0.3 / 5.4 / 0.3 / 5.6			**21** F	0037 / 0632 / 1252 / 1847	0.9 / 5.2 / 1.0 / 5.1		
7 F	0055 / 0705 / 1314 / 1926	0.3 / 5.5 / 0.3 / 5.5			**22** SA	0105 / 0702 / 1319 / 1919	1.0 / 5.1 / 1.1 / 5.0		
8 SA	0135 / 0748 / 1354 / 2010	0.4 / 5.4 / 0.5 / 5.4			**23** SU	0128 / 0733 / 1344 / 1949	1.2 / 5.0 / 1.3 / 4.8		
9 SU	0214 / 0830 / 1434 / 2053	0.6 / 5.3 / 0.7 / 5.1			**24** M	0151 / 0803 / 1407 / 2020	1.3 / 4.9 / 1.5 / 4.6		
10 M	0253 / 0913 / 1516 / 2138	1.0 / 5.1 / 1.1 / 4.8			**25** TU	0212 / 0835 / 1429 / 2053	1.5 / 4.6 / 1.7 / 4.4		
11 TU	0336 / 0959 / 1605 / 2231	1.4 / 4.8 / 1.5 / 4.3			**26** W	0237 / 0912 / 1501 / 2134	1.8 / 4.4 / 1.9 / 4.2		
12 W	0429 / 1100 / 1709 / 2347	1.8 / 4.4 / 1.9 / 4.1			**27** TH	0315 / 0958 / 1551 / 2229	2.0 / 4.3 / 2.1 / 4.0		
13 TH	0550 / 1222 / 1847	2.1 / 4.3 / 2.0			**28** F	0416 / 1059 / 1735 / 2337	2.3 / 4.2 / 2.2 / 3.9		
14 F	0116 / 0731 / 1342 / 2012	4.1 / 2.1 / 4.3 / 1.8			**29** SA	0613 / 1211 / 1858	2.3 / 4.2 / 2.0		
15 SA	0232 / 0842 / 1450 / 2113	4.3 / 1.8 / 4.6 / 1.5			**30** SU	0106 / 0731 / 1335 / 2007	4.1 / 2.0 / 4.4 / 1.6		
					31 M	0235 / 0837 / 1451 / 2109	4.4 / 1.6 / 4.8 / 1.2		

NOVEMBER

Day	Time	m	Time	m	Day	Time	m	Time	m
1 TU	0334 / 0936 / 1549 / 2205	4.8 / 1.2 / 5.1 / 0.9			**16** W	0423 / 1036 / 1637 / 2255	4.9 / 1.3 / 5.0 / 1.1		
2 W	0425 / 1029 / 1642 / 2257	5.1 / 0.8 / 5.3 / 0.6			**17** TH	0459 / 1114 / 1714 / 2332	5.1 / 1.1 / 5.0 / 1.1		
3 TH	0512 / 1121 / 1733 / 2346 ●	5.4 / 0.6 / 5.5 / 0.4			**18** F	0533 / 1152 / 1749 O	5.2 / 1.1 / 5.1		
4 F	0600 / 1210 / 1823	5.5 / 0.4 / 5.5			**19** SA	0006 / 0607 / 1224 / 1825	1.1 / 5.2 / 1.1 / 5.0		
5 SA	0033 / 0645 / 1258 / 1911	0.4 / 5.6 / 0.4 / 5.5			**20** SU	0037 / 0640 / 1255 / 1900	1.1 / 5.2 / 1.2 / 5.0		
6 SU	0120 / 0731 / 1342 / 1957	0.5 / 5.6 / 0.5 / 5.4			**21** M	0105 / 0715 / 1324 / 1935	1.2 / 5.1 / 1.3 / 4.8		
7 M	0202 / 0816 / 1425 / 2043	0.7 / 5.4 / 0.7 / 5.2			**22** TU	0133 / 0748 / 1352 / 2008	1.3 / 5.0 / 1.4 / 4.6		
8 TU	0244 / 0901 / 1509 / 2129	1.0 / 5.2 / 1.0 / 4.9			**23** W	0201 / 0821 / 1422 / 2042	1.5 / 4.9 / 1.5 / 4.5		
9 W	0327 / 0947 / 1555 / 2220	1.3 / 5.0 / 1.4 / 4.5			**24** TH	0231 / 0856 / 1456 / 2121	1.6 / 4.6 / 1.6 / 4.3		
10 TH	0415 / 1040 / 1650 / 2325	1.7 / 4.6 / 1.7 / 4.2			**25** F	0309 / 0939 / 1541 / 2209	1.8 / 4.5 / 1.8 / 4.2		
11 F	0517 / 1152 / 1802	2.0 / 4.4 / 2.0			**26** SA	0359 / 1032 / 1644 / 2307	1.9 / 4.4 / 1.9 / 4.1		
12 SA	0041 / 0642 / 1306 / 1927	4.1 / 2.2 / 4.3 / 1.9			**27** SU	0515 / 1134 / 1809	2.1 / 4.4 / 1.9		
13 SU	0152 / 0801 / 1411 / 2035	4.2 / 2.0 / 4.4 / 1.7			**28** M	0015 / 0644 / 1244 / 1926	4.2 / 2.0 / 4.4 / 1.7		
14 M	0252 / 0901 / 1508 / 2128	4.4 / 1.7 / 4.6 / 1.5			**29** TU	0135 / 0759 / 1402 / 2035	4.4 / 1.7 / 4.6 / 1.4		
15 TU	0341 / 0952 / 1557 / 2214	4.6 / 1.5 / 4.8 / 1.3			**30** W	0252 / 0905 / 1514 / 2136	4.6 / 1.4 / 4.9 / 1.1		

DECEMBER

Day	Time	m	Time	m	Day	Time	m	Time	m
1 TH	0354 / 1005 / 1616 / 2234	5.0 / 1.0 / 5.2 / 0.8			**16** F	0428 / 1044 / 1646 / 2301	4.9 / 1.4 / 4.8 / 1.3		
2 F	0448 / 1100 / 1712 / 2327 ●	5.3 / 0.7 / 5.3 / 0.6			**17** SA	0507 / 1124 / 1727 / 2338	5.0 / 1.3 / 4.9 / 1.2		
3 SA	0540 / 1154 / 1807	5.5 / 0.5 / 5.4			**18** SU	0545 / 1201 / 1807 O	5.1 / 1.2 / 4.9		
4 SU	0018 / 0630 / 1245 / 1857	0.5 / 5.6 / 0.5 / 5.4			**19** M	0014 / 0624 / 1237 / 1845	1.2 / 5.2 / 1.2 / 4.9		
5 M	0108 / 0718 / 1332 / 1947	0.5 / 5.6 / 0.5 / 5.3			**20** TU	0049 / 0702 / 1312 / 1924	1.2 / 5.1 / 1.1 / 4.9		
6 TU	0152 / 0805 / 1417 / 2034	0.6 / 5.5 / 0.6 / 5.2			**21** W	0122 / 0739 / 1344 / 2001	1.2 / 5.1 / 1.2 / 4.8		
7 W	0234 / 0849 / 1458 / 2117	0.8 / 5.4 / 0.8 / 5.0			**22** TH	0154 / 0813 / 1417 / 2036	1.2 / 5.0 / 1.2 / 4.6		
8 TH	0315 / 0931 / 1540 / 2159	1.1 / 5.1 / 1.1 / 4.6			**23** F	0227 / 0846 / 1450 / 2111	1.3 / 4.9 / 1.3 / 4.5		
9 F	0355 / 1013 / 1622 / 2245	1.5 / 4.8 / 1.5 / 4.3			**24** SA	0302 / 0924 / 1528 / 2150	1.4 / 4.8 / 1.4 / 4.4		
10 SA	0441 / 1102 / 1712 / 2346	1.8 / 4.5 / 1.8 / 4.2			**25** SU	0344 / 1009 / 1614 / 2240	1.5 / 4.6 / 1.5 / 4.3		
11 SU	0536 / 1208 / 1815	2.1 / 4.3 / 2.0			**26** M	0436 / 1103 / 1716 / 2340	1.7 / 4.5 / 1.7 / 4.3		
12 M	0054 / 0651 / 1320 / 1932	4.1 / 2.2 / 4.2 / 2.0			**27** TU	0550 / 1207 / 1840	1.8 / 4.4 / 1.7		
13 TU	0200 / 0809 / 1423 / 2041	4.2 / 2.1 / 4.3 / 1.9			**28** W	0050 / 0719 / 1324 / 2001	4.3 / 1.8 / 4.4 / 1.6		
14 W	0258 / 0910 / 1518 / 2135	4.4 / 1.9 / 4.4 / 1.7			**29** TH	0212 / 0837 / 1445 / 2111	4.5 / 1.6 / 4.6 / 1.3		
15 TH	0346 / 1001 / 1605 / 2220	4.6 / 1.6 / 4.6 / 1.5			**30** F	0328 / 0944 / 1557 / 2215	4.9 / 1.2 / 4.9 / 1.1		
					31 SA	0430 / 1046 / 1658 / 2312	5.1 / 0.9 / 5.1 / 0.8		

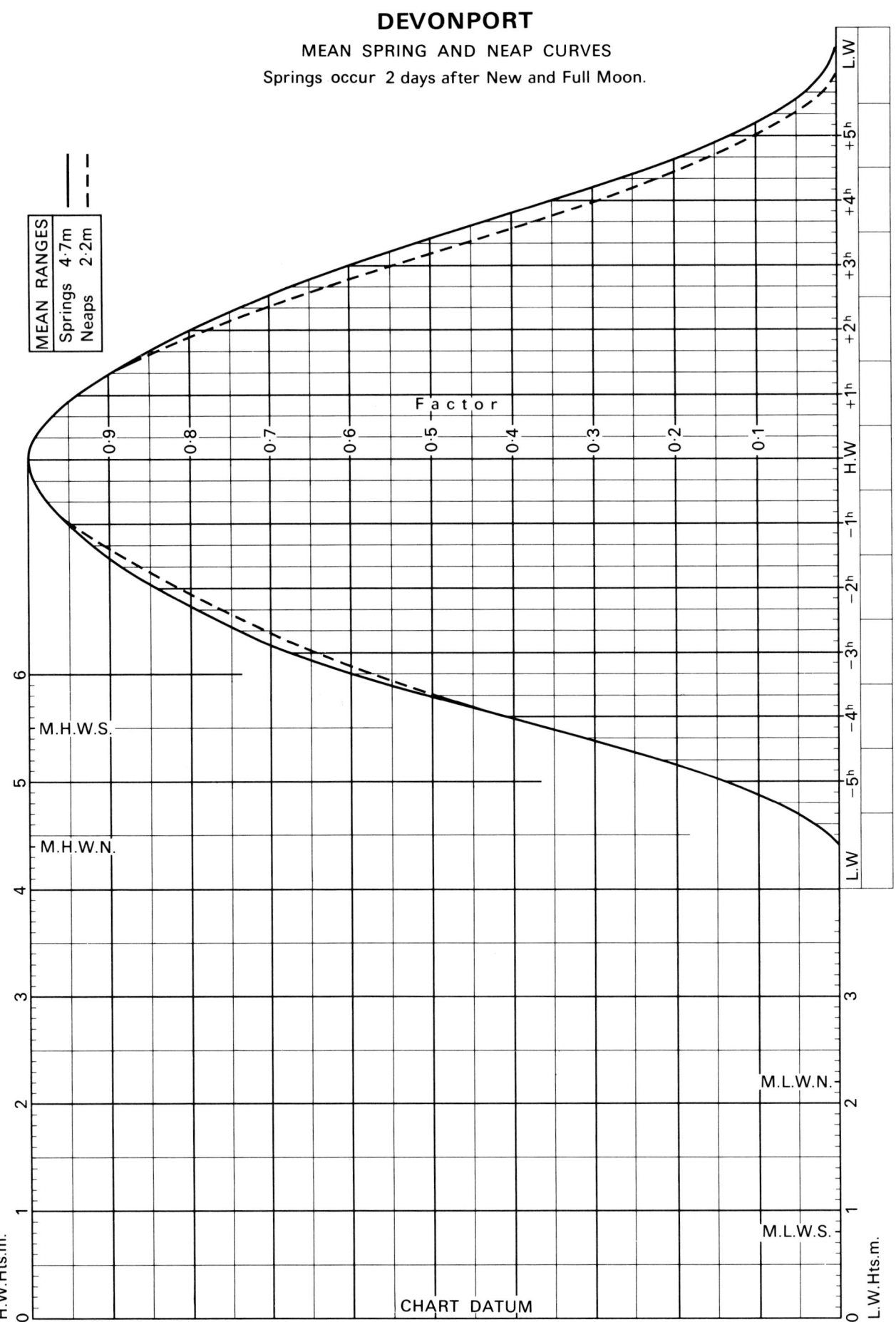

DEVONPORT

MEAN SPRING AND NEAP CURVES

Springs occur 2 days after New and Full Moon.

PLYMOUTH (DEVONPORT)

50°22′N 4°11′W

Times and heights (in metres) of high and low water 1994
Time: GMT. For BST, ADD ONE HOUR in the shaded area
High Water, full and change, 0555

JANUARY

Day	Time	m	Time	m	Day	Time	m	Time	m
1 SA	0139	1.0	0752	5.4	16 SU	0223	1.0	0817	5.3
	1405	0.9	2018	5.2		1442	1.0	2035	5.0
2 SU	0218	1.0	0832	5.4	17 M	0252	1.2	0844	5.2
	1444	1.0	2058	5.1		1510	1.3	2104	4.9
3 M	0257	1.1	0913	5.3	18 TU	0319	1.5	0915	5.0
	1523	1.1	2140	5.0		1539	1.6	2138	4.7
4 TU	0339	1.3	0957	5.1	19 W	0348	1.8	0951	4.8
	1607	1.3	2226	4.8		1610	1.9	2217	4.5
5 W	0428	1.5	1048	4.9	20 TH	0423	2.1	1034	4.5
	1701	1.6	2323	4.7		1656	2.1	2308	4.4
6 TH	0530	1.8	1152	4.7	21 F	0526	2.3	1129	4.3
	1814	1.8				1809	2.3		
7 F	0035	4.6	0654	1.9	22 SA	0015	4.3	0648	2.4
	1309	4.6	1942	1.9		1247	4.2	1923	2.3
8 SA	0154	4.7	0821	1.8	23 SU	0146	4.4	0801	2.2
	1428	4.7	2059	1.7		1425	4.4	2031	2.0
9 SU	0307	4.9	0933	1.6	24 M	0304	4.6	0907	1.9
	1538	4.9	2203	1.4		1534	4.6	2133	1.7
10 M	0409	5.1	1033	1.3	25 TU	0359	4.9	1006	1.6
	1637	5.0	2258	1.2		1625	4.9	2228	1.4
11 TU ●	0501	5.3	1125	1.0	26 W	0446	5.2	1058	1.2
	1727	5.2	2347	1.0		1711	5.1	2318	1.1
12 W O	0548	5.5	1213	0.8	27 TH	0530	5.4	1146	0.9
	1814	5.3				1756	5.2		
13 TH	0032	0.8	0631	5.5	28 F	0005	0.9	0613	5.5
	1257	0.7	1857	5.3		1232	0.7	1840	5.3
14 F	0114	0.8	0712	5.5	29 SA	0049	0.7	0657	5.6
	1336	0.7	1936	5.2		1315	0.6	1923	5.4
15 SA	0150	0.9	0748	5.5	30 SU	0130	0.6	0740	5.6
	1411	0.8	2008	5.1		1354	0.5	2005	5.4
					31 M	0208	0.6	0821	5.6
						1431	0.6	2044	5.3

FEBRUARY

Day	Time	m	Time	m	Day	Time	m	Time	m
1 TU	0245	0.7	0900	5.5	16 W	0246	1.3	0847	5.0
	1508	0.8	2123	5.2		1500	1.4	2105	4.9
2 W	0323	0.9	0941	5.2	17 TH	0307	1.5	0918	4.8
	1547	1.1	2205	5.0		1520	1.6	2139	4.7
3 TH	0406	1.3	1027	4.9	18 F	0329	1.8	0954	4.5
	1633	1.5	2256	4.7		1548	1.9	2220	4.4
4 F	0500	1.7	1127	4.6	19 SA	0408	2.1	1043	4.3
	1736	1.9				1643	2.2	2319	4.3
5 SA	0006	4.5	0617	2.0	20 SU	0551	2.4	1151	4.1
	1248	4.4	1913	2.1		1839	2.3		
6 SU	0130	4.5	0803	2.0	21 M	0040	4.2	0722	2.3
	1413	4.4	2045	1.9		1334	4.2	1956	2.2
7 M	0249	4.7	0923	1.7	22 TU	0223	4.4	0835	2.0
	1528	4.6	2152	1.6		1507	4.5	2104	1.8
8 TU	0354	4.9	1023	1.4	23 W	0331	4.8	0939	1.5
	1627	4.9	2246	1.3		1603	4.8	2205	1.4
9 W	0445	5.2	1112	1.0	24 TH	0422	5.1	1035	1.1
	1713	5.1	2333	1.0		1650	5.1	2258	1.0
10 TH ●	0529	5.4	1157	0.8	25 F	0507	5.4	1126	0.7
	1754	5.2				1735	5.3	2346	0.7
11 F	0015	0.8	0609	5.5	26 SA O	0552	5.6	1212	0.5
	1238	0.6	1832	5.2		1819	5.4		
12 SA	0054	0.7	0647	5.5	27 SU	0031	0.4	0637	5.7
	1315	0.6	1906	5.2		1256	0.3	1902	5.5
13 SU	0128	0.7	0720	5.4	28 M	0113	0.3	0721	5.7
	1346	0.7	1936	5.2		1336	0.3	1944	5.6
14 M	0157	0.8	0749	5.3					
	1414	0.9	2005	5.1					
15 TU	0223	1.0	0817	5.2					
	1438	1.1	2034	5.0					

MARCH

Day	Time	m	Time	m	Day	Time	m	Time	m
1 TU	0152	0.3	0804	5.7	16 W	0154	1.0	0751	5.2
	1414	0.4	2025	5.5		1406	1.1	2006	5.1
2 W	0229	0.5	0845	5.5	17 TH	0216	1.2	0821	5.0
	1451	0.6	2104	5.3		1426	1.3	2036	4.9
3 TH	0307	0.8	0925	5.2	18 F	0235	1.4	0851	4.8
	1529	1.0	2145	5.1		1445	1.5	2107	4.7
4 F	0349	1.2	1010	4.9	19 SA	0258	1.7	0925	4.5
	1612	1.5	2233	4.7		1513	1.8	2145	4.5
5 SA	0440	1.7	1108	4.5	20 SU	0335	1.9	1012	4.3
	1711	2.0	2342	4.5		1559	2.1	2240	4.3
6 SU	0553	2.1	1233	4.2	21 M	0444	2.2	1117	4.1
	1849	2.2				1752	2.2	2353	4.3
7 M	0111	4.4	0748	2.1	22 TU	0647	2.2	1243	4.1
	1401	4.3	2031	2.1		1923	2.2		
8 TU	0231	4.6	0909	1.8	23 W	0127	4.4	0803	1.9
	1515	4.5	2136	1.7		1431	4.4	2034	1.8
9 W	0335	4.8	1005	1.4	24 TH	0253	4.7	0909	1.5
	1610	4.8	2227	1.3		1534	4.8	2137	1.4
10 TH	0425	5.1	1052	1.0	25 F	0351	5.1	1008	1.0
	1652	5.0	2311	1.0		1623	5.1	2232	0.9
11 F	0506	5.3	1134	0.8	26 SA	0440	5.4	1100	0.7
	1729	5.2	2352	0.8		1709	5.3	2322	0.6
12 SA ●	0544	5.4	1213	0.7	27 SU O	0527	5.6	1148	0.4
	1803	5.3				1754	5.5		
13 SU	0028	0.7	0618	5.4	28 M	0008	0.3	0613	5.7
	1248	0.7	1835	5.3		1233	0.2	1838	5.6
14 M	0101	0.7	0650	5.4	29 TU	0053	0.2	0700	5.8
	1318	0.7	1906	5.3		1316	0.2	1923	5.7
15 TU	0129	0.8	0721	5.3	30 W	0134	0.2	0745	5.7
	1343	0.9	1936	5.2		1356	0.4	2005	5.6
					31 TH	0214	0.4	0829	5.5
						1435	0.7	2046	5.4

APRIL

Day	Time	m	Time	m	Day	Time	m	Time	m
1 F	0254	0.7	0912	5.2	16 SA	0214	1.4	0831	4.7
	1515	1.1	2127	5.1		1424	1.5	2043	4.8
2 SA	0337	1.2	0957	4.8	17 SU	0242	1.6	0906	4.6
	1559	1.5	2214	4.8		1456	1.7	2122	4.7
3 SU	0427	1.6	1055	4.5	18 M	0321	1.8	0953	4.4
	1655	2.0	2321	4.5		1544	2.0	2215	4.5
4 M	0536	2.0	1219	4.2	19 TU	0426	2.0	1054	4.2
	1821	2.2				1709	2.2	2321	4.4
5 TU	0049	4.4	0720	2.1	20 W	0611	2.0	1209	4.2
	1340	4.3	2001	2.1		1847	2.1		
6 W	0205	4.5	0840	1.8	21 TH	0040	4.5	0728	1.8
	1448	4.5	2108	1.8		1339	4.4	2000	1.8
7 TH	0307	4.7	0937	1.5	22 F	0205	4.7	0835	1.4
	1541	4.7	2159	1.4		1454	4.7	2105	1.4
8 F	0356	5.0	1023	1.2	23 SA	0313	5.0	0936	1.0
	1623	5.0	2243	1.1		1550	5.1	2203	1.0
9 SA	0437	5.2	1105	0.9	24 SU	0409	5.3	1031	0.7
	1659	5.1	2323	0.9		1640	5.3	2256	0.6
10 SU	0514	5.3	1142	0.8	25 M O	0500	5.5	1122	0.5
	1732	5.2	2359	0.8		1728	5.5	2345	0.4
11 M ●	0548	5.3	1216	0.8	26 TU	0550	5.6	1210	0.3
	1805	5.3				1815	5.7		
12 TU	0031	0.9	0621	5.3	27 W	0032	0.3	0640	5.6
	1246	0.9	1837	5.3		1256	0.3	1902	5.7
13 W	0100	0.9	0655	5.2	28 TH	0118	0.3	0728	5.6
	1312	1.0	1910	5.2		1340	0.5	1948	5.6
14 TH	0126	1.1	0728	5.1	29 F	0202	0.5	0815	5.4
	1337	1.1	1942	5.1		1423	0.7	2031	5.5
15 F	0150	1.2	0800	4.9	30 SA	0244	0.7	0900	5.1
	1400	1.3	2012	5.0		1505	1.1	2114	5.2

PLYMOUTH (DEVONPORT)
50°22′N 4°11′W

Times and heights (in metres) of high and low water 1994
Time: GMT. For BST, ADD ONE HOUR in the shaded area
High Water, full and change, 0555

MAY

Day	Time	m	Day	Time	m
1 SU	0328 / 0946 / 1549 / 2158	1.1 / 4.8 / 1.5 / 4.9	**16** M	0238 / 0856 / 1453 / 2109	1.4 / 4.6 / 1.6 / 4.8
2 M	0416 / 1041 / 1639 / 2256	1.5 / 4.5 / 1.8 / 4.6	**17** TU	0320 / 0940 / 1540 / 2157	1.5 / 4.5 / 1.7 / 4.7
3 TU	0515 / 1153 / 1745	1.8 / 4.3 / 2.1	**18** W	0416 / 1035 / 1644 / 2256	1.7 / 4.4 / 1.9 / 4.6
4 W	0015 / 0632 / 1306 / 1910	4.5 / 2.0 / 4.3 / 2.1	**19** TH	0533 / 1140 / 1806	1.7 / 4.4 / 1.9
5 TH	0128 / 0754 / 1409 / 2024	4.5 / 1.9 / 4.4 / 1.9	**20** F	0005 / 0650 / 1255 / 1922	4.6 / 1.6 / 4.5 / 1.7
6 F	0229 / 0856 / 1502 / 2121	4.6 / 1.7 / 4.6 / 1.7	**21** SA	0122 / 0800 / 1410 / 2031	4.7 / 1.4 / 4.7 / 1.4
7 SA	0320 / 0946 / 1547 / 2208	4.8 / 1.4 / 4.8 / 1.4	**22** SU	0236 / 0904 / 1516 / 2134	4.9 / 1.2 / 5.0 / 1.1
8 SU	0404 / 1029 / 1626 / 2249	4.9 / 1.2 / 5.0 / 1.2	**23** M	0340 / 1004 / 1613 / 2231	5.2 / 0.9 / 5.2 / 0.8
9 M	0442 / 1107 / 1701 / 2326	5.1 / 1.1 / 5.2 / 1.1	**24** TU	0437 / 1058 / 1705 / 2324	5.3 / 0.7 / 5.5 / 0.6
10 TU ●	0518 / 1142 / 1736	5.1 / 1.1 / 5.2	**25** W O	0530 / 1150 / 1755	5.4 / 0.6 / 5.6
11 W	0000 / 0555 / 1214 / 1812	1.1 / 5.1 / 1.1 / 5.2	**26** TH	0015 / 0622 / 1239 / 1844	0.5 / 5.5 / 0.5 / 5.6
12 TH	0032 / 0632 / 1244 / 1849	1.1 / 5.1 / 1.1 / 5.2	**27** F	0104 / 0713 / 1327 / 1933	0.4 / 5.4 / 0.6 / 5.6
13 F	0102 / 0709 / 1314 / 1923	1.1 / 5.0 / 1.2 / 5.1	**28** SA	0150 / 0803 / 1411 / 2018	0.5 / 5.3 / 0.7 / 5.5
14 SA	0133 / 0745 / 1344 / 1956	1.2 / 4.9 / 1.3 / 5.0	**29** SU	0234 / 0848 / 1453 / 2100	0.7 / 5.1 / 1.0 / 5.3
15 SU	0204 / 0819 / 1416 / 2029	1.3 / 4.8 / 1.4 / 4.9	**30** M	0317 / 0932 / 1534 / 2139	1.0 / 4.9 / 1.3 / 5.0
			31 TU	0359 / 1016 / 1617 / 2220	1.3 / 4.6 / 1.6 / 4.8

JUNE

Day	Time	m	Day	Time	m
1 W	0446 / 1107 / 1706 / 2313	1.6 / 4.4 / 1.9 / 4.5	**16** TH	0401 / 1018 / 1622 / 2234	1.3 / 4.6 / 1.5 / 4.8
2 TH	0540 / 1212 / 1806	1.9 / 4.3 / 2.1	**17** F	0458 / 1114 / 1727 / 2335	1.5 / 4.6 / 1.6 / 4.7
3 F	0030 / 0645 / 1317 / 1916	4.4 / 2.0 / 4.3 / 2.1	**18** SA	0610 / 1221 / 1844	1.6 / 4.6 / 1.7
4 SA	0139 / 0754 / 1415 / 2025	4.4 / 1.9 / 4.5 / 2.0	**19** SU	0048 / 0726 / 1335 / 1959	4.7 / 1.5 / 4.7 / 1.5
5 SU	0236 / 0854 / 1505 / 2122	4.5 / 1.7 / 4.6 / 1.7	**20** M	0206 / 0836 / 1447 / 2109	4.8 / 1.4 / 4.9 / 1.3
6 M	0326 / 0944 / 1550 / 2209	4.7 / 1.6 / 4.8 / 1.5	**21** TU	0317 / 0941 / 1550 / 2212	4.9 / 1.1 / 5.1 / 1.1
7 TU	0410 / 1027 / 1631 / 2251	4.8 / 1.4 / 5.0 / 1.4	**22** W	0419 / 1040 / 1646 / 2309	5.1 / 0.9 / 5.3 / 0.8
8 W	0451 / 1106 / 1711 / 2330	4.9 / 1.3 / 5.1 / 1.2	**23** TH O	0514 / 1135 / 1738	5.2 / 0.8 / 5.5
9 TH ●	0532 / 1143 / 1751	5.0 / 1.2 / 5.2	**24** F	0002 / 0606 / 1226 / 1828	0.6 / 5.3 / 0.6 / 5.6
10 F	0007 / 0612 / 1221 / 1830	1.2 / 5.0 / 1.2 / 5.2	**25** SA	0052 / 0658 / 1314 / 1917	0.5 / 5.3 / 0.6 / 5.6
11 SA	0044 / 0654 / 1258 / 1909	1.1 / 5.0 / 1.2 / 5.2	**26** SU	0138 / 0747 / 1357 / 2002	0.5 / 5.2 / 0.7 / 5.5
12 SU	0121 / 0734 / 1334 / 1947	1.1 / 4.9 / 1.2 / 5.1	**27** M	0220 / 0830 / 1436 / 2041	0.6 / 5.1 / 0.8 / 5.3
13 M	0157 / 0813 / 1411 / 2022	1.1 / 4.8 / 1.2 / 5.1	**28** TU	0258 / 0907 / 1513 / 2112	0.8 / 5.0 / 1.1 / 5.1
14 TU	0235 / 0850 / 1449 / 2100	1.2 / 4.8 / 1.3 / 5.0	**29** W	0334 / 0938 / 1549 / 2141	1.1 / 4.8 / 1.4 / 4.9
15 W	0314 / 0931 / 1532 / 2143	1.2 / 4.7 / 1.4 / 4.9	**30** TH	0411 / 1010 / 1627 / 2215	1.4 / 4.6 / 1.7 / 4.7

JULY

Day	Time	m	Day	Time	m
1 F	0452 / 1052 / 1713 / 2301	1.7 / 4.4 / 2.0 / 4.5	**16** SA	0429 / 1050 / 1655 / 2310	1.3 / 4.7 / 1.5 / 4.7
2 SA	0543 / 1150 / 1811	2.0 / 4.3 / 2.1	**17** SU	0532 / 1153 / 1807 / 2335	1.6 / 4.6 / 1.7 / 4.7
3 SU	0006 / 0644 / 1307 / 1917	4.3 / 2.1 / 4.3 / 2.2	**18** M	0022 / 0654 / 1309 / 1934	4.6 / 1.7 / 4.6 / 1.7
4 M	0138 / 0749 / 1418 / 2024	4.3 / 2.0 / 4.4 / 2.0	**19** TU	0146 / 0816 / 1426 / 2053	4.6 / 1.6 / 4.7 / 1.6
5 TU	0248 / 0851 / 1515 / 2125	4.4 / 1.8 / 4.7 / 1.8	**20** W	0303 / 0927 / 1534 / 2201	4.7 / 1.4 / 5.0 / 1.3
6 W	0342 / 0945 / 1604 / 2216	4.6 / 1.6 / 4.9 / 1.5	**21** TH	0407 / 1029 / 1632 / 2259	4.9 / 1.1 / 5.2 / 0.9
7 TH	0428 / 1034 / 1648 / 2303	4.8 / 1.4 / 5.1 / 1.3	**22** F O	0502 / 1123 / 1723 / 2351	5.1 / 0.9 / 5.4 / 0.7
8 F ●	0512 / 1119 / 1731 / 2346	4.9 / 1.2 / 5.2 / 1.1	**23** SA	0552 / 1212 / 1811	5.2 / 0.7 / 5.5
9 SA	0555 / 1202 / 1813	5.0 / 1.1 / 5.2	**24** SU	0038 / 0639 / 1257 / 1857	0.5 / 5.2 / 0.6 / 5.5
10 SU	0029 / 0638 / 1244 / 1855	1.0 / 5.0 / 1.0 / 5.3	**25** M	0121 / 0723 / 1338 / 1938	0.5 / 5.2 / 0.6 / 5.5
11 M	0110 / 0721 / 1324 / 1935	0.9 / 5.0 / 0.9 / 5.3	**26** TU	0159 / 0802 / 1414 / 2013	0.5 / 5.2 / 0.7 / 5.4
12 TU	0148 / 0801 / 1402 / 2013	0.8 / 5.0 / 0.9 / 5.3	**27** W	0233 / 0832 / 1446 / 2039	0.7 / 5.0 / 0.9 / 5.0
13 W	0225 / 0839 / 1439 / 2050	0.8 / 5.0 / 0.9 / 5.2	**28** TH	0304 / 0858 / 1516 / 2105	1.0 / 4.9 / 1.2 / 5.0
14 TH	0301 / 0917 / 1517 / 2130	0.9 / 4.9 / 1.1 / 5.1	**29** F	0333 / 0927 / 1546 / 2136	1.3 / 4.7 / 1.6 / 4.8
15 F	0342 / 0959 / 1601 / 2215	1.1 / 4.8 / 1.3 / 4.9	**30** SA	0405 / 1003 / 1622 / 2213	1.7 / 4.5 / 1.9 / 4.5
			31 SU	0447 / 1049 / 1715 / 2303	2.0 / 4.4 / 2.2 / 4.3

AUGUST

Day	Time	m	Day	Time	m
1 M	0549 / 1151 / 1826	2.2 / 4.2 / 2.3	**16** TU	0006 / 0630 / 1252 / 1919	4.4 / 2.0 / 4.5 / 1.9
2 TU	0016 / 0701 / 1322 / 1938	4.1 / 2.2 / 4.3 / 2.2	**17** W	0137 / 0807 / 1413 / 2047	4.4 / 1.9 / 4.6 / 1.7
3 W	0209 / 0809 / 1443 / 2045	4.2 / 2.0 / 4.5 / 2.0	**18** TH	0257 / 0920 / 1523 / 2153	4.6 / 1.6 / 4.9 / 1.3
4 TH	0318 / 0911 / 1539 / 2146	4.5 / 1.8 / 4.8 / 1.6	**19** F	0401 / 1019 / 1619 / 2247	4.8 / 1.2 / 5.2 / 1.0
5 F	0408 / 1007 / 1626 / 2238	4.7 / 1.5 / 5.0 / 1.3	**20** SA	0451 / 1109 / 1707 / 2335	5.1 / 0.9 / 5.4 / 0.7
6 SA	0453 / 1057 / 1710 / 2326	4.9 / 1.2 / 5.2 / 1.0	**21** SU O	0535 / 1154 / 1751	5.2 / 0.7 / 5.5
7 SU ●	0536 / 1144 / 1753	5.1 / 1.0 / 5.4	**22** M	0018 / 0615 / 1236 / 1831	0.5 / 5.3 / 0.6 / 5.5
8 M	0011 / 0618 / 1228 / 1835	0.8 / 5.2 / 0.8 / 5.4	**23** TU	0058 / 0653 / 1314 / 1908	0.5 / 5.3 / 0.6 / 5.5
9 TU	0053 / 0701 / 1309 / 1918	0.6 / 5.2 / 0.7 / 5.5	**24** W	0133 / 0726 / 1347 / 1939	0.6 / 5.2 / 0.7 / 5.4
10 W	0132 / 0742 / 1347 / 1958	0.6 / 5.2 / 0.6 / 5.5	**25** TH	0203 / 0754 / 1415 / 2005	0.8 / 5.1 / 0.9 / 5.2
11 TH	0209 / 0821 / 1423 / 2036	0.6 / 5.2 / 0.7 / 5.4	**26** F	0230 / 0822 / 1442 / 2032	1.0 / 5.0 / 1.2 / 5.0
12 F	0244 / 0900 / 1500 / 2115	0.7 / 5.1 / 0.9 / 5.2	**27** SA	0254 / 0851 / 1506 / 2102	1.3 / 4.9 / 1.5 / 4.8
13 SA	0322 / 0940 / 1542 / 2157	1.0 / 5.0 / 1.2 / 5.0	**28** SU	0317 / 0925 / 1530 / 2137	1.6 / 4.7 / 1.8 / 4.6
14 SU	0405 / 1028 / 1632 / 2250	1.3 / 4.8 / 1.5 / 4.7	**29** M	0340 / 1005 / 1603 / 2221	2.0 / 4.5 / 2.2 / 4.3
15 M	0503 / 1130 / 1741	1.7 / 4.6 / 1.8	**30** TU	0428 / 1059 / 1736 / 2323	2.3 / 4.3 / 2.4 / 4.1
			31 W	0618 / 1217 / 1901	2.4 / 4.2 / 2.4

PLYMOUTH (DEVONPORT)

50°22'N 4°11'W

Times and heights (in metres) of high and low water 1994
Time: GMT. For BST, ADD ONE HOUR in the shaded area
High Water, full and change, 0555

SEPTEMBER

Day	Time	m	Day	Time	m
1 TH	0115 / 0735 / 1405 / 2013	4.1 / 2.2 / 4.4 / 2.1	**16** F	0251 / 0908 / 1510 / 2139	4.5 / 1.7 / 4.9 / 1.4
2 F	0253 / 0842 / 1512 / 2117	4.4 / 1.9 / 4.7 / 1.7	**17** SA	0351 / 1002 / 1603 / 2229	4.8 / 1.3 / 5.2 / 1.0
3 SA	0347 / 0941 / 1602 / 2213	4.7 / 1.5 / 5.0 / 1.3	**18** SU	0435 / 1049 / 1647 / 2313	5.1 / 1.0 / 5.4 / 0.8
4 SU	0431 / 1033 / 1646 / 2302	5.0 / 1.2 / 5.3 / 0.9	**19** M	0514 / 1131 / 1727 / 2353 O	5.3 / 0.8 / 5.5 / 0.6
5 M ●	0513 / 1121 / 1729 / 2347	5.2 / 0.8 / 5.5 / 0.6	**20** TU	0549 / 1210 / 1803	5.3 / 0.7 / 5.5
6 TU	0555 / 1205 / 1812	5.4 / 0.6 / 5.6	**21** W	0030 / 0621 / 1246 / 1836	0.6 / 5.4 / 0.7 / 5.4
7 W	0030 / 0637 / 1248 / 1855	0.5 / 5.5 / 0.5 / 5.7	**22** TH	0103 / 0652 / 1317 / 1906	0.7 / 5.3 / 0.9 / 5.4
8 TH	0111 / 0719 / 1328 / 1938	0.4 / 5.5 / 0.5 / 5.6	**23** F	0131 / 0721 / 1344 / 1935	0.9 / 5.3 / 1.1 / 5.2
9 F	0150 / 0800 / 1406 / 2019	0.5 / 5.5 / 0.6 / 5.5	**24** SA	0156 / 0750 / 1408 / 2004	1.1 / 5.2 / 1.3 / 5.1
10 SA	0226 / 0841 / 1444 / 2100	0.7 / 5.3 / 0.8 / 5.3	**25** SU	0217 / 0821 / 1430 / 2034	1.4 / 5.0 / 1.5 / 4.8
11 SU	0304 / 0922 / 1526 / 2143	1.0 / 5.1 / 1.2 / 5.0	**26** M	0234 / 0853 / 1448 / 2108	1.7 / 4.8 / 1.8 / 4.6
12 M	0347 / 1009 / 1616 / 2236	1.4 / 4.9 / 1.6 / 4.6	**27** TU	0255 / 0931 / 1517 / 2150	1.9 / 4.6 / 2.1 / 4.4
13 TU	0443 / 1112 / 1725 / 2356	1.9 / 4.6 / 2.0 / 4.3	**28** W	0333 / 1022 / 1615 / 2249	2.2 / 4.4 / 2.4 / 4.2
14 W	0615 / 1238 / 1912	2.2 / 4.5 / 2.1	**29** TH	0521 / 1130 / 1825	2.5 / 4.3 / 2.4
15 TH	0131 / 0758 / 1402 / 2038	4.3 / 2.1 / 4.6 / 1.8	**30** F	0012 / 0701 / 1304 / 1940	4.1 / 2.4 / 4.4 / 2.1

OCTOBER

Day	Time	m	Day	Time	m
1 SA	0217 / 0811 / 1433 / 2045	4.3 / 2.0 / 4.7 / 1.7	**16** SU	0326 / 0937 / 1538 / 2202	4.8 / 1.5 / 5.1 / 1.3
2 SU	0317 / 0912 / 1530 / 2143	4.7 / 1.6 / 5.1 / 1.3	**17** M	0410 / 1023 / 1622 / 2245	5.1 / 1.2 / 5.3 / 1.0
3 M	0404 / 1006 / 1617 / 2234	5.1 / 1.2 / 5.4 / 0.9	**18** TU	0447 / 1104 / 1700 / 2324	5.3 / 1.0 / 5.4 / 0.9
4 TU	0447 / 1055 / 1702 / 2321	5.3 / 0.8 / 5.6 / 0.6	**19** W	0520 / 1142 / 1734 O	5.4 / 0.9 / 5.4
5 W ●	0529 / 1141 / 1747	5.5 / 0.6 / 5.7	**20** TH	0000 / 0551 / 1217 / 1806	0.9 / 5.4 / 1.0 / 5.4
6 TH	0006 / 0612 / 1226 / 1833	0.4 / 5.6 / 0.4 / 5.8	**21** F	0032 / 0622 / 1247 / 1838	1.0 / 5.4 / 1.1 / 5.3
7 F	0050 / 0656 / 1309 / 1918	0.4 / 5.7 / 0.4 / 5.7	**22** SA	0100 / 0653 / 1314 / 1910	1.1 / 5.3 / 1.2 / 5.2
8 SA	0131 / 0740 / 1351 / 2003	0.5 / 5.6 / 0.6 / 5.6	**23** SU	0124 / 0725 / 1340 / 1941	1.3 / 5.2 / 1.4 / 5.0
9 SU	0211 / 0823 / 1432 / 2047	0.7 / 5.5 / 0.8 / 5.3	**24** M	0148 / 0756 / 1404 / 2013	1.4 / 5.1 / 1.6 / 4.9
10 M	0252 / 0907 / 1516 / 2133	1.1 / 5.3 / 1.2 / 5.0	**25** TU	0209 / 0828 / 1427 / 2047	1.6 / 4.9 / 1.8 / 4.7
11 TU	0336 / 0955 / 1606 / 2227	1.5 / 5.0 / 1.6 / 4.6	**26** W	0235 / 0906 / 1500 / 2129	1.9 / 4.7 / 2.0 / 4.5
12 W	0431 / 1057 / 1712 / 2346	1.9 / 4.7 / 2.0 / 4.4	**27** TH	0314 / 0954 / 1552 / 2225	2.1 / 4.6 / 2.2 / 4.3
13 TH	0555 / 1221 / 1851	2.2 / 4.6 / 2.1	**28** F	0418 / 1056 / 1739 / 2335	2.4 / 4.5 / 2.3 / 4.2
14 F	0115 / 0734 / 1341 / 2014	4.4 / 2.2 / 4.6 / 1.9	**29** SA	0618 / 1210 / 1902	2.4 / 4.5 / 2.1
15 SA	0229 / 0843 / 1446 / 2114	4.6 / 1.9 / 4.9 / 1.6	**30** SU	0106 / 0734 / 1334 / 2009	4.4 / 2.1 / 4.7 / 1.7
			31 M	0232 / 0838 / 1447 / 2110	4.7 / 1.7 / 5.0 / 1.3

NOVEMBER

Day	Time	m	Day	Time	m
1 TU	0329 / 0936 / 1544 / 2204	5.0 / 1.3 / 5.3 / 1.0	**16** W	0416 / 1034 / 1630 / 2253	5.1 / 1.4 / 5.2 / 1.2
2 W	0418 / 1028 / 1635 / 2255	5.3 / 0.9 / 5.5 / 0.7	**17** TH	0451 / 1112 / 1706 / 2329	5.3 / 1.2 / 5.2 / 1.2
3 TH ●	0504 / 1118 / 1724 / 2343	5.6 / 0.7 / 5.7 / 0.5	**18** F	0524 / 1148 / 1740 O	5.4 / 1.2 / 5.3
4 F	0550 / 1206 / 1813	5.7 / 0.5 / 5.7	**19** SA	0002 / 0557 / 1220 / 1815	1.2 / 5.4 / 1.2 / 5.2
5 SA	0029 / 0636 / 1253 / 1902	0.5 / 5.8 / 0.5 / 5.7	**20** SU	0032 / 0631 / 1250 / 1851	1.2 / 5.4 / 1.3 / 5.2
6 SU	0115 / 0723 / 1338 / 1950	0.6 / 5.8 / 0.6 / 5.6	**21** M	0100 / 0706 / 1320 / 1927	1.3 / 5.3 / 1.4 / 5.0
7 M	0159 / 0809 / 1423 / 2037	0.8 / 5.6 / 0.8 / 5.4	**22** TU	0129 / 0740 / 1349 / 2001	1.4 / 5.2 / 1.5 / 4.9
8 TU	0242 / 0855 / 1508 / 2124	1.1 / 5.4 / 1.1 / 5.1	**23** W	0158 / 0814 / 1420 / 2036	1.6 / 5.1 / 1.6 / 4.8
9 W	0327 / 0942 / 1556 / 2216	1.4 / 5.2 / 1.5 / 4.8	**24** TH	0229 / 0850 / 1455 / 2116	1.7 / 4.9 / 1.7 / 4.6
10 TH	0417 / 1037 / 1653 / 2323	1.8 / 4.9 / 1.8 / 4.5	**25** F	0308 / 0934 / 1541 / 2205	1.9 / 4.8 / 1.9 / 4.5
11 F	0521 / 1151 / 1807	2.1 / 4.7 / 2.1	**26** SA	0400 / 1028 / 1647 / 2304	2.0 / 4.7 / 2.0 / 4.4
12 SA	0041 / 0646 / 1306 / 1930	4.4 / 2.3 / 4.6 / 2.0	**27** SU	0519 / 1132 / 1814	2.2 / 4.7 / 2.0
13 SU	0150 / 0803 / 1409 / 2036	4.5 / 2.1 / 4.7 / 1.8	**28** M	0014 / 0648 / 1244 / 1929	4.5 / 2.1 / 4.7 / 1.8
14 M	0248 / 0902 / 1504 / 2128	4.7 / 1.8 / 4.9 / 1.6	**29** TU	0134 / 0801 / 1400 / 2036	4.7 / 1.8 / 4.9 / 1.5
15 TU	0336 / 0951 / 1551 / 2213	4.9 / 1.6 / 5.0 / 1.4	**30** W	0248 / 0906 / 1510 / 2136	4.9 / 1.5 / 5.1 / 1.2

DECEMBER

Day	Time	m	Day	Time	m
1 TH	0348 / 1004 / 1610 / 2232	5.2 / 1.1 / 5.4 / 0.9	**16** F	0421 / 1042 / 1639 / 2259	5.1 / 1.5 / 5.0 / 1.4
2 F ●	0441 / 1058 / 1704 / 2324	5.5 / 0.8 / 5.5 / 0.7	**17** SA	0459 / 1121 / 1718 / 2335	5.2 / 1.4 / 5.1 / 1.3
3 SA	0531 / 1150 / 1757	5.7 / 0.6 / 5.6	**18** SU	0536 / 1157 / 1757 O	5.3 / 1.3 / 5.1
4 SU	0014 / 0620 / 1240 / 1848	0.6 / 5.8 / 0.6 / 5.6	**19** M	0010 / 0614 / 1232 / 1836	1.3 / 5.4 / 1.3 / 5.1
5 M	0103 / 0709 / 1328 / 1939	0.6 / 5.8 / 0.6 / 5.5	**20** TU	0044 / 0653 / 1307 / 1916	1.3 / 5.3 / 1.2 / 5.1
6 TU	0149 / 0758 / 1414 / 2027	0.7 / 5.7 / 0.7 / 5.4	**21** W	0118 / 0731 / 1340 / 1954	1.3 / 5.3 / 1.3 / 5.0
7 W	0232 / 0843 / 1457 / 2111	0.9 / 5.6 / 0.9 / 5.2	**22** TH	0151 / 0806 / 1414 / 2029	1.3 / 5.2 / 1.3 / 4.9
8 TH	0314 / 0926 / 1540 / 2155	1.2 / 5.3 / 1.2 / 4.9	**23** F	0225 / 0840 / 1449 / 2105	1.4 / 5.1 / 1.4 / 4.8
9 F	0356 / 1009 / 1624 / 2242	1.6 / 5.0 / 1.6 / 4.6	**24** SA	0301 / 0919 / 1528 / 2146	1.5 / 5.0 / 1.5 / 4.7
10 SA	0443 / 1059 / 1716 / 2344	1.9 / 4.8 / 1.9 / 4.5	**25** SU	0344 / 1005 / 1616 / 2237	1.6 / 4.9 / 1.6 / 4.6
11 SU	0540 / 1207 / 1820	2.2 / 4.6 / 2.1	**26** M	0438 / 1100 / 1720 / 2338	1.8 / 4.8 / 1.8 / 4.6
12 M	0054 / 0655 / 1319 / 1935	4.4 / 2.3 / 4.5 / 2.1	**27** TU	0555 / 1206 / 1844	1.9 / 4.7 / 1.8
13 TU	0158 / 0811 / 1420 / 2042	4.5 / 2.2 / 4.6 / 2.0	**28** W	0050 / 0722 / 1323 / 2003	4.6 / 1.9 / 4.7 / 1.7
14 W	0254 / 0911 / 1514 / 2135	4.7 / 2.0 / 4.7 / 1.8	**29** TH	0210 / 0838 / 1442 / 2112	4.8 / 1.7 / 4.9 / 1.4
15 TH	0341 / 1000 / 1559 / 2219	4.9 / 1.7 / 4.9 / 1.6	**30** F	0323 / 0944 / 1551 / 2214	5.1 / 1.3 / 5.1 / 1.2
			31 SA	0423 / 1044 / 1650 / 2310	5.3 / 1.0 / 5.3 / 0.9

FALMOUTH

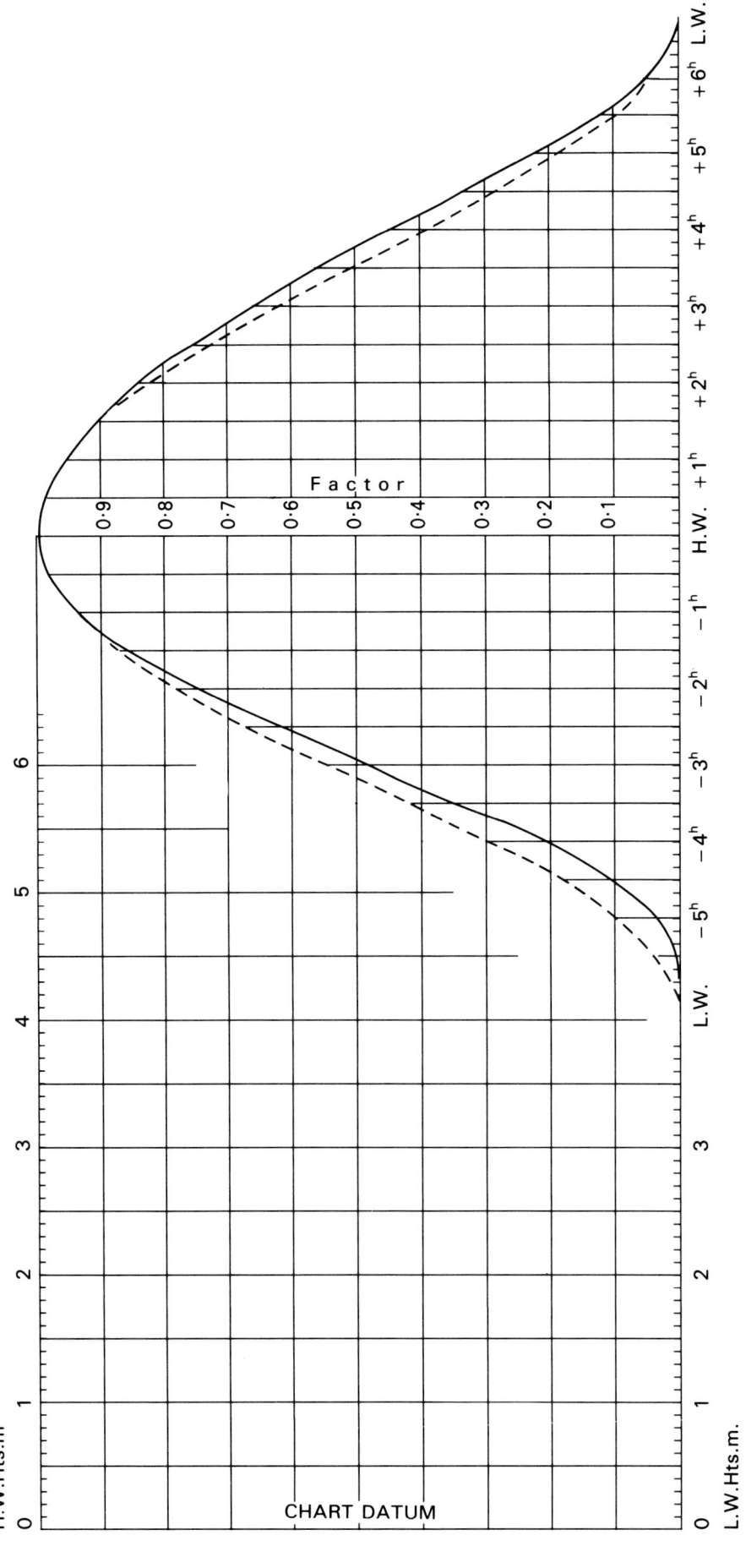

FALMOUTH

50°09′N 5°03′W

Times and heights (in metres) of high and low water 1994
Time: GMT. For BST, ADD ONE HOUR in the shaded area

JANUARY

	Time	m		Time	m
1 SA	0129 0722 1355 1948	0.8 5.2 0.7 5.0	**16** SU	0213 0747 1432 2005	0.8 5.1 0.8 4.8
2 SU	0208 0802 1434 2028	0.8 5.2 0.8 4.9	**17** M	0242 0814 1500 2034	1.0 5.0 1.1 4.7
3 M	0247 0843 1513 2110	0.9 5.1 0.9 4.8	**18** TU	0309 0845 1529 2108	1.3 4.8 1.3 4.5
4 TU	0329 0927 1557 2156	1.1 4.9 1.1 4.6	**19** W	0338 0921 1600 2147	1.5 4.6 1.6 4.3
5 W	0418 1018 1651 2253	1.3 4.7 1.3 4.5	**20** TH	0413 1004 1646 2238	1.8 4.3 1.8 4.2
6 TH	0520 1122 1804	1.5 4.5 1.5	**21** F	0516 1059 1759 2345	2.0 4.1 2.0 4.1
7 F	0005 0644 1239 1932	4.4 1.6 4.4 1.6	**22** SA	0638 1217 1913	2.1 4.0 2.0
8 SA	0124 0811 1358 2049	4.5 1.5 4.5 1.4	**23** SU	0116 0751 1355 2021	4.2 1.9 4.2 1.7
9 SU	0237 0923 1508 2153	4.7 1.3 4.7 1.2	**24** M	0234 0857 1504 2123	4.4 1.6 4.4 1.4
10 M	0339 1023 1607 2248	4.9 1.1 4.8 1.0	**25** TU	0329 0956 1555 2218	4.7 1.3 4.7 1.2
11 TU ●	0431 1115 1657 2337	5.1 0.8 5.0 0.8	**26** W	0416 1048 1641 2308	5.0 1.0 4.9 0.9
12 W	0518 1203 1744	5.3 0.6 5.1	**27** TH O	0500 1136 1726 2355	5.2 0.7 5.0 0.7
13 TH	0022 0601 1247 1827	0.6 5.3 0.5 5.1	**28** F	0543 1222 1810	5.3 0.5 5.1
14 F	0104 0642 1326 1906	0.6 5.3 0.5 5.0	**29** SA	0039 0627 1305 1853	0.5 5.4 0.4 5.2
15 SA	0140 0718 1401 1938	0.7 5.3 0.6 4.9	**30** SU	0120 0710 1344 1935	0.4 5.4 0.3 5.2
			31 M	0158 0751 1421 2014	0.4 5.4 0.4 5.1

FEBRUARY

	Time	m		Time	m
1 TU	0235 0830 1458 2053	0.5 5.3 0.6 5.0	**16** W	0236 0817 1450 2035	1.1 4.8 1.2 4.7
2 W	0313 0911 1537 2135	0.7 5.0 0.9 4.8	**17** TH	0257 0848 1510 2109	1.3 4.6 1.3 4.5
3 TH	0356 0957 1623 2226	1.1 4.7 1.3 4.5	**18** F	0319 0924 1538 2150	1.5 4.3 1.6 4.2
4 F	0450 1057 1726 2336	1.4 4.4 1.6 4.3	**19** SA	0358 1013 1633 2249	1.8 4.1 1.9 4.1
5 SA	0607 1218 1903	1.7 4.2 1.8	**20** SU	0541 1121 1829	2.1 3.9 2.0
6 SU	0100 0753 1343 2035	4.3 1.7 4.2 1.6	**21** M	0010 0712 1304 1946	4.0 2.0 4.0 1.9
7 M	0219 0913 1458 2142	4.5 1.4 4.4 1.3	**22** TU	0153 0825 1437 2054	4.2 1.7 4.3 1.5
8 TU	0324 1013 1557 2236	4.7 1.2 4.7 1.1	**23** W	0301 0929 1533 2155	4.6 1.3 4.6 1.2
9 W	0415 1102 1643 2323	5.0 0.8 4.9 0.8	**24** TH	0352 1025 1620 2248	4.9 0.9 4.9 0.8
10 TH ●	0459 1147 1724	5.2 0.6 5.0	**25** F O	0437 1116 1705 2336	5.2 0.5 5.1 0.5
11 F	0005 0539 1228 1802	0.6 5.3 0.4 5.0	**26** SA O	0522 1202 1749	5.4 0.3 5.2
12 SA	0044 0617 1305 1836	0.5 5.3 0.4 5.0	**27** SU	0021 0607 1246 1832	0.2 5.5 0.1 5.3
13 SU	0118 0650 1336 1906	0.5 5.2 0.5 5.0	**28** M	0103 0651 1326 1914	0.1 5.5 0.1 5.4
14 M	0147 0719 1404 1935	0.6 5.1 0.7 4.9			
15 TU	0213 0747 1428 2004	0.8 5.0 0.9 4.8			

MARCH

	Time	m		Time	m
1 TU	0142 0734 1404 1955	0.1 5.5 0.2 5.3	**16** W	0144 0721 1356 1936	0.8 5.0 0.9 4.9
2 W	0219 0815 1441 2034	0.3 5.3 0.4 5.1	**17** TH	0206 0751 1416 2006	1.0 4.8 1.1 4.7
3 TH	0257 0855 1519 2115	0.6 5.0 0.8 4.9	**18** F	0225 0821 1435 2037	1.2 4.6 1.3 4.5
4 F	0339 0940 1602 2203	1.0 4.7 1.3 4.5	**19** SA	0248 0855 1503 2115	1.4 4.3 1.5 4.3
5 SA	0430 1038 1701 2312	1.4 4.3 1.7 4.3	**20** SU	0325 0942 1549 2210	1.6 4.1 1.8 4.1
6 SU	0543 1203 1839	1.8 4.0 1.9	**21** M	0434 1047 1742 2323	1.9 3.9 2.0 4.1
7 M	0041 0738 1331 2021	4.2 1.8 4.1 1.8	**22** TU	0637 1213 1913	1.9 3.9 1.9
8 TU	0201 0859 1445 2126	4.4 1.5 4.3 1.4	**23** W	0057 0753 1401 2024	4.2 1.6 4.2 1.5
9 W	0305 0955 1540 2217	4.6 1.2 4.6 1.1	**24** TH	0223 0859 1504 2127	4.5 1.3 4.6 1.2
10 TH	0355 1042 1622 2301	4.9 0.8 4.8 0.8	**25** F	0321 0958 1553 2222	4.9 0.8 4.9 0.7
11 F	0436 1124 1659 2342	5.1 0.6 5.0 0.6	**26** SA	0410 1050 1639 2312	5.2 0.5 5.1 0.4
12 SA ●	0514 1203 1733	5.2 0.5 5.1	**27** SU O	0457 1138 1724 2358	5.4 0.2 5.3 0.1
13 SU	0018 0548 1238 1805	0.5 5.2 0.5 5.1	**28** M	0543 1223 1808	5.5 0.0 5.4
14 M	0051 0620 1308 1836	0.5 5.2 0.5 5.1	**29** TU	0043 0630 1306 1853	0.0 5.6 0.0 5.5
15 TU	0119 0651 1333 1906	0.6 5.1 0.7 5.0	**30** W	0124 0715 1346 1935	0.0 5.5 0.2 5.4
			31 TH	0204 0759 1425 2016	0.2 5.3 0.5 5.2

APRIL

	Time	m		Time	m
1 F	0244 0842 1505 2057	0.5 5.0 0.9 4.9	**16** SA	0204 0801 1414 2013	1.2 4.5 1.3 4.6
2 SA	0327 0927 1549 2144	1.0 4.6 1.3 4.6	**17** SU	0232 0836 1446 2052	1.3 4.4 1.4 4.5
3 SU	0417 1025 1645 2251	1.3 4.3 1.7 4.3	**18** M	0311 0923 1534 2145	1.5 4.2 1.7 4.3
4 M	0526 1149 1811	1.7 4.0 1.9	**19** TU	0416 1024 1659 2251	1.7 4.0 1.9 4.2
5 TU	0019 0710 1310 1951	4.2 1.8 4.1 1.8	**20** W	0601 1139 1837	1.7 4.0 1.8
6 W	0135 0830 1418 2058	4.3 1.5 4.3 1.5	**21** TH	0010 0718 1309 1950	4.3 1.5 4.2 1.5
7 TH	0237 0927 1511 2149	4.5 1.3 4.5 1.2	**22** F	0135 0825 1424 2055	4.5 1.2 4.5 1.2
8 F	0326 1013 1553 2233	4.8 1.0 4.8 0.9	**23** SA	0243 0926 1520 2153	4.8 0.8 4.9 0.8
9 SA	0407 1055 1629 2313	5.0 0.7 4.9 0.7	**24** SU	0339 1021 1610 2246	5.1 0.5 5.1 0.4
10 SU	0444 1132 1702 2349	5.1 0.6 5.0 0.6	**25** M O	0430 1112 1658 2335	5.3 0.3 5.3 0.2
11 M ●	0518 1206 1735	5.1 0.6 5.1	**26** TU	0520 1200 1745	5.4 0.1 5.5
12 TU	0021 0551 1236 1807	0.7 5.1 0.7 5.1	**27** W	0022 0610 1246 1832	0.1 5.4 0.1 5.5
13 W	0050 0625 1302 1840	0.7 5.0 0.8 5.0	**28** TH	0108 0658 1330 1918	0.1 5.4 0.3 5.4
14 TH	0116 0658 1327 1912	0.9 4.9 0.9 4.9	**29** F	0152 0745 1413 2001	0.3 5.2 0.5 5.3
15 F	0140 0730 1350 1942	1.0 4.7 1.1 4.8	**30** SA	0234 0830 1455 2044	0.5 4.9 0.9 5.0

53

FALMOUTH
50°09′N 5°03′W

Times and heights (in metres) of high and low water 1994
Time: GMT. For BST, ADD ONE HOUR in the shaded area

MAY

Day	Time	m	Day	Time	m
1 SU	0318 0916 1539 2128	0.9 4.6 1.3 4.7	**16** M	0228 0826 1443 2039	1.2 4.4 1.3 4.6
2 M	0406 1011 1629 2226	1.3 4.3 1.5 4.4	**17** TU	0310 0910 1530 2127	1.3 4.3 1.4 4.5
3 TU	0505 1123 1735 2345	1.5 4.1 1.8 4.3	**18** W	0406 1005 1634 2226	1.4 4.2 1.6 4.4
4 W	0622 1236 1900	1.7 4.1 1.8	**19** TH	0523 1110 1756 2335	1.4 4.2 1.6 4.4
5 TH	0058 0744 1339 2014	4.3 1.6 4.2 1.6	**20** F	0640 1225 1912	1.3 4.3 1.4
6 F	0159 0846 1432 2111	4.4 1.4 4.4 1.4	**21** SA	0052 0750 1340 2021	4.5 1.2 4.5 1.2
7 SA	0250 0936 1517 2158	4.6 1.2 4.6 1.2	**22** SU	0206 0854 1446 2124	4.7 1.0 4.8 0.9
8 SU	0334 1019 1556 2239	4.7 1.0 4.8 1.0	**23** M	0310 0954 1543 2221	5.0 0.7 5.0 0.6
9 M	0412 1057 1631 2316	4.9 0.9 5.0 0.9	**24** TU	0407 1048 1635 2314	5.1 0.5 5.3 0.4
10 TU ●	0448 1132 1706 2350	4.9 0.9 5.0 0.9	**25** W O	0500 1140 1725	5.2 0.4 5.4
11 W	0525 1204 1742	4.9 0.9 5.0	**26** TH	0005 0552 1229 1814	0.3 5.3 0.3 5.4
12 TH	0022 0602 1234 1819	0.9 4.9 0.9 5.0	**27** F	0054 0643 1317 1903	0.2 5.2 0.4 5.4
13 F	0052 0639 1304 1853	0.9 4.8 1.0 4.9	**28** SA	0140 0733 1401 1948	0.3 5.1 0.5 5.3
14 SA	0123 0715 1334 1926	1.0 4.7 1.1 4.8	**29** SU	0224 0818 1443 2030	0.5 4.9 0.8 5.1
15 SU	0154 0749 1406 1959	1.1 4.6 1.2 4.7	**30** M	0307 0902 1524 2109	0.8 4.7 1.1 4.8
			31 TU	0349 0946 1607 2150	1.1 4.4 1.3 4.6

JUNE

Day	Time	m	Day	Time	m
1 W	0436 1037 1656 2243	1.3 4.2 1.6 4.3	**16** TH	0351 0948 1612 2204	1.1 4.4 1.3 4.6
2 TH	0530 1142 1756	1.6 4.1 1.8	**17** F	0448 1044 1717 2305	1.3 4.4 1.3 4.5
3 F	0000 0635 1247 1906	4.2 1.7 4.1 1.8	**18** SA	0600 1151 1834	1.3 4.4 1.4
4 SA	0109 0744 1345 2015	4.2 1.6 4.3 1.7	**19** SU	0018 0716 1305 1949	4.5 1.3 4.5 1.3
5 SU	0206 0844 1435 2112	4.3 1.4 4.4 1.4	**20** M	0136 0826 1417 2059	4.6 1.2 4.7 1.1
6 M	0256 0934 1520 2159	4.5 1.3 4.6 1.3	**21** TU	0247 0931 1520 2202	4.7 0.9 4.9 0.9
7 TU	0340 1017 1601 2241	4.6 1.2 4.8 1.2	**22** W	0349 1030 1616 2259	4.9 0.7 5.1 0.6
8 W	0421 1056 1641 2320	4.7 1.1 4.9 1.0	**23** TH O	0444 1125 1708 2352	5.0 0.6 5.3 0.4
9 TH ●	0502 1133 1721 2357	4.8 1.0 5.0 1.0	**24** F	0536 1216 1758	5.1 0.4 5.4
10 F	0542 1211 1800	4.8 1.0 5.0	**25** SA	0042 0628 1304 1847	0.3 5.1 0.4 5.4
11 SA	0034 0624 1248 1839	0.9 4.8 1.0 5.0	**26** SU	0128 0717 1347 1932	0.3 5.0 0.5 5.3
12 SU	0111 0704 1324 1917	0.9 4.7 1.0 4.9	**27** M	0210 0800 1426 2011	0.4 4.9 0.6 5.1
13 M	0147 0743 1401 1952	0.9 4.6 1.0 4.9	**28** TU	0248 0837 1503 2042	0.6 4.8 0.9 4.9
14 TU	0225 0820 1439 2030	1.0 4.6 1.1 4.8	**29** W	0324 0908 1539 2111	0.9 4.6 1.2 4.7
15 W	0304 0901 1522 2113	1.0 4.5 1.2 4.7	**30** TH	0401 0940 1617 2145	1.2 4.4 1.4 4.5

JULY

Day	Time	m	Day	Time	m
1 F	0442 1022 1703 2231	1.4 4.2 1.7 4.3	**16** SA	0419 1020 1645 2240	1.1 4.5 1.3 4.5
2 SA	0533 1120 1801 2336	1.7 4.1 1.8 4.1	**17** SU	0522 1123 1757 2352	1.3 4.4 1.4 4.4
3 SU	0634 1237 1907	1.8 4.1 1.9	**18** M	0644 1239 1924	1.4 4.4 1.4
4 M	0108 0739 1348 2014	4.1 1.7 4.2 1.7	**19** TU	0116 0806 1356 2043	4.4 1.3 4.5 1.3
5 TU	0218 0841 1445 2115	4.2 1.5 4.5 1.5	**20** W	0233 0917 1504 2151	4.5 1.2 4.8 1.1
6 W	0312 0935 1534 2206	4.4 1.3 4.7 1.3	**21** TH	0337 1019 1602 2249	4.7 0.9 5.0 0.7
7 TH	0358 1024 1618 2253	4.6 1.2 4.9 1.1	**22** F O	0432 1113 1653 2341	4.9 0.7 5.2 0.5
8 F ●	0442 1109 1701 2336	4.7 1.0 5.0 0.9	**23** SA	0522 1202 1741	5.0 0.5 5.3
9 SA	0525 1152 1743	4.8 0.9 5.0	**24** SU	0028 0609 1247 1827	0.3 5.0 0.4 5.3
10 SU	0019 0608 1234 1825	0.8 4.8 0.8 5.1	**25** M	0111 0653 1328 1908	0.3 5.0 0.4 5.3
11 M	0100 0651 1314 1905	0.7 4.8 0.7 5.1	**26** TU	0149 0732 1404 1943	0.3 5.0 0.5 5.2
12 TU	0138 0731 1352 1943	0.6 4.8 0.7 5.1	**27** W	0223 0802 1436 2009	0.5 4.8 0.7 5.0
13 W	0215 0809 1429 2020	0.6 4.8 0.7 5.0	**28** TH	0254 0828 1506 2035	0.8 4.7 1.0 4.8
14 TH	0251 0847 1507 2100	0.7 4.7 0.9 4.9	**29** F	0323 0857 1536 2106	1.1 4.5 1.3 4.6
15 F	0332 0929 1551 2145	0.9 4.6 1.1 4.7	**30** SA	0355 0933 1612 2143	1.4 4.3 1.6 4.3
			31 SU	0437 1019 1705 2233	1.7 4.2 1.9 4.1

AUGUST

Day	Time	m	Day	Time	m
1 M	0539 1121 1816 2346	1.9 4.0 2.0 3.9	**16** TU	0620 1222 1909	1.7 4.3 1.6
2 TU	0651 1252 1928	1.9 4.1 1.9	**17** W	0107 0757 1343 2037	4.2 1.6 4.4 1.4
3 W	0139 0759 1413 2035	4.0 1.7 4.3 1.7	**18** TH	0227 0910 1453 2143	4.4 1.3 4.7 1.1
4 TH	0248 0901 1509 2136	4.3 1.5 4.6 1.3	**19** F	0331 1009 1549 2237	4.6 1.0 5.0 0.8
5 F	0338 0957 1556 2228	4.5 1.3 4.8 1.1	**20** SA	0421 1059 1637 2325	4.9 0.7 5.2 0.5
6 SA	0423 1047 1640 2316	4.7 1.0 5.0 0.8	**21** SU O	0505 1144 1721	5.0 0.5 5.3
7 SU ●	0506 1134 1723	4.9 0.8 5.2	**22** M	0008 0545 1226 1801	0.3 5.1 0.4 5.3
8 M	0001 0548 1218 1805	0.6 5.0 0.6 5.2	**23** TU	0048 0623 1304 1838	0.3 5.1 0.4 5.3
9 TU	0043 0631 1259 1848	0.4 5.0 0.5 5.3	**24** W	0123 0656 1337 1909	0.4 5.0 0.4 5.2
10 W	0122 0712 1337 1928	0.4 5.0 0.4 5.3	**25** TH	0153 0724 1405 1935	0.6 4.9 0.7 5.0
11 TH	0159 0751 1413 2006	0.4 5.0 0.5 5.2	**26** F	0220 0752 1432 2002	0.8 4.8 1.0 4.8
12 F	0234 0830 1450 2045	0.5 4.9 0.7 5.0	**27** SA	0244 0821 1456 2032	1.1 4.7 1.3 4.6
13 SA	0312 0910 1532 2127	0.8 4.8 1.0 4.8	**28** SU	0307 0855 1520 2107	1.3 4.5 1.5 4.5
14 SU	0355 0958 1622 2220	1.1 4.7 1.3 4.5	**29** M	0330 0935 1553 2151	1.7 4.3 1.9 4.1
15 M	0453 1100 1731 2336	1.4 4.4 1.5 4.2	**30** TU	0418 1029 1726 2253	2.0 4.1 2.1 3.9
			31 W	0608 1147 1851	2.1 4.0 2.1

54

FALMOUTH
50°09′N 5°03′W

Times and heights (in metres) of high and low water 1994
Time: GMT. For BST, ADD ONE HOUR in the shaded area

SEPTEMBER

Day	Time	m	Time	m	Time	m	Time	m
1 TH	0045	3.9	0725	1.9	1335	4.2	2003	1.8
16 F	0221	4.3	0858	1.4	1440	4.7	2129	1.2
2 F	0223	4.2	0832	1.6	1442	4.5	2107	1.4
17 SA	0321	4.6	0952	1.1	1533	5.0	2219	0.8
3 SA	0317	4.5	0931	1.3	1532	4.8	2203	1.1
18 SU	0405	4.9	1039	0.8	1617	5.2	2303	0.6
4 SU	0401	4.8	1023	1.0	1616	5.1	2252	0.7
19 M ○	0444	5.1	1121	0.6	1657	5.3	2343	0.4
5 M ●	0443	5.0	1111	0.6	1659	5.3	2337	0.4
20 TU	0519	5.1	1200	0.5	1733	5.3		
6 TU	0525	5.2	1155	0.4	1742	5.4		
21 W	0020	0.4	0551	5.2	1236	0.5	1806	5.2
7 W	0020	0.3	0607	5.3	1238	0.3	1825	5.5
22 TH	0053	0.5	0622	5.1	1307	0.7	1836	5.2
8 TH	0101	0.2	0649	5.3	1318	0.3	1908	5.4
23 F	0121	0.7	0651	5.1	1334	0.9	1905	5.0
9 F	0140	0.3	0730	5.3	1356	0.4	1949	5.3
24 SA	0146	0.9	0720	5.0	1358	1.1	1934	4.9
10 SA	0216	0.5	0811	5.1	1434	0.6	2030	5.1
25 SU	0207	1.2	0751	4.8	1420	1.3	2004	4.6
11 SU	0254	0.8	0852	4.9	1516	1.0	2113	4.8
26 M	0224	1.4	0823	4.6	1438	1.5	2038	4.4
12 M	0337	1.2	0939	4.7	1606	1.3	2206	4.4
27 TU	0245	1.6	0849	4.4	1507	1.8	2120	4.2
13 TU	0433	1.6	1042	4.4	1715	1.7	2326	4.1
28 W	0323	1.9	0952	4.2	1605	2.1	2219	4.0
14 W	0605	1.9	1208	4.3	1902	1.8		
29 TH	0511	2.2	1100	4.1	1815	2.1	2342	3.9
15 TH	0101	4.1	0748	1.8	1332	4.4	2028	1.5
30 F	0651	2.1	1234	4.2	1930	1.8		

OCTOBER

Day	Time	m	Time	m	Time	m	Time	m
1 SA	0147	4.1	0801	1.7	1403	4.5	2035	1.4
16 SU	0256	4.6	0927	1.3	1508	4.9	2152	1.1
2 SU	0247	4.5	0902	1.3	1500	4.9	2133	1.1
17 M	0340	4.9	1013	1.0	1552	5.1	2235	0.8
3 M	0334	4.9	0956	1.0	1547	5.2	2224	0.7
18 TU	0417	5.1	1054	0.8	1630	5.2	2314	0.7
4 TU	0417	5.1	1045	0.6	1632	5.4	2311	0.4
19 W ○	0450	5.2	1132	0.7	1704	5.2	2350	0.7
5 W ●	0459	5.3	1131	0.4	1717	5.5	2356	0.2
20 TH	0521	5.2	1207	0.8	1736	5.2		
6 TH	0542	5.4	1216	0.2	1803	5.6		
21 F	0022	0.8	0552	5.2	1237	0.9	1808	5.1
7 F	0040	0.2	0626	5.5	1259	0.2	1848	5.5
22 SA	0050	0.9	0623	5.1	1304	1.0	1840	5.0
8 SA	0121	0.3	0710	5.4	1341	0.4	1933	5.4
23 SU	0114	1.1	0655	5.0	1330	1.2	1911	4.8
9 SU	0201	0.5	0753	5.3	1422	0.6	2017	5.1
24 M	0138	1.2	0726	4.9	1354	1.3	1943	4.7
10 M	0242	0.9	0837	5.1	1506	1.0	2103	4.8
25 TU	0159	1.3	0758	4.7	1417	1.5	2017	4.5
11 TU	0326	1.3	0925	4.8	1556	1.3	2157	4.4
26 W	0225	1.6	0836	4.5	1450	1.7	2059	4.3
12 W	0421	1.6	1027	4.5	1702	1.7	2316	4.2
27 TH	0304	1.8	0924	4.4	1542	1.9	2155	4.1
13 TH	0545	1.9	1151	4.4	1841	1.8		
28 F	0408	2.1	1026	4.3	1729	2.0	2305	4.0
14 F	0045		0724	1.9	1311	4.4	2004	1.6
29 SA	0608	2.1	1140	4.3	1852	1.8		
15 SA	0159	4.4	0833	1.6	1416	4.7	2104	1.3
30 SU	0036	4.2	0724	1.8	1304	4.5	1959	1.4
31 M	0202	4.5	0828	1.4	1417	4.8	2100	1.1

NOVEMBER

Day	Time	m	Time	m	Time	m	Time	m
1 TU	0259	4.8	0926	1.1	1514	5.1	2154	0.8
16 W	0346	4.9	1024	1.2	1600	5.0	2243	1.0
2 W	0348	5.1	1018	0.7	1605	5.3	2245	0.5
17 TH	0421	5.1	1102	1.0	1636	5.0	2319	1.0
3 TH ●	0434	5.4	1108	0.5	1654	5.5	2333	0.3
18 F ○	0454	5.2	1138	1.0	1710	5.1	2352	1.0
4 F	0520	5.5	1156	0.3	1743	5.5		
19 SA	0527	5.2	1210	1.0	1745	5.0		
5 SA	0019	0.3	0606	5.6	1243	0.3	1832	5.5
20 SU	0022	1.0	0601	5.2	1240	1.1	1821	5.0
6 SU	0105	0.4	0653	5.6	1328	0.4	1920	5.4
21 M	0050	1.1	0636	5.1	1310	1.2	1857	4.8
7 M	0149	0.6	0739	5.4	1413	0.6	2007	5.2
22 TU	0119	1.2	0710	5.0	1339	1.3	1931	4.7
8 TU	0232	0.9	0825	5.2	1458	0.9	2054	4.9
23 W	0148	1.3	0744	4.9	1410	1.3	2006	4.6
9 W	0317	1.2	0912	5.0	1546	1.3	2146	4.6
24 TH	0219	1.4	0820	4.7	1445	1.4	2046	4.4
10 TH	0407	1.5	1007	4.7	1643	1.5	2253	4.3
25 F	0258	1.6	0904	4.6	1531	1.6	2135	4.3
11 F	0511	1.8	1121	4.5	1757	1.8		
26 SA	0350	1.7	0958	4.5	1637	1.7	2234	4.2
12 SA	0011	4.2	0636	2.0	1236	4.4	1920	1.7
27 SU	0509	1.9	1102	4.5	1804	1.7	2344	4.3
13 SU	0120	4.3	0753	1.8	1339	4.5	2026	1.5
28 M	0638	1.8	1214	4.5	1919	1.5		
14 M	0218	4.5	0852	1.5	1434	4.7	2118	1.3
29 TU	0104	4.5	0751	1.5	1330	4.7	2026	1.3
15 TU	0306	4.7	0941	1.3	1521	4.8	2203	1.2
30 W	0218	4.7	0856	1.3	1440	4.9	2126	1.0

DECEMBER

Day	Time	m	Time	m	Time	m	Time	m
1 TH	0318	5.0	0954	0.9	1540	5.2	2222	0.7
16 F	0351	4.9	1032	1.3	1609	4.8	2249	1.2
2 F ●	0411	5.3	1048	0.6	1634	5.3	2314	0.5
17 SA	0429	5.0	1111	1.2	1648	4.9	2325	1.1
3 SA	0501	5.5	1140	0.4	1727	5.4		
18 SU ○	0506	5.1	1147	1.1	1727	4.9		
4 SU	0004	0.4	0550	5.6	1230	0.4	1818	5.4
19 M	0000	1.1	0544	5.2	1222	1.1	1806	4.9
5 M	0053	0.4	0639	5.6	1318	0.4	1909	5.3
20 TU	0034	1.1	0623	5.1	1257	1.0	1846	4.9
6 TU	0139	0.5	0728	5.5	1404	0.5	1957	5.2
21 W	0108	1.1	0701	5.1	1330	1.1	1924	4.8
7 W	0222	0.7	0813	5.4	1447	0.7	2041	5.0
22 TH	0141	1.1	0736	5.0	1404	1.1	1959	4.7
8 TH	0304	1.0	0856	5.1	1530	1.0	2125	4.7
23 F	0215	1.2	0810	4.9	1439	1.2	2035	4.6
9 F	0346	1.3	0939	4.8	1614	1.3	2212	4.4
24 SA	0251	1.3	0849	4.8	1518	1.3	2116	4.5
10 SA	0433	1.6	1029	4.6	1706	1.6	2314	4.3
25 SU	0334	1.3	0935	4.7	1606	1.3	2207	4.4
11 SU	0530	1.9	1137	4.4	1810	1.8		
26 M	0428	1.5	1030	4.6	1710	1.5	2308	4.4
12 M	0024	4.2	0645	2.0	1249	4.3	1925	1.8
27 TU	0545	1.6	1136	4.5	1834	1.5		
13 TU	0128	4.3	0801	1.9	1350	4.4	2032	1.7
28 W	0020	4.4	0712	1.6	1253	4.5	1953	1.4
14 W	0224	4.5	0901	1.7	1444	4.5	2125	1.5
29 TH	0140	4.6	0828	1.4	1412	4.7	2102	1.2
15 TH	0311	4.7	0950	1.4	1529	4.7	2209	1.3
30 F	0253	4.9	0934	1.1	1521	4.9	2204	1.0
31 SA	0353	5.1	1034	0.8	1620	5.1	2300	0.7

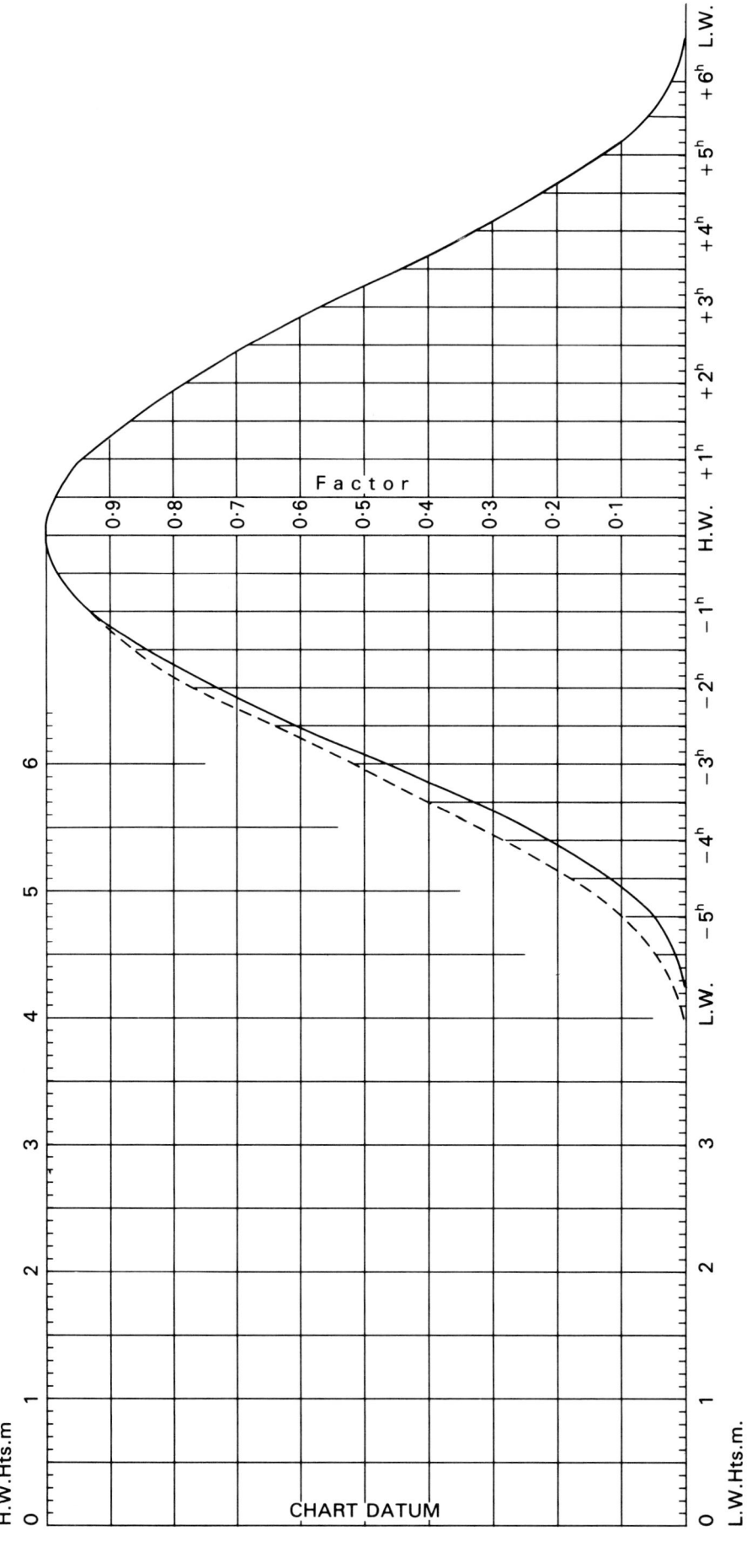

ISLES OF SCILLY – ST. MARY'S
49°55′N 6°19′W

Times and heights (in metres) of high and low water 1994
Time: GMT. For BST, ADD ONE HOUR in the shaded area

JANUARY

Day	Time	m	Day	Time	m
1 SA	0050 / 0654 / 1319 / 1923	0.9 / 5.6 / 0.8 / 5.3	**16** SU	0139 / 0722 / 1400 / 1942	0.9 / 5.4 / 0.9 / 5.1
2 SU	0133 / 0739 / 1402 / 2008	0.9 / 5.6 / 0.9 / 5.2	**17** M	0211 / 0752 / 1431 / 2014	1.1 / 5.3 / 1.2 / 4.9
3 M	0217 / 0825 / 1446 / 2055	1.0 / 5.4 / 1.0 / 5.1	**18** TU	0241 / 0827 / 1504 / 2052	1.4 / 5.1 / 1.4 / 4.7
4 TU	0304 / 0914 / 1535 / 2146	1.2 / 5.2 / 1.2 / 4.8	**19** W	0314 / 0907 / 1538 / 2136	1.6 / 4.8 / 1.7 / 4.4
5 W	0358 / 1010 / 1634 / 2249	1.4 / 4.9 / 1.4 / 4.7	**20** TH	0352 / 0954 / 1629 / 2232	1.9 / 4.4 / 1.9 / 4.3
6 TH	0507 / 1121 / 1752 / 2343	1.6 / 4.7 / 1.6 / 4.2	**21** F	0502 / 1055 / 1748	2.1 / 4.2 / 2.1
7 F	0001 / 0628 / 1231 / 1911	4.6 / 1.7 / 4.6 / 1.7	**22** SA	0622 / 1212 / 1854	2.2 / 4.0 / 2.1
8 SA	0112 / 0746 / 1342 / 2019	4.7 / 1.6 / 4.7 / 1.5	**23** SU	0104 / 0728 / 1339 / 1954	4.3 / 2.0 / 4.3 / 1.8
9 SU	0216 / 0849 / 1444 / 2116	4.9 / 1.4 / 4.9 / 1.3	**24** M	0214 / 0826 / 1440 / 2049	4.6 / 1.7 / 4.6 / 1.5
10 M	0311 / 0943 / 1536 / 2205	5.2 / 1.2 / 5.1 / 1.1	**25** TU	0302 / 0918 / 1526 / 2138	4.9 / 1.4 / 4.9 / 1.3
11 TU ●	0358 / 1029 / 1621 / 2249	5.4 / 0.9 / 5.3 / 0.9	**26** W	0344 / 1005 / 1607 / 2223	5.3 / 1.1 / 5.2 / 1.0
12 W	0439 / 1115 / 1706 / 2336	5.7 / 0.7 / 5.4 / 0.7	**27** TH O	0424 / 1048 / 1646 / 2306	5.6 / 0.8 / 5.3 / 0.8
13 TH	0525 / 1204 / 1754	5.7 / 0.6 / 5.4	**28** F	0505 / 1136 / 1735 / 2355	5.7 / 0.6 / 5.4 / 0.6
14 F	0022 / 0610 / 1247 / 1837	0.7 / 5.6 / 0.6 / 5.3	**29** SA	0554 / 1224 / 1822	5.8 / 0.5 / 5.6
15 SA	0102 / 0650 / 1325 / 1912	0.8 / 5.7 / 0.7 / 5.2	**30** SU	0040 / 0641 / 1306 / 1909	0.5 / 5.8 / 0.4 / 5.6
			31 M	0122 / 0726 / 1348 / 1952	0.5 / 5.8 / 0.5 / 5.4

FEBRUARY

Day	Time	m	Day	Time	m
1 TU	0203 / 0810 / 1429 / 2036	0.6 / 5.7 / 0.7 / 5.3	**16** W	0204 / 0755 / 1420 / 2016	1.2 / 5.1 / 1.3 / 4.9
2 W	0246 / 0856 / 1512 / 2123	0.8 / 5.3 / 1.0 / 5.1	**17** TH	0228 / 0830 / 1442 / 2054	1.4 / 4.8 / 1.4 / 4.7
3 TH	0334 / 0947 / 1603 / 2219	1.2 / 4.9 / 1.4 / 4.7	**18** F	0252 / 0910 / 1514 / 2139	1.6 / 4.4 / 1.7 / 4.3
4 F	0433 / 1053 / 1713 / 2335	1.5 / 4.6 / 1.7 / 4.4	**19** SA	0336 / 1004 / 1614 / 2244	1.9 / 4.2 / 2.0 / 4.2
5 SA	0555 / 1212 / 1845	1.8 / 4.3 / 1.9	**20** SU	0530 / 1120 / 1814	2.2 / 3.9 / 2.1
6 SU	0050 / 0730 / 1328 / 2007	4.4 / 1.8 / 4.3 / 1.7	**21** M	0005 / 0653 / 1254 / 1923	4.0 / 2.1 / 4.0 / 2.0
7 M	0200 / 0840 / 1435 / 2106	4.7 / 1.5 / 4.6 / 1.4	**22** TU	0137 / 0758 / 1416 / 2024	4.3 / 1.8 / 4.4 / 1.6
8 TU	0258 / 0934 / 1527 / 2154	4.9 / 1.3 / 4.9 / 1.2	**23** W	0237 / 0854 / 1506 / 2118	4.8 / 1.4 / 4.8 / 1.3
9 W	0344 / 1018 / 1608 / 2236	5.3 / 0.9 / 5.2 / 0.9	**24** TH	0323 / 0945 / 1548 / 2205	5.2 / 1.0 / 5.2 / 0.9
10 TH ●	0423 / 1057 / 1645 / 2317	5.6 / 0.7 / 5.3 / 0.7	**25** F	0403 / 1030 / 1628 / 2248	5.6 / 0.6 / 5.4 / 0.6
11 F	0500 / 1142 / 1726	5.7 / 0.5 / 5.3	**26** SA O	0443 / 1113 / 1711 / 2335	5.8 / 0.4 / 5.6 / 0.3
12 SA	0000 / 0542 / 1224 / 1804	0.6 / 5.7 / 0.5 / 5.3	**27** SU	0531 / 1203 / 1759	6.0 / 0.2 / 5.7
13 SU	0038 / 0619 / 1258 / 1837	0.6 / 5.6 / 0.6 / 5.3	**28** M	0021 / 0620 / 1247 / 1845	0.2 / 6.0 / 0.2 / 5.8
14 M	0110 / 0651 / 1329 / 1909	0.7 / 5.4 / 0.8 / 5.2			
15 TU	0139 / 0722 / 1355 / 1941	0.9 / 5.3 / 1.0 / 5.1			

MARCH

Day	Time	m	Day	Time	m
1 TU	0104 / 0707 / 1329 / 1931	0.2 / 6.0 / 0.3 / 5.7	**16** W	0106 / 0653 / 1320 / 1910	0.9 / 5.3 / 1.0 / 5.2
2 W	0145 / 0753 / 1410 / 2014	0.4 / 5.7 / 0.5 / 5.4	**17** TH	0131 / 0726 / 1342 / 1943	1.1 / 5.1 / 1.2 / 4.9
3 TH	0228 / 0838 / 1452 / 2100	0.7 / 5.3 / 0.9 / 5.2	**18** F	0152 / 0800 / 1403 / 2018	1.3 / 4.8 / 1.4 / 4.7
4 F	0315 / 0928 / 1540 / 2153	1.1 / 4.9 / 1.4 / 4.7	**19** SA	0218 / 0838 / 1435 / 2100	1.5 / 4.4 / 1.6 / 4.4
5 SA	0411 / 1032 / 1645 / 2310	1.5 / 4.4 / 1.8 / 4.4	**20** SU	0259 / 0930 / 1526 / 2201	1.7 / 4.2 / 1.9 / 4.2
6 SU	0532 / 1159 / 1823	1.9 / 4.0 / 2.0	**21** M	0415 / 1042 / 1731 / 2322	2.0 / 3.9 / 2.1 / 4.2
7 M	0033 / 0716 / 1318 / 1954	4.3 / 1.9 / 4.2 / 1.9	**22** TU	0622 / 1208 / 1854	2.0 / 3.9 / 2.0
8 TU	0144 / 0828 / 1423 / 2052	4.6 / 1.6 / 4.4 / 1.5	**23** W	0047 / 0730 / 1344 / 1957	4.3 / 1.7 / 4.3 / 1.6
9 W	0241 / 0918 / 1512 / 2137	4.8 / 1.3 / 4.8 / 1.2	**24** TH	0204 / 0828 / 1440 / 2053	4.7 / 1.4 / 4.8 / 1.3
10 TH	0326 / 1000 / 1550 / 2217	5.2 / 0.9 / 5.1 / 0.9	**25** F	0255 / 0920 / 1524 / 2142	5.2 / 0.9 / 5.2 / 0.8
11 F	0402 / 1037 / 1623 / 2253	5.4 / 0.7 / 5.3 / 0.7	**26** SA	0339 / 1007 / 1605 / 2226	5.6 / 0.6 / 5.4 / 0.5
12 SA ●	0436 / 1115 / 1653 / 2331	5.6 / 0.6 / 5.4 / 0.6	**27** SU O	0421 / 1049 / 1645 / 2309	5.8 / 0.3 / 5.7 / 0.2
13 SU	0510 / 1154 / 1729	5.6 / 0.6 / 5.4	**28** M	0505 / 1137 / 1732 / 2359	6.0 / 0.1 / 5.8 / 0.1
14 M	0008 / 0546 / 1227 / 1804	0.6 / 5.6 / 0.6 / 5.4	**29** TU	0557 / 1225 / 1822	6.1 / 0.1 / 6.0
15 TU	0039 / 0620 / 1254 / 1837	0.7 / 5.4 / 0.8 / 5.3	**30** W	0044 / 0647 / 1309 / 1909	0.1 / 6.0 / 0.3 / 5.8
			31 TH	0129 / 0735 / 1352 / 1954	0.3 / 5.7 / 0.6 / 5.6

APRIL

Day	Time	m	Day	Time	m
1 F	0213 / 0823 / 1437 / 2040	0.6 / 5.3 / 1.0 / 5.2	**16** SA	0129 / 0738 / 1340 / 1951	1.3 / 4.7 / 1.4 / 4.8
2 SA	0301 / 0914 / 1526 / 2132	1.1 / 4.8 / 1.4 / 4.8	**17** SU	0200 / 0817 / 1416 / 2035	1.4 / 4.6 / 1.5 / 4.7
3 SU	0357 / 1018 / 1628 / 2246	1.4 / 4.4 / 1.8 / 4.4	**18** M	0243 / 0909 / 1509 / 2134	1.6 / 4.3 / 1.8 / 4.4
4 M	0513 / 1147 / 1759	1.8 / 4.0 / 2.0	**19** TU	0356 / 1016 / 1643 / 2246	1.8 / 4.0 / 2.0 / 4.3
5 TU	0013 / 0651 / 1259 / 1928	4.3 / 1.9 / 4.2 / 1.9	**20** W	0550 / 1138 / 1822	1.8 / 4.0 / 1.9
6 W	0121 / 0802 / 1359 / 2027	4.4 / 1.6 / 4.4 / 1.6	**21** TH	0005 / 0658 / 1258 / 1927	4.4 / 1.6 / 4.3 / 1.6
7 TH	0216 / 0853 / 1446 / 2112	4.7 / 1.4 / 4.7 / 1.3	**22** F	0121 / 0758 / 1405 / 2024	4.7 / 1.3 / 4.7 / 1.3
8 F	0259 / 0934 / 1524 / 2152	5.1 / 1.1 / 5.1 / 1.0	**23** SA	0221 / 0852 / 1454 / 2116	5.1 / 0.9 / 5.2 / 0.9
9 SA	0336 / 1011 / 1556 / 2227	5.3 / 0.8 / 5.2 / 0.8	**24** SU	0311 / 0941 / 1539 / 2203	5.4 / 0.6 / 5.4 / 0.5
10 SU	0409 / 1044 / 1625 / 2259	5.4 / 0.7 / 5.3 / 0.7	**25** M O	0357 / 1026 / 1622 / 2247	5.7 / 0.4 / 5.7 / 0.3
11 M ●	0439 / 1118 / 1656 / 2335	5.4 / 0.7 / 5.4 / 0.8	**26** TU	0441 / 1111 / 1707 / 2336	5.8 / 0.2 / 6.0 / 0.2
12 TU	0513 / 1151 / 1731	5.4 / 0.8 / 5.4	**27** W	0535 / 1203 / 1759	5.8 / 0.2 / 6.0
13 W	0007 / 0551 / 1220 / 1808	0.8 / 5.3 / 0.9 / 5.3	**28** TH	0027 / 0628 / 1251 / 1850	0.2 / 5.8 / 0.4 / 5.8
14 TH	0036 / 0628 / 1248 / 1843	1.0 / 5.2 / 1.0 / 5.2	**29** F	0115 / 0720 / 1339 / 1938	0.4 / 5.6 / 0.6 / 5.7
15 F	0102 / 0703 / 1313 / 1916	1.1 / 4.9 / 1.2 / 5.1	**30** SA	0202 / 0810 / 1426 / 2026	0.6 / 5.2 / 1.0 / 5.3

ISLES OF SCILLY – ST. MARY'S

49°55′N 6°19′W

Times and heights (in metres) of high and low water 1994
Time: GMT. For BST, ADD ONE HOUR in the shaded area

MAY

Day	Time	m	Day	Time	m
1 SU	0251	1.0	**16** M	0155	1.3
	0901	4.8		0806	4.6
	1515	1.4		1412	1.4
	2115	4.9		2020	4.8
2 M	0345	1.4	**17** TU	0242	1.4
	1002	4.4		0855	4.4
	1610	1.6		1505	1.5
	2219	4.6		2114	4.7
3 TU	0450	1.6	**18** W	0345	1.5
	1122	4.2		0956	4.3
	1723	1.9		1615	1.7
	2343	4.4		2219	4.6
4 W	0608	1.8	**19** TH	0510	1.5
	1228	4.2		1108	4.3
	1842	1.9		1745	1.7
				2334	4.6
5 TH	0048	4.4	**20** F	0624	1.4
	0722	1.7		1219	4.4
	1325	4.3		1853	1.5
	1948	1.7			
6 F	0143	4.6	**21** SA	0043	4.7
	0816	1.5		0727	1.3
	1412	4.6		1326	4.7
	2039	1.5		1954	1.3
7 SA	0228	4.8	**22** SU	0149	4.9
	0901	1.3		0824	1.1
	1452	4.8		1424	5.1
	2120	1.3		2050	1.0
8 SU	0307	4.9	**23** M	0245	5.3
	0939	1.1		0917	0.8
	1526	5.1		1515	5.3
	2157	1.1		2141	0.7
9 M	0341	5.2	**24** TU	0336	5.4
	1013	1.0		1005	0.6
	1558	5.3		1601	5.7
	2230	1.0		2228	0.5
10 TU ●	0413	5.2	**25** W O	0424	5.6
	1044	1.0		1051	0.5
	1629	5.3		1646	5.8
	2300	1.0		2317	0.4
11 W	0446	5.2	**26** TH	0515	5.7
	1116	1.0		1144	0.4
	1703	5.3		1739	5.8
	2336	1.0			
12 TH	0526	5.2	**27** F	0011	0.3
	1149	1.0		0611	5.6
	1745	5.3		1237	0.5
				1833	5.8
13 F	0009	1.0	**28** SA	0102	0.4
	0607	5.1		0706	5.4
	1222	1.1		1325	0.6
	1822	5.2		1923	5.7
14 SA	0043	1.1	**29** SU	0151	0.6
	0647	4.9		0757	5.2
	1255	1.2		1412	0.9
	1859	5.1		2010	5.4
15 SU	0117	1.2	**30** M	0239	0.9
	0724	4.8		0846	4.9
	1331	1.3		1458	1.2
	1935	4.9		2054	5.1
			31 TU	0326	1.2
				0935	4.6
				1546	1.4
				2139	4.8

JUNE

Day	Time	m	Day	Time	m
1 W	0418	1.4	**16** TH	0328	1.2
	1031	4.3		0937	4.6
	1640	1.7		1551	1.4
	2238	4.4		2154	4.8
2 TH	0518	1.7	**17** F	0431	1.4
	1141	4.2		1039	4.6
	1745	1.9		1703	1.4
	2356	4.3		2302	4.7
3 F	0620	1.8	**18** SA	0549	1.4
	1238	4.2		1149	4.6
	1847	1.9		1819	1.5
4 SA	0058	4.3	**19** SU	0012	4.7
	0722	1.7		0656	1.4
	1330	4.4		1255	4.7
	1949	1.8		1926	1.4
5 SU	0149	4.4	**20** M	0122	4.8
	0815	1.5		0759	1.3
	1414	4.6		1359	4.9
	2039	1.5		2028	1.2
6 M	0233	4.7	**21** TU	0225	4.9
	0859	1.4		0856	1.0
	1454	4.8		1454	5.2
	2121	1.4		2124	1.0
7 TU	0312	4.8	**22** W	0320	5.2
	0937	1.3		0949	0.8
	1531	5.1		1544	5.4
	2159	1.3		2215	0.7
8 W	0349	4.9	**23** TH O	0409	5.3
	1012	1.2		1038	0.7
	1607	5.2		1631	5.7
	2234	1.1		2302	0.5
9 TH ●	0425	5.1	**24** F	0457	5.4
	1045	1.1		1129	0.5
	1642	5.3		1721	5.8
	2308	1.1		2358	0.4
10 F	0503	5.1	**25** SA	0555	5.4
	1123	1.1		1222	0.5
	1724	5.3		1816	5.8
	2349	1.0			
11 SA	0550	5.1	**26** SU	0049	0.4
	1205	1.1		0649	5.3
	1807	5.3		1310	0.6
				1905	5.7
12 SU	0030	1.0	**27** M	0135	0.5
	0634	4.9		0737	5.2
	1244	1.1		1353	0.7
	1849	5.2		1949	5.4
13 M	0110	1.0	**28** TU	0218	0.7
	0718	4.8		0818	5.1
	1325	1.1		1435	1.0
	1928	5.2		2023	5.2
14 TU	0152	1.1	**29** W	0258	1.0
	0808	4.8		0852	4.8
	1408	1.2		1515	1.3
	2010	5.1		2056	4.9
15 W	0236	1.1	**30** TH	0339	1.3
	0845	4.7		0928	4.6
	1456	1.3		1557	1.5
	2058	4.9		2134	4.7

JULY

Day	Time	m	Day	Time	m
1 F	0424	1.5	**16** SA	0359	1.2
	1014	4.3		1012	4.7
	1648	1.8		1628	1.4
	2224	4.4		2234	4.7
2 SA	0521	1.8	**17** SU	0509	1.4
	1119	4.2		1122	4.6
	1750	1.9		1746	1.5
	2335	4.2		2349	4.6
3 SU	0619	1.9	**18** M	0628	1.5
	1229	4.2		1231	4.6
	1848	2.0		1904	1.5
4 M	0057	4.2	**19** TU	0104	4.6
	0717	1.8		0741	1.4
	1333	4.3		1340	4.7
	1948	1.8		2014	1.4
5 TU	0159	4.3	**20** W	0213	4.7
	0812	1.6		0844	1.3
	1423	4.7		1440	5.1
	2042	1.6		2114	1.2
6 W	0247	4.6	**21** TH	0309	4.9
	0900	1.4		0939	1.0
	1507	4.9		1532	5.3
	2127	1.4		2206	0.8
7 TH	0328	4.8	**22** F O	0359	5.2
	0944	1.3		1027	0.8
	1546	5.2		1617	5.6
	2210	1.2		2252	0.6
8 F ●	0408	4.9	**23** SA	0443	5.3
	1024	1.1		1113	0.6
	1624	5.3		1702	5.7
	2248	1.0		2342	0.4
9 SA	0446	5.1	**24** SU	0534	5.3
	1102	1.0		1204	0.5
	1705	5.3		1754	5.7
	2332	0.9			
10 SU	0532	5.1	**25** M	0030	0.4
	1149	0.9		0622	5.3
	1751	5.4		1249	0.5
				1839	5.7
11 M	0018	0.8	**26** TU	0112	0.4
	0620	5.1		0705	5.3
	1233	0.8		1329	0.6
	1836	5.4		1918	5.6
12 TU	0100	0.7	**27** W	0150	0.6
	0704	5.1		0739	5.1
	1315	0.8		1404	0.8
	1918	5.4		1947	5.3
13 W	0141	0.7	**28** TH	0224	0.9
	0747	5.1		0808	4.9
	1357	0.8		1438	1.1
	1959	5.3		2016	5.1
14 TH	0221	0.8	**29** F	0257	1.2
	0829	4.9		0840	4.7
	1439	1.0		1511	1.4
	2044	5.2		2050	4.8
15 F	0307	1.0	**30** SA	0333	1.5
	0916	4.8		0920	4.4
	1528	1.2		1551	1.7
	2134	4.9		2131	4.4
			31 SU	0419	1.8
				1011	4.3
				1650	2.0
				2226	4.2

AUGUST

Day	Time	m	Day	Time	m
1 M	0528	2.0	**16** TU	0607	1.8
	1120	4.0		1216	4.4
	1803	2.1		1850	1.7
	2344	3.9			
2 TU	0634	2.0	**17** W	0056	4.3
	1243	4.2		0733	1.7
	1907	2.0		1328	4.6
				2009	1.5
3 W	0125	4.0	**18** TH	0207	4.6
	0735	1.8		0838	1.4
	1355	4.4		1430	4.9
	2007	1.8		2107	1.2
4 TH	0226	4.4	**19** F	0304	4.8
	0830	1.6		0930	1.1
	1444	4.8		1520	5.3
	2101	1.4		2155	0.9
5 F	0310	4.7	**20** SA	0349	5.2
	0919	1.4		1015	0.8
	1526	5.1		1603	5.6
	2147	1.2		2238	0.6
6 SA	0351	4.9	**21** SU O	0428	5.3
	1004	1.1		1055	0.6
	1606	5.3		1642	5.7
	2230	0.9		2320	0.4
7 SU ●	0429	5.2	**22** M	0507	5.4
	1046	0.9		1140	0.5
	1644	5.6		1725	5.7
	2312	0.7			
8 M	0510	5.3	**23** TU	0005	0.4
	1131	0.7		0549	5.4
	1729	5.6		1222	0.5
	2359	0.5		1806	5.7
9 TU	0558	5.3	**24** W	0043	0.5
	1217	0.6		0626	5.3
	1817	5.7		1259	0.6
				1840	5.6
10 W	0042	0.5	**25** TH	0116	0.7
	0643	5.3		0656	5.2
	1259	0.5		1330	0.8
	1901	5.7		1909	5.3
11 TH	0123	0.5	**26** F	0147	0.9
	0726	5.3		0728	5.1
	1339	0.6		1400	1.1
	1943	5.6		1939	5.1
12 F	0202	0.6	**27** SA	0213	1.2
	0810	5.2		0800	4.9
	1420	0.8		1427	1.4
	2027	5.3		2012	4.8
13 SA	0245	0.9	**28** SU	0239	1.4
	0855	5.1		0838	4.7
	1507	1.1		1454	1.6
	2114	5.1		2051	4.6
14 SU	0333	1.2	**29** M	0305	1.8
	0948	4.8		0923	4.4
	1602	1.4		1530	2.0
	2212	4.7		2140	4.2
15 M	0436	1.5	**30** TU	0358	2.1
	1057	4.6		1022	4.2
	1719	1.6		1713	2.2
	2335	4.3		2249	3.9
			31 W	0556	2.2
				1145	4.0
				1834	2.2

ISLES OF SCILLY – ST. MARY'S
49°55′N 6°19′W

Times and heights (in metres) of high and low water 1994
Time: GMT. For BST, ADD ONE HOUR in the shaded area

SEPTEMBER

Day	Time	m		Day	Time	m
1 TH	0037 / 0705 / 1321 / 1938	3.9 / 2.0 / 4.3 / 1.9		**16** F	0202 / 0827 / 1419 / 2054	4.4 / 1.5 / 4.9 / 1.3
2 F	0204 / 0804 / 1421 / 2035	4.3 / 1.7 / 4.7 / 1.5		**17** SA	0255 / 0915 / 1506 / 2139	4.8 / 1.2 / 5.3 / 0.9
3 SA	0252 / 0856 / 1505 / 2125	4.7 / 1.4 / 5.1 / 1.2		**18** SU	0335 / 0957 / 1545 / 2218	5.2 / 0.9 / 5.6 / 0.7
4 SU	0331 / 0943 / 1544 / 2209	5.1 / 1.1 / 5.4 / 0.8		**19** M	0409 / 1034 / 1621 / 2254	5.4 / 0.7 / 5.7 / 0.5
5 M	0408 / 1026 / 1623 / 2249	5.3 / 0.7 / 5.7 / 0.5		**20** TU	0440 / 1111 / 1653 / 2333	5.4 / 0.6 / 5.7 / 0.5
6 TU	0446 / 1106 / 1703 / 2333	5.6 / 0.5 / 5.8 / 0.4		**21** W	0513 / 1151 / 1730	5.6 / 0.6 / 5.6
7 W	0531 / 1154 / 1751	5.7 / 0.4 / 6.0		**22** TH	0010 / 0548 / 1226 / 1804	0.6 / 5.4 / 0.8 / 5.6
8 TH	0019 / 0618 / 1238 / 1839	0.3 / 5.7 / 0.4 / 5.8		**23** F	0041 / 0620 / 1255 / 1836	0.8 / 5.4 / 1.0 / 5.3
9 F	0102 / 0703 / 1320 / 1924	0.4 / 5.7 / 0.5 / 5.7		**24** SA	0109 / 0652 / 1322 / 1907	1.0 / 5.3 / 1.2 / 5.2
10 SA	0142 / 0749 / 1402 / 2010	0.6 / 5.4 / 0.7 / 5.4		**25** SU	0132 / 0726 / 1347 / 1941	1.3 / 5.1 / 1.4 / 4.8
11 SU	0224 / 0835 / 1449 / 2058	0.9 / 5.2 / 1.1 / 5.1		**26** M	0151 / 0802 / 1407 / 2019	1.5 / 4.8 / 1.6 / 4.6
12 M	0312 / 0927 / 1545 / 2157	1.3 / 4.9 / 1.4 / 4.6		**27** TU	0214 / 0845 / 1439 / 2106	1.7 / 4.6 / 1.9 / 4.3
13 TU	0414 / 1036 / 1701 / 2326	1.7 / 4.6 / 1.8 / 4.2		**28** W	0257 / 0941 / 1544 / 2211	2.0 / 4.3 / 2.2 / 4.0
14 W	0553 / 1204 / 1844	2.0 / 4.4 / 1.9		**29** TH	0456 / 1057 / 1802 / 2341	2.3 / 4.2 / 2.2 / 3.9
15 TH	0051 / 0725 / 1319 / 2001	4.2 / 1.9 / 4.6 / 1.6		**30** F	0634 / 1227 / 1909	2.2 / 4.3 / 1.9

OCTOBER

Day	Time	m		Day	Time	m
1 SA	0132 / 0737 / 1346 / 2007	4.2 / 1.8 / 4.7 / 1.5		**16** SU	0233 / 0853 / 1444 / 2115	4.8 / 1.4 / 5.2 / 1.2
2 SU	0225 / 0831 / 1437 / 2058	4.7 / 1.4 / 5.2 / 1.2		**17** M	0312 / 0934 / 1523 / 2154	5.2 / 1.1 / 5.4 / 0.9
3 M	0307 / 0918 / 1518 / 2144	5.2 / 1.1 / 5.6 / 0.8		**18** TU	0345 / 1011 / 1557 / 2228	5.4 / 0.9 / 5.6 / 0.8
4 TU	0345 / 1003 / 1559 / 2226	5.4 / 0.7 / 5.8 / 0.7		**19** W	0415 / 1044 / 1627 / 2300	5.6 / 0.8 / 5.6 / 0.8
5 W	0423 / 1043 / 1639 / 2307	5.7 / 0.5 / 6.0 / 0.3		**20** TH	0442 / 1119 / 1657 / 2336	5.6 / 0.9 / 5.6 / 0.9
6 TH	0503 / 1129 / 1727 / 2356	5.8 / 0.3 / 6.1 / 0.3		**21** F	0515 / 1152 / 1732	5.6 / 1.0 / 5.4
7 F	0553 / 1217 / 1817	6.0 / 0.3 / 6.0		**22** SA	0007 / 0549 / 1222 / 1808	1.0 / 5.4 / 1.1 / 5.3
8 SA	0041 / 0641 / 1303 / 1906	0.4 / 5.8 / 0.5 / 5.8		**23** SU	0033 / 0625 / 1251 / 1842	1.2 / 5.3 / 1.3 / 5.1
9 SU	0125 / 0729 / 1349 / 1955	0.6 / 5.7 / 0.7 / 5.4		**24** M	0100 / 0659 / 1317 / 1918	1.3 / 5.2 / 1.4 / 4.9
10 M	0211 / 0818 / 1438 / 2047	1.0 / 5.4 / 1.1 / 5.1		**25** TU	0123 / 0734 / 1343 / 1955	1.4 / 4.9 / 1.6 / 4.7
11 TU	0300 / 0911 / 1534 / 2147	1.4 / 5.1 / 1.4 / 4.6		**26** W	0152 / 0817 / 1420 / 2042	1.7 / 4.7 / 1.8 / 4.4
12 W	0401 / 1020 / 1646 / 2314	1.7 / 4.7 / 1.8 / 4.3		**27** TH	0236 / 0910 / 1518 / 2145	1.9 / 4.6 / 2.0 / 4.2
13 TH	0534 / 1149 / 1825	2.0 / 4.6 / 1.9		**28** F	0347 / 1019 / 1717 / 2302	2.2 / 4.4 / 2.1 / 4.0
14 F	0037 / 0704 / 1300 / 1939	4.3 / 2.0 / 4.6 / 1.7		**29** SA	0556 / 1139 / 1835	2.2 / 4.4 / 1.9
15 SA	0143 / 0805 / 1358 / 2032	4.6 / 1.7 / 4.9 / 1.4		**30** SU	0028 / 0704 / 1254 / 1935	4.3 / 1.9 / 4.7 / 1.5
				31 M	0145 / 0801 / 1359 / 2029	4.7 / 1.5 / 5.1 / 1.2

NOVEMBER

Day	Time	m		Day	Time	m
1 TU	0236 / 0852 / 1449 / 2117	5.1 / 1.2 / 5.4 / 0.9		**16** W	0317 / 0944 / 1530 / 2201	5.2 / 1.3 / 5.3 / 1.1
2 W	0319 / 0938 / 1535 / 2203	5.4 / 0.8 / 5.7 / 0.6		**17** TH	0349 / 1018 / 1602 / 2233	5.4 / 1.1 / 5.3 / 1.1
3 TH	0401 / 1023 / 1618 / 2245	5.8 / 0.6 / 6.0 / 0.4		**18** F	0418 / 1049 / 1632 / 2302	5.6 / 1.1 / 5.4 / 1.1
4 F	0441 / 1107 / 1705 / 2332	6.0 / 0.4 / 6.0 / 0.4		**19** SA	0447 / 1122 / 1707 / 2336	5.6 / 1.1 / 5.3 / 1.1
5 SA	0530 / 1159 / 1759	6.1 / 0.4 / 6.0		**20** SU	0525 / 1156 / 1747	5.6 / 1.2 / 5.3
6 SU	0024 / 0622 / 1249 / 1852	0.5 / 6.1 / 0.5 / 5.8		**21** M	0007 / 0604 / 1229 / 1827	1.2 / 5.4 / 1.3 / 5.1
7 M	0112 / 0713 / 1339 / 1944	0.7 / 5.8 / 0.7 / 5.6		**22** TU	0039 / 0641 / 1301 / 1904	1.3 / 5.3 / 1.4 / 4.9
8 TU	0200 / 0804 / 1429 / 2037	1.0 / 5.6 / 1.0 / 5.2		**23** W	0111 / 0719 / 1335 / 1943	1.4 / 5.2 / 1.4 / 4.8
9 W	0250 / 0857 / 1523 / 2135	1.3 / 5.3 / 1.4 / 4.8		**24** TH	0145 / 0759 / 1414 / 2028	1.5 / 4.9 / 1.5 / 4.6
10 TH	0346 / 0958 / 1625 / 2249	1.6 / 4.9 / 1.6 / 4.4		**25** F	0229 / 0848 / 1506 / 2123	1.7 / 4.8 / 1.7 / 4.4
11 F	0456 / 1120 / 1746	1.9 / 4.7 / 1.9		**26** SA	0327 / 0948 / 1619 / 2227	1.8 / 4.7 / 1.8 / 4.3
12 SA	0006 / 0621 / 1228 / 1900	4.3 / 2.1 / 4.6 / 1.8		**27** SU	0454 / 1059 / 1752 / 2342	2.0 / 4.7 / 1.8 / 4.4
13 SU	0108 / 0730 / 1325 / 1959	4.4 / 1.9 / 4.7 / 1.6		**28** M	0622 / 1209 / 1859	1.9 / 4.7 / 1.6
14 M	0159 / 0822 / 1414 / 2045	4.7 / 1.6 / 4.9 / 1.4		**29** TU	0054 / 0728 / 1317 / 1959	4.7 / 1.6 / 4.9 / 1.4
15 TU	0242 / 0905 / 1455 / 2125	4.9 / 1.4 / 5.1 / 1.3		**30** W	0159 / 0825 / 1419 / 2052	4.9 / 1.4 / 5.2 / 1.1

DECEMBER

Day	Time	m		Day	Time	m
1 TH	0252 / 0917 / 1512 / 2142	5.3 / 1.0 / 5.6 / 0.8		**16** F	0322 / 0951 / 1538 / 2206	5.2 / 1.4 / 5.1 / 1.3
2 F	0340 / 1005 / 1601 / 2228	5.7 / 0.7 / 5.7 / 0.6		**17** SA	0356 / 1026 / 1613 / 2238	5.3 / 1.3 / 5.2 / 1.2
3 SA	0424 / 1051 / 1647 / 2316	6.0 / 0.5 / 5.8 / 0.5		**18** SU	0429 / 1057 / 1647 / 2311	5.4 / 1.2 / 5.2 / 1.2
4 SU	0512 / 1145 / 1744	6.1 / 0.5 / 5.8		**19** M	0506 / 1136 / 1730 / 2349	5.6 / 1.2 / 5.2 / 1.2
5 M	0010 / 0607 / 1238 / 1840	0.5 / 6.1 / 0.5 / 5.7		**20** TU	0549 / 1215 / 1815	5.4 / 1.1 / 5.2
6 TU	0101 / 0701 / 1329 / 1933	0.6 / 6.0 / 0.6 / 5.6		**21** W	0027 / 0631 / 1251 / 1856	1.2 / 5.4 / 1.2 / 5.1
7 W	0149 / 0751 / 1417 / 2022	0.8 / 5.8 / 0.8 / 5.3		**22** TH	0103 / 0710 / 1329 / 1935	1.2 / 5.3 / 1.2 / 4.9
8 TH	0236 / 0839 / 1505 / 2111	1.1 / 5.4 / 1.1 / 4.9		**23** F	0141 / 0748 / 1408 / 2016	1.3 / 5.2 / 1.3 / 4.8
9 F	0323 / 0927 / 1553 / 2203	1.4 / 5.1 / 1.4 / 4.6		**24** SA	0221 / 0831 / 1451 / 2101	1.4 / 5.1 / 1.4 / 4.7
10 SA	0414 / 1022 / 1651 / 2312	1.7 / 4.8 / 1.7 / 4.4		**25** SU	0309 / 0923 / 1545 / 2158	1.4 / 4.9 / 1.4 / 4.6
11 SU	0518 / 1136 / 1758	2.0 / 4.6 / 1.9		**26** M	0409 / 1023 / 1655 / 2305	1.6 / 4.8 / 1.6 / 4.6
12 M	0018 / 0629 / 1240 / 1905	4.3 / 2.1 / 4.4 / 1.9		**27** TU	0534 / 1135 / 1819	1.7 / 4.7 / 1.6
13 TU	0115 / 0737 / 1335 / 2004	4.4 / 2.0 / 4.6 / 1.8		**28** W	0014 / 0653 / 1244 / 1930	4.6 / 1.7 / 4.7 / 1.5
14 W	0205 / 0830 / 1422 / 2051	4.7 / 1.8 / 4.7 / 1.6		**29** TH	0126 / 0801 / 1354 / 2031	4.8 / 1.5 / 4.9 / 1.3
15 TH	0246 / 0913 / 1502 / 2130	4.9 / 1.5 / 4.9 / 1.4		**30** F	0230 / 0859 / 1455 / 2126	5.2 / 1.2 / 5.2 / 1.1
				31 SA	0324 / 0953 / 1548 / 2216	5.4 / 0.9 / 5.4 / 0.8

ST HELIER
MEAN SPRING AND NEAP CURVES
Springs occur 2 days after New and Full Moon.

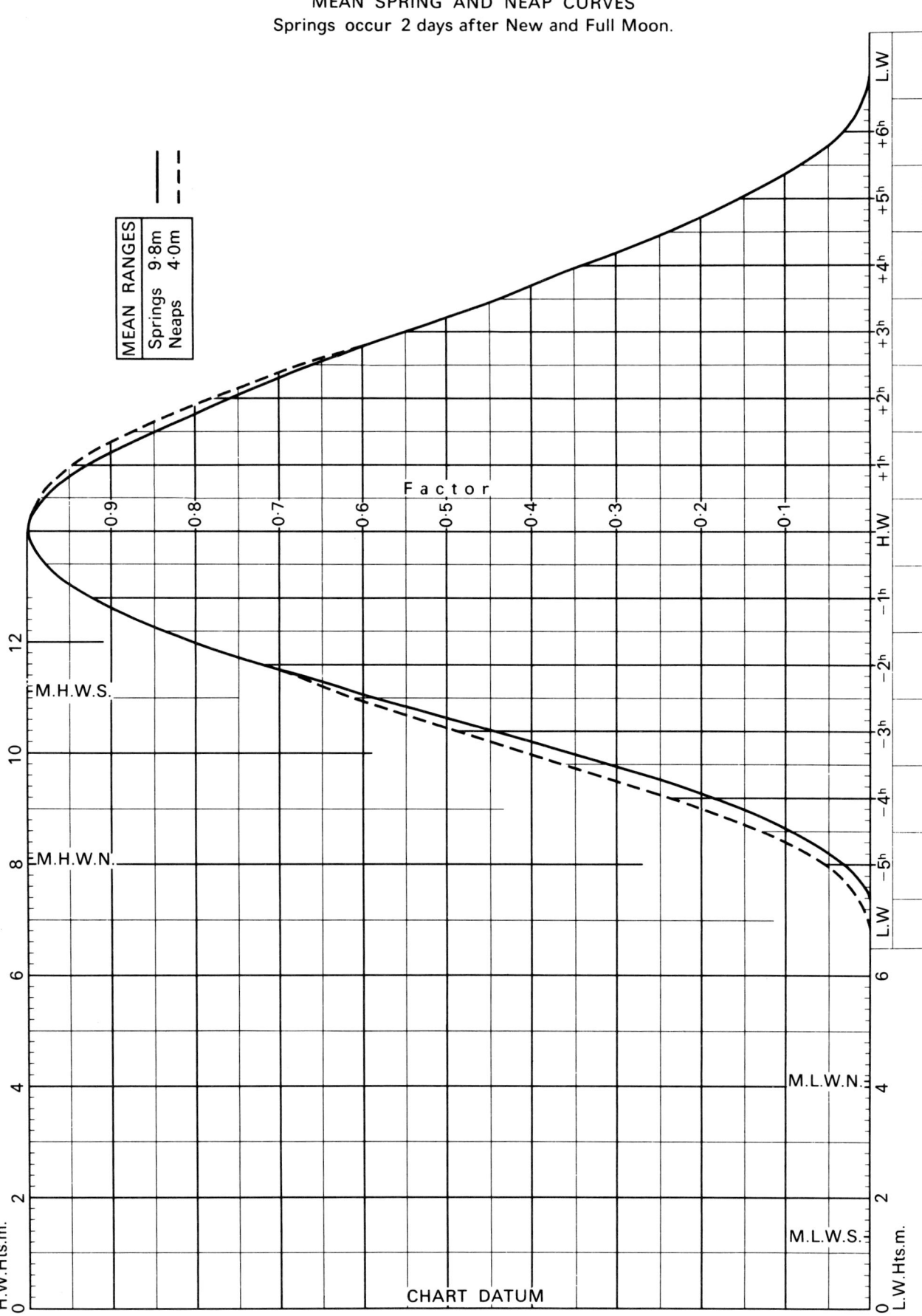

MEAN RANGES
Springs 9·8m
Neaps 4·0m

Factor

0·9 0·8 0·7 0·6 0·5 0·4 0·3 0·2 0·1

L.W +6ʰ +5ʰ +4ʰ +3ʰ +2ʰ +1ʰ H.W −1ʰ −2ʰ −3ʰ −4ʰ −5ʰ L.W

M.H.W.S.

M.H.W.N.

M.L.W.N.

M.L.W.S.

CHART DATUM

H.W.Hts.m.

L.W.Hts.m.

ST. HELIER
49°11′N 2°07′W

Times and heights (in metres) of high and low water 1994
Time: GMT. For BST, ADD ONE HOUR in the shaded area
High Water, full and change, 0632

JANUARY

Day	Time	m	Time	m	Time	m	Time	m
1 SA	0255	1.9	0832	11.1	1519	1.7	2057	10.7
16 SU	0331	2.3	0911	10.7	1549	2.3	2129	10.2
2 SU	0336	2.0	0911	10.9	1600	1.9	2138	10.4
17 M	0400	2.8	0943	10.1	1619	2.7	2200	9.7
3 M	0418	2.3	0953	10.6	1643	2.2	2221	10.0
18 TU	0429	3.2	1014	9.6	1650	3.2	2231	9.2
4 TU	0504	2.6	1039	10.1	1731	2.6	2311	9.6
19 W	0501	3.6	1045	9.1	1726	3.6	2307	8.8
5 W	0556	3.0	1134	9.6	1827	3.0	2354	8.4
20 TH	0540	4.0	1124	8.6	1812	4.0		
6 TH	0012	9.1	0657	3.3	1243	9.1	1933	3.3
21 F	0633	4.3	1221	8.1	1912	4.3		
7 F	0129	8.9	0809	3.5	1407	8.9	2049	3.4
22 SA	0103	8.1	0741	4.5	1349	7.9	2026	4.3
8 SA	0251	9.1	0928	3.3	1530	9.2	2207	3.2
23 SU	0233	8.2	0905	4.3	1521	8.2	2147	4.0
9 SU	0403	9.5	1043	2.8	1637	9.7	2316	2.7
24 M	0351	8.6	1029	3.8	1628	8.8	2258	3.4
10 M	0502	10.2	1146	2.3	1733	10.2		
25 TU	0449	9.4	1133	3.0	1720	9.5	2354	2.7
11 TU ●	0013	2.2	0552	10.7	1240	1.8	1820	10.7
26 W	0538	10.1	1224	2.2	1806	10.3		
12 W O	0102	1.8	0638	11.2	1326	1.4	1903	11.0
27 TH	0042	2.0	0621	10.9	1309	1.6	1847	10.9
13 TH	0146	1.6	0720	11.4	1407	1.4	1944	11.1
28 F	0125	1.5	0702	11.4	1349	1.1	1926	11.3
14 F	0224	1.7	0759	11.4	1444	1.5	2021	10.9
29 SA	0206	1.2	0741	11.7	1429	0.9	2005	11.4
15 SA	0259	1.9	0837	11.1	1518	1.8	2056	10.6
30 SU	0245	1.1	0819	11.7	1507	0.9	2042	11.3
31 M	0324	1.2	0857	11.5	1546	1.2	2121	11.0

FEBRUARY

Day	Time	m	Time	m	Time	m	Time	m
1 TU	0404	1.5	0936	11.1	1626	1.7	2200	10.5
16 W	0355	2.7	0938	9.8	1612	2.8	2151	9.6
2 W	0446	2.0	1019	10.5	1709	2.2	2245	9.9
17 TH	0422	3.1	1003	9.3	1642	3.2	2221	9.1
3 TH	0532	2.6	1107	9.7	1759	2.9	2339	9.2
18 F	0456	3.6	1034	8.8	1721	3.7	2259	8.6
4 F	0628	3.2	1208	8.9	1901	3.4		
19 SA	0542	4.0	1119	8.2	1816	4.1	2356	8.1
5 SA	0051	8.7	0738	3.6	1335	8.4	2018	3.7
20 SU	0647	4.3	1239	7.7	1931	4.3		
6 SU	0225	8.5	0903	3.7	1516	8.5	2147	3.6
21 M	0135	7.8	0815	4.4	1442	7.7	2105	4.2
7 M	0350	9.0	1029	3.2	1629	9.1	2304	3.1
22 TU	0318	8.2	0956	3.9	1603	8.4	2230	3.5
8 TU	0452	9.7	1136	2.6	1723	9.8		
23 W	0425	9.0	1110	3.0	1658	9.3	2332	2.6
9 W	0002	2.4	0540	10.4	1228	1.9	1807	10.4
24 TH	0516	10.0	1203	2.0	1744	10.3		
10 TH ●	0049	1.8	0623	11.0	1310	1.5	1847	10.9
25 F	0022	1.7	0559	10.9	1249	1.2	1825	11.0
11 F	0128	1.5	0702	11.3	1347	1.2	1924	11.1
26 SA O	0106	1.0	0641	11.6	1330	0.6	1905	11.6
12 SA	0203	1.4	0739	11.4	1420	1.3	1958	11.1
27 SU	0147	0.6	0721	12.0	1410	0.3	1943	11.8
13 SU	0235	1.5	0813	11.3	1451	1.5	2029	10.9
28 M	0227	0.4	0800	12.1	1448	0.4	2021	11.7
14 M	0304	1.8	0844	10.9	1520	1.8	2059	10.5
15 TU	0330	2.2	0912	10.4	1546	2.3	2125	10.0

MARCH

Day	Time	m	Time	m	Time	m	Time	m
1 TU	0307	0.6	0838	11.9	1526	0.7	2100	11.4
16 W	0301	1.9	0842	10.3	1515	2.0	2053	10.1
2 W	0346	1.0	0917	11.3	1605	1.3	2139	10.8
17 TH	0326	2.4	0907	9.8	1540	2.5	2118	9.7
3 TH	0427	1.6	0958	10.5	1646	2.0	2222	10.0
18 F	0352	2.8	0931	9.4	1608	2.9	2146	9.3
4 F	0511	2.3	1045	9.6	1734	2.8	2313	9.2
19 SA	0424	3.2	1002	8.8	1645	3.4	2222	8.8
5 SA	0604	3.0	1143	8.7	1833	3.5		
20 SU	0508	3.6	1044	8.3	1737	3.9	2313	8.2
6 SU	0023	8.5	0713	3.6	1311	8.1	1952	3.9
21 M	0610	4.0	1153	7.7	1848	4.2		
7 M	0201	8.2	0839	3.7	1500	8.2	2126	3.8
22 TU	0042	7.8	0732	4.1	1359	7.6	2020	4.1
8 TU	0332	8.6	1010	3.4	1612	8.8	2247	3.2
23 W	0237	8.0	0914	3.7	1528	8.3	2153	3.5
9 W	0433	9.3	1118	2.7	1703	9.5	2343	2.5
24 TH	0351	8.9	1036	2.8	1627	9.2	2301	2.5
10 TH	0520	10.1	1206	2.0	1745	10.2		
25 F	0446	9.9	1133	1.9	1714	10.2	2354	1.6
11 F	0026	1.9	0600	10.7	1245	1.5	1822	10.7
26 SA	0533	10.9	1221	1.1	1758	11.1		
12 SA ●	0103	1.5	0638	11.1	1320	1.2	1857	11.0
27 SU O	0041	0.8	0616	11.6	1305	0.4	1839	11.7
13 SU	0137	1.3	0713	11.2	1352	1.2	1930	11.0
28 M	0125	0.3	0658	12.0	1347	0.1	1920	11.9
14 M	0207	1.3	0745	11.1	1422	1.3	2000	10.9
29 TU	0207	0.1	0739	12.1	1427	0.2	2000	11.9
15 TU	0236	1.6	0816	10.8	1450	1.6	2028	10.5
30 W	0248	0.3	0819	11.8	1507	0.6	2040	11.5
31 TH	0329	0.7	0900	11.2	1547	1.0	2121	10.9

APRIL

Day	Time	m	Time	m	Time	m	Time	m
1 F	0411	1.4	0943	10.4	1629	2.0	2205	10.1
16 SA	0331	2.6	0911	9.3	1546	2.8	2123	9.4
2 SA	0456	2.1	1030	9.5	1716	2.8	2256	9.2
17 SU	0405	2.9	0944	8.9	1623	3.2	2202	9.0
3 SU	0548	2.9	1129	8.6	1814	3.4		
18 M	0449	3.3	1029	8.4	1714	3.6	2253	8.5
4 M	0004	8.5	0653	3.5	1253	8.0	1928	3.9
19 TU	0547	3.6	1135	8.0	1820	3.8		
5 TU	0134	8.2	0813	3.7	1431	8.0	2058	3.9
20 W	0010	8.1	0702	3.7	1316	7.9	1942	3.8
6 W	0300	8.4	0939	3.4	1541	8.5	2217	3.4
21 TH	0150	8.2	0830	3.4	1445	8.4	2110	3.3
7 TH	0402	9.0	1045	2.9	1633	9.2	2313	2.8
22 F	0311	8.9	0953	2.7	1550	9.2	2225	2.5
8 F	0450	9.6	1133	2.3	1715	9.8	2356	2.2
23 SA	0412	9.8	1058	1.9	1643	10.1	2324	1.6
9 SA	0532	10.2	1213	1.8	1752	10.3		
24 SU	0504	10.6	1151	1.1	1730	10.9		
10 SU	0033	1.8	0609	10.6	1249	1.5	1827	10.6
25 M O	0015	0.9	0551	11.3	1240	0.6	1815	11.5
11 M ●	0108	1.5	0644	10.7	1322	1.4	1900	10.8
26 TU	0103	0.4	0637	11.7	1325	0.3	1859	11.8
12 TU	0139	1.5	0717	10.7	1353	1.5	1931	10.7
27 W	0148	0.2	0721	11.8	1409	0.4	1942	11.8
13 W	0209	1.6	0748	10.5	1421	1.7	2000	10.4
28 TH	0232	0.3	0805	11.6	1452	0.7	2025	11.4
14 TH	0236	1.9	0817	10.1	1448	2.1	2026	10.1
29 F	0315	0.7	0848	11.0	1534	1.3	2108	10.9
15 F	0303	2.2	0843	9.7	1515	2.4	2053	9.8
30 SA	0359	1.4	0933	10.3	1618	2.0	2154	10.1

ST. HELIER
49°11′N 2°07′W

Times and heights (in metres) of high and low water 1994
Time: GMT. For BST, ADD ONE HOUR in the shaded area
High Water, full and change, 0632

MAY

Day	Time	m	Time	m	Day	Time	m	Time	m
1 SU	0445	2.1			16 M	0358	2.6		
	1022	9.5				0940	9.2		
	1704	2.7				1614	3.0		
	2244	9.4				2154	9.3		
2 M	0535	2.7			17 TU	0441	2.9		
	1117	8.8				1025	8.8		
	1758	3.4				1703	3.2		
	2344	8.7				2244	9.0		
3 TU	0632	3.3			18 W	0535	3.1		
	1227	8.3				1124	8.5		
	1901	3.8				1803	3.4		
						2348	8.7		
4 W	0058	8.3			19 TH	0640	3.2		
	0739	3.6				1239	8.4		
	1347	8.1				1914	3.4		
	2016	3.9							
5 TH	0216	8.3			20 F	0108	8.7		
	0853	3.6				0754	3.1		
	1457	8.4				1401	8.6		
	2132	3.7				2032	3.2		
6 F	0320	8.6			21 SA	0230	9.0		
	0959	3.2				0911	2.8		
	1552	8.8				1512	9.2		
	2232	3.2				2148	2.6		
7 SA	0413	9.1			22 SU	0339	9.6		
	1052	2.8				1023	2.2		
	1638	9.3				1613	9.9		
	2319	2.8				2254	1.9		
8 SU	0458	9.5			23 M	0438	10.2		
	1136	2.4				1124	1.6		
	1718	9.8				1706	10.6		
						2352	1.3		
9 M	0000	2.3			24 TU	0532	10.8		
	0538	9.9				1218	1.1		
	1215	2.1				1756	11.2		
	1756	10.2							
10 TU ●	0038	2.0			25 W O	0044	0.8		
	0616	10.1				0621	11.2		
	1252	1.9				1309	0.8		
	1831	10.4				1843	11.5		
11 W	0113	1.9			26 TH	0134	0.6		
	0652	10.2				0708	11.4		
	1326	1.9				1356	0.8		
	1905	10.4				1929	11.6		
12 TH	0145	1.9			27 F	0220	0.6		
	0726	10.2				0755	11.3		
	1359	2.0				1441	1.0		
	1937	10.3				2014	11.4		
13 F	0217	2.0			28 SA	0305	0.9		
	0758	10.0				0840	10.9		
	1430	2.2				1525	1.5		
	2008	10.1				2059	10.9		
14 SA	0248	2.2			29 SU	0349	1.4		
	0830	9.7				0925	10.4		
	1502	2.4				1608	2.0		
	2039	9.9				2143	10.4		
15 SU	0321	2.4			30 M	0433	2.0		
	0903	9.5				1011	9.8		
	1535	2.7				1651	2.6		
	2114	9.6				2229	9.7		
					31 TU	0517	2.6		
						1058	9.2		
						1736	3.2		
						2319	9.1		

JUNE

Day	Time	m	Time	m	Day	Time	m	Time	m
1 W	0604	3.1			16 TH	0523	2.7		
	1151	8.7				1107	9.2		
	1825	3.7				1747	3.0		
						2328	9.3		
2 TH	0014	8.6			17 F	0619	2.9		
	0655	3.5				1207	9.0		
	1252	8.3				1849	3.1		
	1922	4.0							
3 F	0119	8.3			18 SA	0034	9.0		
	0754	3.7				0723	3.0		
	1357	8.3				1319	8.9		
	2027	4.0				1959	3.1		
4 SA	0226	8.3			19 SU	0151	9.0		
	0858	3.7				0837	3.0		
	1459	8.4				1436	9.0		
	2134	3.8				2116	2.9		
5 SU	0327	8.5			20 M	0310	9.2		
	0959	3.5				0953	2.7		
	1554	8.8				1547	9.5		
	2234	3.5				2229	2.5		
6 M	0420	8.8			21 TU	0419	9.7		
	1053	3.1				1102	2.2		
	1642	9.2				1649	10.1		
	2325	3.1				2334	1.9		
7 TU	0508	9.2			22 W	0518	10.3		
	1141	2.8				1202	1.7		
	1726	9.6				1743	10.7		
8 W	0009	2.7			23 TH O	0031	1.4		
	0550	9.6				0611	10.7		
	1224	2.4				1256	1.4		
	1806	10.0				1832	11.2		
9 TH ●	0050	2.3			24 F	0123	1.0		
	0631	9.9				0700	11.0		
	1304	2.2				1345	1.2		
	1845	10.2				1919	11.4		
10 F	0128	2.1			25 SA	0210	0.9		
	0709	10.1				0746	11.1		
	1342	2.1				1430	1.2		
	1921	10.4				2003	11.4		
11 SA	0204	2.0			26 SU	0254	1.1		
	0746	10.1				0829	10.9		
	1419	2.1				1513	1.5		
	1957	10.4				2046	11.1		
12 SU	0240	2.0			27 M	0334	1.4		
	0822	10.0				0911	10.6		
	1455	2.2				1552	1.9		
	2032	10.3				2127	10.7		
13 M	0316	2.1			28 TU	0413	1.9		
	0858	9.9				0951	10.1		
	1532	2.4				1629	2.5		
	2108	10.1				2207	10.1		
14 TU	0354	2.2			29 W	0450	2.5		
	0936	9.7				1030	9.6		
	1611	2.5				1705	3.0		
	2148	9.9				2246	9.5		
15 W	0436	2.4			30 TH	0527	3.0		
	1018	9.5				1109	9.1		
	1655	2.8				1743	3.5		
	2234	9.6				2328	8.9		

JULY

Day	Time	m	Time	m	Day	Time	m	Time	m
1 F	0608	3.5			16 SA	0556	2.7		
	1153	8.6				1137	9.2		
	1826	3.9				1824	3.0		
2 SA	0016	8.4			17 SU	0004	9.2		
	0655	3.8				0655	3.1		
	1246	8.3				1244	8.9		
	1918	4.2				1931	3.3		
3 SU	0117	8.1			18 M	0119	8.8		
	0752	4.0				0807	3.3		
	1352	8.2				1405	8.7		
	2023	4.3				2049	3.3		
4 M	0229	8.0			19 TU	0247	8.7		
	0859	4.0				0929	3.2		
	1503	8.3				1529	9.1		
	2137	4.1				2210	3.0		
5 TU	0340	8.3			20 W	0407	9.2		
	1008	3.8				1046	2.8		
	1606	8.7				1638	9.7		
	2247	3.7				2321	2.4		
6 W	0439	8.7			21 TH	0510	9.8		
	1109	3.3				1150	2.2		
	1700	9.2				1734	10.4		
	2343	3.1							
7 TH	0529	9.2			22 F O	0020	1.8		
	1200	2.8				0602	10.4		
	1746	9.7				1244	1.7		
						1822	11.0		
8 F ●	0030	2.6			23 SA	0111	1.3		
	0613	9.7				0648	10.9		
	1246	2.4				1331	1.3		
	1827	10.2				1906	11.3		
9 SA	0113	2.1			24 SU	0154	1.1		
	0654	10.2				0730	11.1		
	1328	2.0				1413	1.3		
	1907	10.6				1947	11.4		
10 SU	0152	1.8			25 M	0234	1.1		
	0732	10.4				0810	11.1		
	1407	1.8				1451	1.4		
	1944	10.8				2026	11.3		
11 M	0230	1.6			26 TU	0310	1.4		
	0810	10.5				0848	10.8		
	1445	1.7				1526	1.8		
	2021	10.8				2103	10.9		
12 TU	0307	1.6			27 W	0344	1.8		
	0846	10.5				0923	10.4		
	1523	1.8				1558	2.3		
	2057	10.8				2137	10.4		
13 W	0344	1.7			28 TH	0415	2.4		
	0923	10.3				0955	9.9		
	1601	2.0				1627	2.8		
	2136	10.5				2210	9.7		
14 TH	0423	2.0			29 F	0445	2.9		
	1002	10.1				1027	9.4		
	1642	2.3				1656	3.3		
	2217	10.2				2243	9.1		
15 F	0506	2.3			30 SA	0518	3.4		
	1045	9.7				1101	8.8		
	1729	2.6				1731	3.8		
	2305	9.7				2320	8.5		
					31 SU	0558	3.9		
						1143	8.4		
						1817	4.2		

AUGUST

Day	Time	m	Time	m	Day	Time	m	Time	m
1 M	0010	8.0			16 TU	0054	8.5		
	0651	4.2				0742	3.6		
	1243	8.0				1343	8.4		
	1919	4.4				2028	3.6		
2 TU	0127	7.7			17 W	0234	8.4		
	0801	4.4				0910	3.6		
	1408	7.9				1518	8.8		
	2042	4.4				2156	3.3		
3 W	0259	7.8			18 TH	0400	8.9		
	0923	4.2				1032	3.1		
	1532	8.2				1627	9.5		
	2212	4.0				2310	2.6		
4 TH	0412	8.3			19 F	0459	9.6		
	1038	3.7				1136	2.4		
	1634	8.9				1720	10.2		
	2319	3.3							
5 F	0506	9.0			20 SA	0006	1.9		
	1137	3.0				0546	10.3		
	1724	9.6				1227	1.8		
						1804	10.9		
6 SA	0010	2.6			21 SU O	0051	1.4		
	0551	9.8				0628	10.8		
	1225	2.3				1310	1.4		
	1806	10.3				1845	11.3		
7 SU ●	0053	1.9			22 M	0131	1.2		
	0632	10.4				0707	11.1		
	1308	1.7				1348	1.2		
	1846	10.9				1923	11.5		
8 M	0133	1.4			23 TU	0206	1.2		
	0711	10.8				0743	11.2		
	1348	1.4				1422	1.3		
	1924	11.3				1959	11.3		
9 TU	0211	1.2			24 W	0239	1.4		
	0748	11.1				0817	11.0		
	1427	1.2				1453	1.7		
	2001	11.4				2032	11.0		
10 W	0248	1.1			25 TH	0308	1.8		
	0825	11.1				0849	10.6		
	1505	1.3				1521	2.1		
	2038	11.3				2104	10.4		
11 TH	0325	1.3			26 F	0336	2.3		
	0901	10.9				0918	10.0		
	1543	1.5				1546	2.6		
	2116	11.0				2132	9.8		
12 F	0403	1.7			27 SA	0401	2.8		
	0939	10.5				0945	9.5		
	1623	1.9				1612	3.2		
	2156	10.5				2159	9.2		
13 SA	0444	2.2			28 SU	0429	3.3		
	1021	10.0				1013	9.0		
	1707	2.4				1643	3.6		
	2242	9.8				2229	8.6		
14 SU	0530	2.7			29 M	0505	3.8		
	1110	9.3				1048	8.5		
	1800	3.0				1726	4.1		
	2337	9.1				2311	8.0		
15 M	0629	3.3			30 TU	0556	4.3		
	1214	8.7				1140	7.9		
	1907	3.4				1827	4.5		
					31 W	0026	7.5		
						0706	4.5		
						1313	7.6		
						1950	4.6		

ST. HELIER
49°11′N 2°07′W

Times and heights (in metres) of high and low water 1994
Time: GMT. For BST, ADD ONE HOUR in the shaded area
High Water, full and change, 0632

SEPTEMBER

Day	Time	m	Day	Time	m
1 TH	0220 / 0838 / 1456 / 2134	7.5 / 4.4 / 8.0 / 4.2	**16** F	0344 / 1016 / 1609 / 2251	8.8 / 3.3 / 9.4 / 2.7
2 F	0342 / 1005 / 1605 / 2249	8.1 / 3.8 / 8.7 / 3.4	**17** SA	0438 / 1116 / 1658 / 2342	9.5 / 2.6 / 10.1 / 2.1
3 SA	0437 / 1108 / 1655 / 2342	9.0 / 3.0 / 9.6 / 2.5	**18** SU	0522 / 1202 / 1740	10.2 / 2.0 / 10.7
4 SU	0523 / 1158 / 1738	9.9 / 2.2 / 10.5	**19** M O	0024 / 0601 / 1242 / 1818	1.6 / 10.7 / 1.5 / 11.1
5 M ●	0026 / 0603 / 1242 / 1818	1.7 / 10.6 / 1.4 / 11.2	**20** TU	0100 / 0637 / 1317 / 1854	1.3 / 11.1 / 1.4 / 11.3
6 TU	0107 / 0642 / 1323 / 1858	1.1 / 11.2 / 1.0 / 11.6	**21** W	0133 / 0712 / 1350 / 1928	1.3 / 11.1 / 1.4 / 11.2
7 W	0145 / 0721 / 1403 / 1936	0.8 / 11.5 / 0.7 / 11.8	**22** TH	0204 / 0744 / 1419 / 2000	1.5 / 11.0 / 1.7 / 10.8
8 TH	0223 / 0758 / 1442 / 2015	0.8 / 11.5 / 0.8 / 11.7	**23** F	0232 / 0814 / 1445 / 2030	1.9 / 10.6 / 2.1 / 10.3
9 F	0301 / 0836 / 1521 / 2053	1.0 / 11.3 / 1.1 / 11.2	**24** SA	0258 / 0841 / 1509 / 2056	2.3 / 10.1 / 2.6 / 9.8
10 SA	0339 / 0915 / 1601 / 2134	1.5 / 10.8 / 1.7 / 10.6	**25** SU	0322 / 0906 / 1535 / 2120	2.8 / 9.6 / 3.1 / 9.2
11 SU	0420 / 0957 / 1646 / 2220	2.1 / 10.1 / 2.3 / 9.7	**26** M	0350 / 0931 / 1606 / 2148	3.3 / 9.1 / 3.5 / 8.7
12 M	0507 / 1047 / 1739 / 2317	2.8 / 9.3 / 3.0 / 8.9	**27** TU	0425 / 1004 / 1648 / 2228	3.8 / 8.6 / 4.0 / 8.1
13 TU	0605 / 1153 / 1847	3.5 / 8.6 / 3.5	**28** W	0513 / 1051 / 1747 / 2334	4.2 / 8.1 / 4.3 / 7.6
14 W	0038 / 0721 / 1328 / 2010	8.2 / 3.9 / 8.3 / 3.7	**29** TH	0622 / 1214 / 1907	4.5 / 7.7 / 4.5
15 TH	0225 / 0853 / 1503 / 2140	8.2 / 3.9 / 8.7 / 3.4	**30** F	0135 / 0751 / 1411 / 2047	7.5 / 4.5 / 7.9 / 4.1

OCTOBER

Day	Time	m	Day	Time	m
1 SA	0303 / 0923 / 1526 / 2209	8.1 / 3.9 / 8.7 / 3.3	**16** SU	0409 / 1048 / 1629 / 2311	9.4 / 2.9 / 9.8 / 2.4
2 SU	0402 / 1032 / 1620 / 2306	9.0 / 3.0 / 9.6 / 2.4	**17** M	0452 / 1133 / 1711 / 2352	10.0 / 2.4 / 10.4 / 2.0
3 M	0449 / 1126 / 1707 / 2353	10.0 / 2.1 / 10.6 / 1.6	**18** TU	0531 / 1211 / 1749	10.5 / 1.9 / 10.8
4 TU	0532 / 1212 / 1750	10.8 / 1.3 / 11.3	**19** W O	0027 / 0606 / 1247 / 1824	1.7 / 10.9 / 1.7 / 10.9
5 W ●	0036 / 0613 / 1256 / 1831	1.0 / 11.5 / 0.8 / 11.8	**20** TH	0101 / 0641 / 1319 / 1858	1.7 / 11.0 / 1.7 / 10.9
6 TH	0118 / 0653 / 1338 / 1912	0.6 / 11.8 / 0.5 / 12.0	**21** F	0132 / 0713 / 1348 / 1931	1.8 / 10.9 / 1.9 / 10.6
7 F	0158 / 0734 / 1419 / 1953	0.6 / 11.8 / 0.6 / 11.8	**22** SA	0200 / 0743 / 1415 / 2000	2.1 / 10.6 / 2.2 / 10.2
8 SA	0238 / 0814 / 1501 / 2034	0.9 / 11.6 / 1.0 / 11.3	**23** SU	0227 / 0810 / 1442 / 2027	2.5 / 10.2 / 2.6 / 9.8
9 SU	0318 / 0855 / 1543 / 2117	1.5 / 11.0 / 1.6 / 10.6	**24** M	0254 / 0836 / 1510 / 2054	2.9 / 9.8 / 3.0 / 9.3
10 M	0401 / 0939 / 1630 / 2205	2.2 / 10.3 / 2.3 / 9.7	**25** TU	0322 / 0904 / 1542 / 2125	3.3 / 9.4 / 3.3 / 8.9
11 TU	0449 / 1031 / 1724 / 2304	2.9 / 9.5 / 3.0 / 8.9	**26** W	0358 / 0938 / 1624 / 2206	3.7 / 9.0 / 3.7 / 8.4
12 W	0548 / 1137 / 1829	3.6 / 8.7 / 3.5	**27** TH	0445 / 1024 / 1720 / 2307	4.0 / 8.5 / 4.0 / 8.0
13 TH	0025 / 0702 / 1308 / 1949	8.3 / 4.0 / 8.4 / 3.7	**28** F	0550 / 1135 / 1833	4.3 / 8.2 / 4.1
14 F	0202 / 0830 / 1436 / 2114	8.3 / 4.0 / 8.6 / 3.5	**29** SA	0044 / 0710 / 1316 / 1958	7.9 / 4.3 / 8.2 / 3.9
15 SA	0316 / 0950 / 1540 / 2221	8.7 / 3.5 / 9.2 / 3.0	**30** SU	0215 / 0836 / 1441 / 2121	8.3 / 3.9 / 8.8 / 3.3
			31 M	0321 / 0951 / 1543 / 2227	9.1 / 3.1 / 9.6 / 2.5

NOVEMBER

Day	Time	m	Day	Time	m
1 TU	0415 / 1052 / 1635 / 2321	10.0 / 2.2 / 10.5 / 1.7	**16** W	0458 / 1140 / 1720 / 2355	10.1 / 2.6 / 10.1 / 2.4
2 W	0502 / 1144 / 1723	10.9 / 1.4 / 11.3	**17** TH	0537 / 1217 / 1757	10.4 / 2.3 / 10.4
3 TH ●	0009 / 0547 / 1232 / 1808	1.1 / 11.5 / 0.9 / 11.7	**18** F O	0031 / 0613 / 1252 / 1833	2.2 / 10.6 / 2.2 / 10.5
4 F	0055 / 0631 / 1318 / 1853	0.8 / 11.9 / 0.6 / 11.9	**19** SA	0105 / 0647 / 1324 / 1907	2.2 / 10.7 / 2.2 / 10.4
5 SA	0139 / 0714 / 1402 / 1937	0.8 / 12.0 / 0.6 / 11.8	**20** SU	0137 / 0720 / 1355 / 1940	2.3 / 10.6 / 2.3 / 10.2
6 SU	0222 / 0758 / 1447 / 2021	1.1 / 11.7 / 1.0 / 11.3	**21** M	0208 / 0750 / 1426 / 2011	2.5 / 10.4 / 2.5 / 9.9
7 M	0305 / 0842 / 1531 / 2107	1.6 / 11.2 / 1.5 / 10.7	**22** TU	0239 / 0820 / 1457 / 2043	2.8 / 10.1 / 2.8 / 9.6
8 TU	0350 / 0928 / 1618 / 2156	2.2 / 10.5 / 2.2 / 9.9	**23** W	0311 / 0852 / 1532 / 2117	3.1 / 9.8 / 3.0 / 9.3
9 W	0438 / 1019 / 1710 / 2252	2.9 / 9.8 / 2.8 / 9.1	**24** TH	0347 / 0928 / 1612 / 2158	3.4 / 9.5 / 3.3 / 9.0
10 TH	0532 / 1119 / 1808	3.5 / 9.1 / 3.4	**25** F	0431 / 1012 / 1703 / 2250	3.6 / 9.2 / 3.5 / 8.7
11 F	0001 / 0636 / 1234 / 1916	8.6 / 4.0 / 8.7 / 3.7	**26** SA	0528 / 1111 / 1806	3.9 / 8.9 / 3.7
12 SA	0121 / 0751 / 1353 / 2030	8.4 / 4.1 / 8.6 / 3.7	**27** SU	0001 / 0637 / 1228 / 1918	8.5 / 3.9 / 8.7 / 3.6
13 SU	0233 / 0908 / 1500 / 2138	8.6 / 3.9 / 8.9 / 3.5	**28** M	0123 / 0754 / 1352 / 2035	8.6 / 3.7 / 8.9 / 3.3
14 M	0330 / 1009 / 1554 / 2232	9.1 / 3.5 / 9.3 / 3.1	**29** TU	0239 / 0911 / 1506 / 2148	9.1 / 3.2 / 9.5 / 2.8
15 TU	0417 / 1058 / 1639 / 2316	9.6 / 3.0 / 9.8 / 2.7	**30** W	0342 / 1020 / 1608 / 2252	9.8 / 2.5 / 10.2 / 2.2

DECEMBER

Day	Time	m	Day	Time	m
1 TH	0437 / 1120 / 1702 / 2347	10.6 / 1.8 / 10.9 / 1.6	**16** F	0509 / 1150 / 1734	9.8 / 3.0 / 9.8
2 F ●	0528 / 1213 / 1753	11.2 / 1.2 / 11.4	**17** SA	0006 / 0549 / 1231 / 1813	2.8 / 10.2 / 2.6 / 10.1
3 SA	0038 / 0615 / 1304 / 1840	1.2 / 11.7 / 0.9 / 11.6	**18** SU O	0045 / 0628 / 1308 / 1851	2.5 / 10.5 / 2.4 / 10.3
4 SU	0126 / 0702 / 1351 / 1927	1.1 / 11.9 / 0.8 / 11.6	**19** M	0122 / 0704 / 1344 / 1927	2.4 / 10.6 / 2.2 / 10.4
5 M	0212 / 0747 / 1437 / 2013	1.2 / 11.8 / 1.0 / 11.4	**20** TU	0158 / 0738 / 1419 / 2001	2.4 / 10.6 / 2.2 / 10.3
6 TU	0257 / 0833 / 1522 / 2058	1.5 / 11.4 / 1.4 / 10.9	**21** W	0232 / 0812 / 1453 / 2035	2.5 / 10.5 / 2.3 / 10.2
7 W	0341 / 0918 / 1607 / 2144	2.0 / 10.9 / 2.0 / 10.3	**22** TH	0307 / 0845 / 1528 / 2110	2.6 / 10.4 / 2.5 / 10.0
8 TH	0425 / 1004 / 1652 / 2232	2.6 / 10.2 / 2.6 / 9.6	**23** F	0343 / 0921 / 1606 / 2148	2.8 / 10.2 / 2.7 / 9.7
9 F	0511 / 1054 / 1740 / 2325	3.2 / 9.6 / 3.2 / 9.1	**24** SA	0424 / 1002 / 1650 / 2232	3.0 / 9.9 / 2.9 / 9.4
10 SA	0601 / 1150 / 1833	3.8 / 9.0 / 3.6	**25** SU	0511 / 1050 / 1742 / 2327	3.3 / 9.6 / 3.2 / 9.1
11 SU	0025 / 0657 / 1255 / 1931	8.7 / 4.1 / 8.6 / 3.9	**26** M	0609 / 1150 / 1844	3.5 / 9.2 / 3.4
12 M	0133 / 0802 / 1405 / 2036	8.5 / 4.3 / 8.5 / 4.0	**27** TU	0035 / 0718 / 1307 / 1956	8.9 / 3.5 / 9.0 / 3.4
13 TU	0238 / 0912 / 1509 / 2140	8.6 / 4.1 / 8.7 / 3.8	**28** W	0155 / 0834 / 1431 / 2114	9.0 / 3.4 / 9.1 / 3.2
14 W	0335 / 1014 / 1604 / 2236	9.0 / 3.8 / 9.0 / 3.5	**29** TH	0312 / 0951 / 1546 / 2228	9.4 / 3.0 / 9.6 / 2.7
15 TH	0425 / 1106 / 1651 / 2323	9.4 / 3.4 / 9.4 / 3.1	**30** F	0418 / 1101 / 1649 / 2332	10.0 / 2.3 / 10.3 / 2.1
			31 SA	0515 / 1201 / 1744	10.8 / 1.7 / 10.9

DIEPPE

MEAN SPRING AND NEAP CURVES
Springs occur 2 days after New and Full Moon.

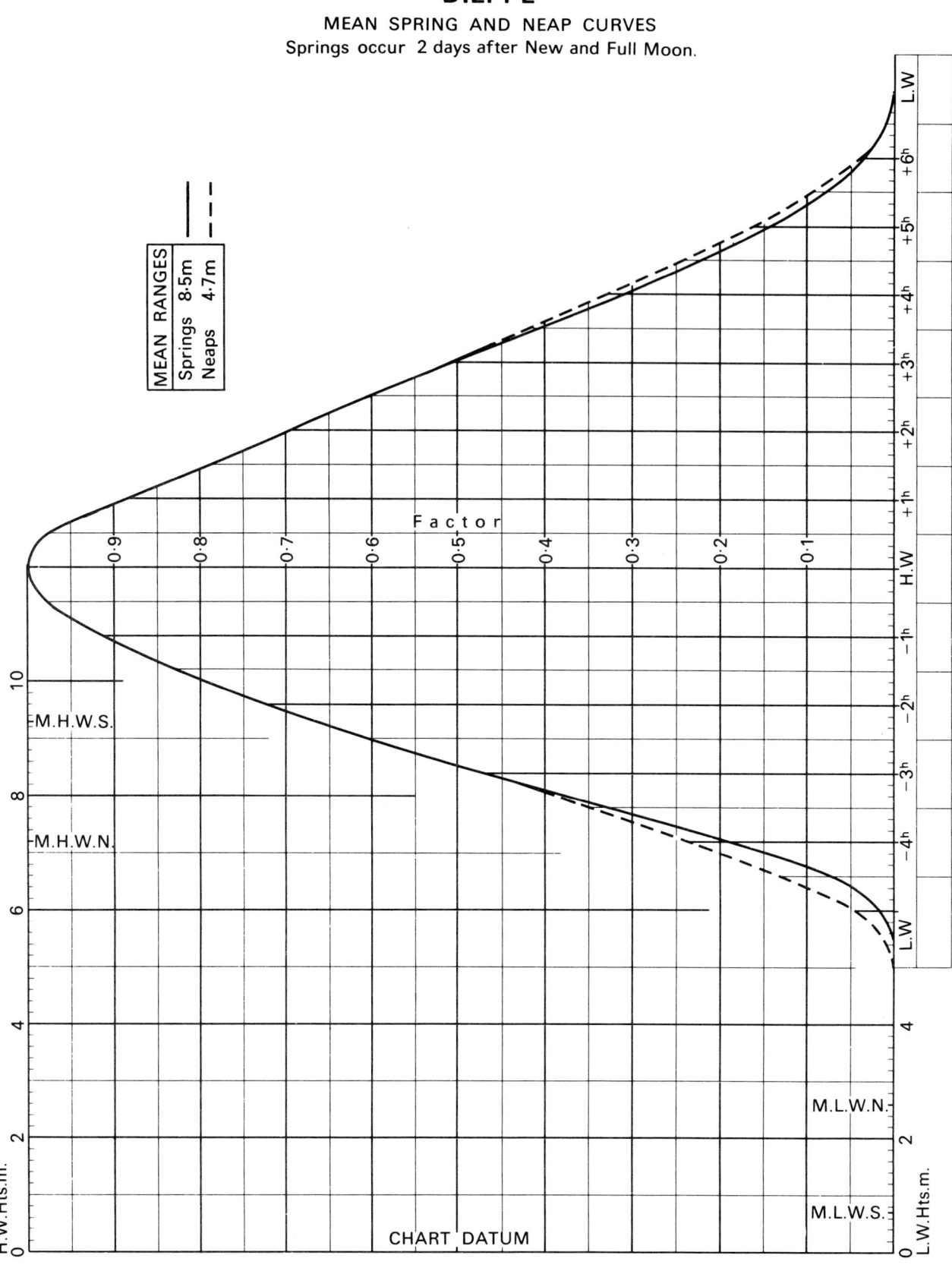

DIEPPE

49°56′N 1°05′E

Times and heights (in metres) of high and low water 1994
Time: French Standard Time. For GMT, SUBTRACT ONE HOUR.
For BST, use unchanged in the shaded area
High Water, full and change, 1206

JANUARY

Day	Time	m	Day	Time	m
1 SA	0135 / 0828 / 1351 / 2053	9.1 / 1.1 / 9.2 / 0.9	**16** SU	0211 / 0904 / 1426 / 2119	8.9 / 1.3 / 8.9 / 1.3
2 SU	0216 / 0909 / 1433 / 2133	9.0 / 1.2 / 9.0 / 1.1	**17** M	0245 / 0932 / 1500 / 2146	8.7 / 1.6 / 8.5 / 1.6
3 M	0259 / 0951 / 1517 / 2214	8.9 / 1.4 / 8.8 / 1.3	**18** TU	0318 / 1001 / 1533 / 2216	8.3 / 1.9 / 8.1 / 2.0
4 TU	0344 / 1035 / 1604 / 2258	8.6 / 1.6 / 8.4 / 1.6	**19** W	0351 / 1036 / 1609 / 2253	7.9 / 2.3 / 7.6 / 2.4
5 W	0435 / 1125 / 1659 / 2352	8.3 / 1.9 / 8.1 / 1.9	**20** TH	0430 / 1116 / 1656 / 2341	7.5 / 2.7 / 7.1 / 2.8
6 TH	0536 / 1227 / 1808	8.0 / 2.1 / 7.8	**21** F	0523 / 1216 / 1804	7.0 / 3.0 / 6.7
7 F	0059 / 0650 / 1342 / 1927	2.2 / 7.8 / 2.2 / 7.7	**22** SA	0045 / 0644 / 1332 / 1935	3.1 / 6.8 / 3.1 / 6.7
8 SA	0220 / 0807 / 1502 / 2043	2.2 / 8.0 / 2.0 / 7.9	**23** SU	0209 / 0811 / 1458 / 2050	3.1 / 7.0 / 2.8 / 7.1
9 SU	0336 / 0917 / 1612 / 2150	1.9 / 8.3 / 1.6 / 8.3	**24** M	0329 / 0916 / 1606 / 2146	2.7 / 7.5 / 2.3 / 7.7
10 M	0442 / 1017 / 1714 / 2247	1.6 / 8.7 / 1.3 / 8.7	**25** TU	0429 / 1007 / 1700 / 2234	2.1 / 8.1 / 1.8 / 8.2
11 TU ●	0540 / 1109 / 1809 / 2336	1.3 / 9.0 / 1.0 / 9.0	**26** W	0520 / 1052 / 1749 / 2317	1.7 / 8.6 / 1.3 / 8.7
12 W	0631 / 1155 / 1857	1.1 / 9.2 / 0.9	**27** TH O	0608 / 1134 / 1836 / 2359	1.3 / 9.0 / 1.0 / 9.0
13 TH	0019 / 0716 / 1236 / 1939	9.1 / 1.0 / 9.3 / 0.8	**28** F	0654 / 1216 / 1921	1.0 / 9.3 / 0.7
14 F	0059 / 0756 / 1315 / 2017	9.2 / 1.0 / 9.3 / 0.8	**29** SA	0040 / 0738 / 1257 / 2004	9.3 / 0.8 / 9.5 / 0.5
15 SA	0136 / 0831 / 1351 / 2050	9.1 / 1.1 / 9.1 / 1.0	**30** SU	0121 / 0820 / 1338 / 2044	9.5 / 0.7 / 9.6 / 0.5
			31 M	0202 / 0900 / 1419 / 2122	9.5 / 0.7 / 9.5 / 0.6

FEBRUARY

Day	Time	m	Day	Time	m
1 TU	0242 / 0939 / 1501 / 2200	9.3 / 0.9 / 9.2 / 0.9	**16** W	0241 / 0927 / 1456 / 2139	8.6 / 1.6 / 8.3 / 1.7
2 W	0324 / 1019 / 1545 / 2239	9.0 / 1.2 / 8.8 / 1.3	**17** TH	0309 / 0956 / 1526 / 2211	8.2 / 1.9 / 7.9 / 2.1
3 TH	0410 / 1103 / 1635 / 2326	8.5 / 1.6 / 8.2 / 1.8	**18** F	0341 / 1033 / 1604 / 2252	7.8 / 2.4 / 7.4 / 2.6
4 F	0506 / 1159 / 1740	8.0 / 2.0 / 7.6	**19** SA	0424 / 1122 / 1659 / 2348	7.2 / 2.8 / 6.8 / 3.0
5 SA	0029 / 0621 / 1315 / 1906	2.3 / 7.6 / 2.3 / 7.3	**20** SU	0530 / 1229 / 1828	6.8 / 3.1 / 6.5
6 SU	0155 / 0749 / 1444 / 2034	2.5 / 7.5 / 2.3 / 7.5	**21** M	0107 / 0715 / 1401 / 2010	3.2 / 6.7 / 3.0 / 6.8
7 M	0322 / 0910 / 1603 / 2146	2.3 / 7.9 / 1.9 / 8.0	**22** TU	0243 / 0840 / 1528 / 2116	2.9 / 7.2 / 2.5 / 7.5
8 TU	0435 / 1012 / 1709 / 2241	1.9 / 8.4 / 1.4 / 8.5	**23** W	0356 / 0939 / 1631 / 2208	2.2 / 7.9 / 1.8 / 8.2
9 W	0534 / 1101 / 1802 / 2326	1.5 / 8.8 / 1.1 / 8.8	**24** TH	0454 / 1028 / 1726 / 2255	1.6 / 8.5 / 1.2 / 8.8
10 TH	0621 / 1143 / 1845	1.2 / 9.1 / 0.9	**25** F	0547 / 1113 / 1816 / 2338	1.1 / 9.1 / 0.8 / 9.2
11 F	0005 / 0701 / 1220 / 1921	9.1 / 1.0 / 9.2 / 0.8	**26** SA O	0636 / 1156 / 1904	0.7 / 9.5 / 0.4
12 SA	0040 / 0736 / 1254 / 1954	9.2 / 0.9 / 9.3 / 0.8	**27** SU	0020 / 0722 / 1238 / 1947	9.6 / 0.5 / 9.7 / 0.2
13 SU	0112 / 0808 / 1327 / 2024	9.2 / 1.0 / 9.2 / 0.9	**28** M	0101 / 0805 / 1320 / 2028	9.8 / 0.5 / 9.8 / 0.2
14 M	0143 / 0836 / 1358 / 2050	9.1 / 1.1 / 9.0 / 1.1			
15 TU	0213 / 0902 / 1428 / 2114	8.9 / 1.3 / 8.7 / 1.3			

MARCH

Day	Time	m	Day	Time	m
1 TU	0142 / 0845 / 1401 / 2106	9.8 / 0.3 / 9.7 / 0.3	**16** W	0142 / 0834 / 1358 / 2045	8.9 / 1.2 / 8.8 / 1.3
2 W	0222 / 0923 / 1443 / 2142	9.6 / 0.5 / 9.4 / 0.7	**17** TH	0210 / 0859 / 1426 / 2110	8.7 / 1.4 / 8.5 / 1.6
3 TH	0303 / 1001 / 1526 / 2220	9.2 / 0.9 / 8.9 / 1.2	**18** F	0237 / 0927 / 1456 / 2140	8.4 / 1.7 / 8.1 / 2.0
4 F	0348 / 1044 / 1615 / 2306	8.6 / 1.4 / 8.2 / 1.9	**19** SA	0309 / 1001 / 1533 / 2219	8.0 / 2.1 / 7.6 / 2.4
5 SA	0442 / 1139 / 1720	7.9 / 2.0 / 7.5	**20** SU	0349 / 1046 / 1622 / 2312	7.4 / 2.5 / 7.1 / 2.9
6 SU	0008 / 0558 / 1255 / 1850	2.4 / 7.3 / 2.4 / 7.1	**21** M	0447 / 1148 / 1738	6.9 / 2.9 / 6.7
7 M	0136 / 0735 / 1428 / 2025	2.7 / 7.2 / 2.4 / 7.3	**22** TU	0025 / 0619 / 1313 / 1924	3.1 / 6.7 / 2.9 / 6.8
8 TU	0310 / 0859 / 1552 / 2134	2.4 / 7.6 / 2.0 / 7.9	**23** W	0158 / 0757 / 1446 / 2040	2.9 / 7.1 / 2.5 / 7.5
9 W	0424 / 0958 / 1656 / 2224	1.9 / 8.2 / 1.5 / 8.4	**24** TH	0319 / 0904 / 1557 / 2137	2.2 / 7.8 / 1.8 / 8.2
10 TH	0520 / 1044 / 1745 / 2306	1.5 / 8.6 / 1.1 / 8.8	**25** F	0422 / 0958 / 1656 / 2226	1.6 / 8.5 / 1.1 / 8.8
11 F	0603 / 1123 / 1823 / 2342	1.2 / 8.9 / 1.0 / 9.0	**26** SA	0519 / 1046 / 1750 / 2312	1.0 / 9.1 / 0.7 / 9.3
12 SA ●	0638 / 1157 / 1856	1.0 / 9.1 / 0.9	**27** SU O	0612 / 1132 / 1840 / 2356	0.6 / 9.5 / 0.3 / 9.7
13 SU	0014 / 0710 / 1229 / 1926	9.1 / 1.0 / 9.1 / 0.8	**28** M	0700 / 1216 / 1925	0.3 / 9.8 / 0.1
14 M	0044 / 0740 / 1300 / 1955	9.1 / 0.9 / 9.1 / 0.9	**29** TU	0038 / 0745 / 1300 / 2008	9.9 / 0.2 / 9.9 / 0.1
15 TU	0114 / 0808 / 1330 / 2021	9.1 / 1.0 / 9.0 / 1.0	**30** W	0121 / 0826 / 1342 / 2047	9.9 / 0.2 / 9.8 / 0.3
			31 TH	0202 / 0906 / 1426 / 2125	9.7 / 0.4 / 9.4 / 0.7

APRIL

Day	Time	m	Day	Time	m
1 F	0245 / 0946 / 1510 / 2205	9.2 / 0.8 / 8.9 / 1.3	**16** SA	0213 / 0906 / 1436 / 2120	8.5 / 1.6 / 8.2 / 1.9
2 SA	0330 / 1029 / 1601 / 2251	8.6 / 1.4 / 8.2 / 1.9	**17** SU	0247 / 0941 / 1514 / 2158	8.1 / 1.9 / 7.8 / 2.3
3 SU	0425 / 1123 / 1705 / 2353	7.9 / 2.0 / 7.5 / 2.5	**18** M	0329 / 1024 / 1602 / 2249	7.7 / 2.3 / 7.3 / 2.6
4 M	0538 / 1236 / 1828	7.3 / 2.4 / 7.1	**19** TU	0423 / 1122 / 1709 / 2356	7.2 / 2.6 / 7.0 / 2.8
5 TU	0116 / 0708 / 1402 / 1958	2.7 / 7.1 / 2.4 / 7.3	**20** W	0541 / 1237 / 1839	7.0 / 2.6 / 7.1
6 W	0242 / 0832 / 1522 / 2107	2.5 / 7.5 / 2.1 / 7.7	**21** TH	0119 / 0711 / 1404 / 1958	2.6 / 7.2 / 2.3 / 7.6
7 TH	0355 / 0931 / 1625 / 2157	2.0 / 8.0 / 1.7 / 8.2	**22** F	0239 / 0824 / 1518 / 2100	2.1 / 7.8 / 1.7 / 8.2
8 F	0449 / 1017 / 1713 / 2238	1.6 / 8.4 / 1.4 / 8.6	**23** SA	0346 / 0923 / 1621 / 2154	1.5 / 8.5 / 1.2 / 8.8
9 SA	0532 / 1056 / 1751 / 2313	1.4 / 8.7 / 1.2 / 8.8	**24** SU	0446 / 1017 / 1719 / 2243	1.0 / 9.0 / 0.7 / 9.3
10 SU	0607 / 1130 / 1824 / 2345	1.2 / 8.8 / 1.1 / 8.9	**25** M O	0543 / 1106 / 1812 / 2330	0.6 / 9.4 / 0.5 / 9.6
11 M ●	0640 / 1201 / 1855	1.1 / 8.9 / 1.0	**26** TU	0635 / 1153 / 1901	0.4 / 9.7 / 0.3
12 TU	0015 / 0711 / 1232 / 1925	8.9 / 1.0 / 8.9 / 1.0	**27** W	0015 / 0723 / 1240 / 1946	9.8 / 0.3 / 9.8 / 0.3
13 W	0045 / 0741 / 1303 / 1954	8.9 / 1.1 / 8.9 / 1.1	**28** TH	0100 / 0808 / 1325 / 2028	9.8 / 0.3 / 9.7 / 0.5
14 TH	0114 / 0809 / 1333 / 2021	8.9 / 1.1 / 8.8 / 1.3	**29** F	0144 / 0850 / 1411 / 2109	9.6 / 0.5 / 9.3 / 0.8
15 F	0143 / 0836 / 1403 / 2048	8.7 / 1.3 / 8.5 / 1.6	**30** SA	0229 / 0932 / 1457 / 2151	9.2 / 0.8 / 8.9 / 1.3

DIEPPE

49°56'N 1°05'E

Times and heights (in metres) of high and low water 1994
Time: French Standard Time. For GMT, SUBTRACT ONE HOUR.
For BST, use unchanged in the shaded area
High Water, full and change, 1206

MAY

	Time	m		Time	m
1 SU	0316 1017 1548 2238	8.6 1.3 8.3 1.8	**16** M	0235 0930 1503 2148	8.3 1.7 8.1 2.0
2 M	0409 1108 1646 2335	8.0 1.8 7.7 2.3	**17** TU	0317 1013 1550 2236	8.0 1.9 7.7 2.2
3 TU	0512 1211 1754	7.5 2.2 7.3	**18** W	0409 1105 1649 2335	7.7 2.1 7.5 2.3
4 W	0044 0627 1321 1911	2.5 7.2 2.4 7.3	**19** TH	0513 1210 1801	7.5 2.2 7.5
5 TH	0156 0745 1431 2023	2.5 7.2 2.2 7.5	**20** F	0045 0629 1324 1916	2.3 7.6 2.1 7.8
6 F	0304 0851 1534 2118	2.2 7.6 2.0 7.9	**21** SA	0200 0743 1439 2022	2.0 7.9 1.7 8.3
7 SA	0402 0941 1627 2202	1.9 8.0 1.7 8.2	**22** SU	0311 0849 1546 2122	1.5 8.4 1.3 8.7
8 SU	0450 1022 1710 2239	1.6 8.3 1.5 8.5	**23** M	0415 0948 1648 2216	1.1 8.8 1.0 9.1
9 M	0531 1059 1748 2314	1.4 8.5 1.4 8.6	**24** TU	0515 1043 1744 2307	0.8 9.2 0.7 9.4
10 TU ●	0608 1133 1824 2346	1.3 8.6 1.3 8.7	**25** W O	0611 1134 1837 2356	0.6 9.4 0.6 9.6
11 W	0642 1207 1857	1.2 8.7 1.2	**26** TH	0703 1223 1926	0.4 9.5 0.6
12 TH	0019 0716 1240 1929	8.8 1.2 8.7 1.3	**27** F	0043 0751 1311 2012	9.6 0.4 9.5 0.7
13 F	0051 0747 1313 2000	8.8 1.2 8.7 1.3	**28** SA	0129 0837 1357 2056	9.4 0.6 9.3 0.9
14 SA	0123 0819 1346 2033	8.7 1.3 8.6 1.5	**29** SU	0215 0920 1444 2139	9.1 0.8 8.9 1.3
15 SU	0157 0853 1423 2108	8.5 1.4 8.3 1.7	**30** M	0301 1003 1530 2222	8.7 1.2 8.5 1.7
			31 TU	0349 1047 1619 2309	8.2 1.6 8.0 2.1

JUNE

	Time	m		Time	m
1 W	0440 1136 1713	7.8 2.0 7.6	**16** TH	0355 1051 1628 2315	8.1 1.7 8.0 1.9
2 TH	0002 0538 1231 1814	2.4 7.4 2.3 7.4	**17** F	0449 1145 1728	7.9 1.8 7.9
3 F	0102 0645 1333 1922	2.5 7.2 2.4 7.3	**18** SA	0015 0554 1249 1837	2.0 7.8 1.9 8.0
4 SA	0206 0755 1436 2026	2.5 7.3 2.3 7.5	**19** SU	0124 0708 1402 1948	1.9 7.9 1.8 8.2
5 SU	0309 0856 1536 2120	2.3 7.5 2.1 7.8	**20** M	0238 0820 1516 2054	1.7 8.1 1.6 8.5
6 M	0405 0946 1628 2204	2.0 7.8 1.9 8.1	**21** TU	0348 0926 1621 2155	1.4 8.5 1.3 8.8
7 TU	0454 1028 1714 2244	1.7 8.1 1.7 8.3	**22** W	0452 1026 1722 2250	1.1 8.8 1.1 9.1
8 W	0537 1107 1755 2321	1.5 8.3 1.5 8.5	**23** TH O	0551 1121 1818 2342	0.8 9.1 0.9 9.3
9 TH ●	0617 1145 1833 2357	1.4 8.5 1.4 8.6	**24** F	0647 1211 1910	0.7 9.3 0.8
10 F	0654 1221 1909	1.3 8.6 1.3	**25** SA	0030 0737 1258 1958	9.4 0.6 9.3 0.8
11 SA	0032 0730 1257 1945	8.7 1.2 8.7 1.3	**26** SU	0116 0823 1343 2041	9.3 0.6 9.2 0.9
12 SU	0108 0807 1334 2022	8.8 1.2 8.7 1.3	**27** M	0159 0905 1425 2121	9.2 0.8 9.0 1.2
13 M	0146 0845 1413 2100	8.7 1.2 8.6 1.4	**28** TU	0241 0943 1506 2158	8.9 1.1 8.7 1.5
14 TU	0225 0924 1454 2140	8.6 1.3 8.4 1.6	**29** W	0322 1018 1547 2234	8.5 1.5 8.3 1.8
15 W	0308 1005 1538 2224	8.4 1.5 8.2 1.8	**30** TH	0404 1054 1629 2315	8.0 1.9 7.9 2.2

JULY

	Time	m		Time	m
1 F	0449 1137 1717	7.6 2.2 7.5	**16** SA	0426 1121 1658 2348	8.3 1.6 8.2 1.8
2 SA	0004 0544 1231 1816	2.5 7.2 2.5 7.2	**17** SU	0525 1219 1805	7.9 1.9 7.9
3 SU	0104 0652 1336 1927	2.7 7.0 2.7 7.1	**18** M	0055 0640 1333 1922	2.0 7.7 2.1 7.9
4 M	0214 0806 1446 2035	2.7 7.1 2.6 7.3	**19** TU	0214 0800 1454 2037	1.9 7.8 1.9 8.1
5 TU	0322 0908 1550 2130	2.4 7.4 2.3 7.7	**20** W	0331 0914 1605 2144	1.7 8.1 1.6 8.5
6 W	0419 0959 1643 2217	2.1 7.8 2.0 8.1	**21** TH	0438 1019 1709 2242	1.3 8.5 1.3 8.9
7 TH	0509 1044 1729 2259	1.7 8.1 1.7 8.4	**22** F O	0541 1113 1807 2333	1.0 8.9 1.1 9.1
8 F ●	0554 1125 1812 2338	1.5 8.4 1.5 8.6	**23** SA	0636 1201 1858	0.8 9.2 0.9
9 SA	0636 1204 1852	1.3 8.7 1.3	**24** SU	0018 0724 1244 1942	9.3 0.7 9.3 0.9
10 SU	0016 0716 1242 1932	8.8 1.1 8.9 1.2	**25** M	0100 0806 1324 2022	9.3 0.7 9.3 0.9
11 M	0054 0757 1320 2012	9.0 1.0 9.0 1.1	**26** TU	0138 0842 1401 2056	9.2 0.8 9.1 1.1
12 TU	0133 0836 1400 2051	9.0 0.9 9.0 1.1	**27** W	0215 0915 1437 2127	9.0 1.0 8.9 1.4
13 W	0213 0915 1440 2130	9.0 1.0 8.9 1.2	**28** TH	0251 0943 1511 2156	8.7 1.4 8.6 1.7
14 TH	0254 0954 1521 2211	8.8 1.1 8.7 1.3	**29** F	0325 1011 1545 2228	8.3 1.7 8.1 2.1
15 F	0337 1034 1606 2255	8.6 1.3 8.5 1.6	**30** SA	0401 1045 1622 2308	7.8 2.2 7.7 2.5
			31 SU	0444 1130 1711	7.2 2.6 7.2

AUGUST

	Time	m		Time	m
1 M	0001 0545 1231 1822	2.8 6.8 3.0 6.9	**16** TU	0034 0622 1314 1905	2.2 7.5 2.4 7.6
2 TU	0112 0712 1352 1949	3.0 6.7 3.0 6.9	**17** W	0200 0752 1442 2029	2.2 7.5 2.3 7.8
3 W	0236 0832 1512 2058	2.8 7.0 2.7 7.3	**18** TH	0323 0912 1558 2140	1.9 7.9 1.9 8.3
4 TH	0347 0932 1613 2151	2.4 7.5 2.2 7.9	**19** F	0434 1014 1703 2235	1.5 8.5 1.4 8.8
5 F	0442 1020 1704 2236	1.9 8.1 1.8 8.3	**20** SA	0535 1104 1758 2321	1.1 8.9 1.1 9.1
6 SA	0531 1103 1750 2318	1.5 8.5 1.4 8.7	**21** SU	0624 1146 1843	0.9 9.2 1.0
7 SU ●	0617 1144 1834 2358	1.1 8.9 1.1 9.0	**22** M	0002 0706 1225 1922	9.3 0.8 9.3 0.9
8 M	0701 1223 1917	0.9 9.1 0.9	**23** TU	0039 0742 1259 1956	9.3 0.8 9.3 0.9
9 TU	0037 0743 1302 1959	9.3 0.7 9.3 0.8	**24** W	0113 0813 1332 2026	9.3 0.9 9.2 1.1
10 W	0116 0823 1341 2038	9.4 0.6 9.4 0.7	**25** TH	0146 0842 1404 2054	9.1 1.1 9.0 1.3
11 TH	0156 0901 1421 2116	9.4 0.7 9.3 0.8	**26** F	0218 0907 1434 2119	8.8 1.3 8.7 1.6
12 F	0236 0938 1501 2154	9.2 0.9 9.1 1.1	**27** SA	0248 0932 1503 2147	8.4 1.7 8.3 2.0
13 SA	0318 1016 1544 2236	8.9 1.2 8.7 1.4	**28** SU	0318 1001 1534 2221	7.9 2.2 7.8 2.4
14 SU	0405 1100 1634 2327	8.4 1.6 8.3 1.8	**29** M	0354 1041 1615 2307	7.4 2.7 7.3 2.8
15 M	0503 1156 1740	7.9 2.1 7.8	**30** TU	0445 1135 1716	6.9 3.1 6.8
			31 W	0011 0608 1253 1855	3.2 6.5 3.3 6.6

66

DIEPPE
49°56′N 1°05′E

Times and heights (in metres) of high and low water 1994
Time: French Standard Time. For GMT, SUBTRACT ONE HOUR.
For BST, use unchanged in the shaded area
High Water, full and change, 1206

SEPTEMBER

Day		Time	m	Time	m	Time	m	Time	m
1	TH	0142	3.1	0753	6.8	1429	3.0	2022	7.1
16	F	0316	2.0	0903	7.9	1551	1.9	2129	8.2
2	F	0310	2.6	0900	7.4	1540	2.4	2121	7.7
17	SA	0425	1.5	1000	8.5	1652	1.5	2220	8.7
3	SA	0411	2.0	0952	8.1	1635	1.8	2209	8.4
18	SU	0520	1.2	1045	8.9	1741	1.2	2302	9.0
4	SU	0503	1.4	1037	8.6	1725	1.3	2253	8.9
19	M	0603	1.0	1125	9.1	1821	1.1	2340	9.2
5	M	0552	1.0	1119	9.1	1812	1.0	2334	9.3
20	TU	0640	0.9	1159	9.2	1855	1.0		
6	TU	0639	0.7	1159	9.4	1857	0.7		
21	W	0013	9.2	0711	0.9	1231	9.2	1926	1.0
7	W	0015	9.5	0722	0.5	1239	9.6	1940	0.6
22	TH	0045	9.2	0745	1.0	1302	9.2	1956	1.1
8	TH	0055	9.7	0803	0.4	1319	9.7	2020	0.5
23	F	0116	9.0	0809	1.2	1332	9.0	2023	1.3
9	F	0136	9.7	0842	0.5	1359	9.6	2058	0.6
24	SA	0146	8.8	0835	1.4	1400	8.7	2048	1.6
10	SA	0217	9.4	0919	0.8	1440	9.3	2137	0.9
25	SU	0215	8.5	0859	1.8	1428	8.4	2114	1.9
11	SU	0300	9.0	0958	1.2	1523	8.8	2219	1.4
26	M	0244	8.1	0928	2.2	1458	7.9	2146	2.3
12	M	0347	8.4	1042	1.8	1614	8.2	2310	1.9
27	TU	0318	7.6	1004	2.6	1536	7.4	2228	2.7
13	TU	0447	7.8	1140	2.3	1723	7.6		
28	W	0405	7.1	1055	3.1	1631	6.9	2327	3.1
14	W	0019	2.3	0611	7.3	1302	2.6	1853	7.4
29	TH	0516	6.7	1206	3.3	1757	6.7		
15	TH	0151	2.4	0745	7.4	1435	2.4	2021	7.7
30	F	0049	3.2	0702	6.7	1340	3.1	1936	7.0

OCTOBER

Day		Time	m	Time	m	Time	m	Time	m
1	SA	0224	2.8	0821	7.3	1501	2.5	2043	7.6
16	SU	0359	1.7	0934	8.3	1626	1.6	2155	8.5
2	SU	0334	2.1	0917	8.1	1601	1.8	2136	8.3
17	M	0451	1.4	1019	8.7	1713	1.4	2237	8.8
3	M	0431	1.4	1005	8.7	1654	1.3	2223	8.9
18	TU	0533	1.3	1057	8.9	1751	1.2	2314	8.9
4	TU	0523	1.0	1049	9.2	1744	0.9	2307	9.4
19	W	0608	1.2	1131	9.0	1825	1.2	2346	9.0
5	W	0612	0.6	1132	9.6	1832	0.6	2350	9.7
20	TH	0640	1.2	1202	9.1	1856	1.2		
6	TH	0658	0.5	1214	9.8	1918	0.4		
21	F	0017	9.0	0710	1.2	1232	9.0	1927	1.2
7	F	0033	9.8	0741	0.4	1256	9.9	2000	0.4
22	SA	0048	8.9	0740	1.3	1302	8.9	1956	1.3
8	SA	0116	9.8	0822	0.5	1338	9.7	2041	0.6
23	SU	0119	8.8	0808	1.5	1332	8.8	2024	1.5
9	SU	0200	9.5	0902	0.8	1422	9.4	2122	0.9
24	M	0149	8.5	0835	1.8	1401	8.5	2051	1.8
10	M	0245	9.1	0943	1.3	1507	8.8	2206	1.4
25	TU	0220	8.2	0904	2.1	1433	8.1	2123	2.1
11	TU	0335	8.4	1029	1.9	1601	8.2	2258	1.9
26	W	0256	7.8	0941	2.5	1512	7.7	2203	2.5
12	W	0436	7.8	1129	2.4	1709	7.6		
27	TH	0340	7.4	1028	2.8	1602	7.2	2256	2.8
13	TH	0007	2.4	0555	7.4	1249	2.7	1833	7.4
28	F	0442	7.0	1132	3.1	1713	7.0		
14	F	0133	2.5	0723	7.4	1415	2.5	1958	7.6
29	SA	0007	2.9	0608	7.0	1252	3.0	1842	7.1
15	SA	0253	2.2	0838	7.8	1528	2.1	2105	8.0
30	SU	0133	2.7	0731	7.4	1414	2.5	1958	7.6
31	M	0251	2.2	0835	8.1	1522	1.9	2058	8.3

NOVEMBER

Day		Time	m	Time	m	Time	m	Time	m
1	TU	0354	1.5	0929	8.7	1620	1.3	2150	8.9
16	W	0456	1.6	1026	8.6	1718	1.5	2245	8.6
2	W	0450	1.1	1018	9.2	1715	0.9	2239	9.3
17	TH	0534	1.5	1102	8.7	1755	1.4	2320	8.7
3	TH	0542	0.7	1105	9.6	1806	0.6	2327	9.6
18	F	0610	1.4	1135	8.8	1830	1.3	2353	8.8
4	F	0632	0.6	1150	9.8	1855	0.5		
19	SA	0644	1.4	1207	8.9	1903	1.3		
5	SA	0013	9.8	0719	0.5	1235	9.9	1942	0.4
20	SU	0025	8.8	0716	1.4	1238	8.9	1935	1.3
6	SU	0059	9.8	0804	0.6	1321	9.7	2026	0.6
21	M	0058	8.8	0747	1.5	1310	8.8	2005	1.5
7	M	0145	9.5	0847	0.9	1407	9.4	2110	0.9
22	TU	0130	8.6	0817	1.7	1343	8.6	2036	1.6
8	TU	0233	9.1	0931	1.3	1455	8.9	2155	1.3
23	W	0204	8.4	0850	1.9	1417	8.3	2110	1.9
9	W	0324	8.6	1019	1.8	1547	8.3	2246	1.8
24	TH	0241	8.1	0927	2.2	1456	8.0	2149	2.1
10	TH	0421	8.0	1115	2.3	1648	7.8	2347	2.3
25	F	0324	7.8	1011	2.4	1543	7.7	2236	2.4
11	F	0527	7.6	1223	2.6	1759	7.4		
26	SA	0416	7.5	1105	2.6	1640	7.4	2334	2.5
12	SA	0058	2.5	0641	7.4	1336	2.6	1916	7.4
27	SU	0523	7.4	1211	2.7	1752	7.4		
13	SU	0209	2.4	0756	7.6	1446	2.3	2026	7.7
28	M	0045	2.5	0640	7.6	1326	2.4	1910	7.6
14	M	0315	2.1	0858	8.0	1546	2.0	2122	8.0
29	TU	0203	2.2	0751	8.0	1441	2.0	2019	8.1
15	TU	0410	1.9	0946	8.3	1636	1.7	2207	8.3
30	W	0315	1.7	0853	8.5	1547	1.5	2119	8.6

DECEMBER

Day		Time	m	Time	m	Time	m	Time	m
1	TH	0418	1.3	0949	9.0	1647	1.1	2215	9.1
16	F	0503	1.9	1034	8.4	1728	1.6	2256	8.4
2	F	0515	1.0	1041	9.4	1743	0.7	2307	9.4
17	SA	0544	1.7	1111	8.6	1807	1.5	2332	8.6
3	SA	0610	0.7	1131	9.7	1837	0.5	2357	9.6
18	SU	0622	1.5	1146	8.7	1844	1.3		
4	SU	0701	0.7	1219	9.8	1927	0.5		
19	M	0007	8.7	0657	1.5	1221	8.8	1919	1.3
5	M	0046	9.6	0749	0.7	1307	9.7	2015	0.5
20	TU	0042	8.8	0731	1.4	1255	8.9	1953	1.3
6	TU	0134	9.5	0836	0.9	1354	9.5	2100	0.8
21	W	0117	8.8	0806	1.5	1330	8.8	2027	1.3
7	W	0221	9.2	0921	1.2	1441	9.1	2144	1.1
22	TH	0152	8.7	0841	1.5	1406	8.7	2102	1.4
8	TH	0308	8.8	1005	1.6	1529	8.6	2228	1.6
23	F	0230	8.5	0917	1.7	1444	8.5	2139	1.6
9	F	0357	8.3	1051	2.0	1619	8.1	2315	2.0
24	SA	0310	8.3	0957	1.9	1526	8.2	2219	1.8
10	SA	0449	7.9	1143	2.4	1715	7.6		
25	SU	0354	8.1	1043	2.1	1614	8.0	2307	2.0
11	SU	0008	2.4	0548	7.5	1242	2.6	1820	7.3
26	M	0447	7.9	1137	2.2	1712	7.7		
12	M	0110	2.6	0657	7.3	1348	2.7	1932	7.2
27	TU	0005	2.2	0553	7.8	1242	2.3	1825	7.7
13	TU	0216	2.6	0808	7.5	1455	2.5	2039	7.5
28	W	0116	2.2	0709	7.9	1400	2.1	1943	7.9
14	W	0321	2.4	0907	7.8	1555	2.2	2133	7.8
29	TH	0237	2.0	0822	8.2	1517	1.7	2054	8.3
15	TH	0416	2.1	0954	8.1	1645	1.9	2217	8.1
30	F	0350	1.6	0926	8.7	1624	1.3	2157	8.7
31	SA	0454	1.2	1024	9.1	1725	0.9	2254	9.1

LE HAVRE
MEAN SPRING AND NEAP CURVES
Springs occur 2 days after New and Full Moon.

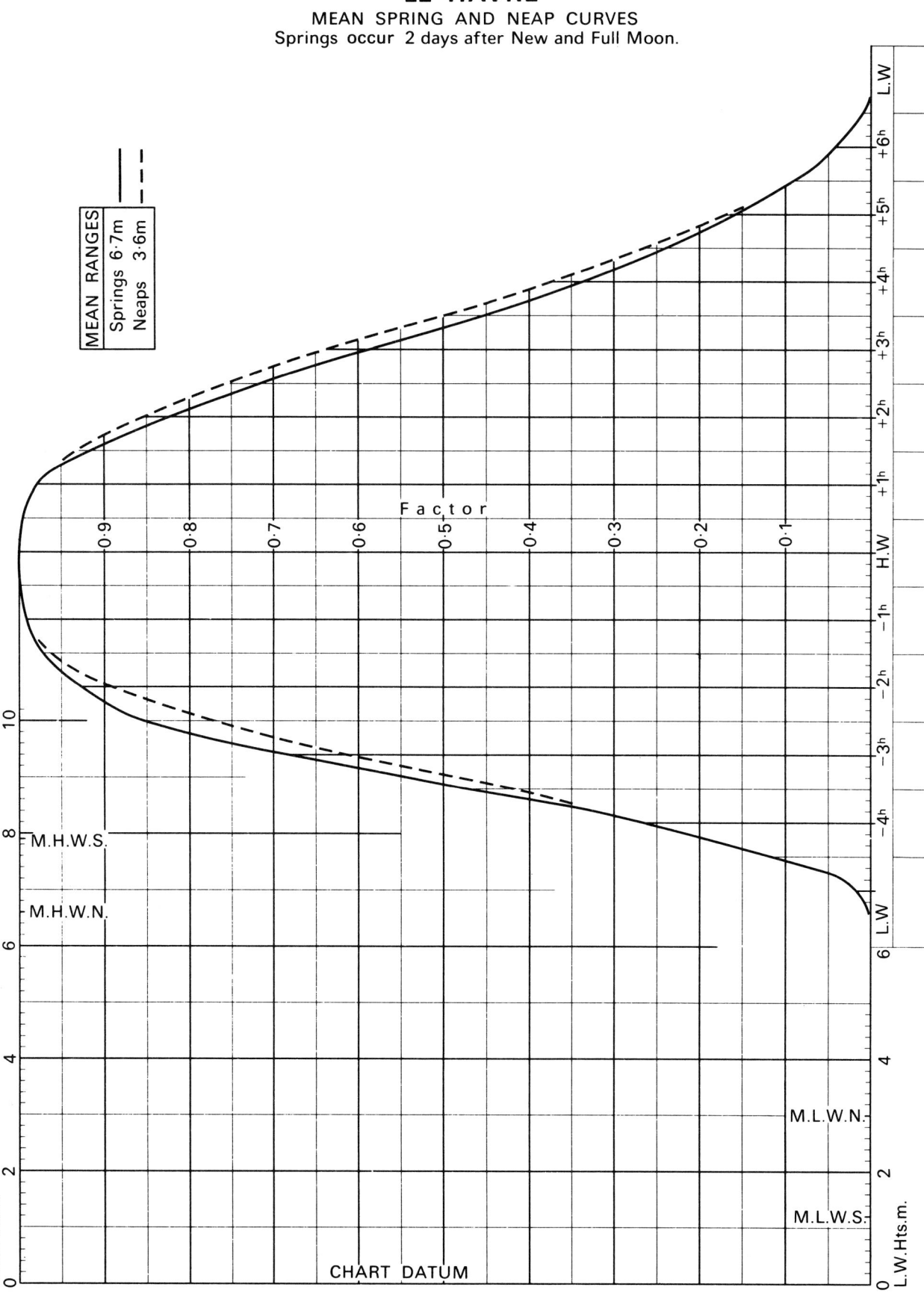

LE HAVRE
49°29'N 0°07'E

Times and heights (in metres) of high and low water 1994
Time: French Standard Time. For GMT, SUBTRACT ONE HOUR.
For BST, use unchanged in the shaded area
High Water, full and change, 1115

JANUARY

Day	Time / m	Day	Time / m
1 SA	0036 7.7 / 0740 1.5 / 1248 7.8 / 2005 1.3	**16** SU	0114 7.6 / 0815 1.7 / 1325 7.6 / 2030 1.6
2 SU	0119 7.7 / 0821 1.6 / 1332 7.7 / 2044 1.4	**17** M	0148 7.4 / 0844 2.0 / 1359 7.3 / 2057 2.0
3 M	0203 7.5 / 0902 1.8 / 1416 7.5 / 2124 1.7	**18** TU	0221 7.1 / 0913 2.3 / 1432 7.1 / 2125 2.3
4 TU	0250 7.4 / 0944 2.0 / 1504 7.3 / 2208 2.0	**19** W	0254 6.9 / 0944 2.6 / 1501 6.8 / 2158 2.7
5 W	0342 7.2 / 1034 2.3 / 1602 7.1 / 2301 2.2	**20** TH	0334 6.6 / 1025 3.0 / 1550 6.4 / 2244 3.1
6 TH	0447 7.0 / 1133 2.5 / 1714 6.9	**21** F	0432 6.4 / 1119 3.3 / 1710 6.2 / 2347 3.3
7 F	0006 2.5 / 0601 7.0 / 1249 2.5 / 1834 6.9	**22** SA	0557 6.3 / 1233 3.3 / 1844 6.2
8 SA	0129 2.5 / 0714 7.1 / 1412 2.4 / 1950 7.0	**23** SU	0111 3.3 / 0719 6.4 / 1404 3.1 / 1957 6.4
9 SU	0247 2.3 / 0822 7.3 / 1523 2.0 / 2057 7.3	**24** M	0238 3.0 / 0820 6.7 / 1516 2.6 / 2052 6.8
10 M	0353 2.0 / 0920 7.5 / 1626 1.7 / 2152 7.5	**25** TU	0340 2.5 / 0908 7.1 / 1611 2.1 / 2138 7.1
11 TU ●	0452 1.7 / 1009 7.7 / 1723 1.4 / 2239 7.7	**26** W	0432 2.1 / 0951 7.4 / 1701 1.7 / 2219 7.4
12 W	0545 1.6 / 1054 7.8 / 1811 1.2 / 2322 7.8	**27** TH O	0521 1.7 / 1032 7.7 / 1748 1.3 / 2300 7.7
13 TH	0629 1.4 / 1135 7.9 / 1852 1.2	**28** F	0607 1.4 / 1112 7.9 / 1833 1.0 / 2341 7.8
14 F	0002 7.8 / 0708 1.4 / 1213 7.9 / 1927 1.2	**29** SA	0650 1.1 / 1154 8.0 / 1915 0.8
15 SA	0039 7.7 / 0742 1.5 / 1250 7.8 / 2000 1.4	**30** SU	0022 7.9 / 0732 1.0 / 1236 8.0 / 1955 0.8
		31 M	0104 8.0 / 0811 1.1 / 1318 8.0 / 2033 1.0

FEBRUARY

Day	Time / m	Day	Time / m
1 TU	0146 7.8 / 0849 1.3 / 1401 7.8 / 2110 1.3	**16** W	0144 7.3 / 0838 2.0 / 1355 7.2 / 2048 2.1
2 W	0229 7.6 / 0928 1.6 / 1445 7.5 / 2149 1.7	**17** TH	0210 7.1 / 0904 2.3 / 1425 6.9 / 2115 2.5
3 TH	0315 7.3 / 1011 2.0 / 1537 7.2 / 2235 2.2	**18** F	0243 6.8 / 0937 2.7 / 1507 6.6 / 2154 2.9
4 F	0414 7.0 / 1105 2.4 / 1647 6.8 / 2336 2.6	**19** SA	0330 6.5 / 1024 3.1 / 1604 6.2 / 2250 3.3
5 SA	0532 6.8 / 1219 2.7 / 1816 6.6	**20** SU	0439 6.2 / 1131 3.3 / 1739 6.1
6 SU	0102 2.8 / 0657 6.8 / 1352 2.6 / 1944 6.7	**21** M	0011 3.4 / 0625 6.2 / 1306 3.3 / 1919 6.2
7 M	0232 2.6 / 0814 7.0 / 1513 2.3 / 2053 7.0	**22** TU	0153 3.2 / 0745 6.5 / 1438 2.8 / 2023 6.6
8 TU	0347 2.3 / 0912 7.3 / 1624 1.9 / 2144 7.3	**23** W	0309 2.6 / 0841 6.9 / 1543 2.2 / 2113 7.1
9 W	0450 1.9 / 0959 7.5 / 1719 1.5 / 2227 7.5	**24** TH	0408 2.0 / 0928 7.3 / 1638 1.6 / 2157 7.5
10 TH ●	0538 1.6 / 1040 7.7 / 1801 1.3 / 2305 7.7	**25** F	0501 1.5 / 1011 7.7 / 1729 1.1 / 2239 7.8
11 F	0616 1.4 / 1116 7.8 / 1834 1.2 / 2340 7.7	**26** SA O	0550 1.1 / 1053 8.0 / 1816 0.8 / 2321 8.0
12 SA	0648 1.3 / 1151 7.9 / 1905 1.2	**27** SU	0634 0.8 / 1136 8.2 / 1858 0.6
13 SU	0013 7.7 / 0719 1.3 / 1224 7.8 / 1934 1.2	**28** M	0002 8.1 / 0716 0.6 / 1218 8.2 / 1938 0.5
14 M	0044 7.7 / 0748 1.5 / 1256 7.7 / 2001 1.4		
15 TU	0115 7.5 / 0814 1.7 / 1327 7.5 / 2024 1.7		

MARCH

Day	Time / m	Day	Time / m
1 TU	0044 8.2 / 0755 0.7 / 1301 8.2 / 2017 0.7	**16** W	0044 7.6 / 0745 1.5 / 1259 7.5 / 1955 1.7
2 W	0126 8.0 / 0833 0.9 / 1344 7.9 / 2053 1.1	**17** TH	0111 7.4 / 0809 1.8 / 1326 7.3 / 2019 2.0
3 TH	0208 7.7 / 0911 1.3 / 1428 7.5 / 2130 1.6	**18** F	0139 7.2 / 0836 2.1 / 1358 7.0 / 2046 2.3
4 F	0252 7.4 / 0951 1.8 / 1519 7.1 / 2213 2.2	**19** SA	0212 6.9 / 0906 2.4 / 1438 6.6 / 2121 2.7
5 SA	0348 6.9 / 1043 2.4 / 1629 6.7 / 2313 2.8	**20** SU	0255 6.6 / 0948 2.8 / 1531 6.3 / 2212 3.1
6 SU	0508 6.6 / 1157 2.8 / 1804 6.4	**21** M	0357 6.3 / 1048 3.1 / 1649 6.1 / 2328 3.4
7 M	0044 3.0 / 0642 6.5 / 1335 2.7 / 1935 6.6	**22** TU	0529 6.2 / 1220 3.2 / 1837 6.2
8 TU	0221 2.8 / 0801 6.7 / 1504 2.4 / 2040 6.9	**23** W	0112 3.2 / 0703 6.4 / 1357 2.7 / 1947 6.6
9 W	0341 2.3 / 0857 7.0 / 1613 1.9 / 2128 7.2	**24** TH	0233 2.6 / 0806 6.8 / 1507 2.1 / 2042 7.1
10 TH	0438 1.9 / 0941 7.3 / 1701 1.6 / 2207 7.4	**25** F	0336 2.0 / 0858 7.3 / 1607 1.5 / 2129 7.5
11 F	0520 1.6 / 1019 7.6 / 1738 1.4 / 2242 7.6	**26** SA	0433 1.4 / 0944 7.7 / 1702 1.0 / 2213 7.9
12 SA ●	0553 1.4 / 1053 7.7 / 1808 1.3 / 2313 7.7	**27** SU O	0525 1.0 / 1030 8.0 / 1751 0.7 / 2256 8.1
13 SU	0623 1.3 / 1125 7.8 / 1838 1.2 / 2344 7.7	**28** M	0612 0.7 / 1114 8.2 / 1836 0.5 / 2340 8.2
14 M	0652 1.3 / 1157 7.7 / 1906 1.3	**29** TU	0656 0.5 / 1159 8.2 / 1919 0.5
15 TU	0014 7.6 / 0720 1.4 / 1228 7.7 / 1931 1.4	**30** W	0023 8.2 / 0738 0.5 / 1244 8.2 / 1958 0.7
		31 TH	0106 8.1 / 0817 0.8 / 1328 7.9 / 2037 1.1

APRIL

Day	Time / m	Day	Time / m
1 F	0149 7.7 / 0856 1.2 / 1414 7.5 / 2115 1.7	**16** SA	0116 7.2 / 0815 1.9 / 1338 7.0 / 2026 2.2
2 SA	0234 7.3 / 0937 1.8 / 1506 7.0 / 2159 2.3	**17** SU	0152 7.0 / 0847 2.2 / 1422 6.8 / 2102 2.6
3 SU	0329 6.9 / 1028 2.3 / 1615 6.6 / 2259 2.8	**18** M	0236 6.7 / 0926 2.5 / 1512 6.5 / 2150 2.9
4 M	0446 6.5 / 1140 2.7 / 1744 6.4	**19** TU	0332 6.5 / 1022 2.8 / 1618 6.3 / 2300 3.1
5 TU	0025 3.0 / 0615 6.4 / 1308 2.7 / 1910 6.5	**20** W	0448 6.3 / 1144 2.9 / 1754 6.4
6 W	0153 2.8 / 0734 6.6 / 1430 2.5 / 2015 6.8	**21** TH	0033 3.0 / 0619 6.5 / 1315 2.6 / 1908 6.8
7 TH	0308 2.4 / 0832 6.9 / 1537 2.1 / 2102 7.1	**22** F	0153 2.5 / 0727 6.9 / 1428 2.1 / 2006 7.2
8 F	0404 2.0 / 0915 7.1 / 1625 1.8 / 2140 7.3	**23** SA	0259 1.9 / 0824 7.3 / 1531 1.5 / 2057 7.6
9 SA	0446 1.7 / 0952 7.4 / 1702 1.6 / 2213 7.5	**24** SU	0400 1.4 / 0916 7.6 / 1629 1.1 / 2145 7.9
10 SU	0521 1.5 / 1026 7.5 / 1736 1.5 / 2244 7.6	**25** M O	0456 1.0 / 1005 7.9 / 1723 0.8 / 2231 8.1
11 M ●	0553 1.4 / 1058 7.6 / 1807 1.4 / 2314 7.6	**26** TU	0548 0.7 / 1053 8.1 / 1812 0.7 / 2317 8.2
12 TU	0624 1.4 / 1130 7.6 / 1836 1.4 / 2345 7.6	**27** W	0635 0.6 / 1141 8.1 / 1857 0.7
13 W	0652 1.4 / 1203 7.5 / 1902 1.5	**28** TH	0002 8.2 / 0720 0.6 / 1228 8.1 / 1940 0.9
14 TH	0015 7.5 / 0719 1.5 / 1234 7.4 / 1929 1.7	**29** F	0047 8.0 / 0802 0.8 / 1315 7.8 / 2022 1.2
15 F	0045 7.4 / 0746 1.7 / 1306 7.3 / 1956 1.9	**30** SA	0132 7.7 / 0843 1.2 / 1402 7.5 / 2103 1.7

LE HAVRE

49°29′ N 0°07′ E

Times and heights (in metres) of high and low water 1994
Time: French Standard Time. For GMT, SUBTRACT ONE HOUR.
For BST, use unchanged in the shaded area
High Water, full and change, 1115

MAY

Day	Time	m	Day	Time	m
1 SU	0219 / 0926 / 1454 / 2148	7.3 / 1.7 / 7.1 / 2.2	**16** M	0139 / 0837 / 1407 / 2053	7.2 / 2.0 / 7.0 / 2.3
2 M	0312 / 1015 / 1555 / 2245	7.0 / 2.2 / 6.7 / 2.7	**17** TU	0223 / 0917 / 1455 / 2140	7.0 / 2.2 / 6.8 / 2.6
3 TU	0418 / 1117 / 1708 / 2354	6.6 / 2.5 / 6.5 / 2.9	**18** W	0314 / 1008 / 1558 / 2242	6.8 / 2.4 / 6.7 / 2.7
4 W	0533 / 1227 / 1825	6.5 / 2.7 / 6.5	**19** TH	0418 / 1117 / 1713 / 2357	6.7 / 2.5 / 6.7 / 2.7
5 TH	0105 / 0649 / 1334 / 1934	2.8 / 6.5 / 2.6 / 6.7	**20** F	0536 / 1234 / 1827	6.7 / 2.4 / 6.9
6 F	0211 / 0753 / 1437 / 2025	2.6 / 6.7 / 2.4 / 6.9	**21** SA	0112 / 0648 / 1347 / 1929	2.4 / 6.9 / 2.1 / 7.2
7 SA	0310 / 0842 / 1532 / 2106	2.3 / 6.9 / 2.1 / 7.1	**22** SU	0223 / 0751 / 1455 / 2026	2.0 / 7.2 / 1.7 / 7.5
8 SU	0400 / 0922 / 1619 / 2141	2.0 / 7.1 / 1.9 / 7.3	**23** M	0328 / 0849 / 1558 / 2118	1.5 / 7.5 / 1.3 / 7.8
9 M	0443 / 0957 / 1659 / 2213	1.8 / 7.3 / 1.8 / 7.4	**24** TU	0428 / 0944 / 1656 / 2209	1.2 / 7.7 / 1.1 / 8.0
10 TU ●	0521 / 1032 / 1735 / 2246	1.6 / 7.4 / 1.7 / 7.5	**25** W O	0524 / 1036 / 1749 / 2258	0.9 / 7.9 / 1.0 / 8.0
11 W	0555 / 1106 / 1807 / 2319	1.6 / 7.4 / 1.7 / 7.5	**26** TH	0616 / 1126 / 1838 / 2345	0.8 / 8.0 / 0.9 / 8.0
12 TH	0626 / 1140 / 1837 / 2351	1.5 / 7.4 / 1.7 / 7.5	**27** F	0704 / 1214 / 1924	0.7 / 7.9 / 1.1
13 F	0656 / 1214 / 1908	1.5 / 7.4 / 1.7	**28** SA	0032 / 0748 / 1302 / 2008	7.9 / 0.9 / 7.8 / 1.3
14 SA	0024 / 0728 / 1250 / 1941	7.4 / 1.6 / 7.3 / 1.9	**29** SU	0117 / 0831 / 1349 / 2051	7.7 / 1.2 / 7.5 / 1.7
15 SU	0059 / 0802 / 1328 / 2015	7.3 / 1.7 / 7.2 / 2.1	**30** M	0203 / 0913 / 1436 / 2134	7.4 / 1.5 / 7.2 / 2.1
			31 TU	0250 / 0956 / 1526 / 2220	7.1 / 2.0 / 6.9 / 2.4

JUNE

Day	Time	m	Day	Time	m
1 W	0343 / 1043 / 1623 / 2313	6.8 / 2.3 / 6.7 / 2.7	**16** TH	0258 / 0958 / 1536 / 2224	7.1 / 2.0 / 7.0 / 2.3
2 TH	0444 / 1137 / 1726	6.6 / 2.6 / 6.6	**17** F	0352 / 1052 / 1637 / 2325	7.0 / 2.2 / 6.9 / 2.4
3 F	0012 / 0551 / 1237 / 1833	2.8 / 6.5 / 2.7 / 6.6	**18** SA	0459 / 1157 / 1748	6.9 / 2.2 / 7.0
4 SA	0115 / 0700 / 1340 / 1936	2.8 / 6.5 / 2.7 / 6.7	**19** SU	0035 / 0614 / 1310 / 1856	2.3 / 6.9 / 2.2 / 7.2
5 SU	0217 / 0800 / 1441 / 2026	2.6 / 6.7 / 2.5 / 6.9	**20** M	0150 / 0724 / 1425 / 1959	2.1 / 7.1 / 2.0 / 7.4
6 M	0315 / 0849 / 1536 / 2108	2.3 / 6.9 / 2.3 / 7.1	**21** TU	0301 / 0830 / 1531 / 2059	1.8 / 7.3 / 1.7 / 7.6
7 TU	0405 / 0930 / 1623 / 2145	2.1 / 7.0 / 2.1 / 7.3	**22** W	0404 / 0930 / 1633 / 2153	1.4 / 7.6 / 1.4 / 7.8
8 W	0449 / 1008 / 1705 / 2222	1.9 / 7.2 / 1.9 / 7.4	**23** TH O	0504 / 1024 / 1730 / 2244	1.2 / 7.7 / 1.3 / 7.9
9 TH	0528 / 1045 / 1741 / 2257 ●	1.7 / 7.3 / 1.8 / 7.5	**24** F	0600 / 1114 / 1823 / 2331	1.0 / 7.8 / 1.2 / 7.9
10 F	0604 / 1122 / 1817 / 2332	1.6 / 7.4 / 1.7 / 7.5	**25** SA	0650 / 1202 / 1911	0.9 / 7.8 / 1.2
11 SA	0639 / 1158 / 1853	1.5 / 7.4 / 1.7	**26** SU	0017 / 0735 / 1246 / 1954	7.9 / 0.9 / 7.8 / 1.3
12 SU	0008 / 0716 / 1236 / 1931	7.5 / 1.5 / 7.4 / 1.7	**27** M	0100 / 0815 / 1329 / 2033	7.8 / 1.1 / 7.6 / 1.5
13 M	0046 / 0754 / 1316 / 2009	7.5 / 1.5 / 7.4 / 1.8	**28** TU	0141 / 0852 / 1410 / 2110	7.6 / 1.4 / 7.4 / 1.9
14 TU	0127 / 0832 / 1358 / 2049	7.4 / 1.6 / 7.3 / 2.0	**29** W	0222 / 0927 / 1451 / 2146	7.3 / 1.8 / 7.1 / 2.2
15 W	0210 / 0913 / 1444 / 2133	7.3 / 1.8 / 7.1 / 2.2	**30** TH	0305 / 1002 / 1535 / 2226	7.0 / 2.2 / 6.9 / 2.5

JULY

Day	Time	m	Day	Time	m
1 F	0353 / 1043 / 1626 / 2313	6.7 / 2.5 / 6.6 / 2.8	**16** SA	0329 / 1029 / 1606 / 2258	7.2 / 2.0 / 7.1 / 2.2
2 SA	0451 / 1134 / 1728	6.4 / 2.8 / 6.5	**17** SU	0430 / 1126 / 1715	7.0 / 2.3 / 7.0
3 SU	0012 / 0600 / 1238 / 1837	3.0 / 6.3 / 3.0 / 6.5	**18** M	0004 / 0549 / 1240 / 1831	2.4 / 6.8 / 2.4 / 7.0
4 M	0122 / 0712 / 1350 / 1942	3.0 / 6.4 / 2.9 / 6.6	**19** TU	0125 / 0708 / 1403 / 1943	2.3 / 6.9 / 2.3 / 7.2
5 TU	0231 / 0815 / 1456 / 2035	2.7 / 6.6 / 2.7 / 6.8	**20** W	0242 / 0821 / 1514 / 2048	2.0 / 7.2 / 2.0 / 7.4
6 W	0329 / 0904 / 1550 / 2120	2.4 / 6.8 / 2.4 / 7.1	**21** TH	0349 / 0923 / 1619 / 2144	1.7 / 7.4 / 1.7 / 7.7
7 TH	0419 / 0947 / 1638 / 2200	2.1 / 7.1 / 2.1 / 7.3	**22** F O	0453 / 1016 / 1720 / 2232	1.4 / 7.6 / 1.5 / 7.8
8 F ●	0504 / 1026 / 1721 / 2237	1.8 / 7.3 / 1.9 / 7.5	**23** SA	0551 / 1102 / 1813 / 2317	1.1 / 7.8 / 1.3 / 7.9
9 SA	0546 / 1104 / 1802 / 2315	1.6 / 7.4 / 1.7 / 7.6	**24** SU	0638 / 1145 / 1856 / 2358	1.0 / 7.8 / 1.3 / 7.9
10 SU	0626 / 1142 / 1842 / 2353	1.4 / 7.5 / 1.5 / 7.7	**25** M	0718 / 1225 / 1934	1.0 / 7.8 / 1.3
11 M	0706 / 1221 / 1922	1.3 / 7.6 / 1.5	**26** TU	0037 / 0752 / 1303 / 2007	7.8 / 1.1 / 7.7 / 1.4
12 TU	0032 / 0746 / 1301 / 2002	7.7 / 1.2 / 7.6 / 1.5	**27** W	0115 / 0823 / 1339 / 2038	7.7 / 1.4 / 7.5 / 1.7
13 W	0113 / 0825 / 1343 / 2041	7.7 / 1.3 / 7.6 / 1.6	**28** TH	0151 / 0852 / 1414 / 2108	7.5 / 1.7 / 7.3 / 2.0
14 TH	0155 / 0903 / 1426 / 2121	7.6 / 1.5 / 7.4 / 1.7	**29** F	0226 / 0919 / 1449 / 2138	7.2 / 2.1 / 7.0 / 2.4
15 F	0240 / 0943 / 1512 / 2205	7.4 / 1.7 / 7.3 / 2.0	**30** SA	0303 / 0949 / 1527 / 2214	6.8 / 2.5 / 6.7 / 2.8
			31 SU	0349 / 1031 / 1618 / 2305	6.5 / 2.9 / 6.5 / 3.1

AUGUST

Day	Time	m	Day	Time	m
1 M	0455 / 1130 / 1734	6.2 / 3.2 / 6.3	**16** TU	0534 / 1219 / 1815	6.7 / 2.7 / 6.8
2 TU	0016 / 0624 / 1252 / 1858	3.2 / 6.1 / 3.3 / 6.3	**17** W	0110 / 0702 / 1351 / 1935	2.5 / 6.8 / 2.6 / 7.0
3 W	0144 / 0740 / 1417 / 2004	3.1 / 6.3 / 3.0 / 6.6	**18** TH	0232 / 0819 / 1507 / 2042	2.2 / 7.0 / 2.3 / 7.3
4 TH	0256 / 0838 / 1521 / 2054	2.7 / 6.7 / 2.6 / 6.9	**19** F	0344 / 0917 / 1615 / 2134	1.8 / 7.3 / 1.9 / 7.6
5 F	0352 / 0924 / 1614 / 2137	2.2 / 7.0 / 2.2 / 7.3	**20** SA	0449 / 1004 / 1714 / 2218	1.5 / 7.6 / 1.6 / 7.8
6 SA	0441 / 1005 / 1701 / 2217	1.8 / 7.3 / 1.8 / 7.5	**21** SU O	0540 / 1046 / 1758 / 2258	1.2 / 7.7 / 1.4 / 7.9
7 SU ●	0528 / 1044 / 1746 / 2255	1.5 / 7.5 / 1.5 / 7.7	**22** M	0619 / 1124 / 1835 / 2335	1.1 / 7.8 / 1.3 / 7.9
8 M	0611 / 1123 / 1828 / 2335	1.2 / 7.7 / 1.3 / 7.9	**23** TU	0653 / 1159 / 1907	1.1 / 7.8 / 1.3
9 TU	0653 / 1203 / 1909	1.0 / 7.8 / 1.1	**24** W	0010 / 0723 / 1233 / 1938	7.9 / 1.2 / 7.7 / 1.4
10 W	0015 / 0732 / 1243 / 1949	7.9 / 0.9 / 7.9 / 1.1	**25** TH	0045 / 0751 / 1305 / 2005	7.7 / 1.4 / 7.6 / 1.6
11 TH	0056 / 0811 / 1324 / 2027	7.9 / 1.0 / 7.8 / 1.2	**26** F	0118 / 0816 / 1337 / 2031	7.5 / 1.7 / 7.4 / 2.0
12 F	0138 / 0848 / 1405 / 2105	7.8 / 1.2 / 7.7 / 1.5	**27** SA	0150 / 0840 / 1406 / 2056	7.2 / 2.1 / 7.1 / 2.3
13 SA	0222 / 0925 / 1449 / 2145	7.6 / 1.6 / 7.4 / 1.8	**28** SU	0216 / 0906 / 1437 / 2127	6.9 / 2.5 / 6.9 / 2.5
14 SU	0309 / 1007 / 1541 / 2234	7.3 / 2.0 / 7.2 / 2.2	**29** M	0255 / 0941 / 1519 / 2211	6.6 / 2.9 / 6.5 / 3.1
15 M	0411 / 1102 / 1651 / 2341	6.9 / 2.4 / 6.9 / 2.5	**30** TU	0348 / 1034 / 1624 / 2315	6.2 / 3.3 / 6.2 / 3.4
			31 W	0527 / 1154 / 1808	6.0 / 3.5 / 6.2

LE HAVRE

49°29′N 0°07′E

Times and heights (in metres) of high and low water 1994
Time: French Standard Time. For GMT, SUBTRACT ONE HOUR.
For BST, use unchanged in the shaded area
High Water, full and change, 1115

SEPTEMBER

Day	Time	m	Time	m	Time	m	Time	m
1 TH	0052	3.3	0704	6.2	1337	3.3	1929	6.4
16 F	0226	2.3	0811	7.0	1502	2.3	2030	7.2
2 F	0221	2.9	0808	6.6	1450	2.7	2025	6.8
17 SA	0337	1.9	0904	7.3	1606	1.9	2118	7.5
3 SA	0323	2.3	0857	7.0	1546	2.2	2110	7.3
18 SU	0434	1.6	0946	7.6	1656	1.6	2159	7.7
4 SU	0415	1.8	0939	7.4	1637	1.7	2152	7.6
19 M O	0517	1.4	1023	7.7	1735	1.5	2236	7.8
5 M ●	0504	1.3	1019	7.7	1724	1.4	2232	7.9
20 TU	0552	1.3	1058	7.8	1807	1.4	2310	7.9
6 TU	0549	1.0	1059	7.9	1808	1.1	2313	8.1
21 W	0622	1.3	1129	7.8	1837	1.4	2342	7.8
7 W	0632	0.8	1139	8.0	1850	0.9	2354	8.1
22 TH	0651	1.3	1201	7.7	1907	1.5		
8 TH	0713	0.7	1220	8.1	1931	0.9		
23 F	0015	7.7	0719	1.5	1232	7.6	1934	1.6
9 F	0037	8.1	0752	0.8	1302	8.0	2009	1.0
24 SA	0047	7.5	0744	1.8	1302	7.4	1959	1.9
10 SA	0120	7.9	0830	1.1	1344	7.8	2048	1.3
25 SU	0117	7.3	0808	2.1	1329	7.2	2025	2.2
11 SU	0204	7.6	0907	1.6	1428	7.5	2128	1.8
26 M	0143	7.0	0835	2.5	1359	6.9	2054	2.6
12 M	0253	7.3	0949	2.1	1520	7.1	2216	2.3
27 TU	0225	6.7	0908	2.9	1441	6.6	2133	3.0
13 TU	0357	6.8	1044	2.6	1633	6.8	2325	2.7
28 W	0315	6.3	0955	3.3	1539	6.3	2230	3.3
14 W	0526	6.6	1208	2.9	1803	6.7		
29 TH	0431	6.1	1107	3.5	1706	6.2		
15 TH	0102	2.7	0657	6.7	1346	2.8	1927	6.9
30 F	0000	3.4	0621	6.2	1251	3.4	1845	6.4

OCTOBER

Day	Time	m	Time	m	Time	m	Time	m
1 SA	0139	3.0	0730	6.6	1413	2.8	1948	6.8
16 SU	0309	2.1	0841	7.2	1538	2.1	2056	7.3
2 SU	0247	2.3	0823	7.1	1513	2.2	2038	7.3
17 M	0402	1.8	0922	7.5	1625	1.8	2136	7.5
3 M	0342	1.8	0908	7.5	1606	1.7	2123	7.7
18 TU	0444	1.7	0957	7.6	1702	1.6	2211	7.7
4 TU	0433	1.3	0950	7.8	1656	1.3	2206	7.9
19 W O	0518	1.6	1030	7.7	1736	1.5	2244	7.7
5 W ●	0522	1.0	1032	8.0	1744	1.0	2249	8.1
20 TH	0550	1.5	1100	7.7	1808	1.5	2316	7.7
6 TH	0608	0.8	1114	8.2	1829	0.8	2333	8.2
21 F	0621	1.6	1131	7.7	1839	1.6	2349	7.6
7 F	0651	0.7	1157	8.2	1912	0.8		
22 SA	0650	1.7	1202	7.6	1907	1.7		
8 SA	0018	8.2	0733	0.9	1241	8.1	1953	0.9
23 SU	0021	7.5	0717	1.9	1231	7.5	1934	1.9
9 SU	0103	8.0	0813	1.2	1325	7.9	2033	1.3
24 M	0052	7.3	0744	2.1	1300	7.3	2002	2.1
10 M	0150	7.7	0853	1.7	1411	7.5	2115	1.8
25 TU	0121	7.1	0813	2.4	1334	7.1	2032	2.4
11 TU	0242	7.2	0937	2.2	1504	7.1	2205	2.3
26 W	0201	6.8	0846	2.8	1416	6.8	2109	2.7
12 W	0347	6.8	1035	2.7	1616	6.7	2315	2.7
27 TH	0250	6.5	0930	3.1	1509	6.5	2159	3.0
13 TH	0512	6.6	1159	3.0	1743	6.6		
28 F	0349	6.4	1033	3.3	1619	6.4	2314	3.2
14 F	0046	2.7	0638	6.7	1328	2.8	1904	6.7
29 SA	0526	6.4	1202	3.3	1751	6.4		
15 SA	0204	2.5	0749	6.9	1439	2.5	2008	7.0
30 SU	0047	2.9	0645	6.7	1326	2.9	1904	6.8
31 M	0203	2.4	0743	7.1	1433	2.3	2000	7.2

NOVEMBER

Day	Time	m	Time	m	Time	m	Time	m
1 TU	0304	1.9	0833	7.5	1532	1.8	2051	7.6
16 W	0403	2.0	0929	7.4	1628	1.9	2146	7.4
2 W	0400	1.4	0919	7.8	1627	1.3	2139	7.9
17 TH	0444	1.9	1002	7.6	1706	1.8	2220	7.5
3 TH ●	0453	1.1	1005	8.1	1719	1.0	2227	8.1
18 F O	0520	1.8	1033	7.6	1741	1.7	2253	7.5
4 F	0543	0.9	1050	8.2	1807	0.8	2314	8.2
19 SA	0554	1.8	1105	7.6	1814	1.7	2327	7.5
5 SA	0630	0.8	1136	8.2	1854	0.8		
20 SU	0625	1.8	1137	7.6	1845	1.7		
6 SU	0002	8.2	0715	1.0	1222	8.1	1938	0.9
21 M	0000	7.5	0656	1.9	1208	7.5	1915	1.8
7 M	0050	8.0	0759	1.3	1308	7.9	2022	1.2
22 TU	0033	7.4	0727	2.1	1241	7.4	1946	1.9
8 TU	0138	7.7	0842	1.7	1356	7.6	2106	1.7
23 W	0108	7.2	0759	2.3	1317	7.3	2019	2.2
9 W	0230	7.3	0929	2.2	1449	7.2	2156	2.1
24 TH	0144	7.0	0835	2.5	1359	7.0	2056	2.4
10 TH	0330	6.9	1024	2.6	1552	6.8	2256	2.5
25 F	0230	6.8	0916	2.8	1447	6.8	2141	2.6
11 F	0442	6.7	1133	2.9	1706	6.6		
26 SA	0323	6.7	1010	2.9	1544	6.7	2241	2.8
12 SA	0008	2.7	0558	6.7	1247	2.9	1823	6.6
27 SU	0435	6.6	1119	3.0	1656	6.6	2355	2.8
13 SU	0119	2.7	0710	6.8	1355	2.7	1932	6.8
28 M	0554	6.8	1235	2.8	1816	6.8		
14 M	0223	2.5	0807	7.0	1455	2.4	2026	7.0
29 TU	0113	2.5	0701	7.1	1351	2.4	1923	7.1
15 TU	0318	2.2	0851	7.3	1545	2.1	2109	7.3
30 W	0225	2.1	0758	7.4	1459	1.9	2022	7.4

DECEMBER

Day	Time	m	Time	m	Time	m	Time	m
1 TH	0329	1.7	0851	7.7	1600	1.5	2117	7.7
16 F	0413	2.2	0936	7.3	1639	2.0	2159	7.3
2 F ●	0427	1.3	0942	8.0	1656	1.1	2209	8.0
17 SA	0455	2.1	1011	7.4	1718	1.8	2234	7.4
3 SA	0522	1.1	1031	8.1	1750	0.9	2300	8.1
18 SU O	0532	1.9	1045	7.5	1754	1.7	2309	7.5
4 SU	0613	1.0	1120	8.2	1840	0.8	2349	8.1
19 M	0607	1.9	1119	7.6	1829	1.6	2344	7.5
5 M	0702	1.1	1208	8.1	1927	0.9		
20 TU	0641	1.8	1152	7.6	1902	1.6		
6 TU	0038	8.0	0748	1.3	1255	8.0	2012	1.1
21 W	0018	7.5	0716	1.8	1227	7.6	1937	1.6
7 W	0126	7.8	0833	1.6	1342	7.7	2056	1.5
22 TH	0055	7.4	0751	1.9	1304	7.5	2013	1.8
8 TH	0214	7.5	0917	2.0	1429	7.4	2139	1.9
23 F	0134	7.3	0828	2.1	1345	7.4	2050	1.9
9 F	0304	7.1	1002	2.4	1520	7.0	2224	2.3
24 SA	0215	7.2	0907	2.3	1428	7.2	2129	2.2
10 SA	0359	6.8	1052	2.7	1619	6.7	2316	2.7
25 SU	0259	7.0	0952	2.5	1516	7.0	2216	2.4
11 SU	0501	6.7	1150	2.9	1726	6.6		
26 M	0354	6.9	1046	2.6	1614	6.9	2314	2.5
12 M	0017	2.9	0611	6.8	1257	3.0	1839	6.5
27 TU	0504	6.9	1151	2.7	1730	6.8		
13 TU	0124	2.9	0719	6.7	1404	2.8	1947	6.7
28 W	0026	2.5	0620	7.0	1308	2.5	1849	6.9
14 W	0229	2.7	0815	6.9	1504	2.6	2040	6.9
29 TH	0147	2.4	0728	7.2	1428	2.2	1959	7.2
15 TH	0325	2.5	0859	7.1	1554	2.3	2122	7.1
30 F	0302	2.0	0830	7.5	1537	1.7	2101	7.5
31 SA	0406	1.6	0926	7.8	1638	1.3	2158	7.8

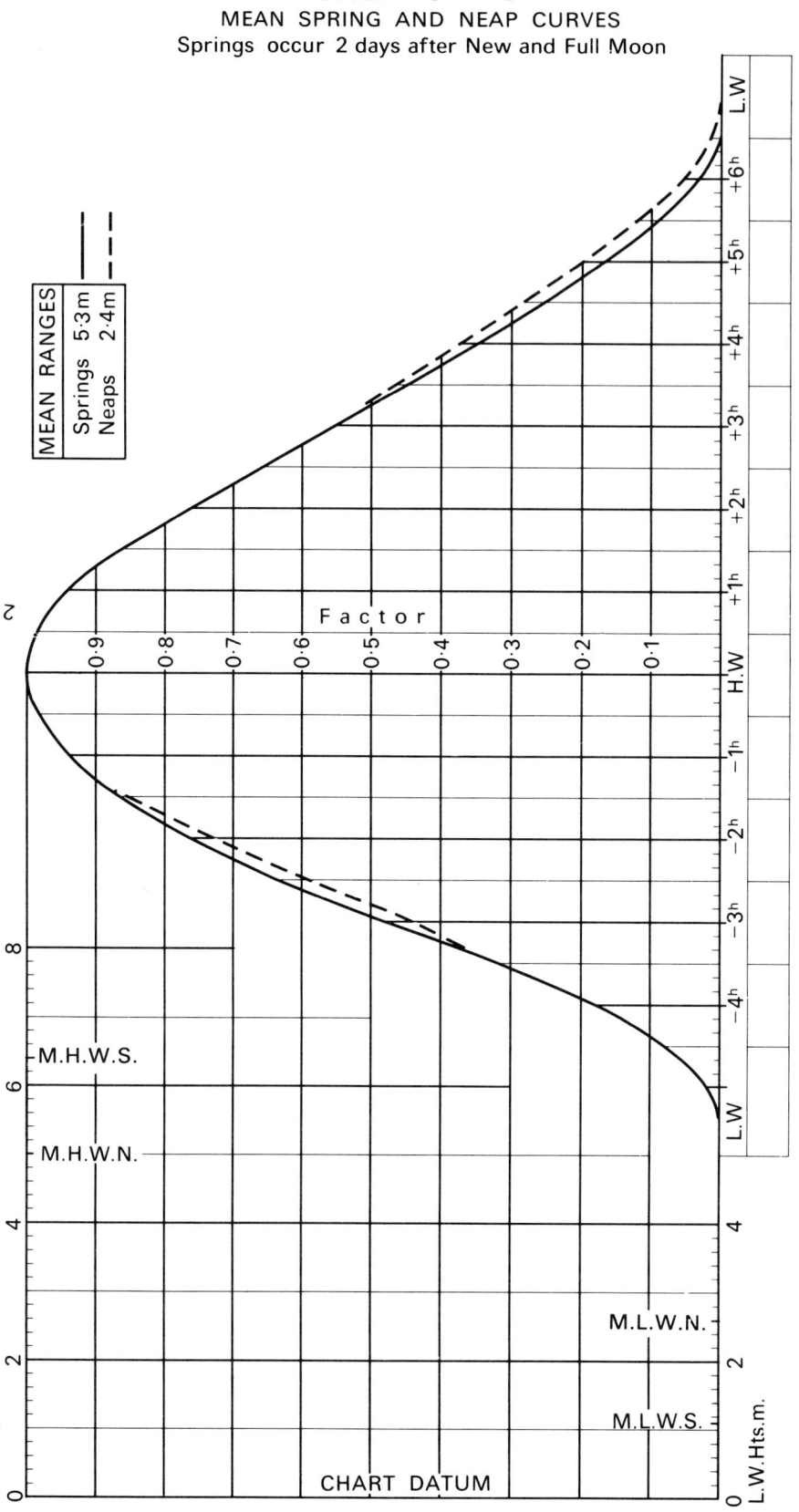

CHERBOURG
MEAN SPRING AND NEAP CURVES
Springs occur 2 days after New and Full Moon

72

CHERBOURG

49°39′N 1°38′W

Times and heights (in metres) of high and low water 1994
Time: French Standard Time. For GMT, SUBTRACT ONE HOUR.
For BST, use unchanged in the shaded area
High Water, full and change, 0905

JANUARY

Day	Time	m	Time	m	Day	Time	m	Time	m
1 SA	0520	1.4			16 SU	0557	1.6		
	1051	6.4				1128	6.1		
	1744	1.1				1814	1.4		
	2321	6.1				2347	5.8		
2 SU	0601	1.4			17 M	0630	1.8		
	1132	6.2				1200	5.9		
	1826	1.2				1846	1.7		
3 M	0004	6.0			18 TU	0018	5.6		
	0645	1.6				0704	2.1		
	1216	6.1				1233	5.5		
	1910	1.4				1919	2.0		
4 TU	0049	5.8			19 W	0051	5.3		
	0733	1.8				0741	2.4		
	1302	5.8				1309	5.2		
	2000	1.7				1958	2.3		
5 W	0140	5.6			20 TH	0132	5.1		
	0827	2.0				0827	2.6		
	1358	5.5				1357	4.9		
	2057	2.0				2047	2.6		
6 TH	0243	5.4			21 F	0229	4.8		
	0932	2.2				0929	2.8		
	1507	5.3				1506	4.7		
	2208	2.2				2156	2.8		
7 F	0358	5.3			22 SA	0349	4.7		
	1049	2.3				1051	2.9		
	1629	5.3				1636	4.7		
	2326	2.2				2321	2.8		
8 SA	0514	5.5			23 SU	0515	4.9		
	1206	2.1				1211	2.6		
	1748	5.4				1754	4.9		
9 SU	0040	2.0			24 M	0034	2.5		
	0621	5.7				0620	5.2		
	1314	1.8				1311	2.3		
	1855	5.7				1852	5.3		
10 M	0142	1.8			25 TU	0130	2.2		
	0721	6.0				0710	5.6		
	1412	1.5				1401	1.9		
	1953	5.9				1940	5.6		
11 TU ●	0236	1.6			26 W	0218	1.8		
	0812	6.2				0755	5.9		
	1503	1.3				1446	1.5		
	2042	6.1				2023	5.9		
12 W	0324	1.4			27 TH O	0302	1.5		
	0857	6.4				0837	6.2		
	1549	1.1				1528	1.1		
	2126	6.2				2105	6.2		
13 TH	0407	1.3			28 F	0345	1.2		
	0939	6.4				0918	6.4		
	1629	1.0				1610	0.9		
	2205	6.2				2146	6.4		
14 F	0446	1.3			29 SA	0427	1.0		
	1017	6.4				0959	6.6		
	1707	1.1				1651	0.7		
	2241	6.2				2227	6.4		
15 SA	0523	1.4			30 SU	0508	0.9		
	1053	6.3				1040	6.6		
	1742	1.2				1731	0.7		
	2315	6.0				2308	6.4		
					31 M	0548	1.0		
						1121	6.6		
						1811	0.8		
						2348	6.3		

FEBRUARY

Day	Time	m	Time	m	Day	Time	m	Time	m
1 TU	0630	1.1			16 W	0629	1.8		
	1201	6.3				1156	5.7		
	1853	1.1				1841	1.8		
2 W	0029	6.1			17 TH	0008	5.5		
	0713	1.4				0700	2.1		
	1243	6.0				1226	5.3		
	1938	1.5				1913	2.2		
3 TH	0114	5.7			18 F	0040	5.2		
	0803	1.8				0737	2.4		
	1333	5.6				1304	5.0		
	2030	1.9				1954	2.5		
4 F	0209	5.4			19 SA	0125	4.9		
	0904	2.2				0828	2.7		
	1439	5.2				1401	4.7		
	2138	2.3				2052	2.8		
5 SA	0326	5.2			20 SU	0236	4.7		
	1023	2.4				0943	2.9		
	1611	5.0				1535	4.5		
	2306	2.5				2220	2.9		
6 SU	0455	5.2			21 M	0421	4.7		
	1152	2.3				1119	2.7		
	1741	5.1				1718	4.7		
						2353	2.7		
7 M	0030	2.3			22 TU	0545	5.0		
	0616	5.4				1236	2.4		
	1307	2.0				1825	5.1		
	1853	5.4							
8 TU	0136	2.0			23 W	0101	2.3		
	0713	5.7				0643	5.4		
	1406	1.6				1333	1.9		
	1948	5.7				1916	5.5		
9 W	0230	1.7			24 TH	0154	1.8		
	0803	6.0				0732	5.8		
	1454	1.3				1422	1.4		
	2032	6.0				2002	5.9		
10 TH ●	0314	1.4			25 F	0241	1.4		
	0847	6.3				0817	6.2		
	1535	1.1				1507	1.0		
	2111	6.1				2045	6.3		
11 F	0353	1.3			26 SA O	0326	1.0		
	0924	6.4				0900	6.6		
	1612	1.0				1550	0.7		
	2145	6.2				2128	6.5		
12 SA	0428	1.2			27 SU	0408	0.7		
	0958	6.4				0943	6.8		
	1645	1.0				1632	0.5		
	2217	6.2				2209	6.7		
13 SU	0500	1.2			28 M	0450	0.6		
	1030	6.4				1024	6.8		
	1716	1.1				1712	0.5		
	2247	6.1				2250	6.7		
14 M	0530	1.3							
	1101	6.2							
	1744	1.3							
	2315	6.0							
15 TU	0559	1.5							
	1129	6.0							
	1812	1.5							
	2341	5.8							

MARCH

Day	Time	m	Time	m	Day	Time	m	Time	m
1 TU	0531	0.6			16 W	0531	1.4		
	1105	6.7				1100	6.0		
	1753	0.6				1742	1.5		
	2329	6.5				2308	5.9		
2 W	0612	0.8			17 TH	0559	1.6		
	1145	6.5				1127	5.7		
	1834	1.0				1810	1.7		
						2335	5.6		
3 TH	0008	6.2			18 F	0629	1.8		
	0655	1.2				1156	5.4		
	1226	6.0				1841	2.1		
	1917	1.5							
4 F	0050	5.8			19 SA	0006	5.4		
	0743	1.7				0704	2.1		
	1314	5.5				1232	5.1		
	2008	2.0				1919	2.4		
5 SA	0143	5.4			20 SU	0047	5.1		
	0842	2.1				0750	2.5		
	1420	5.1				1324	4.8		
	2117	2.5				2013	2.7		
6 SU	0300	5.0			21 M	0149	4.8		
	1004	2.4				0857	2.7		
	1600	4.8				1447	4.5		
	2251	2.7				2135	2.9		
7 M	0438	5.0			22 TU	0327	4.6		
	1139	2.4				1030	2.7		
	1735	5.0				1635	4.7		
						2311	2.7		
8 TU	0020	2.5			23 W	0503	4.9		
	0559	5.2				1155	2.3		
	1255	2.1				1751	5.0		
	1843	5.3							
9 W	0125	2.1			24 TH	0026	2.3		
	0659	5.6				0609	5.3		
	1352	1.7				1259	1.8		
	1932	5.6				1845	5.5		
10 TH	0215	1.8			25 F	0124	1.8		
	0746	5.9				0701	5.8		
	1437	1.4				1352	1.3		
	2013	5.9				1934	6.0		
11 F	0256	1.5			26 SA	0214	1.3		
	0826	6.1				0750	6.2		
	1514	1.2				1440	0.9		
	2048	6.1				2019	6.3		
12 SA ●	0332	1.3			27 SU O	0301	0.9		
	0902	6.3				0837	6.6		
	1548	1.1				1525	0.6		
	2120	6.2				2104	6.6		
13 SU	0404	1.2			28 M	0346	0.6		
	0934	6.3				0922	6.8		
	1618	1.1				1609	0.4		
	2150	6.2				2147	6.8		
14 M	0435	1.2			29 TU	0429	0.5		
	1005	6.3				1006	6.8		
	1647	1.1				1651	0.4		
	2217	6.1				2229	6.8		
15 TU	0503	1.3			30 W	0512	0.5		
	1033	6.2				1048	6.7		
	1715	1.3				1733	0.7		
	2243	6.0				2309	6.6		
					31 TH	0554	0.7		
						1130	6.4		
						1816	1.1		
						2349	6.3		

APRIL

Day	Time	m	Time	m	Day	Time	m	Time	m
1 F	0639	1.1			16 SA	0607	1.7		
	1213	6.0				1139	5.5		
	1901	1.6				1818	2.0		
						2347	5.5		
2 SA	0032	5.8			17 SU	0643	2.0		
	0727	1.6				1217	5.2		
	1302	5.5				1858	2.3		
	1953	2.1							
3 SU	0124	5.4			18 M	0029	5.2		
	0826	2.1				0728	2.2		
	1408	5.0				1307	4.9		
	2101	2.6				1951	2.5		
4 M	0238	5.0			19 TU	0126	4.9		
	0945	2.4				0830	2.4		
	1542	4.8				1418	4.7		
	2232	2.7				2106	2.7		
5 TU	0412	4.9			20 W	0246	4.8		
	1114	2.4				0950	2.4		
	1712	4.9				1551	4.8		
	2355	2.5				2232	2.6		
6 W	0532	5.1			21 TH	0415	4.9		
	1227	2.1				1112	2.2		
	1816	5.2				1710	5.1		
						2347	2.2		
7 TH	0059	2.2			22 F	0527	5.3		
	0631	5.4				1220	1.8		
	1322	1.8				1809	5.5		
	1903	5.5							
8 F	0148	1.9			23 SA	0049	1.8		
	0718	5.7				0626	5.7		
	1407	1.6				1318	1.4		
	1943	5.8				1901	6.0		
9 SA	0229	1.6			24 SU	0144	1.3		
	0758	5.9				0719	6.1		
	1444	1.4				1410	1.0		
	2018	5.9				1950	6.3		
10 SU	0305	1.4			25 M O	0235	0.9		
	0835	6.0				0811	6.5		
	1518	1.3				1459	0.7		
	2051	6.0				2037	6.6		
11 M ●	0337	1.3			26 TU	0323	0.7		
	0908	6.1				0900	6.7		
	1549	1.3				1546	0.6		
	2121	6.1				2123	6.7		
12 TU	0408	1.3			27 W	0409	0.5		
	0939	6.1				0947	6.7		
	1618	1.3				1631	0.6		
	2149	6.1				2207	6.7		
13 W	0437	1.3			28 TH	0455	0.6		
	1008	6.0				1032	6.6		
	1647	1.4				1716	0.9		
	2215	6.0				2250	6.6		
14 TH	0506	1.4			29 F	0540	0.8		
	1036	5.9				1117	6.3		
	1716	1.5				1800	1.2		
	2243	5.9				2333	6.3		
15 F	0536	1.5			30 SA	0625	1.1		
	1106	5.7				1202	5.9		
	1745	1.7				1847	1.7		
	2313	5.7							

CHERBOURG

49°39′N 1°38′W

Times and heights (in metres) of high and low water 1994
Time: French Standard Time. For GMT, SUBTRACT ONE HOUR.
For BST, use unchanged in the shaded area
High Water, full and change, 0905

MAY

Day	Time	m	Time	m	Time	m	Time	m
1 SU	0018	5.9	0714	1.5	1251	5.5	1939	2.1
2 M	0109	5.5	0810	2.0	1351	5.1	2042	2.5
3 TU	0214	5.1	0917	2.2	1506	4.9	2157	2.6
4 W	0331	5.0	1031	2.3	1624	4.9	2312	2.6
5 TH	0452	5.0	1140	2.2	1730	5.1		
6 F	0016	2.3	0550	5.2	1237	2.1	1822	5.3
7 SA	0109	2.1	0641	5.4	1326	1.9	1905	5.6
8 SU	0154	1.9	0726	5.6	1408	1.7	1944	5.8
9 M	0233	1.7	0805	5.8	1445	1.6	2020	5.9
10 TU	0309	1.5	0841	5.9	1519	1.5	●2053	6.0
11 W	0342	1.4	0914	5.9	1551	1.5	2123	6.0
12 TH	0414	1.4	0946	5.9	1623	1.5	2153	6.0
13 F	0446	1.4	1017	5.9	1655	1.6	2225	5.9
14 SA	0519	1.5	1051	5.7	1729	1.7	2300	5.8
15 SU	0553	1.6	1129	5.6	1805	1.9	2338	5.6
16 M	0631	1.7	1210	5.4	1847	2.1		
17 TU	0021	5.4	0716	1.9	1257	5.2	1939	2.3
18 W	0112	5.2	0812	2.1	1357	5.0	2043	2.4
19 TH	0216	5.1	0919	2.1	1510	5.0	2157	2.4
20 F	0331	5.1	1033	2.0	1626	5.2	2309	2.1
21 SA	0445	5.3	1142	1.8	1731	5.5		
22 SU	0015	1.8	0551	5.6	1245	1.5	1829	5.9
23 M	0115	1.4	0651	6.0	1342	1.2	1923	6.2
24 TU	0211	1.1	0748	6.2	1436	1.0	2014	6.5
25 W	0303	0.9	0841	6.4	1526	0.9	O2103	6.6
26 TH	0353	0.7	0932	6.5	1614	0.9	2150	6.6
27 F	0441	0.7	1019	6.4	1701	1.0	2236	6.5
28 SA	0527	0.8	1105	6.2	1747	1.3	2320	6.3
29 SU	0613	1.1	1150	5.9	1833	1.6		
30 M	0005	6.0	0659	1.4	1235	5.6	1921	2.0
31 TU	0051	5.6	0747	1.8	1324	5.3	2013	2.3

JUNE

Day	Time	m	Time	m	Time	m	Time	m
1 W	0143	5.3	0839	2.1	1420	5.1	2112	2.5
2 TH	0242	5.1	0938	2.3	1524	4.9	2218	2.6
3 F	0348	4.9	1042	2.4	1630	5.0	2323	2.5
4 SA	0454	5.0	1144	2.3	1731	5.1		
5 SU	0023	2.3	0558	5.1	1241	2.2	1824	5.3
6 M	0115	2.1	0652	5.3	1330	2.0	1910	5.5
7 TU	0201	1.9	0735	5.5	1413	1.9	1951	5.7
8 W	0241	1.7	0816	5.6	1452	1.7	2028	5.8
9 TH	0318	1.6	0853	5.8	1528	1.6	●2103	5.9
10 F	0354	1.4	0928	5.8	1604	1.6	2136	6.0
11 SA	0429	1.4	1003	5.9	1640	1.6	2212	6.0
12 SU	0506	1.3	1040	5.8	1717	1.6	2250	6.0
13 M	0543	1.4	1119	5.8	1756	1.7	2330	5.9
14 TU	0622	1.4	1201	5.6	1838	1.8		
15 W	0012	5.7	0705	1.6	1246	5.5	1926	2.0
16 TH	0058	5.5	0754	1.7	1336	5.3	2021	2.1
17 F	0151	5.4	0851	1.9	1435	5.3	2125	2.2
18 SA	0255	5.3	0957	1.9	1545	5.3	2235	2.1
19 SU	0408	5.3	1108	1.9	1657	5.5	2346	1.9
20 M	0522	5.5	1217	1.7	1802	5.7		
21 TU	0052	1.6	0631	5.7	1320	1.5	1902	6.0
22 W	0152	1.3	0733	6.0	1418	1.3	1957	6.3
23 TH	0248	1.1	0829	6.2	1512	1.2	O2049	6.4
24 F	0340	0.9	0921	6.3	1601	1.1	2137	6.5
25 SA	0429	0.8	1008	6.3	1648	1.2	2222	6.5
26 SU	0514	0.9	1052	6.2	1732	1.3	2305	6.3
27 M	0556	1.0	1132	6.0	1814	1.5	2346	6.1
28 TU	0636	1.3	1212	5.8	1855	1.8		
29 W	0026	5.8	0716	1.6	1251	5.5	1937	2.1
30 TH	0107	5.5	0756	1.9	1332	5.3	2023	2.3

JULY

Day	Time	m	Time	m	Time	m	Time	m
1 F	0153	5.2	0843	2.2	1421	5.0	2118	2.6
2 SA	0248	4.9	0939	2.5	1523	4.9	2224	2.7
3 SU	0355	4.8	1046	2.6	1635	4.9	2333	2.6
4 M	0509	4.8	1154	2.5	1742	5.0		
5 TU	0036	2.4	0614	5.0	1253	2.3	1838	5.3
6 W	0129	2.1	0707	5.2	1344	2.1	1924	5.5
7 TH	0214	1.9	0752	5.5	1427	1.9	2006	5.8
8 F	0255	1.6	0833	5.7	1508	1.7	●2044	5.9
9 SA	0335	1.4	0912	5.9	1547	1.5	2121	6.1
10 SU	0413	1.2	0949	6.0	1626	1.4	2159	6.2
11 M	0452	1.1	1027	6.0	1705	1.3	2238	6.2
12 TU	0530	1.1	1107	6.0	1744	1.4	2318	6.2
13 W	0608	1.1	1147	6.0	1824	1.4	2358	6.0
14 TH	0649	1.3	1229	5.8	1908	1.6		
15 F	0041	5.8	0733	1.5	1313	5.6	1958	1.8
16 SA	0128	5.6	0825	1.7	1405	5.4	2056	2.0
17 SU	0226	5.4	0927	2.0	1511	5.3	2207	2.2
18 M	0343	5.2	1042	2.1	1631	5.3	2325	2.1
19 TU	0507	5.3	1159	2.0	1746	5.5		
20 W	0038	1.8	0622	5.5	1308	1.8	1850	5.8
21 TH	0142	1.5	0726	5.8	1408	1.6	1949	6.1
22 F	0239	1.2	0822	6.0	1502	1.3	O2039	6.3
23 SA	0330	1.0	0911	6.2	1549	1.2	2125	6.4
24 SU	0415	0.9	0953	6.2	1632	1.2	2207	6.5
25 M	0456	0.9	1032	6.2	1712	1.2	2245	6.4
26 TU	0533	1.0	1108	6.1	1748	1.4	2322	6.2
27 W	0607	1.2	1141	5.9	1823	1.6	2356	6.0
28 TH	0640	1.5	1214	5.7	1857	1.9		
29 F	0029	5.6	0713	1.8	1246	5.4	1934	2.2
30 SA	0105	5.3	0750	2.2	1323	5.1	2019	2.5
31 SU	0148	4.9	0837	2.5	1414	4.9	2119	2.7

AUGUST

Day	Time	m	Time	m	Time	m	Time	m
1 M	0251	4.7	0942	2.8	1528	4.7	2238	2.8
2 TU	0419	4.6	1104	2.8	1658	4.8	2356	2.6
3 W	0542	4.8	1219	2.6	1807	5.1		
4 TH	0058	2.3	0643	5.1	1316	2.3	1859	5.4
5 F	0148	2.0	0729	5.4	1404	1.9	1943	5.7
6 SA	0232	1.6	0812	5.7	1447	1.6	2024	6.0
7 SU	0313	1.3	0852	6.0	1528	1.4	●2103	6.3
8 M	0353	1.0	0931	6.2	1608	1.2	2143	6.4
9 TU	0433	0.9	1010	6.3	1647	1.0	2222	6.5
10 W	0511	0.8	1049	6.3	1726	1.0	2302	6.5
11 TH	0550	0.9	1129	6.3	1806	1.1	2341	6.3
12 F	0630	1.1	1208	6.1	1848	1.4		
13 SA	0022	6.0	0712	1.4	1249	5.8	1935	1.7
14 SU	0108	5.7	0801	1.8	1338	5.5	2032	2.0
15 M	0206	5.3	0903	2.2	1445	5.3	2146	2.3
16 TU	0329	5.1	1024	2.4	1614	5.2	2313	2.3
17 W	0504	5.1	1151	2.3	1740	5.4		
18 TH	0032	2.0	0621	5.4	1303	2.0	1847	5.7
19 F	0136	1.6	0722	5.7	1401	1.7	1940	6.1
20 SA	0230	1.3	0812	6.0	1451	1.4	2027	6.3
21 SU	0316	1.1	0855	6.2	1534	1.3	O2109	6.4
22 M	0356	1.0	0932	6.3	1612	1.2	2145	6.5
23 TU	0431	1.0	1006	6.3	1647	1.3	2220	6.4
24 W	0504	1.1	1038	6.2	1719	1.3	2252	6.3
25 TH	0535	1.2	1107	6.0	1749	1.5	2322	6.0
26 F	0604	1.5	1135	5.8	1819	1.8	2351	5.7
27 SA	0633	1.8	1202	5.6	1851	2.0		
28 SU	0021	5.4	0705	2.2	1233	5.3	1929	2.4
29 M	0058	5.0	0745	2.6	1315	5.0	2018	2.7
30 TU	0152	4.7	0841	2.9	1421	4.7	2135	2.9
31 W	0322	4.5	1009	3.0	1605	4.7	2311	2.8

CHERBOURG

49°39′N 1°38′W

Times and heights (in metres) of high and low water 1994
Time: French Standard Time. For GMT, SUBTRACT ONE HOUR.
For BST, use unchanged in the shaded area
High Water, full and change, 0905

SEPTEMBER

Day	Time	m	Time	m	Time	m	Time	m
1 TH	0507	4.7	1141	2.8	1732	4.9		
2 F	0024	2.5	0612	5.0	1246	2.4	1829	5.3
3 SA	0118	2.0	0701	5.4	1336	2.0	1915	5.8
4 SU	0204	1.6	0745	5.8	1421	1.6	1958	6.1
5 M ●	0247	1.2	0827	6.2	1503	1.2	2040	6.4
6 TU	0328	0.9	0908	6.4	1545	1.0	2121	6.6
7 W	0409	0.7	0948	6.5	1626	0.8	2201	6.7
8 TH	0449	0.7	1027	6.6	1706	0.8	2242	6.7
9 F	0529	0.8	1106	6.5	1746	0.9	2322	6.5
10 SA	0609	1.0	1146	6.3	1829	1.2		
11 SU	0004	6.1	0652	1.4	1227	6.0	1916	1.6
12 M	0051	5.7	0742	1.9	1317	5.6	2014	2.1
13 TU	0152	5.2	0846	2.4	1426	5.2	2132	2.4
14 W	0323	5.0	1016	2.6	1601	5.1	2307	2.4
15 TH	0502	5.0	1146	2.5	1731	5.3		
16 F	0024	2.1	0615	5.3	1254	2.1	1833	5.7
17 SA	0124	1.7	0709	5.7	1348	1.8	1923	6.0
18 SU	0213	1.4	0752	6.0	1433	1.5	2006	6.2
19 M O	0254	1.2	0831	6.2	1512	1.3	2045	6.4
20 TU	0330	1.1	0905	6.3	1547	1.3	2119	6.4
21 W	0403	1.1	0936	6.3	1619	1.3	2151	6.4
22 TH	0433	1.2	1005	6.2	1649	1.4	2221	6.2
23 F	0502	1.4	1033	6.1	1718	1.5	2249	6.0
24 SA	0530	1.6	1058	5.9	1747	1.7	2316	5.8
25 SU	0559	1.9	1125	5.7	1817	2.0	2346	5.5
26 M	0629	2.2	1155	5.4	1851	2.3		
27 TU	0021	5.1	0706	2.6	1235	5.1	1935	2.6
28 W	0111	4.8	0757	2.9	1334	4.8	2041	2.9
29 TH	0232	4.6	0917	3.0	1507	4.7	2216	2.9
30 F	0420	4.6	1056	2.9	1645	4.9	2341	2.5

OCTOBER

Day	Time	m	Time	m	Time	m	Time	m
1 SA	0535	5.0	1209	2.5	1750	5.3		
2 SU	0041	2.1	0627	5.5	1303	2.0	1841	5.7
3 M	0131	1.6	0713	5.9	1351	1.5	1927	6.2
4 TU	0216	1.2	0756	6.3	1436	1.1	2011	6.5
5 W ●	0300	0.9	0839	6.6	1520	0.9	2055	6.7
6 TH	0343	0.7	0921	6.7	1603	0.7	2139	6.8
7 F	0426	0.6	1003	6.8	1645	0.7	2222	6.8
8 SA	0508	0.8	1044	6.7	1728	0.9	2305	6.5
9 SU	0551	1.1	1125	6.4	1812	1.2	2350	6.2
10 M	0636	1.6	1209	6.0	1902	1.6		
11 TU	0039	5.7	0728	2.1	1300	5.6	2001	2.1
12 W	0142	5.2	0834	2.5	1409	5.2	2119	2.4
13 TH	0311	5.0	1003	2.7	1541	5.1	2248	2.4
14 F	0443	5.0	1128	2.6	1705	5.2		
15 SA	0002	2.2	0551	5.3	1233	2.3	1807	5.5
16 SU	0059	1.9	0642	5.6	1324	1.9	1857	5.8
17 M	0145	1.6	0724	5.9	1408	1.7	1939	6.1
18 TU	0225	1.5	0801	6.1	1446	1.5	2017	6.2
19 W O	0301	1.4	0835	6.2	1520	1.4	2051	6.3
20 TH	0333	1.4	0906	6.2	1551	1.4	2123	6.2
21 F	0404	1.4	0935	6.2	1622	1.4	2153	6.1
22 SA	0433	1.5	1002	6.1	1651	1.5	2221	6.0
23 SU	0503	1.7	1028	6.0	1721	1.7	2250	5.8
24 M	0532	1.9	1057	5.8	1751	1.9	2321	5.6
25 TU	0603	2.2	1130	5.6	1825	2.2	2358	5.3
26 W	0640	2.5	1210	5.3	1907	2.4		
27 TH	0046	5.0	0729	2.7	1303	5.0	2004	2.6
28 F	0155	4.8	0838	2.9	1420	4.9	2124	2.7
29 SA	0325	4.8	1005	2.8	1548	4.9	2249	2.5
30 SU	0446	5.0	1124	2.5	1702	5.3	2358	2.1
31 M	0546	5.5	1225	2.1	1800	5.7		

NOVEMBER

Day	Time	m	Time	m	Time	m	Time	m
1 TU	0054	1.7	0636	5.9	1318	1.6	1852	6.1
2 W	0145	1.3	0723	6.3	1408	1.2	1942	6.5
3 TH ●	0233	1.0	0810	6.6	1455	0.9	2030	6.7
4 F	0319	0.8	0855	6.8	1541	0.7	2118	6.8
5 SA	0405	0.8	0940	6.8	1627	0.7	2204	6.7
6 SU	0450	0.9	1024	6.7	1713	0.9	2251	6.5
7 M	0535	1.2	1108	6.5	1800	1.1	2338	6.2
8 TU	0623	1.6	1155	6.1	1850	1.5		
9 W	0028	5.8	0715	2.1	1246	5.7	1946	2.0
10 TH	0127	5.4	0817	2.5	1347	5.4	2053	2.3
11 F	0240	5.1	0932	2.7	1503	5.1	2209	2.4
12 SA	0359	5.0	1049	2.7	1626	5.1	2321	2.4
13 SU	0508	5.2	1155	2.5	1728	5.3		
14 M	0020	2.2	0603	5.4	1250	2.2	1821	5.5
15 TU	0110	2.0	0648	5.7	1336	2.0	1908	5.8
16 W	0152	1.8	0728	5.9	1417	1.8	1949	5.9
17 TH	0231	1.7	0804	6.0	1453	1.6	2025	6.0
18 F O	0305	1.6	0838	6.1	1527	1.6	2059	6.0
19 SA	0338	1.6	0909	6.1	1559	1.5	2130	6.0
20 SU	0410	1.7	0938	6.1	1630	1.5	2200	6.0
21 M	0442	1.7	1008	6.0	1702	1.6	2232	5.9
22 TU	0513	1.9	1040	5.9	1735	1.7	2307	5.7
23 W	0547	2.0	1116	5.8	1810	1.9	2345	5.5
24 TH	0625	2.2	1156	5.5	1850	2.1		
25 F	0030	5.3	0711	2.4	1243	5.3	1940	2.3
26 SA	0126	5.1	0809	2.6	1342	5.1	2043	2.4
27 SU	0235	5.0	0920	2.6	1455	5.1	2157	2.4
28 M	0352	5.1	1035	2.5	1610	5.3	2311	2.2
29 TU	0501	5.4	1145	2.1	1719	5.6		
30 W	0017	1.8	0600	5.8	1247	1.7	1820	5.9

DECEMBER

Day	Time	m	Time	m	Time	m	Time	m
1 TH	0115	1.5	0653	6.2	1342	1.4	1917	6.3
2 F ●	0209	1.2	0745	6.5	1435	1.0	2011	6.5
3 SA	0300	1.0	0834	6.7	1525	0.8	2102	6.6
4 SU	0349	0.9	0923	6.8	1614	0.8	2152	6.6
5 M	0436	1.0	1010	6.7	1702	0.8	2240	6.5
6 TU	0524	1.2	1056	6.6	1749	1.0	2326	6.2
7 W	0610	1.5	1141	6.3	1835	1.4		
8 TH	0013	5.9	0658	1.9	1228	5.9	1924	1.7
9 F	0101	5.6	0749	2.2	1318	5.6	2015	2.1
10 SA	0155	5.3	0846	2.5	1416	5.3	2114	2.4
11 SU	0258	5.1	0952	2.7	1522	5.1	2220	2.5
12 M	0406	5.0	1102	2.7	1632	5.0	2327	2.5
13 TU	0511	5.1	1206	2.5	1743	5.2		
14 W	0027	2.4	0608	5.4	1301	2.3	1837	5.4
15 TH	0118	2.2	0656	5.6	1348	2.0	1924	5.6
16 F	0202	2.0	0737	5.8	1429	1.8	2001	5.8
17 SA	0241	1.9	0815	5.9	1505	1.7	2038	5.9
18 SU O	0317	1.7	0849	6.0	1540	1.5	2112	6.0
19 M	0352	1.7	0921	6.1	1614	1.5	2145	6.0
20 TU	0426	1.7	0954	6.1	1648	1.4	2219	6.0
21 W	0501	1.7	1028	6.1	1723	1.5	2255	5.9
22 TH	0536	1.7	1105	6.0	1758	1.5	2334	5.8
23 F	0613	1.9	1144	5.9	1836	1.7		
24 SA	0015	5.6	0655	2.0	1225	5.7	1920	1.8
25 SU	0100	5.4	0744	2.2	1312	5.5	2011	2.0
26 M	0154	5.3	0842	2.3	1411	5.3	2113	2.2
27 TU	0301	5.2	0951	2.4	1524	5.3	2227	2.2
28 W	0416	5.3	1106	2.2	1643	5.4	2342	2.0
29 TH	0528	5.6	1219	1.9	1756	5.6		
30 F	0050	1.8	0631	5.9	1323	1.6	1901	6.0
31 SA	0151	1.5	0728	6.3	1421	1.2	1959	6.2

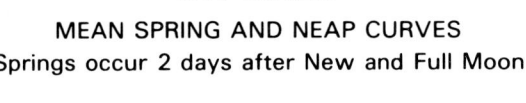

ST. MALO

MEAN SPRING AND NEAP CURVES

Springs occur 2 days after New and Full Moon

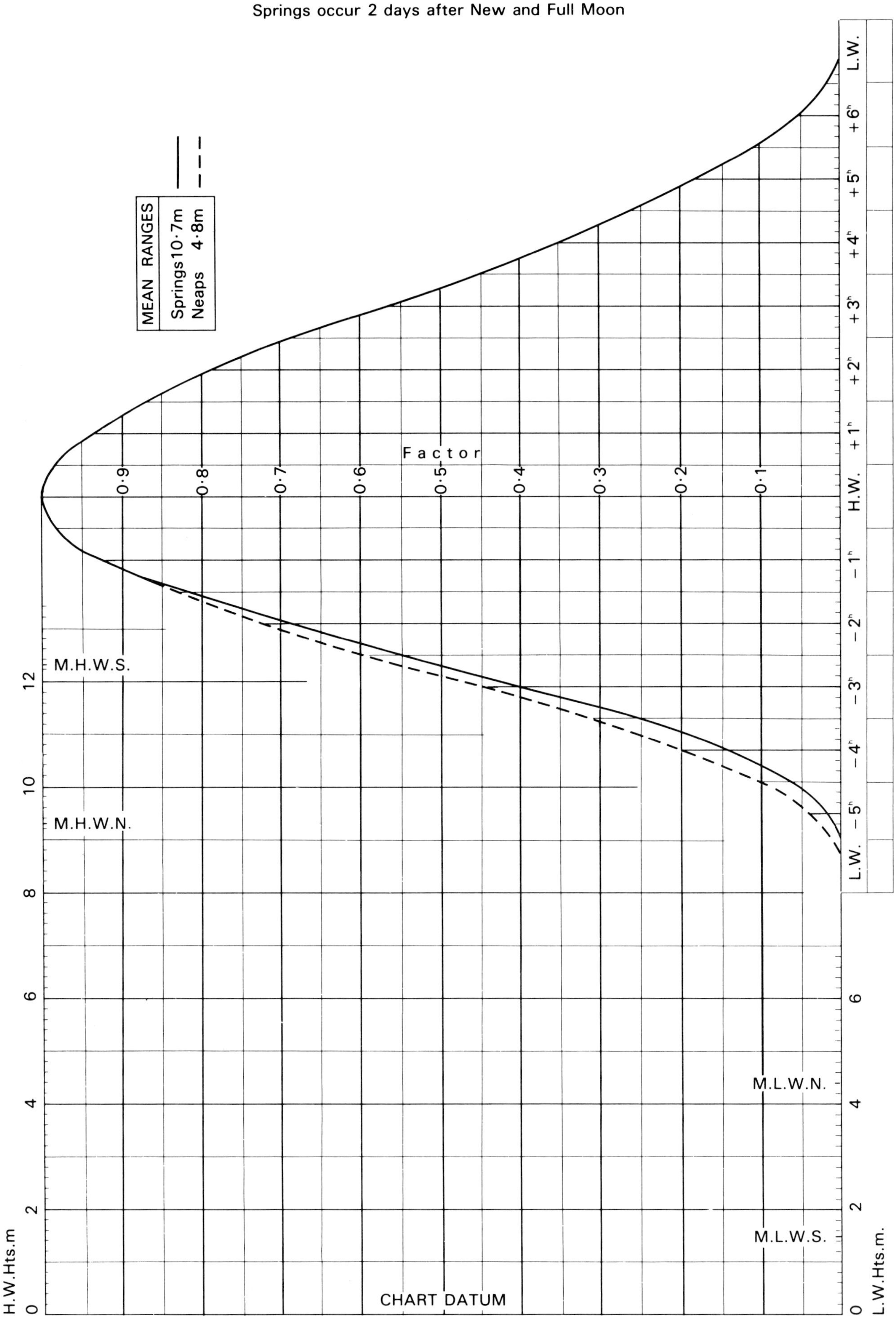

MEAN RANGES
Springs 10·7m ———
Neaps 4·8m – – –

Factor

0·9 0·8 0·7 0·6 0·5 0·4 0·3 0·2 0·1

H.W. −1ʰ −2ʰ −3ʰ −4ʰ −5ʰ L.W.

+6ʰ +5ʰ +4ʰ +3ʰ +2ʰ +1ʰ H.W.

L.W.

H.W.Hts.m.

M.H.W.S.

M.H.W.N.

12

10

8

6

4

2

0 CHART DATUM

M.L.W.N.

M.L.W.S.

L.W.Hts.m.

ST. MALO
48°38′N 2°02′W

Times and heights (in metres) of high and low water 1994
Time: French Standard Time. For GMT, SUBTRACT ONE HOUR.
For BST, use unchanged in the shaded area

JANUARY

Day	Time	m		Day	Time	m
1 SA	0338	2.0		**16** SU	0415	2.4
	0900	12.0			0936	11.6
	1604	2.0			1634	2.5
	2128	11.6			2154	11.2
2 SU	0418	2.1		**17** M	0442	2.9
	0942	11.9			1006	11.1
	1644	2.1			1659	3.0
	2210	11.4			2222	10.7
3 M	0458	2.4		**18** TU	0506	3.4
	1025	11.5			1035	10.5
	1724	2.4			1725	3.5
	2254	11.0			2252	10.2
4 TU	0541	2.8		**19** W	0534	4.0
	1111	11.0			1108	9.9
	1808	2.9			1757	4.1
	2343	10.5			2329	9.6
5 W	0630	3.2		**20** TH	0614	4.5
	1205	10.5			1152	9.2
	1900	3.4			1844	4.6
6 TH	0043	10.0		**21** F	0023	9.0
	0731	3.7			0713	5.0
	1312	10.0			1304	8.7
	2007	3.8			1952	5.0
7 F	0159	9.8		**22** SA	0148	8.7
	0849	3.8			0839	5.1
	1433	9.8			1445	8.6
	2133	3.8			2119	5.0
8 SA	0321	9.9		**23** SU	0325	8.9
	1015	3.6			1007	4.8
	1554	10.1			1607	9.0
	2255	3.5			2237	4.6
9 SU	0433	10.4		**24** M	0434	9.5
	1128	3.1			1114	4.2
	1703	10.5			1705	9.7
					2338	3.9
10 M	0002	3.0		**25** TU	0525	10.2
	0534	11.0			1209	3.5
	1231	2.6			1752	10.4
	1802	11.0				
11 TU ●	0058	2.5		**26** W	0031	3.3
	0625	11.6			0609	10.9
	1325	2.2			1259	2.9
	1852	11.4			1835	11.0
12 W	0147	2.2		**27** TH O	0120	2.6
	0711	11.8			0650	11.6
	1412	1.9			1348	2.2
	1936	11.7			1917	11.6
13 TH	0230	2.0		**28** F	0207	2.1
	0752	12.1			0731	12.1
	1454	1.8			1434	1.7
	2015	11.8			1958	12.0
14 F	0308	1.9		**29** SA	0251	1.6
	0829	12.1			0811	12.5
	1531	1.8			1518	1.4
	2051	11.8			2038	12.3
15 SA	0343	2.1		**30** SU	0333	1.3
	0904	12.0			0852	12.7
	1604	2.0			1558	1.2
	2123	11.6			2118	12.4
				31 M	0412	1.3
					0932	12.6
					1636	1.4
					2158	12.2

FEBRUARY

Day	Time	m		Day	Time	m
1 TU	0449	1.6		**16** W	0436	2.9
	1012	12.2			1002	10.9
	1712	1.9			1649	3.1
	2237	11.7			2215	10.6
2 W	0527	2.2		**17** TH	0459	3.4
	1053	11.5			1029	10.2
	1750	2.6			1716	3.7
	2320	10.9			2244	10.0
3 TH	0610	2.9		**18** F	0530	4.1
	1141	10.6			1102	9.5
	1835	3.4			1753	4.4
					2323	9.2
4 F	0012	10.2		**19** SA	0616	4.7
	0703	3.6			1154	8.7
	1243	9.8			1847	5.0
	1936	4.1				
5 SA	0125	9.5		**20** SU	0029	8.6
	0821	4.2			0726	5.2
	1410	9.3			1340	8.2
	2107	4.4			2011	5.3
6 SU	0259	9.4		**21** M	0229	8.4
	0958	4.1			0908	5.2
	1545	9.4			1533	8.5
	2241	4.1			2150	5.0
7 M	0423	9.9		**22** TU	0400	9.0
	1119	3.5			1036	4.5
	1659	10.0			1639	9.3
	2352	3.4			2305	4.2
8 TU	0526	10.6		**23** W	0458	9.9
	1223	2.9			1140	3.6
	1755	10.7			1729	10.2
9 W	0048	2.8		**24** TH	0005	3.3
	0615	11.3			0546	10.8
	1315	2.4			1237	2.7
	1840	11.2			1815	11.1
10 TH ●	0135	2.3		**25** F	0100	2.4
	0658	11.8			0631	11.7
	1359	2.0			1330	1.9
	1920	11.6			1858	11.9
11 F	0216	2.0		**26** SA O	0151	1.6
	0736	12.1			0714	12.5
	1437	1.7			1419	1.2
	1956	11.9			1941	12.5
12 SA	0251	1.8		**27** SU	0238	1.0
	0810	12.2			0756	13.0
	1510	1.7			1504	0.8
	2028	12.0			2022	12.9
13 SU	0322	1.8		**28** M	0320	0.7
	0842	12.1			0837	13.2
	1540	1.8			1544	0.7
	2057	11.9			2101	13.0
14 M	0350	2.0				
	0910	11.9				
	1605	2.1				
	2124	11.6				
15 TU	0415	2.4				
	0937	11.4				
	1628	2.6				
	2149	11.2				

MARCH

Day	Time	m		Day	Time	m
1 TU	0359	0.7		**16** W	0347	2.1
	0917	13.1			0909	11.5
	1621	1.0			1558	2.3
	2140	12.7			2119	11.4
2 W	0435	1.1		**17** TH	0410	2.5
	0956	12.5			0934	11.0
	1656	1.6			1620	2.8
	2218	12.0			2144	10.9
3 TH	0511	1.9		**18** F	0433	3.1
	1035	11.6			1001	10.3
	1731	2.5			1646	3.4
	2258	11.1			2212	10.2
4 F	0551	2.8		**19** SA	0503	3.7
	1120	10.6			1031	9.6
	1812	3.5			1720	4.1
	2346	10.1			2246	9.5
5 SA	0641	3.7		**20** SU	0542	4.3
	1219	9.5			1113	8.8
	1910	4.3			1808	4.7
					2338	8.7
6 SU	0057	9.3		**21** M	0641	4.9
	0758	4.4			1235	8.2
	1352	8.9			1922	5.1
	2045	4.7				
7 M	0241	9.0		**22** TU	0123	8.3
	0942	4.3			0812	5.0
	1536	9.1			1444	8.4
	2224	4.3			2101	4.9
8 TU	0410	9.6		**23** W	0312	8.8
	1104	3.7			0950	4.5
	1647	9.8			1602	9.2
	2334	3.6			2224	4.1
9 W	0511	10.3		**24** TH	0421	9.7
	1205	3.0			1105	3.5
	1737	10.5			1657	10.2
					2331	3.1
10 TH	0029	2.9		**25** F	0515	10.8
	0557	11.1			1207	2.5
	1254	2.4			1746	11.2
	1819	11.1				
11 F	0114	2.4		**26** SA	0032	2.1
	0637	11.6			0604	11.8
	1336	2.0			1305	1.6
	1856	11.6			1833	12.1
12 SA ●	0153	2.0		**27** SU O	0127	1.3
	0713	11.9			0651	12.6
	1411	1.8			1356	0.9
	1930	11.8			1917	12.8
13 SU	0226	1.8		**28** M	0216	0.7
	0746	12.0			0735	13.2
	1442	1.7			1443	0.5
	2000	11.9			2000	13.2
14 M	0256	1.8		**29** TU	0301	0.4
	0816	12.0			0818	13.3
	1510	1.7			1525	0.5
	2028	11.9			2040	13.2
15 TU	0323	1.9		**30** W	0342	0.5
	0844	11.8			0859	13.1
	1535	1.9			1602	0.8
	2054	11.7			2120	12.8
				31 TH	0420	1.0
					0940	12.4
					1638	1.6
					2158	12.1

APRIL

Day	Time	m		Day	Time	m
1 F	0457	1.7		**16** SA	0415	2.8
	1020	11.5			0942	10.4
	1714	2.5			1626	3.2
	2239	11.1			2151	10.4
2 SA	0536	2.7		**17** SU	0446	3.3
	1105	10.4			1015	9.8
	1755	3.5			1701	3.8
	2327	10.1			2227	9.7
3 SU	0626	3.7		**18** M	0524	3.9
	1203	9.4			1058	9.1
	1851	4.3			1747	4.3
					2318	9.1
4 M	0035	9.2		**19** TU	0617	4.3
	0738	4.3			1207	8.6
	1329	8.8			1853	4.6
	2018	4.7				
5 TU	0212	8.9		**20** W	0039	8.7
	0912	4.4			0734	4.5
	1508	8.9			1349	8.6
	2150	4.4			2019	4.5
6 W	0341	9.3		**21** TH	0216	9.0
	1031	3.9			0905	4.1
	1618	9.6			1514	9.2
	2300	3.8			2142	3.9
7 TH	0442	10.0		**22** F	0334	9.8
	1131	3.2			1025	3.3
	1707	10.3			1618	10.2
	2354	3.1			2254	3.0
8 F	0528	10.7		**23** SA	0437	10.7
	1220	2.7			1134	2.4
	1748	10.9			1713	11.2
					2359	2.0
9 SA	0041	2.6		**24** SU	0533	11.7
	0608	11.2			1235	1.5
	1302	2.3			1803	12.1
	1825	11.3				
10 SU	0121	2.3		**25** M O	0058	1.3
	0645	11.5			0624	12.4
	1339	2.0			1330	0.9
	1859	11.6			1851	12.7
11 M ●	0156	2.1		**26** TU	0152	0.7
	0719	11.7			0713	12.9
	1411	1.9			1419	0.6
	1931	11.7			1936	13.0
12 TU	0227	2.0		**27** W	0240	0.5
	0749	11.7			0758	13.0
	1439	1.9			1503	0.7
	1959	11.7			2019	13.0
13 W	0255	2.0		**28** TH	0323	0.6
	0818	11.5			0842	12.7
	1506	2.0			1543	1.0
	2026	11.6			2100	12.6
14 TH	0321	2.1		**29** F	0404	1.0
	0845	11.3			0925	12.2
	1532	2.2			1621	1.7
	2052	11.4			2141	12.0
15 F	0348	2.4		**30** SA	0444	1.8
	0912	10.9			1008	11.3
	1558	2.6			1659	2.5
	2120	11.0			2224	11.1

ST. MALO
48°38′N 2°02′W

Times and heights (in metres) of high and low water 1994
Time: French Standard Time. For GMT, SUBTRACT ONE HOUR.
For BST, use unchanged in the shaded area

MAY

Day	Time	m	Day	Time	m
1 SU	0525 / 1053 / 1740 / 2311	2.6 / 10.4 / 3.4 / 10.2	16 M	0437 / 1010 / 1652 / 2221	2.9 / 10.1 / 3.3 / 10.2
2 M	0612 / 1146 / 1832	3.5 / 9.6 / 4.1	17 TU	0517 / 1055 / 1737 / 2310	3.4 / 9.6 / 3.7 / 9.7
3 TU	0010 / 0713 / 1254 / 1941	9.5 / 4.1 / 9.0 / 4.5	18 W	0606 / 1153 / 1835	3.7 / 9.3 / 4.0
4 W	0127 / 0826 / 1415 / 2059	9.0 / 4.3 / 8.9 / 4.5	19 TH	0014 / 0710 / 1307 / 1946	9.4 / 3.9 / 9.2 / 4.0
5 TH	0249 / 0938 / 1529 / 2208	9.1 / 4.0 / 9.3 / 4.1	20 F	0131 / 0826 / 1427 / 2103	9.5 / 3.7 / 9.5 / 3.6
6 F	0356 / 1041 / 1625 / 2307	9.6 / 3.6 / 9.9 / 3.5	21 SA	0249 / 0946 / 1538 / 2218	9.9 / 3.2 / 10.2 / 2.9
7 SA	0448 / 1135 / 1710 / 2359	10.1 / 3.1 / 10.4 / 3.1	22 SU	0400 / 1100 / 1640 / 2328	10.6 / 2.5 / 11.0 / 2.2
8 SU	0533 / 1222 / 1750	10.6 / 2.7 / 10.9	23 M	0503 / 1205 / 1735	11.4 / 1.9 / 11.8
9 M	0044 / 0613 / 1303 / 1827	2.7 / 11.0 / 2.4 / 11.2	24 TU	0031 / 0600 / 1304 / 1827	1.6 / 11.9 / 1.4 / 12.3
10 TU ●	0123 / 0650 / 1338 / 1901	2.4 / 11.2 / 2.3 / 11.4	25 W O	0128 / 0653 / 1356 / 1915	1.1 / 12.3 / 1.1 / 12.6
11 W	0157 / 0724 / 1410 / 1933	2.3 / 11.2 / 2.2 / 11.5	26 TH	0220 / 0742 / 1443 / 2001	0.9 / 12.4 / 1.1 / 12.7
12 TH	0229 / 0755 / 1440 / 2002	2.2 / 11.2 / 2.2 / 11.5	27 F	0307 / 0829 / 1526 / 2045	0.9 / 12.3 / 1.3 / 12.4
13 F	0300 / 0826 / 1511 / 2033	2.2 / 11.1 / 2.3 / 11.3	28 SA	0351 / 0913 / 1607 / 2127	1.2 / 11.9 / 1.8 / 12.0
14 SA	0331 / 0857 / 1542 / 2105	2.3 / 10.9 / 2.5 / 11.1	29 SU	0432 / 0956 / 1646 / 2209	1.7 / 11.4 / 2.4 / 11.3
15 SU	0403 / 0931 / 1615 / 2140	2.6 / 10.5 / 2.9 / 10.7	30 M	0513 / 1039 / 1725 / 2252	2.4 / 10.7 / 3.1 / 10.6
			31 TU	0555 / 1123 / 1807 / 2339	3.1 / 10.0 / 3.8 / 9.9

JUNE

Day	Time	m	Day	Time	m
1 W	0640 / 1212 / 1857	3.7 / 9.5 / 4.3	16 TH	0556 / 1137 / 1818 / 2352	3.0 / 10.0 / 3.4 / 10.1
2 TH	0034 / 0734 / 1312 / 2000	9.4 / 4.1 / 9.1 / 4.5	17 F	0648 / 1236 / 1917	3.3 / 9.8 / 3.5
3 F	0142 / 0837 / 1422 / 2108	9.1 / 4.2 / 9.1 / 4.4	18 SA	0057 / 0753 / 1346 / 2027	10.0 / 3.4 / 9.8 / 3.5
4 SA	0255 / 0943 / 1530 / 2215	9.2 / 4.0 / 9.4 / 4.0	19 SU	0212 / 0910 / 1501 / 2147	10.0 / 3.3 / 10.1 / 3.2
5 SU	0401 / 1045 / 1627 / 2314	9.6 / 3.6 / 9.9 / 3.6	20 M	0329 / 1030 / 1611 / 2302	10.3 / 2.9 / 10.7 / 2.6
6 M	0455 / 1140 / 1716	10.0 / 3.3 / 10.4	21 TU	0440 / 1141 / 1713	10.8 / 2.4 / 11.3
7 TU	0006 / 0542 / 1227 / 1758	3.2 / 10.4 / 3.0 / 10.8	22 W	0009 / 0543 / 1242 / 1810	2.1 / 11.3 / 2.0 / 11.8
8 W	0051 / 0625 / 1308 / 1837	2.8 / 10.7 / 2.7 / 11.1	23 TH O	0110 / 0639 / 1337 / 1901	1.6 / 11.7 / 1.7 / 12.2
9 TH ●	0130 / 0703 / 1345 / 1912	2.6 / 10.9 / 2.5 / 11.3	24 F	0204 / 0731 / 1427 / 1948	1.3 / 12.0 / 1.5 / 12.4
10 F	0207 / 0738 / 1420 / 1945	2.4 / 11.0 / 2.4 / 11.4	25 SA	0253 / 0818 / 1512 / 2032	1.2 / 12.0 / 1.5 / 12.3
11 SA	0242 / 0812 / 1456 / 2019	2.3 / 11.0 / 2.3 / 11.4	26 SU	0338 / 0901 / 1552 / 2112	1.3 / 11.9 / 1.7 / 12.1
12 SU	0318 / 0847 / 1532 / 2055	2.2 / 11.0 / 2.4 / 11.4	27 M	0418 / 0941 / 1630 / 2151	1.6 / 11.6 / 2.2 / 11.6
13 M	0355 / 0925 / 1608 / 2133	2.3 / 10.9 / 2.5 / 11.2	28 TU	0455 / 1018 / 1704 / 2228	2.2 / 11.1 / 2.8 / 11.0
14 TU	0433 / 1004 / 1647 / 2214	2.5 / 10.7 / 2.8 / 10.9	29 W	0529 / 1053 / 1736 / 2304	2.8 / 10.5 / 3.4 / 10.3
15 W	0512 / 1048 / 1729 / 2259	2.7 / 10.3 / 3.1 / 10.5	30 TH	0601 / 1130 / 1811 / 2344	3.4 / 10.0 / 4.0 / 9.7

JULY

Day	Time	m	Day	Time	m
1 F	0640 / 1213 / 1857	3.9 / 9.5 / 4.4	16 SA	0627 / 1208 / 1851	3.0 / 10.2 / 3.3
2 SA	0035 / 0733 / 1312 / 2002	9.2 / 4.3 / 9.1 / 4.7	17 SU	0028 / 0724 / 1313 / 1958	10.1 / 3.5 / 9.9 / 3.6
3 SU	0146 / 0842 / 1427 / 2119	8.9 / 4.4 / 9.1 / 4.6	18 M	0144 / 0842 / 1433 / 2124	9.8 / 3.7 / 9.9 / 3.6
4 M	0309 / 0955 / 1543 / 2232	9.0 / 4.3 / 9.4 / 4.2	19 TU	0310 / 1010 / 1553 / 2247	9.9 / 3.5 / 10.2 / 3.1
5 TU	0420 / 1101 / 1644 / 2332	9.4 / 3.9 / 9.9 / 3.7	20 W	0428 / 1125 / 1701 / 2357	10.3 / 3.0 / 10.8 / 2.6
6 W	0516 / 1155 / 1733	9.9 / 3.5 / 10.4	21 TH	0535 / 1229 / 1800	10.9 / 2.5 / 11.5
7 TH	0022 / 0602 / 1242 / 1816	3.3 / 10.4 / 3.1 / 10.9	22 F O	0059 / 0631 / 1325 / 1850	2.0 / 11.4 / 2.0 / 11.9
8 F ●	0106 / 0644 / 1324 / 1854	2.9 / 10.7 / 2.8 / 11.2	23 SA	0153 / 0720 / 1414 / 1935	1.6 / 11.8 / 1.7 / 12.3
9 SA	0148 / 0723 / 1405 / 1931	2.5 / 11.0 / 2.4 / 11.5	24 SU	0240 / 0803 / 1456 / 2016	1.4 / 12.0 / 1.6 / 12.4
10 SU	0229 / 0800 / 1445 / 2007	2.2 / 11.2 / 2.2 / 11.7	25 M	0321 / 0842 / 1534 / 2053	1.4 / 12.0 / 1.7 / 12.2
11 M	0309 / 0837 / 1523 / 2044	2.0 / 11.4 / 2.0 / 11.9	26 TU	0357 / 0917 / 1608 / 2127	1.6 / 11.8 / 1.9 / 11.9
12 TU	0348 / 0914 / 1601 / 2123	1.8 / 11.5 / 1.9 / 11.9	27 W	0429 / 0949 / 1637 / 2158	2.0 / 11.5 / 2.4 / 11.4
13 W	0426 / 0953 / 1638 / 2202	1.9 / 11.4 / 2.1 / 11.6	28 TH	0456 / 1019 / 1702 / 2227	2.6 / 10.9 / 3.1 / 10.7
14 TH	0503 / 1034 / 1717 / 2243	2.1 / 11.1 / 2.4 / 11.2	29 F	0521 / 1048 / 1727 / 2258	3.2 / 10.4 / 3.7 / 10.0
15 F	0542 / 1117 / 1759 / 2330	2.5 / 10.7 / 2.9 / 10.7	30 SA	0549 / 1121 / 1800 / 2337	3.8 / 9.8 / 4.2 / 9.4
			31 SU	0631 / 1209 / 1853	4.4 / 9.2 / 4.7

AUGUST

Day	Time	m	Day	Time	m
1 M	0039 / 0735 / 1324 / 2015	8.8 / 4.8 / 8.8 / 5.0	16 TU	0124 / 0822 / 1415 / 2111	9.4 / 4.2 / 9.5 / 4.0
2 TU	0218 / 0902 / 1501 / 2148	8.5 / 4.9 / 8.9 / 4.8	17 W	0302 / 0959 / 1544 / 2241	9.4 / 4.0 / 9.8 / 3.5
3 W	0350 / 1023 / 1616 / 2300	8.9 / 4.5 / 9.4 / 4.2	18 TH	0425 / 1117 / 1654 / 2351	9.9 / 3.4 / 10.5 / 2.8
4 TH	0452 / 1126 / 1710 / 2355	9.5 / 3.9 / 10.1 / 3.6	19 F	0528 / 1219 / 1749	10.6 / 2.7 / 11.3
5 F	0540 / 1217 / 1754	10.2 / 3.3 / 10.7	20 SA	0049 / 0618 / 1312 / 1836	2.2 / 11.3 / 2.2 / 11.8
6 SA	0043 / 0623 / 1303 / 1835	3.0 / 10.8 / 2.8 / 11.3	21 SU O	0138 / 0702 / 1357 / 1917	1.8 / 11.7 / 1.8 / 12.2
7 SU ●	0129 / 0703 / 1348 / 1914	2.4 / 11.3 / 2.2 / 11.8	22 M	0220 / 0740 / 1436 / 1954	1.5 / 12.0 / 1.7 / 12.3
8 M	0214 / 0742 / 1431 / 1952	1.9 / 11.7 / 1.8 / 12.2	23 TU	0256 / 0815 / 1510 / 2028	1.5 / 12.1 / 1.6 / 12.3
9 TU	0256 / 0820 / 1511 / 2030	1.5 / 12.0 / 1.5 / 12.5	24 W	0328 / 0847 / 1540 / 2058	1.6 / 12.0 / 1.9 / 12.0
10 W	0336 / 0858 / 1549 / 2108	1.3 / 12.2 / 1.4 / 12.5	25 TH	0356 / 0916 / 1606 / 2126	1.9 / 11.7 / 2.3 / 11.5
11 TH	0413 / 0937 / 1626 / 2146	1.4 / 12.1 / 1.5 / 12.2	26 F	0420 / 0942 / 1628 / 2152	2.4 / 11.2 / 2.8 / 10.9
12 F	0449 / 1015 / 1702 / 2226	1.7 / 11.7 / 2.0 / 11.6	27 SA	0441 / 1007 / 1650 / 2218	3.0 / 10.6 / 3.4 / 10.3
13 SA	0525 / 1055 / 1741 / 2310	2.3 / 11.1 / 2.6 / 10.9	28 SU	0505 / 1036 / 1718 / 2249	3.6 / 10.0 / 4.0 / 9.5
14 SU	0607 / 1143 / 1829	3.0 / 10.4 / 3.3	29 M	0540 / 1114 / 1800 / 2337	4.3 / 9.3 / 4.6 / 8.7
15 M	0005 / 0701 / 1247 / 1935	10.0 / 3.7 / 9.8 / 3.9	30 TU	0634 / 1220 / 1908	4.9 / 8.6 / 5.2
			31 W	0120 / 0800 / 1416 / 2052	8.2 / 5.3 / 8.4 / 5.2

ST. MALO
48°38′N 2°02′W

Times and heights (in metres) of high and low water 1994
Time: French Standard Time. For GMT, SUBTRACT ONE HOUR.
For BST, use unchanged in the shaded area

SEPTEMBER

Day	Time	m	Time	m	Time	m	Time	m		Day	Time	m	Time	m	Time	m	Time	m
1 TH	0319	8.5	0940	5.0	1545	8.9	2223	4.6		16 F	0417	9.7	1104	3.5	1641	10.4	2337	3.0
2 F	0425	9.2	1051	4.3	1641	9.8	2323	3.8		17 SA	0513	10.5	1202	2.8	1731	11.1		
3 SA	0513	10.0	1146	3.4	1727	10.6				18 SU	0030	2.4	0557	11.2	1250	2.3	1814	11.7
4 SU	0015	2.9	0556	10.9	1236	2.6	1809	11.4		19 M	0114	1.9	0636	11.6	1332	2.0	1853	12.0
5 M	0104	2.2	0638	11.6	1324	1.9	1850	12.2		20 TU	0152	1.7	0712	11.9	1408	1.8	1927	12.1
6 TU	0152	1.5	0718	12.2	1411	1.4	1931	12.7		21 W	0225	1.6	0745	12.0	1440	1.8	1959	12.1
7 W	0236	1.1	0758	12.6	1453	1.0	2010	13.0		22 TH	0255	1.7	0814	11.9	1509	1.9	2028	11.9
8 TH	0318	0.9	0837	12.7	1533	0.9	2050	12.9		23 F	0322	1.9	0841	11.7	1535	2.2	2054	11.5
9 F	0355	1.0	0916	12.6	1610	1.2	2129	12.5		24 SA	0346	2.3	0907	11.4	1558	2.6	2120	11.0
10 SA	0431	1.5	0954	12.1	1646	1.7	2208	11.8		25 SU	0408	2.9	0932	10.8	1621	3.2	2146	10.4
11 SU	0507	2.2	1034	11.3	1725	2.5	2252	10.8		26 M	0433	3.5	1000	10.2	1649	3.8	2215	9.6
12 M	0548	3.1	1121	10.4	1812	3.4	2347	9.8		27 TU	0505	4.2	1034	9.4	1726	4.4	2255	8.8
13 TU	0643	4.0	1227	9.6	1921	4.1				28 W	0552	4.8	1127	8.7	1822	5.0		
14 W	0112	9.1	0809	4.5	1401	9.2	2103	4.3		29 TH	0013	8.2	0705	5.3	1315	8.3	1950	5.2
15 TH	0257	9.1	0949	4.3	1534	9.6	2232	3.7		30 F	0231	8.2	0846	5.1	1457	8.7	2131	4.8

OCTOBER

Day	Time	m	Time	m	Time	m	Time	m		Day	Time	m	Time	m	Time	m	Time	m
1 SA	0347	9.0	1007	4.4	1600	9.5	2242	3.9		16 SU	0446	10.3	1132	3.2	1704	10.7	2359	2.7
2 SU	0438	9.9	1107	3.5	1651	10.5	2340	2.9		17 M	0528	10.9	1219	2.7	1746	11.3		
3 M	0523	10.9	1202	2.5	1737	11.5				18 TU	0042	2.3	0606	11.4	1301	2.4	1824	11.6
4 TU	0034	2.0	0607	11.8	1255	1.7	1822	12.3		19 W	0119	2.1	0641	11.7	1337	2.2	1858	11.8
5 W	0125	1.3	0650	12.5	1346	1.1	1906	12.9		20 TH	0152	2.0	0714	11.8	1410	2.1	1930	11.8
6 TH	0212	0.8	0732	12.9	1432	0.8	1949	13.2		21 F	0222	2.0	0743	11.8	1439	2.1	2000	11.6
7 F	0256	0.7	0814	13.1	1514	0.7	2030	13.1		22 SA	0250	2.1	0811	11.7	1507	2.3	2027	11.4
8 SA	0336	1.0	0854	12.8	1554	1.1	2112	12.6		23 SU	0316	2.4	0838	11.4	1534	2.6	2054	11.0
9 SU	0413	1.5	0934	12.3	1632	1.7	2153	11.8		24 M	0342	2.8	0906	11.0	1600	3.0	2123	10.5
10 M	0451	2.3	1017	11.4	1713	2.5	2238	10.7		25 TU	0410	3.3	0936	10.4	1630	3.5	2155	9.8
11 TU	0534	3.3	1105	10.4	1802	3.4	2334	9.7		26 W	0443	3.9	1012	9.8	1706	4.1	2235	9.1
12 W	0630	4.1	1210	9.6	1910	4.2				27 TH	0527	4.5	1059	9.1	1755	4.6	2335	8.5
13 TH	0056	9.0	0753	4.6	1340	9.2	2043	4.3		28 F	0629	4.9	1215	8.7	1905	4.8		
14 F	0236	9.0	0924	4.4	1510	9.4	2206	3.9		29 SA	0121	8.4	0752	4.9	1352	8.8	2033	4.6
15 SA	0354	9.5	1036	3.8	1615	10.1	2308	3.3		30 SU	0252	8.9	0915	4.4	1508	9.5	2154	3.9
										31 M	0354	9.8	1024	3.5	1608	10.4	2300	2.9

NOVEMBER

Day	Time	m	Time	m	Time	m	Time	m		Day	Time	m	Time	m	Time	m	Time	m
1 TU	0446	10.8	1126	2.6	1702	11.4				16 W	0003	2.9	0534	10.9	1226	2.9	1753	11.0
2 W	0000	2.0	0535	11.8	1225	1.8	1752	12.2		17 TH	0044	2.6	0611	11.3	1306	2.6	1831	11.3
3 TH	0056	1.4	0622	12.5	1319	1.2	1841	12.7		18 F	0121	2.4	0646	11.5	1341	2.5	1905	11.3
4 F	0147	1.0	0707	12.9	1410	0.8	1928	13.0		19 SA	0153	2.4	0718	11.6	1414	2.4	1937	11.3
5 SA	0234	0.9	0752	13.1	1456	0.8	2013	12.9		20 SU	0224	2.4	0748	11.5	1444	2.4	2007	11.2
6 SU	0317	1.1	0835	12.8	1539	1.1	2057	12.4		21 M	0254	2.5	0817	11.4	1515	2.6	2038	11.0
7 M	0358	1.6	0918	12.3	1622	1.7	2142	11.7		22 TU	0325	2.7	0849	11.2	1546	2.8	2110	10.7
8 TU	0439	2.3	1003	11.6	1705	2.5	2228	10.8		23 W	0357	3.1	0923	10.8	1619	3.2	2146	10.2
9 W	0523	3.2	1051	10.7	1753	3.3	2321	9.9		24 TH	0432	3.5	1000	10.3	1655	3.6	2226	9.7
10 TH	0615	4.0	1149	9.8	1852	4.0				25 F	0513	3.9	1044	9.8	1739	4.0	2316	9.2
11 F	0027	9.2	0722	4.5	1302	9.3	2004	4.3		26 SA	0605	4.3	1140	9.4	1835	4.2		
12 SA	0148	9.0	0839	4.6	1423	9.3	2118	4.2		27 SU	0024	9.0	0710	4.4	1253	9.3	1945	4.2
13 SU	0307	9.2	0950	4.2	1533	9.6	2222	3.8		28 M	0148	9.1	0825	4.2	1412	9.6	2104	3.8
14 M	0407	9.8	1049	3.7	1628	10.1	2316	3.3		29 TU	0305	9.8	0941	3.6	1525	10.3	2220	3.1
15 TU	0453	10.4	1141	3.3	1713	10.6	2329	2.4		30 W	0408	10.6	1052	2.8	1629	11.1		

DECEMBER

Day	Time	m	Time	m	Time	m	Time	m		Day	Time	m	Time	m	Time	m	Time	m
1 TH	0505	11.5	1157	2.1	1727	11.8				16 F	0013	3.2	0545	10.8	1238	3.1	1808	10.8
2 F	0030	1.8	0558	12.2	1256	1.5	1821	12.3		17 SA	0055	2.9	0624	11.1	1319	2.8	1846	11.0
3 SA	0125	1.3	0648	12.7	1351	1.1	1913	12.6		18 SU	0132	2.7	0659	11.3	1354	2.6	1922	11.1
4 SU	0216	1.2	0736	12.8	1442	1.0	2001	12.6		19 M	0206	2.6	0733	11.5	1429	2.5	1955	11.1
5 M	0303	1.3	0822	12.8	1529	1.2	2048	12.3		20 TU	0240	2.5	0805	11.5	1503	2.5	2028	11.1
6 TU	0347	1.6	0907	12.4	1613	1.6	2133	11.8		21 W	0315	2.5	0838	11.5	1538	2.5	2102	11.0
7 W	0429	2.2	0951	11.8	1656	2.2	2217	11.1		22 TH	0350	2.6	0913	11.3	1613	2.7	2138	10.8
8 TH	0511	2.9	1035	11.1	1739	3.0	2301	10.4		23 F	0425	2.9	0950	11.0	1648	2.9	2217	10.5
9 F	0553	3.6	1121	10.3	1823	3.7	2348	9.7		24 SA	0504	3.2	1030	10.6	1727	3.2	2259	10.1
10 SA	0641	4.2	1214	9.6	1913	4.2				25 SU	0547	3.6	1116	10.2	1812	3.6	2350	9.7
11 SU	0045	9.2	0739	4.6	1318	9.2	2013	4.4		26 M	0639	3.8	1213	9.9	1908	3.8		
12 M	0156	9.0	0848	4.7	1432	9.2	2120	4.4		27 TU	0056	9.6	0743	3.9	1326	9.8	2018	3.8
13 TU	0310	9.3	0957	4.4	1542	9.5	2225	4.0		28 W	0217	9.7	0901	3.7	1447	10.0	2143	3.5
14 W	0413	9.8	1059	3.9	1639	9.9	2323	3.6		29 TH	0334	10.2	1023	3.2	1603	10.5	2303	3.0
15 TH	0502	10.3	1152	3.5	1726	10.4				30 F	0442	11.0	1136	2.6	1710	11.2		
										31 SA	0010	2.3	0542	11.7	1240	1.9	1810	11.7

BREST

MEAN SPRING AND NEAP CURVES

Springs occur 2 days after New and Full Moon.

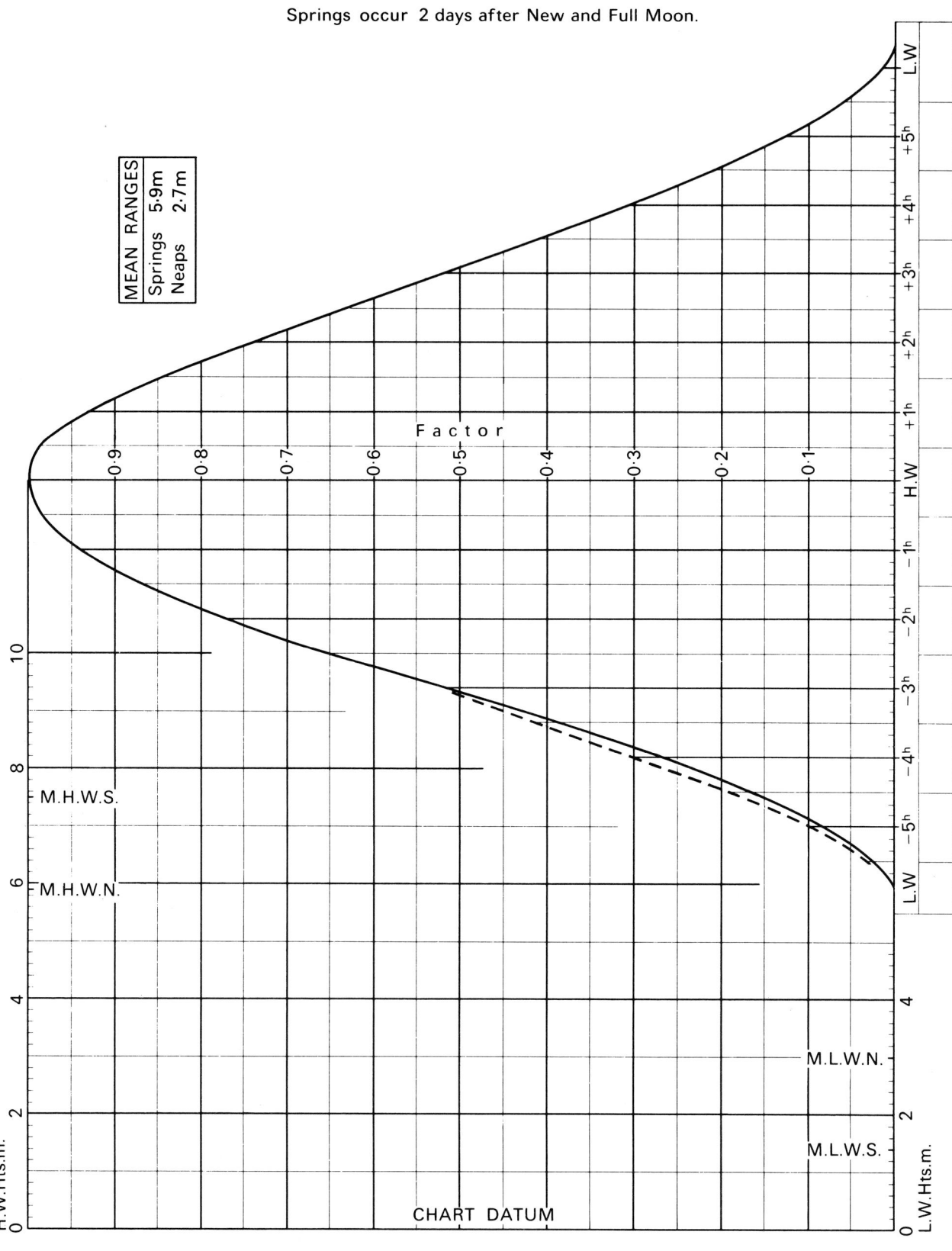

MEAN RANGES
Springs 5·9m
Neaps 2·7m

Factor

CHART DATUM

BREST
48°23′N 4°30′W

Times and heights (in metres) of high and low water 1994
Time: French Standard Time. For GMT, SUBTRACT ONE HOUR.
For BST, use unchanged in the shaded area
High Water, full and change, 0507

JANUARY

Day	Time	m	Time	m	Day	Time	m	Time	m
1 SA	0058 / 0658 / 1324 / 1923	1.8 / 7.4 / 1.7 / 7.1			16 SU	0138 / 0734 / 1358 / 1949	2.0 / 7.1 / 2.0 / 6.7		
2 SU	0140 / 0740 / 1407 / 2007	1.8 / 7.3 / 1.8 / 7.0			17 M	0213 / 0809 / 1433 / 2023	2.3 / 6.8 / 2.3 / 6.4		
3 M	0225 / 0825 / 1453 / 2054	2.0 / 7.1 / 2.0 / 6.7			18 TU	0250 / 0844 / 1509 / 2059	2.6 / 6.4 / 2.7 / 6.1		
4 TU	0314 / 0914 / 1545 / 2148	2.2 / 6.8 / 2.3 / 6.5			19 W	0329 / 0924 / 1551 / 2144	2.9 / 6.1 / 3.0 / 5.8		
5 W	0409 / 1012 / 1644 / 2252	2.5 / 6.5 / 2.6 / 6.3			20 TH	0417 / 1015 / 1643 / 2245	3.2 / 5.8 / 3.3 / 5.6		
6 TH	0513 / 1121 / 1753	2.7 / 6.3 / 2.7			21 F	0518 / 1124 / 1749	3.5 / 5.5 / 3.4		
7 F	0004 / 0626 / 1239 / 1907	6.2 / 2.7 / 6.2 / 2.7			22 SA	0004 / 0634 / 1245 / 1906	5.5 / 3.5 / 5.5 / 3.4		
8 SA	0120 / 0741 / 1356 / 2019	6.3 / 2.6 / 6.4 / 2.5			23 SU	0124 / 0751 / 1359 / 2016	5.7 / 3.3 / 5.8 / 3.1		
9 SU	0228 / 0851 / 1501 / 2121	6.6 / 2.3 / 6.6 / 2.2			24 M	0228 / 0851 / 1456 / 2110	6.0 / 2.9 / 6.1 / 2.7		
10 M	0327 / 0950 / 1556 / 2214	7.0 / 2.0 / 6.9 / 2.0			25 TU	0318 / 0940 / 1543 / 2157	6.4 / 2.5 / 6.5 / 2.3		
11 TU ●	0418 / 1041 / 1644 / 2302	7.3 / 1.7 / 7.1 / 1.8			26 W	0402 / 1024 / 1626 / 2240	6.8 / 2.1 / 6.9 / 1.9		
12 W	0504 / 1126 / 1727 / 2345	7.4 / 1.5 / 7.2 / 1.7			27 TH O	0443 / 1106 / 1706 / 2321	7.2 / 1.7 / 7.2 / 1.6		
13 TH	0546 / 1208 / 1806	7.5 / 1.5 / 7.2			28 F	0523 / 1147 / 1746	7.5 / 1.4 / 7.4		
14 F	0025 / 0624 / 1247 / 1842	1.7 / 7.5 / 1.6 / 7.1			29 SA	0002 / 0603 / 1227 / 1826	1.4 / 7.7 / 1.2 / 7.5		
15 SA	0102 / 0700 / 1323 / 1916	1.8 / 7.3 / 1.7 / 7.0			30 SU	0043 / 0643 / 1308 / 1907	1.3 / 7.8 / 1.2 / 7.5		
					31 M	0125 / 0724 / 1351 / 1948	1.3 / 7.7 / 1.4 / 7.4		

FEBRUARY

Day	Time	m	Day	Time	m
1 TU	0208 / 0807 / 1435 / 2033	1.5 / 7.4 / 1.7 / 7.1	16 W	0213 / 0806 / 1428 / 2017	2.3 / 6.6 / 2.5 / 6.4
2 W	0255 / 0853 / 1523 / 2122	1.9 / 7.0 / 2.1 / 6.7	17 TH	0247 / 0839 / 1504 / 2053	2.7 / 6.2 / 2.8 / 6.0
3 TH	0346 / 0946 / 1619 / 2221	2.3 / 6.5 / 2.5 / 6.3	18 F	0327 / 0921 / 1548 / 2143	3.0 / 5.9 / 3.2 / 5.7
4 F	0448 / 1053 / 1726 / 2336	2.7 / 6.1 / 2.9 / 6.1	19 SA	0420 / 1020 / 1647 / 2256	3.3 / 5.5 / 3.4 / 5.5
5 SA	0603 / 1218 / 1846	2.9 / 5.9 / 3.0	20 SU	0531 / 1145 / 1807	3.5 / 5.4 / 3.5
6 SU	0102 / 0727 / 1347 / 2008	6.1 / 2.8 / 6.0 / 2.8	21 M	0030 / 0700 / 1318 / 1934	5.5 / 3.4 / 5.6 / 3.3
7 M	0220 / 0843 / 1456 / 2113	6.3 / 2.5 / 6.3 / 2.5	22 TU	0151 / 0817 / 1427 / 2040	5.8 / 3.0 / 6.0 / 2.8
8 TU	0319 / 0942 / 1549 / 2205	6.7 / 2.2 / 6.7 / 2.1	23 W	0249 / 0912 / 1518 / 2131	6.3 / 2.5 / 6.5 / 2.3
9 W	0408 / 1030 / 1633 / 2250	7.1 / 1.8 / 7.0 / 1.8	24 TH	0337 / 0959 / 1603 / 2217	6.8 / 2.0 / 7.0 / 1.8
10 TH ●	0451 / 1112 / 1711 / 2329	7.3 / 1.6 / 7.2 / 1.7	25 F	0421 / 1043 / 1645 / 2300	7.3 / 1.5 / 7.4 / 1.4
11 F	0528 / 1149 / 1746	7.5 / 1.5 / 7.2	26 SA O	0503 / 1126 / 1726 / 2342	7.7 / 1.1 / 7.7 / 1.1
12 SA	0005 / 0602 / 1223 / 1817	1.6 / 7.5 / 1.5 / 7.2	27 SU	0544 / 1207 / 1806	8.0 / 0.9 / 7.9
13 SU	0038 / 0634 / 1255 / 1847	1.7 / 7.4 / 1.7 / 7.1	28 M	0024 / 0624 / 1249 / 1847	0.9 / 8.0 / 0.9 / 7.8
14 M	0110 / 0704 / 1326 / 1916	1.8 / 7.2 / 1.9 / 6.9			
15 TU	0141 / 0735 / 1356 / 1946	2.0 / 7.0 / 2.1 / 6.7			

MARCH

Day	Time	m	Day	Time	m
1 TU	0107 / 0706 / 1331 / 1928	1.0 / 7.9 / 1.1 / 7.6	16 W	0112 / 0705 / 1324 / 1915	2.0 / 7.0 / 2.1 / 6.8
2 W	0150 / 0748 / 1415 / 2012	1.2 / 7.6 / 1.5 / 7.3	17 TH	0142 / 0734 / 1355 / 1945	2.2 / 6.7 / 2.4 / 6.5
3 TH	0237 / 0834 / 1503 / 2100	1.7 / 7.1 / 2.0 / 6.8	18 F	0215 / 0807 / 1429 / 2020	2.5 / 6.4 / 2.7 / 6.2
4 F	0328 / 0926 / 1558 / 2159	2.2 / 6.5 / 2.6 / 6.3	19 SA	0254 / 0846 / 1511 / 2105	2.8 / 6.0 / 3.0 / 5.9
5 SA	0429 / 1034 / 1705 / 2316	2.7 / 6.0 / 3.0 / 6.0	20 SU	0342 / 0941 / 1607 / 2211	3.2 / 5.6 / 3.2 / 5.6
6 SU	0545 / 1204 / 1829	3.0 / 5.7 / 3.2	21 M	0447 / 1100 / 1722 / 2340	3.4 / 5.4 / 3.5 / 5.5
7 M	0047 / 0714 / 1338 / 1955	5.9 / 2.9 / 5.9 / 2.9	22 TU	0612 / 1234 / 1850	3.3 / 5.5 / 3.3
8 TU	0207 / 0831 / 1444 / 2059	6.2 / 2.6 / 6.2 / 2.6	23 W	0108 / 0736 / 1351 / 2004	5.8 / 3.0 / 6.0 / 2.8
9 W	0305 / 0927 / 1533 / 2149	6.6 / 2.2 / 6.6 / 2.2	24 TH	0214 / 0838 / 1447 / 2100	6.3 / 2.5 / 6.5 / 2.3
10 TH	0351 / 1012 / 1614 / 2231	6.9 / 1.9 / 6.9 / 1.9	25 F	0307 / 0929 / 1535 / 2149	6.9 / 1.9 / 7.0 / 1.7
11 F	0430 / 1051 / 1649 / 2308	7.2 / 1.7 / 7.1 / 1.7	26 SA	0354 / 1016 / 1619 / 2235	7.4 / 1.4 / 7.5 / 1.3
12 SA ●	0505 / 1125 / 1721 / 2341	7.3 / 1.6 / 7.2 / 1.7	27 SU O	0438 / 1101 / 1702 / 2320	7.8 / 1.0 / 7.8 / 0.9
13 SU	0536 / 1156 / 1750	7.4 / 1.6 / 7.2	28 M	0522 / 1145 / 1744	8.0 / 0.8 / 8.0
14 M	0012 / 0606 / 1226 / 1818	1.7 / 7.3 / 1.7 / 7.2	29 TU	0004 / 0604 / 1228 / 1826	0.8 / 8.1 / 0.9 / 8.0
15 TU	0042 / 0636 / 1255 / 1846	1.8 / 7.2 / 1.8 / 7.0	30 W	0048 / 0647 / 1312 / 1909	0.9 / 7.9 / 1.1 / 7.8
			31 TH	0134 / 0732 / 1358 / 1954	1.2 / 7.5 / 1.5 / 7.3

APRIL

Day	Time	m	Day	Time	m
1 F	0221 / 0819 / 1446 / 2044	1.6 / 7.0 / 2.1 / 6.8	16 SA	0151 / 0744 / 1404 / 1958	2.4 / 6.4 / 2.6 / 6.4
2 SA	0314 / 0913 / 1541 / 2143	2.1 / 6.4 / 2.6 / 6.3	17 SU	0231 / 0825 / 1447 / 2044	2.7 / 6.1 / 2.9 / 6.1
3 SU	0414 / 1020 / 1647 / 2257	2.6 / 5.9 / 3.0 / 6.0	18 M	0318 / 0918 / 1541 / 2145	2.9 / 5.8 / 3.1 / 5.8
4 M	0527 / 1145 / 1807	2.9 / 5.7 / 3.2	19 TU	0418 / 1029 / 1649 / 2303	3.1 / 5.6 / 3.3 / 5.8
5 TU	0023 / 0650 / 1312 / 1929	5.9 / 3.0 / 5.8 / 3.0	20 W	0533 / 1154 / 1809	3.1 / 5.7 / 3.1
6 W	0140 / 0804 / 1417 / 2034	6.1 / 2.7 / 6.1 / 2.7	21 TH	0024 / 0653 / 1310 / 1924	5.9 / 2.9 / 6.0 / 2.8
7 TH	0238 / 0859 / 1506 / 2123	6.4 / 2.4 / 6.4 / 2.3	22 F	0134 / 0800 / 1411 / 2025	6.3 / 2.4 / 6.5 / 2.3
8 F	0324 / 0944 / 1546 / 2205	6.7 / 2.1 / 6.7 / 2.1	23 SA	0233 / 0857 / 1503 / 2119	6.8 / 1.9 / 7.0 / 1.8
9 SA	0403 / 1022 / 1621 / 2241	6.9 / 2.0 / 6.9 / 1.9	24 SU	0324 / 0947 / 1551 / 2209	7.3 / 1.5 / 7.5 / 1.3
10 SU	0437 / 1056 / 1652 / 2314	7.1 / 1.8 / 7.0 / 1.8	25 M O	0413 / 1035 / 1638 / 2257	7.7 / 1.1 / 7.8 / 1.0
11 M ●	0508 / 1127 / 1722 / 2345	7.1 / 1.8 / 7.1 / 1.8	26 TU	0500 / 1122 / 1723 / 2344	7.9 / 1.0 / 7.9 / 0.9
12 TU	0539 / 1157 / 1751	7.1 / 1.8 / 7.1	27 W	0546 / 1208 / 1808	7.9 / 1.0 / 7.9
13 W	0016 / 0609 / 1227 / 1820	1.9 / 7.1 / 1.9 / 7.0	28 TH	0031 / 0631 / 1254 / 1853	1.0 / 7.7 / 1.2 / 7.7
14 TH	0046 / 0639 / 1257 / 1850	2.0 / 6.9 / 2.1 / 6.9	29 F	0118 / 0718 / 1341 / 1940	1.2 / 7.4 / 1.6 / 7.3
15 F	0118 / 0710 / 1328 / 1922	2.2 / 6.7 / 2.3 / 6.7	30 SA	0207 / 0807 / 1430 / 2030	1.6 / 6.9 / 2.1 / 6.9

BREST

48°23'N 4°30'W

Times and heights (in metres) of high and low water 1994
Time: French Standard Time. For GMT, SUBTRACT ONE HOUR.
For BST, use unchanged in the shaded area
High Water, full and change, 0507

MAY

Day	Time	m	Day	Time	m
1 SU	0259	2.1	16 M	0215	2.4
	0900	6.4		0813	6.3
	1524	2.5		1431	2.6
	2127	6.5		2031	6.4
2 M	0356	2.5	17 TU	0301	2.6
	1001	6.0		0903	6.1
	1625	2.9		1523	2.8
	2232	6.1		2126	6.2
3 TU	0500	2.8	18 W	0356	2.8
	1111	5.8		1005	5.9
	1734	3.1		1623	2.9
	2345	5.9		2232	6.1
4 W	0611	2.9	19 TH	0501	2.8
	1228	5.8		1116	5.9
	1848	3.1		1733	2.9
				2344	6.1
5 TH	0057	6.0	20 F	0614	2.7
	0722	2.8		1229	6.1
	1335	5.9		1845	2.7
	1954	2.9			
6 F	0158	6.2	21 SA	0055	6.4
	0820	2.6		0722	2.4
	1428	6.2		1334	6.5
	2047	2.6		1950	2.3
7 SA	0247	6.4	22 SU	0159	6.7
	0907	2.4		0824	2.0
	1511	6.5		1432	6.9
	2131	2.4		2050	1.9
8 SU	0329	6.6	23 M	0257	7.1
	0948	2.3		0920	1.7
	1548	6.7		1525	7.3
	2210	2.2		2145	1.5
9 M	0406	6.8	24 TU	0350	7.4
	1024	2.1		1012	1.4
	1622	6.8		1616	7.6
	2245	2.1		2237	1.2
10 TU ●	0440	6.9	25 W O	0441	7.6
	1057	2.1		1102	1.3
	1654	6.9		1705	7.7
	2319	2.0		2327	1.1
11 W	0513	6.9	26 TH	0531	7.6
	1130	2.0		1151	1.3
	1726	7.0		1753	7.8
	2352	2.0			
12 TH	0546	6.9	27 F	0016	1.1
	1202	2.0		0618	7.5
	1759	7.0		1239	1.4
				1840	7.6
13 F	0025	2.0	28 SA	0105	1.3
	0619	6.8		0705	7.2
	1235	2.1		1326	1.7
	1831	6.9		1927	7.4
14 SA	0059	2.1	29 SU	0152	1.6
	0653	6.7		0752	6.9
	1310	2.3		1413	2.0
	1906	6.8		2014	7.0
15 SU	0135	2.2	30 M	0241	2.0
	0730	6.5		0840	6.5
	1348	2.4		1503	2.4
	1945	6.6		2104	6.6
			31 TU	0331	2.3
				0931	6.2
				1555	2.7
				2158	6.3

JUNE

Day	Time	m	Day	Time	m
1 W	0424	2.7	16 TH	0336	2.4
	1028	5.9		0941	6.3
	1653	3.0		1559	2.6
	2257	6.0		2204	6.4
2 TH	0523	2.9	17 F	0433	2.5
	1131	5.7		1043	6.2
	1756	3.1		1701	2.6
				2308	6.3
3 F	0001	5.9	18 SA	0539	2.6
	0626	3.0		1151	6.2
	1238	5.8		1810	2.6
	1902	3.1			
4 SA	0106	5.9	19 SU	0019	6.3
	0729	2.9		0648	2.5
	1339	5.9		1300	6.4
	2002	2.9		1920	2.4
5 SU	0203	6.0	20 M	0129	6.5
	0824	2.8		0756	2.3
	1431	6.1		1405	6.7
	2054	2.7		2026	2.1
6 M	0252	6.2	21 TU	0235	6.8
	0911	2.6		0858	2.0
	1515	6.4		1505	7.0
	2138	2.5		2126	1.8
7 TU	0335	6.4	22 W	0334	7.0
	0952	2.4		0955	1.7
	1554	6.6		1600	7.3
	2217	2.3		2222	1.5
8 W	0414	6.6	23 TH O	0428	7.2
	1030	2.3		1047	1.5
	1630	6.8		1652	7.5
	2255	2.1		2314	1.3
9 TH ●	0450	6.7	24 F	0518	7.3
	1106	2.1		1137	1.5
	1706	6.9		1740	7.6
	2331	2.0			
10 F	0526	6.8	25 SA	0003	1.3
	1142	2.1		0605	7.3
	1741	7.0		1224	1.5
				1826	7.6
11 SA	0007	2.0	26 SU	0049	1.3
	0602	6.8		0649	7.2
	1218	2.1		1309	1.6
	1817	7.0		1909	7.4
12 SU	0043	2.0	27 M	0134	1.5
	0639	6.8		0731	7.0
	1255	2.1		1352	1.9
	1854	7.0		1952	7.1
13 M	0121	2.0	28 TU	0216	1.8
	0718	6.7		0812	6.7
	1335	2.1		1435	2.2
	1934	6.9		2034	6.8
14 TU	0201	2.1	29 W	0259	2.2
	0800	6.6		0853	6.4
	1417	2.3		1519	2.5
	2018	6.7		2117	6.4
15 W	0245	2.2	30 TH	0343	2.5
	0847	6.4		0938	6.0
	1505	2.4		1606	2.8
	2107	6.5		2205	6.1

JULY

Day	Time	m	Day	Time	m
1 F	0431	2.9	16 SA	0407	2.3
	1031	5.8		1012	6.4
	1700	3.1		1634	2.5
	2301	5.8		2239	6.3
2 SA	0526	3.1	17 SU	0510	2.6
	1133	5.6		1119	6.2
	1803	3.2		1743	2.6
				2352	6.2
3 SU	0006	5.7	18 M	0622	2.6
	0629	3.2		1234	6.2
	1242	5.7		1857	2.6
	1910	3.2			
4 M	0114	5.7	19 TU	0111	6.2
	0735	3.1		0736	2.5
	1347	5.8		1348	6.5
	2013	3.0		2011	2.4
5 TU	0215	5.9	20 W	0224	6.5
	0833	2.9		0845	2.3
	1441	6.1		1454	6.8
	2106	2.8		2117	2.0
6 W	0305	6.1	21 TH	0326	6.7
	0922	2.6		0944	2.0
	1527	6.4		1551	7.1
	2151	2.5		2213	1.7
7 TH	0350	6.4	22 F O	0419	7.0
	1005	2.4		1037	1.7
	1608	6.6		1641	7.4
	2232	2.2		2303	1.5
8 F ●	0430	6.6	23 SA	0506	7.2
	1045	2.2		1124	1.6
	1646	6.9		1726	7.5
	2311	2.0		2349	1.3
9 SA	0508	6.8	24 SU	0549	7.3
	1123	2.0		1207	1.5
	1724	7.1		1808	7.5
	2349	1.8			
10 SU	0546	6.9	25 M	0031	1.4
	1201	1.9		0628	7.2
	1802	7.2		1248	1.6
				1847	7.4
11 M	0027	1.7	26 TU	0109	1.5
	0624	7.0		0704	7.1
	1240	1.8		1326	1.8
	1840	7.2		1923	7.2
12 TU	0105	1.7	27 W	0146	1.8
	0703	7.0		0739	6.8
	1319	1.8		1403	2.0
	1919	7.2		1958	6.9
13 W	0145	1.7	28 TH	0222	2.1
	0744	6.9		0813	6.5
	1401	1.9		1440	2.4
	2001	7.1		2035	6.5
14 TH	0228	1.9	29 F	0259	2.5
	0827	6.8		0850	6.2
	1446	2.1		1520	2.7
	2046	6.9		2114	6.2
15 F	0314	2.1	30 SA	0340	2.8
	0916	6.6		0933	5.9
	1536	2.3		1607	3.1
	2137	6.6		2203	5.8
			31 SU	0429	3.1
				1029	5.6
				1704	3.3
				2306	5.6

AUGUST

Day	Time	m	Day	Time	m
1 M	0530	3.3	16 TU	0604	2.9
	1143	5.5		1219	6.1
	1815	3.4		1845	2.8
2 TU	0023	5.5	17 W	0103	6.0
	0644	3.4		0726	2.8
	1302	5.6		1341	6.3
	1932	3.3		2006	2.5
3 W	0138	5.7	18 TH	0220	6.3
	0756	3.1		0838	2.5
	1409	5.9		1448	6.7
	2035	3.0		2111	2.2
4 TH	0238	6.0	19 F	0319	6.6
	0853	2.8		0936	2.1
	1501	6.3		1542	7.0
	2124	2.6		2204	1.8
5 F	0326	6.3	20 SA	0408	6.9
	0940	2.5		1025	1.8
	1545	6.6		1628	7.3
	2208	2.2		2249	1.6
6 SA	0408	6.7	21 SU O	0450	7.2
	1022	2.1		1108	1.6
	1625	7.0		1709	7.5
	2248	1.9		2330	1.4
7 SU ●	0448	7.0	22 M	0528	7.3
	1102	1.8		1147	1.6
	1704	7.3		1746	7.5
	2328	1.6			
8 M	0527	7.2	23 TU	0007	1.4
	1142	1.6		0602	7.3
	1743	7.5		1223	1.6
				1820	7.4
9 TU	0007	1.4	24 W	0041	1.6
	0605	7.4		0634	7.2
	1221	1.4		1257	1.8
	1821	7.6		1852	7.3
10 W	0046	1.3	25 TH	0113	1.8
	0644	7.4		0704	7.0
	1301	1.4		1330	2.0
	1900	7.6		1923	7.0
11 TH	0126	1.4	26 F	0145	2.1
	0723	7.3		0735	6.7
	1343	1.5		1403	2.3
	1941	7.4		1955	6.6
12 F	0208	1.6	27 SA	0218	2.4
	0806	7.1		0807	6.4
	1427	1.8		1438	2.7
	2025	7.1		2029	6.3
13 SA	0254	1.9	28 SU	0254	2.8
	0852	6.8		0843	6.0
	1516	2.1		1519	3.0
	2115	6.7		2110	5.9
14 SU	0346	2.3	29 M	0337	3.2
	0947	6.4		0931	5.7
	1614	2.5		1610	3.4
	2217	6.3		2208	5.5
15 M	0448	2.7	30 TU	0434	3.4
	1057	6.2		1043	5.5
	1724	2.8		1720	3.5
	2335	6.0		2331	5.4
			31 W	0552	3.5
				1214	5.5
				1847	3.4

82

BREST

48°23′N 4°30′W

Times and heights (in metres) of high and low water 1994
Time: French Standard Time. For GMT, SUBTRACT ONE HOUR.
For BST, use unchanged in the shaded area
High Water, full and change, 0507

SEPTEMBER

Day	Time	m		Day	Time	m
1 TH	0101	5.5		16 F	0212	6.2
	0716	3.3			0828	2.6
	1334	5.8			1436	6.6
	2001	3.1			2059	2.3
2 F	0209	5.9		17 SA	0306	6.6
	0822	2.9			0922	2.2
	1431	6.2			1526	7.0
	2055	2.6			2147	1.9
3 SA	0259	6.3		18 SU	0350	6.9
	0912	2.5			1008	1.9
	1518	6.7			1609	7.3
	2140	2.2			2229	1.7
4 SU	0343	6.8		19 M	0429	7.1
	0956	2.0			1048	1.7
	1600	7.1			1646	7.4
	2222	1.7		O	2306	1.6
5 M	0424	7.2		20 TU	0503	7.2
	1038	1.6			1124	1.7
●	1640	7.5			1720	7.4
	2303	1.4			2340	1.6
6 TU	0503	7.5		21 W	0534	7.3
	1119	1.3			1157	1.7
	1720	7.8			1751	7.4
	2344	1.2				
7 W	0542	7.7		22 TH	0011	1.7
	1159	1.2			0604	7.2
	1759	7.9			1228	1.8
					1821	7.2
8 TH	0024	1.1		23 F	0042	1.9
	0621	7.7			0633	7.0
	1241	1.2			1259	2.0
	1839	7.8			1851	7.0
9 F	0105	1.2		24 SA	0112	2.1
	0702	7.6			0702	6.8
	1324	1.3			1331	2.3
	1921	7.6			1922	6.7
10 SA	0148	1.5		25 SU	0143	2.5
	0745	7.3			0733	6.5
	1409	1.7			1404	2.6
	2007	7.2			1954	6.3
11 SU	0235	1.9		26 M	0217	2.8
	0832	6.9			0807	6.2
	1500	2.1			1442	3.0
	2058	6.6			2032	6.0
12 M	0328	2.4		27 TU	0257	3.1
	0929	6.5			0851	5.9
	1559	2.6			1529	3.3
	2203	6.1			2125	5.6
13 TU	0432	2.9		28 W	0351	3.4
	1042	6.1			0955	5.6
	1712	2.9			1633	3.5
	2327	5.8			2243	5.4
14 W	0552	3.1		29 TH	0504	3.6
	1210	6.0			1124	5.5
	1838	2.9			1757	3.5
15 TH	0059	5.9		30 F	0017	5.5
	0717	3.0			0631	3.4
	1333	6.3			1251	5.8
	1958	2.6			1919	3.2

OCTOBER

Day	Time	m		Day	Time	m
1 SA	0132	5.9		16 SU	0243	6.5
	0744	3.0			0900	2.4
	1355	6.2			1502	6.8
	2020	2.7			2123	2.1
2 SU	0226	6.4		17 M	0326	6.8
	0839	2.5			0944	2.1
	1445	6.7			1544	7.1
	2108	2.2			2204	2.0
3 M	0313	6.9		18 TU	0403	7.0
	0926	2.0			1023	2.0
	1531	7.2			1620	7.2
	2153	1.7			2240	1.9
4 TU	0356	7.3		19 W	0437	7.1
	1011	1.6			1058	1.9
	1614	7.6			1653	7.2
	2237	1.3		O	2312	1.9
5 W	0437	7.7		20 TH	0507	7.2
	1054	1.2			1131	1.9
●	1656	7.9			1724	7.2
	2319	1.1			2343	1.9
6 TH	0519	7.9		21 F	0537	7.2
	1138	1.0			1202	2.0
	1738	8.0			1755	7.1
7 F	0002	1.0		22 SA	0013	2.0
	0600	7.9			0606	7.1
	1221	1.1			1233	2.1
	1821	7.9			1825	6.9
8 SA	0046	1.2		23 SU	0044	2.2
	0643	7.8			0636	6.9
	1307	1.3			1305	2.3
	1905	7.6			1856	6.7
9 SU	0131	1.5		24 M	0115	2.5
	0728	7.5			0708	6.7
	1355	1.6			1338	2.6
	1953	7.1			1929	6.4
10 M	0219	2.0		25 TU	0149	2.7
	0818	7.0			0742	6.4
	1447	2.1			1415	2.8
	2047	6.6			2008	6.1
11 TU	0314	2.5		26 W	0230	3.0
	0917	6.5			0825	6.1
	1548	2.6			1500	3.1
	2153	6.1			2057	5.8
12 W	0419	2.9		27 TH	0320	3.3
	1030	6.2			0922	5.8
	1659	2.9			1557	3.3
	2314	5.8			2205	5.6
13 TH	0536	3.1		28 F	0425	3.4
	1153	6.1			1037	5.7
	1820	2.9			1709	3.3
					2329	5.6
14 F	0041	5.9		29 SA	0543	3.4
	0658	3.0			1200	5.9
	1312	6.2			1830	3.1
	1936	2.7				
15 SA	0150	6.2		30 SU	0047	5.9
	0806	2.7			0659	3.1
	1413	6.5			1311	6.2
	2035	2.4			1938	2.7
				31 M	0148	6.4
					0801	2.6
					1409	6.7
					2033	2.2

NOVEMBER

Day	Time	m		Day	Time	m
1 TU	0239	6.9		16 W	0335	6.8
	0854	2.1			0956	2.3
	1500	7.2			1553	6.9
	2123	1.8			2211	2.2
2 W	0327	7.3		17 TH	0410	6.9
	0943	1.6			1033	2.2
	1547	7.6			1628	7.0
	2210	1.4			2246	2.1
3 TH	0412	7.7		18 F	0443	7.0
	1030	1.3			1107	2.1
	1634	7.8			1701	7.0
●	2256	1.2		O	2318	2.1
4 F	0457	7.9		19 SA	0514	7.1
	1118	1.1			1140	2.1
	1720	7.9			1733	7.0
	2342	1.1			2350	2.1
5 SA	0542	8.0		20 SU	0546	7.0
	1205	1.1			1213	2.1
	1806	7.8			1806	6.9
6 SU	0028	1.3		21 M	0023	2.2
	0628	7.9			0618	7.0
	1253	1.2			1245	2.2
	1853	7.5			1839	6.7
7 M	0116	1.6		22 TU	0056	2.4
	0715	7.6			0651	6.8
	1342	1.6			1320	2.4
	1942	7.1			1913	6.6
8 TU	0206	2.0		23 W	0131	2.5
	0806	7.1			0727	6.6
	1435	2.0			1357	2.6
	2036	6.7			1952	6.3
9 W	0259	2.4		24 TH	0211	2.7
	0903	6.7			0808	6.4
	1532	2.5			1439	2.8
	2136	6.2			2038	6.1
10 TH	0400	2.8		25 F	0258	2.9
	1008	6.3			0858	6.2
	1636	2.8			1530	2.9
	2246	5.9			2134	5.9
11 F	0508	3.1		26 SA	0353	3.1
	1120	6.1			0959	6.0
	1747	3.0			1630	3.0
					2243	5.9
12 SA	0002	5.9		27 SU	0459	3.1
	0622	3.1			1110	6.0
	1234	6.1			1741	3.0
	1858	2.9			2357	6.0
13 SU	0113	6.0		28 M	0612	3.0
	0731	2.9			1224	6.2
	1338	6.3			1853	2.7
	2000	2.7				
14 M	0209	6.3		29 TU	0106	6.3
	0827	2.7			0721	2.7
	1430	6.5			1330	6.6
	2051	2.5			1957	2.4
15 TU	0256	6.5		30 W	0205	6.7
	0916	2.5			0822	2.2
	1514	6.7			1430	7.0
	2134	2.3			2054	2.0

DECEMBER

Day	Time	m		Day	Time	m
1 TH	0300	7.2		16 F	0346	6.6
	0918	1.8			1009	2.4
	1525	7.3			1605	6.7
	2147	1.6			2222	2.3
2 F	0351	7.6		17 SA	0422	6.8
	1011	1.4			1046	2.2
	1616	7.6			1641	6.8
●	2237	1.4			2257	2.2
3 SA	0440	7.8		18 SU	0456	7.0
	1102	1.2			1121	2.1
	1706	7.7			1716	6.9
	2326	1.3		O	2332	2.1
4 SU	0529	7.9		19 M	0530	7.1
	1152	1.1			1155	2.1
	1754	7.7			1750	6.9
5 M	0015	1.3		20 TU	0006	2.1
	0616	7.9			0604	7.1
	1241	1.2			1230	2.0
	1842	7.5			1825	6.9
6 TU	0103	1.5		21 W	0040	2.1
	0704	7.7			0638	7.1
	1330	1.5			1304	2.1
	1930	7.2			1900	6.8
7 W	0151	1.8		22 TH	0116	2.2
	0752	7.3			0714	7.0
	1419	1.8			1341	2.2
	2018	6.8			1938	6.7
8 TH	0240	2.2		23 F	0155	2.3
	0842	6.9			0753	6.8
	1509	2.2			1421	2.3
	2109	6.4			2020	6.5
9 F	0332	2.6		24 SA	0238	2.5
	0935	6.5			0837	6.6
	1602	2.6			1506	2.5
	2205	6.1			2107	6.3
10 SA	0429	2.9		25 SU	0327	2.7
	1034	6.2			0927	6.4
	1701	2.9			1558	2.7
	2308	5.9			2204	6.2
11 SU	0533	3.1		26 M	0423	2.8
	1139	6.0			1028	6.2
	1805	3.1			1700	2.8
					2311	6.1
12 M	0017	5.8		27 TU	0530	2.9
	0642	3.2			1139	6.2
	1248	6.0			1810	2.8
	1912	3.1				
13 TU	0125	5.9		28 W	0024	6.2
	0747	3.0			0643	2.7
	1350	6.1			1255	6.3
	2012	2.9			1923	2.6
14 W	0220	6.2		29 TH	0134	6.5
	0842	2.8			0754	2.4
	1442	6.3			1405	6.6
	2101	2.7			2029	2.3
15 TH	0306	6.4		30 F	0238	6.9
	0928	2.6			0858	2.0
	1526	6.5			1508	7.0
	2144	2.5			2129	1.9
				31 SA	0335	7.3
					0957	1.6
					1604	7.3
					2223	1.6

TIDAL STREAM CHARTS - ENGLISH CHANNEL

Based on HW DOVER   indicate weak stream ⟶ indicate strong stream ⟶ rates shown in 1/10th knot

5 HOURS BEFORE HW DOVER	Date	Ship's time	Ship's time	Date	Ship's time	Ship's time

(Tidal stream chart of the English Channel — 5 hours before HW Dover, with labelled locations including Milford Haven, Swansea, Cardiff, Avonmouth, Watchet, Barnstaple, Exmouth, Portland, Poole, Southampton, Portsmouth, Littlehampton, Shoreham, Newhaven, Dover, Chatham, Boulogne, Dieppe, Le Havre, Cherbourg, Alderney, Guernsey, Jersey, St Helier, St Malo, Tréguier, L'Aberwrac'h, Morlaix, Brest, I d'Ouessant, Falmouth, Devonport, Eddystone, Scilly Is, Seven Stones, Wolf Rk, Bann Sh. Chart references NP 256, NP 249, NP 233, NP 251, NP 337, NP 267, NP 264.)

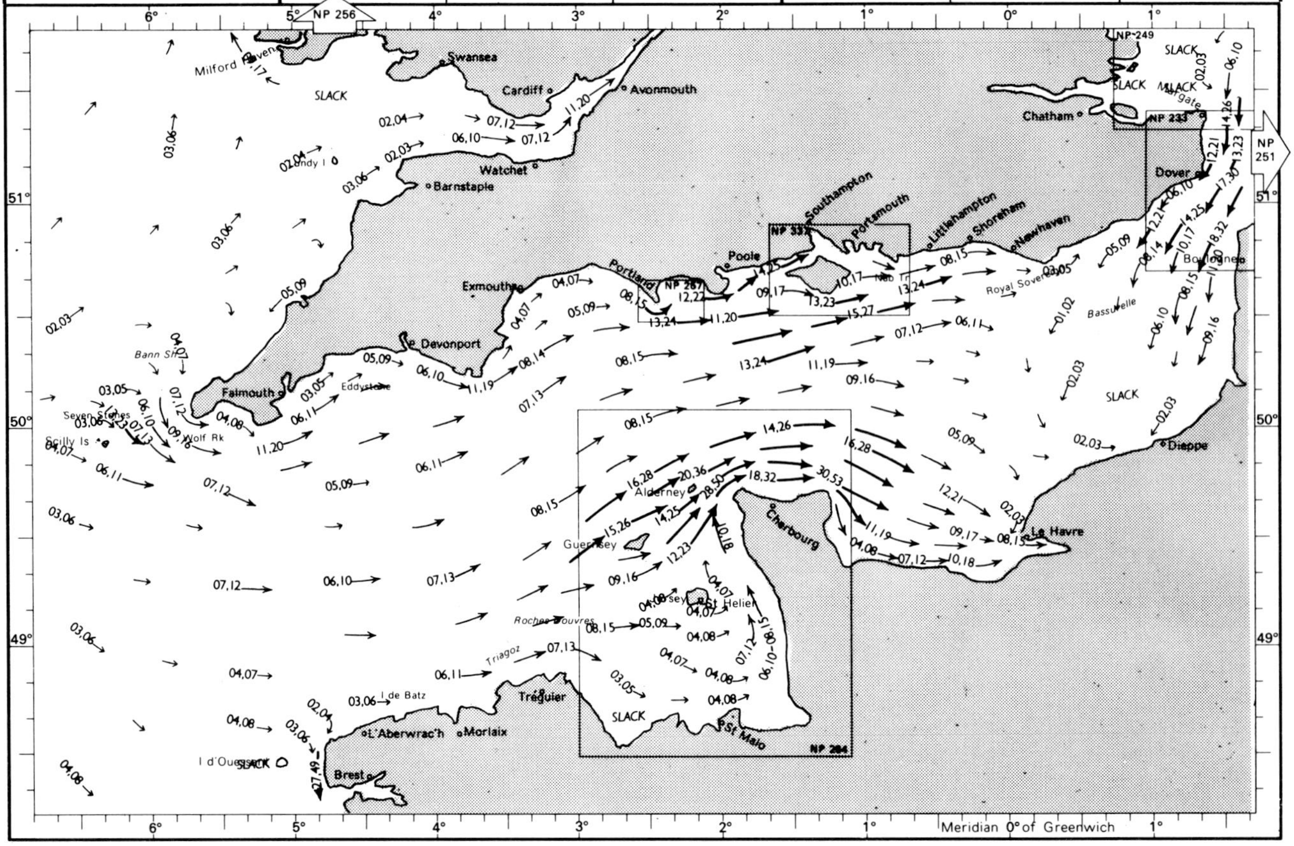

4 HOURS BEFORE HW DOVER	Date	Ship's time	Ship's time	Date	Ship's time	Ship's time

(Tidal stream chart of the English Channel — 4 hours before HW Dover, with the same labelled locations and chart references.)

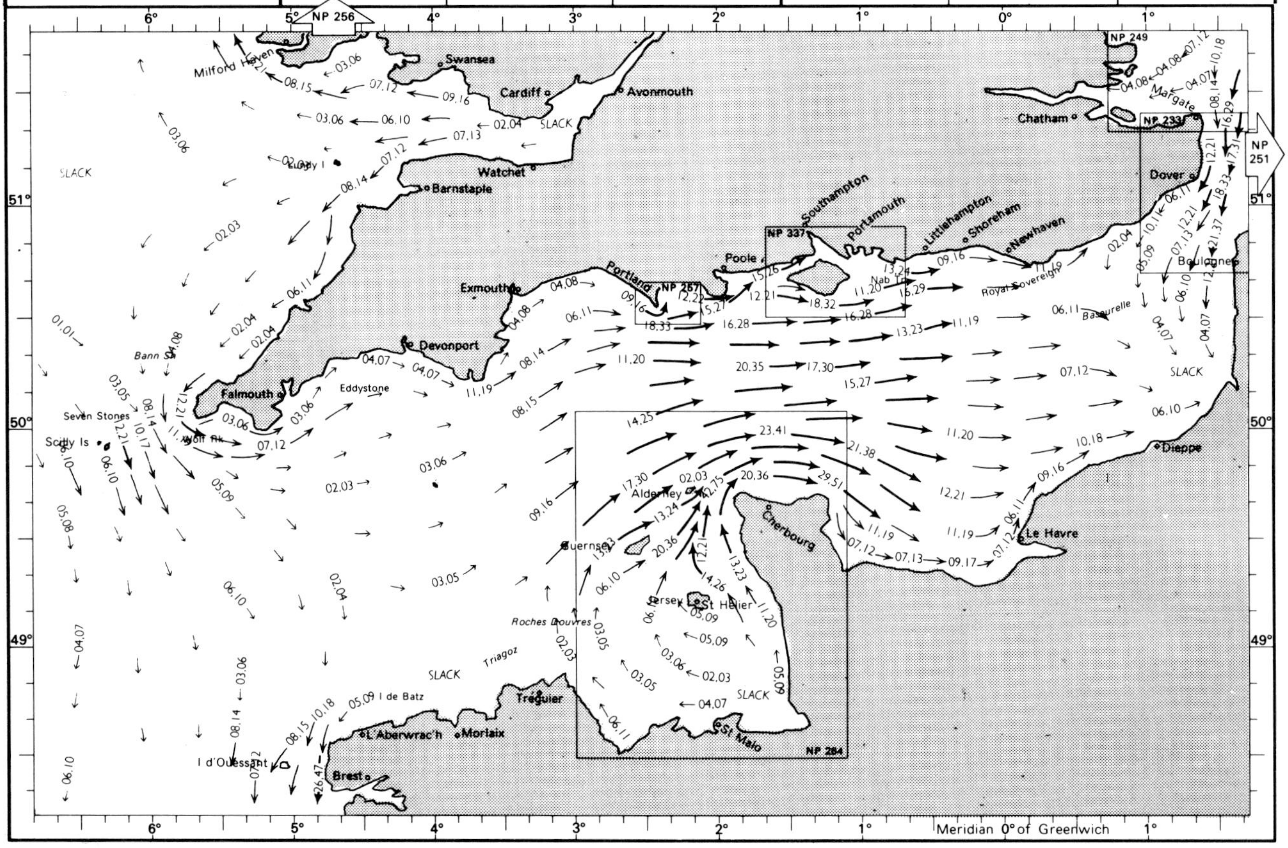

85

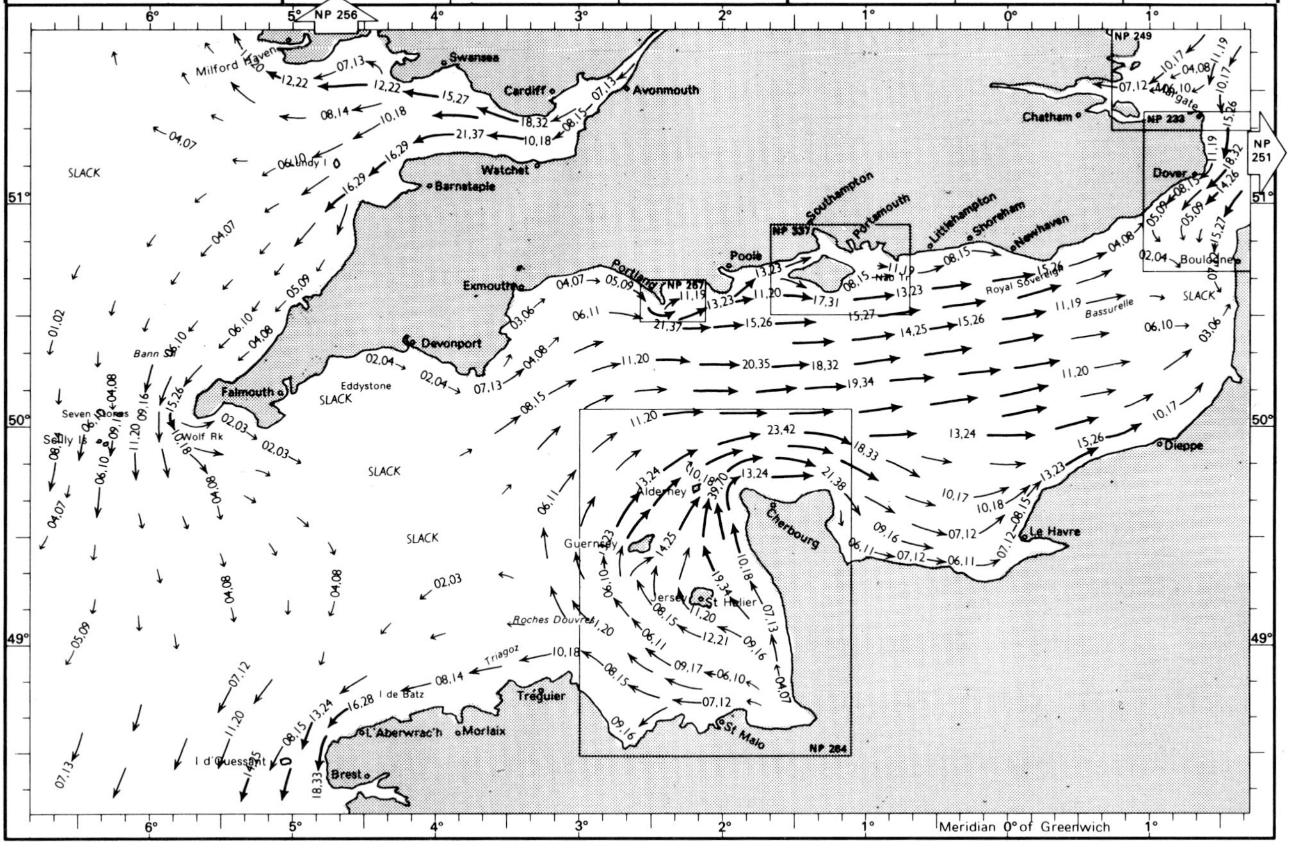

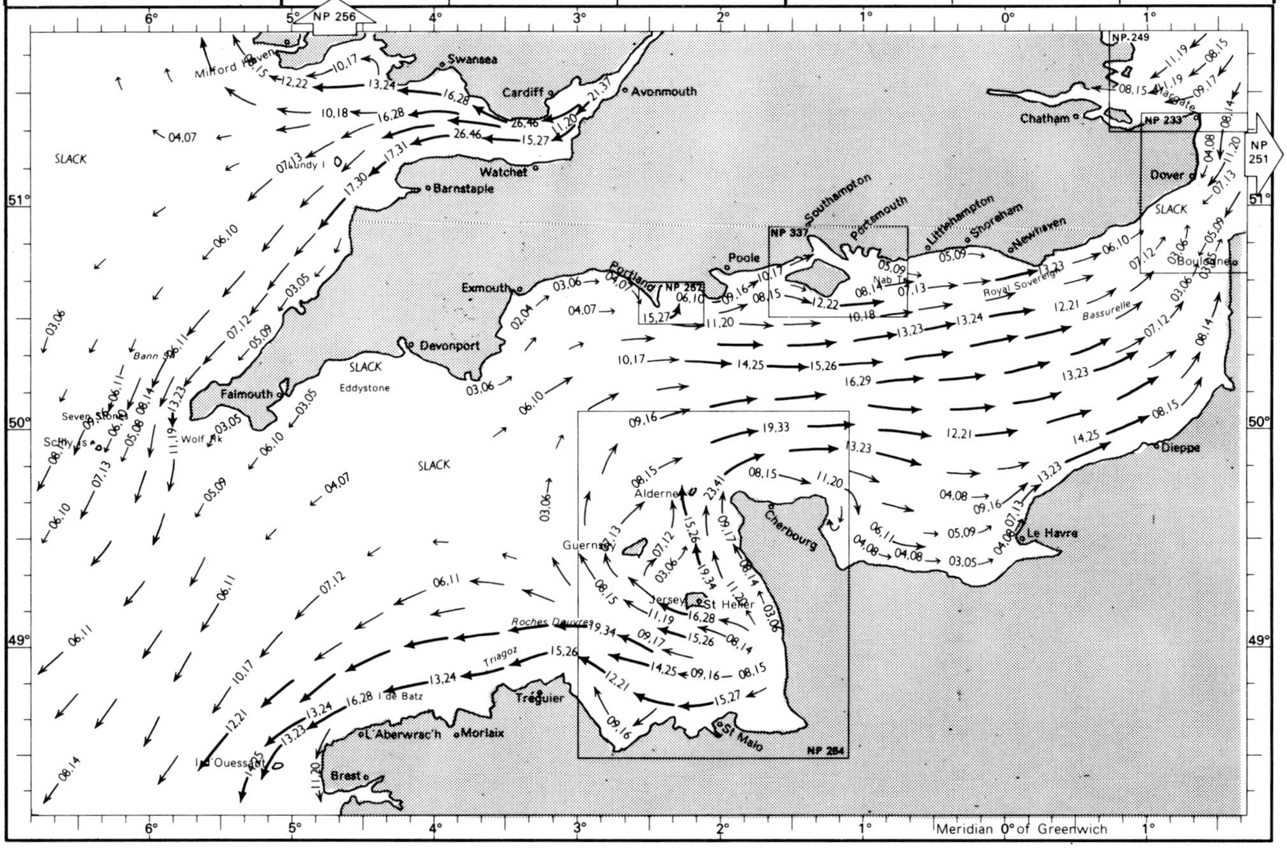

1 HOUR BEFORE HW DOVER	Date	Ship's time	Ship's time	Date	Ship's time	Ship's time

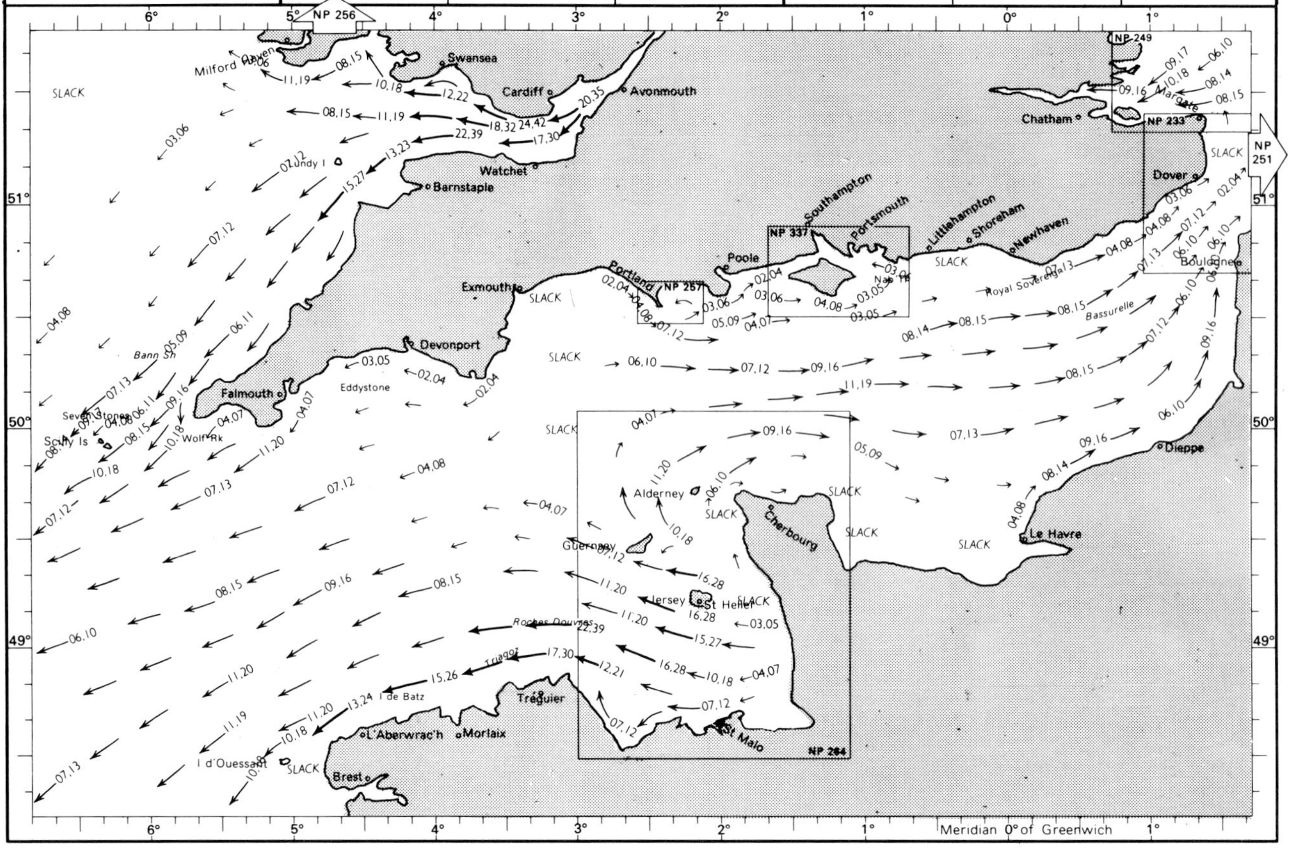

HW DOVER	Date	Ship's time	Ship's time	Date	Ship's time	Ship's time

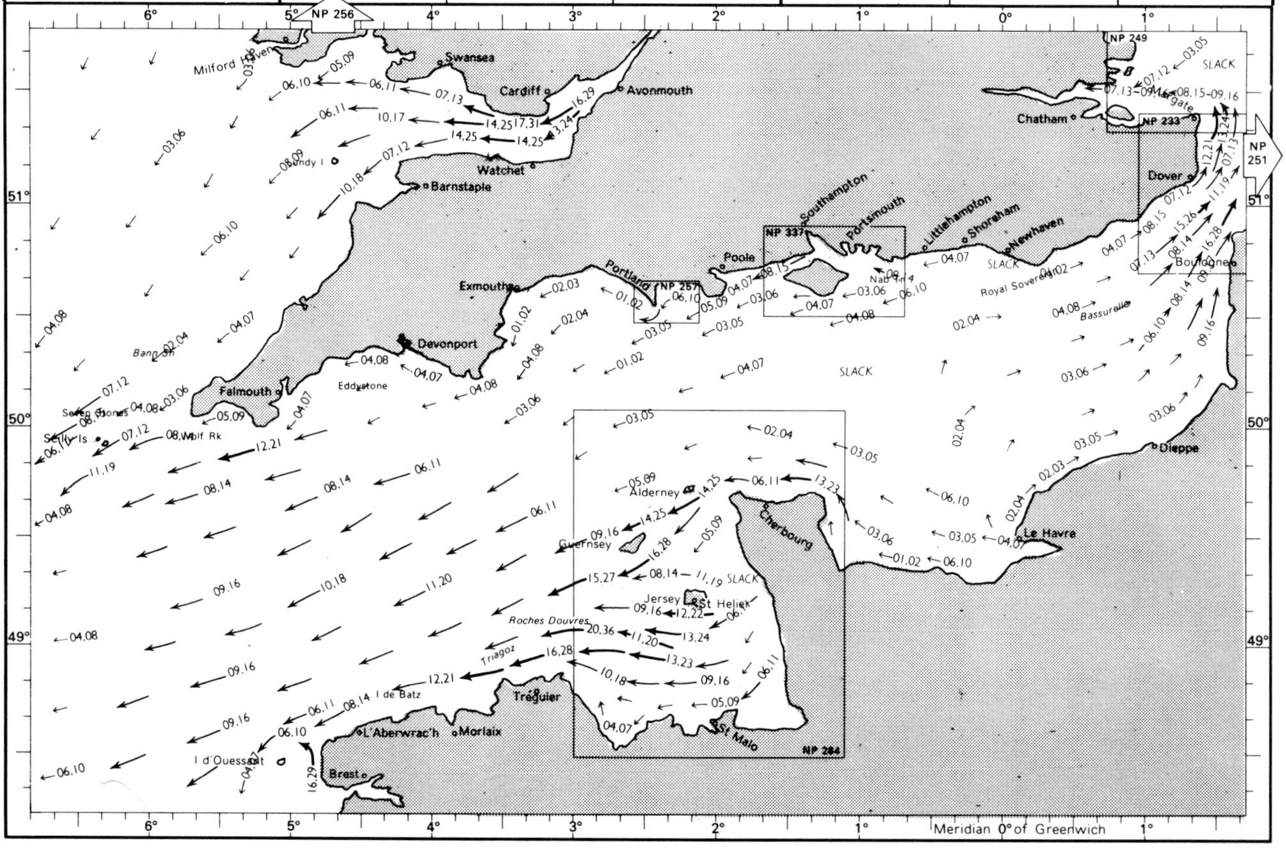

1 HOUR AFTER HW DOVER	Date	Ship's time	Ship's time	Date	Ship's time	Ship's time

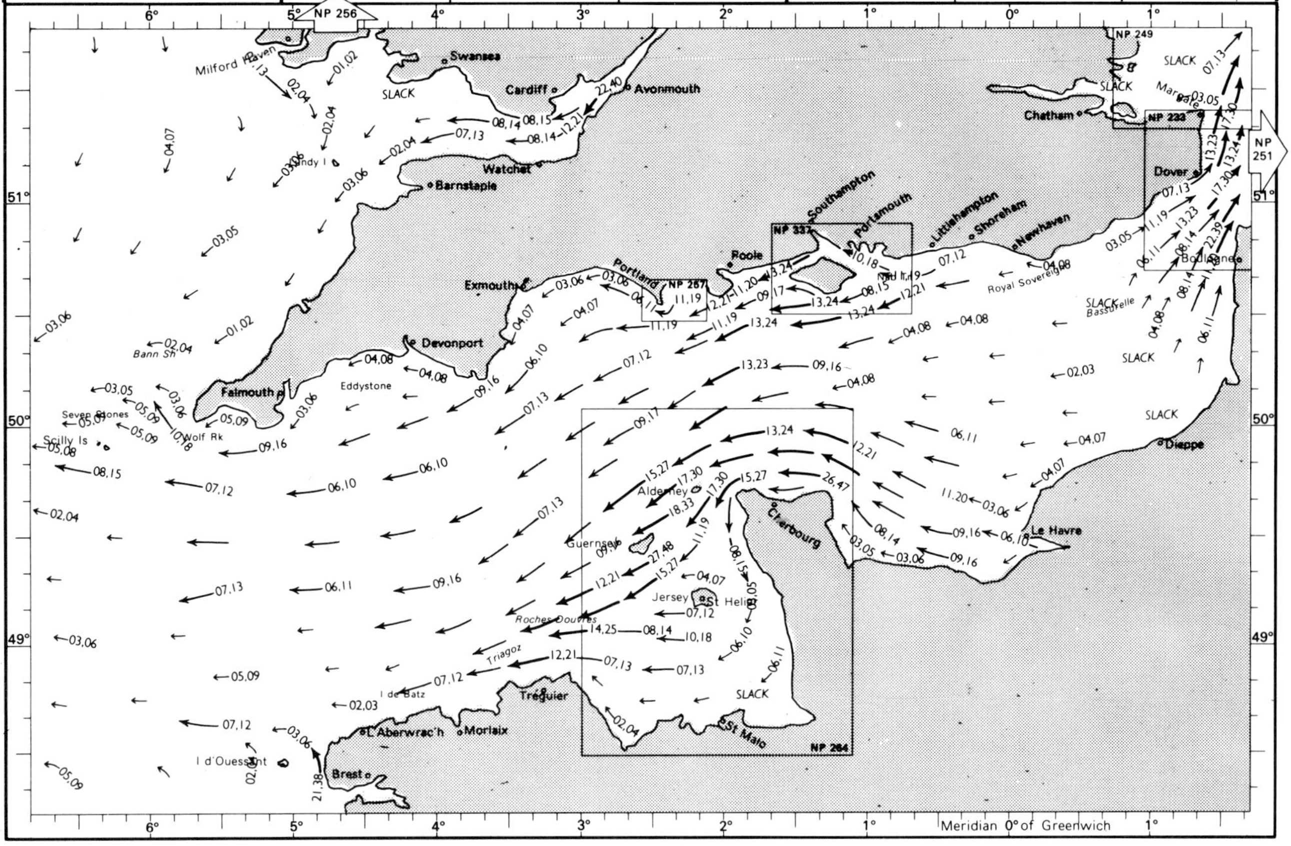

NP 256
NP 249
NP 233
NP 251
NP 337
NP 257
NP 264
Milford Haven
Swansea
Cardiff
Avonmouth
Lundy I
Watchet
Barnstaple
SLACK
Chatham
Margate
Dover
Boulogne
Southampton
Portsmouth
Littlehampton
Shoreham
Newhaven
Poole
Portland
Exmouth
Royal Sovereign
Bassurelle
Devonport
Bann Sh
Falmouth
Eddystone
Seven Stones
Scilly Is
Wolf Rk
Dieppe
Alderney
Cherbourg
Le Havre
Guernsey
Jersey
St Helier
Roches Douvres
Triagoz
I de Batz
Treguier
L'Aberwrac'h
Morlaix
St Malo
I d'Ouessant
Brest
Meridian 0° of Greenwich

2 HOURS AFTER HW DOVER	Date	Ship's time	Ship's time	Date	Ship's time	Ship's time

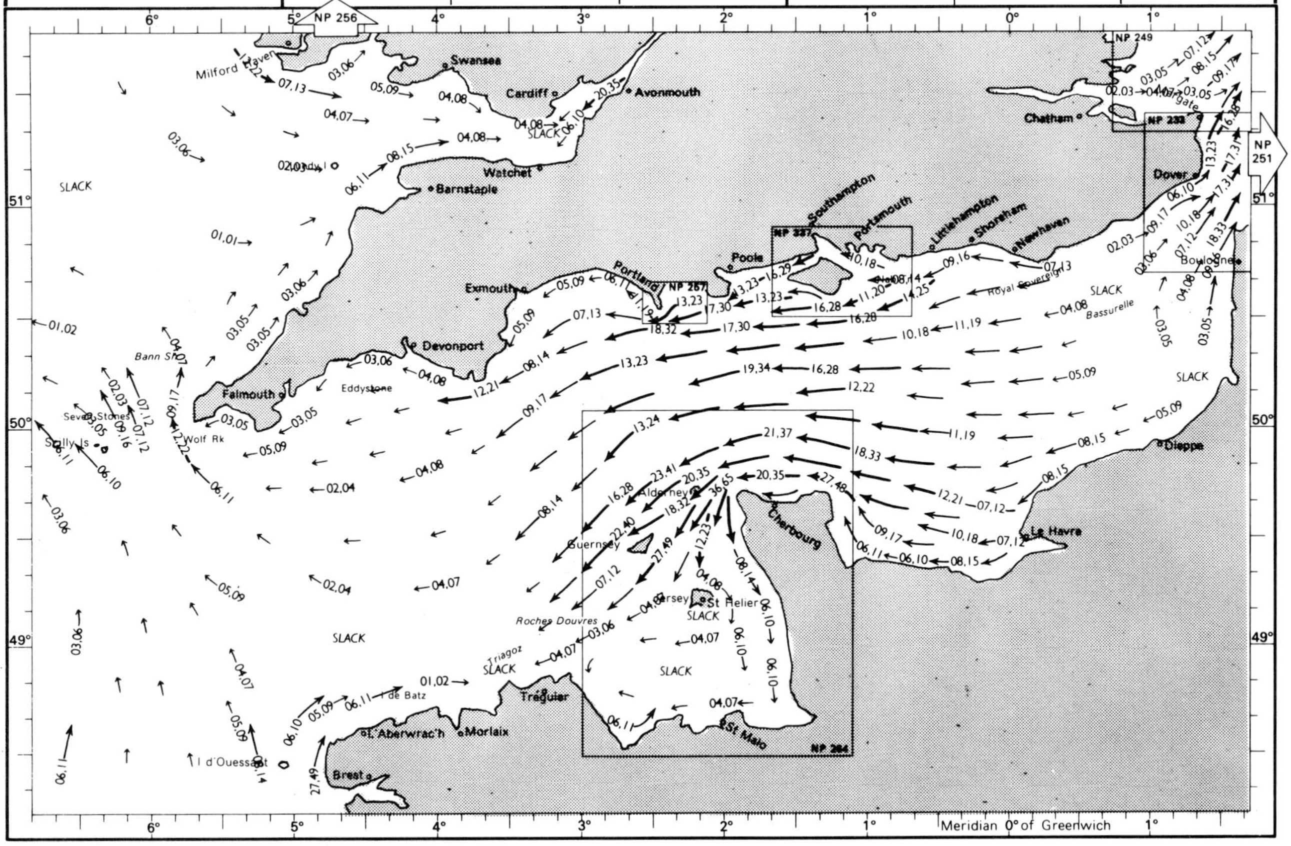

NP 256
NP 249
NP 233
NP 251
NP 337
NP 257
NP 264
Milford Haven
Swansea
Cardiff
Avonmouth
Lundy I
Watchet
Barnstaple
SLACK
Chatham
Margate
Dover
Boulogne
Southampton
Portsmouth
Littlehampton
Shoreham
Newhaven
Poole
Portland
Exmouth
Royal Sovereign
Bassurelle
Devonport
Bann Sh
Falmouth
Eddystone
Seven Stones
Scilly Is
Wolf Rk
Dieppe
Alderney
Cherbourg
Le Havre
Guernsey
Jersey
St Helier
Roches Douvres
Triagoz
I de Batz
Treguier
L'Aberwrac'h
Morlaix
St Malo
I d'Ouessant
Brest
Meridian 0° of Greenwich

3 HOURS AFTER HW DOVER	Date	Ship's time	Ship's time	Date	Ship's time	Ship's time

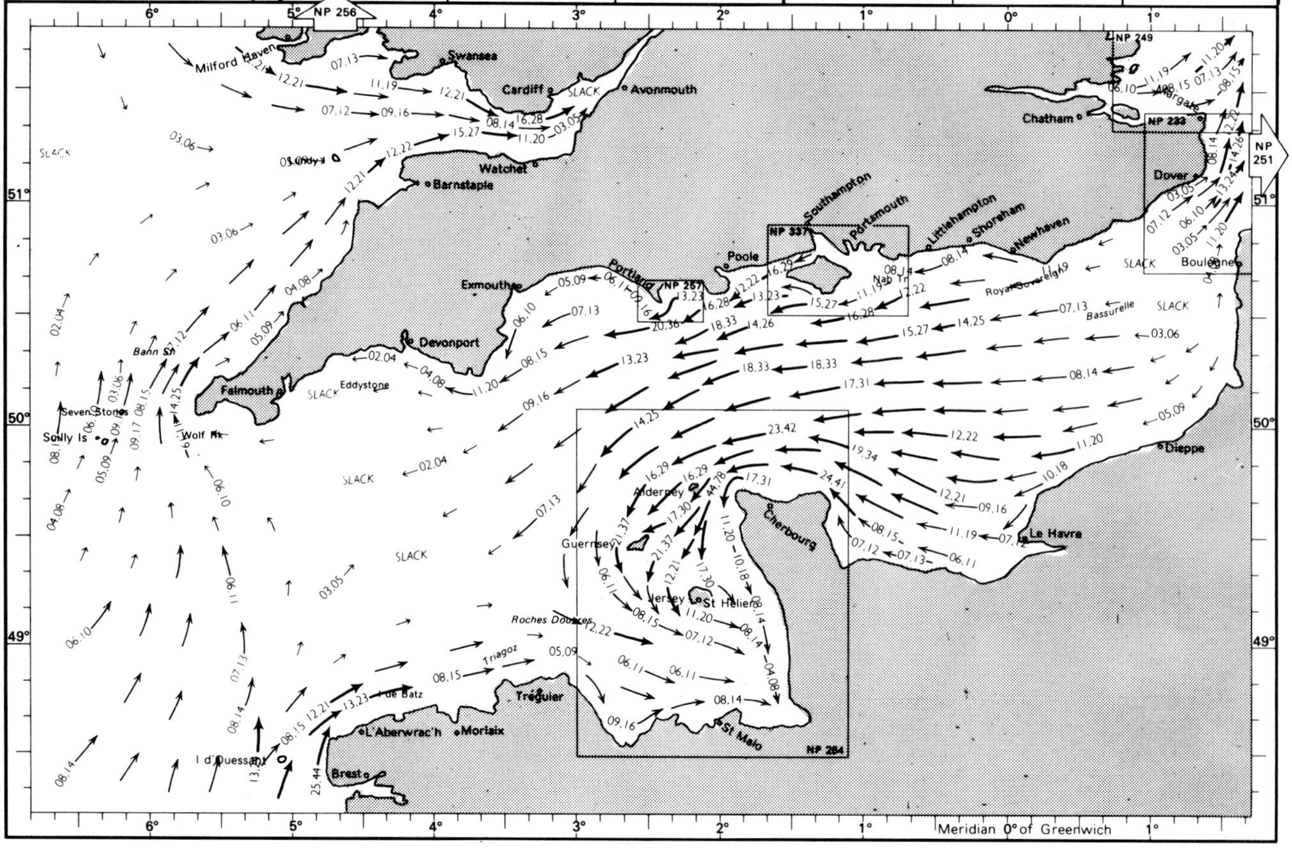

4 HOURS AFTER HW DOVER	Date	Ship's time	Ship's time	Date	Ship's time	Ship's time

88

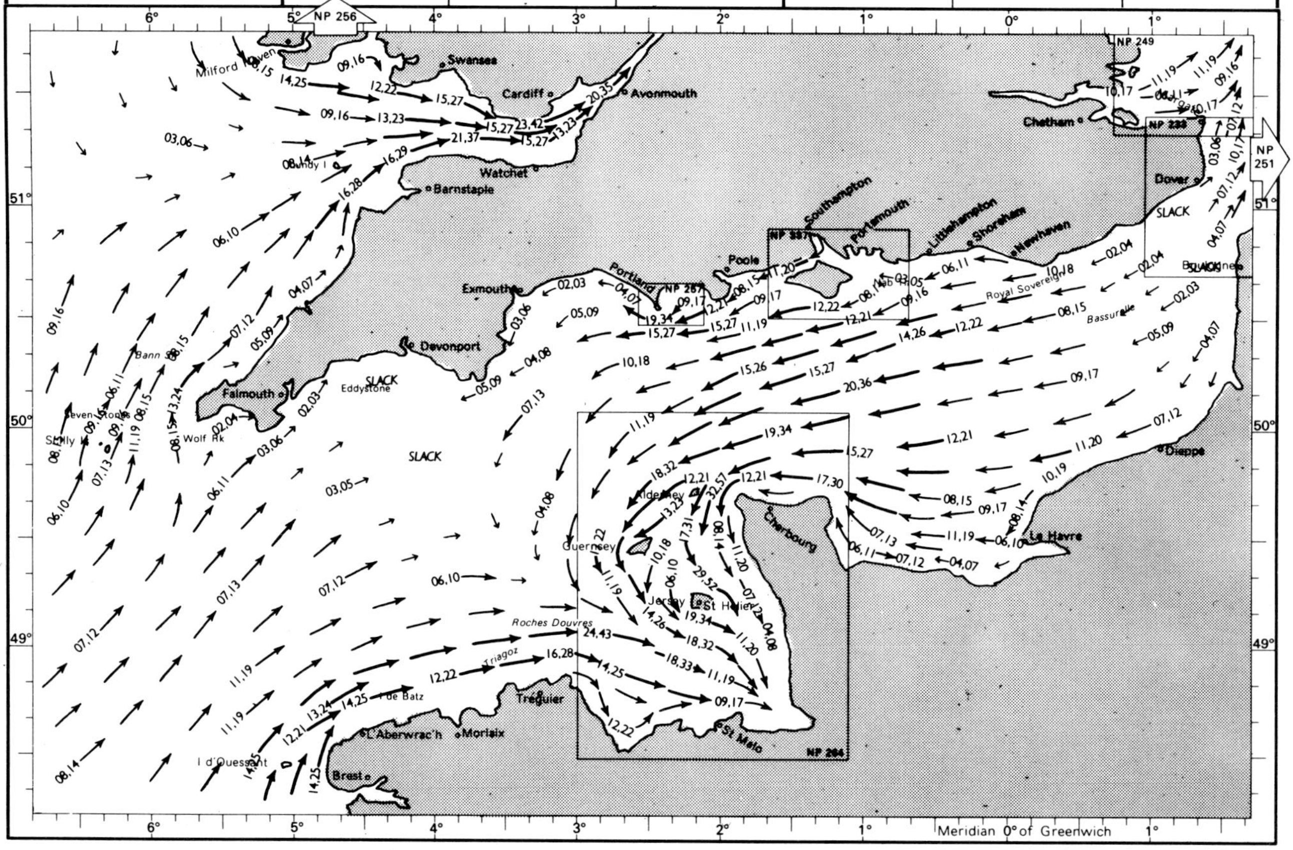

5 HOURS AFTER HW DOVER	Date	Ship's time	Ship's time	Date	Ship's time	Ship's time

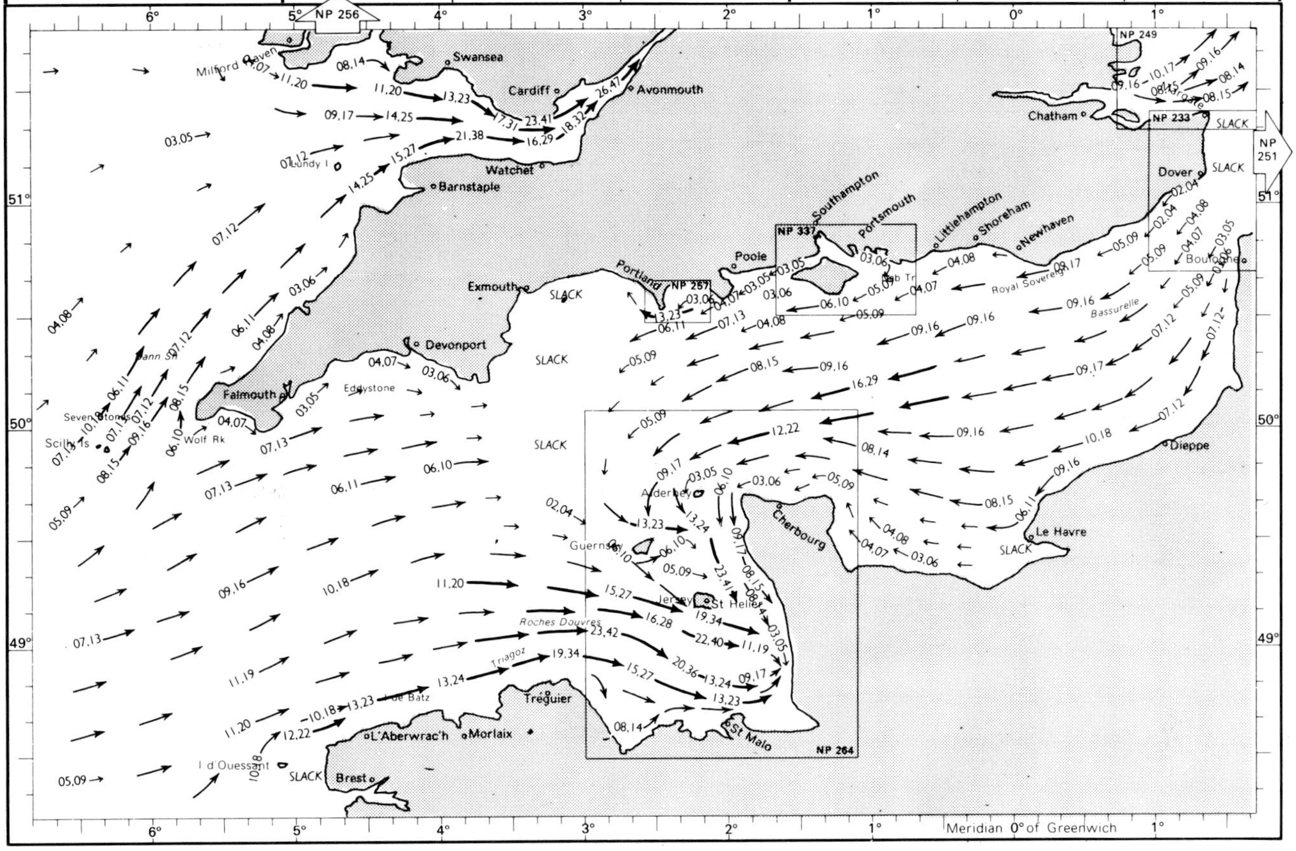

6 HOURS AFTER HW DOVER	Date	Ship's time	Ship's time	Date.	Ship's time	Ship's time

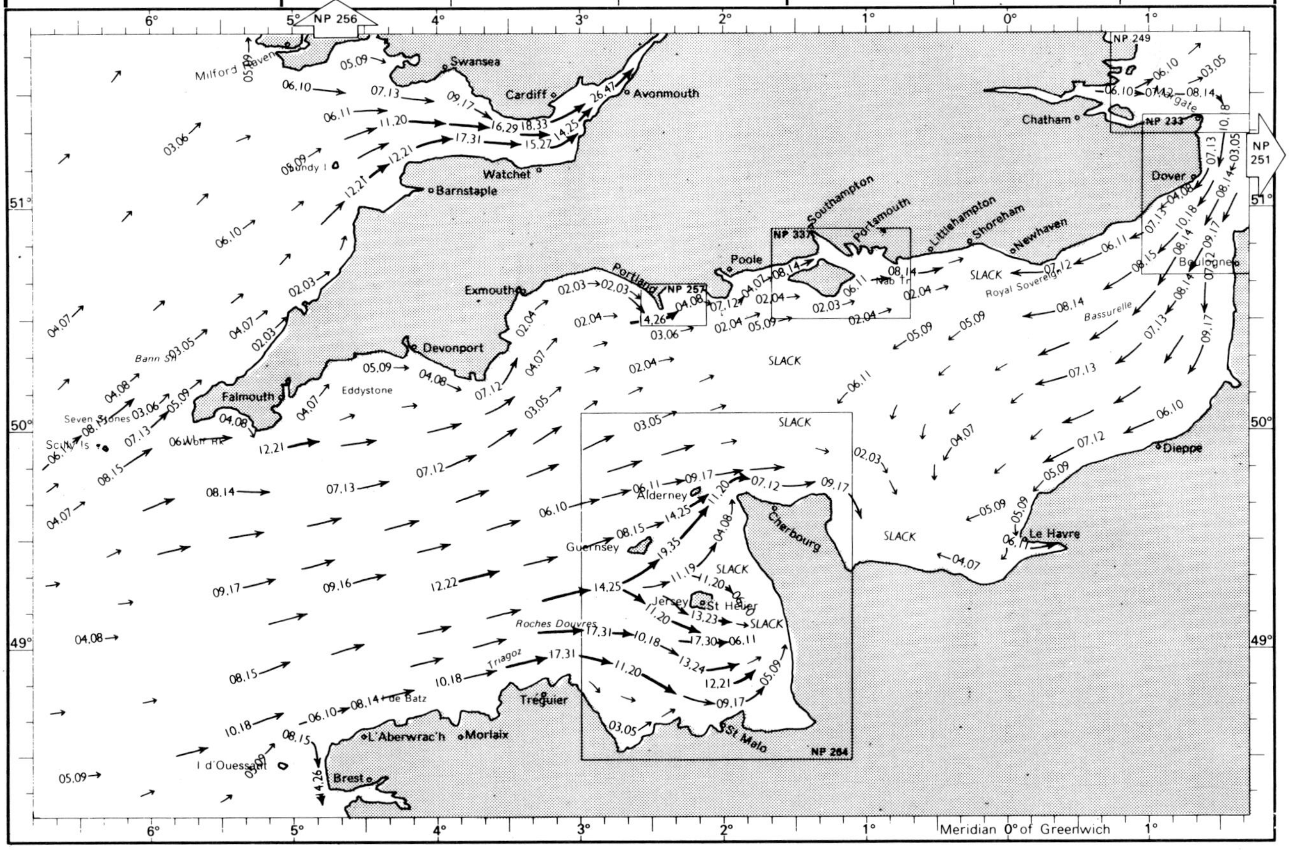

TIDAL STREAM CHARTS - SOLENT

indicate weak stream ⟶ indicate strong stream ⟶ rates shown in 1/10th knot

5h BEFORE HW PORTSMOUTH 4h 40min BEFORE HW DOVER	Date	Ship's time	Ship's time	Date	Ship's time	Ship's time

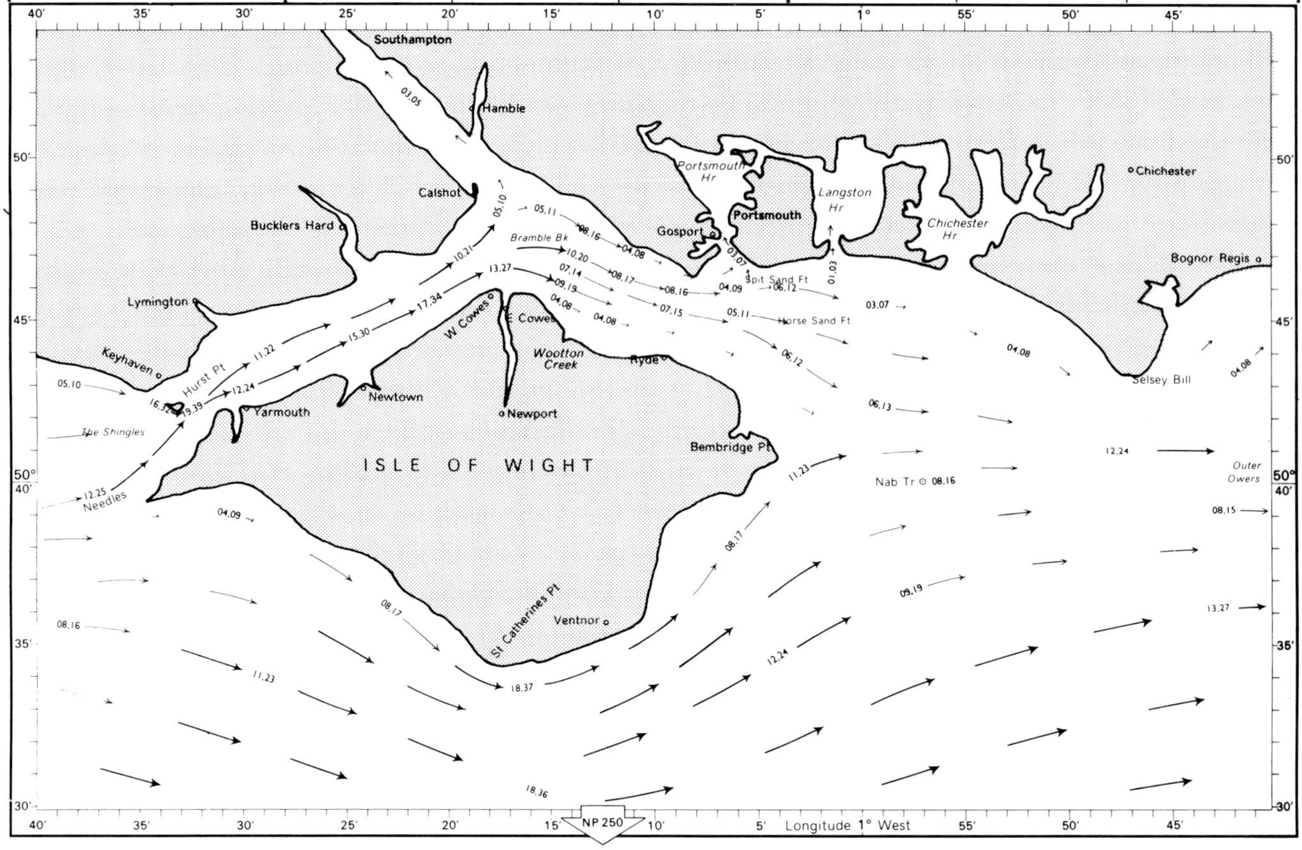

4h BEFORE HW PORTSMOUTH 3h 40min BEFORE HW DOVER	Date	Ship's time	Ship's time	Date	Ship's time	Ship's time

90

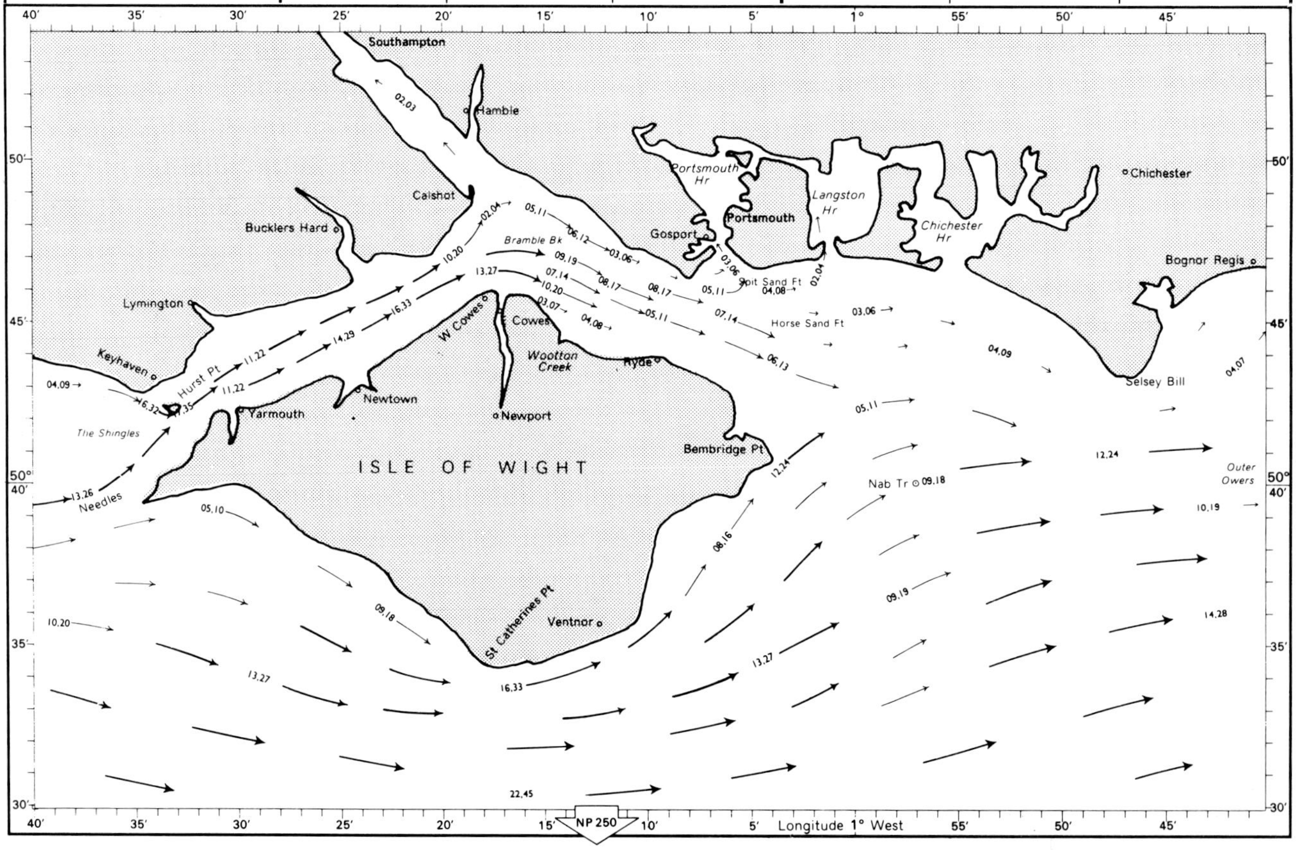

91

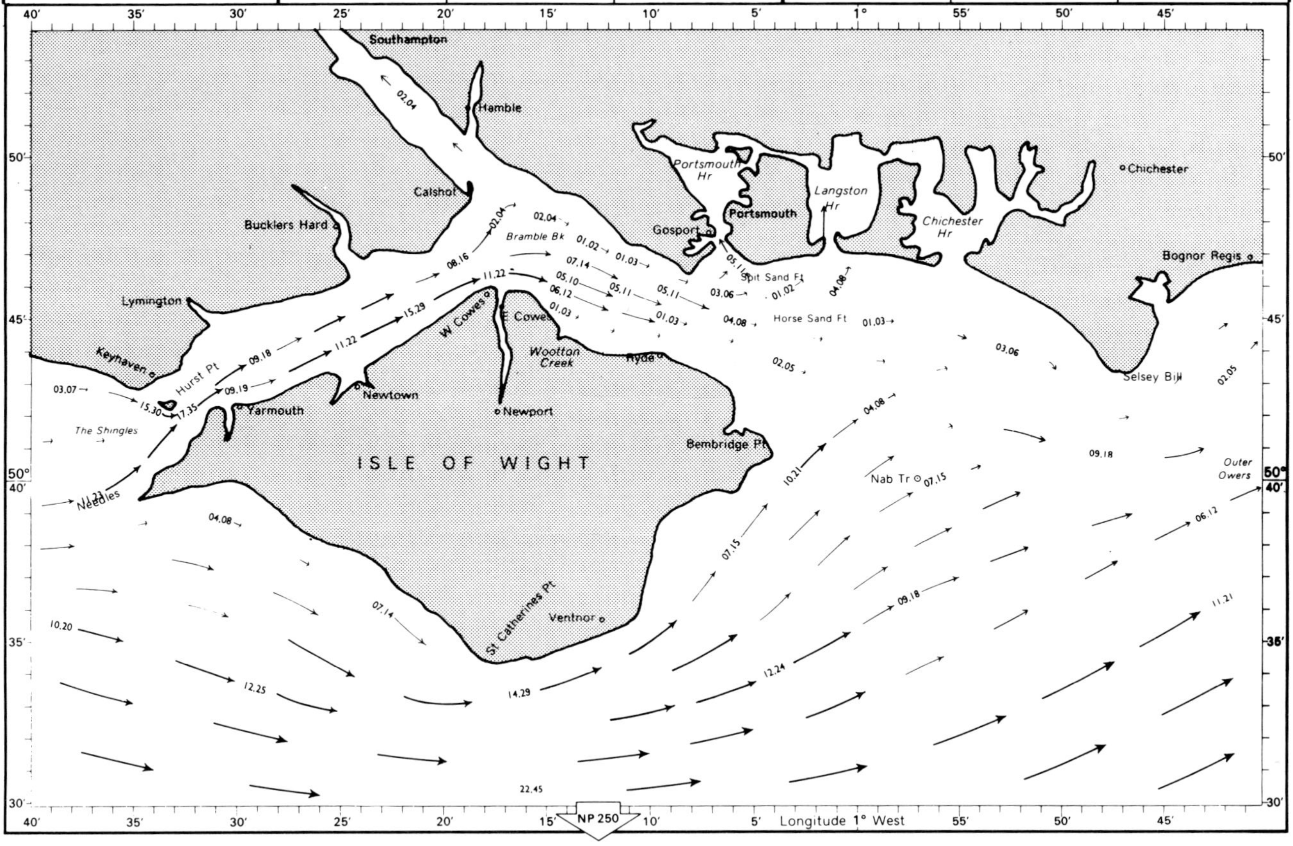

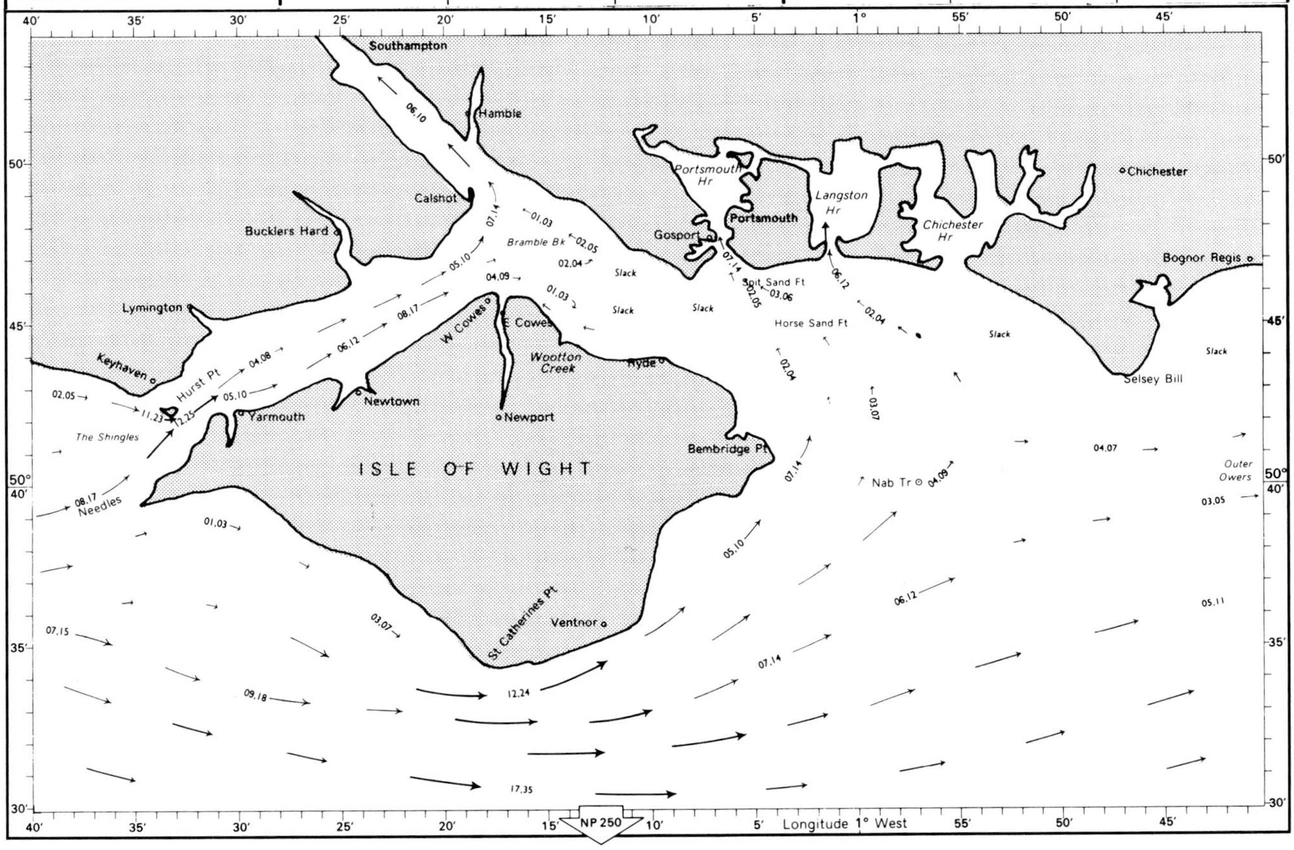

1h BEFORE HW PORTSMOUTH 0h 40min BEFORE HW DOVER	Date	Ship's time	Ship's time	Date	Ship's time	Ship's time

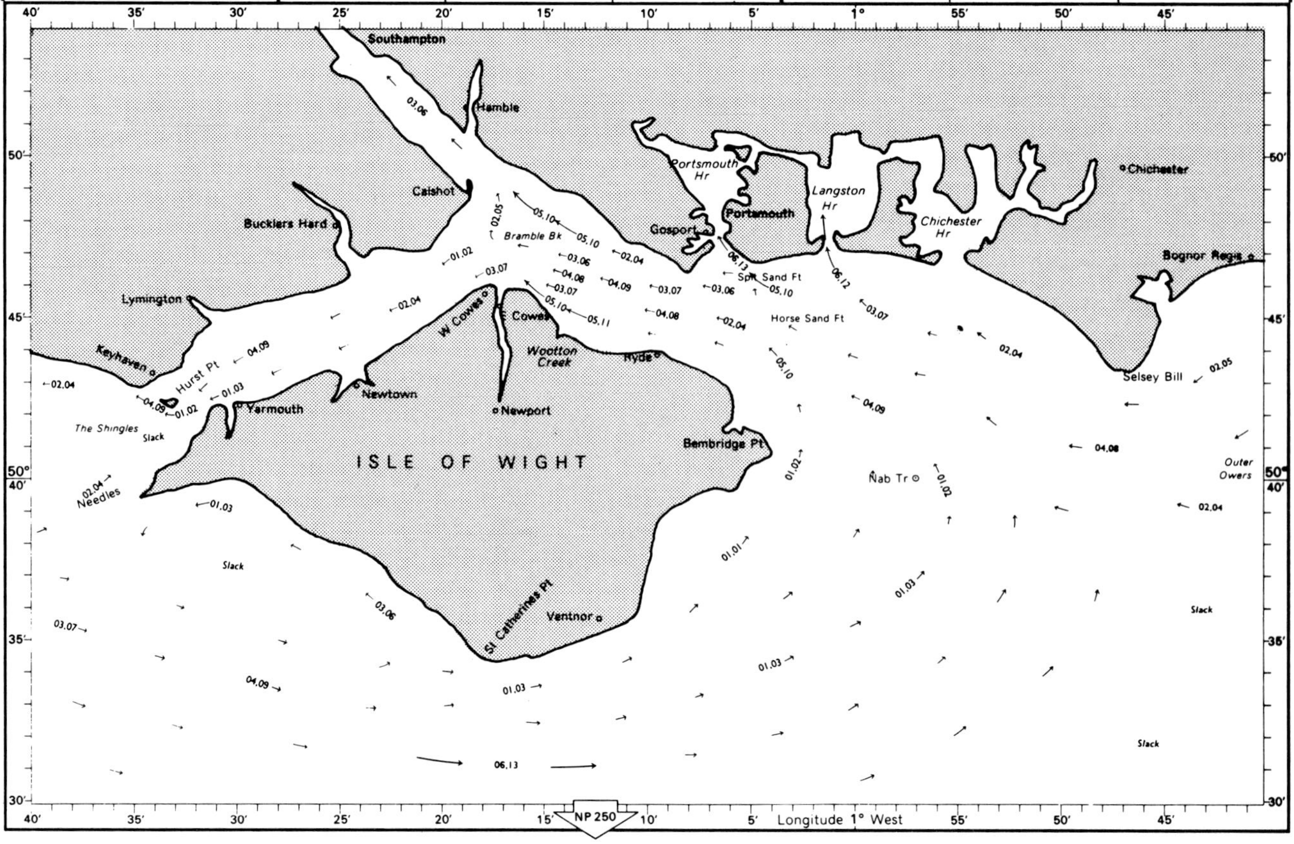

HW PORTSMOUTH 0h 20min AFTER HW DOVER	Date	Ship's time	Ship's time	Date	Ship's time	Ship's time

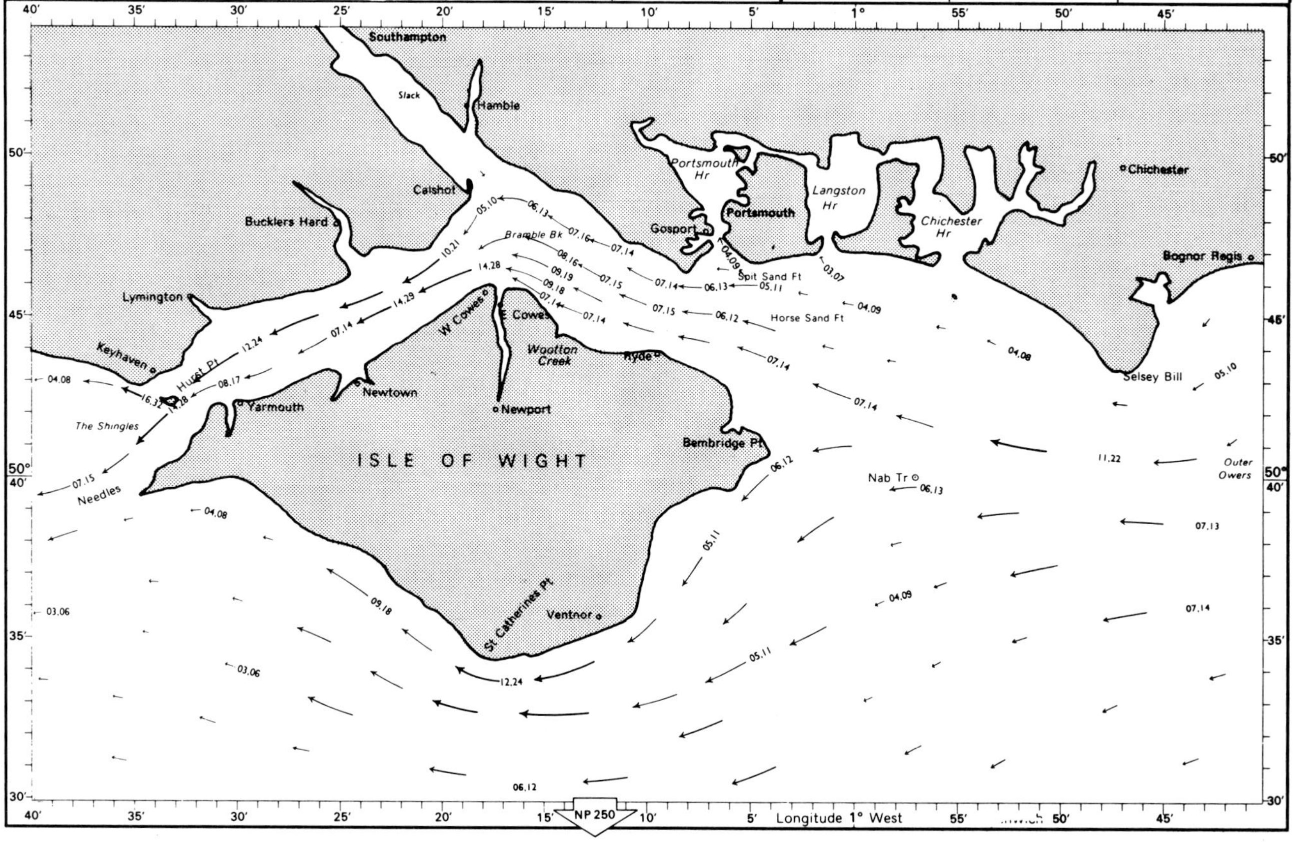

1h AFTER HW PORTSMOUTH 1h 20min AFTER HW DOVER	Date	Ship's time	Ship's time	Date	Ship's time	Ship's time

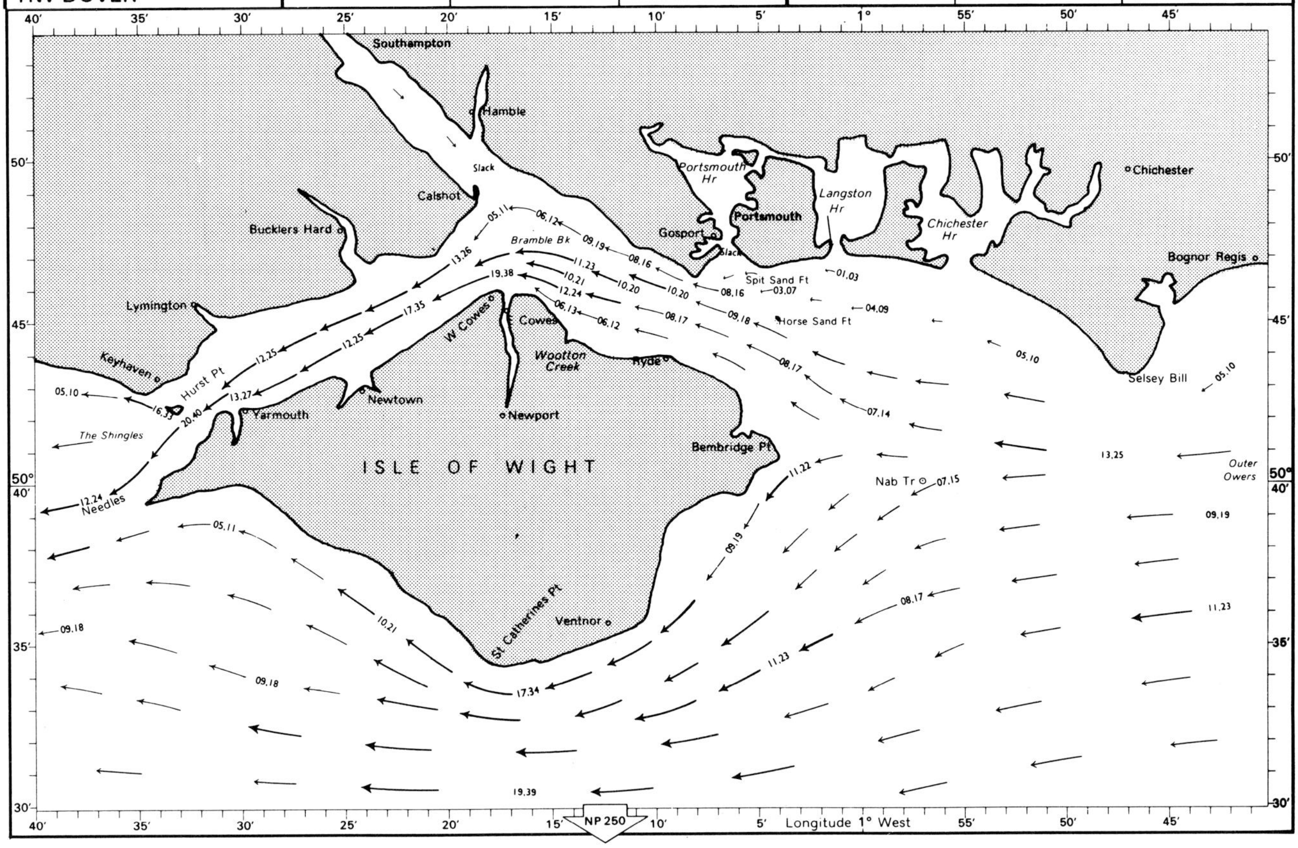

40′
35′
30′
25′
20′
15′
10′
5′
1°
55′
50′
45′
50°
Southampton
Hamble
Slack
Calshot
Bucklers Hard
Portsmouth Hr
Portsmouth
Gosport
Langston Hr
Chichester Hr
Chichester
Bognor Regis
Bramble Bk
Spit Sand Ft
Horse Sand Ft
Lymington
Keyhaven
Hurst Pt
The Shingles
W Cowes
Cowes
Wootton Creek
Ryde
Newtown
Yarmouth
Newport
ISLE OF WIGHT
Bembridge Pt
Nab Tr
Selsey Bill
Outer Owers
Needles
St Catherines Pt
Ventnor
NP 250
Longitude 1° West

2h AFTER HW PORTSMOUTH 2h 20min AFTER HW DOVER	Date	Ship's time	Ship's time	Date	Ship's time	Ship's time

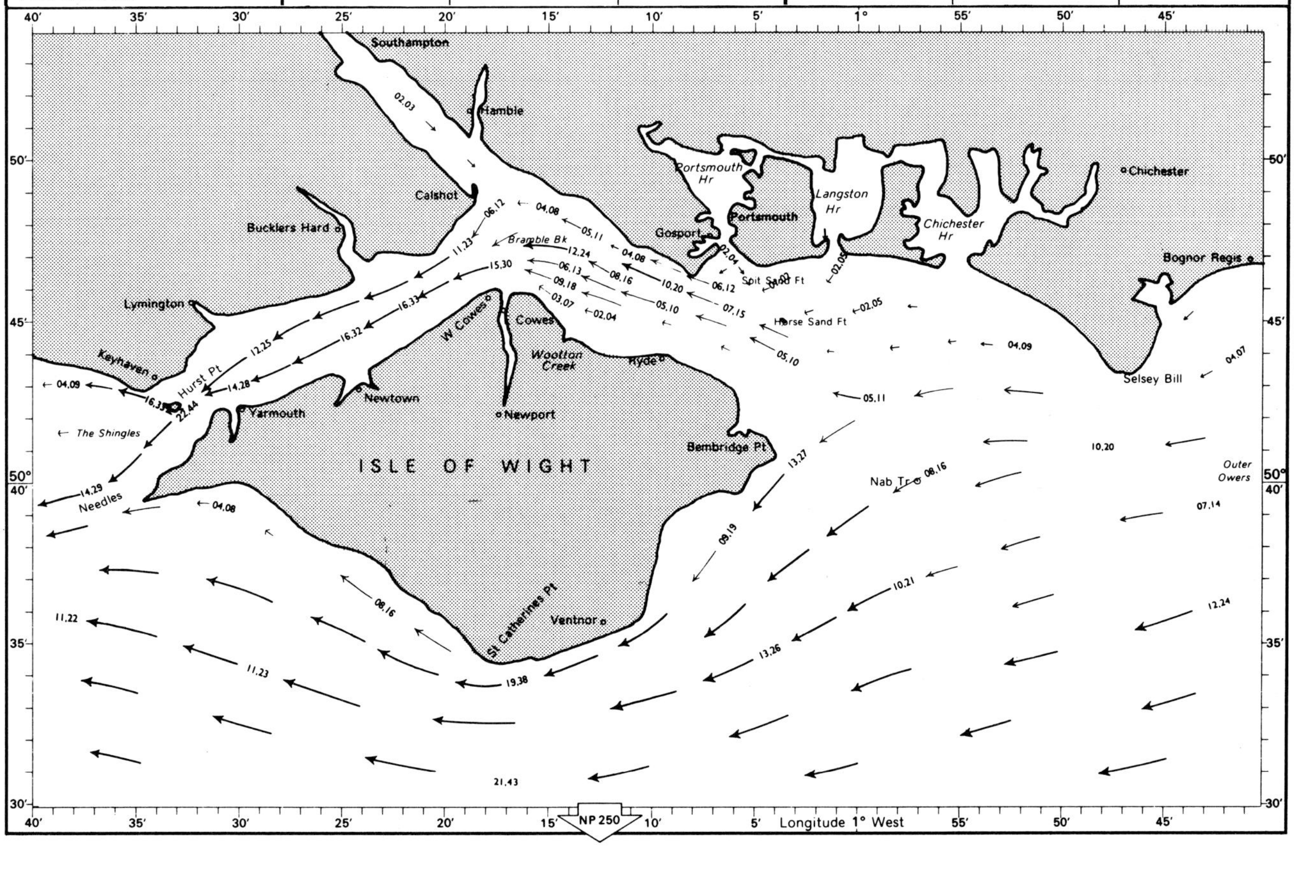

40′
35′
30′
25′
20′
15′
10′
5′
1°
55′
50′
45′
50°
Southampton
Hamble
Calshot
Bucklers Hard
Portsmouth Hr
Portsmouth
Gosport
Langston Hr
Chichester Hr
Chichester
Bognor Regis
Bramble Bk
Spit Sand Ft
Horse Sand Ft
Lymington
Keyhaven
Hurst Pt
The Shingles
W Cowes
Cowes
Wootton Creek
Ryde
Newtown
Yarmouth
Newport
ISLE OF WIGHT
Bembridge Pt
Nab Tr
Selsey Bill
Outer Owers
Needles
St Catherines Pt
Ventnor
NP 250
Longitude 1° West

3h AFTER HW PORTSMOUTH 3h 20min AFTER HW DOVER	Date	Ship's time	Ship's time	Date	Ship's time	Ship's time

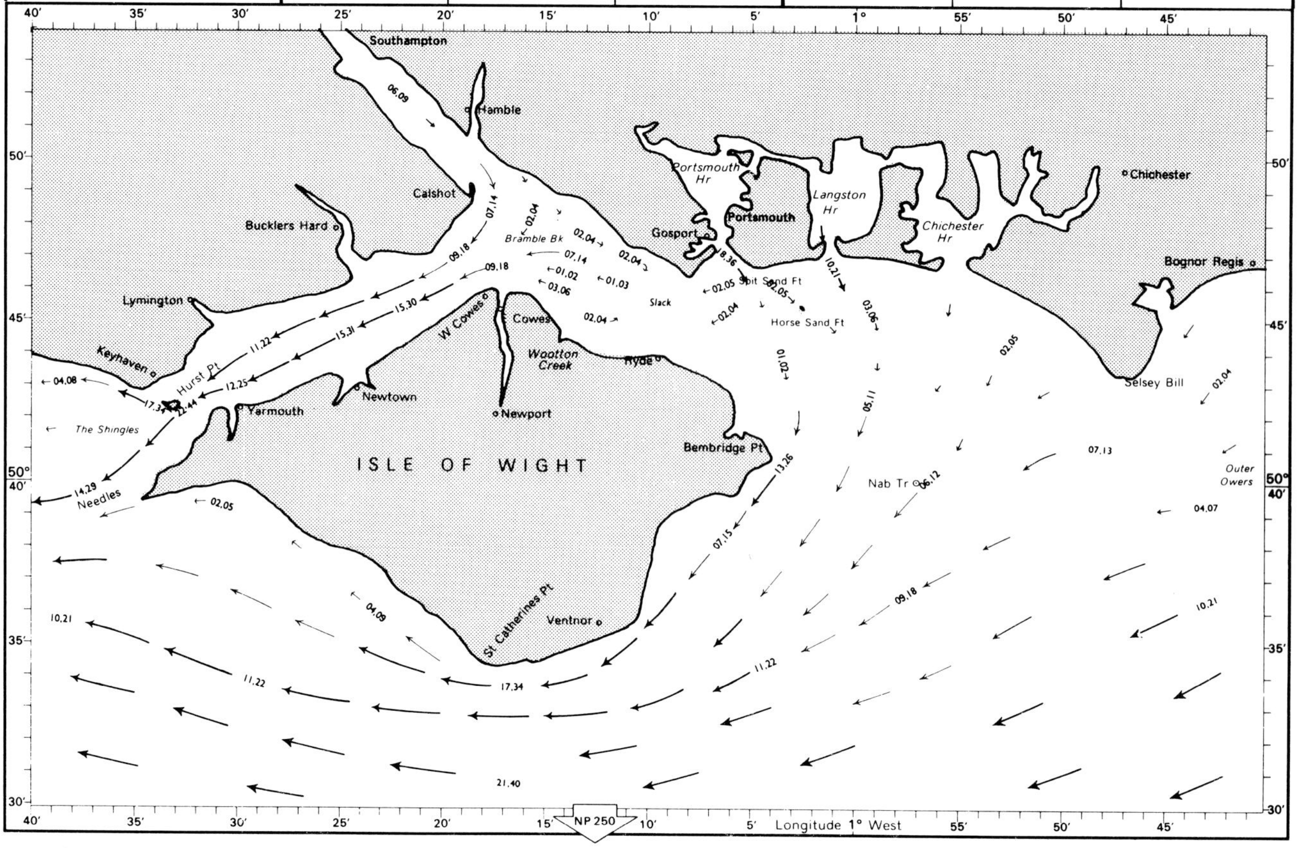

4h AFTER HW PORTSMOUTH 4h 20min AFTER HW DOVER	Date	Ship's time	Ship's time	Date	Ship's time	Ship's time

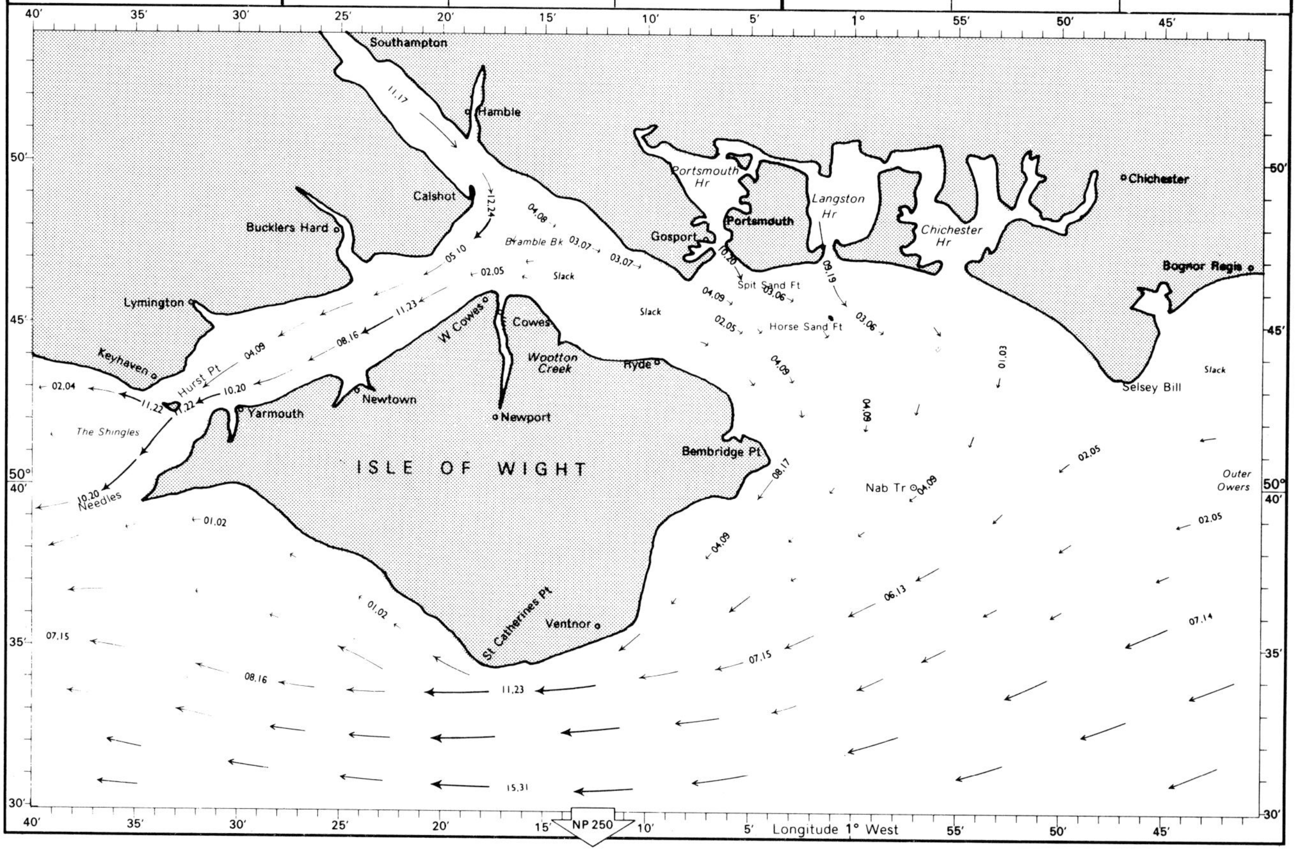

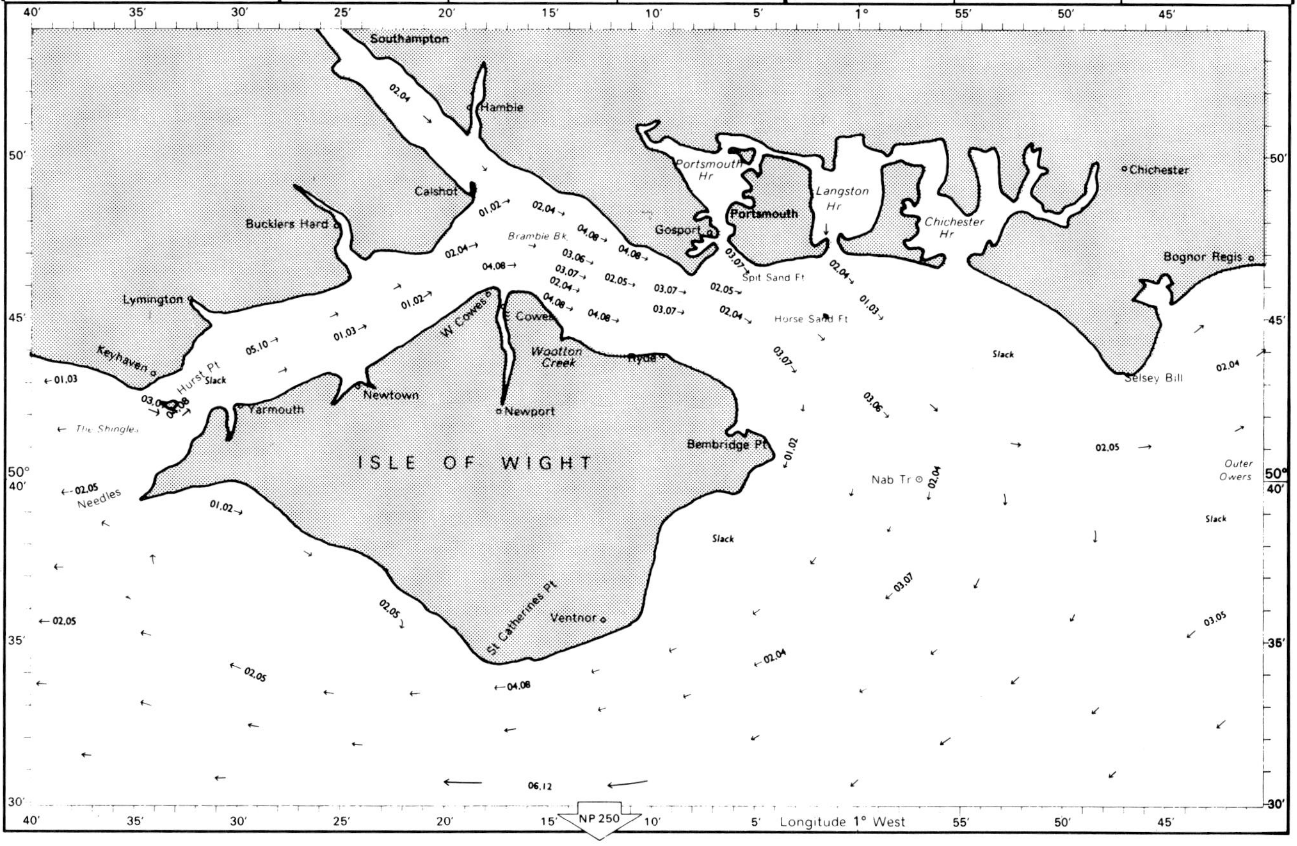

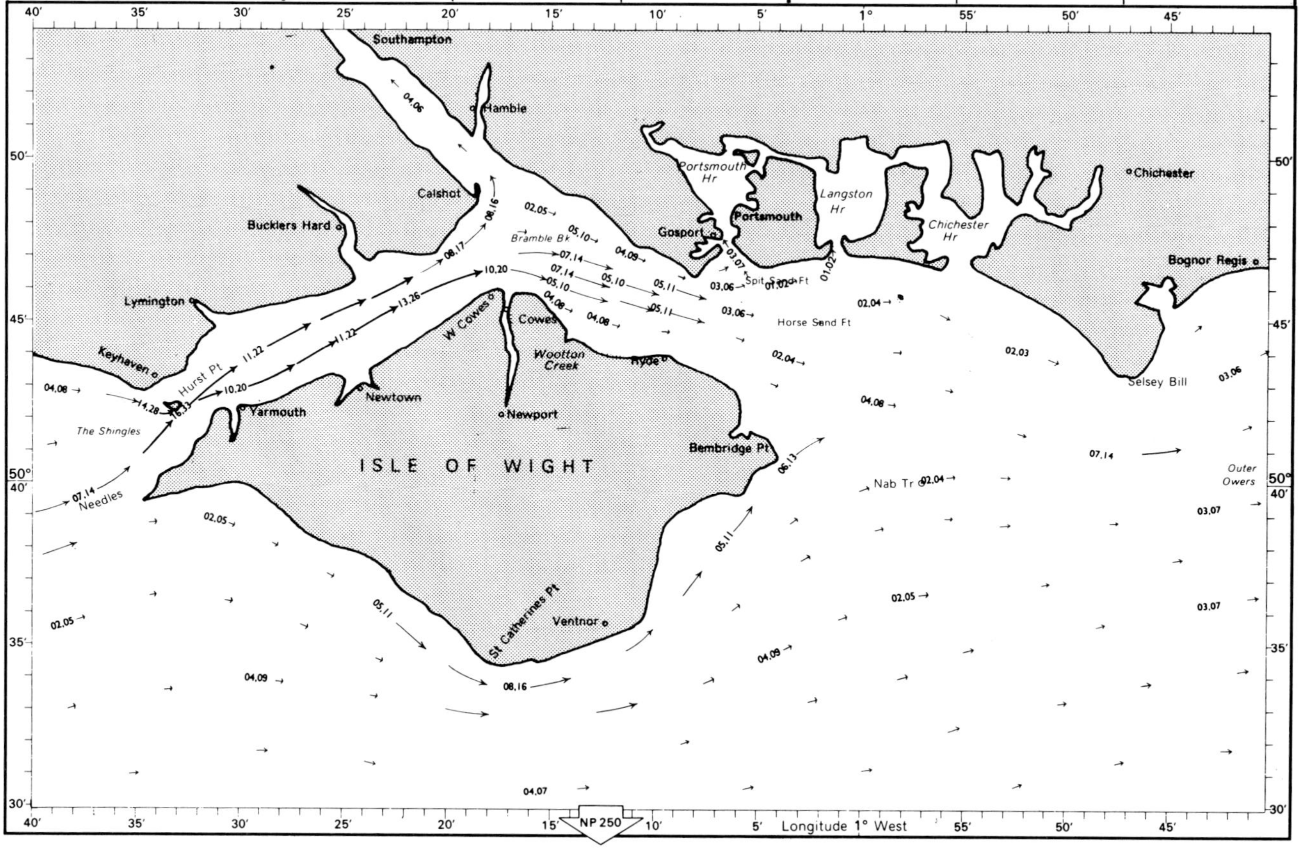

TIDAL STREAM CHARTS - PORTLAND BILL

indicate weak stream ⟶ indicate strong stream ⟶ rates shown in 1/10th knot

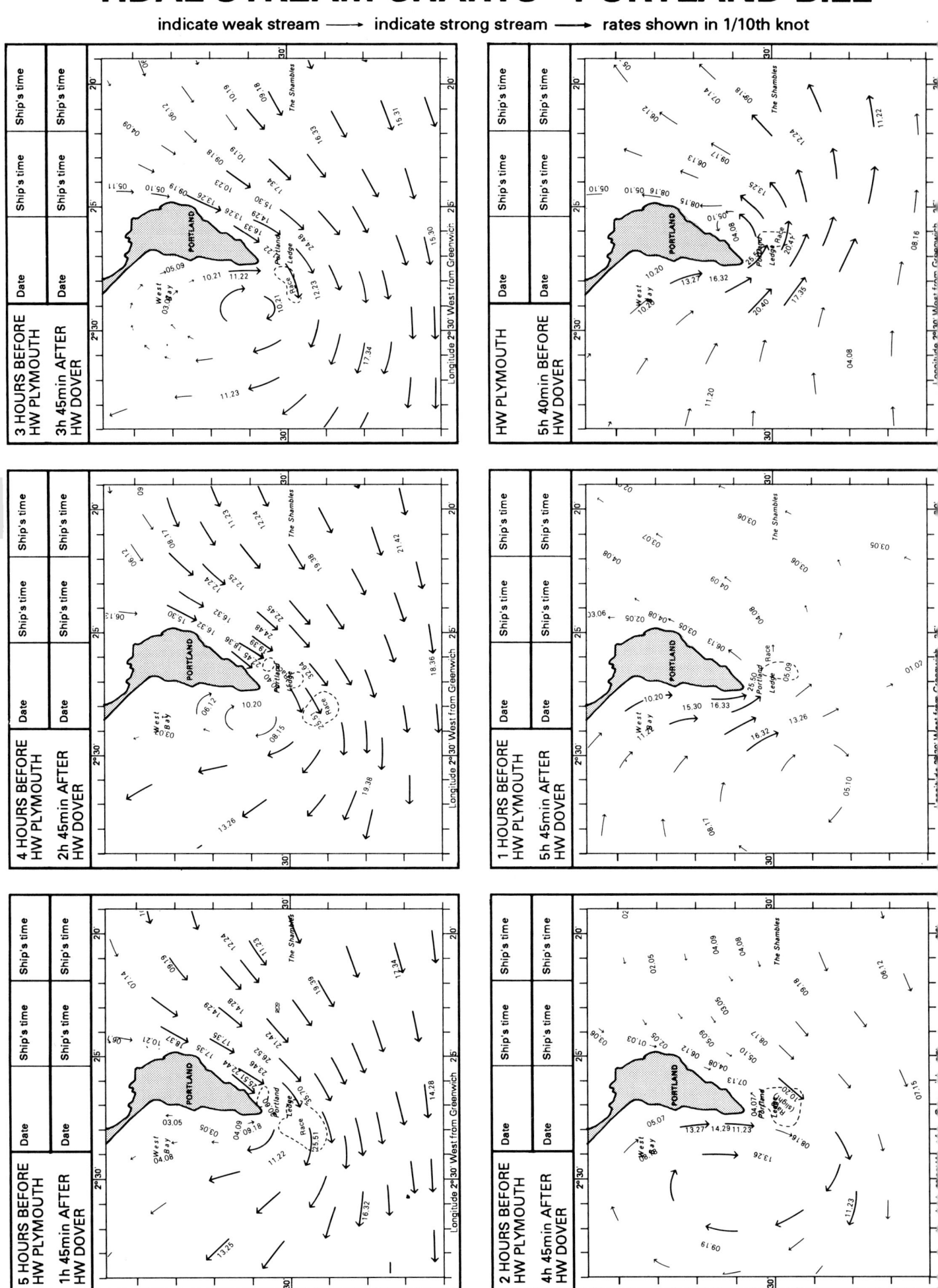

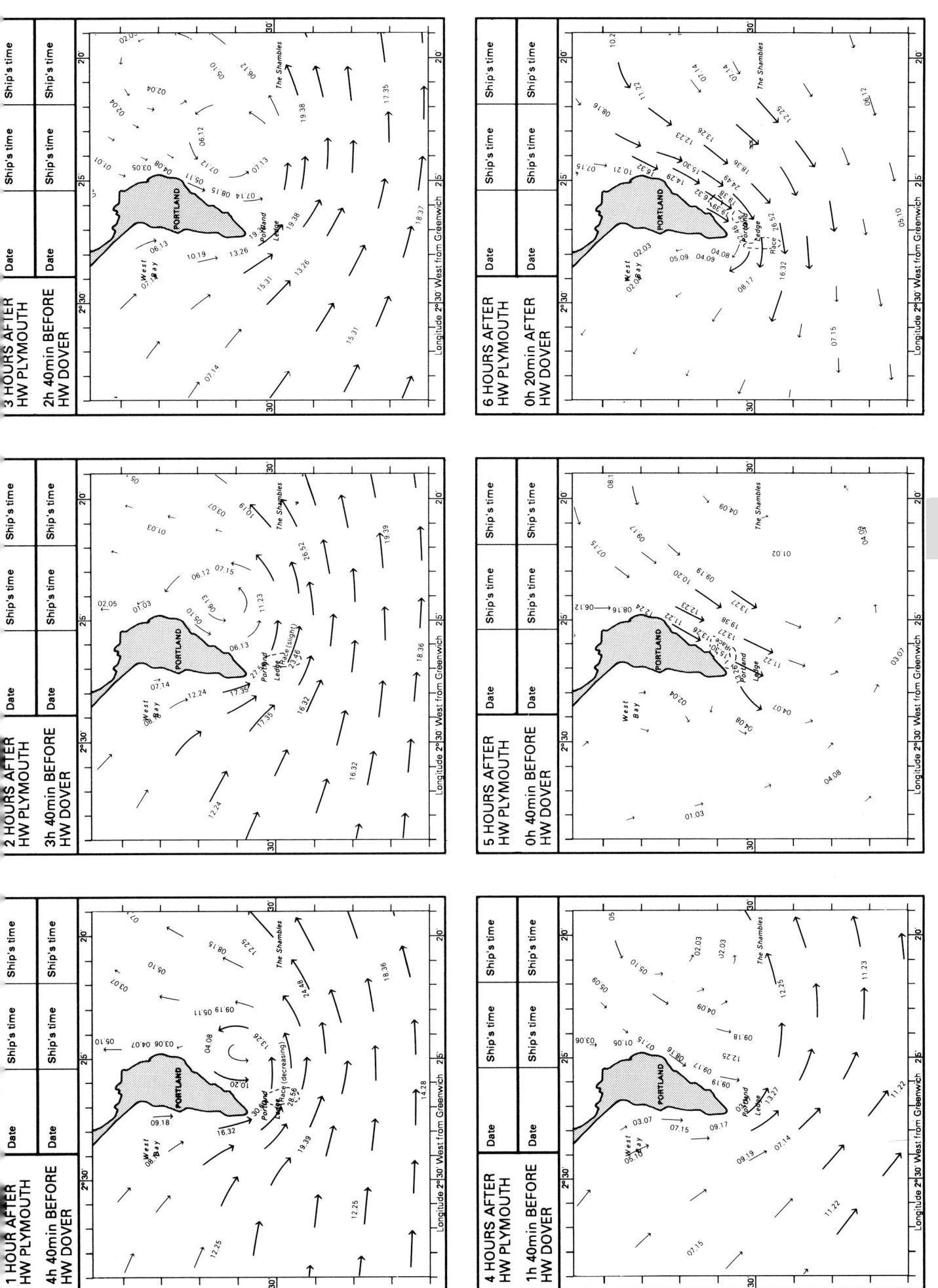

TIDAL STREAM CHARTS
CHANNEL ISLANDS AND
ADJACENT COASTS OF FRANCE

See also passage notes.

Tidal streams in this area are notoriously fast and tides must be worked with care on all passages.

indicate weak stream ⟶ indicate strong stream ⟶ rates shown in 1/10th knot

See page 85 for table to compute rates between spring and neap tides.

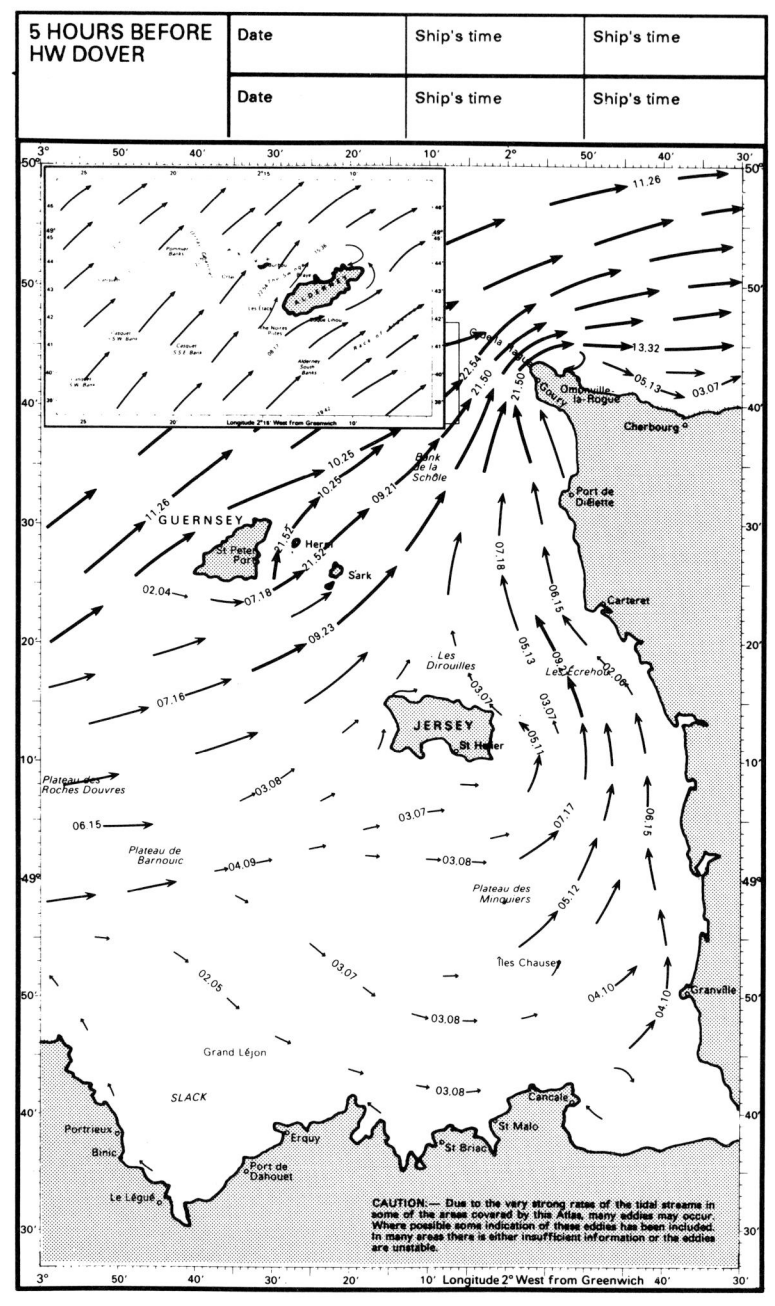

5 HOURS BEFORE HW DOVER	Date	Ship's time	Ship's time
	Date	Ship's time	Ship's time

CAUTION:— Due to the very strong rates of the tidal streams in some of the areas covered by this Atlas, many eddies may occur. Where possible some indication of these eddies has been included. In many areas there is either insufficient information or the eddies are unstable.

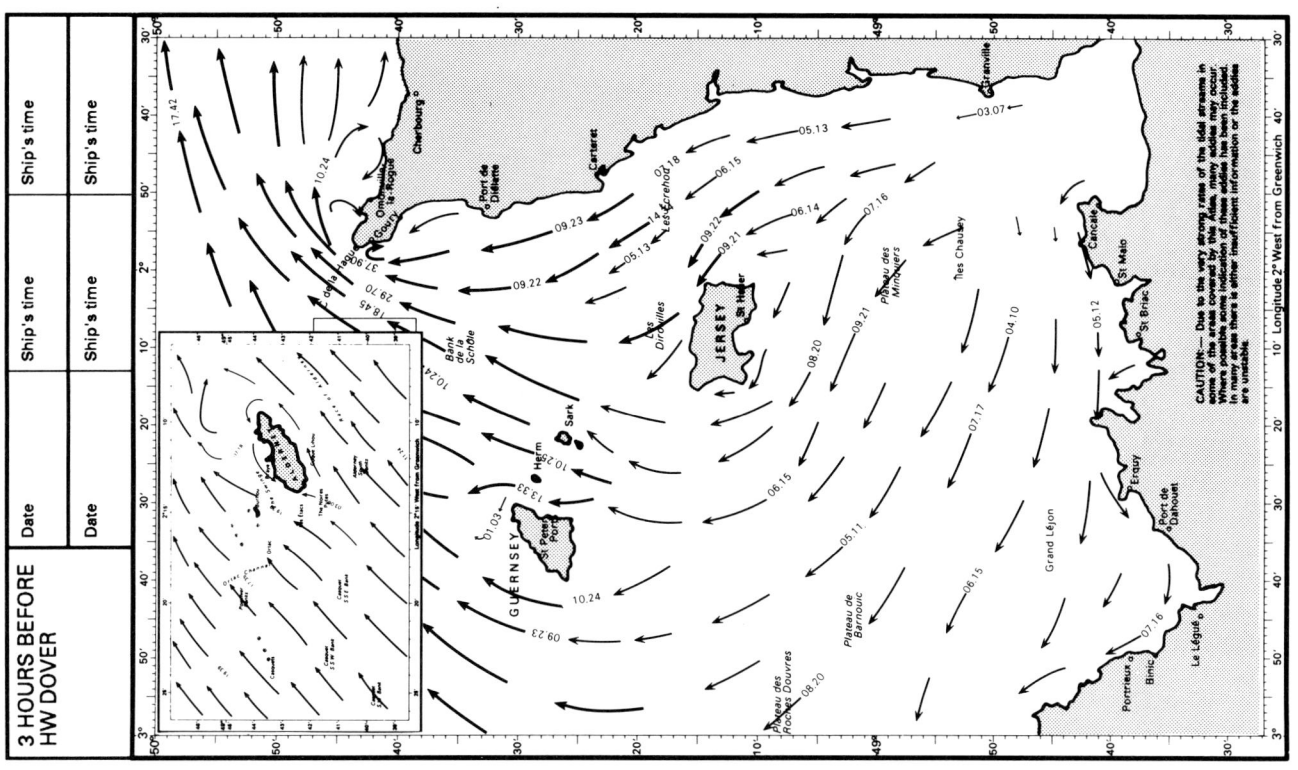

3 HOURS BEFORE HW DOVER	Date		Ship's time	
	Date		Ship's time	

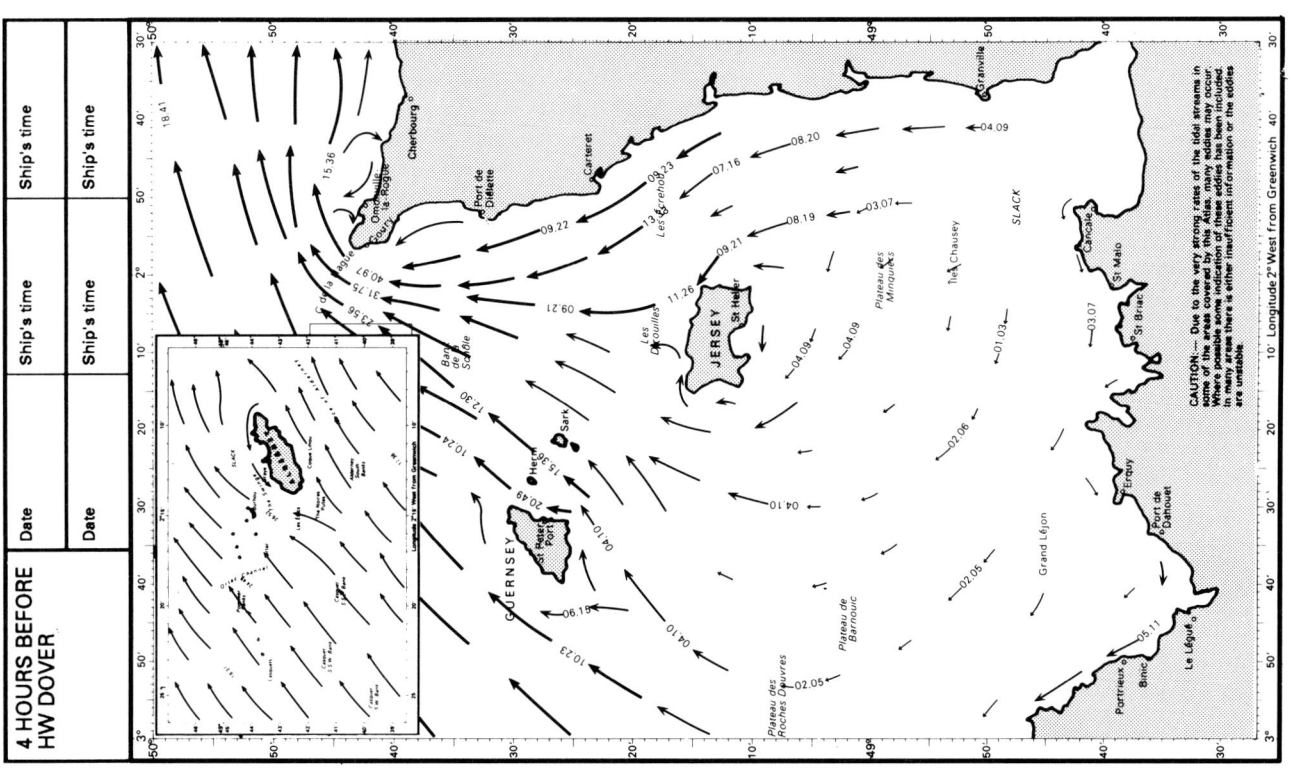

4 HOURS BEFORE HW DOVER	Date		Ship's time	
	Date		Ship's time	

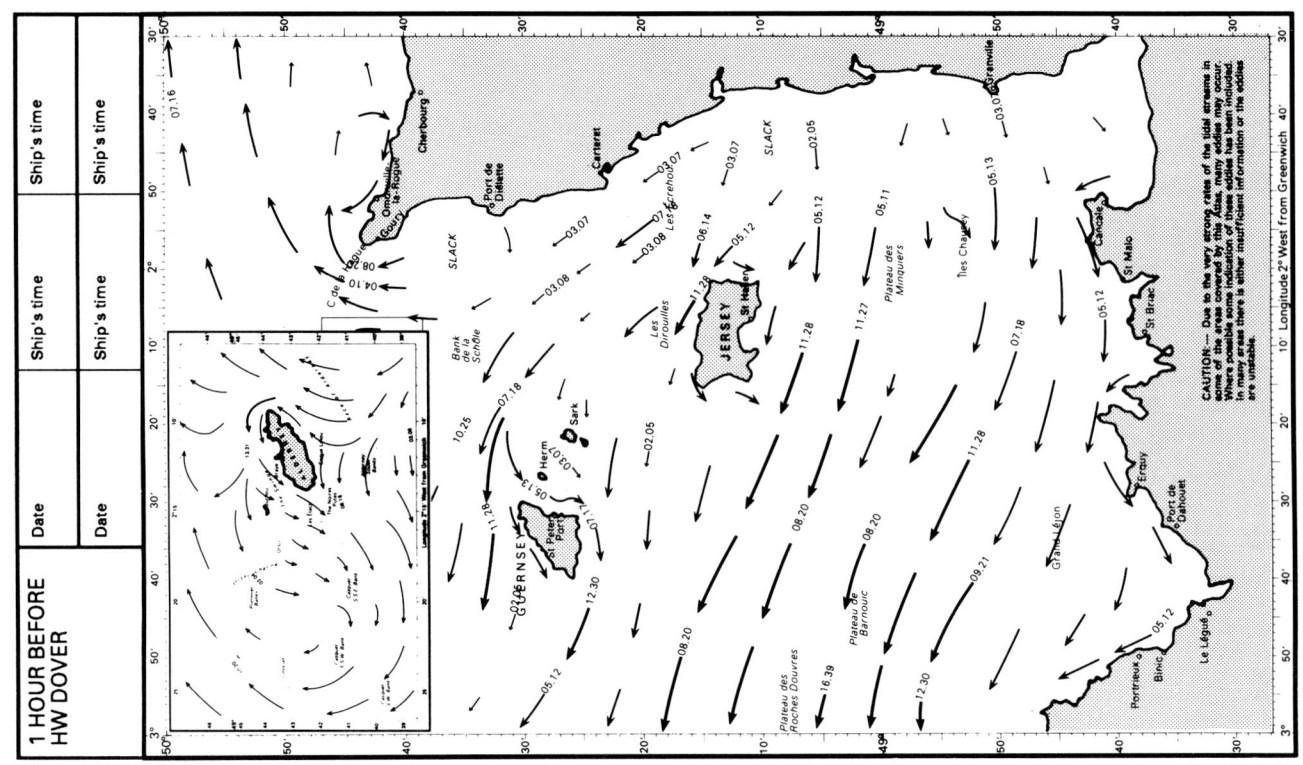

1 HOUR BEFORE HW DOVER

Date	Ship's time	Ship's time	Ship's time
Date	Ship's time	Ship's time	Ship's time

CAUTION:— Due to the very strong rates of the tidal streams in some of the areas covered by this Atlas, many eddies may occur. Where possible some indication of these eddies has been included. In many areas there is either insufficient information or the eddies are unstable.

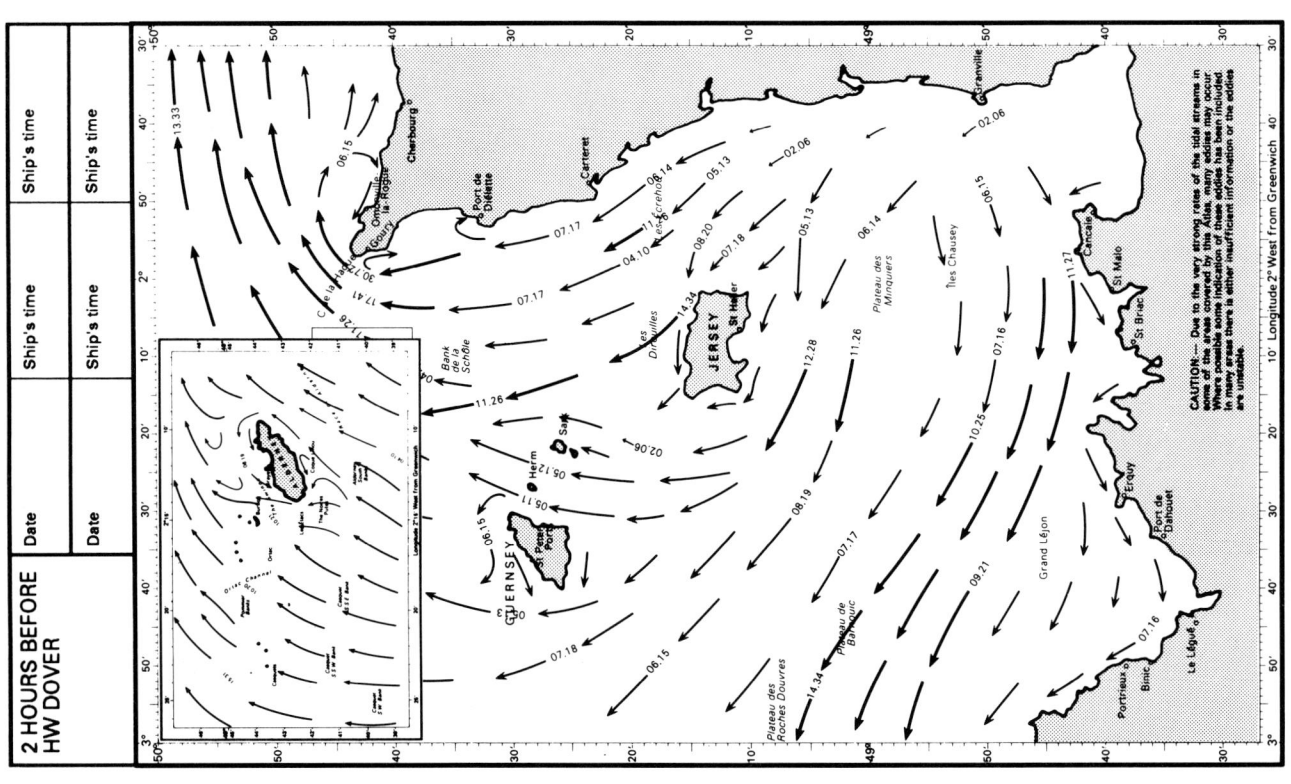

2 HOURS BEFORE HW DOVER

Date	Ship's time	Ship's time	Ship's time
Date	Ship's time	Ship's time	Ship's time

CAUTION:— Due to the very strong rates of the tidal streams in some of the areas covered by this Atlas, many eddies may occur. Where possible some indication of these eddies has been included. In many areas there is either insufficient information or the eddies are unstable.

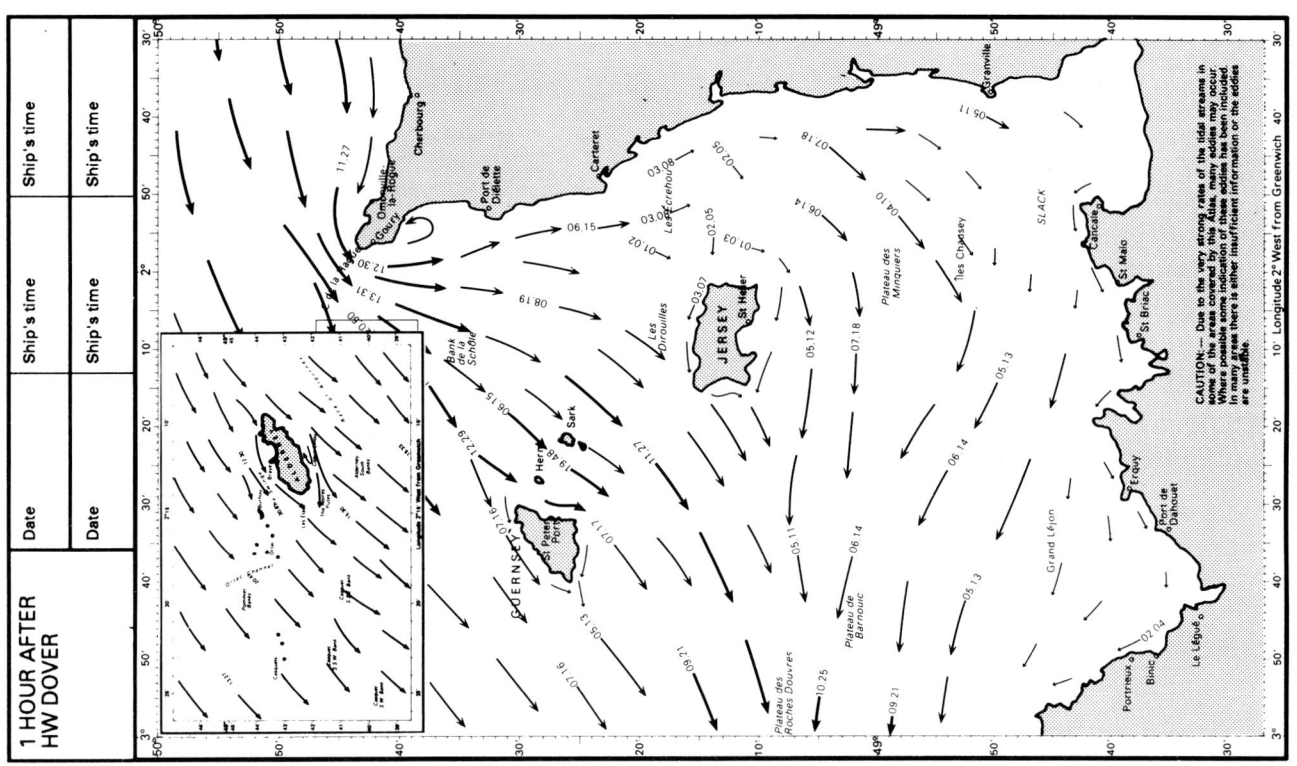

Date		Ship's time		Ship's time		Ship's time
Date		Ship's time		Ship's time		Ship's time

CAUTION.— Due to the very strong rates of the tidal streams in
some of the areas covered by this Atlas many eddies may occur.
Where possible some indication of these eddies has been included.
In many areas there is either insufficient information or the eddies
are unstable.

Longitude 2° West from Greenwich

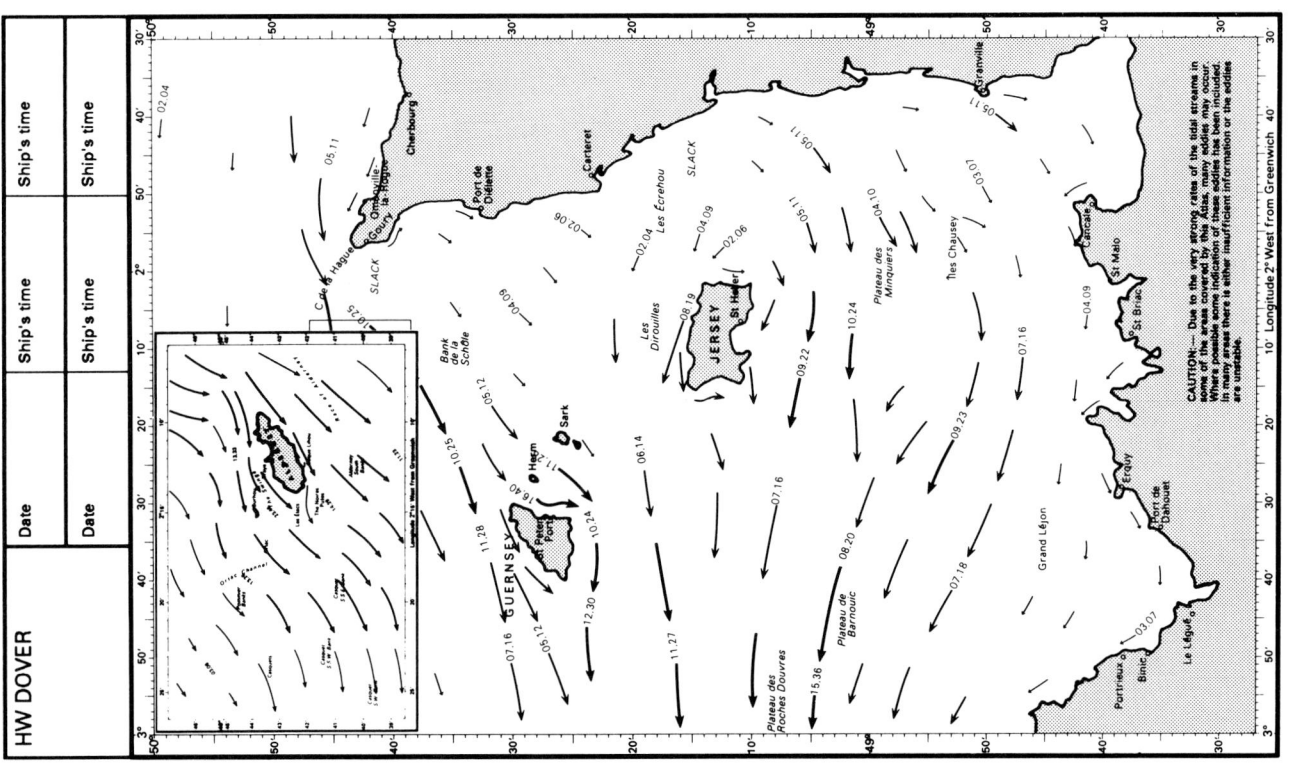

Date		Ship's time		Ship's time		Ship's time
Date		Ship's time		Ship's time		Ship's time

CAUTION.— Due to the very strong rates of the tidal streams in
some of the areas covered by this Atlas many eddies may occur.
Where possible some indication of these eddies has been included.
In many areas there is either insufficient information or the eddies
are unstable.

Longitude 2° West from Greenwich

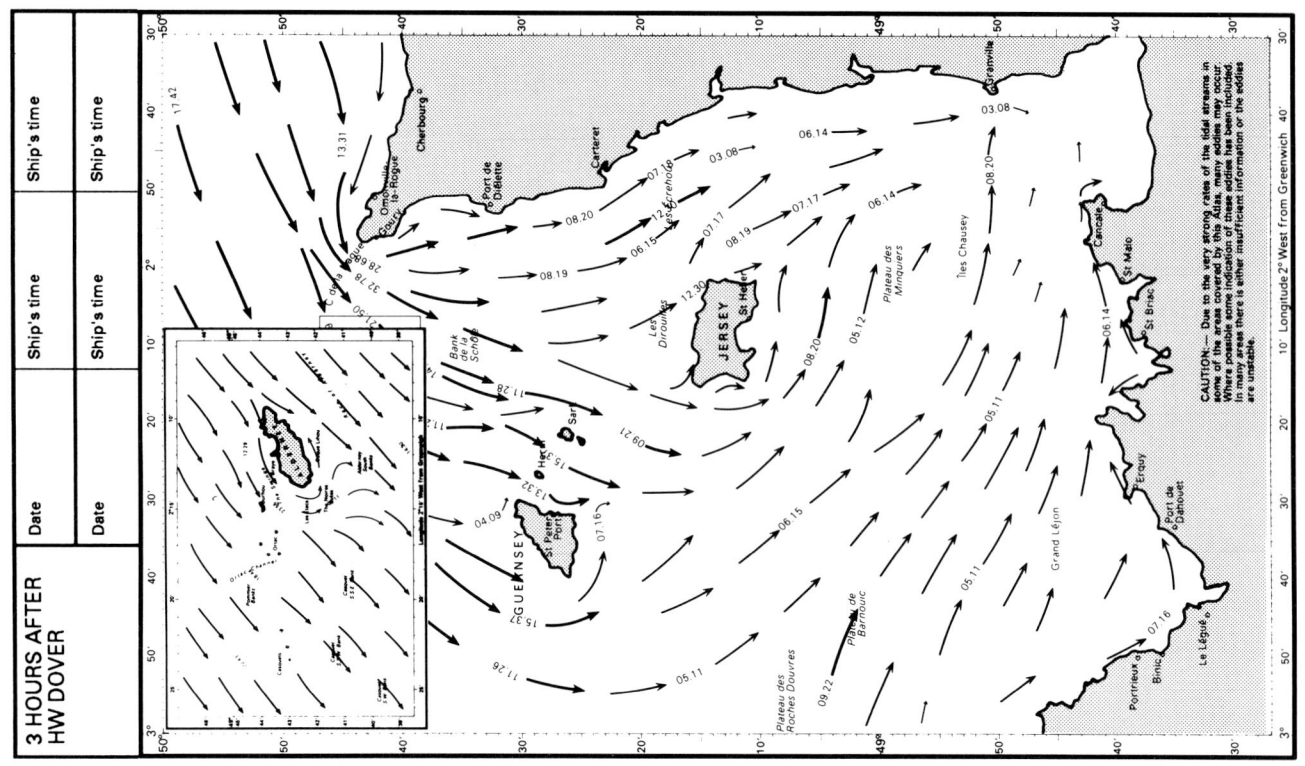

| 3 HOURS AFTER HW DOVER | Date | Ship's time | Ship's time |
| | Date | Ship's time | Ship's time |

CAUTION:— Due to the very strong rates of the tidal streams in some of the areas covered by this Atlas, many eddies may occur. Where possible some indication of these eddies has been included. In many areas there is either insufficient information or the eddies are unstable.

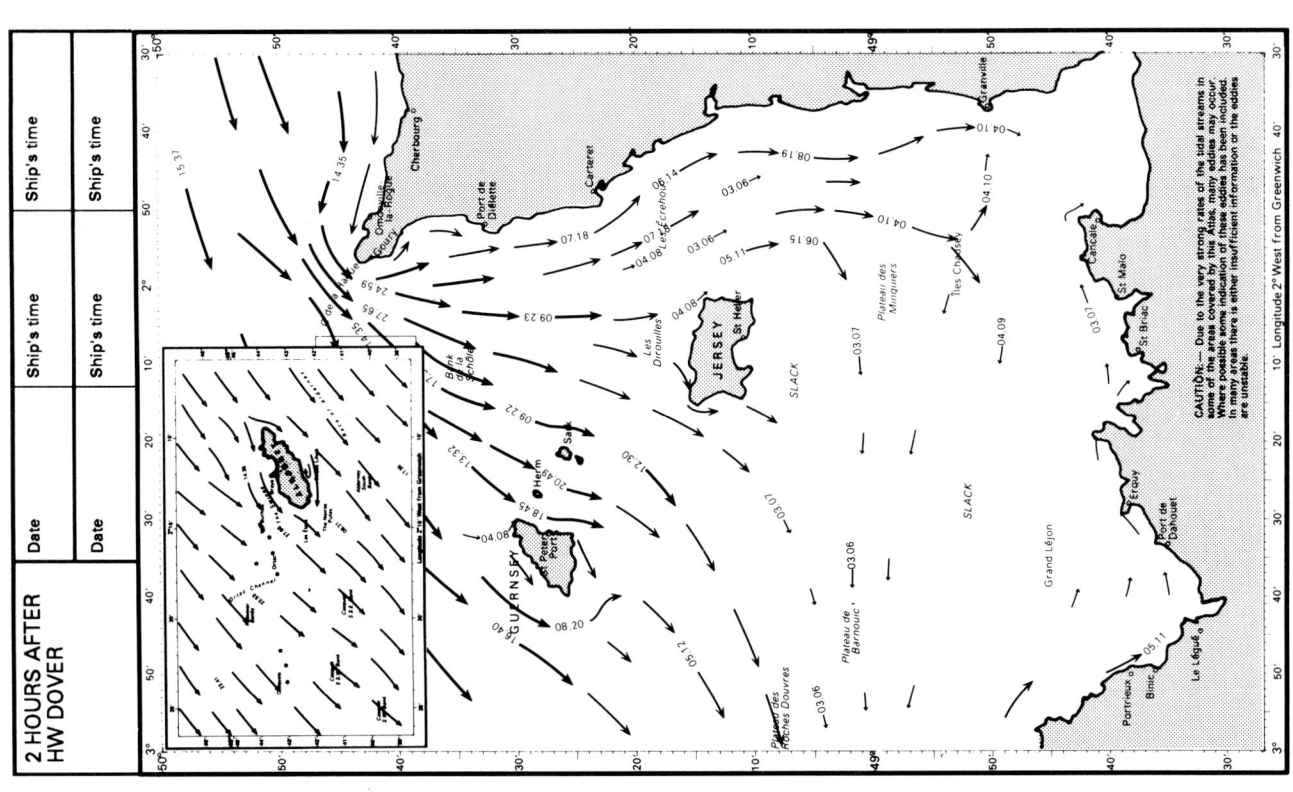

| 2 HOURS AFTER HW DOVER | Date | Ship's time | Ship's time |
| | Date | Ship's time | Ship's time |

CAUTION:— Due to the very strong rates of the tidal streams in some of the areas covered by this Atlas, many eddies may occur. Where possible some indication of these eddies has been included. In many areas there is either insufficient information or the eddies are unstable.

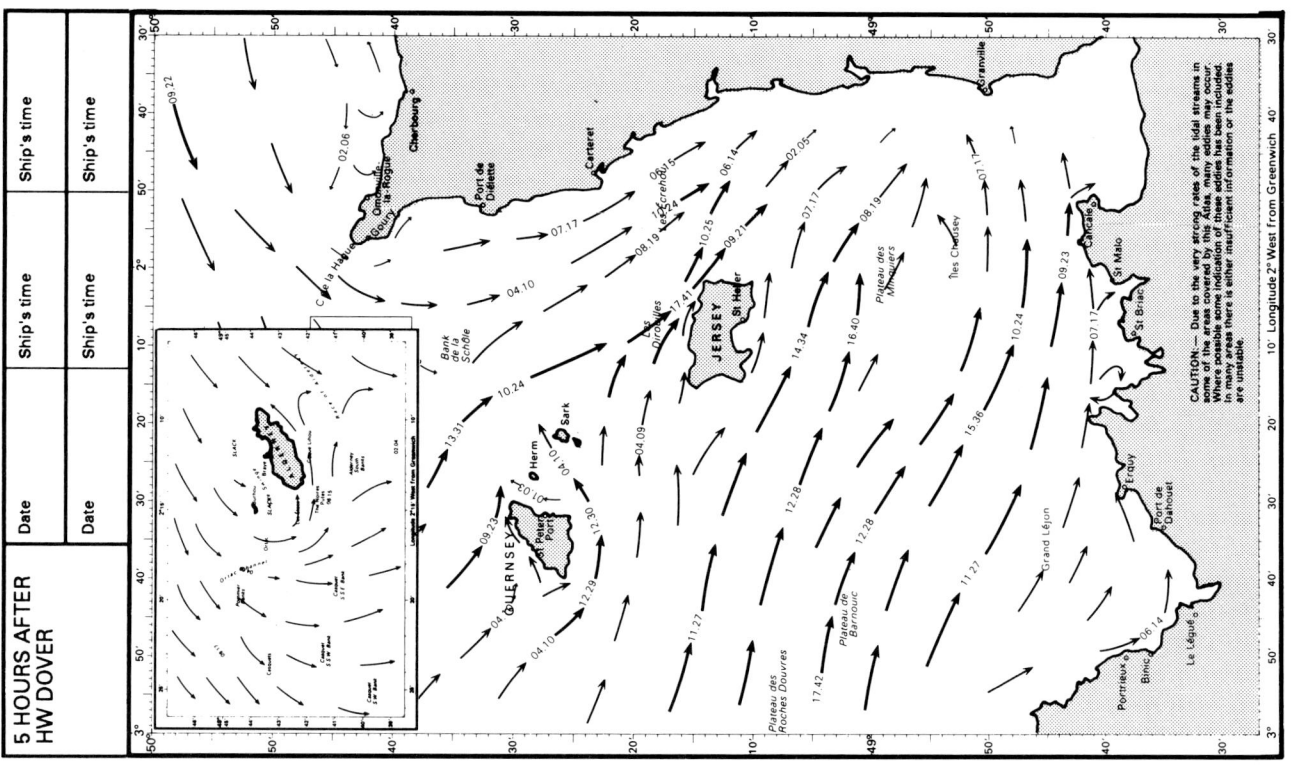

CAUTION:— Due to the very strong rates of the tidal streams in some of the areas covered by this Atlas, many eddies may occur. Where possible some indication of these eddies has been included. In many areas there is either insufficient information or the eddies are unstable.

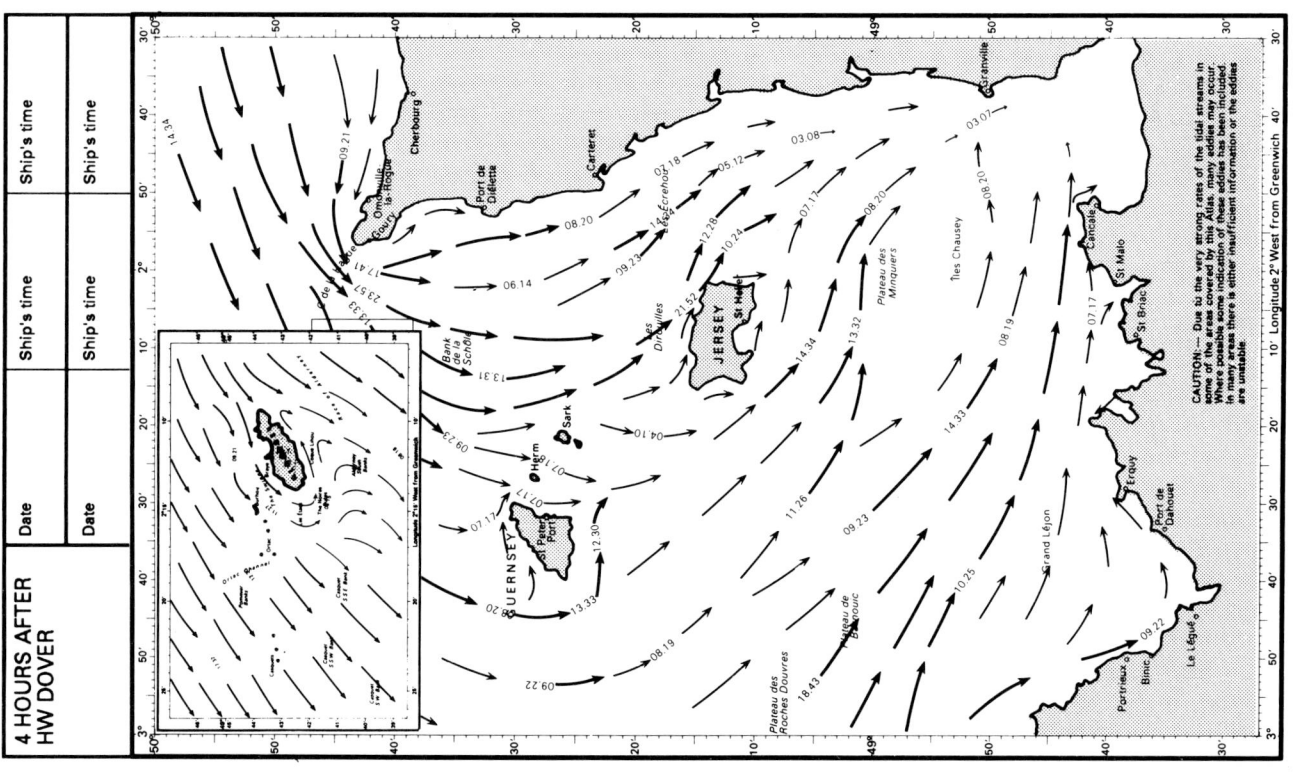

CAUTION:— Due to the very strong rates of the tidal streams in some of the areas covered by this Atlas, many eddies may occur. Where possible some indication of these eddies has been included. In many areas there is either insufficient information or the eddies are unstable.

6 HOURS AFTER HW DOVER	Date	Ship's time	Ship's time
	Date	Ship's time	Ship's time

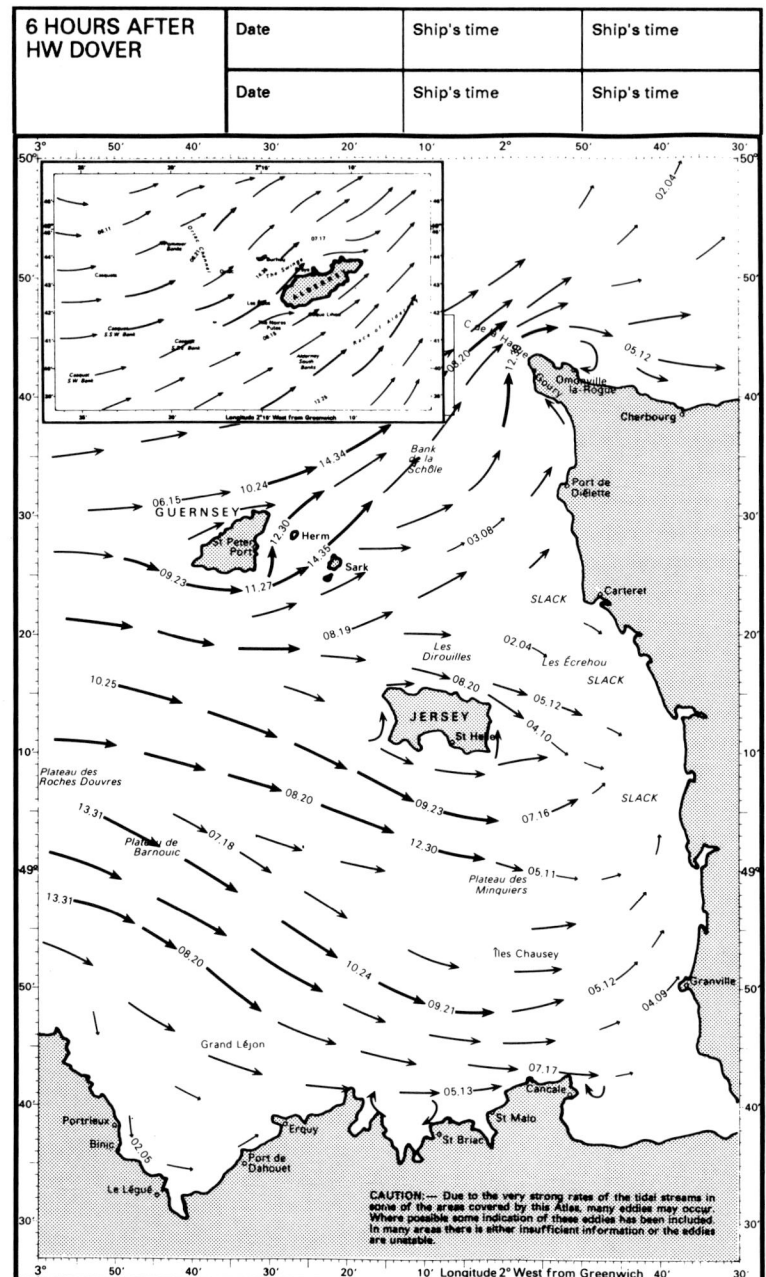

CAUTION:— Due to the very strong rates of the tidal streams in some of the areas covered by this Atlas, many eddies may occur. Where possible some indication of these eddies has been included. In many areas there is either insufficient information or the eddies are unstable.

TIDAL STREAM CHARTS - USHANT

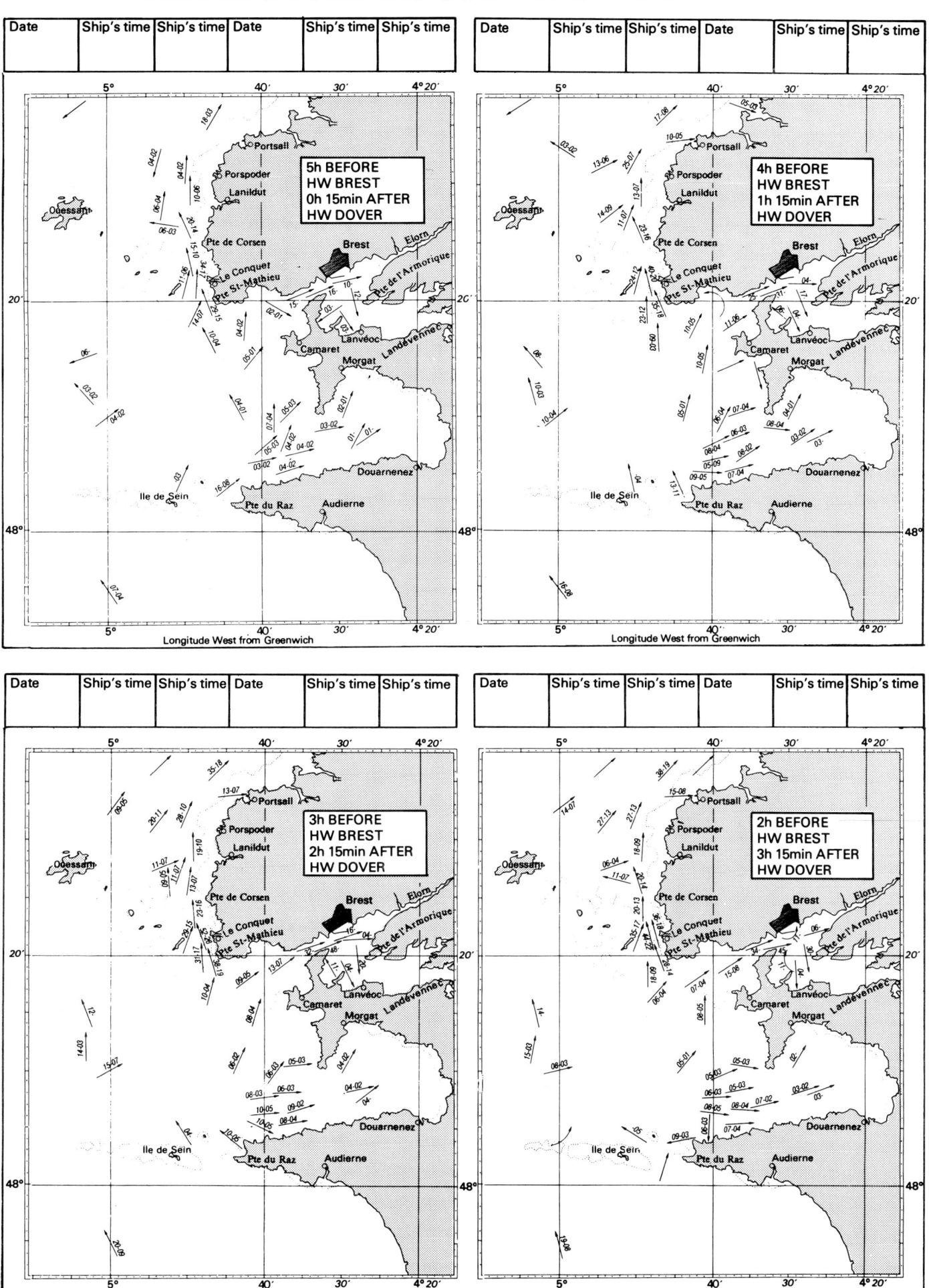

Date	Ship's time	Ship's time	Date	Ship's time	Ship's time

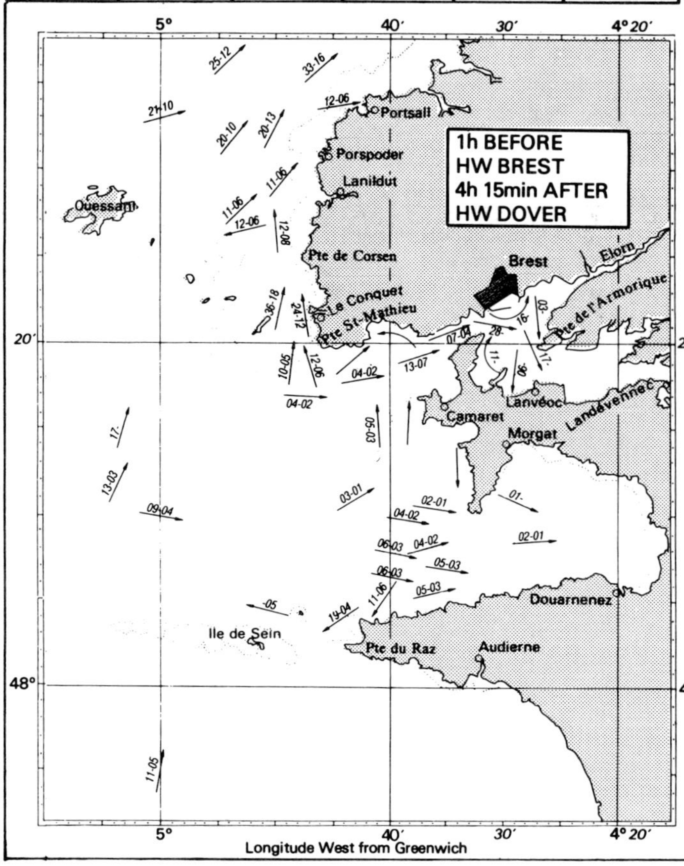

Date	Ship's time	Ship's time	Date	Ship's time	Ship's time

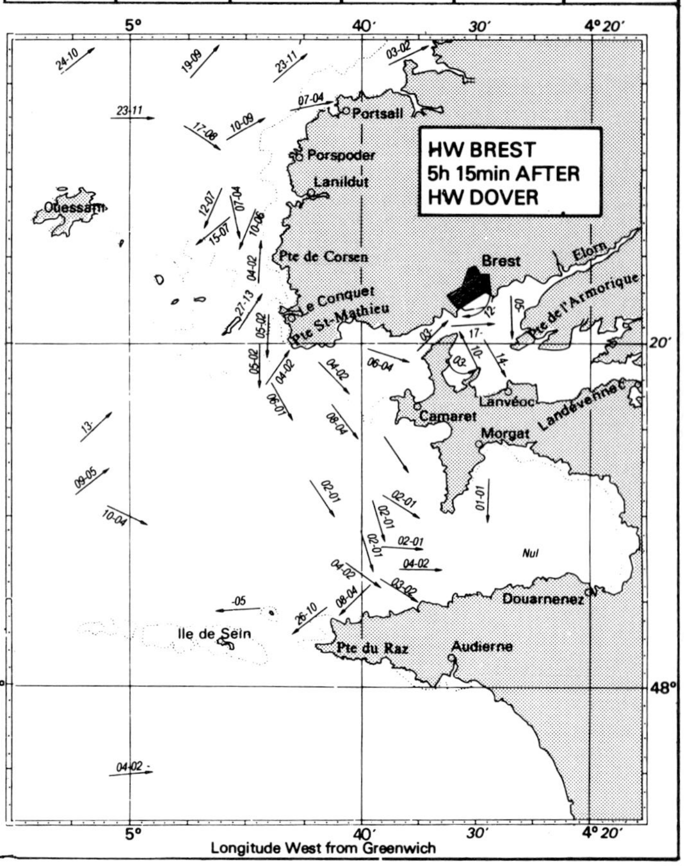

Date	Ship's time	Ship's time	Date	Ship's time	Ship's time

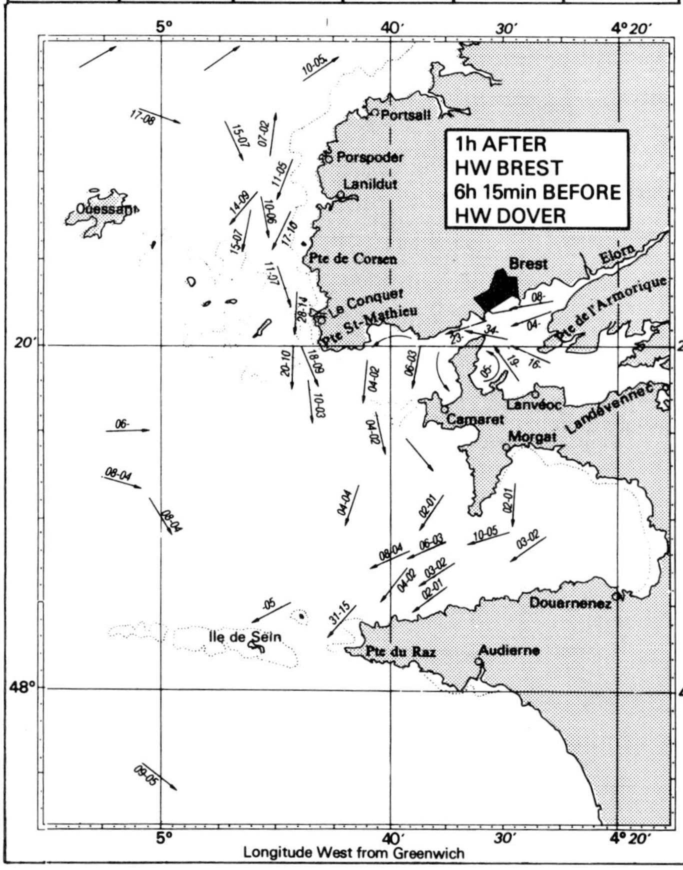

Date	Ship's time	Ship's time	Date	Ship's time	Ship's time

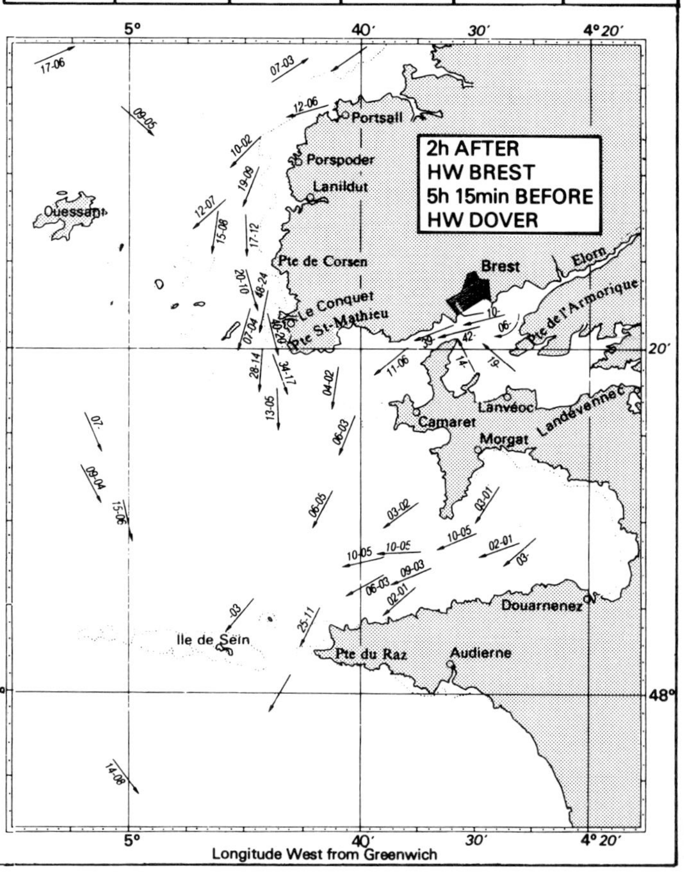

Date	Ship's time	Ship's time	Date	Ship's time	Ship's time

Date	Ship's time	Ship's time	Date	Ship's time	Ship's time

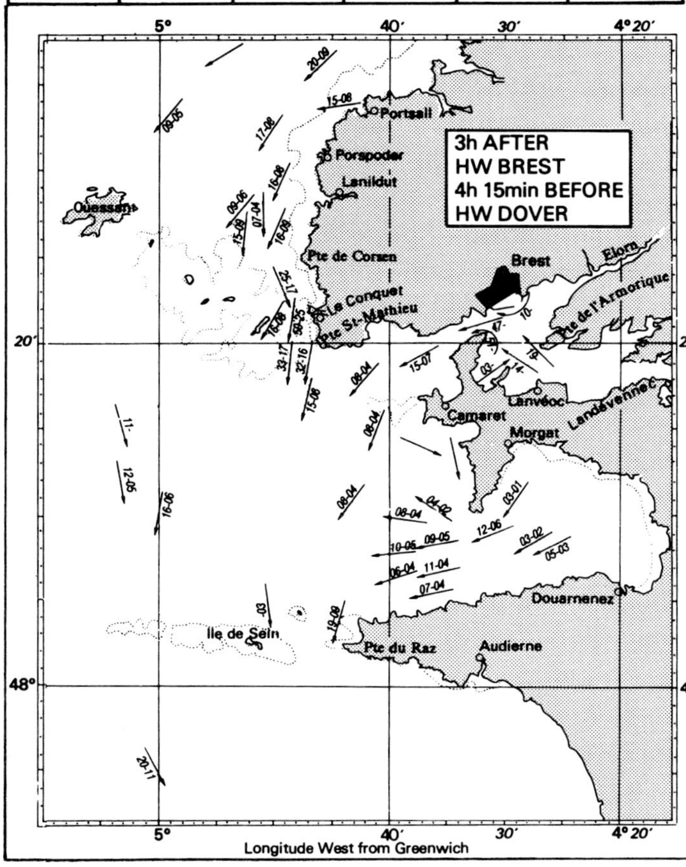

3h AFTER
HW BREST
4h 15min BEFORE
HW DOVER

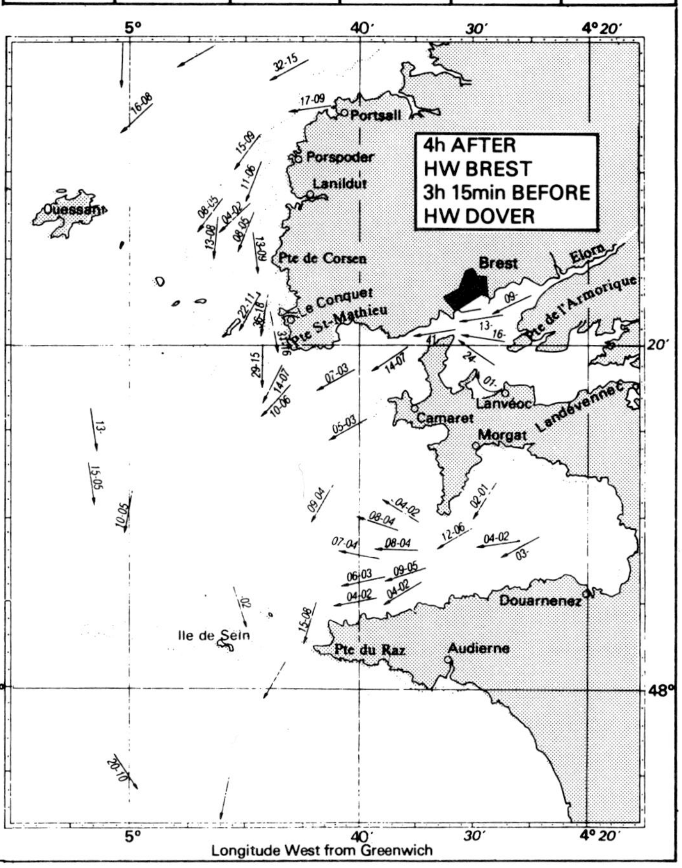

4h AFTER
HW BREST
3h 15min BEFORE
HW DOVER

Date	Ship's time	Ship's time	Date	Ship's time	Ship's time

Date	Ship's time	Ship's time	Date	Ship's time	Ship's time

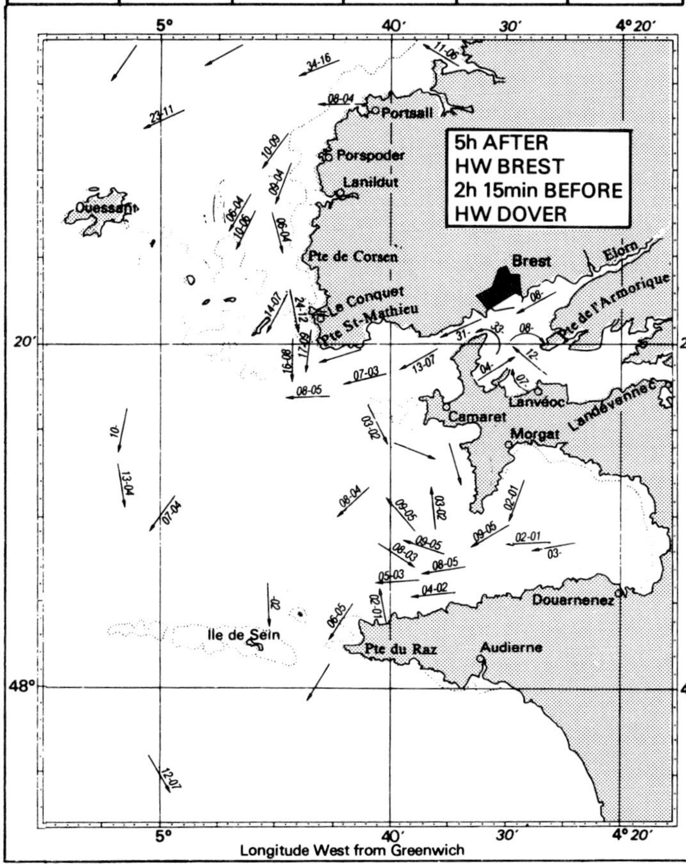

5h AFTER
HW BREST
2h 15min BEFORE
HW DOVER

6h AFTER
HW BREST
1h 15min BEFORE
HW DOVER

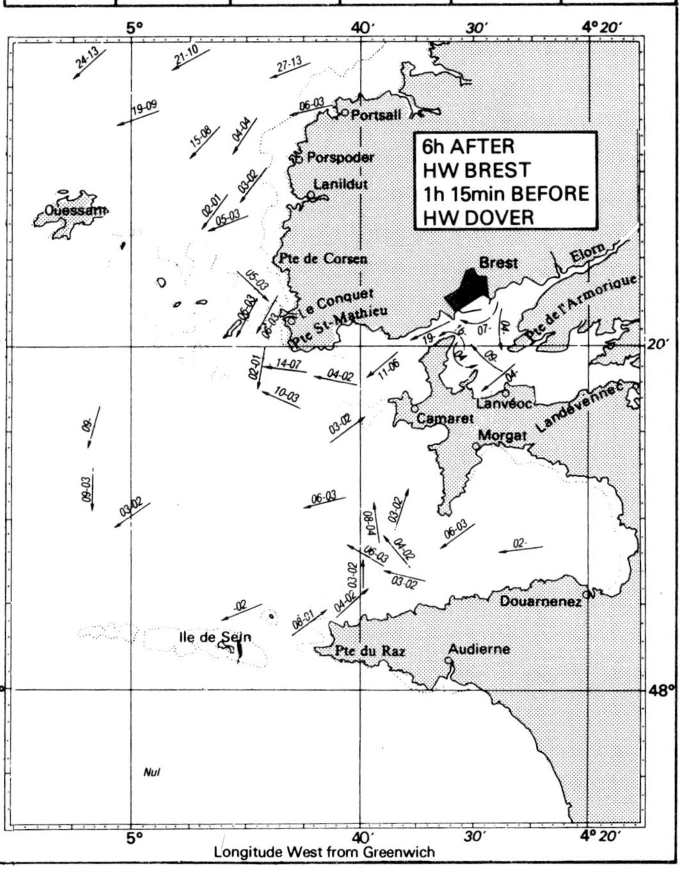

NOTES ON CHANNEL TIDES

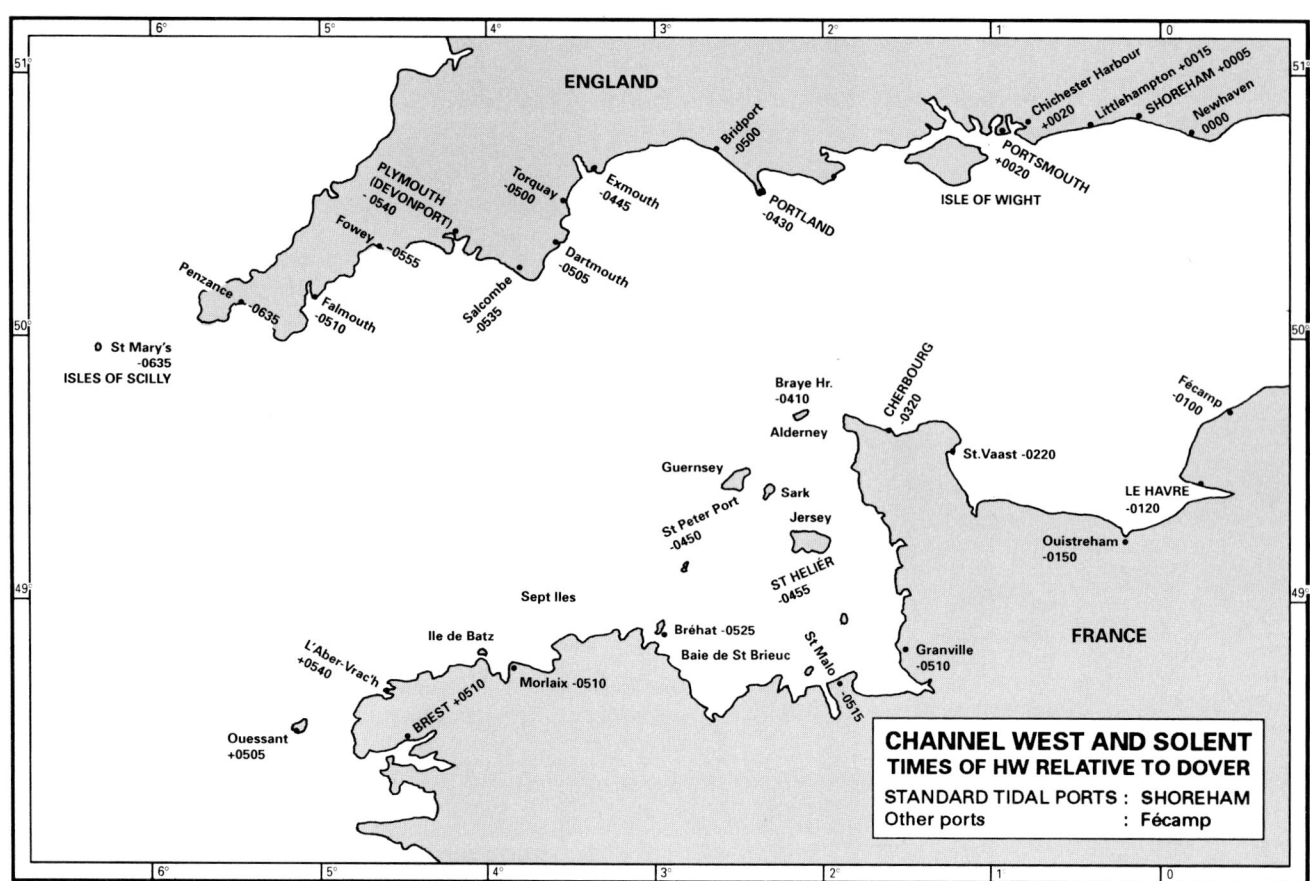

It is sometimes a useful aid to planning a cruise to be able to relate tide to a single datum and we reproduce a chart here of ports related to Dover. For more accurate predictions, see the tide tables and Standard/Secondary port relationships.

NOTE: Predictions derived from the charted differences will be in the same Zone Time as those for Dover.

Between Start Point and Portland the tidal curve gradually becomes more and more distorted, especially on the rising tide; the rise is relatively fast for the first hour after low water and there is then a noticeable slackening in the rate of rise for the next 1½ hours, after which the rapid rate of rise is resumed. There is often a "stand" at high water, which, while not very noticeable at Start Point, lasts for about an hour at Torquay and for 1½ hours at Lyme Regis.

Double low waters occur between Portland and Lulworth Cove. Data for Lulworth refer to the first low water.

Owing to the complicated variations in the tide between Portland and Portsmouth, the time and height differences for these places will only give approximate predictions. A more accurate representation of the tidal curves at these places can be obtained from the diagrams.

From Swanage to Christchurch double high waters occur except at neaps; at neaps the earlier time differences may represent only the beginning of a "stand" or a point at which the rate of rise decreases noticeably.

Tidal levels at Christchurch are for a position inside the bar; outside the bar the tide falls about 0.6m lower at Springs.

Within the Western Solent double high waters occur at or near springs; on other occasions there is a stand which lasts about 2 hours. Where two high water time differences are given these may, therefore, represent the beginning and end of the stand; where only one HW time difference is given, this represents approximately the middle of the stand.

From Totland Bay to Freshwater double high waters occur except at neaps; at neaps the earlier time differences may represent only the beginning of a "stand" or a point at which the rate of rise decreases noticeably.

With a NE gale and a high barometer, tidal heights at Southampton may be as much as 0.6m less than predictions.

Tidal heights inside Littlehampton Harbour are affected by the water coming down the River Arun; the tide seldom falls lower than 0.7m above datum.

LIGHTS AND BEACONS

RADIO BEACONS

These are arranged geographically. English coast, east to west, then French coast and Channel Islands, east to west. Aero beacons are listed separately.

English coast, east to west

Station	Lat/Long	Morse Indentn		Mode	Freq (kHz)	Range (M)
Dungeness	**50°54'.77N 0°58'.67E**	DU	– • • • • –	**A1A**	**300.5**	**50**
Brighton Marina	50°48'.67N 0°05'.95W	BM	– • • • – –	A1A	294.5	10
St Catherine's	**50°34'.52N 1°17'.80W**	CP	– • – • • – – •	**A1A**	**293**	**50**
Portland Bill	**50°30'.82N 2°27'.32W**	PB	• – – • – • • •	**A1A**	**313**	**50**
Lizard	**49°57'.58N 5°12'.07W**	LZ	• – • • – – • •	**A1A**	**284.5**	**70**
Round Island	**49°58'.70N 6°19'.33W**	RR	• – • • – •	**A1A**	**298.5**	**150**

French coast and Channel Islands, east to west

Station	Lat/Long	Morse Indentn		Mode	Freq (kHz)	Range (M)
Cap d'Alprech	50°41'.95N 1°33'.83E	PH	• – – • • • • •	A1A	294	20
Pte d'Ailly	**49°55'.00N 0°57'.55E**	AL	• – • – • •	**A1A**	**305.5**	**50**
Cap d'Antifer	**49°41'.07N 0°10'.00E**	TI	– • •	**A1A**	**300**	**50**
Pte de Ver	49°20'.47N 0°31'.15W	ÉR	• • – • • • – •	A1A	310	20
Port en Bessin	49°21'.00N 0°45'.60W	BS	– • • • • • •	A1A	290	5
Pte de Barfleur	**49°41'.87N 1°15'.87W**	FG	• • – • – – •	**A1A**	**297**	**70**
Cherbourg	49°40'.50N 1°38'.87W	RB	• – • – • • •	A1A	302	20
St Peter Port	49°27'.37N 2°31'.37W	GY	– – • – • – –	A1A	304.5	10
St Helier Hr	49°10'.62N 2°07'.50W	EC	• – • – •	A1A	306	10
La Corbière	49°10'.85N 2°14'.90W	CB	– • – • – • • •	A1A	295.5	20
Le Grand Jardin	48°40'.27N 2°04'.90W	GJ	– – • • – – –	A1A	306.5	10
Cap Fréhel Lt	48°41'.10N 2°19'.07W	FÉ	• • – • • • – • •	A1A	286.5	20
Rosédo Lt, Île Bréhat	49°51'.50N 3°00'.32W	DO	– • • – – –	A1A	287.5	10
Roches Douvres	**49°06'.47N 2°48'.65W**	RD	• – • – • •	**A1A**	**308**	**70**
Roscoff/Bloscon	49°43'.30N 3°57'.63W	BC	– • • • – • – •	A1A	304.5	10
Île Vierge	**48°38'.38N 4°33'.97W**	VG	• • • – – – •	**A1A**	**314**	**70**
Pt de Créac'h	**48°27'.63N 5°07'.57W**	CA	– • – • • –	**A1A**	**301**	**100**
Ouessant SW Lanby	48°31'.68N 5°49'.10W	SW	• • • • – –	A1A	305.5	10
St Mathieu	48°19'.85N 4°46'.17W	SM	• • • – –	A1A	292.5	50
Île de Sein, NW	48°02'.70N 4°51'.95W	SN	• • • – •	A1A	289.5	70
Penmarc'h	47°47'.95N 4°22'.35W	UH	• • – • • • •	A1A	312	50
Pte de Combrit	47°51'.92N 4°06'.70W	CT	– • – • –	A1A	288.5	20

AERO BEACONS

English coast, east to west

Station	Lat/Long	Morse Indentn		Mode	Freq (kHz)	Range (M)
Fawley/Hythe	50°51'.95N 1°23'.44W	FAW	• • – • • – • – –	NON A2A	370	20
Bournemouth/Hurn	**50°47'.97N 1°43'.68W**	HRN	• • • • • – • – •	**NON A2A**	**401.5**	**35**
Exeter	50°45'.12N 3°17'.62W	EX	• – • • –	NON A2A	337	15
Berry Head	50°23'.88N 3°29'.55W	BHD	– • • • • • • • – • •	NON A2A	318	25
Penzance Heliport	50°07'.67N 5°31'.00W	PH	• – – • • • • •	NON A2A	333	15
St Mary's	49°54'.82N 6°17'.43W	STM	• • • – – –	NON A2A	321	15

French coast and Channel Islands, east to west

Station	Lat/Long	Morse Indentn		Mode	Freq (kHz)	Range (M)
Le Touquet	50°32'.13N 1°35'.37E	LT	• – • • –	A2A	358	20
Le Havre/Octeville	49°35'.75N 0°11'.00E	LHO	• – • • • • • • – – –	A2A	346	15
Jersey East	**49°13'.18N 2°38'.30W**	JEY	• – – – • – • – –	**NON A2A**	**367**	**75**
Alderney	**49°42'.58N 2°11'.90W**	ALD	• – • – • • – • •	**NON A2A**	**383**	**50**
Jersey West	49°12'.37N 2°13'.30W	JW	• – – – • – –	NON A2A	329	25
Guernsey	**49°26'.12N 2°38'.30W**	GRB	– – • • – • – • • •	**NON A2A**	**361**	**30**
Granville	48°55'.10N 1°28'.87W	GV	– – • • • • –	A1A	321	25
St Brieuc	**48°34'.10N 2°46'.90W**	SB	• • • – • • •	**A1A**	**353**	**25**
Lannion	48°43'.25N 3°18'.45W	LN	• – • • – •	A1A	345	50
Lanvéoc, Poulmic	**48°17'.07N 4°26'.00W**	BST	– • • • • • • –	**A1A**	**316**	**80**

LIGHTS

Definitions

Alt	Alternating colours
Dir	Direction light
F	Fixed, ie continuous and steady
Fl	Flashing
Intens	Intensified sector
Iso	Isophase, ie equal light and dark
L	Long flashing
Ldg Lts	Leading lights
LtV	Light vessel
Mo	Morse code
Obsc	Obscured
Oc	Occulting, ie longer light than dark
Q	Quick flashing
Vis	Visible
T	Temporary
TD	Fog signal temporarily discontinued
TE	Light temporarily extinguished

All bearings are from seaward

(eg a sector quoted as 180°-270° occupies the north-east quadrant from the light)

Colours

Bu	Blue
G	Green
R	Red
Vi	Violet
W	White
Y	Yellow

(3) eg represents a group of three, thus Fl(3) means a triple flash. Some of these types of light emission may be combined.

m	metres, in this context, the height of the light
M	sea miles, in this context, the maximum distance at which a light can be seen
Dia	Diaphone using compressed air, usually a powerful, low pitched sound
Horn	A diaphragm vibrated by electricity or compressed air. Varies considerably
Siren	Uses compressed air. Varies considerably
Reed	A weak, high pitched sound using compressed air

Mode

A1A	Continuous wave telegraphy, Morse code
A2A	Telegraphy by the on-off keying of a tone modulated carrier, Morse code: double sideband
NON	Unmodulated continuous wave emission

DF accuracy and reliability

Inaccuracies in a 'fix' can be caused by:
1. Failure to calibrate the set
2. Atmospheric effects, including sunrise, sunset and night effects
3. Coast refraction if the beam cuts a coast
4. Convergency due to the radio wave following a great circle track. Not important over short ranges.

Only three bearing fixes with a small 'cocked hat' should be considered satisfactory. Two bearing fixes should not be trusted over much.

LIGHTS

with a listed range of ONE MILE and above; bearings are given from seaward.

International no. with prefix 'A' for lights to Les Pierres Noires and 'D' thereafter
name/Lat, Long
description,
height, range and fog signal
Description of structure (height)
Remarks

ENGLAND - ISLES OF SCILLY

0002	**Bishop Rock 49°52'.3N 6°26'.7W** Fl(2)W 15s 44m 24M Horn Mo(N) 90s, Racon Grey round granite tr (49m) *Ptly obsc 204°-211°(7°),obsc 211°-233°(22°),236°-259°(23°)*
	ST MARY'S
0006	**- Peninnis Head 49°54'.2N 6°18'.2W** Fl W 20s 36m 17M W round metal tr on black metal frame, black cupola (14m) *Vis 231°-117°(246°),ptly obsc 048°-083°(35°) within 5M*
0008	- St Mary's Pool. Pier. Head 49°55'.1N 6° 19'.0W F G 4m 3M Building, W roof (3m) *Vis 072°-192°(120°)*

0018	**Round Island 49°58'.7N 6°19'.3W** Fl W 10s 55m 24M Horn(4) 60s W round tr (19m) *Vis 021°-288°(267°)*
0020	**Seven Stones LtF 50°03'.6N 6°04'.3W** Fl(3)W 30s 12m 25M Horn(3) 60s, Racon R hull, lt tr amidships
	ENGLAND - SOUTH COAST
0028	**Longships 50°04'.0N 5°44'.8W** Iso WR 10s 35m 19/18/15M Horn 10s Grey round granite tr (35m) *R189°-208°(19°), R(unintens)208°-307°(99°),* *R307°-327°(20°), W327°-189°(222°)*
0030	**Wolf Rock 49°56.7N 5°48'.5W** Fl W 15s 34m 23M Horn 30s, Racon Grey round granite tr, black lantern (41m)

0032	**Tater-du 50°03'.1N 5°34'.6W** Fl(3)W 15s 34m 23M Horn(2) 30s F R 31m 13M W round tr (15m) *W vis 241°-074° (193°), R vis 060°-074° (14°) over Runnel stone and in places 074°-077° (3°) within 4M*
0034	Mousehole N pier. Head 50°04'.9N 5°32'.2W 2 F G (vert) 8m 4M Grey metal mast (3m) *2m apart. Replaced by a F R when harbour is closed*
	NEWLYN HARBOUR
0038	- S pier. Head 50°06'.1N 5°32'.5W Fl W 5s 10m 9M Siren 60s W round metal tr, R base and cupola (10m) *Vis 253°-336° (83°)*
0040	- N pier. Head 50°06'.1N 5°32'.6W F WG 4m 2M R metal post on pedestal *G238°-248° (10°), W over harbour*
0042	- Mary Williams Pier. Head. 50°06'.1N 5°32'.7W 2 FR (vert) 8m 2M Grey metal column (4m) *2m apart*
	PENZANCE HARBOUR
0046	- S pier. Head 50°07'.0N 5°31'.6W Fl WR 5s 11m 17/12 M W round tr, black base (9m) *R(unintens) 159°-224° (65°), R224°-268° (44°), W268°- 344.5° (76.5°), R344.5°-shore TE 1993*
0048	- Albert Pier. Head. 50°07'.1N 5°31'.7W 2 F G (vert) 11 m 2M Grey metal column (6m) *2m apart*
0051	- Wet Dock. N Arm 50°07'.0N 5°31'.8W 2 F R (vert) 6m 2M Column (4m)
	PORTHLEVEN HARBOUR
0056	- S pier 50°04'.9N 5°19'.1W FG 10m 4M G metal column (6m) *When harbour is open to shipping*
0057	- Inside harbour 50°05'.0N 5°18'.9W F G 10m 4M Set in stone wall. Vis 033°-067° (34°)
0060	**Lizard 49°57'.6N 5°12'.1W** Fl W 3s 70m 25M Siren Mo(N) 60s W 8-sided tr at E end of building (19m) *Vis 250°-120° (230°), ptly vis 235°-250° (15°)*
0062	**St Anthony Head 50°08'.4N 5°00'.9W** Oc WR 15s 22m 22/20/20M Horn 30s W 8-sided tr (19m) *W295°-004° (69°), R004°-022° (18°) over Manacle rocks, W(unintens) 022°-100° (78°) W100° -172° (72°). Fog Det Lt LFl W 5 min 18m 16M. Vis 148.2°-151.3° (2.5°). Shown 24 hours*
	FALMOUTH HARBOUR
0064	- Outer hr. E brkwtr. Head 50°09'.3N 5°02'.9W Fl R 2s 20m 3M Grey mast (17m)
0065	- - N arm. E head 50°09'.4N 5°03'.2W Q W 19m 3M Grey mast (16m)
0071	- - Falmouth Yacht Marina. Pontoon 50°09'.9N 5°04'.9W 2 F R (vert) 4m 1 M Pile *2m apart*
0071.2	- - - 50°09'.9N 5°04'.9W VQ(3)W 5s 1M E cardinal on pile
0071.4	- - - 50°09'.9N 5°05'.1W Fl Y 2s 1M Yellow x on pile *Marks NW limit of dredged area*
0078	Mevagissey Harbour S. pier Head 50°16'.1N 4°46'.9W Fl(2)W 10s 9m12M Horn 30s W metal tr (8m) *Temporary FW 1990*
	CHARLESTON HARBOUR
0080	- N Breakwater 50°19'.8N 4°45'.3W 2 F G (vert) 5m 1M
0080.2	- S Breakwater 50°19'.8N 4°45'.3W 2 F R (vert) 5m 1M
	FOWEY HARBOUR
0082	- Fowey 50°19'.6N 4°38'.8W LFl WR 5s 28m 11/9M W 8-sided tr, R lantern (6m) *R284°-295° (11°), W295°-028° (93°), R028°-054° (26°)*
0083	- St Catherines Pt. NE Side. 50°19.7N 4°38'.6W F R 15m 2M Lamp box. *Vis 150°-295° (145°)*
0083.5	- Lamp Rock. 50°19'.7N 4°38'.3W Fl G 5s 7m 2M Lamp box. *Vis 010°-205° (195°)*
0084	- Whitehouse Pt 50°20'.0N 4°38'.2W Iso WRG 3s 11m 11/8/8M R metal column (4m) *G017°-022° (5°), W022°-032° (10°), R032°-037° (5°)*
0086	- - N pier. Head 50°20'.0N 4°38'.1W 2 F R (vert) 4m 8M R post (2m)
0090	- Spy House Point 50°19'.8N 4°30'.6W Iso WR 6s 30m 7M W concrete pillar (3m) *W288°-060° (132°), R060°-288° (228°)*
0092	Polperro Tidal Basin. W pier. Head 50°19'.8N 4°30'.9W F W or R 4m 4M Post (3m) *R when harbour is closed*
	LOOE HARBOUR
0094	**- Banjo Pier. Head 50°21'.0N 4°27'.0W** Oc WR 3s 8m 15/12M R metal column (6m) *W013°-207° (194°), R207°-267° (60°), W267°-313° (46°), R313°-332° (19°)*
0095	- Nailzee Pt fog signal (fishing) 50°21'.0N 4°27'.0W Siren (2) 30s
0098	**Eddystone 50°10'.8N 4°15'.9W** Fl(2)W 10s 41m 24M Horn(3) 60s F R 28m 13M, Racon Grey granite tr R lantern (49m) *F R vis 112°-129° (17°) over Hand deeps*
	PLYMOUTH SOUND 'QY indicates mains failure' to the following lts: 0111.2, 0112, 0116, 0117, 0119, 0119.1, 0122, 0162, 0164, 0170, 0172, 0173, 0174, 0178, 0184, 0193
0111.2	- Whidbey 50°19'.5N 4°07'.2W Oc(2) G10s 29m 3M Or and W metal col *Vis 000°-160° (160°)*
0112	- Hooe Lake Pt. Maker 50°20'.5N 4°10'.8W Fl(2)WRG 10s 16m 11/6/6M W metal frame tr (5m) *G270°-330° (60°), W330°-004° (34°), R004°-050° (46°)*
0114	**- Plymouth brkwtr. W head 50°20'.0N 4°09'.5W** Fl WR 10s 19m 15/12M Bell(1) 15s Iso W 4s 12m 12M W round granite tr (23m) *W262°-208° (306°), R208°-262° (54°) Iso W vis 031°- 039° (8°)*
0114.5	- - E Head 50° 20'.0N 4° 08'.2W Iso WR 5s 9m 8M *R190°-353° (163°), W353°-001° (8°), R001°-018° (17°), W018°-190° (172°)*
0116	- Bovisand Pier 50°20'.2N 4°07'.6W Oc(2) G 15s 17m 3M W metal col
0117	- Withyhedge. Dir Lt 070° 50°20'.7N 4°07'.4W Dir WRG 13m 13/5/5M W ▽, orange stripe, on column *F G060°-065° (5°), Al WG065°-069° (4°), F W069°-071° (2°), Al WR071°-075° (4°), F R075°-080° (5°). Fl(2)Bu 5s10M Vis120°-160° (40) Shown 24 hours*
0119	- Ldg Lts 349°. Mallard Shoal. Front 50°21'.6N 4°08'.3W Q WRG 5m 10/3/3M *In fog, Fl W 5s vis 232°-110° (238°)* W △ on W column, Or bands *G233°-043° (170°), R043°-067° (24°), G067°- 087° (20°), W087°-099° (12°), Ldg sector R099°-108° (9°)*
0119.1	- - Hoe. Rear 396m from front 50°21'.8N 4°08'.3W Oc G 1.3s 11m 3M W ▽, orange stripe, on column *vis 310°-040° (90°)*
0122	- Dir Lt 315.5°W Hoe Beacon 50°21'.8N 4°08'.8W Dir WRG 9m 13/5/5M Orange ▽. *In fog, FW vis 313.5°-316.5° (3°)* *F G 309°-311° (2°), Al WG 311°-314° (3°), F W314°-317° (3°), Al WR 317°-320° (3°), F R 320°-329° (9°). Shown 24 hours.*
0124	- Mount Batten Breakwater. Head 50°21'.5N 4°08'.0W Fl(3)G 10s 7m 4M Metal col
0132	- Cattewater. Q Anne's Bty. DirLt 048°30' 50°21'.9N 4°07'.7W. Dir Oc WRG 7.5s 14m 3M. W tr on R roofed bldg. *G038°-047.2° (9.2°), W047.2°-049.7° (2.5°), R049.7°-060.5° (10.8°)*
0134	- - Fisher's Nose 50°21'.8N 4°08'.0W Fl(3)R 10s 6m 4M Metal column (4m)
0136	- - Cattedown Appr. Dir Lt 102° 50°21'.7N 4°07'.2W Dir F WRG 27m 8M R ▽ on R column *G090.7°-100.7° (10°), W100.7°-103.2° (2.5°), R103.2°- 113.2° (10°) TE 1993*
0137	- - Victoria pier. Head 50°21' 8N 4°07'.5W 2 F R (vert) 8m 4M R metal column (5m)
0138	- - Turnchapel Appr. Dir Lt 128°30' 50°21'.4N 4°06'.9W Dir F WRG 49m 8M R △, W stripe, *G117.8°-127.8° (10°), W127.8°-129.2° (1.4°), R129.2°-139.2° (10°)*
0140	- - Sparrows Quay 50°21'.7N 4°07'.3W 2 F R (vert) 8m 6M Column
0146	- - Baltic Wharf. Elphinstone Quay 50°21'.8N 4°08' 0W Fl R 2s 8m 5M

0148   - - Queen Anne's Breakwater. Knuckle 50°21'.8N 4°07'.9W
      OcG 8s 5m 2M Silver metal col (3m)

0148.5   - - - Head 50°21'.9N 4°07'.9W
      Fl(2)G 5s 5m 2M Silver metal col (3m)
      2 F G (vert) 2M on head of floating piers A-E inside marina

0150   - Sutton Hr W pier. Head 50°21'.9N 4°07'.9W
      Fl R 3s 5m 2M
      Silver post (3m)

0151   - - E pier. Head 50°21'.9N 4°07'.9W
      Fl G 3s 5m 2M
      Silver post (3m)

0154   - - Whitehouse pier 50°22'.0N 4°08'.0W
      2 F R (vert) 4m 1M
      Metal column (3m) *At each end*

0156   - - Wharf. Head 50°22'.1N 4°08'.0W
      2 F R (vert) 5m 1M
      Mast (3m)

0162   - W King. Dir Lt 271° 50°21'.6N 4°09'.7W
      Dir WRG, 14m 13/5/5M
      W ▽, orange stripe, on column
      F G264°-266° (2°), Al WG266°-270° (4°), F W270°-272° (2°),
      Al WR272° -276° (4°), F R276°-284° (8°).
      Shown 24 hours

0164   - Mill Bay. Dir Lt 048°30' 50°21'.7N 4°09'.0W
      Dir Q WRG 12m 11/3/3M
      W △ on W mast, Or bands
      G006.5°-045.5° (39°), W045.5°-051.5° (6°),
      R051.5°-071.5° (20°), W321.5°-329.5° (8°), R329.5°-006.5° (37°)

0166   - - Millbay pier. Head 50°21'.7N 4°09'.1W
      Q G 10m 2M
      Concrete column (8m)

0167   - - Camber jetty. Head 50°21'.7N 4°09'.2W
      Q R 5m 2M
      Grey metal column (5m)

0168   - - Trinity pier. Head 50°21'.8N 4°09'.1W
      2 F G (vert) 8m 2M
      Concrete column (8m) *2m apart*

0169   - - RoRo Ferry Terminal. Head 50°21'.8N 4°09'.3W
      2 F R (vert) 6m 2M
      Dolphin *2m apart*

0169.2   - - - W side 50°21'.9N 4° 09'.3W
      2 F R (vert) 6m 2M Dolphin *2m apart*

0170   - Ravenness. Dir Lt 225° 50°21'.1N 4°10'.0W
      Dir WRG 11m 13/5/5M (24 hours)
      W ▽, orange stripe, on column
      F G217°-221° (4°), Al WG221°-224° (3°), F W224°-226° (2°),
      Al WR226°-229° (3°), FR229°-237° (8°).
      In fog, Fl(2)W 15s vis 160°-305° (145°)

0172   - Mount Wise pier. Root. Dir Lt 343° 50°21'.9N 4°10'.3W
      Dir WRG 7m 13/5/5M (24 hours)
      W ▽, orange stripe on W hut
      F G331°-338° (7°), Al WG338°-342° (4°), F W342°-344° (2°),
      Al WR344°-348° (4°), FR348°-351° (3°).
      In fog, FW vis 341.5°-344.5° (3°)

0173   - Bridge 50°21'.0N 4°09'.8W
      Fl(2)Bu 5s 5m 3M
      W ▽, orange stripe, on column
      Vis 140°-210° (70°)

0174   - Devil's Pt 50°21'.6N 4°10'.0W
      Q G 5m 3M *In fog Fl W 5s.*
      Or and W concrete column

0178   - Hamoaze. Ocean Court Dir Lt 085°
      50°21'.8N 4°10'.0W
      Dir Q WRG 15m 11/3/3M
      In fog, Fl W 5s vis 270°-100° (190°)
      Orange ▽ on W structure (3m)
      G010°-080° (70°), W080°-090° (10°), R090°-100° (10°)

0179   - - Marina. Pontoon F 50°21'.7N 4°10'.0W
      2 F R (Vert) 2M W metal column (4m)

0180   - - - - Pontoon B 50°21'.8N 4°09'.9W
      2 FR (vert) 2M W metal column (4m)

0182   - - Mutton Cove. Landing Stage 50°21'.9N 4°10'.5W
      2 F G (vert) 5m 1M Metal column (3m)

0184   - - Millbrook 50°21'.3N 4°11'.3W
      Q WG 11m 11/3M
      W △, orange stripe, on column
      G165°-180° (15°), W180°-230° (50°)

0185   - - Sango Point 50°21'.7N 4°12'.3W
      QW 8m 5M
      Beacon *Vis 215°-289° (74°)*

0186   - - N corner. Landing Stage 50°22'.3N 4°11'.0W
      2 F G (vert) 2m 2M Metal column

0193   - - NW corner 50°23'.4N 4°11'.5W
      Q WRG 12m 11/3/3M *In fog, Fl W 5s vis 310°-*
      220° (270°) Column
      W340°-355° (15°), R355°-025° (30°), G025°-055° (30°),
      W055°-110° (55°), R110°-140° (30°), W140°-230° (90°)

      SALCOMBE HARBOUR
0220   - Sandhill Pt. Dir Lt 000° 50°13'.7N 3°46'.6W

      Dir Fl WRG 2s 27m 10/7/7M
      R and W diamond on W mast (12m)
      R002.5°-182.5° (180°), G182.5°-357.5° (175°), W357.5°-
      002.5° (5°)

0221   - Blackstone Rock 50°13'.5N 3°46'.4W
      Q(2)G 8s 4m 2M G and W Beacon

0222   - Ldg Lts 042°30'. Front 50°14'.5N 3°45'.2W
      Q W 5m 8M Mast

0222.1   - - Rear. 180m from front 50°14'6N 3°45'.1W
      Q W 45m 8M
      Stone column (2m)

0224   - Landing Stage 50°14'.1N 3°45'.9W
      F R 4m 3M W metal column (3m)

0228   **Start Pt 50°13'.3N 3°38'.5W**
      Fl(3)W 10s 62m 25M Horn 60s
      F R 55m 12M
      W round granite tr (28m)
      Fl W vis 184°-068° (244°), F R vis 210°-255° (45°) over
      Skerries bank

      DARTMOUTH HARBOUR
0236   - Kingswear 50°20'.8N 3°34'.0W
      Iso WRG 3s 9m 8M
      W round GRP tr
      G318°-325° (7°), W325°-331° (6°), R331°-340° (9°)
      Temp extinguished (1989)

0237   - - 50°20'.6N 3°33'.7W
      F W 5m 9M R lantern
      Vis 102°-107° (5°)

0238   - Dartmouth. Bayards Cove 50°20'.8N 3°34'.6W
      Fl WRG 2s 5m 6M W stripe on rock
      G280°-289° (9°), W289°-297° (8°), R297°-shore

0244   **Berry Head 50°24'.0N 3°28'.9W**
      Fl(2)W 15s 58m 18M W tr (5m)
      Vis 100°-023° (283°)

      TORBAY
0246   - Brixham. Victoria brkwtr. Head 50°24'.3N 3°30'.7W
      Oc R 15s 9m 6M
      W tr (6m)

0247.4   - - Prince William Marina. Wave Screen. SW end.
      50°23'.9N 3°30'.5W
      2 FlR 5s (vert) 4m 2M Mast (4m) *2m apart*

0247.6   - - - - E end. 50°24'.1N 3°30'.4W
      2FlG 5s (vert) 4m 2M Mast (4m) *2m apart*

0248   - - New pier. Head 50°23'.8N 3°30'.6W
      Q G 6m 3M
      W metal structure (1m)

0249   - - Fish Market pier. Head. SW corner. 50°23'.9N 3°30'.6W
      2FG(vert) 5m 1M. On building *2m apart*

0249.2   - - - - NW corner. 50°23'.9N 3°30.6N
      2FG(vert) 5m 1M.
      On building *2m apart*

0250   - Paignton. E quay 50°25'.9N 3°33'.3W
      Fl R 7m 3M
      R metal column (5m)

0252   - Torquay Harbour. Princess pier. Head 50°27'.4N 3°31'.7W
      Q R 9m 6M
      Metal column (7m)

0254   - - Haldon pier. Head 50°27'.4N 3°31'7W
      Q G 9m 6M
      Metal column (7m)

0256   - - S pier. Head 50°27'.5N 3°31'.5W
      2 F G (vert) 6m 5M
      Metal structure (1m) *Temp extinguished (1991)*

      TEIGNMOUTH HARBOUR
0262   - The Den. Ldg Lts 334°. Front 50°32'.5N 3°29'.7W
      F R 10m 6M
      Grey round stone tr (6m)
      Vis 225°-135° (270°)

0262.1   - - Powderham Terr. Rear. 62m from Front
      50°32'.5N 3°29.7W
      F R 11m 3M
      Black column (6m)

0263   - Training Wall. Middle. Ph. Lucette bn
      50°32'.3N 3°29'.8W
      Oc R 5.5s 4m 2M
      W stone column, black base

      EXMOUTH HARBOUR
0270   - Straight Pt 50°36'.5N 3°21'.7W
      Fl R 10s 34m 7M
      Metal mast (7m)

0274   - Ldg Lts 305°. Front 50°36'.9N 3°25'.3W
      F Y 6m 7M
      W metal column (2m)
      Difficult to distinguish by day

0274.1   - - Custom House. Rear 57m from front
      50°36'.9N 3°25'.3W
      F Y 12m 7M
      Black mast (10m)

0275	- Exmouth pier. S corner 50°36'.9N 3°25'.4W 2 F G (vert) 7m 3M Aluminium column (5m) *2m apart Temp extinguished (1991)*
0277	River Exe. Turf Lock. Entrance. E side 50°39'.6N 3°27'.7W 2 F R (vert) 7m 3M Aluminium column (5m) *2m apart*
0282	Axmouth. Pier. Hd. 50°42'.1N 3°03'.2W Fl W 5s 7m 2M △ on metal col
	LYME REGIS
0284	- Ldg Lts 296°. Victoria pier. Head. Front 50°43'.2N 2°56'.1W Oc WR 8s 6m 9/7M Blue metal column (5m) R296°-116°(180°) W116°-296°(180°)
0284.1	- - Rear 240m from Front 50°43'.2N 2°56'.2W F G 8m 9M On building
	BRIDPORT HARBOUR
0288	- E pier. Head 50°42'.5N 2°45'.7W F G 3m 2M On pier capping *Occasional*
0290	- W pier. Head 50°42'.5N 2°45'.8W F R 3m 2M On pier capping *Occasional*
0290.2	- - Root 50°42'.6N 2°45'.8W Iso R 2s 9m 5M Harbour Master's office
0294	**Portland Bill 50°30'.8N 2°27'.3W** Fl(4)W 20s 43m 25M Dia 30s F R 19m 13M W round tr, R band (41m) *W grad changes from Fl(1) to Fl(4) 221°-244°(23°), Fl(4) 244°-117°(233°), grad changes from Fl(4) to Fl(1) 117°-141°(24°) R vis 271°-291°(20°) over The Shambles*
	PORTLAND HARBOUR
0302	- Outer brkwtr. D Head 50°34'.1N 2°25'.1W Oc R 30s 12m 5M Frame tr on concrete hut (8m)
0308	- - 530m from N end. Bn E 50°34'.8N 2°24'.8W 2 F W (vert) 7m 2M o on beacon (5m) *Obsc from seaward . 2m apart*
0310	- - N end. Fort Head 50°35'.1N 2°24'.8W Q R 14m 5M Metal frame tr (2m) *Vis 013°-268°(255°)*
0314	**- NE brkwtr. SE end. A Head 50°35'.1N 2°25'.0W** Fl W 10s 22m 20M W metal tr (22m)
0320	- - - NW end. B Head 50°35'.6N 2°25'.8W Oc R 15s 11m 5M Grey metal column (2m)
0322	- Northern Arm. SE end. C Head 50°35'.7N 2°25'.9W Oc G 10s 11m 5M Grey metal column (2m)
0323	- - Torpedo pier. Head 50°35'.9N 2°26'.8W Fl G 5s 7m 2M Pedestal. *Obsc when brg less than 290°*
0325	- Naval Air Station 50°34'.2N 2°27'.5W OcG 15s 14m 10M Frame tr
0326	- Camber jetty. E. arm 50°34'.1N 2°25'.9W 2 F R (vert) 4m 2M Metal column (2m)
0326.2	- - N arm 50°34'.1N 2°25'.9W 2 F R (vert) 4m 2M Metal column (2m)
0326.5	- Loading Jetty. N end 50°34'.1N 2°26'.0W QW 4m 2M Metal column
0327	- Coaling pier. Catwalk. Head 50°34'.3N 2°25'.8W VQ(3)W 5s 2M Dolphin
0327.2	- - NE corner 50°34'.2N 2°25'.8W FR 5m 2M
0327.5	- - Deep water berth. E end 50°34'.3N 2°25'.9W 2 F R (vert) 5m 2M Metal column
0327.6	- - - W end 50°34'.2N 2°26'.0W 2FR (vert) 5m 2M Metal column
0330	- Q pier. Head. N corner 50°34'.3N 2°26'.2W Fl R 5s 5m 5M Metal frame tr (3m)
0332	- - - S corner 50°34'.3N 2°26'.2W Fl G 5s 5m 5M Metal frame tr (3m)
0334	- - Elbow 50°34'.3N 2°26'.3W Fl R 2s 6m 2M Metal frame tr (3m)
0339	- New Entrance 50°34'.9N 2°27'.6W L Fl W 10s 3m 5M W square on metal pile
339.4	- Ferrybridge Ldg Lts 288° Front 50°35'.0N 2°28'.1W QG 3m 2M Post
0339.41	- - Rear 63m from front 50°35'.0N 2°28'.1W IsoG 4s 5m 2M On bridge
0340	- Wellworthy Bn 50°35'.3N 2°27'.7W Fl(4)W 10s 3m 5M W square on metal pile
	WEYMOUTH HARBOUR
0346	- S pier. Head 50°36'.5N 2°26'.4W Q W 10m 9M W mast on grey metal platform (8m)
0348	- Ldg Lts 239°45'. Ballast quay. Front 50°36'.4N 2°26'.8W F R 5m 4M R diamond on W post (3m)
0348.1	- - Rear 17m from front 50°36'.4N 2°26'.8W F R 7m 4M R diamond on W mast (5m)
0354	- N pier. Head 50°36'.5N 2°26'.6W 2 F G (vert) 9m 6M Bell (when vessels expected) G column *2m apart*
0356	- - Ro Ro Ferry Terminal. 50°36'.5N 2°26'.7W 2 F G (vert) 10m 2M Dolphin *2m apart*
0496	**Anvil Pt 50°35'.5N 1°57'.5W** Fl W 10s 45m 24M W round tr and dwelling (12m) *Vis 237°-076°(199°) shown 24 hours*
0498	Swanage pier. Head 50°36'.5N 1°56'.9W 2 F R (vert) 6m 3M Mast (3m)
	POOLE HARBOUR
0507	- R Motor YC. E Brkwater 50°41'.3N 1°56'.7W 2 FG (vert) 2M *2m apart*
0507.2	- - W Brkwater 50°41'.3N 1°56'.7W 2 FG (vert) 2M *2m apart*
0508	- Bullpit Beacon 50°41'.7N 1°56'.6W Q(9) W 15s 7m 4M W cardinal mark on yelllow dolphin, black band, name on side
0510.4	- - Salterns Marina. Outer brkwtr. Head 50°42'.2N 1°57'.0W 2 F R (vert) 2M *2m apart Traffic signals*
0510.6	- - - Inner brkwtr. Head 50°42'.2N 1°57'.0W 2 F G (vert) 3M *2m apart*
0513	- Starting platform 50°42'.3N 1°58'.0W Q W 8m lM Hut on dolphin
0515	- New Quay. LCT S End. 50°42'.5N 1°59'.1W 2 F G (vert) 2M Dolphin *2m apart*
0521	Bournemouth. Pier. Head 50°42'.8N 1°52'.4W 2 F R (vert) 9m 1M Reed(2) 120s Bell *2m apart* W column (4m) *Fog signals when vessel is expected*
0522	Boscombe. Pier. Head 50°43'.1N 1°50'.5W 2 F R (vert) 7m 1M R column (3m)
	NEEDLES CHANNEL
0528	**- Needles 50°39'.7N 1°35'.4W** Oc(2) WRG 20s 24m 17/17/14/14M Horn (2) 30s Round granite tr, R band, R lantern (31m) *R shore-300°, W300°-083°(143°), R(unintens(083°- 212°(129°), W212°-217°(5°), G217°-224°(7°), R224°-shore*
0534	- Totland Bay. Pier. Head 50°41'.0N 1°32'.7W 2 F G (vert) 6m 2M.
0538	- Hurst Pt Ldg Lts 042°. Front 50°42'.4N 1°33'.1W Iso W 4s 15m 14M R square tr (16m) *Vis 029°-053°(24°)*
0538.1	- - Rear 215m from front 50°42'.5N 1°32'.9W Iso WR 6s 23m 14/13/11M W round tr (26m) *W(unintens)080°-104°(24°), W234°-244°(10°), R244°- 250°(6°), W250°-053°(163°)*
	LYMINGTON RIVER
0542	- Entrance Ldg Lts 319°30'. Front 50°45'.2N 1°31'.6W F R 12m 8M Metal column (11m) *Vis 309.5°-329.5°(20°)*
0542.1	- - Rear 363m from front 50°45'.3N 1°31'.7W F R 17m 8M Metal column (17m) *Vis 309.5°-329.5°(20°)*

0543	- Cross Boom. No. 2 50°44'.3N 1°30'.5W Fl R 2s 4m 3M R square on pile (8m)
0544	- No 1 50°44'.4N 1°30'.4W Fl G 2s 2m 3M G △ on pile (6m)
0545	- No 3 50°44'.4N 1°30'.5W Fl G 2s 2m 3M G △ on pile (6m)
0546	- No 7 50°44'.7N 1°30'.9W Fl G 2s 2m 1 M G △ on pile (5m)
0548	- Cocked Hat 50°45'.0N 1°31'.1W Fl R 2s 3m 3M R stripe on pile (5m)
0549	- Cage Boom. No 9 50°45'1N 1°31'.1W Fl G 2s 4m 3M G △ on pile
0550	- Harper's Post 50°45'.1N 1°31'.4W Q(3)W 10s 5m 1M E cardinal on black pile yellow band (7m)
0551	- Car Ferry. Pier. Head 50°45'.4N 1°31'.6W 2 F G (vert) 5m 3M Post (3m)
0554	Beaulieu Spit. E end 50°46'.8N 1°21'.7W Fl R 5s 3M R dolphin W band *Vis 277°-037° (120°)*

ENGLAND - SOUTH COAST - ISLE OF WIGHT

0555	Victoria. Pier. Head 50°42'.4N 1°31'.1W 2 F G (vert) 4M Column *2m apart*
	YARMOUTH
0558	- Pier. Head. Centre 50°42'.5N 1°29'.9W 2 F R (vert) 2M High intens F W (occas) G metal column *2m apart*
0560	- Jetty. Head 50°42'.4N 1°29'.9W FR 4m 2M Second FR shows when hr is full. *In fog FY* W wooden mast
0561	- Ferry terminal 50°42'.4N 1°30'.0W 2 FR (vert) 5m 2M Dolphin *2m apart*
0562	- Ldg Lts 187°34'. Front 50°42'.3N 1°30'.0W F G 5m 2M W diamond, black band on W metal post
0562.1	- - Rear 63m from front 50°42'.3N 1°30'.0W F G 9m 2M W diamond, black band on W mast

ENGLAND - SOUTH COAST
OFF STANSORE POINT

0575	- 50°46'.7N 1°20'.7W QR 4m 1M R diamond, W band, on R pile *Marks cables*
0575.2	- 50°46'.8N 1°20'.5W QR 4m 1M R diamond, W band, on R pile *Marks cables*
0575.4	- 50°46'.9N 1°20'.4W QR 4m 1M R diamond, W band, on R pile *Marks cables Rep missing (1985)*

ENGLAND - SOUTH COAST - SOUTHAMPTON WATER

0576	Calshot Spit Lt F 50°48'.3N 1°17'.5W Fl W 5s 12m 11M Horn (2) 60s R hull, Lt tr amidships
0577	Outfall 50°48'.2N 1°18'.7W Iso R 10s 6m 5M Horn 20s 4 F R 4m 1M Metal column on square concrete structure. *1 F R on each corner*
	CONTROLLED ANCHORAGE
0581.9	- Inshore Lts in line 326°07'. Front 50°51'.3N 1°20'.2W 0.53M from rear Fl W 2s 14m 3M Yellow △, R border, on metal tr
0582	- - Common rear 50°51'.7N 1°20'.7W LFl Y 6s 17m 5M Yellow diamond, R border, on metal tr
0582.1	- - Offshore Lts in line 327°25'. Front 50°51'.3N 1°20'.2W 0.53M from rear Fl W 2s 14m 3M Yellow o, R border, on metal tr
0586	Esso Marine Terminal. SE end 50°50'.0N 1°19'.3W 2 F R (vert) 9m 10M Whis(2) 20s *2m apart*
0588.5	- AGWI Pier. Head 50°50'.2N 1°19'.7W 2 F R (vert) 4m 2M *2m apart*

	RIVER HAMBLE
0590	- Ldg Lts 345°.30'. No. 6. Front 50°50'.6N 1°18'.7W Oc(2) R 12s 4m 2M R square on beacon
0590.01	- - Hamble. Rear 50°51'.0N 1°18'.9W 820m from front QR 12m W mast
0590.14	- No 1 50°50'.3N 1°18'.6W Fl G 3s 3M G △ on beacon
0590.16	- No 2 50°50'.4N 1°18'.7W Q (3)W 10s 3M E cardinal on beacon
0594	BP Hamble Jetty 50°50'.8N 1°19'.4W 2 F G (vert) 5m 2M Grey posts on dolphins (1m) *2m apart*
0601	Hythe pier. Head 50°52'.5N 1°23'.5W 2 F R (vert) 12m 5M Mast (9m) *2m apart*
0602	Queen Elizabeth II Terminal. S end 50°53'.0N 1°23'.6W 4 F G (vert) 16m 3M Frame tr (16m) *2m apart*
	RIVER ITCHEN
0605	- E side. No 2 50°53'.2N 1°23'.3W Fl G 5s 2M G △ on beacon
0610	- Empress Dock. S head 50°53'.3N 1°23'.6W 2 F R (vert) 8m 3M R ▽ on grey metal frame tr
0612	- - N head 50°53'.3N 1°23'.5W 2 F G (vert) 8m 3M Yellow △ on grey metal frame tr (6m) *Vis 246°-000° (114°)*
0614	- No 4 50°53'.6N 1°23'.1W Q G 4m 2M G △ on W pile, black base
0618.2	- Woolston. Bridge W pier 50°53'.9N 1°23'.0W 2 F R (vert) 2M *On N and S sides of bridge 2m apart*
0618.4	- - E pier 50°53'.9N 1°23'.0W 2 F G (vert) 2M *On N and S sides of bridge 2m apart*
0620.5	- Crosshouse Bn 50°54'.0N 1°23'.1W Oc R 5s 5m 2M R square on R pile structure
0620.7	- Chapel Bn 50°54'.1N 1°23'.1W Fl G 3s 5m 3M G △ on beacon (5m)
0621.4	- Jetty. Head 50°54'.7N 1°22'.5W 2 F R (vert) 5m 1 M Metal column *2m apart*
0621.6	- Kemps Marina Jetty. Head 50°54'.8N 1°22'.6W 2 F G (vert) 5m 1M Metal column *2m apart*
	RIVER TEST
0626	- Town Quay. Ldg Lts 329°. Front 50°53'.5N 1°24'.2W F Y 12m 3M, 2 F G (vert) W △, G border, on metal frame tr *Neon △*
0626.1	- - Rear. 410m from front 50°53'.7N 1°24'.4W FY 22m 2M W diamond, R border, on metal frame tr (23m) *Neon diamond*
0628	- Royal pier. SE head 50°53'.6N 1°24'.4W 2 F G (vert) 8m 2M Metal column (8m)
0633	- - Husbands Jetty. Off head 50°53'.8N 1°25'.5W 2 F R (vert) 9m 2M Dolphin *2m apart*
0633.2	- - - Elbow 50°53'.9N 1°25'.6W 2 F R (vert) 9m 2M Mast *2m apart*

ENGLAND - SOUTH COAST - ISLE OF WIGHT
COWES HARBOUR

0652	- Ldg Lts 164°. Front 50°45'.9N 1°17'.8W Iso W 2s 3m 6M Post
0652.1	- - Rear 290m from front 50°45'.7N 1°17'.7W Iso R 2s 5m 3M Dolphin *Vis 120°-240° (120°)*
0654	- E brkwtr. Head 50°45'.8N 1°17'.4W Fl R 3s 3M
0656	- C Lallow Slipway. Head 50°45'.6N 1°17'.6W 2 F G (vert) 3m 1M Wooden post
0661.3	- River Medina CEGB Wharf 50°44'.7N 1°17'.2W 2 F R (vert) 2M
0661.5	- - Medham 50°44'.3N 1°17'.2W VQ(3)W 5s 4m 3M
0661.7	- - W side. South Folly 50°43'.8 1°16'.8W Q G 3m 1M G post

0662   - - Newport. Ldg Lts 192°15'. Front
50°42'.4N 1°17'.3W
2 F R (hor) 7m 2M
W diamond on beacon

0662.1   - - Rear 37m from front 50°42'.4N 1°17'.3W
2 F R (hor) 11 m 2M
W diamond on beacon

0664   Wootton Beacon 50°44'.5N 1°12'.0W
QW 1M
N cardinal beacon

0669   Ryde Harbour E side 50°44.1N 1°09'4W
2 F R (vert) 7m 1M metal mast (6m) *2m apart*
On same structure, tidal lts FY when depth of
water more than1m in harbour and 2 FY (vert)
when depth of water greater than 1.5m

0669.2   - - W side 50°.44'1N 1°09'.4W
2 F G (vert)
7m 1M metal mast (6m) *2m apart*

ENGLAND - SOUTH COAST
0680   Fort Gilkicker 50°46'.4N 1°08'.4W
Oc G 10s 7M
Signal mast

0684   Submerged barrier, S side of passage
50°46'.0N 1°04'.0W
Q R 6m 2M
Dolphin (6m)

0686   South Parade pier. Head 50°46'.6N 1°04'.5W
2 F G (vert) 5m 1M
Posts (3m). *At each corner*

ENGLAND - SOUTH COAST - PORTSMOUTH HARBOUR
0688   Spit Sand Fort 50°46'.2N 1°05'.8W
Fl R 5s 18m 7M
Large round stone structure

0691   Southsea Castle and Dir Lt 001°30'
50°46'.7N 1°05'.3W
Iso W 2s 16m 11 M
Dir WRG, 11m 13/5/5M
W stone tr, black band (l0m)
Iso W vis 339°-066°(87°), F G351.5°-357.5°(6°),
Al WG357.5°-000°(2.5°) W phase incr with bearing, F W000°-003°(3°),
Al WR003°-005.5°(2.5°) R phase incr with bearing, F R005.5°-011.5°(6°).
Shown 24 hours.

0692.5   Fort Blockhouse Dir Lt 320° 50°47'.3N 1°06'.6W
Dir WRG 6m 13/5/5M
Base of mast
Oc G310°-316°(6°), AlWG 316°-318.5°(2.5°) W phase incr
with bearing, OcW 318.5°-321.5°(3°), AlWR 321.5°-
324°(2.5°) R phase incr with bearing, OcR 324°-330°(6°).
Shown 24H. 2 F R (vert) 20m E

0692.8   Harbour Entrance Dir Lt 50°47'.8N 1°06'.9W
Dir WRG 2m 1M, concrete dolphin (4m)
IsoG 2s 322.5°-330°(7.5°), AlWG 330°-332.5°(2.5°), IsoW
2s 332.5°-335°(2.5°), AlWR 335°-337.5°(2.5°), IsoR 2s
337.5°-345°(7.5)

0698   Victoria Pile 50°47'.3N 1°06'.4W
Oc G 15s 1M
G pile

0700   The Point 50°47'.5N1°06'.5W
Q G 2M
Pile (5m)

0704   Railway Landing Stage. S end 50°47'.7N 1°06'.5W
2 F G (vert) 5m 3M
Post (2m)

0704.4   - Near N end 50°47'.8 1°06'.5W
2 F G (vert) 5m 3M
Post

0706   North Corner Jetty 50°48'.4N 1°06'.6W
Fl G 2s 11m 2M on roof of building (9m)

0733   Gosport Marina S Breakwater.
Head 50°47'.8N 1°06'.9W 2 F R (vert)
5m 3M Mast *2m apart*

0733.2   - - Floating Breakwater. S End 50°47'.8N
1°06'.9W 2 F G (vert) 4m 3M Mast *2m apart*

0733.4   - - - N End 50°47'.9 1°06'.9W 2 F R (vert)
4m 3M Mast *2m apart*

0734   - Landing Stage. Head 50°47'.6N 1°06'.9W
2 F R (vert) 6m 2M
Mast (5m) at each end *2m apart*

ENGLAND - SOUTH COAST
0750   **Horse Sand Fort 50°45'.0N 1°04'.3W**
Fl W 10s 21m 15M
Large round stone structure

0752   **No Man's Land Fort 50°44'.4N 1°05'.6W**
Fl W 5s 21m 15M
Large round stone structure

ENGLAND - SOUTH COAST - ISLE OF WIGHT
0760   St Helen's Fort 50°42'.3N 1°05'.0W
Fl(3)W 10s 16m 8M
Large round stone structure

0762   Bembridge Harbour Channel Entr. W side 50°42'.4N
1°04'.9W
Fl Y 2s 1M X on Y pile

0768   Sandown pier. Head 50°39'.0N 1°09'.0W
2 F R (vert) 7m 2M *2m apart*

0772   Ventnor pier 50°35'.4N 1°12'.2W
2 F R (vert) 10m 3M
Post (3m)

0774   **St Catherine's Pt 50°34'.5N 1°17'.8W**
Fl W 5s 41m 27M
F R 35m 17M
W 8 sided castellated tr and dwelling (26m)
Fl W vis 257°-117° (220°), F R vis 099°-116°(17°)

0780   **NAB 50°40'.0N 0°57'.1W**
Fl(2) W 10s 27m 15M Horn (2) 30s Racon
R lantern on concrete and metal tr. Wind generators *Vis 300°-120° (180°)*

ENGLAND - SOUTH COAST
LANGSTONE HARBOUR
0782   - Eastney Pt. Drain bn 50°47'.2N 1°01'.6W
Q R 2m 2M
Concrete dolphin

0782.08   - - Outfall Jetty. Head 50°47'.3N 1°01'.6W
2 F R (vert) 5m 5M *2m apart*

0782.65   - Langstone Channel South Lake 50°49'.5N 0°59'.7W
Fl G 3s 3m 2M
Pile

0782.67   - - Binness 50°49'.6N 0°59'8W
Fl R 3s 3m 2M
Pile

0783.4   Chichester Bar 50°45'.9N 0°56'.4W
Fl WR 5s 14m 7/5M
W frame tr R sq topmark
W322°-080°(118°), R080°-322°(242°)
Fl(2)R 10s 7m 2M vis 020°-080°(60°)

0789   Selsey Bill. Lifeboat station 50°43'.6N 0°46'.6W
F R 3M *Occas*

0790   **Owers Lanby 50°37'.3N 0°40'.6W**
Fl(3)W 20s 12m 22M Horn(3) 60s
R tubular superstructure on circular buoy

LITTLEHAMPTON HARBOUR
0800   - West pier. Head 50°47'.8N 0°32'.4W
2 F R (vert) 7m 6M
R square on beacon *2m apart*

0801   - East pier. Ldg Lts 346°. Front 50°48'.1N 0°32'.4W
F G 6m 7M
Black metal column

0801.1   - - Rear 64m from front 50°48'.1N 0°32'.4W
Oc WY 7.5s 9m 10M
W concrete tr
W290°-356°(66°) Y356°-042° (46°)

0804   - Norfolk Wharf. NW corner 50°48'.4N 0° 32'.6W
Fl G 3s 4m 5M
Black metal column (3m)
Vis 320°-032° (72°)

0808   - Bridge. SW fendering 50°48'.6N 0°32'.9W
2 F R (vert) 3m 2M *1m apart*

0808.2   - - NE fendering 50°48'.6N 0°32'.9W
2 F G (vert) 3m 2M *1m apart*

0810   Worthing pier. Head 50°48'.4N 0°22'.0W
2 F R (vert) 6m 1 M
Column (4m)

SHOREHAM HARBOUR
0812   - W brkwtr. Head 50°49'.4N 0°14'.8W
Fl R 5s 7m 7M
R concrete column (3m)

0813   - E brkwtr. Head 50°49'.5N 0°14'.7W
Fl G 5s 7m 8M Siren 120s
G concrete column (3m)

0814   - Ldg Lts 355°. Middle pier. Front 50°49'.7N 0°14'.8W
OcW 5s 8m 10M Traffic signals Horn 20s
W watch house, R base (6m)

0814.1   **- - Rear 192m from front 50°49'.8N 0°14'.8W**
Fl W 10s 13m 15M
Grey round stone tr (12m) *Vis 283°-103°(180°)*

BRIGHTON
0820   - West pier. Head 50°49'.1N 0°09'.0W
Fl R 10s 13m 2M Bell(1) 13s
Mast *Bell at SW end when vessels expected*

0822   - Marine Palace pier. Head 50°48'.8N 0°08'.1W
2 F R (vert) 10m 2M
Mast on hut (7m)

0825   - Marina. E brkwtr 50°48'.6N 0°06'.3W
Fl(4)WR 20s 16m 10/8M
W pillar, G bands
R260°-295°(35°) W295°-100°(165°)

0825.2   - - - Head 50°48'.6N 0°06'.3W
Q G 8m 7M

0826	- - W brkwtr. Head 50°48'.5N 0°06'.3W Q R 10m 7M Horn(2) 30s W round structure, R bands
0830	NEWHAVEN HARBOUR - Brkwtr. Head 50°46'.5N 0°03'.6E Oc(2)W 10s 17m 12M Horn 30s Concrete tr (14m)
0832	- E pier. Head 50°46'.8N 0°03'.7E Iso G 5s 12m 6M W metal frame tr (12m)
0833	- - Inner End. 50°46'.9N 0°03'.6E 2 FG (vert) 6m 2M *2m apart*
0833.4	- E Quay. S End 50°47'.0N 0°03'.5E 2 FG (vert) 6m 2M *2m apart*
0839	**Greenwich Lanby 50°24'.5N 0°00'.0** Fl W 5s 12m 21M Horn 30s R tubular superstructure on circular buoy. Racon
0840	**Beachy Head 50°44'.0N 0°14'.6E** Fl(2)W 20s 31m 25M Horn 30s W round tr R band and lantern (43m) *Vis 248°-101°(213°)* *Fog Det Lt Fl W 4-7 times every 4 min, 6s intervals, vis 085.5°-265.5°(180°)*
0843	**Royal Sovereign 50°43'.4N 0°26'.2E** Fl W 20s 28m 28M Dia(2) 30s W tr R band on W cabin on concrete column
0846	Eastbourne pier. Head 50°45'.9N 0°17'.8E 2 F R (vert) 8m 2M Metal column (3m)
1244	**FRANCE - NORTH COAST** **FÉCAMP.** **-Jetée Nord 49°46'.0N 0°21'.9E** Fl(2)W 10s 15m 16M Horn(2) 30s Grey tr R top (14m). *Fog signal -2.1/2HW+2*
1245	- - Root 49°46'.0N 0°21'.7E QR 10m 4M R circle on W mast (7m) *In line 082° with 1246*
1246	- Jetée Sud. Head 49°45'.9N 0°21'.9E Q G 14m 9M Grey tr, G top (10m) *Obsc on bearings more than 217°*
1250	**Cap d'Antifer 49°41'.1N 0°10'.0'E** Fl W 20s 128m 29M Grey 8-sided tr, G top (38m) *Vis 021°-222°(201°)*
1250.2	PORT D'ANTIFER - Approach Ldg Lts 127°30'. Front 49°38'.3N 0°09'.2E Dir OcW 4s 105m 22M; by day Dir FW 33M W pylon G top (7m) *Dir OcW vis 127°-128°(1°), Dir FW vis 126.5°-128.5°(2°).* *Occas*
1250.21	- - - Rear 430m from front 49°38'.2N 0°09'.4E Dir OcW 4s 124m 22M; by day Dir FW 33M W pylon, G top (13m) *Vis: as 1250.2*
1250.8	- 49°39'.5N 0°09'.2E Dir Oc WRG 4s 24m 15/13/13M W pylon, black top (20m) *G068.5°-078.5°(10°), W078.5°-088.5°(10°), R088.5° 098°.5(10°)*
1251	- Bassin de Caux. Mole Ouest. Head 49°39'.0N 0°08'.8E Fl R 4s 13m 5M W mast, R top (8m)
1251.2	- - - Elbow Dir Lt 018°30' 49°39'.3N 0°09'.0E Dir Oc WRG 4s 11m 15/11/11M Pylon (5m) *G006.5°-17.5°(11°), W17.5°-19.5°(2°), R19.5°-36.5°(17°)*
1251.4	- - Jetée Est. Head 49°39'.0N 0°09'.0E Fl G 4s 13m 5M W mast, G top (8m)
1251.6	- Digue M Thieullent. NE corner 49°40'.3N 0°08'.2E F Vi 15m 5 M W pylon, purple top (8m)
1251.62	- - NW corner 49°40'.3N 0°07'.4E F Vi 15m 5M W pylon, purple top (8m)
1251.7	- - Post 2 49°40'.3N 0°08'.1E Dir Oc(2)WRG 6s 24m 15/13/13M W pylon, R top (17m) *G334.5°-346.5°(12°), W346.5°-358.5°(12°), R358.5°-004.5°(6.5°)*
1251.8	- - Post 3 49°40'.3N 0°07'.7E Dir Oc WRG 4s 21m 15/13/13M W pylon, R top (17m) *R352.5°-358°.5(6°), W358.5°-010.5°(12°), G010.5°-022.5°(12°)*
1251.84	- - Head 49°39'.8N 0°07'.1E Q R 20m 7M W structure, R top (17m)
1254	**LHA Lanby 49°31'.7N 0°10'.2W** Q(2)R 10s 10m 20M W buoy, R stripes. Racon

1256	**Cap de la Heve 49°30'.8N 0°04'.2E** Fl W 5s 123m 24M W 8-sided tr, R top (32m). *Vis 225°-196°(331°)*
1260	LE HAVRE - Ldg Lts 106°48'. Quai R Meunier. Front 49°29'.0N 0°06'.5E Dir F W 36m 25M Grey tr, G top (35m) *Intens 106°-108°(2°). Shown 24 hours*
1260.1	- - Quai J Couvert. Rear 0.73M from front 49°28'.8N 0°07'.6E Dir F W 78m 25M Grey tr G top (77m) *Intens 106°-108°(2°). Shown 24 hours*
1261	- Ldg Lts 090°. Front 49°29'.6N 0°05'.9E Dir F R 21m 19M W tr, R top (18m) *Intens 089°-091°(2°). Occas*
1261.1	- - Rear 680m from front 49°29'.6N 0°06'.4E Dir F R 43m 19M R lantern, square base on house (41m) *Intens 089°-091°(2°) Occas*
1262	**- Digue Nord. Head 49°29'.2N 0°05'.5E** Fl R 5s 15m 21M Horn 15s W tr, R top (15m) FlR 4s 8m (T) 1992
1264	- Digue Sud. Head 49°29'.1N 0°05'.4E VQ(3)G 2s 15m 11M W tr, G top (14m)
1266	- Yacht hr. Digue A Normand 49°29'.3N 0°05'.6E Q(2)G 5s 5m 2M W metal pole G top(3m)
1266.2	- - Breakwater. Head 49°29'.3N 0°05'.6E Fl(2)R 6s 3M W metal support R top
1268	- Quai des Abeilles. Head 49°29'.1N 0°06'.2E Q R 9m 7M Bell(1) 2.5s W and R metal mast (6m)
1269	- Quai R Meunier. W corner 49°29'.0N 0°06'.4E Fl(3) W 15s 4m 23M G lantern (3m) *Occas.*
1270	- - Quai de la Marine. Head. 49°29'.1N 0°06'.6E VQ(9)W 10s 7m 7M West cardinal on yellow pylon, Black band
1274	- Bassin Th Ducrocq. Môle Nord 49°28'.9N 0°06'.4E Oc(2) R 6s 7m 7M Horn (2) 20s W metal structure, R top (5m)
1274.4	- - Môle Sud 49°28'.8N 0°06'.3E Oc(2)G 6s 7m 7M W structure, G top (5m)
1274.6	- - Dir Lt 192° 49°28'.5N 0°07'.0E Dir Oc WRG 4s 15m 12/11/11M Structure, W top (13m) *G183°-190°(7°), W190°-194°(4°), R194°-201°(7°), Shown 24 hours*
1280.7	- - Digue Ch Laroche, Dir Lt 119°30' 49°28'.1N 0°08' 3E Dir Oc WRG 4s 8m 12/11/11M W pyramidal tr, G top (6m) *G118°-119°(1°), W119°-120°(1°), R120°-121°(1°), Shown 24 hours*
1282	TROUVILLE-SUR-MER - W jetty 49°22'.4N 0°04'.2E Fl WG 4s 10m 12/9M Black pylon G top (16m) *W005°-176°(171°), G176°-005°(189°)*
1282.2	- E jetty 49°22'.3N 0°04'.4E Fl(4)WR 12s 8m 7/4M W pylon, R top on dolphin (15m) *W131°-175°(44°), R175°-131°(316°)*
1283	- - Ldg Lts 148°. Front 49°22'.1N 0°04'.6E Oc R 4s 11m 12M Horn(2) 30s (TD 1993) W tr, R top (11m) *Vis 330°-150°(180°), Fog signal -3 HW +3*
1283.1	- - - Rear 217m from front 49°22'.0N 0°04'.7E Oc R 4s 17m 10M W pylon, R top (15m) *Synch with Front. Vis 120°-170°(50°)*
1284	- Jetée Ouest 21m from head 49°22'.1N 0°04'.4E Q G 11m 9M W tr G top (10m)
1285	- Brkwtr. Head. W side 49°22'.2N 0°04'.3E Iso G 4s 9m 5M G mast (7m)
1286	HONFLEUR - Digue du Ratier. Head 49°26'.0N 0°06'.7E VQ W 8m 4M N cardinal on black col (10m)
1289	- - Spillway 49°25'.8N 0°12'.8E VQ (9)W 10s 15m 7M West cardinal top mark on Y beacon with black band
1290	**- Falaise des Fonds 49°25'.5N 0°12'.9E** Fl(3) WRG 12s 15m 17/13/13M W tr G top (18m) *G040°-080°(40°), R080°-084°(4°), G084°-100°(16°)* *W100°-109°(9°), R109°-162°(53°), G162°-260°(98°)*
1293	- Digue Est. Head 49°25'.7N 0°14'.0E Q W 9m 9M Horn(5) 40s N cardinal pylon (8m)

1294	- Jetée Est 25m from Head 49°25'.5N 0°14'1E Oc(2)R 6s 12m 6M W tr R top (12m)
1296	- Digue Ouest. 49°25'.7N 0°13'.9E Q G 10m 6M G pylon (8m)
1297	- Jetée du Transit 49°25'.3N 0°14'.2E F Vi 10m 1M W pylon, black bands (8m)
1300	- Quay. W 49°25'.7N 0°14'.9E 2 F G (vert) 6m 5M Grey metal mast (4m)
1301	- - E 49°25'.7N 0°15'.0E 2 F G (vert) 6m 5M Grey metal mast (4m)
1306	LA SEINE MARITIME - La Risle. Digue Sud. Km 346.0 49°26'.3N 0°22'.0E Iso G 4s11m 7M W pylon G top (9m)
1308	-Tourelle Ygou. Digue Nord. Km 343.4 49°27'.1N 0°24'.1E. VQ R 7m 3M R lantern on grey tank (13m)
1312	- Epi de la Roque. Km 342.2 49°27'.1N 0°25'.2E Q G 8m 6M W column, G top (8m)
1314	- Marais-Vernier. Km 339.9 49°27'.8N 0°26'.9E Fl G 4s 8m 5M Platform on W and G column (7m)
1316	- Tancarville. Digue Nord. Km 337.4 49°28'.8N 0°28'.2E Q R 9m 6M W column, R top (9m)
1374	Dives-sur-Mer 49°17'.8N 0°05'.2W Oc(2 + 1)WRG 12s 6m 12/9/9M R hut (5m) G124°-156°(32°), W156°-160°(4°), R160°-193°(33°)
1377	OUISTREHAM - **Main Light 49°16'.8N 0°14'.9W** Oc WR 4s 37m 17/13M W tr, R top (38m) R115°-151°(36°), W151°-115°(324°)
1377.4	- OC Buoy 49°19'.9N 0°14'.6W Iso W 4s 8m 8M Whis Ball on R buoy, W stripes
1378	- Enrochements Est. Head 49°18'.1N 0°14'.5W Oc(2)R 6s 7m 8M W pylon, R top (11m)
1378.3	- Banc de Île 49°18'.1N 0°14'.7W Iso G 4s 7m 4M W pylon G top (11m)
1378.5	- 49°17'.8N 0°14'.6W VQ(3)R 5s 9m 4M R pylon (9m)
1378.6	- 49° 17'.8N 0°14'.7W VQ(3)G 5s 9m 4M G pylon (9m)
1379	-Enrochements Ouest. Head 49°17'.6N 0°14'.7W Iso G 4s 11m 7M Horn 10s Platform on W column G top (19m)
1379.3	- Banc des Corbeilles 49° 17'.6N 0° 14'.6W Iso R 4s 11m 8M R pylon (16m)
1381	- Ldg Lts 185°. Jetée Est. Head. Front 49°17'.2N 0°14'.7W DirOc(3 + 1)R 12s 10m 17M. Intens 183.5°-186.5°(3°) W pylon, R top (8m)
1381.1	- - Rear 610m from front 49°16'.9N 0°14'.8W Dir Oc(3 + 1)R 12s 30m 17M Tripod, R top (28m) Synch with front. Intens 183.5°-186.5°(3°)
1390	PORT DE COURSEULLES-SUR-MER - Jetée Est. Head 49°20'.3N 0°27'.4W Oc(2)R 6s 9m 7M Brown pylon, R top (12m)
1391	- Jetée Ouest. Head 49°20'.4N 0°27'.4W Iso WG 4s 7m 9/6M Horn 30s Brown pylon on dolphin, G top (14m) W135°-235°(100°), G235°-135°(260°) Horn sounded -2 HW +2
1396	**Ver 49°20'.5N 0°31'.1W** Fl(3)W 15s 42m 26M W tr, grey top (16m) Obsc when brg more than 275°
1400	PORT-EN-BESSIN - Ldg Lts 204°. Front 49°21'.0N 0°45'.5W Oc(3)W 12s 25m 10M Siren 20s W pylon (8m) G top W hut Vis 069°-339°(270°) Siren sounded over a sector of 90° on each side of leading line, continuous in western sector, interrupted In eastern. Temp discontinued (1988)
1400.1	- - Rear 93m from front 49°21'.0N 0°45'.5W Oc(3)W 12s 42m 11M W and grey house (12m) Synch with front. Vis 114°-294°(180°)
1403	- Môle Est. Head 49°21'.2N 0°45'.4W Oc R 4s 14m 7M R pylon (10m)
1404	- Môle Ouest. Head 49°21'.2N 0°45'.4W Fl WG 4s 14m 10/7M G pylon (9m) G065°-114.5°(49.5°), W114.5°-065°(310.5°) Oc(2)R 6s and Fl(2)G 6s mark the heads of the piers
1406	GRANDCAMP - Perré 49°23'.4N 1°02'.5W Oc W 4s 8m 12M G pylon on W hut (7m) Vis 083°-263°(180°). In line 221° with 1410
1408	- Jetée Est. Head 49°23'.5N 1°02'.9W Oc(2)R 6s 10m 9M Siren Mo(N) 30s W column, R top (8m), Fog signal temp discontinued 1988
1409	- Jetée Ouest. Head 49°23'.5N 1°03'.0W Fl G 4s 9m 6M W column, G top (14m)
1410	La Maresquerie 49°23'.2N 1°02'.7W Oc W 4s 28m 12M W mast (12m) Vis 090°-270°(180°)
1411	- Ldg Lts 146°. Front 49°23'.4N 1°02'.8W Dir Q W 9m 15M Platform on W mast R top (7m) Vis 144.5°-147.5°(3°)
1411.1	- - Rear. 102m from front 49°23'.4N 1°02'.8W Dir QW 12m 15M W mast R daymark (11m) Vis 144.5°-147.5°(3°)
1412	ISIGNY-SUR-MER - Ldg Lts 172°30'. Front 49°19'.6N 1°06'.7W Dir Oc(2 + 1)W 12s 7m 18M W mast (7m) Intens 170.5°-174.5°(4°)
1412.1	- - Rear 625m from front 49°19'.3N 1°06'.8W Dir Oc(2 + 1)W 12s 19m 18M W pylon, black top (23m) Synch with front. Intens 170.5°-174.5°(4°)
1418	CARENTAN - Ldg Lts 209°30'. Front 49°20'.5N 1°11'.1W Dir Oc(3)R 12s 6m 17M W mast, R top (6m) Intens 208.2°-210.7°(2.5°)
1418.1	- - Rear 723m from front 49°20'.2N 1°11'.5W Oc(3)W 12s 14m 11M W gantry, G top (15m) Vis 120°-005°(245°). Synch with front
1424	Îles St- Marcouf. Île du Large 49°29'.9N 1°08'.8W VQ(3)W 5s 18m 9M Square grey tr, G top (17m)
1428	MORSALINES - Ldg Lts 267°. La Hougue. Front 49°34'.3N 1°16'.3W Oc W 4s 9m 10M W pylon, G top (7m)
1428.1	- - Rear 1.8M from front 49°34'.3N 1°19'.2W Oc(3 + 1)WRG 12s 90m 12/9/8M W 8-sided tr, G top (13m) W171°-316°(145°), G316°-321°(5°), R321°-342°(21°) W342°-355°(13°)
1434	SAINT VAAST-LA-HOUGUE - Jetty. Head 49°35'.2N 1°15'.4W Oc(2)WRG 6s 12m 12/8/8M Siren Mo(N) 30s W 8 sided tr, R top (11m) R219°-237°(18°), G237°-310°(73°), W310°-350°(40°), R350°-040°(50°)
1436	- NE side. Brkwtr. Head 49°35'.3N 1°15'.6W Iso G 4s 6m 5M W tank. G top (6m)
1438	- SW side. Groyne. Head 49°35'.2N 1°15'.6W Oc(4)R 12s 6m 7M W hut, R top (6m) obscured 278°-018°(100°) (T 1993)
1442	RÉVILLE Pte de Saire 49°36'.4N 1°13'.7W Oc(2 + 1)W 12s 11m 13M W tr, G top (10m)
1444	BARFLEUR - Ldg Lts 219°30'. Front 49°40'.2N 1°15'.5W Oc(3)W 12s 7m 10M W square tr (7m)
1444.1	- Rear. 288m from front 49°40'.1N 1°15'.8W Oc(3)W 12s 13m 10M Grey and W square, tr G top (13m) Vis 085°-355°(270°). Synch with front
1448	- Jetée Est. Head 49°40'.4N 1°15'.4W Oc R 4s 5m 6M W hut, R top (4m)
1450	- Jetée Ouest. Head 49°40'.4N 1°15'.5W Fl G 4s 8m 6M W pylon, G top (7m)

1454	**Pte de Barfleur-Gatteville 49°41'.8N 1°15'.9W** Fl(2)W 10s 72m 29M Horn (2) 60s Grey tr, black top (75m) *Obsc when brg less than 088°*
1455	Les Equets. Buoy 49°43'.7N 1°18'.3W Q W 8m 4M N cardinal
1456	Basse du Renier. Buoy 49°44'.9N 1°22'.1W VQ W 8m 8M Whis N Cardinal
	ANSE DE VICQ
1458	- Ldg Lts 158°. Front 49°42'.3N 1°23'.9W F R 8m 8M △ on W pylon, R top (5m)
1458.1	- Rear. 403m from front 49°42'.0N 1°23'.8W F R 14m 8M △ on W pylon, R top (8m)
1460	La Pierre Noire. Buoy 49°43'.6N 1°29'.1W Q(9)W 15s 8m 7M W cardinal
1462	**Cap Lévi 49°41'.8N 1°28'.4W** Fl R 5s 36m 22M Grey square tr, W top (28m)
1463	Port de Lévi 49°41'.3N 1°28'.2W F WRG 7m 11/8/8M W and grey hut, W lantern (6m) *G050°-109°(59°), R109°-140°(31°), W140°-184°(44°)*
	LE BECQUET
1466	- Ldg Lts 186°30'. Front 49°39'.3N 1°32'.8W Dir Oc(2 +1)W 12s 8m 10M W 8-sided tr (6m) *Intens 183°-190°(7°)*
1466.1	- - Rear 49m from front 49°39'.3N 1°32'.8W Dir Oc(2 + 1)R 12s 13m 7M W 8-sided tr, R top (10m) *Synch with front. Intens 183°-190°(7°)*
	CHERBOURG
1469	- CH1 Buoy 49°43'.3N 1°42'.1W LFlW 10s 8m 7M Ball on R buoy, W stripes. Whis
1470	- Passe de l'Est. Forte d'Île Pelée 49°40'.2N 1°35'.0W Oc(2) WR 6s 19m 11/8M W and R pedestal, on fort (8m) *W055°-120°(65°), R120°-055°(295°)*
1471	- - Fort des Flamands 49°39'.1N 1°35'.6W Dir Q WRG 13m 12/10/10M W pedestal, R top (1m) *G173.5°-176°(2.5°), W176°-183°(7°), R183°-193°(10°)*
1472	- Passe Collignon. S side 49°39'.6N 1°34'.2W Fl(2)R 6s 5m 4M W tank, R top (4m)
1476	- Fort de l'Est 49°40'.3N 1°35'.9W Iso WG 4s 19m 13/10M W pylon. G top (9m) *W008°-229°(221°), G229°-008°(139°)*
1478	- Fort Central 49°40'.5N 1°37'.0W VQ(6) + LFl W 10s 5m 4M Black column, Y top (3m) *Vis 322°-032°(70°)*
1480	**- Fort de L'Ouest 49°40'.5N 1°38'.8W** Fl(3)WR 15s 19m 24/20MHorn(3) 60s Grey tr, R top on fort (9m) *W122°-355°(233°), R355°-122°(127°)*
1482	- Digue de Querqueville. Head 49°40'.5N 1°39'.7W Oc(3)WG 12s 8m 8/5M W column, G top (7m) *W120°-290°(170°), G290°-120°(190°)*
1484	-Lts in line 140°18' and 142°.12'. Jetée du Homet. Front 49°39'.6N 1°37'.9W Dir Q W (2 horiz) 5m 15M W △ on parapet at root of jetty (4m) *63m apart. Intens 137.3°-143.3° (6°) and 139.2°-145.2° (6°)* Marks SW/NE limit of dredged channel
1484.1	- - Gare Maritime. Rear 0.99M from front 49°38'.8N 1°37'.0W Dir QW 35m 21M Grey pylon with W △ on building (35m) *Intens 140°-142.5° (2.5°)*
1486	- Lts in line 124°18'. Jetée du Homet. Head. Front 49°39'.5N 1°36'.9W F G 10m 9M Horn(2 + 1)60s W pylon, G top, on blockhouse (9m) *Intens 114°.3°-134.3°(20°)*
1486.1	- - Terre-plein de Mielles. Rear 0.75M from front 49°39'.1N 1°35'.9W Iso G 4s 16m 12M W column, black bands, W top (15m) *Intens 114.3°-134.3°(20°)*
1488	- Lts in line 192°. Front 49°39'.6N 1°38'.4W Dir Q G 11m 14M W pylon *Intens 190°-194°(4°)*
1488.1	- - Rear 652m from front 49°39'.3N 1°38'.6W Dir Q G 26m 15M G pedestal on roof of Rochambeau barracks (17m) *Intens 189°-195°(6°)*

1490	- Port Militaire. N side 49°39'.2N 1°37'.9W F G 11m 6M W pylon G top (8m)
1491	- - Avant Port. Pier. Head. S 49°39'.2N 1°37'.8W F R 11m 6M. W pylon R top (8m)
1492	- - - Bassin Napoléon III 49°39'.2N 1°38'.4W QW 16m 11M Grey pylon, W top (14m) *Vis 250°-280°(30°). In line 261°18' and 267°48'with 1490 and 1491, forms transits for turning in Petite Rade.*
1495	- Darse Transatlantique. Quai Est. Head 49°39'.1N 1°36'.7W Oc R 4s 9m 8M W structure R top (3m)
1496	- - Gare Maritime. NW corner 49°39'.0N 1°37'.1W Q R 6m 6M W col, R lantern (6m)
1498	- - - NE corner 49°39'.0N 1°37'.0W Fl G 4s 2m 6M G pedestal (1 m)
1498.5	- - - Quai Ouest. Head 49°38'.8N 1°37'.1W Oc(2)R 6s 3m 4M R support (1m) *Vis 006°-186°(180°)*
1499	- Marina. Môle. Head 49°38'.9N 1°37'.2W Oc(2)G 6s 7m 6M G pylon (6m)
1499.5	- Avant-Port-de-Commerce. Jetée Ouest. Head 49°38'.7N 1°37'.2W Iso G 4s 4m 2M W pylon G top (3m)
1504	- Darse des Mielles. Car ferry. Mole. 49°39'.0N 1°36'.6W F Vi 11m 6M Purple Col (4m)
1508	Omonville-la-Rogue 49°42'.3N 1°50'.2W Iso WRG 4s 13m 11/8/8M W pylon, R top (8m) *G180°-252°(72°), W252°-262°(10°), R262°-287°(25°)*
1510	Basse Brefort. Buoy 49°43'.8N 1°51'.1W VQ W 8m 6M Whis N cardinal
1512	**Cap de la Hague 49°43'.4N 1°57'.3W** Fl W 5s 48m 23M Horn 30s Grey tr, W top (51m)
1514	La Plate 49°44'.0N 1°55'.7W Fl(2 + 1)WR 12s 11m 9/6M N cardinal on yellow 8-sided tr, black top (19m) *W115°-272°(157°), R272°-115°(203°)*
1516	Goury Ldg Lts. 065°12' Front. 49°42'.9N 1°56'.7W QR 5m 7M R square on W square on pier
1516.1	- - Rear. 116m from front 49°43'.0N 1°56'.6W QW 11m 8M W pylon on hut. *Intens 057°-075° (18°)*
	ENGLISH CHANNEL
1518	- Lanby. SW 48°31'.7N 5°49'.1W Fl W 4s 10m 20M R and W striped buoy. Racon
1519	- Buoy NE 48°45'.9N 5°11'.6W LFl W 10s 9m 8M Whis R and W striped buoy. Racon
1520	**- Channel Lt F 49°54'.4N 2°53'.7W** Fl W 15s 12m 25M Horn 20s R hull, lt tr amidships. Racon
1521	- E Channel 49°58'.7N 2°28'.9W FlY 5s. X on HFP buoy. Whis. Racon
1522	EC1 Buoy 50°05'.9N 1°48'.3W Fl Y 2.5s Whis X on Y HFP buoy. *Racon*
1523	EC2 Buoy 50°12'.1N 1°12'.4W Fl(4)Y 15s Whis X on Y HFP buoy. *Racon*
1524	EC3 Buoy 50°18'.3N 0°36'.1W Fl Y 5s Whis X on Y HFP buoy. *Racon*
1532	**CHANNEL ISLANDS** **Casquets 49°43'.4N 2°22'.7W** Fl(5)W 30s 37m 24M Horn(2) 60s W tr (23m). *Racon*. 24hours
1536	**ALDERNEY** **- Alderney 49°43'.8N 2°09'.8W** Fl(4)W 15s 37m 28M Siren(4) 60s W round tr, black band (32m) *Vis 085°-027°(302°)*
1537	- Chateau a L'Etoc Pt 49°44'.0N 2°10'.6W Iso WR 4s 20m 10/7M W column (20m) *R071°-111°(40°), W111°-151°(40°) In line 111° with 1536*
1538	- Braye Ldg Lts 215°. Elbow of old pier. Front 49°43'.4N 2°11'.8W Q W 8m 17M Metal post on W concrete base (2m) *Vis 210°-220°(10°)*

1538.1	- - Rear 335m from front 49°43'.2N 2°12'.0W Iso W 10s17m 18M Metal post on W column, brick base (5m) *Vis 210°-220°(10°)*
1538.5	-Breakwater. Head 49°43'.8N 2°11'.5W LFI(2) 10s 13m 7M
1539	- - Quay. Head 49°43'.6N 2°11'.9W 2FR(vert) 14m 5M
	SARK
1544	**- Pt Robert 49°26'.2N 2°20'.7W** Fl W 15s 65m 28M Horn(2) 30s W 8-sided tr *Vis 138°-353°(215°)*
1545	- Corbée du Nez 49°27'.1N 2°22'.1W Fl(4) WR 15s14m 8M W wooden structure on rock (1m). *Wind generator close by.* *W057°-230°(173°), R230°-057°(187°)*
1545.5	Big Russel. Noire Pute 49°28'.3N 2°24'.9W Fl(2)WR 15s 8m 6M On rock *Destroyed (Temporary) (1987)* *W220°-040°(180°), R040°-220°(180°)*
	GUERNSEY
1548	**- Platte Fougère 49°30'.9N 2°29'.0W** Fl WR 10s 15m 16M Horn 45s W 8-sided tr, black band (25m) *W155°-085°(290°), R085°-155°(70°). Racon*
1548.5	- Tautenay 49°30'.2N 2°26'.7W Q(3)WR 6s 7m 7/6M Black and W beacon *W050°-215°(165°), R215°-050°(195°)*
1550	- Platte 49°29'.1N 2°29'.5W Fl WR 3s 6m 7/5M Green conical stone tr (9m) *R024°-219°(195°), W219°-024°(165°)*
1552	- Roustel. S end 49°29'.3N 2°28'.9W Q W 8m 7M Black and W chequered stone tr, G lantern (10m)
1554	- St Sampson Hr. Crocq pier. Head 49°29'.0N 2°31'.1W F R 11m 5M R column (6m) *Vis 250°-340°(90°) Traffic signals*
1557	- - N pier. Head 49°29'.0N 2°30'.7W F G 3m 5M Post(2m) *Vis 230°-340°(110°)*
1558	- - S pier. Head. Ldg Lts 286°. Front 49°28'.9N 2°30'8W F R 3m 5M Post (2m) *Vis 230°-340°(110°)*
1558.1	- - - Rear. 390m from front 49°29'.0N 2°31'.0W F G 13m Clock tr (12m) *2 FR (vert) on two chimneys 300m N*
1559	- Brehon 49°28'.3N 2°29'.2W Iso W 4s 19m 9M Beacon on round tr
1560	**- St Peter Port Ldg Lts 220°. Castle brkwtr. Head. Front 49°27'.4N 2°31'.4W** Al WR 10s 14m 16M Horn 15s Dark round granite tr, W on NE side (12m) *Vis 187°-007°(180°)*
1560.1	- - - Belvedere. Rear 49°26'.9N 2°31'.9W Oc W 10s 61m 14M W square, orange stripe, on W tr (4m) *Vis 179°-269°(90°)*
1562	- - White Rock pier. Head. 49°27'.4N 2°31'.5W Oc G 5s 11m 14M Round stone tr (10m). *Intens 174°-354°(180°)*
1564	- - New Jetty. Head 49°27'.4N 2°31'.7W F G 1m 5M *One at each corner (1m)*
1565	- - - 49°27'.4N 2°31'.7W 2 F G (vert) 7m 3M *2m apart*
1566	- - - St Julians Emplacement. Head. No 7 Berth. E end 49°27'.5N 2°31'.8W F G 5m 1M Column (3m)
1566.2	- - - - W end 49°27'.5N 2°31'.9W F G 5m 1M Column (3m)
1569	- Victoria Marina Ldg Lts 265°. Front. S pier. Head 49°27'.4N 2°31'.9W Oc R 5s10m 14M W frame tr, R lantern (7m)
1569.1	- - - - Rear 160m from front. 49°27'.4N 2°32'.1W Iso R 2s 22m 3M
1570	- - Queen Elizabeth II Marina Dir Lt 270° 49°27'.8N 2°31'.8W Dir Oc WRG 3s 5m 6M *G258°-268°(10°), W268°-272°(4°) R272°-282°(10°)*
1574	- St Martin's Pt 49°25'.3N 2°31'.7W Fl(3)WR 10s 15m 14M Horn(3) 30s Flat-roofed W concrete building (5m) *R185°-191°(6°), W191°-011°(180°)R011°-081°(70°)*

1580	**- Les Hanois 49°26'.2N 2°42'.1W** Q(2)W 5s 33m 23M Horn(2) 60s Grey round granite, tr, black lantern (33m) *Vis 294°-237°(303°)*
	JERSEY
1584	**- Sorel Pt 49°15'.7N 2°09'.4W** LFI WR 7.5s 50m 15M Black and W chequered round concrete tr (3m) *W095°-112°(17°), R112°-173°(61°), W173°-230°(57°) R230°-269°(39°), W269°-273°(4°)*
1585	- Bonne Nuit Bay, Ldg Lts 223°. Pier. Head. Front 49°15'.1N 2°07'.0W F G 7m 6M
1585.1	- - - Rear 170m from front 49°15'.1N 2°07'.2W F G 34m 6M
1585.5	- Rozel Bay. Dir Lt 245°. 49°14'.3N 2°02'.7W Dir F WRG 11m 5M *G240°-244°(4°), W244°-246°(2°), R246°-250°(4°)*
1586	- St Catherine Bay. Verclut Brkwtr. Head 49°13'.4N 2°00'.5W Fl W 1.5s 18m 13M W frame tr (9m)
1588	- Gorey Ldg Lts 298°. Pier. Head. Front 49°11'.9N 2°01'.3W Oc RG 5s 8m 12M W metal frame tr (5m) *R304°-352°(48°), G352°-304°(312°)*
1588.1	- - - Rear 490m from front 49°12'.0N 2°01'.6W Oc R 5s 24m 8M W ☐ orange sides on stone wall (1m)
1594	- Ldg Lts 082°. La Gréve d'Azette. Front 49°10'.2N 2°05'.0W Oc W 5s 23m 14M R vert stripe on W metal frame tr (20m) *Vis 034°-129°(95°)*
1594.1	- - Mont Ubé. Rear 49°10'.3N 2°03'.5W Oc R 5s 46m 12M W metal frame tr (14m) *Vis 250°-095°(205°) Racon*
1598	- Demie de Pas 49°09'.1N 2°06'.0W Mo(D)WR 12s11m 14/10M Horn(3) 60s Black tr,Y top. *Racon* *R130°-303°(173°), W303°-130°(187°)*
1604	- St Helier. Small Roads. Ldg Lts 022°40'. Elizabeth E Berth. Dolphin. Front 49°10'.7N 2°06'.8W Oc G 5s 10m 11M R vert stripe on metal frame tr
1604.1	- - - - Albert Pier. Elbow. Rear 230m from front 49°10'.8N 2°06'.8W Oc R 5s 18m 12M R vert stripe on metal frame tr (15m) *Synch with Front*
1606	- - Platte Rock 49°10'.2N 2°07'.3W Fl R 1.5s 6m 5M R metal column
1614	- St Aubin hr. N pier. Head Dir Lt 252° 49°11'.2N 2°09'.9W Iso R 4s 12m 10M Dir F WRG 5m Metal column (10m) *G246°-251°(5°), W251°-253°(2°), R253°-258°(5°)*
1614.2	- - Fort. Pierhead 49°11'.2N 2°09'.5W Fl(2) Y 5s 8m 1M
1616	- Noirmont Pt 49°10'.0N 2°10'.0W Fl(4)W 12s 18m 13M Black tr, W band (10m)
1620	**-La Corbière 49°10'.8N 2°14'.9W** Iso WR 10s 36m 18/16M Horn Mo(C) 60s Round stone tr (19m) *W shore-294°, R294°-328°(34°), W328°-148°(180°), R148°-shore*
1622	**- Grosnez Pt 49°15'.5N 2°14'.7W** Fl(2)WR 15s 50m 19/17M W concrete hut *W081°-188°(107°), R188°-241°(53°)*
	FRANCE - NORTH COAST **DIÉLETTE**
1632	- Ldg Lts 125°30'. Jetée Ouest. Head. Front 49°33'.2N 1°51'.8W Oc WRG 4s 12m 8/5/5M W tr,G top (11m) *G shore-072°, W072°-138°(66°), R138°-206°(68°), G206°-shore*
1632.1	- - Rear. 460m from front 49°33'.1N 1°51'.4W Dir FR 23m 11M W dwelling (7m) *Intens 121°-130°(9°)*
1638	**Cap de Carteret 49°22'.4N 1°48'.4W** Fl(2 + 1)W 15s 81m 26M Horn(3) 60s Grey tr G top (18m)
1640	- Carteret. Jetée Ouest. Head 49°22'.2N 1°47'.4W Oc R 4s 6m 8M W column, R top (5m)
1641	- Training Wall. Head 49°22'.3N 1°47'.3W Fl(2)G 5s 1M W mast G top

1644	PORT DE PORTBAIL - Ldg Lts 042°. La Caillourie. Front 49°19'.8N 1°42'.5W QW 14m 11M W pylon, R top (8m)
1644.1	- - Rear. 870m from front 49°20'.2N 1°41'.9W QW 4s 20m 9M Belfry (35m)
1646	- Training wall. Head 49°19'.5N 1°43'.0W Q(2)R 5s 5m 2M W mast, R top (7m)
1648	Le Sénéquet 49°05'.5N 1°39'.7W Fl(3)WR 12s 18m 13/10M W tr (26m) R083.5°-116.5° (33°), W116.5°-083.5° (327°)
1650	REGNÉVILLE - Pte d'Agon 49°00'.2N 1°34'.6W Oc(2)WR 6s 12m 10/7M W tr, R top, W dwelling (12m) R063°-110° (47°), W110°-063° (313°)
1651	- Dir Lt 028°49°00'.7N 1°33'.3W Dir Oc WRG 4s 9m 9/7/7M House (6m) G024°-027° (3°), W027°-029° (2°), R029°-033° (4)
1654	ÎLES CHAUSEY - Îles Chausey. Grande Île 48°52'.2N 1°49'.3W FlW 5s 39m 23M Horn 30s Grey square tr (19m)
1655	- La Crabière Est 48°52'.5N 1°49'.4W Oc WRG 4s 5m 9/6/6M S cardinal, on black metal frame tr, Y top (11m) W079°-291° (212°), G291°-329° (38°), W329°-335° (6°), R335°-079° (104°)
1656	Le Pignon 48°53'.5N 1°43'.4W Oc(2) WR 6s 10m 11/8M E cardinal on black tr, Y band (20m) R005°-150° (145°), W150°-005° (215°)
1660	PORT DE GRANVILLE - Pte du Roc 48°50'.1N 1°36'.8W Fl(4)W 15s 49m 23M Grey tr, R top (16m)
1662	- Jetée Ouest. Head 48°49'.9N 1°36'.3W Iso R 4s 12m 6M R pylon (9m)
1664	- Jetée Est. Head 48°50'.0N 1°36'.2W Iso G 4s 11m 6M W pylon, G top, on hut (8m)
1666	- Le Loup 48°49'.6N 1°36'.2W Fl(2)W 6s 8m 11M 2 balls on black tr R band (24m)
1668	- Hérel. Marina. Digue Principale. Head 48°49'.9N 1°35'.9W Fl R 4s 12m 8M Horn(2) 40s W round tr, R top (9m)
1668.2	- - - Secondary Mole. Head 48°50'.0N 1°35'.9W Fl G 4s 4m 5M G structure (13m)
1668.4	- - Entrance to Basin. W side 48°50'.0N 1°35'.9W Oc R 4s 4m 5M Grey pylon, R top (13m)
1668.6	- - - E side. 48°50'.0N 1°35'.9W OcG 4s 4m 5M Grey pylon, G top (13m)
1670	La Pierre-de-Herpin 48°43'.8N 1°48'.9W Oc(2)W 6s 20m 17M Siren Mo(N) 60s W tr, black top and base (28m)
1672	La Houlle-sous-Cancale. Jetty. Head 48°40'.1N 1°51'.1W Oc(3)G 12s 12m 7M W pylon, G top, G hut (11m) Obsc when brg less than 223°
1674	PORT SAINT MALO - Les Courtis 48°40'.5N 2°05'.8W Fl(3)G 12s 14m 8M G tr (21m)
1675	- La Plate 48°40'.8N 2°01'.9W FlWRG 4s 11m 11/8/8M N cardinal on Y tr, black top (22m) W140°-203° (63°), R203°-210° (7°), W210°—225° (15°) G225°-140° (275°)
1676	-Ldg Lts 089°. Le Grand Jardin. S end. Front 48°40'.2N 2°05'.0W Fl(2)R 10s 24m 15M Grey tr, R top (38m) In line 130° with 1686.1 leads through the channel of Petite Port. Obsc when brg less than 097°, 220°-233° (13°), 241°-243° (2°) and when brg more than 251°
1676.1	- - Rochebonne. Rear 4.2M from front 48°40'.3N 1°58'.7W Dir FR 40m 24M Grey square tr, W face W, R top (20m) Intens 088.2°-089.7° (1.5°)
1680	- Le Buron 48°39'.4N 2°03'.7W Fl(2)G 6s 15m 8M G tr (23m)

1682	- Môles des Noires. Head 48°38'.6N 2°01'.9W Fl R 5s 11m 13M Horn(2) 20s W tr, R top (10m) Obsc 155°-159° (4°), 171°-178° (7°) and when brg more than 192°
1686	- Ldg Lts 128°42'. Les Bas-Sablons. Front 48°38'.2N 2°01'.2W Dir F G 20m 18M W square tr, black top (20m) Intens 127.5°-130.5° (3°)
1686.1	- - La Balou. Rear 0.9M from front 48°37'.7N 2°00'.2W Dir F G 69m 24M Grey square tr (37m) Intens 128.2°-129.7° (1.5°). See 1676
1687	- Ecluse du Naye. Ldg Lts 070°42'. Front 48°38'.6N 2°01'.5W F R 6m 3M W o purple border (4m)
1687.1	- - Rear 48°38'.8N 2°00'.7W FR 23m 8M W o, R border on W col (23m) Vis 030°-120° (90°)
1688	- Bas-Sablons Marina Mole. Head 48°38'.5N 2°01'.7W Fl G 4s 7m 5M Grey mast (5m)
1692	LA RANCE - La Jument 48°37'.5N 2°01'.8W Fl(5)G 20s 6m 5M G tr (15m)
1693	- Tidal Barrage. NW wall 48°37'.1N 2°01'.8W Fl G 4s 6m 5M G pylon on dolphin (4m) Vis 191°-291° (100°)
1693.2	- - NE 48°37'.1N 2°01'.8W Fl(2)R 6s 6m 5M R pylon on dolphin (5m) Vis 040°-200° (160°)
1695	St Briac. Embouchure du Frémur. Dir Lt 125° 48°37'.1N 2°08'.2W Dir Iso WRG 4s 10m 13/11/11M W mast on hut (6m) G121.5°-124.5° (3°), W124.5°-125.5° (1°), R125.5°-129.5° (4°)
1697	St Cast. Mole. Head 48°38'.4N 2°14'.6W Iso WG 4s 11m 11/8M G and W structure (9m) W204°-217° (13°), G217°-233° (16°), W233°-245° (12°), G245°-204° (319°)
1698	Cap Fréhel 48°41'.1N 2°19'.2W Fl(2)W 10s 85m 29M Horn(2) 60s (400m NNE) Brown square tr G lantern (33m)
1701	Erquy. Mole. S end. Head 48°38'.1N 2°28'.8W Oc(2 + 1)WRG 12s 11m 11/8/8M W tr, R top (10m) R055°-081° (26°), W081°-094° (13°), G094°-111° (17°) W111°-120° (9°), R120°-134° (14°)
1702	- Inner Jetty. Head 48°38'.1N 2°28'.4W Fl R 2.5s 10m 3M R and W tr (10m)
1703	Le Rohein 48°38'.9N 2°37'.8W VQ(9)WRG 10s 13m 10/8/8M W cardinal on Y tr, black band (15m) R072°-105° (33°), W105°-180° (75°), G180°-193° (13°), W193°-237° (44°), G237°-282° (45°), W282°-301° (19°), G301°-330° (29°), W330°-072° (102°)
1704	Dahouet. La Petite-Muette 48°34'.9N 2°34'.3W Fl WRG 4s 10m 9/6/6M Δ on G and W tr (17m) G055°-114° (59°), W114°-146° (32°), R146°-196° (50°) Fl(2)G 6s Vis 156°-286° (130°) 240m SE
1708	Le Légué. Pt à l'Aigle. Jetty 48°32'.2N 2°43'.1W Q G 13m 8M W tr, G top (14m) Vis 160°-070° (270°)
1709	- Custom House Jetty 48°31'.9N 2°43'.5W Iso G 4s 6m 8M W column, G top (9m)
1710	Binic. Mole de Penthièvre. Head 48°36'.1N 2°49'.0W Oc(3)W 12s 12m 12M W tr, G gallery (12m) Unintens 020°-110° (90°)
1712	PORTRIEUX - Port d'echouage. N Môle. Head 48°38'.7N 2°49'.4W FlG 2.5s 11m 2M W and G 8-sided tr (12m) Vis 265°-155° (250°)
1713	- - S Môle. Head 48°38'.7N 2°49'.4W Fl R 2.5s 9m 2M W mast, R top (8m)
1713.5	- Port en eau profonde. NE Môle. Head 48°38'.9N 2°48'.9W Fl(3) G 12s 2M G tr (6m)
1713.55	- - - Elbow 48°39'.0N 2°49'.1W Dir Iso WRG 4s 15/11/11M Concrete tr (12m) W159°-179° (20°), G179°-316° (137°), W316°-320.5° (4.5°), R320.5°-159° (198.5°)

1713.6 - - SE Môle. Head 48°38'.9N 2°49'.1W
FI(3) R 12s 2M R tr (6m)

ROCHES DE SAINT-QUAY
1714 - Île Hr. 48°40'.0N 2°48'.5W
Oc(2)WRG 6s 16m 11/8/8M
W tr and dwelling R top (13m)
R011°-133° (122°), G133°-270° (137°),
R270°-306° (36°), G306°-358° (52°), W358°-011° (13°)

1714.5 - Herflux. Dir Lt 130° 48°39'.1N 2°47'.9W
Dir FI(2) WRG 6s 8/6/6M
S cardinal on black tr, Y top G115°-125° (10°), W125°-135° (10°)
R 135°-145° (10°)

1716 Le Grand Léjon 48°44'.9N 2°39'.9W
FI(5)WR 20s 17m 18/14M
R tr, W bands (24m)
R015°-058° (43°), W058°-283° (225°), R283°-350° (67°),
W350°-015° (25°)

1720 L'Ost-Pic 48°46'.8N 2°56'.5W
Oc WR 4s 20m 11/8M
2 W trs, R tops (15m)
W105°-116° (11°), R116°-221° (105°), W221°-253° (32°),
R253°-291° (38°), W291°-329° (38°). Obsc when brg less than 162°

PAIMPOL
1722 - Pte de Porz-Don 48°47'.5N 3°01'.6W
Oc(2) WR 6s 13m 15/11M
W house (8m)
W269°-272° (3°), R272°-279° (7°)

1724 - Kernoa. Ldg Lts 264°12'. Front
48°47'.1N 3°02'.4W
F R 5m 7M
W and R hut (4m)

1724.1 - - - Rear 370m from front 48°47'.1N 3°02'.6W
Dir F R 12m 14M
W pylon, R top (10m)
Intens 260.2°-264.2° (4°)

1726 La Horaine 48°53'.5N 2°55'.3W
FI(3)W 12s 13m 11M
Grey 8-sided tr on black hut (20m)

1730 Barnouic 49°01'.7N 2°48'.4W
VQ(3)W 5s 15m 9M
E cardinal on black 8-sided tr, Y band, W base (19m)

1734 **Roches Douvres 49°06'.5N 2°48'.8W**
FI W 5s 60m 28M Siren 60s
Pink tr with green roof on dwelling (65m)

1738 **Les Héaux de Bréhat 48°54'.5N 3°05'.2W**
Oc(3)WRG 12s 48m 17/12/12M
Grey round tr (57m)
R227°-247° (20°), W247°-270° (23°), G270°-302° (32°)
W302°-227° (285°)

ÎLE DE BRÉHAT
1740 - N end. Le Paon 48°52'.0N 2°59'.2W
F WRG 22m 12/9/9M
Y tr (12m)
W033°-078° (45°), G078°-181° (103°), W181°-196° (15°)
R196° -307° (111°), W307°-316° (9°), R316°-348° (32°)

1742 **- NW side. Rosédo 48°51'.5N 3°00'.3W**
FI W 5s 29m 20M
W tr G gallery (13m)

1744 - Men-Joliguet 48°50'.2N 3°00'.2W
Iso WRG 4s 6m 13/10/10M
Y tr, black band (8m)
R255°-279° (24°), W279°-283° (4°), G283°-175° (252°)

1745 - Chenal de Ferlas. Roche Quinonec. Dir Lt
257°21' 48°49'.4N 3°03'.7W
Dir Q WRG 12m 10/8/8M
Grey tr (6m)
G254°-257° (3°), W257°-257.7° (0.7°), R257.7°-260.7° (3°)

1745.4 - - Embouchure du Trieux. Dir Lt 271°
48°49'.6N 3°05'.2W
Dir FI WRG 2s 16m 10/8/8M
W structure (2m)
G267°-270° (3°), W270°-272° (2°), R272°-274° (2°)

LE TRIEUX
1746 - Rocher Men-Grenn 48°51'.3N 3°03'.9W
Q(9) W 15s 7m 8M
Y tr, black band (9m)

1748 - Ldg Lts 224°42'. La Croix. Front 48°50'.3N 3°03'.3W
Dir Oc W 4s 15m 19M
2 grey round trs W on NE side, R tops (18m)
Intens 215°-235° (20°)

1748.1 - - Bodic. Rear 2.1M from front 48°48'.8N 3°05'.4W
Dir Q W 55m 22M
W house with G gable (23m)
Intens 221°-229° (8°)

1752 - Coatmer Ldg Lts 218°42'. Front 48°48'.3N 3°05'.8W
F RG 16m 9/9M
W gable (11m)
R200°-250° (50°), G250°-053° (163°)

1752.1 - - - Rear 660m from front 48°48'.0N 3°06'.0W
F R 50m 9M
W gable (8m)
Vis 197°-242° (45°)

1758 - Les Perdrix 48°47'.8N 3°05'.8W
FI(2)WG 6s 5m 6/3M
G tr(11m)
G165°-197° (32°), W197°-202.5° (5.5°), G202.5°-040° (197.5°)
3 F Bu mark marina pontoons 750m SSW

RIVIÈRE DE TRÉGUIER
1760 - La Corne 48°51'.4N 3°10'.7W
FI(3)WRG 12s 14m 11/8/8M
W tr, R base (23m)
W052°-059° (7°), R059°-173° (114°), G173°-213° (40°)
W213°-220° (7°), R220°-052° (192°)

1762 - Grande-Passe. Ldg Lts 137°. Port de la Chaîne.
Front 48°51'.6N 3°07'.9W
Oc W 4s 12m 12M
W house (5m) Vis 042°-232° (190°)

1762.1 - - - Sainte Antoine. Rear. 0.75M from front 48°51'.1N 3°07'.0W
Dir Oc R 4s 34m 15M
R and W house (6m)
Intens 134°-140° (6°)

1768 Port-Blanc. Le Voleur 48°50'.2N 3°18'.5W
FI WRG 4s 17m 14/11/11M
W tr (12m)
G140°-148° (8°), W148°-152° (4°), R152°-160° (8°)

PERROS GUIREC
1770 - Passe de l'Ouest. Kerjean. Dir Lt 143°36'
48°47'.8N 3°23'.4W
Dir Oc(2 + 1)WRG 12s 78m 15/13/13M
W tr, black top (16m)
G133.7°-143.2° (9.5°), W143.2°-144.8° (1.6°)
R144. 8°-154.3° (9.5°)

1774 - Passe de l'Est. Ldg Lts 224°30'. Le Colombier.
Front 48°47'.9N 3°26'.7W
Dir Oc(4)W 12s 28m 18M
W house (7m) Intens 214.5°-234.5° (20°)

1774.1 - - - Kerprigent. Rear 1.5M from front 48°46'.9N 3°28'.2W
Dir Q W 79m 22M
W tr (14m) Intens 221°-228° (7°)

1780 - Jetée Est (Linkin). Head 48°48'.3N 3°26'.3W
FI(2)G 6s 4m 9M
W pile, G top (4m)

1782 - Môle Ouest. Head 48°48'.2N 3°26'.5W
FI(2)R 6s 4m 9M
W pile, R top (4m)

1784 Ploumanac'h. Men-Ruz 48°50'.3N 3°29'.0W
Oc WR 4s 26m 13/10M
Pink square tr (15m)
W226°-242° (16°), R242°-226° (344°). Obsc when brg less
than 080°, ptly obsc 156°-207° (51°) and 264°-278° (14°)

1786 **Les Sept-Îles. Île-aux-Moines 48°52'.8N 3°29'.5W**
FI(3)W 15s 59m 24M
Grey tr and dwelling (20m)
Obsc 237°-241° (4°) and when brg less than 039°

1790 Les Triagoz. Rocher Guen Bras 48°52'.3N 3°38'.8W
Oc(2)WR 6s 31m 15/11M
Grey square stone tr, R lantern (30m)
W010°-339° (329°), R339°-010° (31°). Ptly obsc
258°-268° (10°)

1792 Beg-Léguer 48°44'.4N 3°32'.9W
Oc(4)WRG 12s 60m 13/10/10M
West face of W house, R lantern (8m)
G007°-084° (77°), W084°-098° (14°), R098°-129° (31°)

LOCQUÉMEAU
1794 - Ldg Lts 121°. Front 48°43'.5N 3°34'.4W
F R 21m 6M
W pylon, R top (19m) Vis 068°-228° (160°)

1794.1 - - Rear 484m from front 48°43'.4N 3°34'.1W
Oc(2 + 1)R 12s 39m 7M
W gabled house R gallery (6m)
Vis 016°-232° (216°)

ANSE DE PRIMEL
1796 - Ldg Lts 152°. Front 48°42'.5N 3°49'.1W
F R 35m 6M
W square, R stripe, on pylon (7m)
Vis 134°-168° (34°)

1796.1 - - Rear 172m from front 48°42'.5N 3°49'.0W
F R 56m 6M
W square, R stripe on wall (4m)

1796.4 - Marina. Jetty. Head 48°42'.8N 3°49'.5W
FI G 4s 6m 7M
W column, G top on hut (5m)

BAIE DE MORLAIX
1799.9 - Ldg Lts 190°30'. Île Noire. Front 48°40'.4N 3°52'.6W
Oc(2) WRG 6s 15m 11/8/8M
W square tr, R top (13m)
G051°-135° (84°), R135°-211° (76°), W211°-051° (200°). Obsc
in places

1800 **- - La Lande. Common Rear 48°38'.2N 3°53'.1W**
FI W 5s 85m 23M
W square tr, black top (19m)
Obsc when brg more than 204°

1800.1	- Ldg Lts 176°24'. Île Louet. Front 48°40'.5N 3°53'.4W Oc(3)WG 12s 17m 15/10M W square tr, black top (12m) *W305°-244°(299°), G244°-305°(61°), Vis 139°-223°(84°)* *from offshore except where obsc by islands*
1804	- La Menk 48°43'.3N 3°56'.7W. Q(9)WR 15s 6m 5/3M W cardinal on Y tr, black band (11m) *W160°-188°(28°) R188°-160°(322°)*
1805	PORT DE ROSCOFF BLOSCON - Jetty. Head. 48°43'.3N 3°57'.6W Fl WG 4s 9m 10/7M In fog F W 2s W round tr, G top (5m) *W206°-216°(10°), G216°-206°(350°)*
1808	Ar-Chaden 48°44'.0N 3°58'.3W Q(6) + LFl WR 15s 14m 8/6M S cardinal on black conical masonry tr, Y top (22m) *R262°-289.5°(27.5°), W289.5°-293°(4.5°), R293°-326°(33°),* *W326°-110°(144°)*
1810	Men-Guen-Bras 48°43'.8N 3°58'.1W Q WRG 14m 9/6/6M N cardinal on Y masonry tr, black top (20m) *W068°-073°(5°), R073°-197°(124°), W197°-257°(60°),* *G257°-068°(171°)*
1811	PORT DE ROSCOFF - Approaches - Buoy 'Astan' 48°44'.9N 3°57'.7W VQ(3) W 5s 9m 6M, E cardinal, Whis
1812	- Ldg Lts 209°. Môle Nord. Front 48°43'.6N 3°58'.6W Oc(2 + 1)G 12s 7m 7M W column, G top (7m) *Vis 078°-318°(240°)*
1812.1	- - Rear 430m from front 48°43'.4N 3°58'.7W Oc(2 + 1)W 12s 24m 15M Grey square tr, W on NE side (24m) *Vis 062°-242°(180°)*
1813	- Jetty. Head 48°44'.0N 3°59'.0W F Vi 5m 1M W and purple column (14m)
1816	Île de Batz 48°44'.8N 4°01'.6W Fl(4)W 25s 69m 23M F R 65m 7M Grey tr, black lantern (43m) *F R vis 024°-059°(35°)*
1816.3	- Slip. S end 48°44'.3N 4°00'.5W VQ(6) + LFlW 10s 3m 7M S Cardinal on black bn, Y top (12m)
1818	PORT DE MOGUÉRIEC - Ldg Lts 162°. Jetty. Head. Front 48°41'.4N 4°04'.5W Iso WG 4s 9m 11/6M W tr, G top (10m) *W158°-166°(8°), G166°-158°(352°)*
1818.1	- - Rear. 440m from front 48°41'.2N 4°04'.3W F G 22m 7M W column, G top (11m) *Vis 142°-182°(40°)*
1820	Pontusval. Pointe de Beg-Pol 48°40'.7N 4°20'.8W Oc(3)WR 12s 16m 10/7M W tr, black top, W dwelling (15m) *W shore-056°, R056°-096°(40°), W096°-shore*
1820.6	Aman-ar-Ross. Buoy 48°41'.9N 4°27'.0W Q W 9m 7M Whis N cardinal
1821.3	Lizen-ven-Ouest. Buoy 48°40'.6N 4°33'.7W VQ(9)W 10s 8m 8M Whis W cardinal
1822	Île-Vierge 48°38'.4N 4°34'.1W Fl W 5s 77m 27M Siren 60s Grey tr (83m) *Vis 337°-325°(348°)*
1825	L'ABER VRAC'H - Libenter. Buoy 48°37'.5N 4°38'.4W Q(9)W 15s 8m 6M Whis W cardinal
1826	- 1st Ldg Lts 100°. Île Vrac'h. Front 48°36'.9N 4°34'.6W Q R 20m 7M W square tr, orange top, dwelling (15m)
1826.1	- - Lanvaon. Rear 1.63M from front 48°36'.7N 4°32'.0W Dir Q W 55m 12M W square tr, orange △ on top (27m) *Intens 090°-110°(20°)*
1831	- Dir Lt 128° N brkwater 48°35'.9N 4°33'.9W Dir Oc(2)WRG 6s 5m 13/11/11 M W structure (4m) *G125.7°-127.2°(1.5°), W127.2°-128.7°(1.5°)* *R128.7°-130.2°(1.5°)*
1832	- Breac'h Ver 48°36'.7N 4°35'.4W Fl G 2.5s 6m 3M △ on tr (13m)
1836	Corn-Carhai 48°35'.2N 4°43'.9W Fl(3)W 12s 19m 9M W 8-sided tr, black top (20m)
1837	Grande basse de Portsall. Buoy 48°36'.7N 4°46'.2W VQ(9)W 10s 9m 8M Whis. W cardinal

1838	Portsall 48°33'.9N 4°42'.3W Oc(4) WRG 12s 9m 13/10/10M W column, R top (7m) *G058°-084°(26°), W084°-088°(4°), R088°-058°(330°)*
1842	FRANCE - WEST COAST OUESSANT - Le Stiff 48°28'.5N 5°03'.4W Fl(2)R 20s 85m 24M 2 adjoining W trs (32m) *FR(QW by day occas) on Radar tr* *1862 Lts in line 293°30'*
1843	- Port du Stiff. Môle Est. Head 48°28'.2N 5°03'.2W Q WRG 11m 10/7/7M W tr, G top (6m) *G251°-254°(3°), W254°-264°(10°), R264°-267°(3°)*
1844	- Créac'h 48°27'.6N 5°07'.8W Fl(2)W 10s 70m 34M Horn(2) 120s. Racon W tr, black bands (55m) *Obsc 247°-255°(8°)*
1846	- An-Ividig (Nividic) 48°26'.8N 5°09'.1W VQ(9)W 10s 28m 9M W 8-sided tr, R bands (36m) *Obsc 225°-290°(65°)*
1848	- La Jument 48°25'.4N 5°08'.1W Fl(3)R 15s 36m 22M Horn(3) 60s Grey 8-sided tr, R top (48m) *Obsc 199°-241°(42°)*
1849	Pierres-Vertes. Buoy 48°22'.2N 5°04'.7W VQ(9)W 10s 9m 8M Whis W cardinal
1850	- Kéréon (Men-Tensel) 48°26'.3N 5°01'.6W Oc(2 + 1) WR 24s 38m 17/7M Horn (2 + 1) 120s Grey tr (41m) *W019°-248°(229°), R248°-019°(131°)*
1852	- Men-Korn 48°28'.0N 5°01'.4W VQ(3)WR 5s 21m 8/8M E cardinal on black round tr, Y band (29m) *W145°-040°(255°), R040°-145°(105°)*
1854	CHENAL DU FOUR (N PART) - Le Four 48°31'.4N 4°48'.3W Fl(5)W 15s 28m 18M Siren (3 + 2) 75s Grey round tr (28m)
1856	- L'Aberildut 48°28'.3N 4°45'.6W Dir Oc(2)WR 6s 12m 25/20M W buildings (5m) *W081°-085°(4°), R085°-087°(2°)*
1859	Valbelle. Buoy 48°26'.5N 4°50'.0W Fl(2)R 6s 8m 5M Whis R Buoy
1860	- Les Plâtresses 48°26'.3N 4°50'.9W Fl RG 4s 17m 6M W 8 sided tr (23m) *R343°-153°(170°), G153°-333°(180°)*
1862	CHENAL DE LA HELLE - Le Faix 48°25'.8N 4°53'.9W VQ W 16m 8M Y tr, black top (21m) *1842 Lts in line 293°30'*
1870	Les Trois-Pierres 48°24'.7N 4°56'.8W Iso WRG 4s 15m 9/6/6M W column(16m) *G070°-147°(77°), W147°-185°(38°), R185°-191°(6°)* *G191°-197°(6°), W197°-213°(16°), R213°-070°(217°)*
1871	ÎLE DE MOLÈNE - Molène. Old Mole. Head. Dir Lt 191° 48°23'.9N 4°57'.3W Dir Fl(3)WRG 12s 6m 9/7/7M Column on hut (5m) *G183°-190°(7°), W190°-192°(2°), R192°-203°(11°)*
	- - Chenal des Las. Dir Lt 261° Dir Fl(2)WRG 6s 9m 9/7/7M Same structure as 1871 *G252.5°-259.5°(7°), W259.5°-262.5°(3°), R262.5°-269.5°(7°)*
1872	La Grande Vinotière 48°22'.0N 4°48'.5W Oc R 6s 15m 5M R 8-sided tr (24m)
1873	Port du Conquet. Môle Ste Barbe 48°21'.6N 4°47'.1W Oc G 4s 5m 6M G mast (4m)
1873.9	CHENAL DU FOUR (S PART) - Ldg Lts 007°. Trézien. Rear 48°25'.4N 4°46'.8W Dir Oc(2)W 6s 84m 20M Grey tr, W on S side (37m) *Intens 003°-011°(8°)*
1874	- - Kermorvan. Front 48°21'.7N 4°47'.4W Fl W 5s 20m 22M Horn 60s W square tr (20m) *Obsc when brg less than 341°. Front Ldg Lt 137°30' for* *Chenal de la Helle with 1880*

1874.1 **- Ldg Lts 158°30'. St Mathieu. Rear**
48°19'.8N 4°46'.3W
Fl W 15s 56m 29M
Dir F W 54m 28M
W tr, R top (37m)
Intens F W 157.5°-159.5°(2°)

1875 - - 54m 291° 49°19'.8N 4°46'.3W
Q WRG 26m 14/11/11M
W tr (6m)
G085°-107°(22°), W107° -116°(9 °), R116°-134°(18°)

1876 - Corsen 48°24'.9N 4°47'.7W
Dir Q WRG 33m 12/8/8M
W hut (3m)
R008°-012°(4°), W012°-015°(3°), G015°-021°(6°)

1880 Lochrist 48°20'.6N 4°45'.7W
Dir Oc(3)W 12s 49m 22M
W 8 sided tr, R top (17m)
Intens 135°-140.°(5°)
Rear Ldg Lt 137.9° for Chenal de la Helle with 1874

1884 Les Vieux-Moines 48°19'.4N 4°46'.5W
Fl R 4s 16m 5M
R 8-sided tr (19m)
Vis 280°-133°(213°)

1886 **Les Pierres Noires 48°18'.7N 4°54'.9W**
Fl R 5s 27m 19M Horn(2) 60s
W tr, R top (28m)

FRANCE - WEST COAST
GOULET DE BREST
Ouessant SW Lanby 48°31'.7N 5°49'.1W
Fl 45 20M RW Lanby

0790 **Pointe du Petit-Minou 48°20'.2N 4°36'.9W**
Fl(2)WR 6s 32 m 19/15M
Grey round tr, W on SW side, R top (26m)
R Shore-252°, W252°-260°(8°), R260-307°(47°)
W (unintens) 307°-015°(68°), W015°-065.5°(50.5°),
W070.5° - shore.

- Ldg Lts 068°. Front
Dir Q W 30m 23M Horn 60s
Intens 065.5°-070.5°(5°)
Fog Det Lt FG
Intens 036.5°-039.5°(3°) 420m NE

0790.1 **- - Pointe due Portzic 48°21'.6N 4°32'.0W**
Oc(2)WR 12s 56m 19/15M
Grey 8-sided tr (35m)
R219°-259°(40°), W259°-338°(79°), R338°-000°(22°)
W000°-065.5°(65.5°), W070.5°-219°(148.5°).
Vis 041°-069 (28°) in W of Goulet.

- - Rear
Dir Q W 54m 23M
Intens 065°-071°(6°)

0790.2 **- 48°21'.6N 4°32'.0W**
Dir Q(6) + LFl W 15s 54m 24M
Intens 045°-050(5°)

0792 Roche Mengam 48°20'.4N 4°34'.5W
Fl(3)WR 12s 11m 11/8M on R tower, black bands (15m)
R034°-054°(20°), W054°-034°(340°)

0794 I.F.R.E.M.E.R. 48°21'.6N 4°33'.0W
Fl R 2s 1m 2M Dolphin (2m)

PORT DE BREST
0796 - PORT MILITAIRE. Jetée Sud. Head 48°22'1N 4°29'.5W
Q R 10m 5M W tr, R top (9m)
Vis 094°-048°(314°)

0798 - - Jetée Est. Head 48°22'2N 4°29'.2W
Q G 10m 5M W tr, G top (10m)
Vis 299°-163°(224°)

0799 - - - Terre-pleine du Château 48°22'.9N 4°29'.5W
Dir Oc(2)WRG 6s 19m 11/8/8M On roof of building
G335°-344°(9°), W344°-350°(6°), R350°-014°(24°)

0800 - LA PENFELD. Pointe de la Rose 48°22'.9N 4°29'8W
Iso G 3s 11m 7M W pylon, G top (8m)
Vis 316°-180°(224°)

0800.4 - - Quai de l'Artillerie 48°22'.7N 4°29'.6W
Iso R 3s 8m 7M W support, R top (8m)
Vis 144°-350°(206°)

0802 - PORT DE COMMERCE. E entrance. S side
48°22'.7N 4°28'5W
Oc(2)R 6s 8m 5M W pylon, R top (7m)
Vis 018°-301°(283°)

0803 - - Quai Est. No 5. Head 48°22'.8N 4°28'.6W
Oc(2)G 6s 8m 7M W metal framework tr, G top (9m)

0804 - - Jetée Ouest. Head 48°22'.7N 4°29'.0W
Iso R 4s 10m 7M W column, R top (11m)

0806 - - Jetée du Sud W Head 48°22'.6N 4°29'.2W
Fl G 4s 10m 6M W column, G top (10m)
Vis 022°-257°(235°)

0810 - S. Nicolas. Quai de la Pyrotechnie 48°24'.1N 4°22'.2W
Fl R 4s 5M R mast

0811 - - 48°24'.6N 4°21'.7W
Dir Fl(2)WRG 6s 9/7/7M Masonry hut
R014°-018°(4°), W018°-022°(4°), G022°-026°(4°)

CAMARET-SUR-MER
0816 - Môle Nord. Head. 48°16'.9N 4°35'.3W
Iso WG 4s 7m 12/8M W pylon, G top (7m)
W135°-182°(47°), G182°-027°(205°). Obscured when
bearing more than 187°

0817 - Môle Sud Head. 48°16'.7N 4°35'.4W
Fl(2)R 6s 9m 5M R pylon (8m)
Obscured when bearing less than 143°
and when bearing more than 185°.

0818 **Pointe du Toulinguet 48°16'.8N 4°37'.8W**
Oc(3)WR 12s 49m 15/11M W square tr on building (14m)
W shore-028°, R028°-090°(62°), W090°-shore.
Fog Det Lt F G. R Lt on mast 450m SE

FRANCE - WEST COAST
0820 La Parquette 48°15'.9N 4°44'.3W
Fl RG 4s 17m 6/6M
W 8-sided tr, black diagonal stripes (25m)
R244°-285°(41°), G285°-244°(319)°

0821 Basse du Lis. Buoy 48°13'.1N 4°44'.6W
Q(6)+LFl W 15s Whis 9m 8M S cardinal

BAIE DE DOUARNENEZ
0826 **- Pointe de Morgat 48°13'.2N 4°29'.9W**
Oc(4)WRG 12s 77m 15/11/10M W square tr, R top
W dwelling (15m)
W shore-281°, G281°-301°(20°),W301°-021°(80°),
R021°-043°(22°) Obsured when bearing more than 027°

0828 - Morgat. Môle. Head 48°13'.6N 4°29'.9W
Oc(2)WR 6s 8m 9/6M W and R metal framework tr (6m)
W007°-257°(250°), R257°-007°(110°). Marina Pontoons
marked by Fl G 4s at E end and Fl R 4s at W end 320m E

0829 - Basse Vieille. Buoy 48°08'.3N 4°35'.7W
Fl(2)W 6s Whis 8m 8M on black HFPB, red bands

DOUARNENEZ
0830 - Île Tristan 48°06'.2N 4°20'.3W
Oc(3)WR 12s 35m 13/10M Grey tower, W band, black top (11m)
W shore-138°, R138°-153°(15°), W153°-shore. Obscured when
bearing less than 111°

0831 - Bassin Nord. N Mole. E Head 48°06'.0N 4°19'.3W
Iso G 4s 9m 4M W and G pylon (8m)

0831.2 - - S Mole. N Head 48°05'.9N 4°19'.3W
Oc(2)R 6s 6m 6M W and R pylon (5m)

0832 - - - Elbow. Môle de Rosmeur. Head 48°05'.8N 4°19'.2W
Oc G 4s 6m 6M W pylon. G top (6m)
Vis 170°-097°(287°)

0834 - Tréboul. Pointe Biron. Head 48°06'.1N 4°20'.4W
Q G 7m 6M W column, G top (7m)

0836 **- Pointe du Millier 48°05'.9N 4°27'.9W**
Oc(2)WRG 6s 34m 16/12/11M W house (8m)
G080°-087°(7°), W087°-113°(26°), R113°-120°(7°),
W120°-129°(9°), G129°-148°(19°), W148°-251°(103°),
R251°-258°(7°). Obscured 255.5°-081.5°(186°)

CHAUSSÉE DE SEIN
0850 - 'Chaussée De Sein' Buoy 48°03'.8N 5°07'.7W
VQ(9)W 10s Whis 9m 8M W cardinal. Racon

0852 **- Ar-men 48°03'.0N 4°59'.9W**
Fl(3)W 20s Siren(3) 60s 29m 24M W tr, black top. dark base (37m)

0856 **- Main light. Île de Sein. NW point 48°02'.6N 4°52'.1W**
Fl(4)W 25s 49m 29M W tr, black top (51m)

0858 - Ar Guéveur 48°02'.0N 4°51'.4W
Dia 60s 20m W tr (16m)

0860 - Men-Brial. 48°02'.3N 4°51'.0W
Oc(2)WRG 6s 16m 12/9/7M G and W tr (14m)
G149°-186°(37°), W186°-192°(6°), R192°-221°(29°),
W221°-227°(6°), G227°-254°(27°)

RAZ DE SEIN
0862 - Le Chat 48°01'.5N 4°48'.8W
Fl(2)WRG 6s 27m 9/6/6M on black tower, Y top (31m)
G096°-215°(119°), W215°230°(15°), R230°-271°(41°),
G271°-286°(15°), R286°-096°(170°)

0866 - Tévennec 48°04'.3N 4°47'.6W
Q WR 28m 9/6M W tr and dwelling (15m)
W090°-345°(255°), R345°-090°(105°)

- - Dir Lt Dir Iso W 4s 24m 12M (9m)
Intens 324°-332°(8°)

0870 **- La Vieille 48°02'.5N 4°45'.4W**
Oc(2+1) WRG 12s 33m17/14/13M
Grey tr, black top (27m) Horn (2+1) 60S
W290°-298°(8°), R298°-325°(27°), W325°-355°(30°),
G355°-017°(22°), W017°-035°(18°), G035°-105°(70°),
W105°-123°(18°) R123°-158°(35°), W158°-295°(47°).
R light on radio mast 3.4M ENE

0872 - La Plate 48°02'.4N 4°45'.5W
VQ(9)W 10s 19m 8M on yellow tr, black band (26m)

AUDIERNE
0874 - Pointe de Lervily 48°00'.1N 4°34'.0W
Fl(2+1)WR 12s 20m 14/11M W round tr, R top (12m)
W211°-269°(58°), R269°294(25°), W294°-087°(153°),
R087°-121°(34°)

0875	- Jetée de Saint-Évette. Head 48°00'.3N 4°33'.1W Oc(2)R 6s 2m 7M R lantern (1m) *Vis 090°-000°(270°)*
0877	- Passe de l'Est. Ldg Lts 331°. Jetée de Raoulic. Head. Front 48°00'.6N 4°32'.5W Oc(2+1) WG 12s 11m 14/9M W round tr (11m) *W shore-034°, G034°-shore but may show W037°-055°(18°)*
0877.1	- - Rear. 0.5M from front 48°01'.0N 4°32'.8W Dir F R 44m 9M W 8-sided tower, R top (15m) *Intens 321°-341°(20°)*
	- Kergadec. Dir Lt 006° Dir Q WRG 43m 12/9/9M *G000°-005.3°(5.3°), W005.3°-006.7°(1.4°), R006.7°-017°(10.3°)*
0884	Pors-Poulhan. W side of entrance 47°59'.1N 4°28'.0W Q R 14m 9M W square tr, R top (6m)
	SAINT GUÉNOLÉ
0885	- Ldg Lts 026°30'. Front 47°49'.1N 4°22'.6W Q R 8m 4M R mast (13m)
0885.1	- - Rear. 51m from front 47°49'.1N 4°22'.6W Q R 12m 4M Mast, R and W bands (10m) *Synchronised with front*
0886	- Chenal de Groumilli. Ldg Lts 123°. Front 47°48'.2N 4°22'.6W F G 9m 9M Orange ○ on W tr, black bands (11m)
0886.1	- - - Rear. 300m from front 47°48'.1N 4°22'.4W F G 13m 9M Orange ○ on W tower, black bands (14m)
0887	- Ldg Lts 055°24'. Front. 47°48'.7N 4°22'.7W VQ W 5m 2M Platform on G and W metal column
0887.1	- - Rear. 320m from front 47°48'.9N 4°22'.4W F Vi 12m 1M Platform on G and W metal column *Vis 040°-070°(30°)*
	POINTE DE PENMARC'H
0890	**- Eckmühl 47°47'.9N 4°22'.4W** Fl W 5s Siren 60s 60m 24M Grey 8-sided tr (65m)
0892	- Men Hir 47°47'.8N 4°23'.9W Fl(2)WG 6s 19m 8/5M W tr, black band (21m) *G135°-315°(180°), W315°-135°(180°)*
0893	- Scoedec 47°48'.5N 4°23'.1W Fl G 2.5s 6m 3M G tr (7m)
0894	- Locarec 47°47'.3N 4°20'.3W Iso WRG 4s 11m 9/6/6M W tank on rock (8m) *G063°-068°(5°), R068°-271°(203°), W271°-285°(14°), R285°-298°(13°), G298°-340°(42°),R340°-063°(83°)*
0895	Kérity. Men Hir 47°47'.3N 4°20'.6W Fl R 2.5s 6m 2M R □ on beacon
0895.4	- Detached Breakwater. Head 47°47'.6N 4°20'.9W Fl(2)G 6s 5m 1M G metal mast (4m)
	PORT DE GUILVINEC
0896	- Ldg Lts 053°. Môle de Léchiagat. Spur. Front 47°47'.5N 4°17'.0W Q W 7m 8M W pylon (6m) *Vis 233°-066°(193°)*
0896.05	- - Rocher Le Faoutés. Middle. 210m from front 47°47'.6N 4°16'.9W Q WG 12m 14/11M R ○ on W pylon (11m) *W006°-293°(287°), G293°-006°(73°). Synchronised with front*
0896.1	- - Rear. 0.58m from front 47°47'.8N 4°16'.3W Dir Q W 26m 8M R ○ on W pylon (23m) *Vis 051.5°-054.5°(3°). Synchronised with front*
0898	- Lost-Moan 47°47'.1N 4°16'.7W Fl(3) WRG 12s 8m 9/6/6M □ on W tr, R top (13m) *R327°-014°(47°), G014°-065°(51°), R065°-140°(75°), W140°-160°(20°), R160°-268°(108°), W268°-273°(5°), G273°-317°(44°), W317°-327°(10°)*
0899	- Môle de Léchiagat. Head 47°47'.5N 4°17'.1W Fl G 4s 5m 7M W hut, G top (3m)
0899.2	- - Spur 47°47'.5N 4°17'.0W Fl(2)G 6s 4m 5M G structure (2m) *Vis 078°-258°(180°)*
0900	- Môle. Head 47°47'.6N 4°17'.0W Fl R 4s 11m 9M W tr, R top (10m)
0901	- Outer Breakwater. Head 47°47'.5N 4°17'.1W Fl(2)R 6s 4m 5M R structure (2m)
	LESCONIL
0902	- Men-ar-Groas 47°47'.8N 4°12'.6W Fl(3)WRG 12s 14m 13/9/9M W tr, G top (11m) *G268°-313°(45°), W313°-333°(20°), R333°-050°(77°)*
0904	- E Breakwater. Head 47°47'.8N 4°12'.6W Q G 5m 6M G tr (4m)
0904.5	- S Breakwater. Head 47°47'.7N 4°12'.6W Oc R 4s 5m 6M R tripod (3m)
	LOCTUDY
0906	**- Point de Langoz 47°49'.9N 4°09'.6W** Fl(4)WRG 12s 12m 15/11/11M W tr, R top (13m) *W115°-257°(142°), G257°-284°(27°), W284°-295°(11°), R295°-318°(23°), W318°-328°(10°), R328°-025°(57°)*

0908	- Les Perdrix 47°50'.3N 4°10'.0W Fl WRG 4s 15m 11/8/8M ∆ on black and W chequered tr (18m) *G090°-285°(195°), W285°-295°(10°), R295°-090°(155°)*
0909	- Karek-Saoz 47°50'.1N 4°09'.3W Q R 3m 1M R truncated tr (10m)
0910	- Le Blas 47°50'.3N 4°10'.1W Fl(3)G 12s 5m 1M G ∆ on truncated column (11m)
	BÉNODET. RIVIÈRE ODÉTÉ
0913.9	**- Ldg Lts 345°30' Pointe du Coq. Front. 336m from rear** **47°52'.4N 4°06'.6W** Dir Oc(2+1)G 12s 11m 17M W round tr, G stripe (13m) *Intens 345°-347°(2°)*
0914	- - Common rear. Pyramide 47°52'.5N 4°06'.8W Oc(2+1)W 12s 48m 11M W tr, G top (39m) *Sychronised with 0913.9. Vis 338°-016°(38°)*
0914.1	- Lts in line. 000°30'. Pointe de Combrit. Front. 0.63M from rear 47°51'.9N 4°06'.7W Oc(3+1)WR 12s 19m 12/9M W square tr, grey corners (17m) *W325°-017°(52°), R017°-325°(308°)*
0915	- Pointe de Toulgoet 47°52'.3N 4°06'.8W Fl R 2s 2m 2M R mast (4m)
	ÎLES DE GLÉNAN
0918	**- Ile-aux-Moutons 47°46'.5N 4°01'.7W** Oc(2)WRG 6s 18m 15/11/11M W tr and dwelling (17m) *W035°-050°(15°), G050°-063°(13°), W063°-081°(18°), R081°-141°(60°),W141°-292°(151°), R292°-035°(103°)*
	- - Auxiliary light Dir Oc(2) W 17m 24M *Sychronised with main light. Intens 278.5°-283.5°(5°)*
0922	**- Penfret 47°43'.3N 3°57'.2W** Fl R 5s 36m 21M W square tr, R top (24m) *5 F R on wind generator 2.12M W*
	- - Auxiliary light Dir Q W 34m 12M *Vis 295°-315°(20°)*
0922.4	- Jument de Glenan. Buoy 47°38'.8N 4°01'.3W Q(6)+LFl W 15s Whis 10m 8M S cardinal
0922.6	- Basse Perennes. Buoy 47°41'.1N 4°06'.3W Q(9)W 15s Whis 8m 8M W cardinal
0923	- Île Cigogne 47°43'.1N 3°59'.6W Q(2)RG 5s 2M R tripod (1m) *G106°-108°(2°), R108°-262°(154°), G262°-268°(6°). Shown May 1 to Oct 1*
0923.4	- Rouge de Glénan. Buoy 47°45'.5N 4°03'.9W VQ(9)W 10s Whis 8m 8M W cardinal
0924	Beg-Meil. Quay. Head 47°51'.7N 3°58'.8W Fl R 2s 6m 2M R and W column (4m) *Aero obstruction light on tr 0.5M SE*
	LA FORÊT-FOUESNANT
0925	- Cap Coz. Shelter mole. Head 47°53'.5N 3°58'.1W Fl(2)R 6s 5m 6M R lantern, on grey post, W hut (3m)
0925.4	- Port de la Forêt. Kerleven. Shelter mole. Head 47°53'.6N 3°58'.1W Fl G 4s 8m 6M G lantern on grey mast, W hut (7m)
0925.6	- - Inner shelter mole. Head 47°54'.0N 3°58'.2W Iso G 4s 5m 5M G lantern on grey mast, W hut (4m)
	CONCARNEAU
0928	- Ldg Lts 028°30'. La Croix. Front 47°52'.2N 3°55'.1W Oc(3)W 12s 14m 13M R and W tr (12m) *Vis 006.5°-093°(86.5°)*
0930	**- - Beuzec. Rear. 1.34M from front 47°53'.4N 3°54'.0W** Dir Q W 87m 23M Belfry (32m) *Intens 026.5°-030.5°(4°)*
0932	- Lanriec 47°52'.1N 3°54'.6W Q G 13m 8M G stripe on W gable (8m) *Vis 063°-078°(15°)*
0933	- La Médée 47°52'.1N 3°54'.9W Fl R 2.5s 9m 4M R tr (16m)
0934	- Passage de Lanriec 47°52'.3N 3°54'.8W Oc(2)WR 6s 4m 8/6M R tr (5m) *R209°-354°(145°), W354°-007°(13°), R007°-018°(11°). Fl R 4s and Q(6)+LFl R 6s shown on W side, Fl G 4s and Fl(2)G 6s on E side of passage*
0936	- Le Cochon 47°51'.5N 3°55'.5W Fl(3)WRG 12s 5m 9/6/6M G tr (11m) *G048°-205°(157°), R205°-352°(147°), W352°-048°(56°)*
0937	- Basse du Chenal 47°51'.6N 3°55'.6W Q R 6m 5M R tr (12m) *Vis 180°-163°(343°)*

SUGGESTED WAYPOINTS

WARNING:
THESE WAYPOINTS DO NOT NECESSARILY GIVE SAFE PASSAGE FROM EVERY DIRECTION – ALWAYS PLOT A SAFE TRACK
NOTE THAT MOST WAYPOINTS ALLOW FOR A SAFE OFFING

Bearing (T) and dist (nm) FROM		Waypoint	
180/2.0	Bishop Rock	49 50.3N	6 26.7W
135/1.0	Peninnis Head	49 53.5N	6 17.5W
000/1.0	Round Island	49 59.7N	6 19.3W
*	St Mary's (Isles of Scilly)	49 53.7N	6 18.1W
-	Seven Stones LtV	50 03.5N	6 04.4W
225/1.0	Longships	50 03.3N	5 45.9W
180/2.0	Wolf Rock	49 54.7N	5 48.4W
*	Newlyn	50 06.4N	5 31.2W
*	Penzance	50 06.8N	5 31.0W
180/2.0	Lizard	49 55.6N	5 12.1W
*	Helford River	50 05.7N	5 04.1W
*	Falmouth	50 07.6N	5 01.5W
*	Mevagissey	50 16.1N	4 46.4W
*	Fowey	50 19.1N	4 39.0W
*	Looe	50 20.8N	4 25.8W
000/1.0	Eddystone	50 11.8N	4 15.9W
180/1.0	Eddystone	50 09.8N	4 15.9W
*	Plymouth	50 20.2N	4 10.0W
*	Yealm River	50 18.0N	4 05.6W
*	Salcombe	50 12.1N	3 46.4W
135/2.0	Start Pt	50 11.9N	3 36.4W
*	Dartmouth	50 20.0N	3 33.3W
*	Teignmouth	50 32.2N	3 28.7W
090/1.0	Berry Head	50 24.0N	3 27.2W
*	Brixham	50 24.4N	3 30.8W
*	Torquay	50 27.0N	3 31.7W
*	Exmouth	50 36.0N	3 22.3W
180/1.0	Straight Pt	50 35.5N	3 21.7W
*	Lyme Regis	50 42.9N	2 55.2W
*	Bridport (West Bay)	50 42.4N	2 46.0W
180/0.3	Portland Bill	50 30.5N	2 27.3W
180/3.0	Portland Bill	50 27.8N	2 27.3W
*	Portland Harbour	50 35.7N	2 25.0W
*	Weymouth	50 36.7N	2 26.1W
180/0.5	St Alban's Hd	50 34.0N	2 03.2W
135/1.0	Anvil Pt	50 34.8N	1 56.6W
090/1.0	Handfast Pt	50 38.5N	1 53.6W
*	Poole Harbour	50 39.3N	1 55.1W
*	Christchurch	50 43.4N	1 43.5W
-	Needles Fairway By	50 38.2N	1 38.9W
-	Solent Forts Entr	50 44.7N	1 04.9W
180/2.0	St Catherine's Pt	50 32.5N	1 17.8W
*	Lymington	50 44.2N	1 30.5W
*	Beaulieu River	50 46.6N	1 21.4W
*	River Hamble	50 50.1N	1 18.6W
*	Portsmouth Harbour	50 47.0N	1 06.3W
*	Yarmouth	50 42.7N	1 29.9W
*	Newtown River	50 43.7N	1 24.9W
*	Cowes	50 46.4N	1 17.5W
*	Wootton Creek	50 44.5N	1 12.0W
*	Bembridge Harbour	50 42.5N	1 05.2W
090/0.1	Bembridge Ledge by	50 41.1N	1 02.6W
090/0.1	W Princessa by	50 40.1N	1 03.4W
*	Langstone Harbour	50 46.3N	1 01.3W
-	Chichester Bar Beacon	50 45.9N	0 56.4W
-	Nab	50 40.0N	0 57.1W
-	Owers Lanby	50 37.3N	0 40.6W
*	Littlehampton	50 47.3N	0 32.1W
*	Shoreham	50 49.0N	0 14.7W
*	Brighton Marina	50 47.5N	0 06.2W
*	Newhaven	50 46.3N	0 04.0E
090/5.0	E Channel Lt Float	49 58.7N	2 21.0W
270/2.0	Channel LtV	49 54.4N	2 57.0W
-	EC1	50 05.9N	1 48.5W
-	EC2	50 12.1N	1 12.2W
-	EC3	50 18.4N	0 36.0W
270/1.0	Greenwich Lanby	50 27.0N	0 01.6W

Bearing (T) and dist (nm) FROM		Waypoint	
*	Fécamp	49 45.9N	0 21.1E
315/2.0	Cap d'Antifer	49 42.4N	0 07.8E
*	Le Havre	49 29.5N	0 04.5E
-	Le Havre Lt By	49 31.7N	0 09.8W
*	Honfleur	49 25.8N	0 14.0E
270/1.0	Cap de la Heve	49 30.8N	0 02.6E
*	Deauville	49 22.7N	0 02.6E
*	Ouistreham	49 20.48N	0 14.73W
*	Courseulles	49 21.3N	0 27.6W
*	Grandcamp	49 25.2N	1 04.5W
*	Carentan	49 25.5N	1 07.0W
*	St Vaast La Hougue	49 34.3N	0 14.73W
*	Barfleur	49 41.2N	1 14.3W
045/2.0	Pte de Barfleur	49 43.2N	1 13.7W
000/2.0	Cap Levi	49 43.8N	1 28.4W
-	Cherbourg, W Hr Entr	49 40.5N	1 39.4W
315/2.0	Cap de la Hague	49 45.0N	1 58.5W
315/2.0	Casquets	49 44.8N	2 24.9W
*	Alderney, Braye Harbour	49 44.4N	2 10.8W
-	Sark, Blanchard by	49 25.4N	2 17.5W
090/1.0	Plat Fougere	49 30.9N	2 27.5W
270/1.0	Guernsey, Les Hanois	49 26.2N	2 43.6W
*	Guernsey, St Peter Port	49 27.6N	2 31.0W
-	Banc Desormes by	49 19.0N	2 18.1W
270/1.0	Jersey, La Corbiere	49 10.8N	2 16.4W
*	Jersey, St Helier	49 08.7N	2 08.2W
-	NW Minquiers by	48 59.6N	2 20.5W
-	SW Minquiers by	48 54.4N	2 19.3W
*	Granville	48 49.6N	1 36.5W
-	Le Vieux Banc, N Cardinal by	48 42.5N	2 09.4W
*	St Malo	48 41.4N	2 07.2W
000/1.0	Cap Fréhel	48 42.1N	2 19.1W
*	Le Légué	48 34.4N	2 41.1W
000/3.0	Roche Douvres	49 09.5N	2 48.8W
090/3.0	Roche Douvres	49 06.5N	2 44.3W
270/3.0	Roche Douvres	49 06.5N	2 53.3W
*	Binic	48 36.5N	2 44.8W
*	St Quay-Portrieux	48 40.7N	2 49.8W
*	Paimpol (East)	48 47.7N	2 56.0W
*	Paimpol (West)	48 49.9N	2 57.7W
*	Rievère de Trieux	48 53.9N	2 57.7W
000/2.0	Les Heaux de Brehat	48 56.5N	3 05.2W
000/0.5	Ile de Brehat, Rosedo	48 52.0N	3 00.3W
*	Tréguier	48 55.5N	3 12.0W
*	Perros-Guirec (West)	48 51.7N	3 31.5W
*	Perrs-Guirec (North)	48 53.0N	3 23.0W
000/2.0	Les Sept Iles	48 54.8N	3 29.5W
000/2.0	Les Triagoz	48 54.3N	3 38.8W
*	Morlaix	48 43.0N	3 53.5W
*	Roscoff and Ile de Batz (East)	48 45.3N	3 56.5W
*	Roscoff and Ile de Batz (West)	48 44.7N	4 04.0W
315/2.0	Ile-Vierge	48 39.8N	4 36.3W
*	L'Aber Vrac'h	48 37.6N	4 38.4W
*	Le Conquet	48 23.2N	4 49.0W
000/2.0	Ouessant, Le Stiff	48 30.5N	5 03.4W
270/2.0	Ouessant, Creac'h	48 27.6N	5 10.8W
*	Port de Moulin-Blanc (Brest)	48 22.8N	4 25.9W
*	Camaret	48 17.2N	4 35.0W
*	Morgat	48 13.7N	4 29.0W
*	Douarnanez	48 06.5N	4 20.2W
*	Audierne	47 59.1N	4 33.8W
*	Loctudy	47 50.0N	4 05.8W
*	Benodet	47 50.0N	4 05.8W
*	Port-la-Forêt	47 50.0N	3 56.8W
*	Concarneau	47 50.0N	3 56.8W

*See Port Information for description of Waypoint

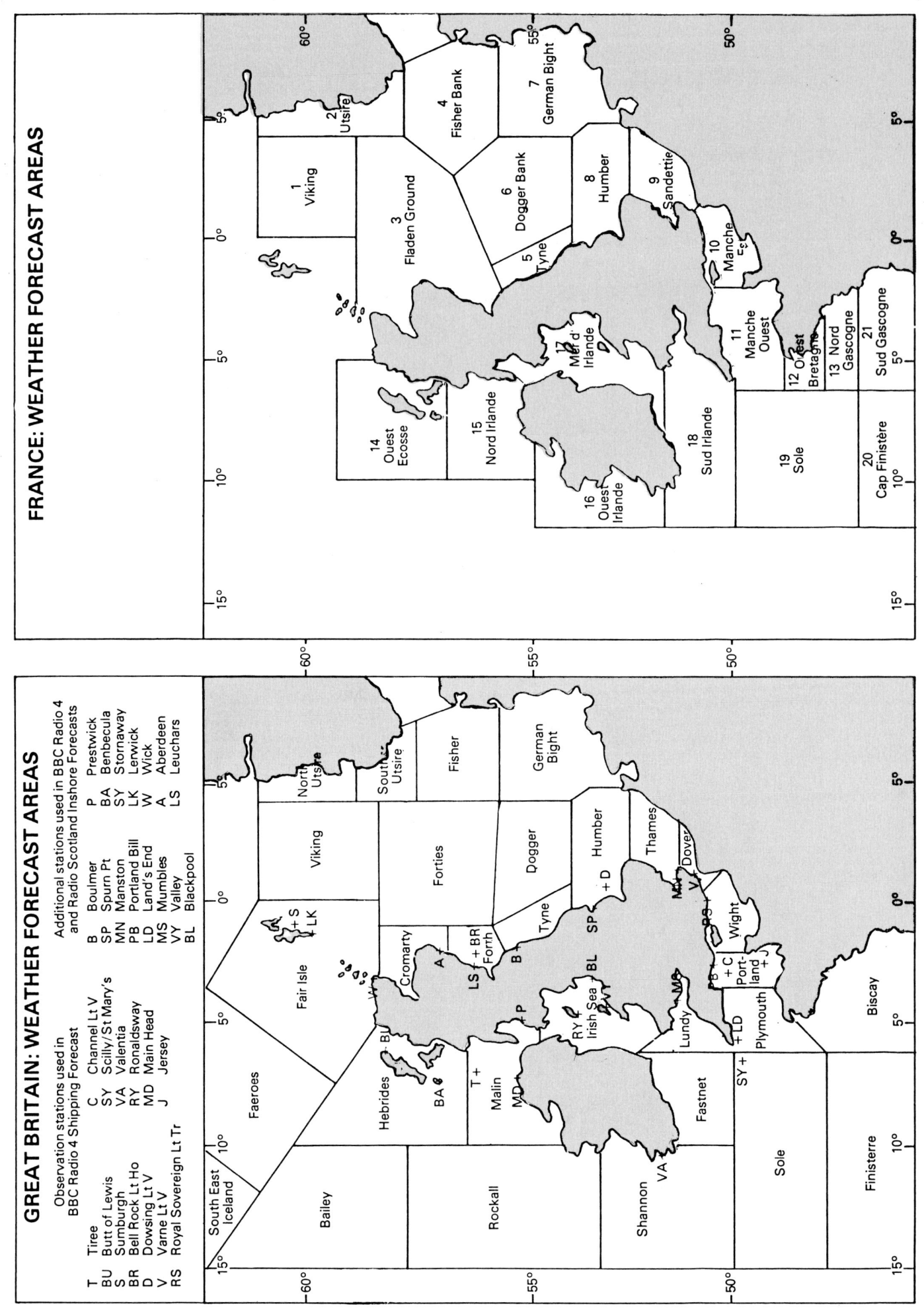

FRANCE: WEATHER FORECAST AREAS

1 Viking
2 Utsire
3 Fladen Ground
4 Fisher Bank
5 Tyne
6 Dogger Bank
7 German Bight
8 Humber
9 Sandettié
10 Manche Est
11 Manche Ouest
12 Ouest Bretagne
13 Nord Gascogne
14 Ouest Ecosse
15 Nord Irlande
16 Ouest Irlande
17 Mer d'Irlande
18 Sud Irlande
19 Sole
20 Cap Finistère
21 Sud Gascogne

GREAT BRITAIN: WEATHER FORECAST AREAS

Observation stations used in
BBC Radio 4 Shipping Forecast

T	Tiree	C	Channel Lt V		
BU	Butt of Lewis	SY	Scilly/St Mary's		
S	Sumburgh	VA	Valentia		
BR	Bell Rock Lt Ho	RY	Ronaldsway		
D	Dowsing Lt V	MD	Main Head		
V	Varne Lt V	J	Jersey		
RS	Royal Sovereign Lt Tr				

Additional stations used in BBC Radio 4
and Radio Scotland Inshore Forecasts

B	Boulmer	P	Prestwick
SP	Spurn Pt	BA	Benbecula
MN	Manston	SY	Stornaway
PB	Portland Bill	LK	Lerwick
LD	Land's End	W	Wick
MS	Mumbles	A	Aberdeen
VY	Valley	LS	Leuchars
BL	Blackpool		

Faeroes
South East Iceland
Bailey
Rockall
Shannon
Fair Isle
Hebrides
Malin
Viking
Cromarty
Forties
Tyne
Dogger
German Bight
Forth
Humber
Thames
Dover
Wight
Portland
Plymouth
Lundy
Irish Sea
Fastnet
Sole
Finisterre
Biscay
North Utsire
South Utsire
Fisher

126

WEATHER

The RYA publishes a useful booklet (G5/92) on weather forecasts. Join the RYA - 0703 629962

BEAUFORT SCALE

No	Wind Speed (Knots)	Official Term	Sea State
0	1 or less	Calm	Mirror like sea.
1	1–3	Light air	Gentle scaly ripples.
2	4–6	Light breeze	Small wavelets. May have glassy crests but these will not break.
3	7–10	Gentle breeze	Large wavelets. Crests begin to break. Possibly some white horses.
4	11–16	Moderate breeze	Waves becoming longer with white horses.
5	17–21	Fresh breeze	Moderate waves with white horses and possibly occasional spray.
6	22–27	Strong breeze	Large waves forming with extensive white crests and spray.
7	28–33	Near gale	Sea heaps up and foam from breaking waves blows in streaks.
8	34–40	Gale	Moderately high waves. Edge of crests break into spindrift. Well marked streaks.
9	41–47	Severe gale	High waves. Confused breaking crests. Spray affects visibility.
10	48–55	Storm	Very high waves with long overhanging crests. Sea surface becomes white.
11	56–63	Violent storm	Exceptionally high waves hiding ships from view. Sea covered in white foam.
12	64 plus	Hurricane	Air full of driving spray. Very bad visibility.

Decisions based on estimates or forecasts of Beaufort Scale wind strength should be made with caution. Sea state descriptions are based on open sea conditions and may well be different and more dangerous inshore or in shallow waters, where they can change suddenly. A slow or disturbed sea can often precede a blow by several hours.

Glossary of common terms French/English

prévision	forecast	avis de coup de vent:	
Nord	north	néant (coastal	
Sud	south	stations MW)	no gale
Est	east	dépression	low
Ouest	west	anticyclone	high
six heures	six hours	pluie	rain
douze heures	twelve hours	bruine	drizzle
dix-huit heures	eighteen hours	averse	shower
vingt-quatre heures	twenty-four hours	brouillard	fog
aujourd'hui	today	brume	mist
demain	tomorrow	vent	wind
les prochain jours	next few days	rafale	gust
avis de coup de vent	gale warning	léger (faible)	slight
pas d'avis de coup de vent en cours ou prévu (Radio France 164 Khz)	no gale in force or forecast	modéré	moderate
		lourd (gros)	heavy
		fort	strong
		mauvais	poor
		bon	good

RADIO WEATHER SHIPPING FORECAST ROUND THE CLOCK

GALE WARNINGS

'Gale warnings' are issued when winds of force 8 or more are expected. They remain in force until cancelled or amended but if the gale persists for more than 24 hours after the time or origin, the warning will be reissued. 'Imminent' means within 6 hours. 'Soon' means between 6 and 12 hours.

All times are LOCAL except those marked * which are UT.

Storm warning are broadcast as soon as possible after receipt.

HM Coastguard broadcast weather forecasts at regular intervals and gale and strong wind forecasts on receipt. Listen on Ch 16 and then switch to Ch 67 when advised.

Solent: 0040, 0440, 0840, 1240, 1640, 2040

Portland: 0220 and every four hours

Brixham: 0050 and every four hours

Falmouth: 0140 and every four hours

plus every two hours when forecasting winds of force 6 and above.

Local Time (except*=UT)	Station	MHz/ kHz/Ch
0033	BBC Radio 4	198
0150*	CROSS Le Stiff (English and French)	Ch 79
0333*	CROSS Cap Frehel (English and French)	Ch 79
0348*	CROSS Ile de Batz (English and French)	Ch 79
0450*	CROSS Le Stiff (English and French)	Ch 79
0555	BBC Radio 4	198
0604	BBC Radio Solent (Mon-Fri)	96.1
0610	BBC Radio Cornwall (Mon-Fri)	96.0
0625	BBC Radio Cornwall (Mon-Fri)	96.0
0633*	Dieppe Radio (French)	Ch 02
0633*	Le Havre Radio (French)	Ch 26
0633*	Port en Bessin Radio (French)	Ch 03
0633*	Cherbourg Radio (French)	Ch 27
0633*	St Malo Radio (French)	Ch 02
0633*	Paimpol Radio (French)	Ch 84
0633*	Plougasnou Radio (French)	Ch 81
0633*	Ouessant Radio (French)	Ch 82
0633	BBC Radio Devon (Mon-Sat)	103.4
0633	BBC Radio Solent (everyday)	96.1
0645*	Jersey Radio	CH 25 82
0645	BBC Radio Cornwall (Mon-Fri)	96.0
0655	BBC Radio 3	90.2–92.4
0658	BBC Radio Sussex (Mon-Fri)	95.3
0700	BBC Radio Jersey (Mon-Fri)	88.8
0705	BBC Radio Sussex (Sat)	95.3
0709	BBC Radio Solent (everyday)	103.4
0715	BBC Radio Cornwall (Mon-Sat)	96.0
0732	BBC Radio Guernsey (Summer Mon-Fri)	93.2
0733*	Land's End Radio	Ch 27
0733*	Start Point Radio	Ch 26
0733*	Pendennis Radio	Ch 62
0733*	Hastings Radio	Ch 07
0733*	Niton Radio	Ch 28
0733*	Weymouth Bay Radio	Ch 05
0733	BBC Radio Devon (Mon-Fri)	103.4
0733	BBC Radio Solent (everyday)	96.1

Local Time (except*=UT)	Station	MHz/ kHz/Ch
0735	BBC Radio Jersey (Mon-Fri)	88.8
0745*	Jersey Radio	Ch 25 82
0745	BBC Radio Cornwall (everyday)	96.0
0745	BBC Radio Solent (everyday)	96.1
0750*	CROSS Le Stiff (English and French)	Ch 79
0758	BBC Radio Sussex (Mon-Fri)	95.3
0800	BBC Radio Jersey (Sat)	88.8
0805	BBC Radio Jersey (Sun)	88.8
0809	BBC Radio Solent (everyday)	96.1
0810	BBC Radio Guernsey (Sat)	93.2
0810	BBC Radio Jersey (Mon-Sat)	88.8
0815	BBC Radio Cornwall (Mon-Fri, Sun)	96.0
0815	BBC Radio Jersey (Sun)	88.8
0829	BBC Radio Jersey (Mon-Fri)	88.8
0830	BBC Radio Jersey (Sat)	88.8
0832	BBC Radio Guernsey (Summer Mon-Fri)	93.2
0833	BBC Radio Devon (everyday)	103.4
0833	BBC Radio Solent (Mon-Sat)	96.1
0845	BBC Radio Cornwall (everyday)	96.0
0845	BBC Radio Sussex (Mon-Fri)	95.3
0900	BBC Radio Jersey (Mon-Fri)	88.8
0903	BBC Radio Jersey (Sat)	88.8
0904	BBC Radio Solent (everyday)	96.1
0910	BBC Radio Guernsey (Sat)	93.2
0912	BBC Radio Jersey (Sun)	88.8
0915	BBC Radio Cornwall (Sun)	96.0
0930	BBC Radio Sussex (Sun)	95.3
1004	BBC Radio Solent (Mon-Fri, Sun)	96.1
1005	BBC Radio Guernsey (Sun)	93.2
1028	BBC Radio Sussex (Sat)	95.3
1050*	CROSS Le Stiff (English and French)	Ch 79
1104	BBC Radio Solent (everyday)	96.1
1204	BBC Radio Solent (everyday)	96.1
1205	BBC Radio Guernsey (Sun)	93.2
1245*	Jersey Radio	Ch 25 82
1245	BBC Radio Cornwall (Mon-Fri)	96.0

Local Time (except*=UT)	Station	MHz/ kHz/Ch
1259	BBC Radio Jersey (Sun)	88.8
1304	BBC Radio Solent (Sat, Sun)	96.1
1305	BBC Radio Jersey (Sat)	88.8
1308	BBC Radio Cornwall (Sun)	96.0
1309	BBC Radio Solent (Mon-Fri)	96.1
1310	BBC Radio Devon (everyday)	103.4
1310	BBC Radio Cornwall (Sat)	96.0
1310	BBC Radio Jersey (Mon-Fri)	88.8
1313	BBC Radio Cornwall (Mon-Fri)	96.0
1328	BBC Radio Solent (Mon-Fri)	96.1
1350*	CROSS Le Stiff (English and French)	Ch 79
1355	BBC Radio 4	198
1404	BBC Radio Solent (Mon-Sat)	96.1
1433*	Dieppe Radio (French)	Ch 02
1433*	Le Havre Radio (French)	Ch 26
1433*	Port en Bessin Radio (French)	Ch 03
1433*	Cherbourg Radio (French)	Ch 27
1433*	St Malo Radio (French)	Ch 02
1433*	Paimpol Radio (French)	Ch 84
1433*	Plougasnou Radio (French)	Ch 81
1433*	Ouessant Radio (French)	Ch 82
1500	BBC Radio Solent (Sat)	96.1
1504	BBC Radio Solent (Mon-Fri, Sun)	96.1
1604	BBC Radio Solent (Mon-Fri)	96.1
1628	BBC Radio Sussex (Mon-Fri)	95.3
1650*	CROSS Le Stiff (English and French)	Ch 79
1709	BBC Radio Solent (Mon-Fri)	96.1
1715	BBC Radio Cornwall (Mon-Fri)	96.0
1728	BBC Radio Sussex (Mon-Fri)	95.3
1732	BBC Radio Guernsey (Mon-Fri)	93.2
1733	BBC Radio Solent (Mon-Fri)	96.1
1735	BBC Radio Devon (Mon-Fri)	103.4
1735	BBC Radio Jersey (Mon-Fri)	88.8
1740	BBC Radio Cornwall (Mon-Fri)	96.0
1750	BBC Radio 4	198
1758	BBC Radio Solent (Sat)	96.1
1804	BBC Radio Solent (Mon-Fri)	96.1
1805	BBC Radio Jersey (Sat)	88.8
1825	BBC Radio Sussex (Sat)	95.3
1828	BBC Radio Sussex (Mon-Fri)	95.3
1845*	Jersey Radio	Ch 25 82
0933*	Land's End Radio	Ch 27
0933*	Start Point Radio	Ch 26
0933*	Pendennis Radio	Ch 62
0933*	Hastings Radio	Ch 07
0933*	Niton Radio	Ch 28
0933*	Weymouth Bay Radio	Ch 05
1950*	CROSS Le Stiff (English and French)	Ch 79
2033*	CROSS Cap Frehel (French)	Ch 79
2048*	CROSS Ile de Batz	Ch 79
2204	BBC Radio Solent (Mon-Fri)	96.1
2205	BBC Radio Jersey (Mon-Fri)	88.8
2245*	Jersey Radio	Ch 25 82
2250*	CROSS Le Stiff (English and French)	Ch 79
2300	BBC Radio Solent (Mon-Fri)	96.1

IN ADDITION TO THE ABOVE

2 Counties Radio (Poole) broadcasts weather information on the hour and on the half hour on 102.3 MHz

CROSS (Centres Regionaux Operationnels de Surveillance et de Sauvetage) provides weather forecasts on request as follows:

East Channel	CROSS GRIS NEZ	Ch 11
Mid Channel	CROSS JOBUOURG	Ch 80

Marinecall Weather Forecasts

Local weather forecasts (2 days) are available for inshore waters for Channel East 0891 500 456, Mid-Channel 0891 500 457 and SW Channel 0891 500 458. A 5 day forecast for the Channel Waters is also available on 0891 500 450.

MetFAX Marine Weather Forecasts

Call on a FAX machine for forecasts and charts. A menu is available on 0366 400 401 and in particular, 2 day forecasts and charts are available for Channel East 0336 400 456, Mid-Channel 0336 400 457, SW Channel 0336 400 458 and the Channel Waters 0336 400 491. Forecasts and charts are available for days 3 to 5 for the Channel Waters on 0336 400 471.

Marinecall and MetFAX Marine cost 36p per minute cheap rate and 48p per minute at all other times.

Telephone Forecasts (France)

Boulogne	21/31 79 90
Le Havre (auto)	42 12 19 and 21 14 35
Le Havre	42 12 06 and 21 16 11
Deauville	88 84 22
Cherbourg	53 11 55
Granville	50 10 00
St Malo	46 18 77
Lézardrieux	96/20 01 77
Brest	84 60 64
Brest (auto)	84 63 00

In general an automatic forecast for local areas is given on (36) 65 08 08

Telephone Weather Information
(prevailing conditions, not forecasts)

Dover CG	(0304) 210008
St. Catherine's Point	(0983) 730284
MRSC Solent	(0705) 552100
MRSC Portland	(0305) 760439
Portland Bill L.H.	(0305) 820495
MRSC Brixham	(0803) 882704/5
MRCC Falmouth	(0326) 317575
Lizard L.H.	(0326) 290431

PORT INFORMATION

INDEX

PLACE	TIME DIFFERENCES				HEIGHT DIFFERENCES (IN METRES)			
	High Water		Low Water		MHWS	MHWN	MLWN	MLWS
SHOREHAM (see page 14)	**0500** and **1700**	**1000** and **2200**	**0000** and **1200**	**0600** and **1800**	**6.3**	**4.9**	**2.0**	**0.6**
Newhaven	−0015	−0010	0000	0000	+0.4	+0.2	0.0	−0.2
Brighton	−0010	−0005	−0005	−0005	+0.3	+0.1	0.0	−0.1
Littlehampton	+0010	0000	−0005	−0010	−0.4	−0.4	−0.2	−0.2

Newhaven

Way Point
50° 46'.3N 0° 04'.0E (3.2 cables SE of breakwater light)
Charts
Admiralty No 2154
Adlard Coles Pilot Pack Vol I No 126
Tides
See above for corrections from standard port of Shoreham
Harbour Lights
See 0830/0833.4 p.116
Cautions
1 There may be a breaking sea in strong onshore winds. In these circumstances, it may be advisable to keep close to the breakwater.
2 Dredgers are often working.
3 Heaving off warps or wires may be run off across the harbour.
Berthing
Marina on west side of harbour
VHF Ch 16; 12 (24 hrs)
  Newhaven Marina Ch M; 80

Telephones
Harbour Master: (0273) 514131
HM Coastguard: (0273) 514008
MRSC: (0705) 552100
HM Customs: (0703) 229251 or Freephone Customs Yachts
Medical: (0273) 696955 (Hospital)
Marina: (0273) 513881
Newhaven and Seaford YC: (0323) 890077
Newhaven YC: (0273) 513770

Brighton Marina

Way Point
50° 47'.5N 0° 06'.2W (1 mile S of entrance)
Charts
Admiralty No 1991
Adlard Coles Pilot Pack Vol I No 127
Tides
See above for corrections from standard port of Shoreham

Harbour Lights
See 0820/0826 p.115/116
Beacon
50° 48'.67N 0° 05'.95W BM 10M 294.5 kHz
Cautions
1 Strong onshore winds can make the entrance dangerous.
2 The entrance is subject to shoaling.
Berthing
The visitor reception pontoon is immediately on the port hand on passing through the inner entrance.
VHF   Ch M; 80
Telephones
Harbour Master: (0273) 693636 ex 69
HM Coastguard: (0705) 552100
MRSC: (0705) 552100
HM Customs: (0703) 229251 or Freephone Customs Yachts
Medical: (0273) 696955 (Hospital)
Brighton Marina YC: (0273) 609235

Shoreham

Way Point
50° 49'.0N 0° 14°.7W (4.4 cables S of entrance)
Charts
Admiralty No 2044
Adlard Coles Pilot Pack Vol I No 128
Tides
Standard Port - see p.14
Harbour Lights
See 0812/0814.1 p.115
Cautions
1 A shallow entrance, 2.1m.
2 Onshore winds cause rough seas.
3 Dredging is almost always in operation.
Berthing
Lady Bee Marina is approached through lock on the E side of the harbour - opens - 4 HW+4. Berthing limited.
VHF   Ch 14; 16; (24 hrs)
           Lady Bee Marina: Ch M; 80
Telephones
Harbour Master: (0273) 592366
HM Coastguard: (0705) 552100
MRSC: (0705) 552100
HM Customs: (0703) 229251 or Freephone Customs Yachts
Medical: (0903) 205111
Lady Bee Marina: (0273) 593801
Sussex Motor YC: (0273) 453078
Sussex YC: (0273) 464868

Littlehampton

Way Point
50° 47'.3N 0° 32'.1W (5.8 cables SSE of entrance)
Charts
Admiralty No 1991
Adlard Coles Pilot Pack Vol I No 129
Tides
See p.130 for corrections from Standard Port of Shoreham
Harbour Lights
See 0800/0808.2 p.115
Cautions
1 Entry dangerous in strong SE winds, especially on the ebb.
2 The training wall on the E side of the entrance covers at half tide.
3 The stream runs strongly in the river.
Berthing
Apply to the Harbour Office on the E side just opposite Arun YC, for berthing. Arun YC berths are entirely occupied by members. The marina is above the opening footbridge (3.6m when closed) which will be opened on request to the Harbour Master. Request must be made not later than 1630 on the day before.
VHF   Littlehampton Marina: Ch M; 80
Telephones
Harbour Master: (0903) 721215
HM Coastguard: (0705) 552100
MRSC: (0705) 552100
HM Customs: (0703) 229251 or Freephone Customs Yachts

Medical: (0903) 714113 (Doctor)
Littlehampton Marina: (0903) 713553
Ship and Anchor Marina: (0243) 551262
Arun YC: (0903) 714553
Littlehampton S & MBC: (0903) 715859

Chichester Harbour

Way Point
50° 45'.9N 0° 56'.4W (Chichester Bar Bn)
Charts
Admiralty No 3418
Adlard Coles Pilot Pack Vol 2 Nos 201 and 202
Tides
Standard Port - see p.18
Harbour Lights
See 0783.4 p.115
Cautions
1 Onshore winds, especially nearing LW with an ebb tide, can create a dangerous sea.
2 Speed limit: 8 knots.
3 Chichester bar is hard and a yacht touching may be wrecked.
4 Depths in the entrance to Chichester Harbour may alter by as much as 1m.
5 The ebb stream runs strongly.
6 There is a gunnery range at Eastney Point in use during the week. Firing takes place when a R flag is flown from the range building, Hayling Island SC, the Harbour Master's offices at Itchenor and Langstone and S Parade Pier, Southsea. Call (0705) 822351 ext 6420 for details.
Berthing
There are a number of marinas and safe anchorages. See charts.
VHF   Harbour Master: Ch 14 (call CHICHESTER)
           Northney Marina: Ch M; 80
           Sparkes Marina: Ch M; 80
           Chichester Yacht Basin: Ch M; 80
           Emsworth Yacht Harbour: Ch M; 80
Telephones
Harbour Master: (0243) 512301
HM Coastguard: (0705) 552100
MRSC: (0705) 552100
HM Customs: (0703) 229251 or Freephone Customs Yachts
Medical: (0243) 788122 (Hospital)
Northney Marina: (0705) 466321
Sparkes Marina: (0705) 466075
Chichester Yacht Basin: (0243) 512731
Emsworth Yacht Harbour: (0243) 375211
Birdham Pool: (0243) 512310
Itchenor SC: (0243) 512400
Hayling Island SC: (0705) 463768
Mengham Rythe SC: (0705) 463337
Birdham YC: (0243) 512642
Bosham SC: (0243) 572341
Chichester YC: (0243) 512918
Dell Quay SC: (0243) 785080
Emsworth SC: (0243) 373065
Emsworth Slipper SC: (0243) 372523

Langstone Harbour

Way Point
50° 46'.3N 1° 01'.3W (Langstone Fairway Buoy)
Charts
Admiralty No 3418
Adlard Coles Pilot Pack Vol 2 No 201
Tides
Generally as Chichester - p.18
Harbour Lights
See 0782/0782.67 p.115
Cautions
1 Speed limit: 10 knots.
2 There is a gunnery range at Eastney Point in use during the week. Firing takes place when a R flag is flown from the range building, Hayling Island SC, the Harbour Master's offices at Itchenor and Langstone and S Parade Pier, Southsea. Call (0705) 822351 ext 6420 for details.

Berthing

Langstone Marina offers deep water berths, otherwise anchor as practical though landing is not very convenient.

VHF Harbour Master: Ch 16 then 12 (call LANGSTONE HARBOUR)

Langstone Marina: Ch M; 80

Telephones

Harbour Master: (0705) 463419
HM Coastguard: (0705) 552100
MRSC: (0705) 552100
HM Customs: (0703) 229251 or Freephone Customs Yachts
Medical: (0243) 788122 (Hospital)
Langstone Marina: (0705) 822719
Langstone SC: (0705) 484577
Eastney CA: (0705) 734103
Solartron & Lock SC: (0705) 829833
Tudor SC: (0705) 862002

Bembridge Harbour

Way Point

50° 42'.5N 1° 05'.2W (Tide Gauge Fl Y 2s 1M. Steer SSW for buoyed channel)

Charts

Admiralty No 2022
Adlard Coles Pilot Pack Vol 2 No 207

Tides

See p.133 for corrections from Standard Port of Portsmouth

Harbour Lights

Apart from the Tide Gauge, above, the harbour is unlit

Cautions

Anchoring and fishing is prohibited within 1 cable of St Helen's Fort.

Berthing

There is room for only a few visiting yachts in the marina at the head of the harbour. Bilge keel yachts may find room to moor to two anchors inside the point but will dry out.

VHF Bembridge Marina: Ch M; 80

Telephones

Harbour Master: (0983) 872828
HM Coastguard: (0983) 872886
MRSC: (0705) 552100
HM Customs: (0703) 229251 or Freephone Customs Yachts
Medical: (0983) 872614 (Doctor)
Bembridge Marina: (0983) 874436
Bembridge SC: (0983) 872237
Brading Haven YC: (0983) 872289

Wootton Creek

Way Point

50° 44'.5N 1° 12'.0W (Wootton Bn QW)

Charts

Admiralty No 2022
Adlard Coles Pilot Pack Vol 2 No 208

Tides

See Ryde, p.133 for corrections from Standard Port of Portsmouth

Harbour Lights

See 0664 p.115

Cautions

The car ferries to Portsmouth move in and out at all hours.

Berthing

The boatman of the R Victoria YC will always try to find a mooring for visiting yachts but generally the harbour is full with local boats.

Telephones

HM Coastguard: (0983) 872886
HM Customs: (0703) 229251 or Freephone Customs Yachts
Medical: (0983) 882542(Doctor)
R Victoria YC: (0983) 882325

Cowes

Way Point

50° 46'.4N 1° 17'.5W (Prince Consort Buoy)

Charts

Admiralty No 2793

Adlard Coles Pilot Pack Vol 2 No 209

Tides

See p.133 for corrections from Standard Port of Portsmouth

Harbour Lights

See 0652/0662.1 p.114/115

Cautions

1 There is a speed limit of 6 knots within the harbour.
2 The chain ferry gives way to vessels but, in case of doubt, call 'CHAIN FERRY' on VHF Ch 69.
3 Avoid the Shrape mud and enter via the buoyed channel. Do not sail through the moorings or pick up a harbour mooring without permission.

Berthing

There are a few visitors' moorings off the Parade, plenty of visitors' piles, clearly marked, in the river, a short-stay visitors' pontoon just above Shepards Wharf, two marinas accessible at all states of tide and one, Medina Yacht Harbour, accessible -3HW +3 and more piles off the Folly Inn. Newport offers pontoons for bilge keel yachts; deep draft yachts will find a berth alongside the wall. If intending to visit Newport, try to arrive 2 hrs before HW.

VHF Cowes Harbour: Ch 16, then 69

Chain Ferry: Ch 69
Newport Harbour: Ch 16, then 69
Folly Harbour: Ch 16, then 69
West Cowes Marina: Ch M; 80
Cowes Marina (East Cowes): Ch M; 80
Shepards Wharf: Ch M; 80
Medina Yacht Harbour: Ch M; 80

Telephones

Harbour Master (Cowes): (0983) 293952
Harbour Master (Newport): (0983) 525994
MRSC: (0705) 552100
HM Customs: (0703) 229251 or Freephone Customs Yachts
Medical: (0983) 295251 (Cowes Health Centre)
Cowes Yacht Haven: (0983) 299975
Cowes Marina (East Cowes): (0983) 293983
Medina Yacht Harbour: (0983) 526733
Souter's Marina: (0983) 294711
R Yacht Squadron: (0903) 292743
R London YC: (0983) 299727
R Corinthian YC: (0983) 294278
Island SC: (0983) 296621
Cowes Corinthian YC: (0983) 296333
Cowes Combined Clubs (Cowes Week): (0983) 295744
JOG: (0983) 280279 (Secretary)
Gurnard SC: (0983) 297672 (Secretary)
Medina Mariners Assn: (0983) 294622 (Secretary)

Newtown River

Way Point

50° 43'.7N 1° 24'.9W (Unlit R spher entrance buoy)

Charts

Admiralty No 2022
Adlard Coles Pilot Pack Vol 2 No 210

Tides

Generally as Lymington - p.32

Cautions

Avoid oyster beds.

Berthing

Anchor anywhere clear of oyster beds or moorings or pick up a visitors' mooring.

Telephones

Harbourmaster: (0983) 378424
MRSC: (0705) 552100
HM Customs: (0703) 229251 or Freephone Customs Yachts
Medical: (0983) 760434 (Doctor)

Yarmouth

Way Point

50° 42'.7N 1° 29'.9W (3 cables N of entrance, on leading line)

Charts

Admiralty No 2021
Adlard Coles Pilot Pack Vol 2 No 211

	TIME DIFFERENCES				HEIGHT DIFFERENCES (IN METRES)			
PLACE	High Water		Low Water		MHWS	MHWN	MLWN	MLWS
PORTSMOUTH (see page 24)	**0000** and **1200**	**0600** and **1800**	**0500** and **1700**	**1100** and **2300**	**4.7**	**3.8**	**1.9**	**0.8**
Bembridge Harbour	−0010	+0005	+0020	0000	−1.6	−1.5	−1.4	−0.6
Ryde	−0010	+0010	−0005	−0010	−0.2	−0.1	0.0	+0.1
Cowes	−0015	+0015	0000	−0020	−0.5	−0.3	−0.1	0.0
Bucklers Hard	−0040	−0010	+0010	−0010	−1.0	−0.8	-0.2	−0.3
Christchurch (Entrance)	−0230	+0030	−0035	−0035	−2.9	−2.4	−1.2	−0.2

Tides
Generally as Lymington - p.32
Harbour Lights
See 0558/0562.1 p.114
Cautions
1 There are frequent ferry movements between Yarmouth and Lymington.
2 There are four large mooring buoys to the E of the entrance; only the end ones are lit.
3 Black Rock dries.
4 Speed limit: 4 knots.
Berthing
Yarmouth provides excellent shelter with pile moorings. It is very popular on summer weekends, so much so that the harbour may be closed to visitors, in which case a red flag will be flown. In this event, anchor off to the NW of the entrance or, by arrangement with the R Solent YC, use one of their moorings to the E. The Yar bridge opens in summer at 0800, 0900, 1000, 1200, 1400, 1600, 1730, 1830, 2000.
VHF (Port operations) Ch 68
(Yacht berths) Ch M
Telephones
Harbour Master: (0983) 760321 or (Berthing) 760300
MRSC: (0705) 552100
HM Customs: (0703) 229251 or Freephone Customs Yachts
Medical: (0983) 760434 (Doctor)
R Solent YC: (0983) 760239
Yarmouth SC: (0983) 755778 (Secretary)

Portsmouth Harbour

Way Point
50° 47'.0N 1° 06'.3W (No 4 Harbour buoy QR)
Charts
Admiralty No 2625 and 2631
Adlard Coles Pilot Pack Vol 2 No 212
Tides
Standard Port - see p.24
Harbour Lights
See 0688/0734 p.115
Cautions
1 There is much naval and ferry traffic, the latter including high speed catamarans and hovercraft. Keep a sharp look out.
2 The deep water channel is reserved for large vessels above No 4 buoy and yachts should use the small boat passage to the SW of the channel or keep well over to the starboard hand on entering. Yachts with engines must use them between No 4 buoy and Ballast Buoy.
3 Listen on VHF Ch 11 for shipping movements.
Berthing
There is a large marina (C and N) to the W of the entrance, Port Solent in the NE corner and a smaller one at Fareham (access -3HW+3) and occasional space on a visitors' mooring or a temporarily vacant mooring.
VHF Queen's Harbour Master: Ch 11
Portsmouth Harbour Radio: Ch 11
Camper & Nicholsons Marina: Ch M; 80
Fareham Yacht Harbour: Ch M; 80
Port Solent: Ch M; 80
Telephones
Queen's Harbour Master: (0705) 822351 Ext 23694

Portsmouth Commercial Port: (0705) 297395
MRSC: (0705) 552100
HM Customs: (0703) 229251 or Freephone Customs Yachts
Medical: Portsmouth side: (0705) 379451; Gosport side: (0705) 584255 (Hospitals)
Camper & Nicholsons: (0705) 524811
Fareham Yacht Harbour: (0329) 232854
Port Solent: (0705) 210765
RNC and R Albert YC: (0705) 825924
Fareham S & MB Club: (0329) 232160 (Hon Secretary)
Hardway SC: (0705) 581875
Portchester SC: (0705) 379525 (Secretary)
Portsmouth SC: (0705) 820596

River Hamble

Way Point
50° 50'.1N 1° 18'.6W (Hamble Point buoy Q(6) + LFl 15s at entrance)
Charts
Admiralty No 2022
Adlard Coles Pilot Pack Vol 2 Nos 213
Tides
See p.134 for corrections from Standard Port of Southampton
Harbour Lights
See 0590/0590.42 p.114
Cautions
1 Anchoring is prohibited.
2 The river is very busy, especially at weekends.
3 Use great care at night as there are many unlit obstructions.
Berthing
The River Hamble has a number of large marinas.
VHF Hamble Harbour Master: Ch 68, or afloat Ch 16, 68
Hamble Point Marina: Ch M; 80
Mercury Yacht Harbour: Ch M; 80
Moody's Marina: Ch M; 80
Port Hamble: Ch M; 80
Telephones
Harbour Master: (0489) 576387
MRSC: (0705) 552100
HM Customs: (0703) 229251 or Freephone Customs Yachts
Medical: (0489) 573110 (Doctor)
Hamble Point Marina: (0703) 452464
Mercury Yacht Harbour: (0703) 455994
Swanwick Marina: (0489) 885262
Port Hamble Marina: (0703) 452741
R Southern YC: (0703) 453271 (Sec) or 452231 (Sailing Sec)
Royal Air Force YC: (0703) 452208
Hamble River SC: (0703) 452070
Warsash SC: (0489) 583575

Southampton Water

Charts
Admiralty Nos 1905 and 2041
Adlard Coles Pilot Pack Vol 2 No 214
Tides
Standard Port - see p.28
Harbour Lights
See 0576/0586 and 0605/0633.2 p.114

	TIME DIFFERENCES				HEIGHT DIFFERENCES (IN METRES)			
PLACE	High Water		Low Water		MHWS	MHWN	MLWN	MLWS
SOUTHAMPTON (see page 28)	**0400** and **1600**	**1100** and **2300**	**0000** and **1200**	**0600** and **1800**	**4.5**	**3.7**	**1.8**	**0.5**
River Hamble	+0020	+0010	+0010	0000	0.0	+0.1	+0.1	+0.3

Beacon
Fawley, Hythe (Aero) 50° 51'.95N 1° 23'.44W FAW 20M 370 kHz
Caution
An 'Area of Concern' exists in the Channel between Prince Consort and Gurnard buoys and Black Jack and Reach buoys. Vessels over 150m long are given a 'Moving Prohibited Zone' of 1000m ahead and 100m on either side into which small vessels under 20m long are prohibited from entering. Listen on VHF Ch 12.
Berthing
See Marinas below.
VHF Southampton (Call SOUTHAMPTON VTS): Ch 12, 14, 16
Marinas listed below: Ch M; 80
Telephones
Harbour Master (Operations Room): (0703) 330022 x 2440 (Office hrs) 339733 (other times)
MRSC: (0705) 552100
HM Customs: (0703) 229251 or Freephone Customs Yachts
Medical: (0703) 777222(Hospital)
R Southampton YC: (0703) 223352
Marinas
Shamrock Quay (R Itchen): (0703) 229461
Ocean Village: (0703) 229385
Town Quay Marina: (0703) 234397
Kemps Quay: (0703) 632323
Itchen Marine Ltd: (0703) 631500
Hythe Marina Village: (0703) 207073

Beaulieu River

Way Point
50° 46'.6N 1° 21'.4W (AFN London Y spherical racing mark (Apr - Oct) 3 cables SSE of entrance)
Charts
Admiralty No 2021
Adlard Coles Pilot Pack Vol 2 No 215
Tides
See p.133 for corrections from Standard Port of Portsmouth
Harbour Lights
See 0554 p.114
Cautions
1 Do not anchor below beacon No 14 or in the vicinity of the river entrance owing to the presence of telephone and electricity cables on the sea bed.
2 The old half tide passage at Needs Ore Pt has been closed with a causeway.
3. Gull Island is a nature reserve.
4 There is a 5 knot speed limit.
Berthing
There is plenty of room between Inchmery House and Needs Ore Point for anchoring and also a marina at the head.
Telephones
Harbour Master: (0590) 616200
MRSC: (0705) 552100
HM Customs: (0703) 229251 or Freephone Customs Yachts
Medical: (0703) 845955(Doctor)
Bucklers Hard Marina: (0590) 616200
R Southampton YC: (0590) 63213

Lymington

Way Point
50° 44'.25N 1° 30'.5W (Jack in the Basket beacon FlR 2s at entrance)
Charts
Admiralty No 2021
Adlard Coles Pilot Pack Vol 2 No 216

Tides
Standard Port - see p.32
Harbour Lights
See 0542/0551 p.113/114
Cautions
1 The river is used by car ferries which need nearly the whole width to manoeuvre and which have right of way at all times.
2 There is no fixed speed limit but care must be taken to avoid damage by excessive wash.
3 Do not approach too closely to the marker posts - some of them dry out.
Berthing
There are two marinas and a berth may be found at the Town Quay. Anchoring is not possible as the river is full of moorings and the fairway busy with the Isle of Wight ferries.
VHF Lymington Yacht Haven: Ch M; 80
Lymington Marina: Ch M; 80
Telephones
Harbour Master: (0590) 672014
MRSC: (0705) 552100
HM Customs: (0703) 229251 or Freephone Customs Yachts
Medical: (0590) 677011 or 672953 (Doctor)
Lymington Marina (Berthons): (0590) 673312
Lymington Yacht Haven: (0590) 677071
R Lymington YC: (0590) 672677
Lymington Town SC: (0590) 674514

Christchurch

Way Point
50° 43'.4N 1° 43'.5W (4.5 cables WSW of entrance)
Charts
Admiralty No 2172
Adlard Coles Pilot Pack Vol 2 No 218
Tides
See p.133 for corrections from Standard Port of Portsmouth and p.36 for curves
Cautions
1 Entrance is best between -2HW and HW. Do not attempt to enter after HW + 1/2 as the ebb runs very strongly. The bar shifts and varies in depth but the buoys (which may be shifted by bad weather and lifted out of season) are moved to suit.
2 Speed limit 5 knots.
Berthing
There are a few visitors' moorings and anchoring in the fairways is not allowed so yachts must be prepared to take the ground.
Telephones
Harbour Master: (0425) 274933
HM Coastguard: (0202) 425204
MRSC: (0705) 552100
HM Customs: (0703) 229251 or Freephone Customs Yachts
Medical: (0202) 486361
Christchurch SC: (0202) 483150

Poole Harbour

Way Point
50° 39'.31N 1° 55'.10W (No 1 Bar buoy)
Charts
Admiralty No 2175 and 2611
Adlard Coles Pilot Pack Vol 2 Nos 219 and 220
Tides
Standard Port - see p.36
Harbour Lights
See 0507/0515 p.113

Cautions

1 The chain ferry works day and night at Sandbanks.

2 Use the Small Craft Channel S of the Middle Ship Channel or, preferably one of the other channels which are clear of merchant ships.

Berthing

Room to anchor in the quieter spots clear of moorings. Alongside berths may be found at the Town Quay or in Poole Harbour YC Marina, or through the bridge (opens 0930, 1130, 1430, 1630, 1830, 2130 (weekdays) and 0730, 0930, 1130, 1330, 1530, 1730, 1930, 2130, 2330 (weekends) at Cobb's Quay.

VHF Poole Harbour Control: Ch 16; 14
Salterns Marina Ch M; 80
Cobb's Quay Marina: Ch M; 80

Telephones

Harbour Master: (0202) 685261
MRSC: (0305) 760439
HM Customs: (0703) 229251 or Freephone Customs Yachts
Medical: (0202) 675100 (Hospital)
Salterns Marina: (0202) 709971
Cobb's Quay: (0202) 674299
Poole YC: (0202) 672687
Poole Harbour YC: (0202) 707321
Parkstone YC: (0202) 743610
R Motor YC: (0202) 707227
Cobbs's Quay YC: (0202) 673690

Weymouth

Way Point

50° 36'.7N 2° 26'.1W (2 cables off entrance on leading lights)

Charts

Admiralty No 2255 and 2172
Adlard Coles Pilot Pack Vol 2 Nos 223 and 224

Tides

Generally as Portland - see p.40

Harbour Lights

See 0346/0356.2 p.113

Cautions

1 Commercial vessels, which berth on the N side, may warp off using wires across the harbour.

Berthing

Weymouth offers good shelter and all facilities but is often crowded in the season. Yachts usually moor on the S side of the harbour in the Cove, though there is deeper water on the other side. Access to the marina is through the bridge which indicates the headroom by a gauge or which opens at 2 hrs notice to the Harbour Master; may not be accessible to visitors.

VHF Harbour: Ch 16, 12 (when vessel expected)

Telephones

Harbour Master: (0305) 206421
MRSC: (0305) 760439
HM Customs: (0305) 774747 or Freephone Customs Yachts
Medical: (0305) 772211 (Hospital)
R Dorset YC: (0305) 786258
Weymouth SC: (0305) 785481
Castle Cove SC: (0305) 783708

Portland Harbour

Way Point

50° 35'.7N 2° 25'.0W (5 cables E of North Ship Channel)

Charts

Admiralty Nos 2255 and 2268
Adlard Coles Pilot Pack Vol 2 No 223

Tides

Standard Port - see p.40

Harbour Lights

See 0302/0340 p.113

Beacon

Portland Bill 50°30'.82N 2°27'.30W PB 50M 313kHz

Cautions

1 Note the prohibited anchorages.

2 Torpedoes are fired seawards from the NE breakwater when a R flag is flown from the firing point.

3 There is much naval traffic and the entrances must be approached with care.

4. There is a speed limit of 12 knots.

5 Yachts should keep watch on VHF Ch 13 when within 3M of 'A' Head and advise QHM Portland when approaching or leaving Portland or Weymouth harbours.

Berthing

Portland is a naval base and only suitable for those who find Weymouth too crowded for comfort. The usual place to anchor is off Castle Cove, clear of the moorings, but in a S wind, off Castletown to the W of the prohibited anchorage sector is better.

VHF Portland Naval Base: Ch 13, 14

Telephones

Queen's Harbour Master: (0305) 820311
MRSC: (0305) 760439
HM Customs: (0305) 71189 or Freephone Customs Yachts
Medical: (0305) 820311 or Coastguard CH 69
Castle Cove SC: (0305) 783708

Bridport (West Bay)

Way Point

50° 42'.4N 2° 46'.0W (280m SSW of entrance)

Charts

Admiralty No 3315
Adlard Coles Pilot Pack Vol 3 No 301

Tides

See p.136 for corrections from Standard Port of Plymouth

Harbour Lights

See 0288/0290.2 p.113

Cautions

1 The entrance is impossible in strong onshore winds and must not be attempted.

2 Do not attempt to enter at night.

Berthing

Berth as directed by the Harbour Master, either against the quay, to starboard, or round the corner. It is possible to anchor off, but keep clear of the leading line and the sewer pipe.

VHF Ch 16; 11

Telephones

Harbour Master: (0308) 23222
MRSC: (0305) 760439
HM Customs: (0305) 71189 or Freephone Customs Yachts
Medical: (0308) 23771 (Doctor)

Lyme Regis

Way Point

50° 42'.9N 2° 55'.2W (6 cables SE of entrance on leading line)

Charts

Admiralty No 3315
Adlard Coles Pilot Pack Vol 3 No 302

Tides

See p.136 for corrections from Standard Port of Plymouth

Harbour Lights

See 0284/0284.1 p.113

Cautions

1 Do not attempt to enter in strong onshore winds.

2 There are many fishing floats in the area.

Berthing

It is advisable to arrange a berth with the Harbour Master before entering as space is very limited. There are 12 berths for visiting craft on Victoria Pier. If it is decided to anchor off, take advice, if possible, as holding varies.

VHF Ch 16; 14

Telephones

Harbour Master: (0297) 442137
MRSC: (0305) 760439
Medical: (0297) 445777 (Doctor)
Lyme Regis SC: (0297) 443573
Lyme Regis Power Boat Club: (0297) 443788

PLACE	TIME DIFFERENCES				HEIGHT DIFFERENCES (IN METRES)			
	High Water		Low Water		MHWS	MHWN	MLWN	MLWS
PLYMOUTH (see page 48)	**0100** and **1300**	**0600** and **1800**	**0100** and **1300**	**0600** and **1800**	**5.5**	**4.4**	**2.2**	**0.8**
Bridport (West Bay)	+0025	+0040	0000	0000	−1.4	−1.4	−0.6	−0.2
Lyme Regis	+0040	+0100	+0005	−0005	−1.2	−1.3	−0.5	−0.2
Exmouth (Approaches)	+0030	+0050	+0015	+0005	−0.9	−1.0	−0.5	−0.3
Teignmouth (Approaches)	+0025	+0040	0000	0000	−0.7	−0.8	−0.3	−0.2
Torquay	+0025	+0045	+0010	0000	−0.6	−0.7	−0.2	−0.1
Dartmouth	+0015	+0025	0000	−0005	−0.6	−0.6	−0.2	−0.2
Salcombe	0000	+0010	+0005	−0005	−0.2	−0.3	−0.1	−0.1

Exmouth

Way Point
50° 36'.0N 3° 22'.3W (E.Exe E.Cardinal buoy)
Charts
Admiralty No 2290
Adlard Coles Pilot Pack Vol 3 Nos 303 and 304
Tides
See above for corrections from Standard Port of Plymouth
Harbour Lights
See 0270/0277 p.112/113
Beacon
Aero RC Exeter 50° 45'.12N 3° 17'.62W EX 337 kHz 15M
Cautions
The entrance is perfectly safe, given water and fine weather, but should not be used in strong onshore winds.
Berthing
There is a small tidal dock approached via a swing bridge with the possibility of finding a mooring or space to anchor in the river. There is a canal up to Exeter.
VHF Ch 16; 6; 12
Telephones
Dock Master (Exmouth): (0395) 272009
Harbour Master (Exeter): (0392) 74306
MRSC: (0803) 882704
HM Customs: (0752) 220661 or Freephone Customs Yachts
Medical: (0395) 273001 (Doctor)
Exe SC: (0395) 264607
Starcross YC: (0626) 890470

Teignmouth

Way Point
50° 32'.2N 3° 28'.7W (5 cables E of entrance)
Charts
Admiralty No 26
Adlard Coles Pilot Pack Vol 3 No 305
Tides
See above for corrections from Standard Port of Plymouth
Harbour Lights
See 0262/0263 p.112
Cautions
1 Unfortunately, there is little room for visiting craft and the approach is also discouraging.
2 The bar shifts constantly and, though marked with buoys, requires local knowledge unless there is plenty of water and fine weather.
Berthing
Do not anchor within the harbour but apply to the Harbour Master for a mooring.
VHF Ch 12; 16
Telephones
Harbour Master: (0626) 774044 or outside office hours 772892
MRSC: (0803) 882704
HM Customs: (0752) 220661 or Freephone Customs Yachts
Medical: (0626) 774355 (Doctor) or 772161 (Hospital)
Teign Corinthian YC: (0626) 772734

Torquay

Way Point
50° 27'.0N 3° 31'.7W (4 cables S of entrance)
Charts
Admiralty No 26
Adlard Coles Pilot Pack Vol 3 No 306
Tides
See above for corrections from Standard Port of Plymouth
Harbour Lights
See 0252/0256 p.112
Cautions
1 A controlled area up to about 2 cables off the beach and marked with Y spherical buoys is for swimming and there is a speed limit of 5 knots within it.
2 The entrance may be busy with tripper boats.
Berthing
There is a large marina with visitors' pontoons on the eastward side.
VHF Torquay Harbour: Ch 14; 16 (Office hours)
Torquay Marina: Ch M
Telephones
Harbour Master: (0803) 292429
MRSC: (0803) 882704
HM Customs: (0752) 220661 or Freephone Customs Yachts
Medical: (0803) 298441 (Doctor)
Torquay Marina: (0803) 214624
R Torbay YC: (0803) 292006

Brixham

Way Point
50° 24'.4N 3° 30'.8W (1 cable NNW of entrance)
Charts
Admiralty No 26
Adlard Coles Pilot Pack Vol 3 No 307
Tides
Generally as Torquay. See above for corrections from Standard Port of Plymouth
Harbour Lights
See 0246/0249.2 p.112
Beacon
Aero RC Berry Head 50° 23'.88N 3° 29'.55W BHD 318 kHz 25M
Cautions
1 Strong NW winds make the outer harbour dangerous.
Berthing
There is a large marina at the SE end of the harbour.
VHF Ch 14; 16
Prince William Marina: M; 80
Telephones
Harbour Master: (0803) 853321
MRSC: (0803) 220661
HM Customs: (0752) 220661 or Freephone Customs Yachts
Medical: (0803) 882731 (Doctor)
MDL Brixham Marina: (0803) 882711 or 882929
Brixham YC: (0803) 853332

	TIME DIFFERENCES				HEIGHT DIFFERENCES (IN METRES)			
PLACE	High Water		Low Water		MHWS	MHWN	MLWN	MLWS
PLYMOUTH (see page 48)	**0000** and **1200**	**0600** and **1800**	**0000** and **1200**	**0600** and **1800**	**5.5**	**4.4**	**2.2**	**0.8**
River Yealm (Entrance)	+0006	+0006	+0002	+0002	−0.1	−0.1	−0.1	−0.1
Looe	−0010	−0010	−0005	−0005	−0.1	−0.2	−0.2	−0.2
Fowey	−0010	−0015	−0010	−0005	−0.1	−0.1	−0.2	−0.2
Mevagissey	−0010	−0015	−0005	+0005	−0.1	−0.1	−0.2	−0.1
Helford River (Entrance)	−0030	−0035	−0015	−0010	−0.2	−0.2	−0.3	−0.2
Penzance (Newlyn)	−0040	−0105	−0045	−0020	+0.1	0.0	−0.2	0.0

Dartmouth

Way Point
50° 20'.0N 3° 33'.3W
Charts
Admiralty No 2253
Adlard Coles Pilot Pack Vol 3 No 308
Tides
See above for corrections from Standard Port of Plymouth
Harbour Lights
See 0236/0238 p.112
Cautions
1 The area between the Mewstone and the land is littered with fishing lines.
2 Both sides of the entrance have dangerous rocks. Do not cut the corners.
3 The lower ferry has right of way.
Berthing
It is possible to anchor off, but there is often a nasty swell. The marinas from seaward are: Darthaven (starboard), Dart (port) and Kingswear (starboard). The HM may be able to offer a mooring or it may be possible to come alongside the pontoons temporarily at the R Dart YC (starboard) or the Dartmouth YC (port). Anchoring within the river, even off the fairway, is not recommended owing to the presence of mooring chains on the bottom.
VHF Dartmouth Harbour: Ch 11
Dartmouth Marina: Ch M; 80
Dart Marina: Ch M; 80
Kingswear Marina (Call DART MARINA FOUR): Ch M; 80
Telephones
Harbour Master: (0803) 832337 and 833767
MRSC: (0803) 882704
Medical: (0803) 832212 (Doctor)
Darthaven Marina: (080425) 545
Dart Marina: (0803) 833351
Kingswear Marina: (0803) 833351
R Dart YC: (080425) 272
The Dartmouth YC: (0803) 832305

Salcombe

Way Point
50° 12'.1N 3° 46'.4W
Charts
Admiralty No 28
Adlard Coles Pilot Pack Vol 3 No 310
Tides
Standard Port - see p.44
Harbour Lights
See 0220/0224 p.112
Cautions
1 Dangerous breaking seas may occur on the bar (about 1.2m charted depth) on onshore winds or swell, especially on the ebb or below half tide. Boats have been lost even in quite an innocent looking swell.
2 Anchoring is prohibited due to cables in the area 3 cables above Biddlehead Point
3 Speed limit - 8 knots.

Berthing
There are plenty of visitors' moorings, a visitors' pontoon and a fuel barge.
VHF Ch 16: 14
Island Cruising Club: Ch M (base or Egremont)
Fuel barge: Ch 6
Telephones
Harbour Master: (0548) 843791
MRSC: (0803) 882704
HM Customs: (054 884) 2835 (Local Office), or to clear call (0752) 220661 or Freephone Customs Yachts
Medical: (0548) 842284 (Health Centre, 24 hrs)
Fuel Barge: (0836) 775644
Salcombe YC: (0548) 842872
Island Cruising Club: (0548) 843481

Yealm River

Way Point
50° 18'.0N 4° 05'.6W (on 023° safe approach to St Weburgh's Ch 6 cables before altering course 088° on leading line)
Charts
Admiralty No 30
Adlard Coles Pilot Pack Vol 3 No 311
Tides
See above for corrections from Standard Port of Plymouth
Harbour Lights
The river is not lit
Cautions
1 The whole area is to be avoided in strong SW winds, which create a breaking sea over the shoal patches in Wembury Bay and over the bar.
2 The bar extends nearly the whole way across the entrance to the Yealm from the N.
3 There is a firing range at Wembury Point. Firing is indicated by R flags and information can be obtained from HMS Cambridge on VHF Chs 16; 10; 11 or by telephone Range Officer (0752) 862779 (office hours), QM (0752) 553740 Ext 77406 (other times).
Berthing
There is an anchorage in Cellar Bay, just over the bar and visitors' moorings.
Telephones
Harbour Master: (0752) 872533
MRCC: (0803) 882704
HM Customs: (0752) 220661 or Freephone Customs Yachts
Medical: (0752) 880392 (Doctor)
Yealm YC: (0752) 872291

Plymouth

Way Point
50° 20'.2N 4° 10'.0W (Queens Ground Buoy at W entrance to Plymouth Sound)
Charts
Admiralty Nos 1967, 1901, 1902, 30 and 871
Adlard Coles Pilot Pack Vol 3 Nos 312, 313, 314, 315 and 316
Tides
Standard Port - see p.48

Harbour Lights
See 0111.2/0193 p.111/112
Cautions
1 Large vessels use the port and should be given a wide berth.
2 There are bathing and diving areas N and S of Fort Bovisand.
3 There is a firing range at Wembury Point -see Yealm River.
Berthing
There are four marinas, listed below. In addition anchorages may be found in the Rivers Lynher and Tamar.
VHF Long Room Port Control: Ch 16; 8; 12; 14
Mill Bay Docks: Ch 16; 12; 14
Sutton Marina Radio: Ch 16; M; 80
Queen Anne's Battery Marina: Ch M; 80
Sutton Harbour Marina: Ch M; 80
Mayflower Marina: Ch M; 80
Telephones
Queen's Harbour Master: (0752) 663225
Harbour Master, Cattewater: (0752) 665934
Harbour Master, Mill Bay Docks: (0752) 662191
MRSC: (0803) 882704
Medical: (0752) 53533 (Doctor) or 668080 (Hospital)
Sutton Harbour and Marina: (0752) 664186
Queen Anne's Battery: (0752) 671142
Mayflower Marina: (0752) 556633
R Western YC of England: (0752) 660077
R Plymouth Corinthian YC: (0752) 664327
Mayflower SC: (0752) 662526
Cawsand SC: (0752) 822429
Saltash SC: (0752) 2826
Torpoint Mosquito SC: (0752) 812508
Weir Quay SC: (0822) 840474

Looe

Way Point
50° 20'.8N 4° 25'.8W (8 cables ESE of entrance)
Charts
Admiralty No 147
Adlard Coles Pilot Pack Vol 3 No 317
Tides
See p.137 for corrections from Standard Port of Plymouth
Harbour Lights
See 0094 p.111
Cautions
1 Do not attempt to enter in strong SE winds which produce a breaking sea.
2 The safest approach is to keep St Mary's Church (East Looe) bearing about 290° or, at night, keep within the W sector of the light.
Berthing
Yachts should anchor off or go alongside the W wall above the cables and pipelines near St Nicholas Church (West Looe) where there is between 2.6m and 3.1m at MHWS.
Telephones
Harbour Master: (050 36) 2839
MRCC: (0803) 882704
HM Customs: (0752) 220661 or Freephone Customs Yachts
Medical: (050 36) 3195 (Doctor)
Looe SC: (050 36) 2559

Fowey

Way Point
50° 19'.1N 4° 39'.0W (5 cables SSW of entrance)
Charts
Admiralty No 31
Adlard Coles Pilot Pack Vol 3 No 319
Tides
See p.137 for corrections from Standard Port of Plymouth
Harbour Lights
See 0082/0090 p.111
Cautions
1 There is a speed limit of 6 knots.
2 There is considerable commercial traffic.
3 Care must be taken if anchoring. Keep clear of the fairway and buoy the anchor.
4 Strong onshore winds may cause a heavy swell which may be

avoided by moving further up the harbour.
Berthing
There are visitors' moorings and pontoons on the E side about half a mile inside the entrance.
VHF Fowey Harbour: Ch 16; 11; 12
Polruan Ferry (water taxi): Ch 6
Telephones
Harbour Master: (0726) 832471/2
MRCC: (0803) 882704
HM Customs: (0752) 220661 or Freephone Customs Yachts
Medical: (0726) 832451 (Doctor)

Mevagissey

Way Point
50° 16'.1N 4° 46'.4W (5 cables E of entrance)
Charts
Admiralty No 147
Adlard Coles Pilot Pack Vol 3 No 321
Tides
See p.137 for corrections from Standard Port of Plymouth
Harbour Lights
See 0078 p.111
Cautions
1 Do not approach in strong winds.
2 Be prepared to move to Fowey or Falmouth if the wind strengthens or shifts E.
3. Speed limit - 3 knots.
Berthing
Mevagissey is a fishing port and popular tourist resort with little space for visiting craft. However it may be possible to lie to two anchors in about 1.5m on the N side of the outer harbour or berth alongside the S pier. The inner harbour dries and is reserved for fishing boats. Good shelter in offshore winds but unsuitable in anything E as a big swell builds up.
VHF Harbour Master: Ch 16; 14
Telephones
Harbour Master: (0726) 843305
MRSC: (0803) 882704
HM Customs: (0752) 220661 or Freephone Customs Yachts
Medical: (0726) 843701 (Doctor)

Falmouth and St Mawes

Way Point
50° 07'.6N 5° 01'.5W (9 cables S of entrance)
Charts
Admiralty No 32
Adlard Coles Pilot Pack Vol 3 No 322 and 323
Tides
Standard Port - see p.52
Harbour Lights
See 0064/0071.4 p.111
Cautions
1 See note below about oyster beds.
2 Large vessels use the port of Falmouth and caution is necessary at the entrance.
3 Black Rock lies in the middle of the entrance but is guarded by an E cardinal lit buoy.
4 Lugo Rock lies on the N side of the entrance to St Mawes but is guarded by a S cardinal unlit buoy.
5 The bottom of the harbour off Falmouth is foul; buoy the anchor
Berthing
Falmouth offers all facilities for yachts, three marinas and a number of visitors' moorings. St Mawes offers all facilities except fuel. There are no visitors' moorings but boats may anchor anywhere clear of moorings and the oyster beds which are laid on both sides of the Percuil River above Polvarth Pt.
VHF Falmouth Hr Radio: Ch 16; 12; 13; 14
Customs Launch: Ch 16; 6; 9;10; 12; 14
Falmouth Yacht Marina: Ch M; 80
R Cornwall YC: Ch M
Telephones
Harbour Master (Falmouth): (0326) 312285 and (0326) 314379
Harbour Master (St Mawes): (0326) 750553
MRCC: (0326) 317575
HM Customs: (0752) 220661 or Freephone Customs Yachts

Medical: (0326) 312033 (Doctor)
Falmouth Yacht Marina: (0326) 316620
Visitors' Yacht Haven: (0326) 312285
Port Pendennis Marina: (0326) 211819
R Cornwall YC: (0326) 311105
Flushing SC: (0326) 374043
St Mawes SC: (0326) 270686

Mylor and Truro River

Way
Admiralty No 32
Adlard Coles Pilot Pack Vol 3 No 324 and 325
Tides
Generally as Falmouth - see p.52
Cautions
1 There are concrete mooring blocks which dry 3 cables S and half a cable N of the King Harry ferry crossing.
2 There may be other obstructions in entrance to Ruan Creek.
Berthing
There is a marina at Mylor.
VHF Mylor Yacht Harbour: Ch M; 80
Telephones
Harbour Master (Truro): (0872) 72130
Medical: (0326) 312033 (Doctor)
Mylor Yacht Harbour: (0326) 372121
Mylor YC: (0326) 374391

Helford River

Way Point
50° 05'.7N 5° 04'.1W (5 cables E of entrance)
Charts
Admiralty No 147
Adlard Coles Pilot Pack Vol 3 No 326
Tides
See p.137 for corrections from Standard Port of Plymouth
Cautions
1 Keep clear of oyster beds.
2 Though there is generally plenty of water, bars exist at the entrance to Navas Creek and the mud bank off Helford is very steep.
3 Speed limit: 6 knots.
4 The only danger on approach is the Gedges Rock on the N side of the entrance.
Berthing
Anchor as convenient, keeping clear of oyster beds in Navas Creek and W of its entrance. There are also visitors' buoys off Helford and visitors' pontoons in Navas Creek.
VHF Helford River SC: Ch M; 80
Gweek Quay (yard and supplies): Ch M; 80
Telephones
Harbour Master: (0326) 280422
MRCC: (0326) 317575
Medical: (0326) 572151 (Hospital)
Helford River SC: (0326) 23460

Penzance

Way Point
50° 06'.8N 5° 31'.0W (5 cables ESE of entrance)
Charts
Admiralty No 2345
Adlard Coles Pilot Pack Vol 3 No 327
Tides
See p.137 for corrections from Standard Port of Plymouth
Harbour Lights
See 0046/0051 p.111
Beacon
Aero RC (Penzance Heliport) 50° 07'.67N 5° 31'.00W PH 333 kHz 15M
Cautions
1 Mount's Bay is open to SE winds and Penzance should not be approached in strong winds from this quarter.
2 The entrance shoals on the N side.
3 In S gales, seas break over the S arm.

4 There is a speed limit of 5 knots within the harbour.
5 There is a ledge about 1m wide all round the inside of the wet dock wit 1.4m at MLWS.
Berthing
Anchor off to the NNE of the entrance or make fast alongside either the Albert or Lighthouse Piers if space is available until the dock gates open (-2HW+1). Traffic signals on FS on N arm of dock: 2 balls (hor) or 2 R Lts (Vert) - dock open; 2 balls (vert) or R Lt over G Lt - dock closed. Wait until signalled to proceed by the dockmaster who will allocate a berth.
VHF Penzance Harbour: Ch 16; 9; 12 (-2HW+1 and office hrs)
Telephones
Harbour Master: (0736) 66113 or (0736) 61119 outside office hours
Berthing Master: (0736) 65974 outside office hours
MRCC: (0326) 317575
HM Customs: (0752) 220661 or Freephone Customs Yachts
Medical: (0736) 63866 (Doctor)
Penzance SC: (0736) 64989

Newlyn

Way Point
50° 06'.4N 5° 31'.2W (9 cables ENE of entrance)
Charts
Admiralty No 2345
Adlard Coles Pilot Pack Vol 3 No 328
Tides
See p.137 for corrections from Standard Port of Plymouth
Harbour Lights
See 0038/0042 p.111
Cautions
1 The approach is clear of dangers except for the Gear Rock to the NE.
2 There is a speed limit of 3 knots.
Berthing
Newlyn provides good shelter but should only be used for an overnight stay except by arrangement with the Harbourmaster. Unless told otherwise, berth outside a fishing boat but be prepared to move at short notice.
VHF Newlyn Harbour: Ch 16; 12 (office hrs)
Telephones
Harbour Master: (0736) 62523 or outside office hours (0736) 61017
MRCC: (0326) 317575
HM Customs: (0752) 220661 or Freephone Customs Yachts
Medical: (0736) 63866 (Doctor)

St Mary's (Isles of Scilly)

Way Point
49° 53'.7N 6° 18'.1W (4 cables S of Penninis Head)
Charts
Admiralty No 883
Adlard Coles Pilot Pack Vol 3 No 330
Tides
Standard Port - see p.56
Harbour Lights
See 0006/0008 p.110
Beacons
Aero RC St Mary's 49° 54'.82N 6° 17'.43W STM 321 kHz 15M
 Round Island 49° 58'.70N 6° 19'.33W RR 298.5 kHz 150M
Cautions
1 Great care is needed to approach and to sail within the Isles. Apart from the principal lights there are few others and pilotage is achieved by leading lines which require daylight.
2 There are many rock pinnacles.
3 The tides run strongly with confusing eddies and some overfalls.
Berthing
Consult the charts for suitable anchorages.
VHF St Mary's Harbour: Ch 16; 14 (office hours)
Telephones
St Mary's Harbour Master: (0720) 22768
MRCC: (0326) 317575
HM Customs: (0720) 22571
Medical: (0720) 22628 (Doctor)
Isles of Scilly YC: (0720) 22352

	TIME DIFFERENCES				HEIGHT DIFFERENCES (IN METRES)			
PLACE	High Water		Low Water		MHWS	MHWN	MLWN	MLWS
ST HELIER (see page 60)	**0300** and **1500**	**0900** and **2100**	**0200** and **1400**	**0900** and **2100**	**11.1**	**8.1**	**4.1**	**1.3**
Alderney	+0050	+0040	+0025	+0105	−4.8	−3.4	−1.5	−0.5
St Peter Port	0000	+0012	−0008	+0002	−1.8	−1.1	−0.5	+0.2

CHANNEL ISLAND PORTS

Customs restrictions still exist between the UK and Channel Islands. Consult HM Customs and Excise Notices 1 and 8B.

Alderney

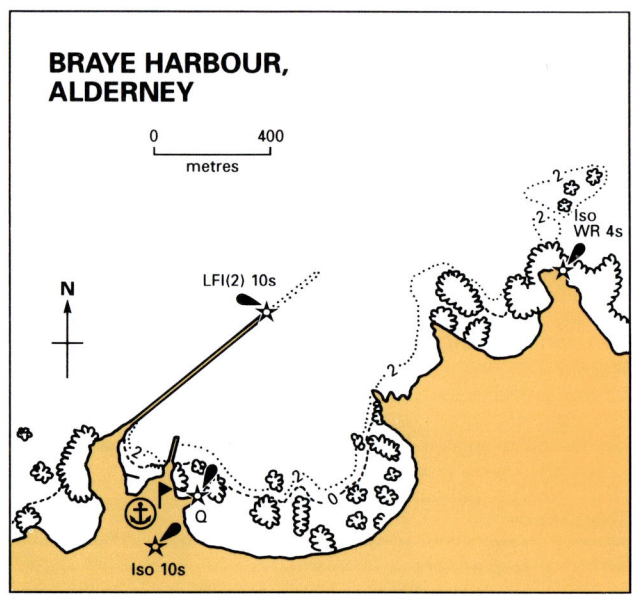

BRAYE HARBOUR, ALDERNEY

Way Point
49° 44'.4N 2° 10'.8W (on leading line into Braye Harbour, 7 cables off)
Charts
Admiralty Nos 60 and 2845
Adlard Coles Pilot Pack Vol 2 No 241
Tides
See above for corrections from Standard Port of St Helier
Harbour Lights
See 1536/1538.1 p.118/119
Beacon
Aero RC 49° 42'.58N 2° 11'.90W ALD 383 kHz 50M
Cautions
1 The strength of the stream in the Alderney Race and the Swinge cannot be overemphasised.
2 There are the remains of the foundations extending NE from the end of the breakwater for about 3 cables with 1.8m at the extremity.
3 Berthing alongside anywhere, except for fuel in the inner (Little Crabby) harbour is not allowed.
Berthing
Once inside Alderney Harbour breakwater, there are lots of moorings for visitors and a water taxi will pick up and return at all reasonable hours. There is usually a swell in the harbour, particulary in N to NE winds and the mooring lines should be substantial and protected against chafe.
VHF Alderney Radio: Ch 16; 12; 74
        Mainbrayce (Water Taxi, fuel etc): Ch 80; M
Telephones
Harbour Master: (0481) 822620
Customs: (0481) 822620
Medical: (0481) 822822 (Hospital)
Alderney SC: (0481) 822758

St Peter Port (Guernsey)

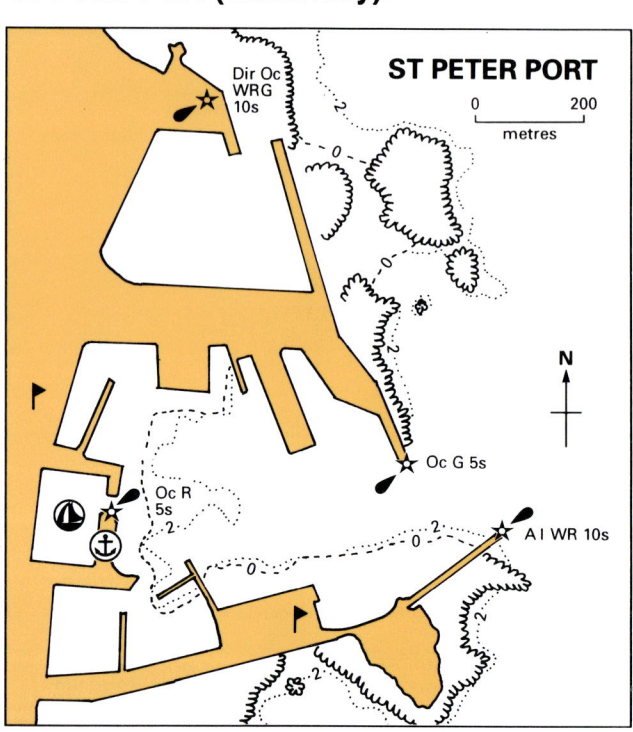

ST PETER PORT

Way Point
49° 27'.6N 2° 31'.0W (3 cables NE of entrance)
Charts
Admiralty Nos 808 and 3140
Adlard Coles Pilot Pack Vol 2 No 243
Tides
See above for corrections from Standard Port of St Helier
Harbour Lights
See 1560/1570 p.119
Beacon
RC Castle Breakwater Lt 49° 27'.37N 2° 31'.37W GY 304.5 kHz 10M
Aero RC Guernsey 49° 26'.12N 2° 38'.30W GRB 361 kHz 30M
Cautions
1 The tidal range is high and the streams run strongly.
Berthing
The new Queen Elizabeth II Marina on the N side of St Peter Port harbour is for locals only; visiting yachts must lie to visitors' buoys in the harbour or pass over the sill (4.2m above datum) into Victoria marina.
VHF Port Control: Ch 12
Telephones
Harbour Master: (0481) 720229
Customs: (0481) 26911
Medical: (0481) 25211
St Peter Port Marina: (0481) 25987
R Channel Islands YC: (0481) 25500
Guernsey YC: (0481) 22838

St Helier (Jersey)

Way Point
49° 08'.7N 2° 08'.2W
Charts
Admiralty Nos 1137 and 3278
Adlard Coles Pilot Pack Vol 2 No 248
Tides
Standard Port - see p.60
Harbour Lights
See 1604/1616 p.119
Beacon
Elizabeth Castle 49° 10'.62 2° 07'.50W EC 306 kHz 10M
Cautions
1 There are many off-lying dangers.
2 The rise and fall is considerable.
Berthing
Visiting yachts will be directed to move into the marina which has a 5m sill, or, if there is insufficient water, to pick a mooring or make fast temporarily in La Collette yacht basin.
VHF St Helier Port Control: Ch 14
Telephones
Harbour Master: (0534) 34451
Customs: (0534) 30232
Medical: (0534) 59000 (Hospital)
St Helier Marina: (0534) 79549
La Collette Yacht Basin: (0534) 69147
St Helier YC: (0534) 32229
R Channel Islands YC (St Aubin): (0534) 41023

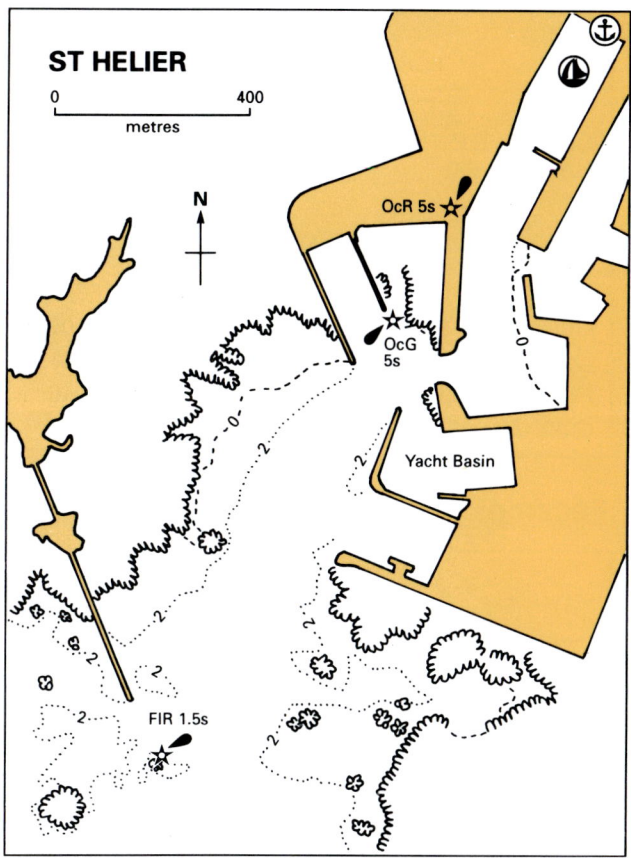

FRENCH PORTS
EAST TO WEST

New customs rules came into effect in 1993. Consult HM Customs and Excise Notices 1 and 8B. Generally speaking there is free traffic unless you are carrying pets or prohibited or restricted goods or immigrants.

PLACE	TIME DIFFERENCES				HEIGHT DIFFERENCES (IN METRES)			
	High Water		Low Water		MHWS	MHWN	MLWN	MLWS
DIEPPE (see page 64)	**0100** and **1300**	**0600** and **1800**	**0100** and **1300**	**0700** and **1900**	9.3	7.3	2.6	0.8
Fécamp	−0022	−0018	−0034	−0043	−0.9	−0.5	+0.3	+0.4

	TIME DIFFERENCES				HEIGHT DIFFERENCES (IN METRES)			
PLACE	High Water		Low Water		MHWS	MHWN	MLWN	MLWS
LE HAVRE (see page 68)	**0000** and **1200**	**0500** and **1700**	**0000** and **1200**	**0700** and **1900**	7.9	6.6	3.0	1.2
Honfleur	−0140	−0135	+0005	+0040	−0.1	−0.2	−0.1	+0.2
Deauville	−0035	−0015	0000	−0010	−0.2	−0.2	−0.2	−0.1
Dives	−0055	⊙	⊙	−0115	−0.5	−0.5	−0.6	−0.4
Ouistreham	−0007	−0007	−0005	−0005	−0.3	−0.3	−0.3	−0.3
Courseulles	−0025	−0015	−0020	−0025	−0.5	−0.5	−0.2	−0.1
Port-en-Bessin	−0045	−0040	−0040	−0045	−0.7	−0.7	−0.4	−0.1

⊙ *No data*

Fécamp

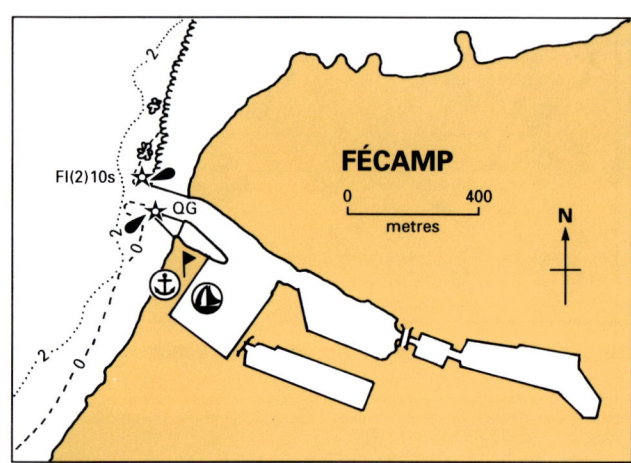

Way Point
49° 45'.9N 0° 21'.1E (5 cables W of entrance)
Charts
Admiralty No 1352
Adlard Coles Pilot Pack Vol 1 No 149
Tides
See p.141 for corrections from Standard Port of Dieppe
Harbour Lights
See 1244/1246 p.116
Cautions
1 The entrance is dangerous at low water in strong W to NW winds.
2 The flood stream sets strongly across the harbour mouth.
3 There is a strong scend in the entrance channel.
Berthing
There is a marina in the Avant Port
VHF Port of Fécamp: Ch 12; 16 (-2.1/2 HW +1/2)
Port de Plaisance: Ch 9 (0800 to 2000 local time)
Telephones
Harbour Master (Port de Plaisance): (35) 28 16 35
Customs: (35) 28 19 40
Medical: (35) 28 05 13 (Hospital)
British Consul: (35) 42 27 47
Société des Régates de Fécamp: (35) 28 08 44

Le Havre

Way Point
49° 29'.5N 0° 04'.5E (LH 16 buoy 7 cables WNW of entrance)
Charts
Admiralty No 2990
Adlard Coles Pilot Pack Vol 1 No 150
Tides
Standard Port - see p.68
Harbour Lights
See 1260/1280.7 p.116

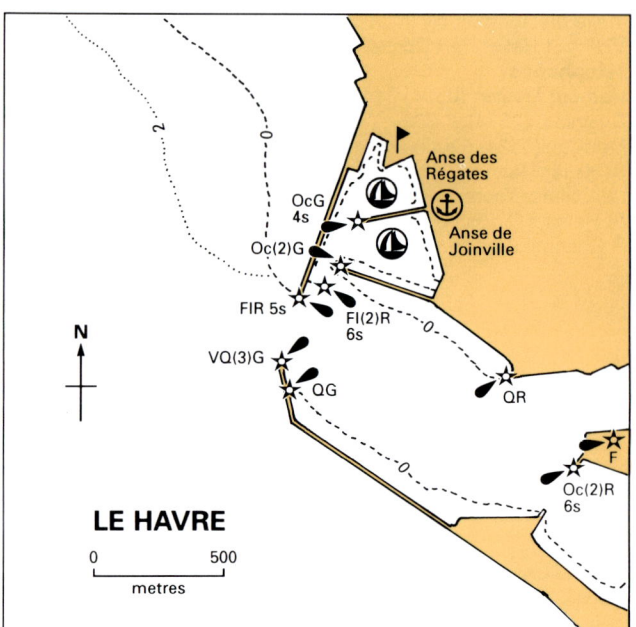

Beacons
RC Cap d'Antifer Lt 49° 41'.07N 0° 10'.00E Tl 300 kHz 50M
Aero RC Le Havre, Octeville 49° 35'.75N 0° 11'.00E LHO 346 kHz 15M
Cautions
1 Keep clear of the deep water channel which has heavy commercial traffic and is well marked.
Berthing
There is a large marina but also good berths in the Basin du Commerce at HW and after special request. Le Havre provides entry to the Tancarville Canal and hence the River Seine.
VHF Call: HAVRE PORT: Ch 12; 16; 20; (24 hrs)
Marina: Ch 9
Telephones
Harbour Master (Port de Plaisance): (35) 21 23 95
Customs: (35) 41 24 34
Medical: (35) 41 23 61 (Doctor)
British Consul: (35) 42 27 47
Société des Régates du Havre: (35) 42 41 21
Société Nautique du Havre: (35) 21 01 41

Honfleur

Way Point
49° 25'.8N 0° 14'.0E (Entrance)
Charts
Admiralty No 2994
Adlard Coles Pilot Pack Vol 1 No 151
Tides
See above for corrections from Standard Port of Le Havre
Harbour Lights
See 1286/1301 p.116/117

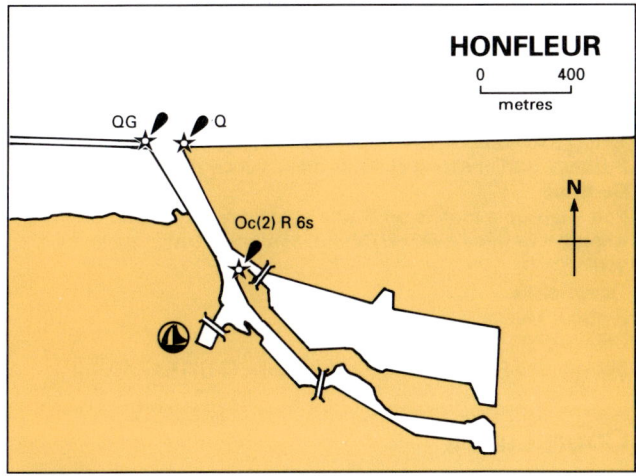

Cautions
1 Be prepared to take the ground in the Avant Port if you miss the lock opening, or go back to Le Havre.
2 Dredging is frequently in operation.
3 Sluicing, lasting for 5 hrs, takes place from the Bassin de Retenue at springs during which time the channel must be avoided.

Berthing
The marina is in the Vieux Bassin (Bassin de l'Ouest) -1 blast on the horn requests entry. The lock opens between -1 HW +1 (HW +2 in summer) but the bridge only opens at HW -1, HW and HW + 1 (HW +2 in summer)

VHF Call: PR: Ch 12; 16 (-2 HW +4 Le Havre)

Telephones
Harbour Master: (31) 89 20 02
Customs: (31) 89 12 13
Medical: (31) 89 34 05 (Doctor), (31) 89 07 74 (Hospital)
British Consul: (35) 42 27 47
Vieux Bassin Yacht Harbour: (31) 89 01 85
Cercle Nautique de Honfleur: (31) 98 87 13

Deauville

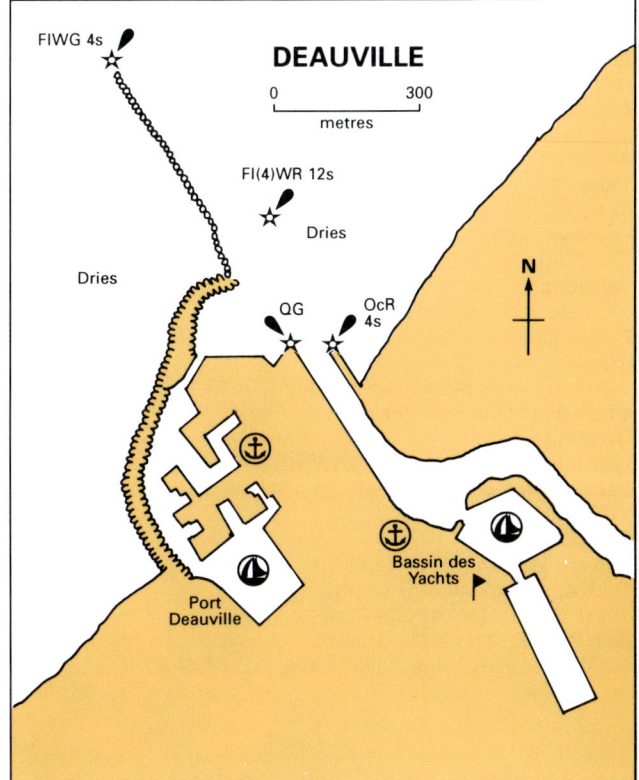

Way Point
49° 22'.7N 0° 02'.6E (Trouville SW buoy, 1M WNW of entrance)
Charts
Admiralty No 1349
Adlard Coles Pilot Pack Vol 1 No 152
Tides
See p.142 for corrections from Standard Port of Le Havre
Harbour Lights
See 1282/1285 p.116
Cautions
1 Dangerous entry in NW gales.
2 There are strong tidal streams across the entrance.
3 Suction dredging may be in operation.
4 There may be difficult eddies at the entrance to the Bassin des Yachts.
5 The approach dries at LW. Simplified traffic signals are shown from the E breakwater. Entry LW +2 but in strong onshore winds, -2 HW +2.
Berthing
Visiting yachts have the choice between the Port Deauville (2.5m minimum) on the starboard side (Lock opens -3 HW +5 approx) or the cheaper Bassin des Yachts (Lock opens -2 HW +2.1/2), less modern but more interesting and more convenient to the town.
VHF Yacht Basin: Ch 11
Marina: Ch 9
Telephones
Harbour Master (Port Deauville): (31) 98 30 01
Habour Master (Yacht Basin): (31) 98 50 40
Customs: (31) 85 35 29
Medical: (31) 88 23 57 (Doctor), (31) 88 14 00 (Hospital)
British Consul: (35) 42 27 47
Deauville YC: (31) 88 38 19

Ouistreham

Way Point
49°20'.48N 0°14'.73W (Ouistreham E cardinal pillar buoy)
Charts
Admiralty No 1349
Adlard Coles Pilot Pack Vol 1 No 154
Tides
See p.142 for corrections from Standard Port of Le Havre
Harbour Lights
See 1377/1381.1 p.117
Cautions
1 The approaches are littered with wrecks and block ships.
Berthing
Temporary berth on the E side of the Avant Port until the lock opens. Yachts usually use the E lock. Departure -2HW +1.3/4; entry -1.1/2HW +2.1/4, longer in busy periods - check with the YC. Traffic signals do not apply to yachts which may only enter lock when W Lt is shown at bottom of light panel. There is a marina at Ouistreham and a canal to Caen where there is another marina.
VHF Call: OUISTREHAM PORT: Ch 12; 16; 68
(-2 HW +3)
Call: CAEN PORT: Ch 8; 68
Société des Régates de Caen-Ouistreham: Ch 9
Caen Marina: Ch 12; 68
Telephones
Harbour Master (Ouistreham): (31) 97 14 43
Harbour Master (Caen): (31) 95 24 47
Customs: (31) 96 89 10
Medical: (31) 96 12 86 (Doctor), (31) 94 81 12 (Hospital)
British Consul: (35) 42 27 47
Ouistreham Marina: (31) 97 13 05
Caen Marina: (31) 95 24 47
Société des Régates de Caen-Ouistreham: (31) 97 13 05

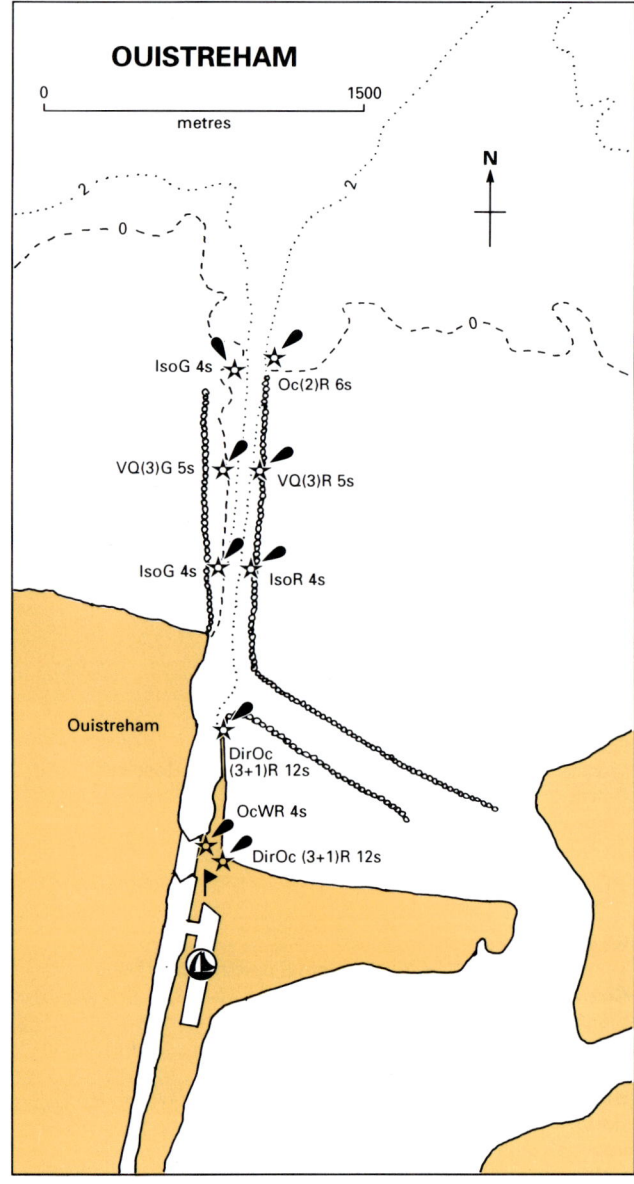

Dives

Way Point
49°20'.0N)°06'.5W (2.3M off in W sector of light)
Charts
Admiralty No 2146
Adlard Coles Pilot Pack Vol 1 No 153

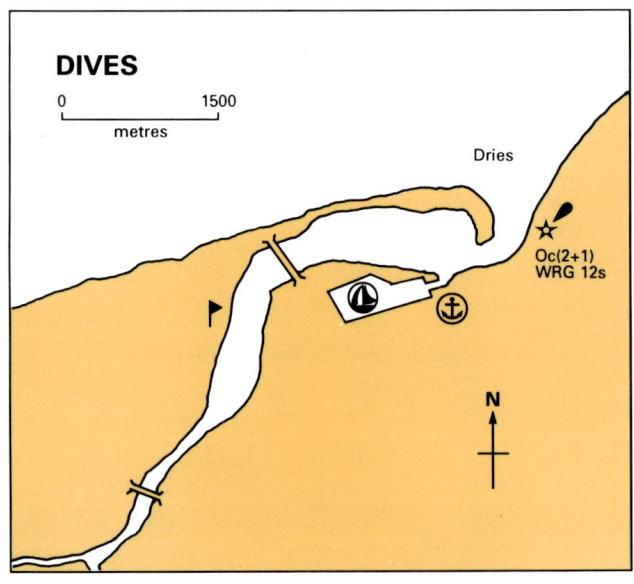

Tides
See p.142 for corrections from Standard Port of Le Havre
Harbour Lights
See 1374 p.117
Cautions
1 Approach dries at LW
2 Heavy Surf in strong N winds makes entry dangerous
Berthing
Port Guillaume marina on S side of estuary. Lock gate opens when 2m or more over cill (about -3HW+3). Traffic lights
VHF Ch 9
Telephones
Harbour Master: (31) 24 48 00
Cabourg YC: (31) 91 23 55
Société des Régates de Dives Houlgate: (31) 91 47 10

Courseulles

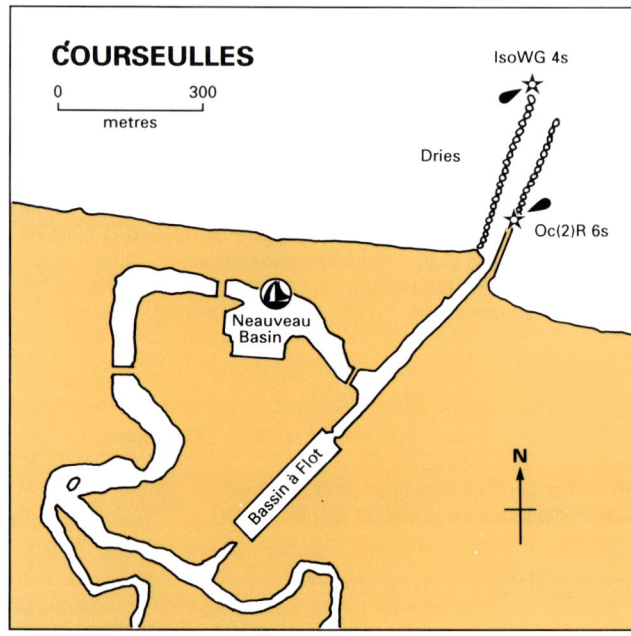

Way Point
49° 21'.3N 0° 27'.6W (Safe Water Buoy. Steer 134°T for 5.7 cables then 198°T to entrance)
Charts
Admiralty No 1349
Adlard Coles Pilot Pack Vol 1 No 155
Tides
See p.142 for corrections from Standard Port of Le Havre
Harbour Lights
See 1390/1391 p.117
Cautions
1 Dangerous in strong onshore winds.
2 Approach with care due to shifting banks, rocks and the old extension to the W breakwater.
3 Sluicing takes place at springs signalled 24 hrs in advance by a blue flag at the dock gates.
Berthing
Lock into the Bassin à Flot (-2HW +2) or go into the Neauveau Bassin over the sill (-3HW +3, 2.5m at HW).
VHF Courseulles: Ch 9
Telephones
Harbour Master: (31) 37 51 69
Medical: (31) 37 45 24 (Doctor)
British Consul: (35) 42 27 47
Both Basins: (31) 37 46 03
Société des Régates de Courseulles: (31) 37 47 42

	TIME DIFFERENCES				HEIGHT DIFFERENCES (IN METRES)			
PLACE	High Water		Low Water		MHWS	MHWN	MLWN	MLWS
CHERBOURG (see page 72)	**0300** and **1500**	**1000** and **2200**	**0400** and **1600**	**1000** and **2200**	**6.4**	**5.0**	**2.6**	**1.1**
St Vaast	+0105	+0055	+0120	+0100	+0.2	+0.4	−0.3	−0.2
Barfleur	+0110	+0055	+0050	+0050	+0.1	+0.3	0.0	+0.1

Grandcamp

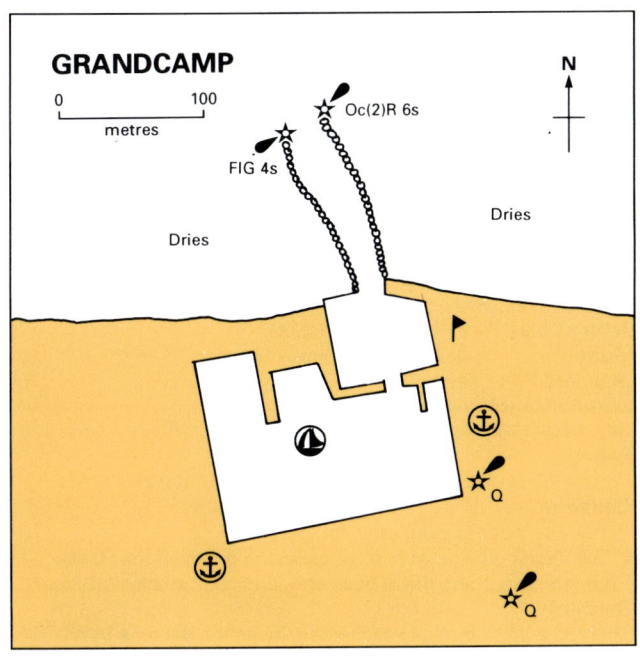

Way Point
49° 25'.2N 1° 04'.5W (2M NW of entrance)
Charts
Admiralty No 2073
Adlard Coles Pilot Pack Vol 1 Nos 157 and 158
Tides
Generally as Port-en-Bessin. See p.142 for corrections from Standard Port of Le Havre
Harbour Lights
See 1406/1409 p.117
Cautions
1 Dangerous approach in strong onshore winds.
2 Sluicing takes place at springs and is signalled by a blue flag 24 hrs in advance.
Berthing
The basin sill dries 2m but there is 2.5m inside; the gates open -2.1/2HW + 2.1/2. Visitors' berth at the outer end of the N finger pontoon.
VHF Ch 9; 11
Telephones
Harbour Master: (31) 22 63 16
Medical: (31) 22 60 50
British Consul: (35) 42 27 47
Marina: (31) 22 63 16

Carentan and Isigny

Way Point
49° 25'.5N 1° 07'.0W (CI Buoy)
Charts
Admiralty No 2073
Adlard Coles Pilot Pack Vol 1 No 158
Tides
Generally as Port-en-Bessin. See p.142 for corrections from Standard Port of Le Havre
Harbour Lights

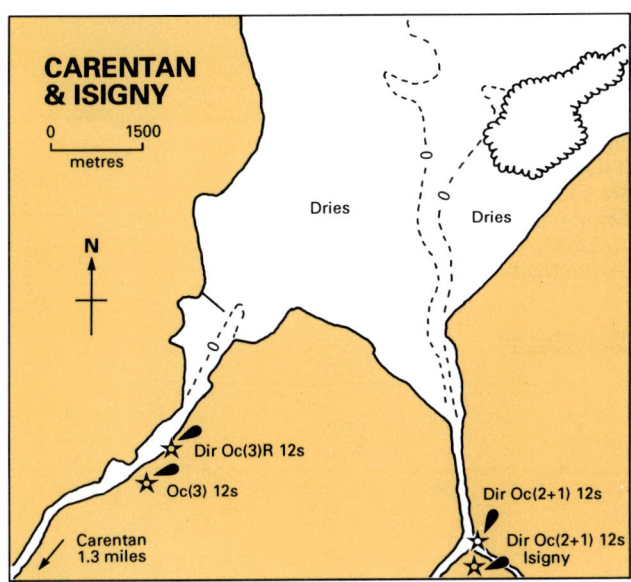

See 1412/1418.1 p.117
Cautions
1 Dangerous in strong onshore winds.
2 There are strong tidal streams.
Berthing
Lock in at Carentan between -2HW +3. There is a drying berth at Isigny, accessible -3HW +3.
VHF Carentan: Ch 9 (0800 to 1800 and when lock is operated) Isigny: Ch 9
Telephones
Harbour Master (Carentan): (33) 42 24 44
Harbour Master (Isigny): (31) 22 10 67
Customs: Port-en-Bessin (for Isigny) (31) 21 71 09
       Valognes (for Carentan) (33) 40 23 27
Medical: (33) 42 14 12 (Hospital)
CFCC: (33) 34 40 50

St Vaast la Hougue

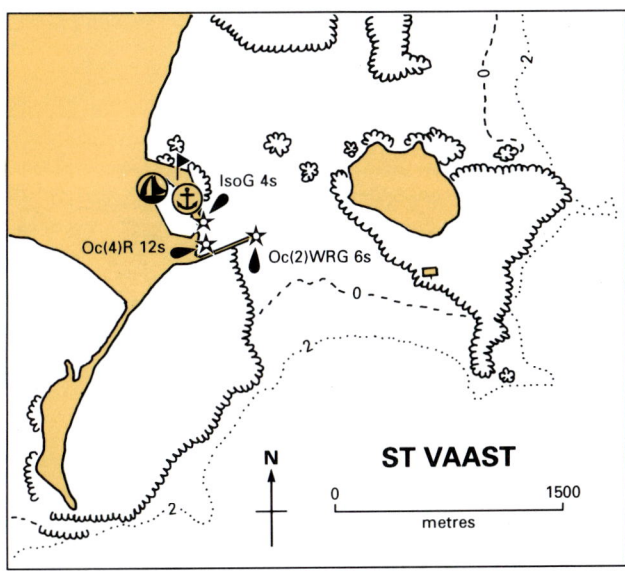

St Vaast la Hougue

Way Point
49° 34'.3N 1° 14'.3W (1.2M SE of entrance)
Charts
Admiralty No 1349
Adlard Coles Pilot Pack Vol 2 No 225
Tides
See above for corrections from Standard Port of Cherbourg
Harbour Lights
See 1434/1438 p.117
Cautions
An easy approach protected from all but strong NE to SE winds which can create a considerable swell.
Berthing
The lock is open between -2.1/4HW +3 to 3.1/2. The Harbour Master will indicate a berth as the yacht passes through the lock.
VHF Ch 9
Telephones
Harbour Master: (33) 54 48 81
Medical: (33) 54 43 42
British Consul: (33) 44 20 13
Cercle Nautique de la Hougue: (33) 54 55 73

Barfleur

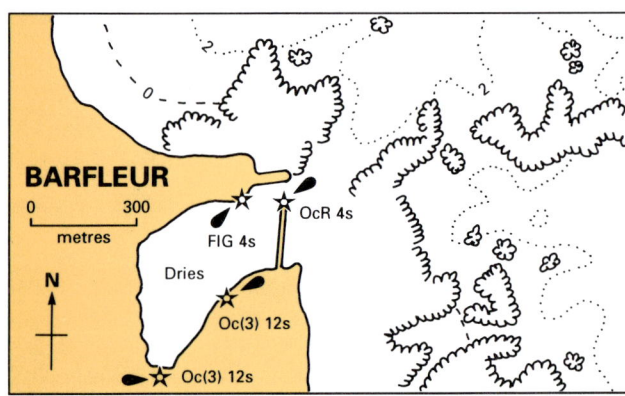

Way Point
49° 41'.2N 1° 14'.3W (1.1M NE of entrance)
Charts
Admiralty No 1349
Adlard Coles Pilot Pack Vol 2 No 226
Tides
See p.145 for corrections from Standard Port of Cherbourg
Harbour Lights
See 1444/1450 p.117
Beacon
Pointe de Barfleur Lt 49° 41'.87N 1° 15'.87W FG 297 kHz 70M
Cautions
1 The Barfleur race should be avoided either by going right inshore past La Jamette (E cardinal beacon 1/4M east of Pte de Barfleur) or by standing off at least 4M.
2 Avoid the rocky S side of the harbour.
Berthing
Yachts usually lie to the SW end of the NW wall on the direction of the Harbour Master from his white office hut by the church. It is feasible to anchor off in settled weather. A marina is reported (1990) as being planned.
Telephones
Harbour Master: (33) 54 08 29
Medical: (33) 54 00 02 (Doctor)
British Consul: (33) 44 20 13
Cercle Maritime de Plaisance: (33) 54 08 60

Cherbourg

Way Point
49° 40'.5N 1° 39'.4W (West entrance)
Charts
Admiralty No 2602
Adlard Coles Pilot Pack Vol 2 No 228
Tides
Standard Port - see p.72
Harbour Lights
See 1469/1504 p.118
Beacon
Fort de l'Ouest Lt 49° 40'.50N 1° 38'.87W RB 302 kHz 20M
Cautions
1 The approach is clear of all dangers.
2 The Digue du Homet and the basins to the W of the Petite Rade are part of the naval base and landing is strictly forbidden.
Berthing
There is a large marina which does, however, become very crowded in summer weekends and it may be necessary to berth alongside a holding pontoon or to anchor off in the Petite Rade, just N of the marina and well clear of the ferries.
VHF Port Chantereyne (Marina): Ch 9
Telephones
Harbour Master: (33) 53 75 16 (Marina)
Customs: (33) 53 79 65
Medical: (33) 53 05 68 (Doctor)
British Consul: (33) 44 20 13
YC de Cherbourg: (33) 53 02 83

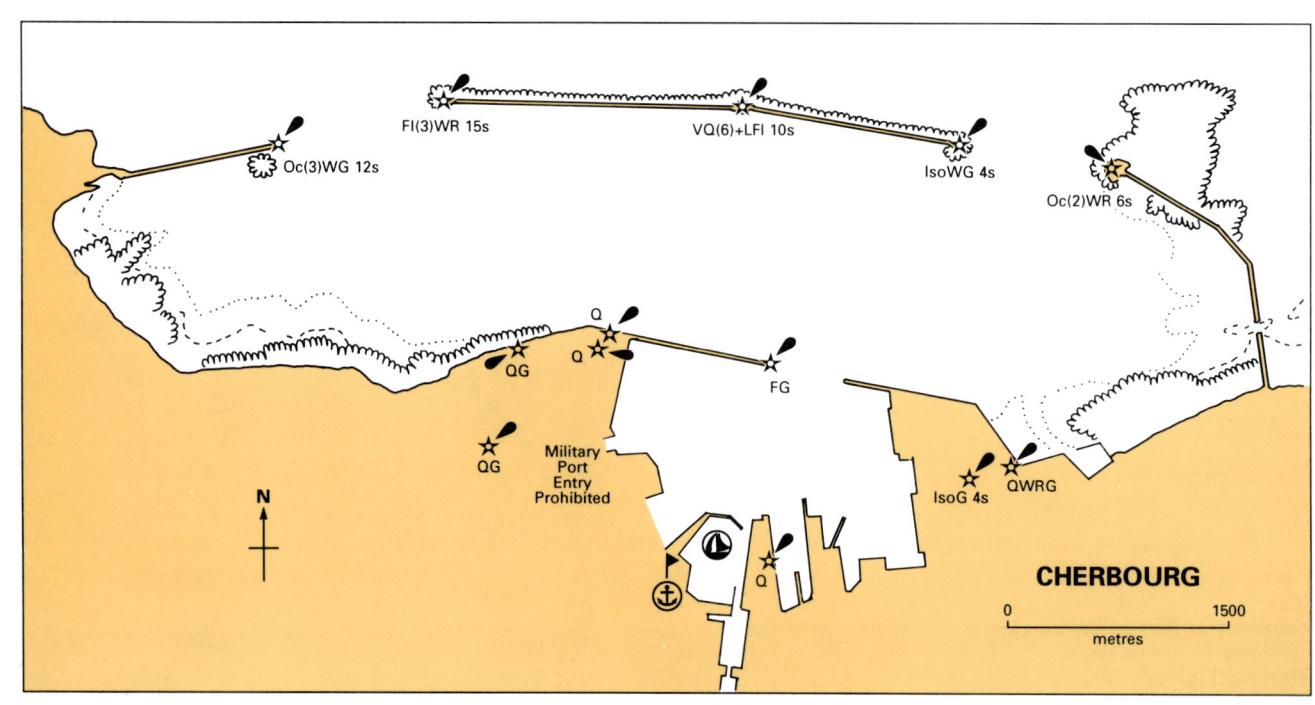

PLACE	TIME DIFFERENCES				HEIGHT DIFFERENCES (IN METRES)			
	High Water		Low Water		MHWS	MHWN	MLWN	MLWS
ST MALO (see page 76)	**0100** and **1300**	**0800** and **2000**	**0300** and **1500**	**0800** and **2000**	**12.2**	**9.2**	**4.4**	**1.5**
Granville	+0010	+0010	+0025	+0020	+0.8	+0.6	+0.2	−0.1
Dahouet	−0005	−0005	−0025	−0015	−0.9	−0.6	−0.4	−0.3
Le Légué	−0005	−0005	−0020	−0010	−0.8	−0.5	−0.3	−0.1
Binic	−0005	−0005	−0020	−0010	−0.7	−0.6	−0.4	−0.3
Portrieux	−0005	−0005	−0020	−0010	−0.9	−0.6	−0.4	−0.2
Paimpol	−0010	−0005	−0035	−0035	−1.3	−0.9	−0.5	−0.1
Lezardrieux	−0010	−0005	−0050	−0035	−1.7	−1.2	−0.6	−0.2
Tréguier	−0035	−0035	−0130	−0050	−2.4	−1.7	−1.1	−0.4
Perros-Guirec	−0035	−0035	−0115	−0105	−2.8	−1.9	−0.9	−0.3

Granville

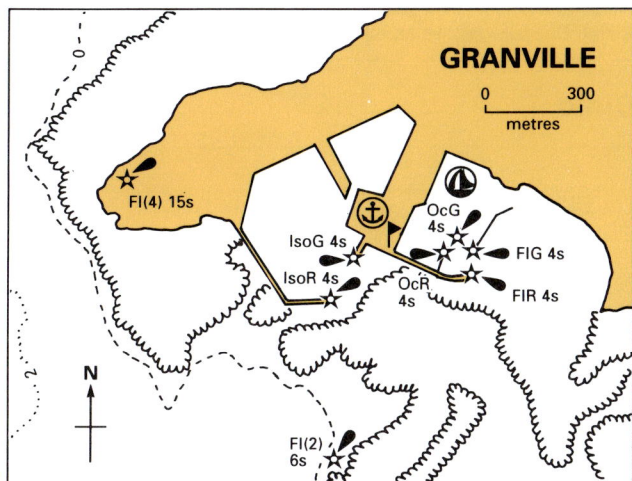

Waypoint
48°49'.6N 1°36'.5W (6 cables SW of Port de Hérel entrance)
Charts
Admiralty No 3672
Adlard Coles Pilot Pack Vol 2 No 233
Tides
See above for corrections from Standard Port of St Malo
Harbour Lights
See 1660/1668.6 p.120
Beacon
Aero RC Granville 48° 55'.10N 1° 28'.87W GV 321 kHz 25M
Cautions
1 Keep away in poor visibility or strong onshore winds.
2 There are some isolated shoal patches to the SW and some drying rocks off Pointe du Roc.
Berthing
The depth over the sill is given in metres (white) and decimetres (orange) on an illuminated tide gauge near the end of the breakwater. Zero means absolutely no entry. Turn sharply to port after passing the breakwater end for the entrance. 'G' pontoon is reserved for visitors.
VHF Herel Marina: Ch 9
Granville Harbour: Ch 16, 12
Telephones
Harbour Master (Hérel): (33) 50 20 06
Harbour Master (Granville): (33) 50 17 75
Customs: (33) 50 19 90
Medical: (33) 50 00 07 (Doctor)
British Consul: (33) 44 20 13
YC de Granville: (33) 50 04 25

St Malo

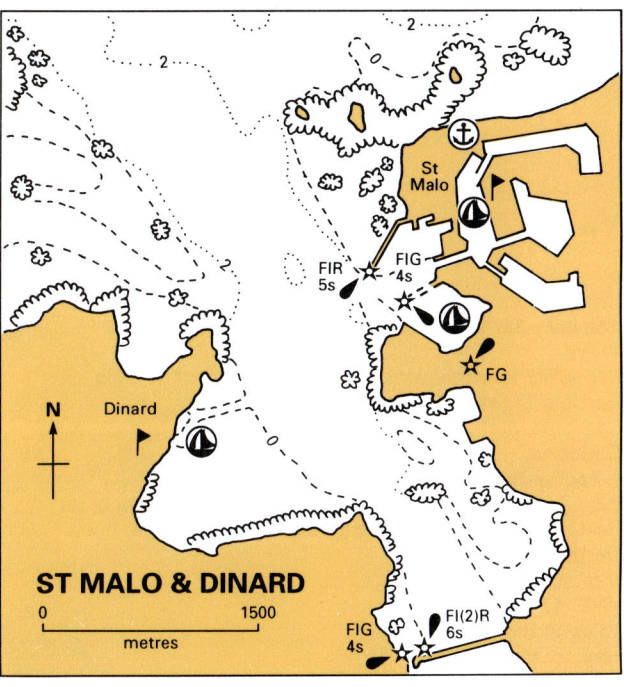

Way Point
48° 41'.4N 2° 07'.2W (Safe Water Buoy)
Charts
Admiralty No 2700
Adlard Coles Pilot Pack Vol 2 No 236
Tides
Standard Port - see p.76
Harbour Lights
See 1674/1688 p.120
Beacon
Le Grand Jardin Lt 48° 40'.27N 2° 04'.90W GJ 306.5 kHz 10M
Cautions
1 The tidal stream runs hard.
2 There are numerous rocks in the area.
3 There are alternative approaches but these are unsuitable in the dark or bad weather or without experience.
Berthing
St Malo has unlimited space for yachts in the Bassins Vaubin and Duguay-Trouin, either alongside the wall or on pontoons at the N end of Bassin Vaubin. In addition there is a large marina, Bas-Sablons, entered over a sill. For shopping and the old town, use Bassin Vaubin. The lock normally opens -2HW +2.
VHF St Malo Port: Ch 12, 16
Bas-Sablons Marina: Ch 9
Vaubin Marina: Ch 9
Grand Jardin Lt Ho: Ch 12; 16

Telephones
Harbour Master (St Malo): (99) 56 51 91
Harbour Master (Bas-Sablons): (99) 81 71 34
Harbour Master (Dinard): (99) 46 65 55
Customs: (99) 81 65 90
Medical: (99) 81 60 40
British Consul: (99) 46 18 68
Société Nautique de la Baie de St Malo: (99) 40 84 42
YC de Dinard: (99) 46 14 32

Dahouet

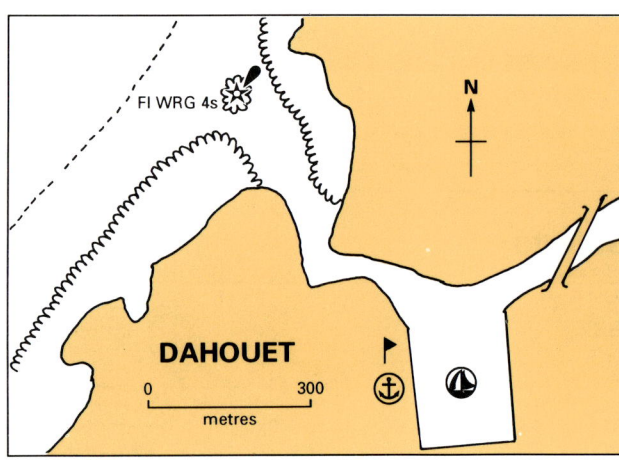

Way Point
48°35'.3N 2°34'.8W (5 cables NW of La Petite Muette Bn at entrance)
Charts
Admiralty 3674
Tides
See p.147 for corrections from Standard Port of St Malo
Harbour Lights
See 1704 p.120
Cautions
1 Approach dries at LW.
2 Le Dahouet Rock (dries 0.3m) just S of white sector of La Petite Mouette Bn is marked by unlit N Cardinal Spar buoy.
Berthing
Marina Accessible -2HW+2, maximum length 14m.
VHF Ch 9
Telephones
Harbour Master: (96) 72 82 85
Dahouet Nautical Centre Clubhouse: (96) 72 95 28

Le Légué and St Brieuc

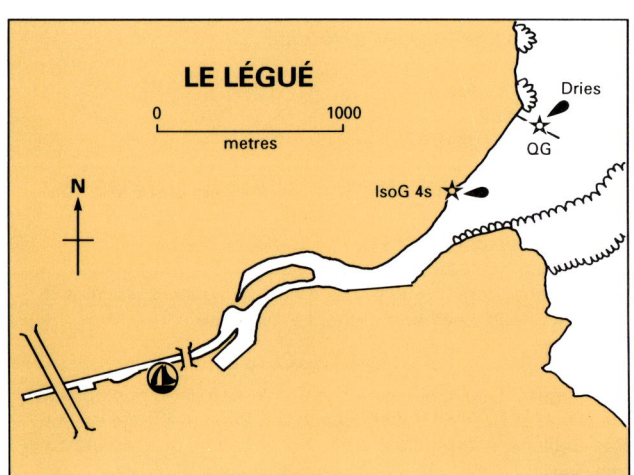

Way Point
48° 34'.4N 2° 4'.1W (Le Légué Safe Water Buoy 2.3M NNE of No 1 Channel Buoy)
Charts
Admiralty No 3674
Adlard Coles Pilot Pack Vol 3 No 332
Tides
See p.147 for corrections from Standard Port of St Malo
Harbour Lights
See 1708/1709 p.120
Beacon
Aero RC St Brieuc 48° 34'.10N 2° 46'.90W SB 353 kHz 25M
Cautions
1 Keep clear in strong northerlies.
2 A blue flag at the lock indicates that sluicing is imminent.
3 There are numerous shell fish beds in the bay.
Berthing
Le Légué has two wet docks divided by a swing bridge and yachts use the innermost.
VHF Le Légué Port: Ch 16; 12 (about 1.1/2 hrs either side of HW)
Telephones
Harbour Master: (96) 33 35 41
Medical: (96) 61 49 07 (Doctor)
British Consul: (99) 46 26 64

Binic

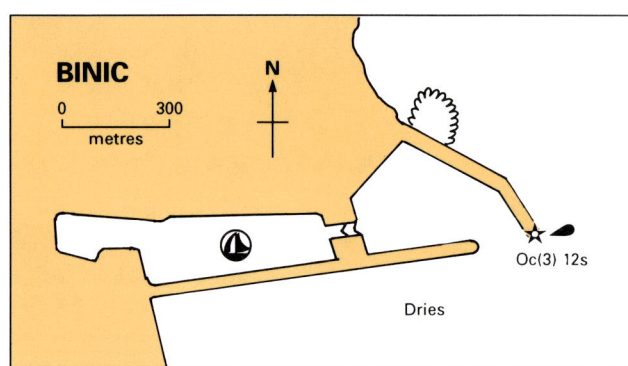

Way Point
48° 36'.5N 2° 44'.8W (2.7M E of entrance. **CAUTION**: Île Harbour and its outlying rocks extend for several miles to the N of this way point. Plot your approach track)
Charts
Admiralty No 3674
Adlard Coles Pilot Pack Vol 3 No 333
Tides
See p.147 for corrections from Standard Port of St Malo
Harbour Lights
See 1710 p.120
Beacon
Aero RC St Brieuc 48° 34'.10 2° 46'.90W SB 353 kHz 25M
Caution
1 A strong E wind makes access difficult.
Berthing
Binic has a drying outer harbour, with good drying berths and a locked inner harbour with pontoon berths for 500 plus 50 visitors' berths alongside the quay immediately to port. Most facilities in the season.
VHF Ch 9
Telephones
Harbour Master: (96) 73 61 86
Medical: (96) 42 61 05 (Doctor)
British Consul: (99) 46 26 64
Club Nautique du Binic: (96) 42 62 72

St Quay - Portrieux

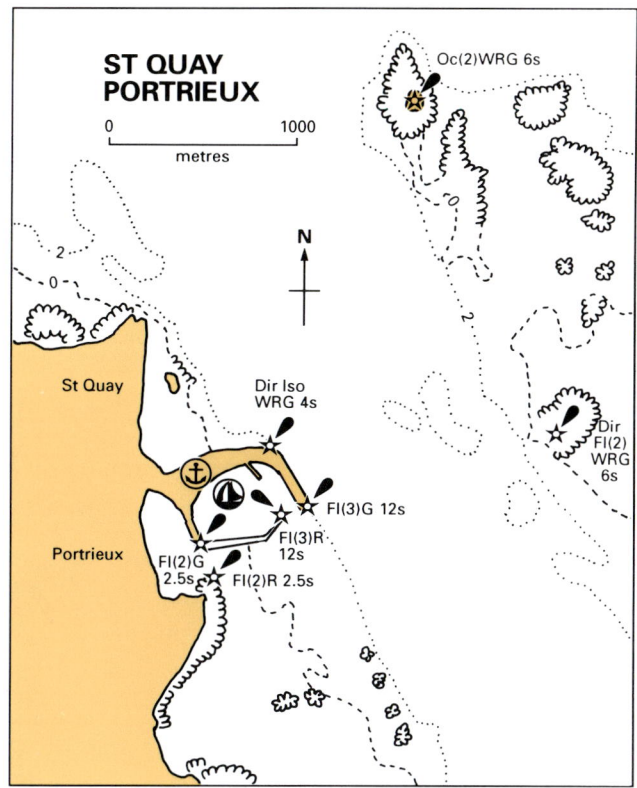

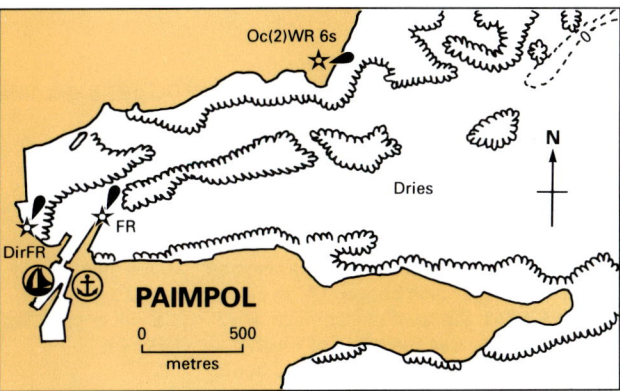

yachts berth in the first basin (No 2) where there is between 3.0 and 4.6m depending on the range of tide.

VHF Ch 9
Telephones
Harbour Master: (96) 20 80 77
Customs: (96) 20 95 38
Medical: (96) 20 80 04
British Consul: (99) 46 26 64
Port de Plaisence: (96) 20 80 15 or (96) 20 47 65

Way Point
48° 40'.7N 2° 49'.8W (2M N of entrance. **CAUTION**: Only suitable for approach from N as the Île Harbour blocks the approach from the E. Plot your track).
Charts
Admiralty No 3672
Adlard Coles Pilot Pack Vol 3 No 334
Tides
See p.147 for corrections from Standard Port of St Malo
Harbour Lights
See 1712/1713.6 p.120/121
Cautions
1 Île Harbour and its outlying rocks prevent approach from the E.
Berthing
The marina has 100 berths for visitors
VHF Ch 9
Telephones
Harbour Master: (96) 70 49 51
Medical: (96) 70 41 31
British Consul: (99) 46 26 64
Cercle de Voile de Portieux: (96) 70 41 76

Paimpol

Way Point
48° 47'.7N 2° 56'.0W (Entrance to Chenal de la Jument)
48° 48.9N 2° 57'.7W (Entrance to Chenal du Dénou)
Charts
Admiralty No 3673
Adlard Coles Pilot Pack Vol 3 No 335
Tides
See p.147 for corrections from Standard Port of St Malo
Harbour Lights
See 1722/1724.1 p.121
Cautions
1 When both lock gates are open, the flood may be up to 2 knots through the lock.
2 The approach is marked with unlit buoys and beacons and care should be taken to avoid the many rocks, especially to the N of the channel.
3 There are numerous oyster beds on both sides of the approach.
Berthing
The lock usually opens for yachts -1 1/2 HW + 1 1/2. Visiting

Rivière de Trieux and Lézardrieux

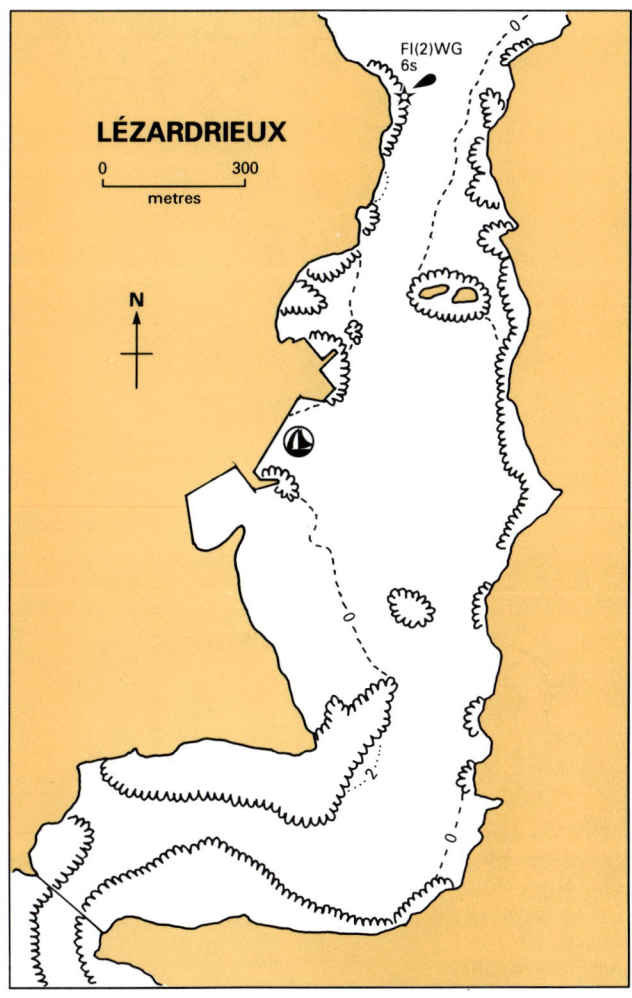

Way Point
48° 53'.9N 2° 57'.7W (On 225° (T) leading line about 2M from the entrance of the river)
Charts
Admiralty No 3673
Adlard Coles Pilot Pack Vol 3 No 337
Tides
See p.147 for corrections from Standard Port of St Malo

Harbour Lights
See 1740/1758 p.121
Beacons
Rosédo Lt, Île Bréhat 48° 51'.50N 3° 00'.32W DO 287.5 kHz 10M
Cautions
1 Streams run strongly.
2 Note the cable area across the Rade and at the head of La Chambre where anchoring is forbidden.
3 There are many oyster beds in the area.
Berthing
Lézardrieux has a marina and moorings off. Above Lézardrieux there is a suspension bridge, 17.7m clearance, and then, after about 6 miles, the town of Pontrieux which has a wet dock, 3.9m, formed by the river, the gates of which open -1HW +1.
VHF Lézardrieux Port: Ch 9 (office hours)
Telephones
Harbour Master: (96) 20 14 22
Medical: (96) 20 10 30 (Doctor)
British Consul: (99) 46 26 64
YC de Trieux: (96) 20 10 39

Tréguier

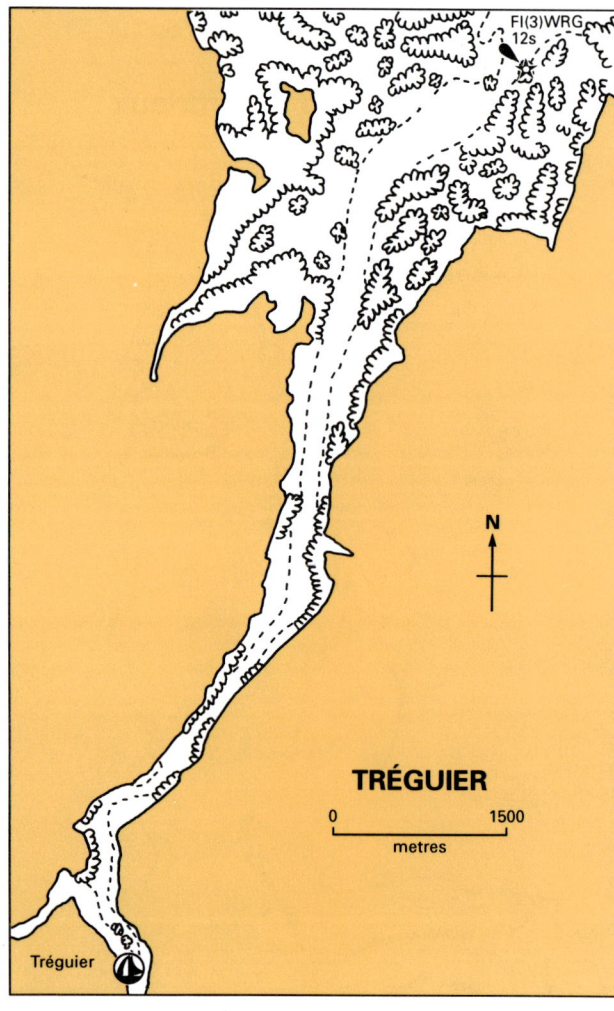

Way Point
48° 55'.5N 3° 12'.0W (1.3M NNW of Basse Crublent Buoy)
Charts
Admiralty No 3672
Adlard Coles Pilot Pack Vol 3 No 340
Tides
See p.147 for corrections from Standard Port of St Malo
Harbour Lights
See 1760/1762.1 p.121
Cautions
1 The stream runs very strongly, through the marina.
2 There are many oyster beds in the area.
Berthing
There is a marina but it is also possible to anchor in the river clear of oyster beds.
VHF Ch 9
Telephones
Harbour Master: (96) 92 42 37
Customs: (96) 20 81 87
Medical: (96) 92 32 14
British Consul: (99) 46 26 64
Club Nautique du Trégor: (96) 92 42 08

Perros - Guirec

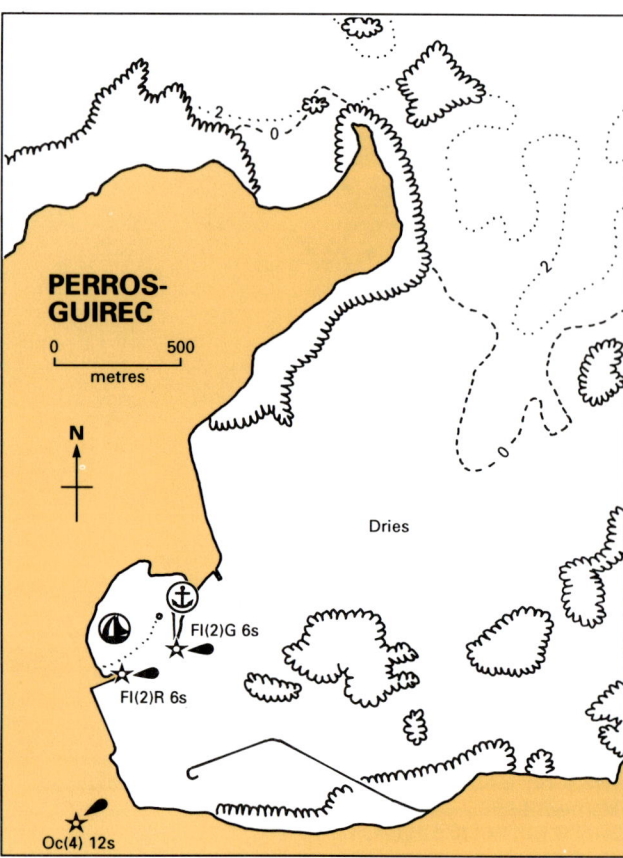

Way Points
48° 51'.7N 3° 31'.5W (W approach) 48° 53'.0N 3° 23'.0W (N approach) CAUTION: The approach is guarded by Les Sept Îles and Île Tomé. Plot your track.
Charts
Admiralty No 3672
Adlard Pilot Pack Vol 3 No 342 and 343
Tides
See p.147 for corrections from Standard Port of St Malo
Harbour Lights
See 1770/1782 p.121
Cautions
1 There are two approaches, E and W, both lit. Both have isolated rocks very near the leading lines, so care is needed.
Berthing
Peros-Guirec offers excellent shelter and a good anchorage off. The marina has 600 berths, maximum 15m LOA, with 50 reserved for visitors. The lock opens between -2HW +1 at springs and -1HW approaching neaps, though it is possible to be locked in for up to three days at neaps. There is at least 2m in the marina.
VHF Ch 9; 16
Telephones
Harbour Master: (96) 23 37 82
Lock Master and Marina: (96) 23 19 03
Medical: (96) 23 20 01
British Consul: (99) 46 26 64
Société des Régates Perrosienne: (96) 91 12 65

	TIME DIFFERENCES				HEIGHT DIFFERENCES (IN METRES)			
PLACE	High Water		Low Water		MHWS	MHWN	MLWN	MLWS
BREST (see page 80)	0000 and 1200	0600 and 1800	0000 and 1200	0600 and 1800	7.5	5.9	3.2	1.6
Morlaix (Chateau du Taureau)	+0100	+0110	+0110	+0100	+1.5	+1.1	+0.3	−0.3
Roscoff	+0055	+0105	+0105	+0100	+1.4	+1.1	+0.2	−0.3
Ile de Batz	+0050	+0105	+0105	+0055	+1.4	+1.1	+0.3	−0.2
L'Aber Vrac'h	+0035	+0030	+0040	+0040	+0.3	+0.2	−0.4	−0.6
Le Conquet	−0005	0000	+0010	0000	−0.3	−0.3	−0.3	−0.2
Camaret	−0010	−0010	−0015	−0010	−0.5	−0.4	−0.4	−0.2
Morgat	−0010	−0010	−0020	−0010	−0.6	−0.5	−0.4	−0.3
Douarnenez	−0015	−0010	−0015	−0010	−0.6	−0.5	−0.4	−0.2
Audierne	−0025	−0030	−0040	−0020	−2.3	−1.8	−1.2	−0.8
Loctudy	−0010	−0030	−0030	−0025	−2.5	−1.9	−1.3	−0.8
Benodet	−0010	−0035	−0040	−0015	−2.6	−2.2	−1.5	−1.0
Concarneau	−0005	−0030	−0030	−0020	−2.5	−2.0	−1.3	−0.8

Morlaix

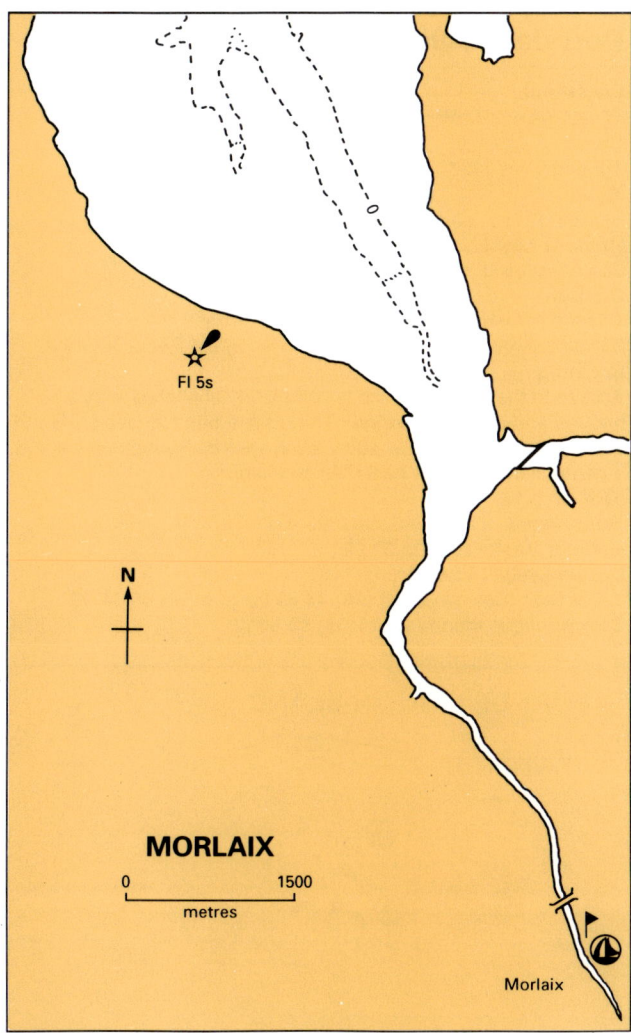

Way Point
48° 43'.0N 3° 53'.5W (1.4M N of entrance)
Charts
Admiralty No 2745
Adlard Coles Pilot Pack Vol 3 No 345 and 346
Tides
See above for corrections from Standard Port of Brest
Harbour Lights
See 1799.9/1800.1 p.121/122

Caution
The approach requires care.
Berthing
The lock opens 1 1/2 hours before, at and 1 hour after HW during daylight, but in the season, probably more often.
VHF Port de Morlaix: Ch 9
Telephones
Harbour Master: (98) 62 13 14
Lockmaster: (98) 88 54 92
Medical: (98) 88 40 22 (Hospital)
British Consul: (99) 46 26 64
YC de Morlaix: (98) 88 38 00

Roscoff and Île de Batz

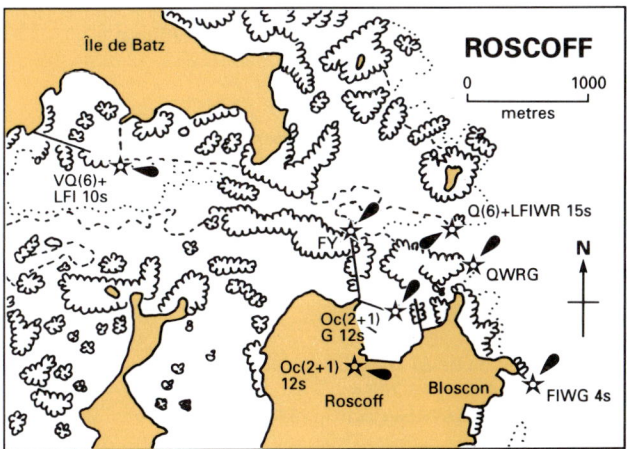

Way Point
48° 45'.3N 3° 56'.5W (from E, 1.8M NNE of entrance to Roscoff)
48° 44'.7N 4° 04'.0W (from W, 5 cables W of entrance to Chenal de l'Île de Batz)
Charts
Admiralty No 2745
Adlard Coles Pilot Pack Vol 3 No 348
Tides
See above for corrections from Standard Port of Brest
Harbour Lights
See 1805/1816.3 p.122
Beacon
Roscoff, Bloscon Jetty Lt 48° 43'.30N 3° 57'.62W BC 304.5 kHz 10M
Cautions
1 Keep clear of the port limits of Bloscon.
2 The stream runs very strongly in the channel, nearly four knots, and 'wind against tide' produces an uncomfortable berth.

3 The whole area is encumberd with isolated rocks and rocky ledges. Great care is needed.

Berthing

Roscoff is a drying harbour, somewhat difficult of access but with good shelter except in strong NE winds; all facilities. Bloscon is a ferry port and closed to yachts (except by special permission from the Harbour Master), though a deep water anchorage is available S of the port limits. On the Île de Batz, there is a small drying harbour, Porz Kernoch, with limited facilities and a ferry service to Roscoff.

VHF Roscoff and Bloscon: Ch 12; 16

Telephones

Harbour Master (Port de Plaisance): (98) 69 76 37
Harbour Master (Roscoff): (98) 61 27 84
Customs: (98) 61 27 86
Medical: (98) 69 71 18 (Doctor)
British Consul: (99) 46 26 64
Cercle Nautique de Roscoff: (98) 69 72 79

L'Aber Vrac'h

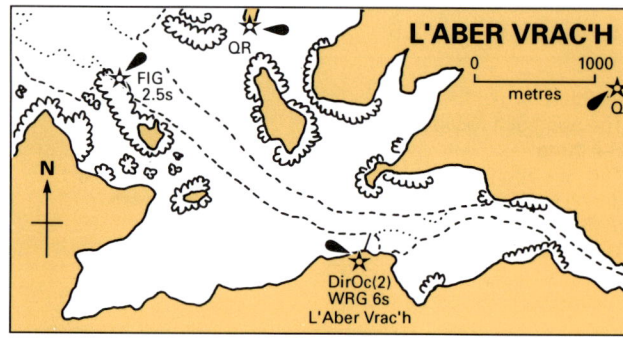

Way Point

48° 37'.6N 4° 38'.4W (W Cardinal Whistle Buoy)

Charts

Admiralty No 1432
Adlard Coles Pilot Pack Vol 3 No 350

Tides

See p.151 for corrections from Standard Port of Brest

Harbour Lights

See 1825/1832 p.122

Cautions

1 There are oyster beds to be avoided.
2 Note the dangers on either side of the approach line.

Berthing

L'Aber Vrac'h provides good shelter, pontoon berths and an anchorage.

VHF L'Aber Vrac'h: Ch 9 (0700 to 2100 local time)

Telephones

Harbour Master: (98) 04 91 62
Customs: (98) 44 35 20
Medical: (98) 04 91 87 (Doctor)
British Consul: (99) 46 26 64
Centre de Voile de l'Aber Vrac'h: (98) 04 90 64

Le Conquet

Way Point

48° 23'.2N 4° 49'.0W (St Pierre pillar buoy (unlit) 2M NW on leading line)

Charts

Admiralty No 3345
Adlard Coles Pilot Pack Vol 3 No 354

Tides

See p.151 for corrections from Standard Port of Brest

Harbour Lights

See 1873/1876 p.122/123

Cautions

1 The streams run strongly across the entrance.

Berthing

Anchor in 2m behind the outer mole, or further up in neaps or with a shallow draft yacht. Do not berth alongside the mole as that is in constant use by the ferry. There are a number of visitors' buoys.

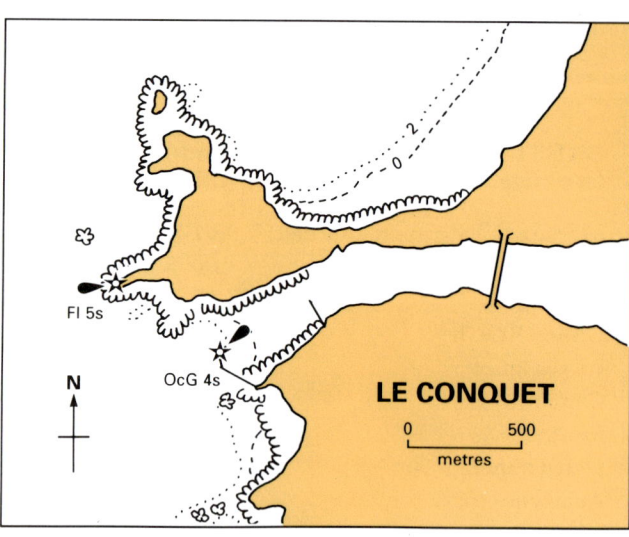

VHF St Mathieu Signal Station: Ch 16; 8

Telephones

Harbour Master: (98) 89 08 07
Medical: (98) 89 01 86 (Doctor)
British Consul: (99) 46 26 64

Port de Moulin-Blanc (Brest)

Way Point

42°22'.8N 4°25'.9W (Moulin Blanc Buoy)

Charts

Admiralty No 3427 and No 3428 (plan)

Tides

Standard Port - see p.80

Harbour Lights

See 0790/0811 p.123

Cautions

1 There is an unmarked wreck off La Cormorandiere.
2 Note the many prohibited anchorages in the Rade de Brest.

Berthing

Access to the marina, which is completely sheltered is by a buoyed and dredged channel. The marina has two basins, North and South with berths for 100 visiting yachts. Reception is at No 1 pontoon in the North basin. All services.

VHF Ch 9,16

Telephones

Harbour Master (98) 02 20 02
Customs (98) 44 35 20
Yacht Club (Bay de Brest) (98) 44 63 32 and (98) 02 11 93
Club Nautique Marine Brest (98) 80 80 80

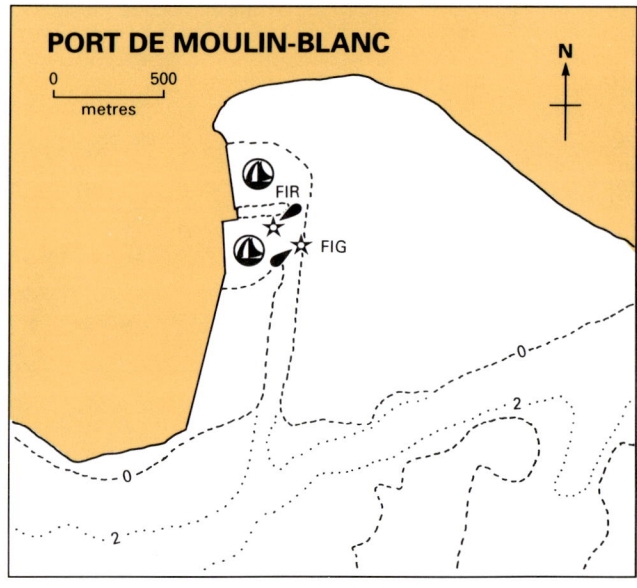

Port de Camaret

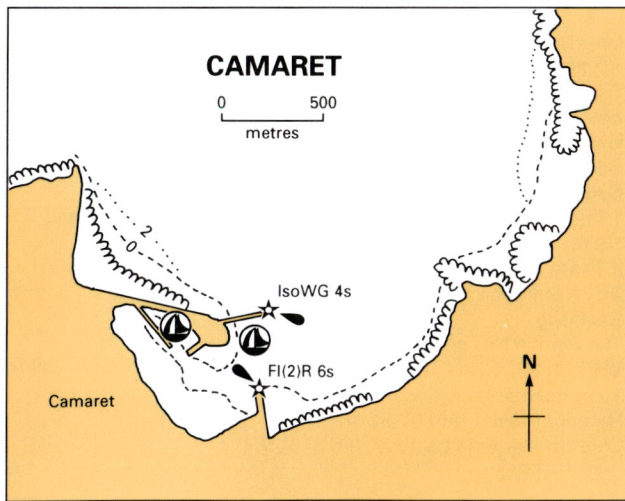

CAMARET

0   500
metres

IsoWG 4s

Fl(2)R 6s

Camaret

N

Way Point
48°17'.2N 4°35'.0W (3 cables NNE of North Mole head)
Charts
Admiralty No 2694 and No 3427 or No 798
Tides
See p.151 for corrections from Standard Port of Brest
Harbour Lights
See 0816/0817 p.123
Caution
1 Anchoring is forbidden within the port except by permission.
Berthing
There are berths for visiting yachts in the Avant-Port (though this is exposed), a number of moorings and some berths in the inner harbour.
VHF Ch 9
Telephones
Harbour Master (98) 27 95 99
Customs (98) 27 93 02
Club Leo-Lagrange (98) 27 90 49 and (98) 27 92 20
Centre APAS (98) 27 93 14 and (98) 27 91 47

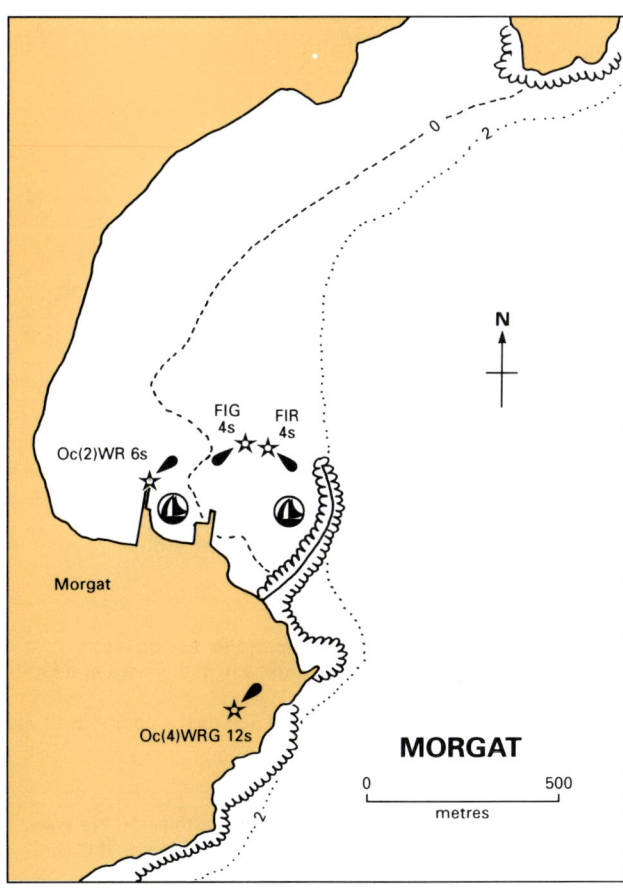

FIG
4s

FIR
4s

Oc(2)WR 6s

N

Morgat

Oc(4)WRG 12s

MORGAT

0   500
metres

Port de Crozon Morgat

Way Point
48°13'.7N 4°29'.0W (4 cables E of harbour entrance)
Charts
Admiralty No 798 (incl plan)
Tides
See p.151 for corrections from Standard Port of Brest
Harbour lights
See 0826/0829 p.123
Caution
1 Anchoring is forbidden within the port.
Berthing
There is a 500 berth marina with 50 places reserved for visitors.
Fuel and slips but limited services otherwise.
VHF Ch 9
Telephones
Harbour Master (98) 27 01 97
Customs (at Camaret) (98) 27 93 02
Centre Nautique Crozon Morgat: (98) 27 01 98

Douarnenez/Tréboul

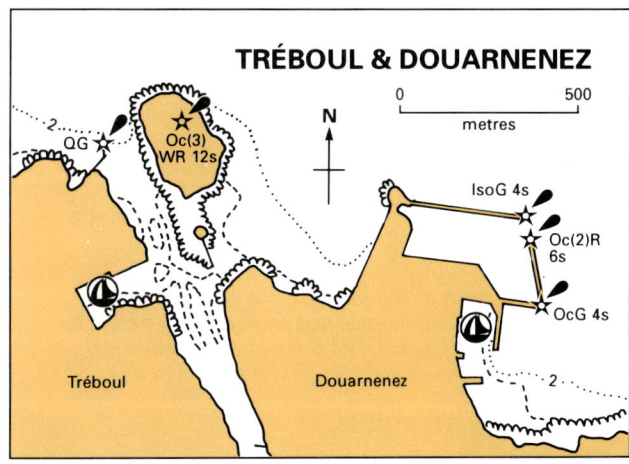

TRÉBOUL & DOUARNENEZ

0   500
metres

QG

Oc(3)
WR 12s

N

IsoG 4s

Oc(2)R
6s

OcG 4s

Tréboul   Douarnenez

Way Point
48°06'.5N 4°20'.2W (2.5 cables NNE of entrance to Grande Passe)
Charts
Admiralty No 798 (incl plan)
Tides
See p.151 for corrections from Standard Port of Brest
Harbour Lights
See 0830/0836 p.123
Cautions
1 There is a 1.8m shoal patch 4 cables NNW of entrance to Grande Passe.
Berthing
There is a 445 berth marina, with 30 berths for visitors, at Tréboul. There are also visitors moorings in the Grande Passe and an anchorage in the Rade de Guet.
VHF Ch 9
Telephones
Harbour Master. Tréboul (98) 74 02 56
Customs (at Quimper) (98) 55 02 19
Medical: (98) 92 25 00 (Hospital)
Yacht Clubs (98) 74 13 79

Port d'Audierne

Way Point
47°59'.1N 4°33'.8W (1M south of Pte de Lervily)
Charts
Admiralty No 2351 and No 3640 (plan)
Tides
See p.151 for corrections from Standard Port of Brest
Harbour Lights
See 0874/0877.1 p.123/124
Cautions
1 The entrance is dangerous in strong onshore winds.

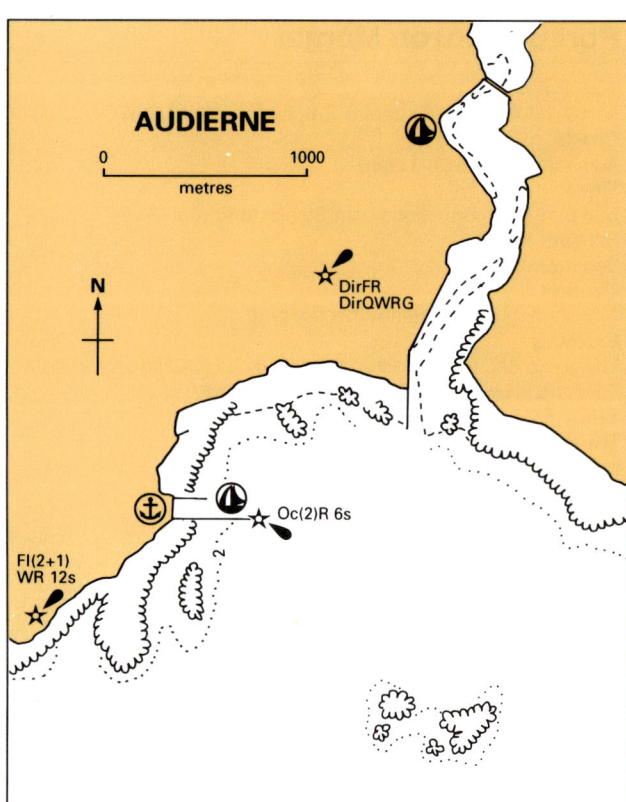

AUDIERNE

0   1000
metres

N

DirFR
DirQWRG

Oc(2)R 6s

Fl(2+1)
WR 12s

2 La Gamette rocks and drying wrecks lie 8 cables SE of the entrance.
Berthing
Anchor in the Anse de Ste Evette, moderate holding and sheltered from W and N winds and largely from S except for swell. Not much room and a lot of moorings. Alternatively, proceed up the river -1.¹/₂HW+1.¹/₂ to the small marina.
Telephones
Harbour Master: (98) 70 03 33
Customs: (98) 70 70 97
Club Nautique de la Baie d'Audienne: (98) 70 21 69

Loctudy

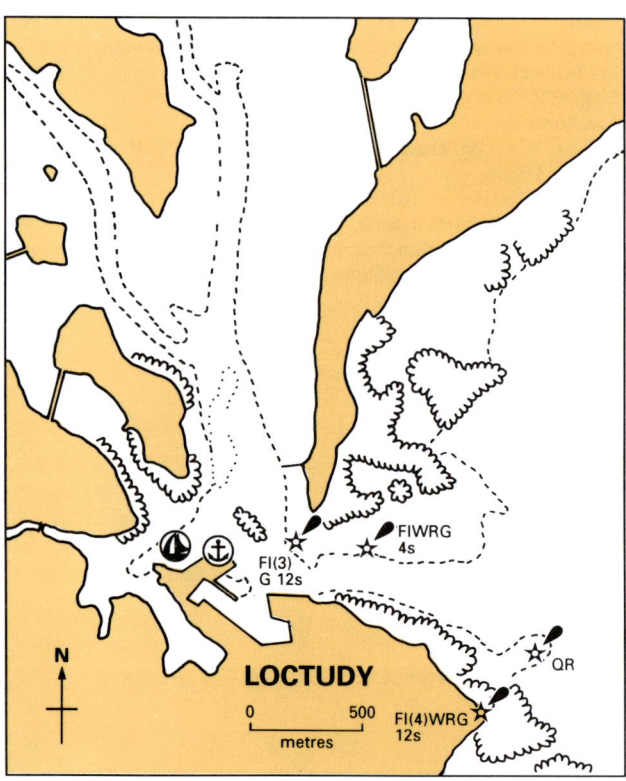

Fl WRG
4s

Fl(3)
G 12s

N

LOCTUDY

0   500
metres

QR

Fl(4)WRG
12s

Way Point
47°50'.0N 4°05.8W (2.5M east of entrance, on Bénodet Leading Line)
Charts
Admiralty No 2351, No 2352 and No 3641 (plan)
Tides
See p.151 for corrections from Standard Port of Brest
Harbour Lights
See 0906/0910 p.124
Cautions
1 Entry and departure restricted to yachts between 1700 and 1800.
2 There are many outlying dangers.
3 The entrance is dangerous in strong onshore winds.
Berthing
The marina has 400 berths and 60 berths for visitors.
VHF Ch 9
Telephones
Harbour Master (98) 87 51 36
Club Nautique de Loctudy (98) 87 92 64

Port de Bénodet

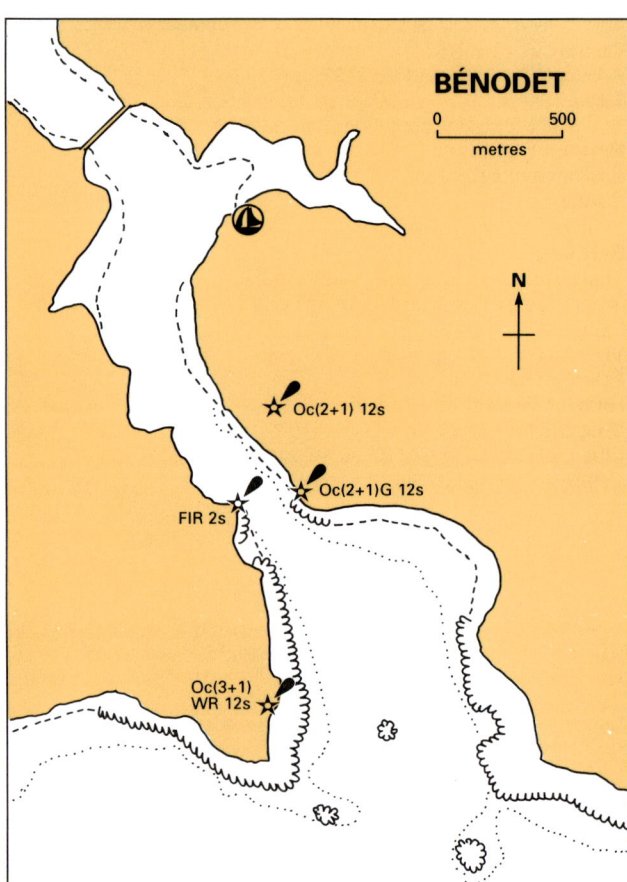

BÉNODET

0   500
metres

N

Oc(2+1) 12s

Oc(2+1)G 12s

Fl R 2s

Oc(3+1)
WR 12s

Way Point
47°50'.0N 4°05'.8W (1.9M SSE of entrance on Leading Line)
Charts
Admiralty No 2351, No 2352 and No 3641 (plan)
Tides
See p.151 for corrections from Standard Port of Brest
Harbour Lights
See 0913.9/0916.2 p.124
Cautions
1 There is a 3 knot speed limit between Pte du Coq and Cornouaillie bridge. Anchoring is forbidden in this area and for about 100m above the bridge.
2 The stream runs strongly especially across the pontoons of Ste Marine marina.
3 There are many outlying dangers.
Berthing
There are marina berths on both sides of the river, on the West bank at Bénodet and on the East bank at Ste Marine. It is

possible to anchor above the bridge, selecting a spot clear of the shipping and with a decent (ie not rock) holding ground. Quimper may be visited by dinghy if the yacht's mast cannot be lowered.
VHF Ch 9 for either Ste Marine or Bénodet
Telephones
Harbour Master (Ste Marine) (98) 56 38 72
Harbour Master (Bénodet) (98) 57 05 78
Customs (at Concarneau) (98) 97 01 73
YC de l'Odet (98) 57 26 09

Port-la-Forêt

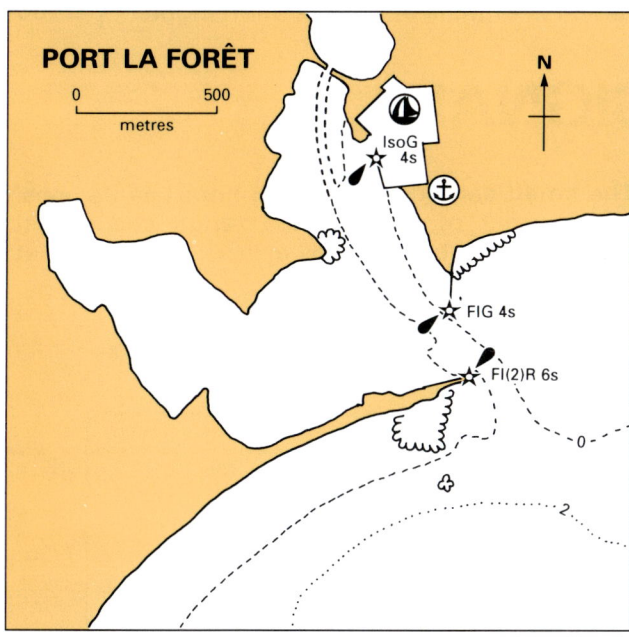

Way Point
47°50'.0N 3°56'.8W (3.6M SSE of Cap-Coz on Concarneau Leading Line)
Charts
Admiralty No 2352 and No 3641 (plan)
Tides
See p.151 for corrections from Standard Port of Brest
Harbour Lights
See 0925/0925.6 p.124
Cautions
1 There are many off lying rocks and a fish farm.
Berthing
There is a marina with 950 berths and 50 moorings, allowing 100 berths for visitors. It is possible to anchor off the beach at Cap Coz except in strong SE to SW winds. All facilities.
VHF Ch 9
Telephones
Harbour Master (98) 56 98 45
Customs (at Concarneau) (98) 97 01 73
Assn Nautique de Port-la-Forêt (98) 56 84 13

Concarneau

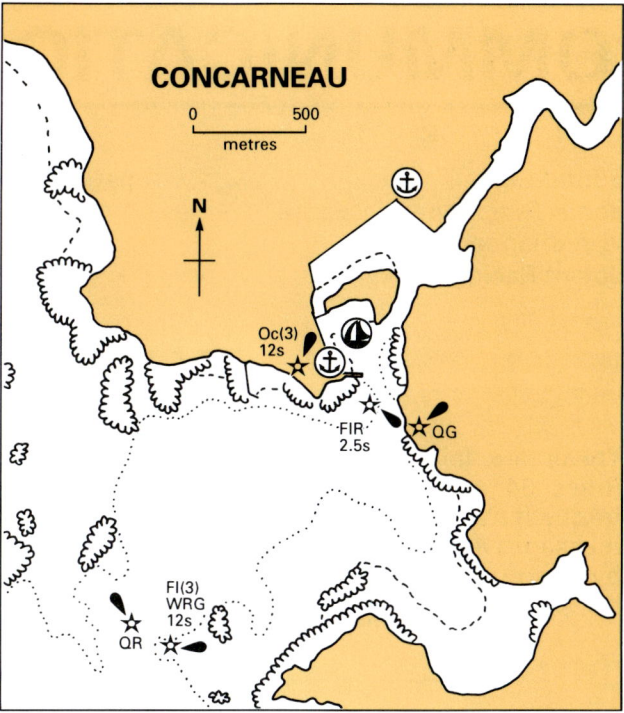

Way Point
47°50'.0N 3°56'.8W (1.8M SSW of Le Cochon and Basse du Chenal beacons)
Charts
Admiralty No 2352 and No 3641 (plan)
Tides
See p.151 for corrections from Standard Port of Brest
Harbour Lights
See 0928/0937 p.124
Cautions
1 There are off lying rocks
Berthing
The marina is in the Avant Port but there is a pontoon for large deep-draft yachts in the less attractive Arrière Port. It is also possible to anchor in the Anse de Kersos, though there are a large number of moorings.
VHF Ch 9
Telephones
Harbour Master (98) 97 57 96
Customs (98) 97 01 73
Sociète Nautique de Concarneau (98) 97 14 84

COMMUNICATIONS AND BUOYAGE

SOUND SIGNALS

These are laid down in Collision Regulations, Rules 34 and 35, and are generally the most frequent means of communicating simple, urgent messages and the most common should be learnt by heart.

The small aerosol type of fog horn has its uses, but is only of very limited range and would probably only be heard by another yacht close at hand.

Short Blast ◄█ : about 1 second   Prolonged Blast ◖████ : about 5 seconds

---

VESSELS IN SIGHT OF ONE ANOTHER

◄█	I am turning to STARBOARD
◄█ ◄█	I am turning to PORT
◄█ ◄█ ◄█	My engines are going ASTERN
◄█ ◄█ ◄█ ◄█ ◄█ (at least)	LOOK OUT

In a narrow channel

◖████ ◖████ ◄█	I intend to overtake on your STARBOARD side
◖████ ◖████ ◄█ ◄█	I intend to overtake on your PORT side
◖████ ◄█ ◖████ ◄█	In response to the above two signals— AGREED (Morse "C"—affirmative)

Approaching a bend in the channel or a harbour wall which restricts visibility

◖████	Look out—I am coming
◖████	Reply to above—so am I

VESSELS IN FOG

◖████	Power vessel under way (2 mins)
◖████ ◖████	Power vessel stopped (2 mins)
◖████ ◄█ ◄█	All the lame ducks—not under command, restricted, sailing, fishing, or towing. (2 mins) (Morse "D"—I am manoeuvring with difficulty)
◖████ ◄█ ◄█ ◄█	Last vessel in tow (immediately after tug signal)
🔔 (5 secs)	At anchor (Bell, every min)
🔔 (5 secs) + (gong) (5 secs)	At anchor over 100 metres (Bell forward, gong aft, every min)
◄█ ◖████ ◄█	At anchor. In addition to above, to warn approaching vessel.

Yachts under 12 metres are not obliged to sound the fog signals listed above, but, if they do not, they MUST make some efficient noise every two minutes.

INTRODUCTION TO RADIO TELEPHONY

Radio sets suitable for small yachts have become so cheap and reliable over the past few years that owners should consider very carefully before not fitting one.

They have the following uses:

MAYDAY calls for help — or to receive and respond to such calls.

PAN PAN calls for assistance or to receive and respond to such calls.

Calls to HM Coastguard or Coast Radio Stations to provide reassurance to relatives and friends ashore, especially in bad weather, and to provide information to Search and Rescue services.

Link telephone calls for private or business purposes.

Race control.

The vast majority of radio sets in use in yachts are VHF (Very High Frequency) with a relatively short range (say 20 miles). MF (Medium Frequency) sets with a much greater range (say 200 miles) are becoming available to meet a relaxed, yachting, specification at prices which make them worth considering for serious offshore work. **Double sideband transmissions are prohibited except for emergency-only equipment operating on 2182 kHz.**

References and further reading

VHF Radio Telephony for Yachtsmen
RYA Publication G22/78 — very concise and useful
Handbook for Radio Operators
HMSO — mostly for big ships, but the standard work
Notices to Ship Wireless Stations
obtainable as Notices to Mariners — complete and up-to-date practical information.

Radio Telephone (Link) Calls

Coast Radio Stations may now be contacted direct on a working frequency. Listen in until you find a free channel, then call. When your call has activated the automatic system, you will hear a series of pips. As soon as a radio officer is free, he will then take your call.

Certain radiotelephone calls may be charged to your home account. Quote YTD and then your home telephone number.

Licences

A yacht with VHF transmitting equipment must have the following licences

A Ship Licence
This is granted by the Home Office after inspection of the equipment by an official of the Post Office.

Authorisation to use Channel 'M' (the Marina channel — 157.850 MHz) obtainable as the Ship Licence with no extra fee or inspection. VHF only.

Applications for any of the above licences should be made to:

The Home Office
Licencing Branch
Radio Regulatory Division
Waterloo Bridge House
London SE1 8UA

The Operator's Certificate of Competence
In the case of a VHF installation this will probably be a 'Restricted Certificate of Competence in Radiotelephony (VHF only)' and must be held by someone on board before the equipment can be properly used. Examinations are now handled by the RYA through centres at Plymouth, Warsash, Cowes and London.

RADIO TELEPHONE PROCEDURE

Brisk, business-like transmissions take up least air-time and are most easily understood. The basis for such transmissions is correct procedure. Operators should take a pride in the workmanlike way they use their sets as in any other aspect of running a yacht.

Listening watch

A listening watch on Ch 16 can be very valuable. Coast Guard weather information and navigation warnings are easily monitored. You will pick up any incoming calls and, most important, any distress calls.

Do's and don'ts

DO
Listen before transmitting to avoid butting in on another transmission. Think of exactly what you want to say — say it and get off the air.

DO NOT
Chat.
Use high power when low power will do.
Continue to call a station ceaselessly. Call twice at an interval of not less than a minute but if you do not get a reply, repeat your call only after an interval of at least three minutes.
Make test calls on Ch 16.

Procedure card

A useful reminder to the operator, who in an emergency might not be trained or experienced, should be provided in the form of a card placed near the set with a brief summary of procedure, the ship's call sign and an example of a distress call.

Phonetic alphabet

Practise using the proper phonetics so that important parts of your messages are transmitted smoothly and accurately.

Examples of procedures

These examples are based on VHF procedure. MF procedure is exactly the same except that MF frequencies are worked instead of VHF channels.

Call sign
> Yachts should identify themselves with their name. If this might cause difficulty due to its unusual character or common use, add the International call sign assigned to the yacht until communications are established and then revert to the yacht's name.
> TRANSMISSIONS WITHOUT IDENTIFICATION ARE FORBIDDEN.

Repeat
> Important parts of the message may be repeated eg
> "There is sev-en metre REPEAT sev-en metre depth of water"

Position
> Use latitude and longitude *or*
> bearing and distance FROM a mark

Bearings
> Use 360° True notation. Though the bearing should be FROM a mark, it does no harm to make this unmistakable as
> "My position is 186 degrees three miles FROM St Catherine's light"
> Of course, in an emergency, you may prefer to reverse this and, if you do, *make it quite clear as:*
> "St Catherine's light bears 006° FROM me"

Time
> Time should be in 24 hour notation and should indicate GMT, BST or whatever.

THIS IS
> is the introduction to the call sign, as
> "THIS IS Dolly Dolly"

OVER
> is the invitation to reply

OUT
> signifies the end of working. Thus the phrase OVER AND OUT is rubbish.

Example
'Dolly' needs a marina berth:
She transmits on Channel 80
> "Mudhole Marina Mudhole Marina—THIS IS Dolly Dolly. OVER"
> "Dolly —THIS IS Mudhole. Over".

> "Mudhole Dolly - I require a berth tonight please - I am
> too six feet REPEAT too six feet long. OVER"
> "Dolly Mudhole — berth Bravo ait REPEAT Bravo ait. OUT"

Example
'Dolly' on passage through Needles Channel.
She transmits on Channel 67
> "Solent Coast Guard - THIS IS Dolly. OVER."
> "Dolly — Solent Coast Guard. OVER."
'Dolly ' reports he intentions and ETA her intended destination.

Example
'Dolly' wishes to make a link telephone call. She calls on a working Channel.
> "Niton Radio Niton Radio THIS IS Dolly Dolly — one link call please. OVER"
> "Dolly THIS IS Niton Radio — Channel 28 (for example) and
> stand by. OVER"
> "Niton Radio THIS IS Dolly — Channel 28. OVER"
'Dolly' now waits for Niton Radio to call her on Channel 28.
> "Dolly THIS IS Niton Radio - what number do you want? OVER"
> "Niton Radio THIS IS Dolly MIKE OSCAR LIMA WHISKEY —
> I have a call for 071-493 5252. OVER"
> "Dolly THIS ID Niton Radio - stand by. OVER"
Niton will then set up the call and advise 'Dolly' when ready.

Traffic List

Listen on Channel 16 to any Coast Radio Station within range to hear if there is a call for you. The list is broadcast at the times shown in Notices to Ship Wireless Stations. Example
> "All ships THIS IS Niton Radio Niton Radio — listen for my traffic list on Channel 28."
Switch to Channel 28 and hear:
> "All ships THIS IS Niton Radio Niton Radio — I have traffic for the following ships — Annie Oakley — Champagne — (and so on using the ship's name or her call sign). OUT"
If you hear your name, call the Coast Radio Station on a working Channel.

Garbled calls

If you are trying to establish communications with or expecting a call from a Coast Radio Station and hear a garbled message which you think might be yours, do not reply — wait until the transmission is clear and understood.

If you hear someone calling you but cannot identify the caller, reply
> "Station calling Dolly — Station calling Dolly — THIS IS Dolly — SAY AGAIN. OVER"

DISTRESS PROCEDURE

A radio transmitter is of special value in emergency but it is at such times that proper procedure becomes even more important.

MF Distress frequency

The distress and calling frequency is 2182 kHz. All transmissions on 2182 kHz, except for Distress and Urgency communications, must cease during the three minute 'silence periods' commencing at the hour and half hour.

VHF Distress channel

Channel 16 is used for distress, safety and calling. There are no silence periods on Channel 16 as there are on the medium frequency 2182 kHz.

Navigational warnings

Navigational warnings are transmitted as follows:

Station	Ch	Times GMT
Hastings	07	0033, 0433, 0833, 1233, 1633, 2033
Niton	28	0233, 0633, 1033, 1433, 1833, 2233
Weymouth Bay	05	0233, 0633, 1033, 1433, 1833, 2233
Start Point	26	0033, 0433, 0833, 1233, 1633, 2033
Pendennis	62	0033, 0433, 0833, 1233, 1633, 2033
Lands End	27	0033, 0433, 0833, 1233, 1633, 2033
Scillies	61	0033, 0433, 0833, 1233, 1633, 2033

Listening watch

Yachts should maintain a listening watch on Channel 16 VHF or 2182 kHz MF, especially during the silence period.

HM Coastguard keeps a constant distress watch on Channel 16 at the Centres listed below after which Channel 67 should be used. UK Post Office Radio Stations provide a constant distress watch on 2182 kHz.

MRSC Solent – tel (0705) 552100
MRSC Portland – tel (0305) 820441
MRSC Brixham – tel (08045) 58292
MRCC Falmouth – tel (0326) 317575

Coastguard VHF DF

Coastguard VHF DF is provided to assist in locating vessels in distress. The following stations are in operation:

Newhaven	50°47'N 00°03'E	Ch 67
Fairlight	50°52'N 00°39'E	Ch 67
Selsey Bill	50°44'N 00°48'W	Ch 67
Stenbury Down	50°37'N 01°15'W	Ch 67
Hengistbury Head	50°43'N 01°46'W	Ch 67
Grove Point	50°33'N 02°25'W	Ch 67
Berry Head	50°24'N 03°29'W	Ch 67
East Prawle	50°13'N 03°42'W	Ch 67
Rame Head	50°19'N 04°13'W	Ch 67
Trevose Head	50°33'N 05°02'W	Ch 67
Pendeen	50°08'N 05°38'W	Ch 67
St.Mary's, Isle of Scilly	49°56'N 06°18'W	Ch 67
Guernsey	49°26'N 02°36'W	Ch 67
Jersey	49°11'N 02°14'W	Ch 82

Distress call

The signal is MAYDAY and is given absolute priority over all other transmissions.

Example

Note the PROCEDURE WORDS IN CAPITALS
"MAYDAY MAYDAY MAYDAY — THIS IS Dolly Dolly Dolly — MAYDAY Dolly — close by Atherfield Ledge[1] — am aground[2] — require lifeboat or helicopter[3] — am firing red flares[4]. OVER"
[1] Position
[2] Nature of distress
[3] Assistance required
[4] Other information useful to rescuers

Acknowledgement of distress message

If a yacht hears a distress call, the sensible thing is to wait to see what acknowledgement is heard from other ships, Coast Radio Station or Coastguard. If no acknowledgement is heard, you have to decide whether you can be of any direct assistance without hazarding your own vessel or whether to re-transmit the distress call as a MAYDAY RELAY.

If you can be of any assistance, acknowledge the call and do what you can to help. For example:
"MAYDAY Dolly Dolly Dolly — THIS IS Flame Flame Flame — I see your flares and will be with you in too zero minutes. OVER"

MAYDAY RELAY example

"MAYDAY RELAY MAYDAY RELAY MAYDAY RELAY — THIS IS Flame Flame Flame — MAYDAY Dolly — close by Atherfield Ledge — aground — require lifeboat or helicopter — firing red flares. OVER"

URGENCY AND SAFETY

When serious and immediate danger threatens but a MAYDAY is not justified, the urgency signal PAN PAN — PAN PAN — PAN PAN must be used. Transmitted on Channel 16, it takes priority immediately behind a MAYDAY message. As for example:
"PAN PAN — PAN PAN — PAN PAN — all stations all stations — THIS IS Dolly Dolly Dolly — wun ait zero Start Point fife miles — dismasted and require tow. OVER"
PAN PAN calls for medical advice may be linked directly to a Doctor or hospital.

A navigational warning or other safety signal may be preceded by SÉCURITÉ (pronounced SAY-CURE-E-TAY) and after the initial call, a working frequency is used.
As for example, first on Channel 16:
"SECURITE SECURITE SECURITE — all stations all stations — THIS IS Hastings Radio Hastings Radio — Navigational warning — change to Channel 7"
then on Channel 7
"SECURITE SECURITE SECURITE — all stations all stations — THIS IS Hastings Radio Hastings Radio — Rye Harbour East Pierhead leading lights are damaged and out of action until further notice. OUT"

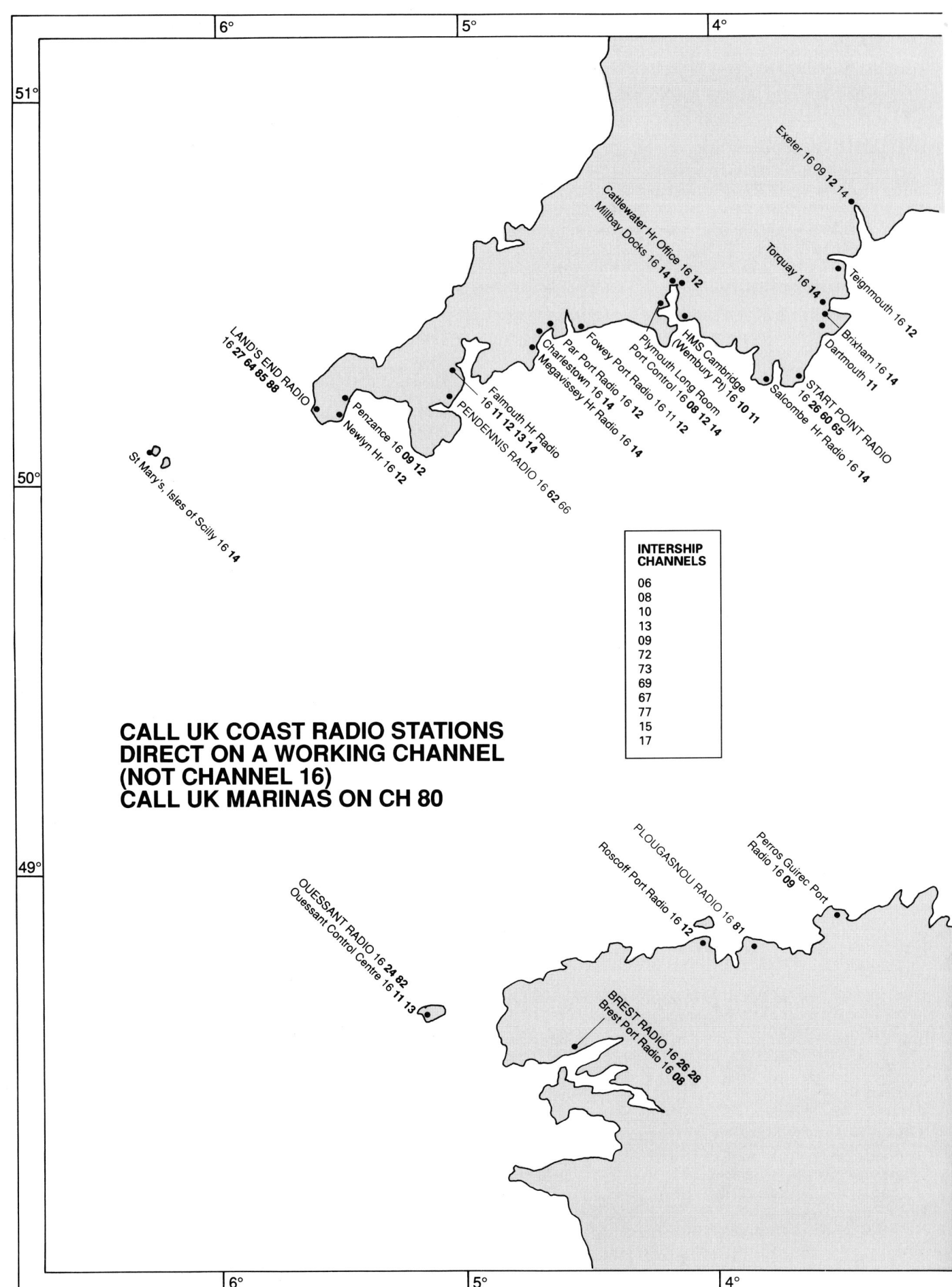

Exeter 16 09 **12 14**

Cattlewater Hr Office 16 **12**
Millbay Docks 16 **14**

Torquay 16 **14**

Teignmouth 16 **12**

Brixham 16 **14**

Dartmouth **11**

HMS Cambridge
(Wembury Pt)
Plymouth Long Room
Port Control 16 **08 12 14**
Port Control 16 11 **12**

LAND'S END RADIO
16 **27 64 85 88**

START POINT RADIO
16 **26 60 65**

Salcombe Hr Radio 16 **14**

Fowey Port Radio 16 **12**
Par Port Radio 16 **14**
Charlestown 16 **12**
Megavissey Hr Radio 16 **14**

Penzance 16 **09 12**
Newlyn Hr 16 **12**

Falmouth Hr Radio
16 **11 12 13 14**
PENDENNIS RADIO 16 **62** 66

St Mary's, Isles of Scilly 16 **14**

INTERSHIP CHANNELS

06
08
10
13
09
72
73
69
67
77
15
17

**CALL UK COAST RADIO STATIONS
DIRECT ON A WORKING CHANNEL
(NOT CHANNEL 16)
CALL UK MARINAS ON CH 80**

PLOUGASNOU RADIO 16 **81**

Perros Guirec Port
Radio 16 **09**

Roscoff Port Radio 16 **12**

OUESSANT RADIO 16 **24 82**
Ouessant Control Centre 16 **11 13**

BREST RADIO 16 **26 28**
Brest Port Radio 16 **08**

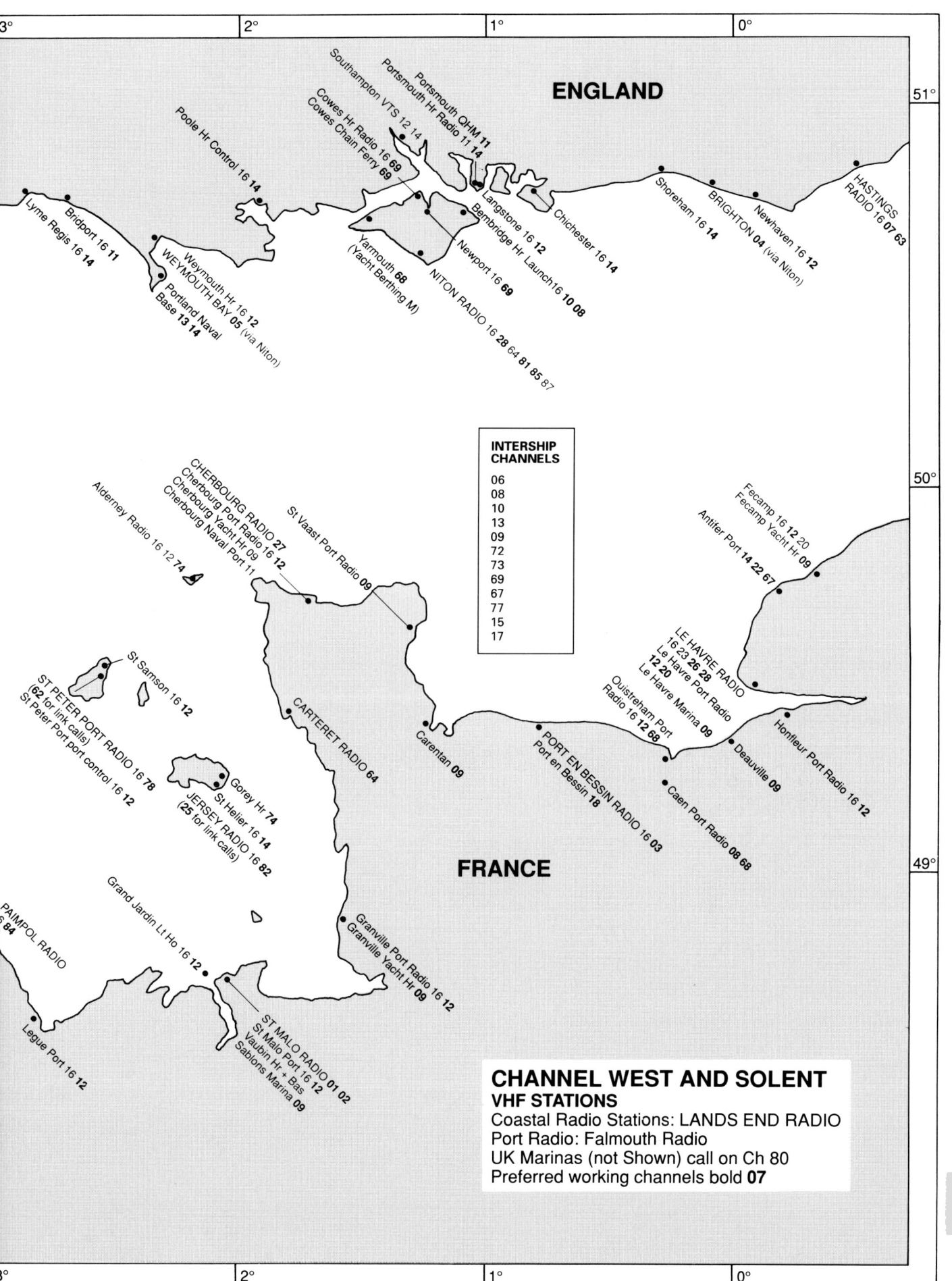

ENGLAND

51°

Poole Hr Control 16 **14**

Southampton VTS 12 14
Cowes Hr Radio 16 **69**
Cowes Chain Ferry **69**
Portsmouth Hr Radio 11 **14**
Portsmouth QHM **11**
Langstone 16 **12**
Chichester 16 **14**

Shoreham 16 **14**
BRIGHTON **04** (via Niton)
Newhaven 16 **12**
HASTINGS RADIO 16 **07 63**

Lyme Regis 16 **14**
Bridport 16 **11**
Weymouth Hr 16 **12**
WEYMOUTH BAY **05** (via Niton)
Portland Naval Base **13 14**
Yarmouth **68** (Yacht Berthing M)
Bembridge Hr Launch 16 **10 08**
Newport 16 **69**
NITON RADIO 16 **28** 64 **81 85** 87

50°

INTERSHIP
CHANNELS

06
08
10
13
09
72
73
69
67
77
15
17

Alderney Radio 16 12 74

CHERBOURG RADIO **27**
Cherbourg Port Radio 16 **12**
Cherbourg Yacht Hr 09
Cherbourg Naval Port 11

St Vaast Port Radio 09

Fecamp 16 **12** 20
Fecamp Yacht Hr **09**

Antifer Port **14 22** 67

LE HAVRE RADIO 16 23 **26 28**
Le Havre Port Radio **12 20**
Le Havre Marina **09**
Le Havre **20**

St Samson 16 **12**

ST PETER PORT RADIO 16 **78** (**62** for link calls)
St Peter Port port control 16 **12**

CARTERET RADIO **64**

Carentan 09

Ouistreham Port Radio 16 **12 68**

Honfleur Port Radio 16 **12**

Deauville **09**

PORT EN BESSIN RADIO 16 **03**
Port en Bessin **18**

Caen Port Radio 08 **68**

Gorey Hr **74**
St Helier 16 **14**
JERSEY RADIO 16 **82** (**25** for link calls)

FRANCE

49°

PAIMPOL RADIO 16 **84**

Grand Jardin Lt Ho 16 **12**

Granville Port Radio 16 **12**
Granville Yacht Hr **09**

Legue Port 16 **12**

ST MALO RADIO 16 **01 02**
St Malo Port 16 **12**
Vaubin Hr + Bas Sablons Marina **09**

CHANNEL WEST AND SOLENT
VHF STATIONS
Coastal Radio Stations: LANDS END RADIO
Port Radio: Falmouth Radio
UK Marinas (not Shown) call on Ch 80
Preferred working channels bold **07**

SOLENT RACING MARKS

	Lat N ° '	Lat W ° '
Air Canada	50 47.30	01 16.75
Beken	50 45.45	01 19.40
Bembridge Ledge by	50 41.11	01 02.75
Berthon	50 44.18	01 29.13
Bob Kemp	50 45.15	01 09.55
Bowring	50 47.28	01 12.00
Bridge	50 39.59	01 37.20
Browndown	50 46.54	01 10.87
Cathead	50 50.59	01 19.18
Champagne Mumm	50 45.60	01 23.03
Chilling	50 49.17	01 17.38
Clipper	50 48.41	01 15.65
Cutter	50 49.47	01 16.83
Daks Simpson	50 45.50	01 14.30
DB Marine	50 46.13	01 13.00
Deck	50 48.60	01 16.57
Durns	50 45.40	01 25.80
East Bramble	50 47.20	01 13.55
East Knoll	50 47.93	01 16.76
East Lepe	50 46.09	01 20.81
East Winner	50 45.07	01 00.00
Elephant	50 44.60	01 21.80
Frigate	50 46.10	01 22.10
Gurnard	50 46.18	01 18.76
Gurnard Ledge	50 45.48	01 20.50
Hamstead Ledge	50 43.83	01 26.10
Hill Head	50 48.02	01 15.92
Hook	50 49.48	01 18.21
Horse Elbow	50 44.23	01 03.80
Jackson	50 44.40	01 28.05
Jardines	50 48.10	01 14.55
Jib	50 52.93	01 22.95
Kelvin Hughes	50 47.30	01 14.50
Lucas	50 46.24	01 08.67
Marina Developments	50 46.12	01 16.55
Mark	50 49.55	01 18.90
Meon	50 49.12	01 15.63
Mother Bank	50 45.46	01 11.13
Nab Tower	50 40.05	00 57.06
Newtown	50 44.15	01 23.70
Norris	50 45.94	01 15.42
North East Gurnard	50 47.04	01 19.33
North East Ryde Middle	50 46.18	01 11.80
North East Shingles	50 41.94	01 33.32
North Head	50 42.64	01 35.42
North Ryde Middle	50 46.57	01 14.28
North Thorn	50 47.88	01 17.75
Outer Spit	50 45.55	01 05.40
Peel Bank	50 45.47	01 13.25
Prince Consort	50 46.38	01 17.48
Quinnell	50 47.03	01 19.78
Ratsey	50 47.63	01 13.57
Reach	50 49.03	01 17.56
Royal London	50 46.55	01 21.37
Royal Thames	50 47.78	01 19.17
Saltmead	50 44.49	01 22.95
Sconce	50 42.50	01 31.35
Seascope	50 47.23	01 15.82
South Bramble	50 46.95	01 17.65
South East Ryde Middle	50 45.90	01 12.00
South Ryde Middle	50 46.10	01 14.07
South West Shingles	50 39.44	01 37.28
Spanker	50 47.08	01 17.99
Spit Sand Area		
Alpha	50 46.40	01 07.80
Beta	50 46.80	01 07.25
Delta	50 46.12	01 06.33
Echo	50 46.05	01 05.66
Gamma	50 46.48	01 05.87
Starting Buoy	50 47.05	01 06.68
Sposa	50 49.65	01 17.51
Sunsail	50 46.40	01 15.00
Tesco	50 45.08	01 27.25
Thorn Knoll	50 47.47	01 18.35
Trap (approximate only)	50 46.13	01 17.50
Warden	50 41.45	01 33.47
Warner	50 43.83	01 03.90
West Bramble	50 47.15	01 18.57
West Knoll	50 47.52	01 17.70
West Lepe	50 45.20	01 24.00
West Ryde Middle	50 46.45	01 15.70
Yarmouth No.2	50 42.72	01 29.53

Symbols		
⊡	Yarmouth No.2	Full Stop
%	Berthon	Percent
☆	Tesco	Star
$	Hamstead Ledge	Dollar
A	West Lepe	
B	Champagne Mumm	
C	Saltmead	
D	Frigate	
E	Elephant	
F	Royal London	
G	East Lepe	
H	Gurnard Ledge	
J	Quinnell	
K	Beken	
L	Royal Thames	
M	Gurnard	
N	Spanker	
O	South Bramble	
P	Prince Consort	
Q	West Knoll	
R	East Knoll	
T	Deck	
U	Marina Developments	
V	Air Canada	
W	Hill Head	
X	Norris	
Y	Clipper	
1	West Ryde Middle	
2	Seascope	
3	Daks Simpson	
4	Jardines	
5	Ratsey	
6	South Ryde Middle	
7	North Ryde Middle	
8	East Bramble	
9	Peel Bank	
◣	DB Marine	Steep Hill
£	Bowring	Pound
↗	South East Ryde Middle	SE Arrow
↘	North East Ryde Middle	NE Arrow
♡	Browndown	Heart
÷	Mother Bank	Divide
=	Bob Kemp	Equals
↑	Meon	One Way
&	Outer Spit	Ampersand
♣	Warner	Club
Ø	Sunsail	Zero
❖	Lucas	Chequer
♂	Kelvin Hughes	Mars

INTERNATIONAL CODE

* Signals with letters marked * when made by sound may only be made in compliance with
the Collision Regulations, Rules 34 and 35

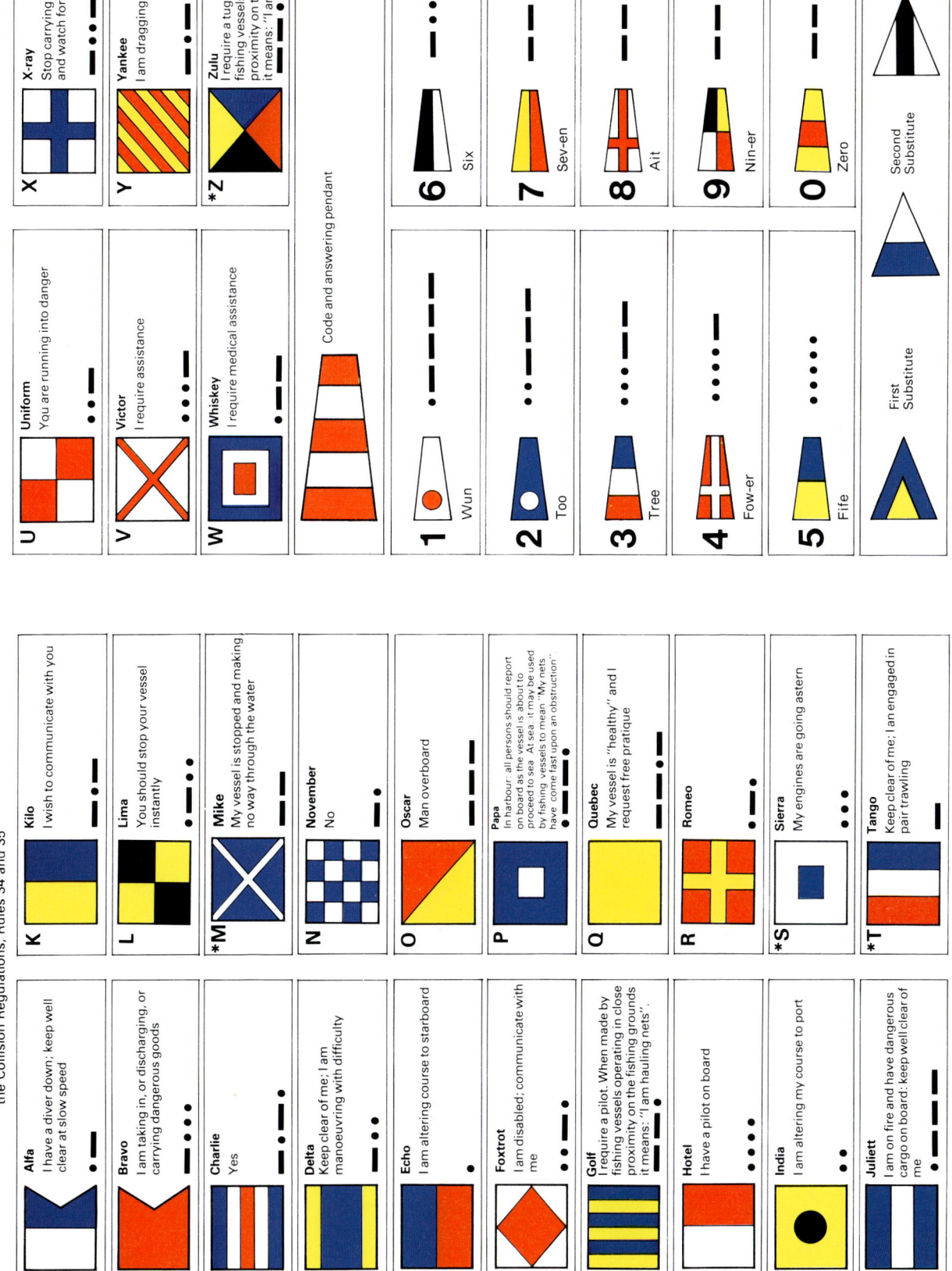

A — Alfa — I have a diver down; keep well clear at slow speed

*B — Bravo — I am taking in, or discharging, or carrying dangerous goods

*C — Charlie — Yes

*D — Delta — Keep clear of me; I am manoeuvring with difficulty

*E — Echo — I am altering course to starboard

F — Foxtrot — I am disabled; communicate with me

*G — Golf — I require a pilot. When made by fishing vessels operating in close proximity on the fishing grounds it means: "I am hauling nets".

*H — Hotel — I have a pilot on board

*I — India — I am altering my course to port

J — Juliett — I am on fire and have dangerous cargo on board: keep well clear of me

K — Kilo — I wish to communicate with you

L — Lima — You should stop your vessel instantly

*M — Mike — My vessel is stopped and making no way through the water

N — November — No

O — Oscar — Man overboard

P — Papa — In harbour: all persons should report on board as the vessel is about to proceed to sea. At sea: it may be used by fishing vessels to mean "My nets have come fast upon an obstruction".

Q — Quebec — My vessel is "healthy" and I request free pratique

R — Romeo

*S — Sierra — My engines are going astern

*T — Tango — Keep clear of me; I am engaged in pair trawling

U — Uniform — You are running into danger

V — Victor — I require assistance

W — Whiskey — I require medical assistance

Code and answering pendant

X — X-ray — Stop carrying out your intentions and watch for my signals

Y — Yankee — I am dragging my anchor

*Z — Zulu — I require a tug. When made by fishing vessels operating in close proximity on the fishing grounds it means: "I am shooting nets"

1 — Wun

2 — Too

3 — Tree

4 — Fow-er

5 — Fife

6 — Six

7 — Sev-en

8 — Ait

9 — Nin-er

0 — Zero

First Substitute

Second Substitute

Third Substitute

163

IALA SYSTEM 'A'

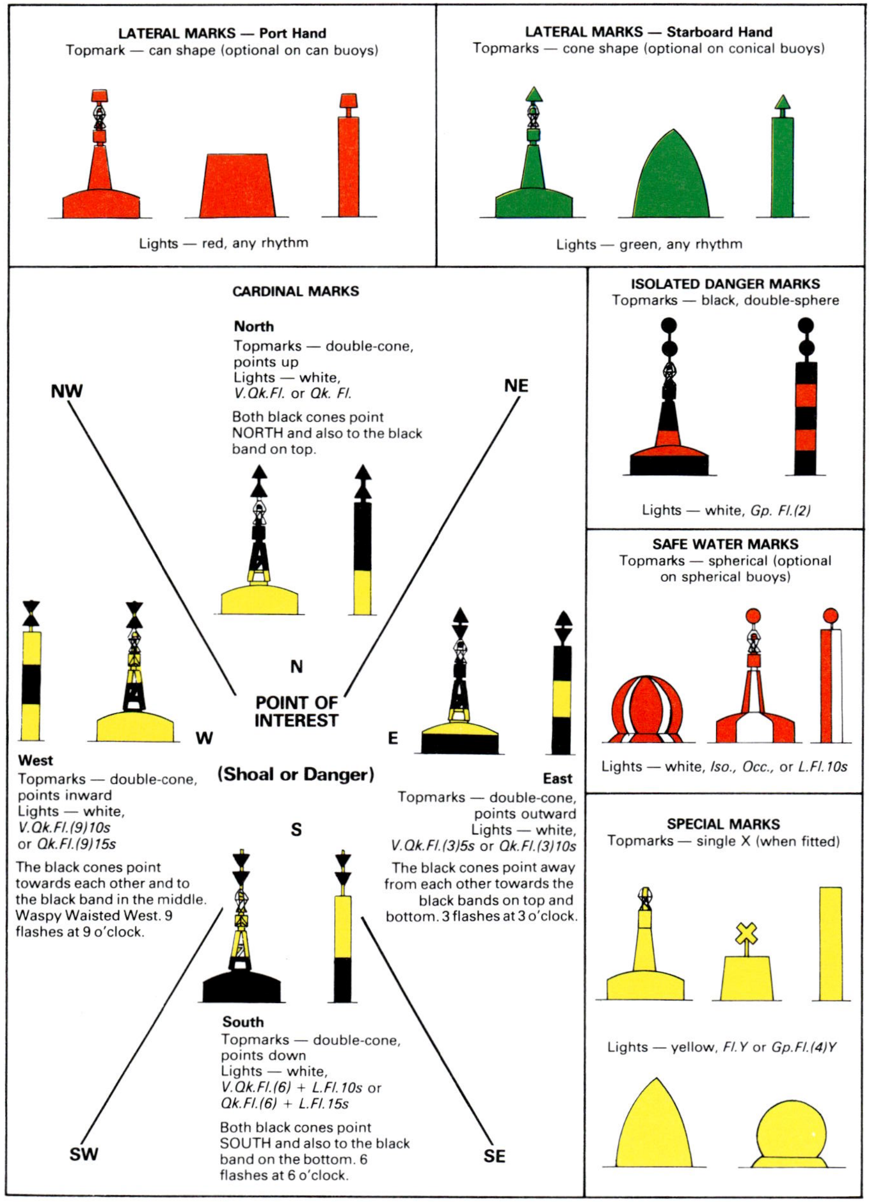

THE I.A.L.A. MARITIME BUOYAGE SYSTEM 'A'

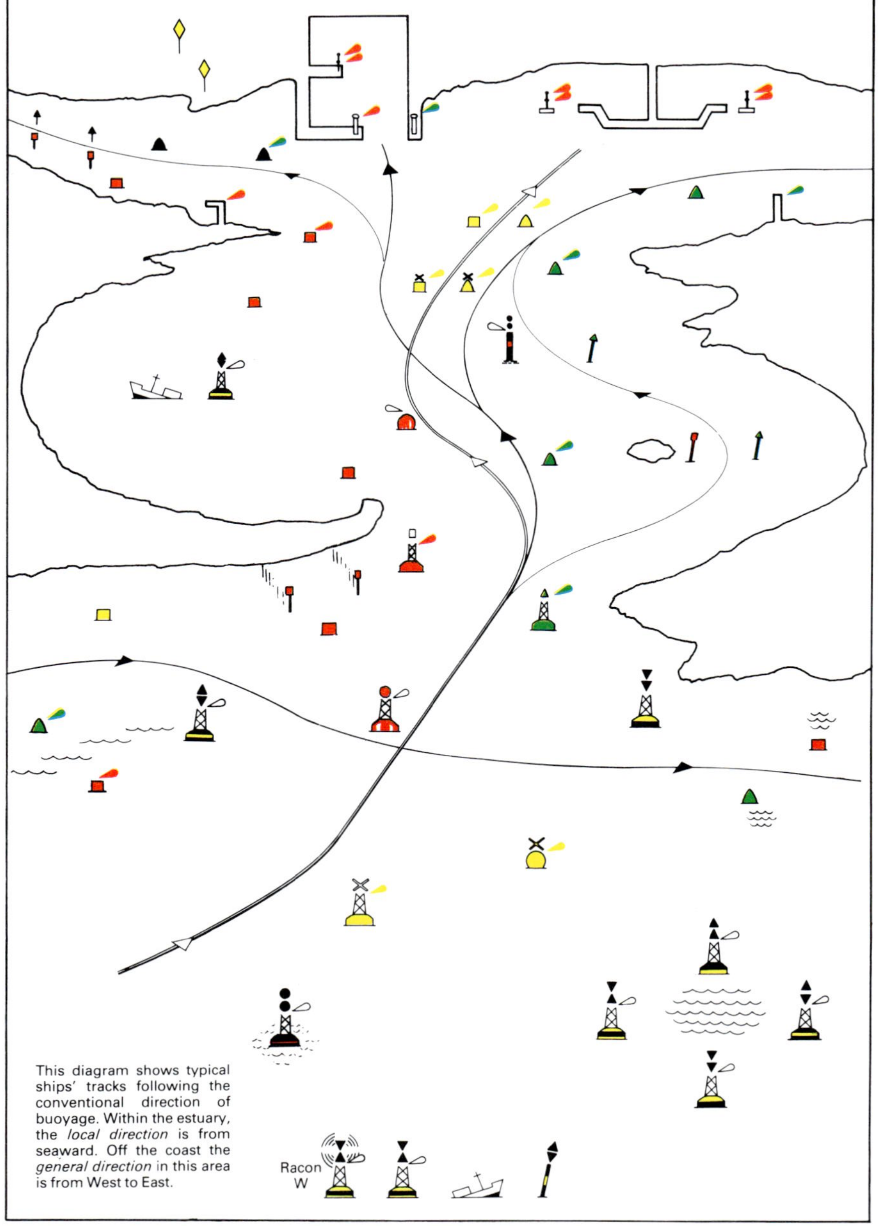

This diagram shows typical ships' tracks following the conventional direction of buoyage. Within the estuary, the *local direction* is from seaward. Off the coast the *general direction* in this area is from West to East.

Racon W

LATERAL MARKS — Port Hand
Topmark — can shape (optional on can buoys)

Lights — red, any rhythm

LATERAL MARKS — Starboard Hand
Topmarks — cone shape (optional on conical buoys)

Lights — green, any rhythm

ISOLATED DANGER MARKS
Topmarks — black, double-sphere

Lights — white, Gp. Fl.(2)

SAFE WATER MARKS
Topmarks — spherical (optional on spherical buoys)

Lights — white, Iso., Occ., or L.Fl.10s

SPECIAL MARKS (when fitted)
Topmark — single X

Lights — yellow, Fl.Y or Gp.Fl.(4)Y

CARDINAL MARKS

POINT OF INTEREST (Shoal or Danger)

NE   N   NW   W   SW   S   SE   E

North
Topmarks — double-cone, points up
Lights — white,
V.Qk.Fl. or Qk. Fl.
Both black cones point NORTH and also to the black band on top.

East
Topmarks — double-cone, points outward
Lights — white,
V.Qk.Fl.(3)5s or Qk.Fl.(3)10s
The black cones point away from each other towards the black bands on top and bottom. 3 flashes at 3 o'clock.

South
Topmarks — double-cone, points down
Lights — white,
V.Qk.Fl.(6) + L.Fl.10s or
Qk.Fl.(6) + L.Fl.15s
Both black cones point SOUTH and also to the black band on the bottom. 6 flashes at 6 o'clock.

West
Topmarks — double-cone, points inward
Lights — white,
V.Qk.Fl.(9)10s
or Qk.Fl.(9)15s
The black cones point towards each other and to the black band in the middle. Waspy Waisted West. 9 flashes at 9 o'clock.

164

LIGHTS AND SHAPES

These are specified in the Collision Regulations and the most common ones are shown below.
They may be combined together e.g. a restricted tug.

lights	shape	indicates	If risk of collision exists, action to be taken by	
			sailing vessel	power vessel
(white, white, red)		Towing vessel (Port side)	Stand on (or Rule 17)	Keep clear (Rule 15)
(white white white)	◆	Towing vessel length of tow over 200m (Starboard side)	Stand on (or Rule 17)	Stand on (or Rule 17)
(red white red, green)	● ◆ ●	Restricted vessel (plus usual lights if making way)	Keep clear (Rule 18)	Keep clear (Rule 18)
(white, white red red)	▐	Vessel constrained by her draught (Starboard side)	Keep clear (Rule 18)	Keep clear (Rule 18)
(white, red red)	● ●	Vessel not under command (plus usual lights if making way)	Keep clear (Rule 18)	Keep clear (Rule 18)
Proper power lights	▶	Sailing vessel under sail AND power	Stand on	Apply power to power rules
	●	Vessel at anchor	Keep clear	Keep clear
	(blue/white flag)	Diving	Keep clear	Keep clear
	(signal flags)	As appropriate	Slow down when passing	Slow down when passing

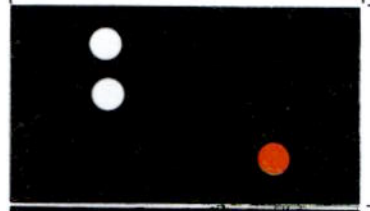

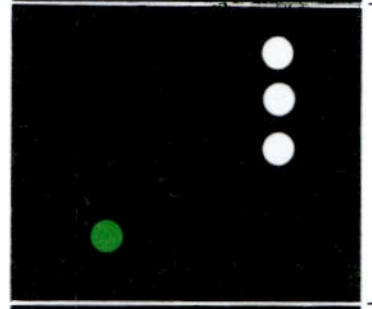

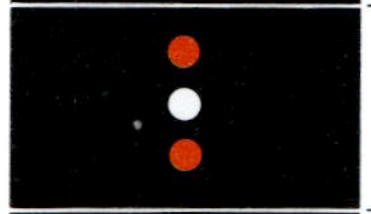

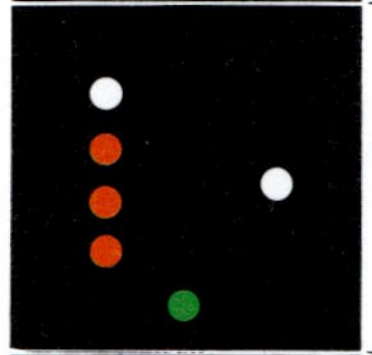

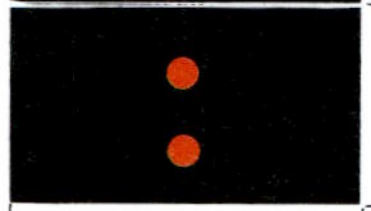

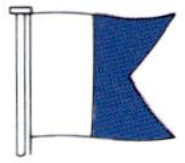

lights	shape	indicates	If risk of collision exists, action to be taken by	
			sailing vessel	power vessel
(red)		Sailing vessel (Port side)	Apply Rule 12	Keep clear (Rule 18)
(green)		Sailing vessel (Starboard side)	Apply Rule 12	Keep clear (Rule 18)
(red, green)		Sailing vessel (Head-on)	Apply Rule 12	Keep clear (Rule 18)
(white)		Stern light of any vessel (Probably, but may be many other things)	Keep clear (Rule 13)	Keep clear (Rule 13)
(white, red)		Power vessel under 50 m (Port side)	Stand on (or Rule 17)	Keep clear (Rule 15)
(white, red)		Power vessel (Port side) *Notice that the foremost white is the lower*	Stand on (or Rule 17)	Keep clear (Rule 15)
(green, white)		Power vessel under 50 m (Starboard side)	Stand on (or Rule 17)	Stand on (or Rule 17)
(white, green)		Power vessel (Starboard side) *Notice that the foremost white is the lower*	Stand on (or Rule 17)	Stand on (or Rule 17)
(white white, red)		Power vessel (Head-on)	Stand on (or Rule 17)	TURN TO STARBOARD (Rule 14)
(green white, white)	⧓ or (net shape) if below 20 m	Trawler (Starboard side)	Keep clear (Rule 18)	Keep clear (Rule 18)
(red white)		Fishing vessel (Not making way)	Keep clear (Rule 18)	Keep clear (Rule 18)

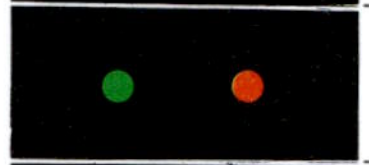

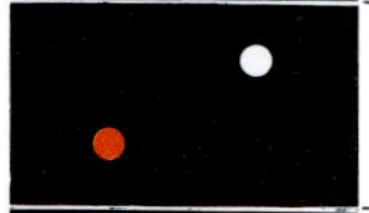

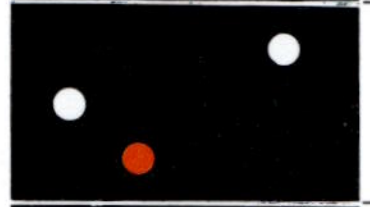

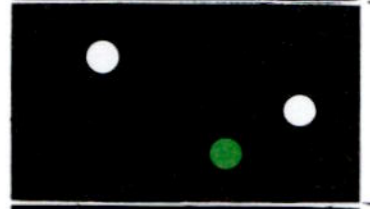

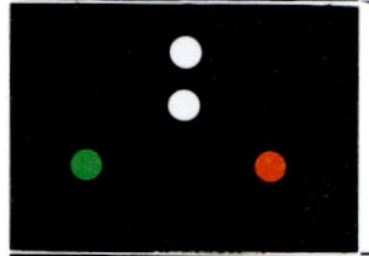

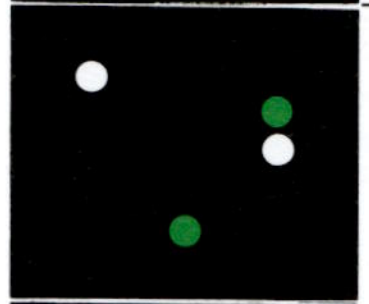

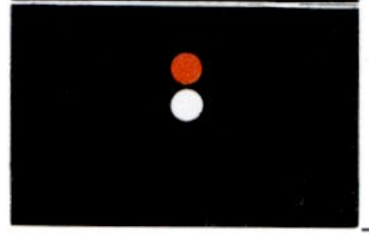

165

LIGHTS AND SHAPES TO BE CARRIED BY YACHTS

Lights

Definitions (Rule 21):

Masthead light: White light from right ahead to
(motor yachts or 22½° abaft the beam on either
sailing yachts side
under power)

Sidelight: Red to port and green to
(all yachts) starboard from right ahead to
22½° abaft the beam

Sternlight: White light from 67½° from
(all yachts) right aft on either side

Rule 22 carefully specifies the visibility of these lights, but for yachts below 20 metres, the sensible light is not the minimum required, but one which enables you to be seen.

Suitable wattages are as follows:

Coloured lights: 25 watts
White lights: 10 watts

It is, of course, important to keep the batteries supplying these lights fully charged and to ensure that the cables used are not so thin as to reduce the voltage excessively between the battery and the light.

Strobe lights are not permitted.

Shapes

All vessels must carry a black ball (which might double as a fender) to act as a day signal when they are at anchor. Sailing yachts with auxiliaries must carry a black cone for use when motor sailing.

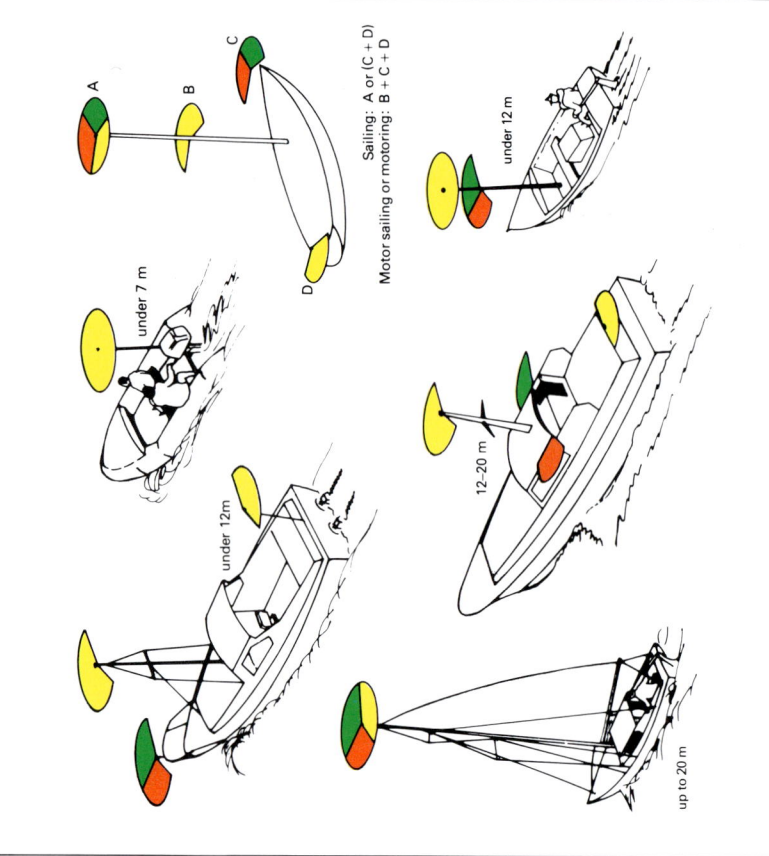

A
B
C
D

under 7 m
under 12m
12–20 m
up to 20 m
under 12 m

Sailing: A or (C + D)
Motor sailing or motoring: B + C + D

DISTRESS SIGNALS

These signals are listed in Annex IV of the Collision Regulations and those particularly applicable to small yachts are illustrated below.
They mean no less than that LIFE IS IN DANGER

It is the duty of amateur yachtsmen, no less than professional seamen, to try to assist any vessel in distress if this can be done without endangering the yacht. Keep a good look-out; if equipped with VHF, this should always be left on at sea, tuned to Channel 16.

If you see or hear anything indicating distress, act as best you can to help. Exact times, bearings, details of any messages, your own position and so on will be essential to the search and rescue services if they are to act on your report.

Red flares or rockets

Orange smoke signals
Flames and smoke as from
an oil barrel

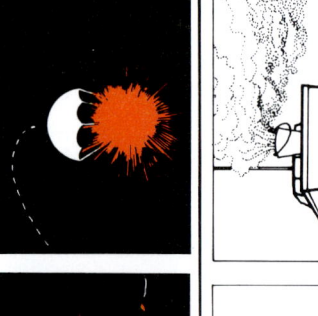

MAY DAY by radio
SOS by lamp or any other
signalling method

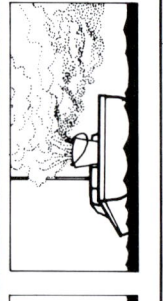

International code flags NC
A square flag having above it
or below it a ball or anything
like a ball

Continuous sounding of the
fog-horn
Slowly and repeatedly raising
and lowering arms outstretched
to each side

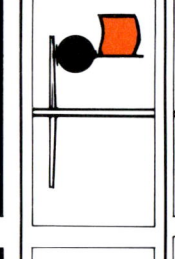

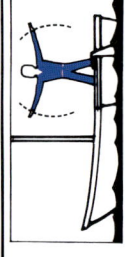

There are lesser degrees of emergency and some signals to indicate these are shown below. They may be made by any means.

F •••—•   I am disabled; communicate
with me (Example: yacht with
steering or engine defect with
plenty of sea-room)

V •••—   I require assistance
(Example: yacht asking for
navigational or other advice)

U ••—   You are running into danger

CALLS FOR MEDICAL ASSISTANCE
By lamp or flag: W •——
By radio: PAN PAN (see p. 180)

166

CHANNEL WEST & SOLENT 1994
AMENDMENT SERVICE

Valid only to 31st December 1994

Send to: The Editor, Channel West and Solent, 18 Bath Road, Cowes, Isle of Wight PO31 7QN

The amendment booklet for CHANNEL WEST AND SOLENT is up-dated weekly, and so is always absolutely up to date and complete.

Booklets are provided free of charge on receipt of this form, completed below together with a stamped and addressed C5 envelope (9" x 6³/₈", 229mm x 162mm).

Requests received during any one week are usually processed early in the next, using the latest Weekly Notices to Mariners and other sources.

In returning this form, please help us and other readers by offering suggestions and drawing our attention to errors:

Name _____

Address _____

_____

_____

Post Code _____

_____

Suggestions/Errors _____

_____

_____

_____

_____

_____

_____

_____

Contents found most useful: _____

_____

Contents found least useful: _____

_____

LIST OF YACHTSMAN'S PILOT BOOKS AND CRUISING GUIDES FOR ENGLISH CHANNEL AND SOLENT AREAS

Author	Title	Price	Order Code
Bowskill, Derek	THE SOLENT - Selsey Bill to Needles	£19.95	PIL0035
Brackenbury, Mark	NORMANDY AND CHANNEL ISLANDS PILOT (7th Edition Revised)	£25.00	PIL0060
Bray, Andrew	SOUTH COAST FROM THE AIR	£12.95	PIL0020
Bruce, Peter	INSHORE ALONG THE DORSET COAST	£9.95	PIL0225
	SOLENT HAZARDS	£5.95	PIL0230
	WIGHT HAZARDS	£5.95	PIL0240
Coles, Adlard	CHANNEL HARBOURS AND ANCHORAGES (7th Edition)	£25.00	PIL0259
Coles/Sylvester	CREEKS AND HARBOURS OF THE SOLENT (11th Edition)	£21.99	PIL0260
Coles/RCC	NORTH BRITTANY PILOT (6th Edition)	£29.95	PIL0270
Coote, John	SHELL PILOT TO ENGLISH CHANNEL: VOL I: ENGLISH COAST, RAMSGATE TO SCILLIES	£17.50	PIL0280
	SHELL PILOT TO ENGLISH CHANNEL: VOL II: FRENCH COAST, DUNKIRK TO BREST	£17.50	PIL0281
Cumberlidge, Peter	CHANNEL CROSSINGS	£16.95	PIL0405
Fishwick, Mark	WEST COUNTRY CRUISING	£13.95	PIL0457
Goulder, Brian	PILOT PACK VOL I: GT YARMOUTH TO LITTLEHAMPTON & IJMUIDEN TO CARENTAN	£25.00	PIL0480
	PILOT PACK VOL II: CHICHESTER TO PORTLAND, & ST VAAST TO ERQUY INC. CHANNEL ISLANDS	£25.00	PIL0481
	PILOT PACK VOL III: BRIDPORT TO SCILLY, & LES LEGUES TO USHANT	£25.00	PIL0482
Jefferson, David	BRITTANY & CHANNEL ISLAND CRUISING GUIDE	£17.99	PIL0580
Robson, Malcolm	CHANNEL ISLANDS PILOT (4th Edition)	£27.50	PIL0730
Thompson, T & D	NORTH FRANCE PILOT: CALAIS TO CHERBOURG	£14.95	PIL0825
Cumberlidge, Peter	BRITTANY & CHANNEL ISLANDS CRUISING GUIDE	£25.00	PIL0407

TO ORDER

By Telephone	KELVIN HUGHES MAIL ORDER HOTLINE: (0703) 223722
By Post	KELVIN HUGHES MAIL ORDER DEPT. ROYAL CRESCENT ROAD SOUTHAMPTON, SO9 1WB

Please quote your credit card number and expiry date.
Please note: Minimum post & packing charge £3.00
Please use the order code shown here for each title.
Prices may change with reprints or new editions.

NOTES